Practical WPF Graphics Programming

Advanced .NET Graphics Development with the Windows Presentation Foundation

Practical WPF Graphics Programming

Advanced .NET Graphics Development with
the Windows Presentation Foundation

Jack Xu, Ph.D

UniCAD Publishing

Practical WPF Graphics Programming

Copyright © 2007 by Jack Xu, Ph.D
Printed and bound in the United States of America 9 8 7 6 5 4 3 2 1UC

Editor: Anna Hsu

The publisher offers excellent discounts on this book when ordered in quantity for bulk purchases or special sales, which may include electronic versions and /or custom covers and content particular to your business, training goals, marketing focus, and branding interests. For more information, please contact:

sales@unicadpublish.com
Visit us on the website: www.unicadpublish.com

Published by UniCAD Publishing.
Phoenix, USA
ISBN-13: 978-0-9793725-1-3
ISBN-10: 0-9793725-1-8

Publisher's Cataloging-in-Publication Data

Xu, Jack
Practical WPF Graphics Programming – Advanced .NET Graphics Development with the Windows Presentation Foundation / Jack Xu
– 1st ed.
p.cm.
ISBN 978-0-9793725-1-3

1. Windows Presentation Foundation. 2. Graphics Programming. 3. .NET Applications
I. Title. II. Title III Title: Practical WPF Graphics Programming

For my wonderful family

Contents

Introduction xvii

    Overview.. xvii

    What this Book Includes xix

    Is This Book for You?.. xix

    What Do You Need to Use This Book?............................xx

    How the Book Is Organized..xx

    Using Code Examples... xxii

    Customer Support xxii

Chapter 1 Overview of WPF Programming................1

    New Features in WPF 1

    XAML basics...2

        Why XAML Needed? 2

        Creating XAML Files.. 3

        Code-Behind Files.. 4

    Your first WPF Program...5

        Properties in XAML.. 6

        Event Handlers in Code-Behind Files..................... 7

    Code-Only Example...8

    XAML-Only Example 10

Chapter 2 WPF Graphics Basics in 2D 13

    2D Coordinate Systems in WPF 13

        Default Coordinates... 13

        Custom Coordinates 16

        Custom Coordinates for 2D Charts 22

            2D Viewport 27

            Zooming and Panning.................................... 29

Basic 2D Graphics Shapes 31
    Lines 31
    Rectangles and Ellipses 33
    Polylines 37
    Polygons 38

Chapter 3 2D Transformations 43

Basics of Matrices and Transforms..............................43
    Vectors and Points.. 44
    Scaling.. 44
    Reflection 45
    Rotation 46
    Translation.. 47
Homogeneous Coordinates 47
    Translation in Homogeneous Coordinates 48
    Scaling in Homogeneous Coordinates 48
    Rotation in Homogeneous Coordinates.................. 49
    Combining Transforms 50
Vector and Matrix in WPF..51
    Vector Structure 51
    Matrix Structure 53
    Matrix Operations 54
    Matrix Transforms... 57
    Creating Perpendicular Lines 64
Object Transforms in WPF 69
    MatrixTransform Class 71
    ScaleTransform Class... 75
    TranslateTransform Class 79
    RotateTransform Class 80
    SkewTransform Class 81
    Composite Transforms 83

Chapter 4 Geometry and 2D Drawing 87

Path and Geometry Classes...87
    Line, Rectangle, and Ellipse Geometries 88
    GeometryGroup Class 89
    CombinedGeometry Class....................................... 92
    PathGeometry Class 96
        Lines and Polylines................................ 97

Arcs 97
Bezier Curves 98
Geometry and Mini-Language 100
Interactive 2D Drawing 103
Mouse Events 114
Creating and Combining Shapes 115
Dragging and Moving Shapes 116
Hit Testing 117
Custom Shapes 121
Star Shape 121
Arrow Line 125
Testing Custom Shapes 131

Chapter 5 Colors and Brushes 137

Colors 137
System Colors 138
Color Picker 142
Brushes 150
SolidColorBrush 151
LinearGradientBrush 153
Custom Colormap Brush 158
RadialGradientBrush 165
Custom Radial Colormap Brush 169
ImageBrush 175
DrawingBrush 181
VisualBrush 187
Bitmap Effects 189
Opacity Masks 194
Brush Transforms 196
LinearGradientBrush Transform 204
RadialGradientBrush Transform 206
ImageBrush Transform 207
Drawing and Visual Brush Transform 207

Chapter 6 Animation 209

WPF Animation Basics 209
Property-Based Animation 210
A Simple Animation in Code 211
Animation and Storyboard 213

Storyboard and Event Trigger 213
Storyboard Animation in Code 215
Animation and Timing Behavior............................ 217
    Duration 218
    RepeatBehavior.. 220
    AutoReverse 220
    BeginTime 221
    Speed Controls.. 221
Interactive Control.. 224
Animation and Transform..................................228
    Animating Translation................................. 228
    Rolling Balls.. 231
    Combining Transform Animations 236
Path Animation 240
Frame-Based Animation 244
    Key-Frame Animation................................. 244
    Spline Key-Frame Animation 247
Custom Animation 249
    Custom Animation Class............................... 250
    Per-Frame Animation 254
    Animation Using Timer 256

Chapter 7 Physics and Games in WPF 263

Ordinary Differiential Equations 263
    Fourth-Order Runge-Kutta Method 264
    Higher-Order ODEs 265
    ODE Solver 265
Pendulum 267
    Equation of Motion 267
    Pendulum Simulator.................................... 268
Coupled-Spring System 274
    Equations of Motion.................................... 275
    Coupled Spring Simulator 275
Projectiles..287
    Aerodynamic Drag Force 287
    Projectile Equations of Motion 288
    Golf Game 289
Collision...296
    Bouncing Ball Physics 297

Bouncing Ball Simulator 299
Fractals 306
    Binary Tree 307
    Snowflake 310
    Mandelbrot Set 315
    Julia Set 323

Chapter 8 Charts in WPF **331**

Simple Line Charts 331
    Creating Simple Line Charts 332
    How It Works 334
Line Charts with Data Collection 334
    Chart Style 335
    Data Collection 336
    Data Series 337
    Creating Charts 339
Gridlines and Labels 342
    XAML Layout 342
    ChartStyleGridlines Class 344
    Testing Project 349
Legend 351
    Legend Class 352
    Testing Project 355
Chart User Control 358
    Creating Chart Control 359
        Defining Dependency Properties 361
        Chart Style for Chart Control 366
        Data Collection and Data Series 371
    Using Chart Control 372
        Creating Simple Chart 373
        Creating Multiple Charts 375

Chapter 9 3D Transformations **379**

3D Matrices in WPF 379
    3D Points and Vectors 379
    Matrix3D Structure 382
    Matrix3D Operations 383
    Matrix3D Transforms 387
    Rotation and Quaternion 391

Projections...394
   Orthographic Projections.............................. 395
      Multi-View Projections 395
      Axonometric Projections 396
   Perspective Projections 399
      One-Point Perspective Projections 400
      Two-Point Perspective Projections............. 400
      Three-Point Perspective Projections........... 401
      Perspective Projection Matrix.................... 401
Views and Projections in WPF 402
   View Transform 403
   Perspective Projection 406
      View Frustum 406
      Perspective Transform Matrix 406
      Implementing Perspective Transforms........ 409
      Testing Perspective Projections................. 411
   Orthographic Projection 415
      Orthographic Transform Matrix 416
      Implementing Orthographic Transforms 417
      Testing Orthographic Projections............... 418
Object Transforms in WPF 420
   ScaleTransform3D Class............................... 421
   TranslateTransform3D class 425
   RotateTransform3D Class.............................. 426
   MatrixTransform3D Class.............................. 428
   Combining Transforms 429

Chapter 10 WPF Graphics Basics in 3D 433

3D Graphics Basics..433
   Viewport3D.. 434
   3D Objects in WPF 435
   Geometry and Mesh 436
   GeometryModel3D and Surfaces.................... 438
   Illuminating the Scene.................................. 440
   Camera Position 441
   Simple Triangle in 3D 442
Basic 3D Shapes 444
   Coordinate Axes and Wireframe.................... 445
   Creating Cube.. 447

Creating Sphere 453
Creating Cylinder 456
Creating Cone 461
Creating Torus 464

Chapter 11 Custom 3D Geometries 469

Cube Geometry 469
  CubeGeometry Class 469
  Tesing CubeGeometry 473
Ellipsoid Geometry 477
  EllipsoidGeometry Class 477
  Testing EllipsoidGeometry 480
Cylindrical Geometry 482
  CylinderGeometry Class 483
  Testing CylinderGeometry 486
Cone Geometry 489
  ConeGeometry Class 490
  Testing ConeGeometry 493
Torus Geometry 497
  TorusGeometry Class 497
  Testing TorusGeometry 501
Icosahedron Geometry 505
  IcosahedronGeometry Class 506
  Testing IcosahedronGeometry 509
Dodecahedron Geometry 512
  DodecahedronGeometry Class 513
  Testing DodecahedronGeometry 519
Soccer Ball Geometry 521
  SoccerGeometry Class 522
  Testing SoccerGeometry 529

Chapter 12 Custom 3D Shapes 535

Deriving from UIElement3D 535
Cube Shape 538
  Cube Shape Class 538
  Testing Cube Shape 540
Ellipsoid Shape 544
  Ellipsoid Shape Class 544
  Testing Ellipsoid Shape 547

Cylinder Shape 548
    Cylinder Shape Class 549
    Testing Cylinder Shape 551
Cone Shape 552
    Cone Shape Class 553
    Testing Cone Shape 555
Torus Shape 556
    Torus Shape Class 557
    Testing Torus Shape 559
Icosahedron Shape 560
    Icosahedron Shape Class 561
    Testing Icosahedron Shape 563
Dodecahedron Shape 563
    Dodecahedron Shape Class 563
    Testing Dodecahedron Shape 564
Soccer Shape 565
    Soccer Shape Class..565
    Testing Soccer Shape 569
Combining Shape 569
    Combining Shape Class 570
    Testing Combining Shape 573

Chapter 13 3D Surfaces **575**

Simple Surfaces 575
    Rectangular Meshes 576
    SimpleSurface Class..577
    Creating Simple Surfaces 581
Parametric Surfaces 584
    ParametricSurface Class..585
    Creating Parametric Surfaces 589
        Helicoid Surface 589
        Sphere Surface 590
        Torus Surface..591
        Quadric Surfaces...592
Extruded Surfaces 593
    ExtrudeSurface Class 594
    Creating Extruded Surfaces.....................................598
Surfaces of Revolution..599
    RotateSurface Class...600

Creating Surfaces of Revelution............................ 604
Surface Shading 606
SurfaceShading Class.. 606
Creating Shaded Surfaces..................................... 610

Chapter 14 3D Model Manipulation 615

Lighting and Shading......................................615
Light Sources.. 616
Testing Light Sources............................ 617
Shading.. 620
Materials 621
Diffuse Materials.................................... 622
Specular and Emissive Materials 624
Texture Mapping..627
Using LinearGradientBrush........................ 627
Using RadialGradientBrush........................ 630
Using Image and Tile Brushes.................... 633
2D Elements on 3D Surfaces 634
Viewport2DVisual3D Class 635
Using Viewport2DVisual3D 635
Interacting with 3D Models 641
Hit-Testing for 3D Geometries.................... 642
Hit-Testing for 3D Shapes......................... 645
Rotating 3D Objects with Mouse 649

Index 653

Introduction

Overview

Welcome to *Practical WPF Graphics Programming*. This book will provide all the tools you need to develop professional graphics applications using the Windows Presentation Foundation (WPF) and C# based on the .NET framework. I hope this book would be useful for WPF and C# programmers of all skill levels.

As a C# programmer, you are probably already familiar with Windows Forms, the mature and full-featured development tool. Windows Forms is built on top of the .NET framework and uses the Windows API to create the visual appearance of standard user interface elements. It provides all kinds of tools for laying out windows, menus, dialogs, and controls. You can also develop graphics applications based on Windows Forms using the Graphical Device Interface (GDI+). However, creating a feature-rich graphics application using Windows Forms can be a difficult and tedious task. For example, Windows Forms provides no tools for creating three-dimensional (3D) graphics applications. Even a 3D point, the simplest of 3D graphics objects, must be defined first in a suitable 3D coordinate system before it can be used as a 3D graphics object.

WPF completely changes the landscape for graphics programming. At first, you may think that WPF is just another way to create windows, menus, dialogs, and controls. However, WPF has much more to offer than any other Windows programming framework does. It integrates three basic Windows elements – text, controls, and graphics – into one single programming model, and puts these three elements into the same element tree in the same manner.

Without WPF, developing a graphics application might have involved using a number of different technologies, ranging from GDI/GDI+ for 2D graphics to Direct3D or OpenGL for 3D graphics. On the contrary, WPF is designed as a single model for graphics application development, providing seamless integration between such services within an application. Similar constructs can be used for creating animation, data binding, and 3D models.

To take further advantage of new powerful graphics hardware technologies, WPF implements a vector-based graphics model. This allows for graphics to be scaled based on screen-specific resolution without the loss of image quality, something nearly impossible with fixed-size raster graphics. In addition, WPF leverages Direct3D for vector-based rendering and makes use of the graphics processing unit on any video card that implements DirectX in hardware.

With WPF, graphics elements can be easily integrated into any part of your user interface. For example, WPF provides 2D shape elements that can be involved in the user interface (UI) tree like other elements can. You are free to mix these shapes with any other kind of element, such as a button. The WPF 3D model is based on the Direct3D technology and allows you to create a custom 3D shape library that can be reused in your projects. The main benefits that WPF offers in 3D are its ease of use and its ability to integrate 3D content anywhere in a WPF application.

As you may have already noticed, there are many WPF programming books available in bookstores. The vast majority of these books are general-purpose user guides and tutorials, which explain the basics of WPF and how to use it to implement simple WPF applications. To take full advantage of WPF graphics features, however, there is a need for a book to provide an in-depth introduction specifically to WPF graphics programming.

This book is written with the intention of providing you with a complete and comprehensive explanation of the WPF graphics capability, and pays special attention to the code implementation details, which will be useful when you create your own real-world WPF graphics Applications. This book includes over 120 code examples, which cover broad array of topics on WPF graphics programming. Much of this book contains original work based on my own programming experience when I was developing commercial Computer Aided Design (CAD) packages. Without WPF and the .NET framework, developing advanced graphics is a difficult and time-consuming task. To add even simple charts or graphs to your applications, you often have to waste effort creating a chart program, or buy commercial graphics and chart add-on packages.

Practical WPF Graphics Programming provides everything you need to create advanced graphics in your WPF applications. It shows you how to create a variety of graphics, ranging from simple 2D shapes to complex 3D surfaces and interactive 3D models. I'll try my best to introduce you to WPF graphics programming in a simple way – simple enough to be easily followed by a beginner who has never had experience developing WPF graphics applications before. You can learn from this book how to create a full range of 2D and 3D graphics applications and how to implement custom 3D geometries and shapes that can be reused in your WPF projects.

What this Book Includes

This book and its sample code listings, which are available for download at my website at www.authors.unicadpublish.com/~jack_xu, provide you with:

- A complete, in-depth instruction on practical WPF graphics programming. After reading this book and running the example programs, you will be able to add various sophisticated graphics to your WPF applications.

- Over 120 ready-to-run example programs that allow you to explore the graphics techniques described in the book. These examples can be used to better understand how graphics algorithms work. You can modify the code examples or add new features to them to form the basis of your own projects. Some of the example code listings provided in this book are already sophisticated graphics packages that can be used directly in your own real-world WPF applications.

- Many classes in the sample code listings that you will find useful in your WPF graphics programming. These classes contain matrix manipulation, coordinate transformation, color maps, chart controls, and the other useful utility classes. You can extract these classes and plug them into your own applications.

Is This Book for You?

You don't have to be an experienced WPF developer or an expert to use this book. I designed this book to be useful to people of all levels of WPF programming experience. In fact, I believe that if you have some experience with the programming language C#, Windows Forms, HTML, and the .NET framework, you will be able to sit down in front of your computer, start up Microsoft Visual Studio 2008 and .NET 3.5, follow the examples provided in this book, and quickly become familiar with WPF graphics programming. For those of you who are already experienced WPF developers, I believe this book has much to offer as well. There is a great deal of information in this book about graphics programming not available in other WPF tutorial and reference books. In addition, most of the example programs in this book can be used directly in your own real-world application development. This book will provide you with a level of detail, explanation, instruction, and sample program code that will enable you to do just about anything WPF graphics-related.

The majority of the example programs in this book can be used routinely by WPF developers and technical professionals. Throughout the book, I'll emphasize the *usefulness* of WPF graphics programming to real-world applications. If you follow the instructions presented in this book closely, you'll be able to easily develop various practical WPF graphics applications, from 2D graphics and charts to a sophisticated 3D model libraries. At the same time, I'll not spend too much time discussing programming style, execution speed, and code optimization, because there is a plethora of books out there that already deal with such topics. Most of the example programs you'll find in this book omit error handlings. This makes the code easier to understand by focusing only on the key concepts and practical applications.

What Do You Need to Use This Book?

You'll need no special equipment to make the best use of this book and understand the algorithms. To run and modify the sample programs, you'll need a computer that is capable of running either Windows Vista or Windows XP. The software installed on your computer should include Visual Studio 2008 and the .NET 3.5 standard edition or higher. If you have Visual Studio 2005 and .NET 3.0, you can also run most of the sample code with few modification. Please remember, however, that this book is intended for Visual Studio 2008 and .NET 3.5, and that all of the example programs were created and tested on this platform, so it is best to run the sample code on the same platform.

How the Book Is Organized

This book is organized into fourteen chapters, each of which covers a different topic about WPF graphics programming. The following summaries of each chapter should give you an overview of the book's content:

Chapter 1, *Overview of WPF Programming*

This chapter introduces the basics of WPF and reviews some of the general aspects of WPF programming, including XAML files used to define user interfaces.

Chapter 2, *WPF Graphics Basics in 2D*

This chapter reviews some fundamental concepts of the 2D graphics and the 2D drawing model in WPF. It introduces coordinate systems and basic 2D shapes.

Chapter 3, *2D Transformations*

This chapter covers the mathematical basics for 2D graphics programming. 2D vectors, matrices, and transformations in the homogeneous coordinate system, including translation, scaling, reflection, and rotation, are discussed. These 2D matrices and transformations allow WPF applications to perform a wide variety of graphical operations on graphics objects in a simple and consistent manner.

Chapter 4, *Geometry and 2D Drawing*

This chapter introduces WPF's Geometry classes and demonstrates why you need them to create complex 2D graphics objects. It also shows you how to create interactive 2D drawing programs and custom shapes.

Chapter 5, *Colors and Brushes*

This chapter covers the color system and brushes that WPF uses to paint graphics objects. It introduces a variety of brushes and their transformations. You'll learn how to create exotic visual effects using different brushes, including the gradient, tile, and image brushes.

Chapter 6, *Animation*

This chapter describes WPF animation facilities, which allow most of the properties and transformations of the graphics objects (such as position, size, translation, rotation, etc.) to be animated. It also describes how to create a custom animation class that can be used in physics-based animation.

Chapter 7, *Physics and Games in WPF*

This chapter covers topics related to real-world WPF applications. You'll learn how to create and simulate physics models by solving ordinary differential equations with the Runge-Kutta method, and how to incorporate physics models into real-world games in WPF. This chapter discusses several physics models and games, including a pendulum, a coupled spring system, a golf ball (projectiles), ball collision, and fractals.

Chapter 8, *Charts in WPF*

This chapter contains instructions on creating 2D line charts in WPF. It introduces basic chart elements including the chart canvas, text canvas, axes, title, labels, ticks, and legend. From this chapter, you'll also learn how to put a 2D chart application into a custom user control and how to reuse this control in your WPF applications.

Chapter 9, *3D Transformations*

This chapter extends the concepts described in Chapter 3 into the third dimension. It explains how to define 3D graphics objects and how to translate, scale, reflect, and rotate these 3D objects. It also describes transformation matrices that represent projection and transformations, which allow you to view 3D graphics objects on a 2D screen. You'll also learn how WPF defines 3D vectors, matrices, and projections.

Chapter 10, *WPF Graphics Basics in 3D*

This chapter explores the basics of 3D models in WPF. It introduces Viewport3D, the 3D geometry and the mesh model, lighting, camera, etc. You'll also learn how to create basic 3D shapes directly in WPF.

Chapter 11, *Custom 3D Geometries*

This chapter explains how to create custom geometries for various 3D shapes. These custom geometry classes can be used as resources in XAML files, and these resources can be used in your markup with a data binding.

Chapter 12, *Custom 3D Shapes*

This chapter shows how to implement custom 3D shape classes. Unlike custom 3D geometry classes, which can only be used as shareable resources, these custom 3D shape classes can be used directly in your XAML files in the same way as the 2D shapes, such as the Line, Rectangle, and Ellipse. You can use these custom 3D shape classes to create a powerful 3D model library.

Chapter 13, *3D Surfaces*

This chapter explains how to create various 3D surfaces, from simple surfaces to complex surfaces, using rectangular meshes and different techniques, including parametric, extrusion, and revolution approaches. It also describes how to add lighting and shading effects to these surfaces.

Chapter 14, *3D Model Manipulation*

This chapter covers broad array of topics on manipulating 3D models in WPF. It describes how to create various 3D special effects using different materials, different light sources, and texture maps. It also explains how to place interactive 2D elements on 3D surfaces and how to rotate 3D graphics objects with the mouse using the virtual trackball method.

Using Code Examples

You may use the code in this book in your applications and documentation. You don't need to contact the author or the publisher for permission unless you are reproducing a significant portion of the code. For example, writing a program that uses several chunks of code from this book doesn't require permission. Selling or distributing the example code listings does require permission. Incorporating a significant amount of example code from this book into your applications and documentation also requires permission. Integrating the example code from this book into commercial products isn't allowed without written permission of the author.

Customer Support

I am always interested in hearing from readers, and would like to hear your thoughts on this book. You can send me comments by e-mail to jxu.authors@unicadpublish.com. I also provide updates, bug fixes, and ongoing support via my website:

www.authors.unicadpublish.com/~jack_xu

You can also obtain the complete source code for all of examples in this book from the above website.

Chapter 1
Overview of WPF Programming

Windows Presentation Foundation (WPF) is a next generation graphics platform which is included in the Microsoft .NET Framework 3.0 and 3.5. It allows you to build advanced user interfaces (UI) that incorporate documents, media, 2D and 3D graphics, animations, and web-like characteristics. Built on the .NET framework 3.0 and 3.5, WPF provides a managed environment for developing applications using the Windows operating system. Like other features of the .NET Framework 3.0 and 3.5, WPF is available for Windows Vista, Windows XP, and Windows Server 2003.

In a pre-WPF world, developing a Windows application might have required the use of several different technologies. For instance, in order to add forms and user controls to your application, you needed to use the Windows Forms that is part of the .NET framework. You had to use GDI+ to create images and 2D graphics. To add 3D graphics, you probably needed to use Direct3D or OpenGL, a standard part of Windows.

WPF is designed to be a unified solution for the application development, providing a seamless integration of different technologies. With WPF, you can create vector graphics or complex animations and incorporate media into your applications to address all of the areas listed above.

New Features in WPF

There are several new features in WPF that you can take advantage of when you develop your WPF applications. First, to utilize powerful new graphics hardware, WPF implements a vector graphics model based on the Direct3D technology. This allows graphics to scale according to screen-specific resolution without losing image quality, which is impossible to do with fixed-size raster graphics. WPF leverages Direct3D for vector-based rendering, and uses the graphics processing unit on any video card with built-in DirectX implemented. In anticipation of future technology, such as high-resolution display, WPF uses a floating-point logical pixel system and supports 32-bit ARGB colors.

Furthermore, to easily represent UI and user interaction, WPF introduces a new XML based language, called XAML. XAML allows applications to dynamically parse and manipulate user interface elements at either design-time or runtime. It uses the code-behind model, similar to ASP.NET programming, allowing designers and developers to work in parallel and to seamlessly combine their work to create a compelling user experience. Of course, WPF also provides you the option to not use XAML files when you develop WPF applications, meaning that you can still develop your applications entirely in code such as C#, C++, or Visual Basic.

Another new feature is related to the resolution-independent layout. All WPF layout dimensions are specified using device-independent pixels. A device-independent pixel is one ninety-sixth of an inch in size and resolution-independent, so you'll get similar results regardless of whether you are rendering to a 72-DPI (dots per inch) monitor or a 19,200-DPI printer.

WPF is also based on a dynamic layout. This means that a UI element arranges itself on a window or page according to its content, its parent layout container, and the available screen area. Dynamic layout facilitates localization by automatically adjusting the size and position of UI elements when the strings they contain change length. By contrast, the layout in Windows Forms is device-dependent and more likely to be static. Typically, Windows Forms controls are positioned absolutely on a form using dimensions specified in hardware pixels.

XAML basics

As mentioned previously, using XAML to create UI is a new feature in WPF. In this section, I'll present an introduction to XAML, and consider its structure and syntax. Once you understand the basics of XAML, you can use it to easily create UI and layout in WPF applications.

Why XAML Needed?

Since WPF applications can be developed entirely in code, you may ask a perfectly natural question – why do we need XAML in the first place? The reason can be traced back to the question of efficiently implementing complex, graphically rich applications. A long time ago, developers realized that the most efficient way to develop these kinds of applications was to separate the graphics portion from the underlying code. In this way, the designers could work on the graphics, while the developers could work on the code behind the graphics. Both parts could be designed and refined separately, without any versioning headaches.

Before WPF, it was impossible to separate the graphics content from the code. For example, when you work with Windows Forms, you define every form entirely in C# code or any other language. As you add controls to the UI and configure them, the program needs to adjust the code in corresponding form classes. If you want to decorate your forms, buttons, and other controls with graphics developed by designers, you must extract the graphic content and export it to a bitmap format. This approach works for simple applications; however, it is very limited for complex, dynamic applications. Plus, graphics in bitmap format can lose their quality when they get resized.

The XAML technology introduced in WPF resolves these issues. When you develop a WPF application in Visual Studio, the window you are creating isn't translated into code. Instead, it is serialized into a set of XAML tags. When you run the application, these tags are used to generate the objects that compose the UI.

XAML isn't a must in order to develop WPF applications. You can implement your WPF applications entirely in code. However, the windows and controls created in code will be locked into the Visual Studio environment and available only to programmers; there is no way to separate the graphics portion from the code.

In orther words, WPF doesn't require XAML. However, XAML opens up world of possibilities for collaboration, because many design tools understand the XAML format.

Creating XAML Files

There are some standard rules for creating a XAML file. First, every element in a XAML file must relate to an instance of a .NET class. The name of the element must match the name of the class exactly. For example, <TextBlock> tells WPF to create a TextBlock object.

In a XAML file, you can nest one element inside another. In this way, you can place an element as a child of another element. For example, if you have a Button inside a Canvas, this means that your UI contains a Canvas that has a Button as its child. You can also set the properties of each element through attributes.

Let's look at a simple XAML structure:

```
<Window x:Class="Chapter01.Window1"
    xmlns="http://schemas.microsoft.com/winfx
        /2006/xaml/presentation"
    xmlns:x="http://schemas.microsoft.com/winfx/2006/xaml"
    Title="Chapter1" Height="300" Width="300">
    <Grid>
        <TextBlock>Hello, WPF!</TextBlock>
    </Grid>
</Window>
```

This file includes three elements: the top-level Window element, which represents the entire window; the Grid; and a TextBlock that is placed inside the Grid as a child. You can use either a Window or a Page as the top-level element in WPF. The Page is similar to the Window, but is used for navigable applications. WPF also involves an Application file that defines application resources and startup settings. If you start with a new WPF Window (or Page) project, Visual Studio will automatically generate an Application file called App.xaml. In this book, I'll use Window as the top-level WPF element, although Page can be used without any difficulty.

The starting tag for the Window element includes a class name and two XML namespaces. The xmlns attribute is a specialized attribute in XML, which is reserved for declaring namespaces. The two namespaces in the above XAML file will appear in every WPF XAML file. You only need to know that these namespaces simply allow the XAML parser to find the right classes. You can also see three properties within the tag: Title, Height, and Width. Each attribute corresponds to a property of the Window class. These attributes tells WPF to create a 300 x 300 window with the title Chapter01.

Inside the Window tag, there is a Grid control that in turn contains a TextBlock with its Text property setting to "Hello, WPF!". You can create the same TextBlock using the following snippet:

```
<TextBlock Text="Hello, WPF!"/>
```

Code-Behind Files

As mentioned previously, XAML is used to create the UI for your application, but in order to make the application functioning, you need to attach event handlers to the UI. XAML makes this easy using the Class attribute:

```
<Window x:Class="Chapter01.Window1".....>
```

The x namespace prefix places the Class attribute in the XAML namespace, which means that this is a more general part of the XAML language. This example creates a new class named Chapter01.Window1, which derives from the base Window class.

When you create a WPF Window application, Visual Studio will automatically create a partial class where you can place your event handling code. In the previous example, you created a WPF Window application named Chapter01 (the project name) which contained a window named Window1. Visual Studio will automatically generate the following code-behind file:

```
Namespace Chapter01
{
    /// <summary>
    /// Interaction logic for Window1.xaml
    /// </summary>

    public partial class Window1 : Window
```

```
    {
        public Window1()
        {
            InitializeComponent();
        }
    }
}
```

When you compile this application, XAML is translated into a CLR type declaration which is merged with the logic in the code-behind class file (Window1.xaml.cs in this example) to form one single unit.

The above code-behind file only contains a default constructor, which calls the InitializeComponent method when you create an instance of the class. This is similar to the C# class in Windows Forms.

Your first WPF Program

Let's consider a simple WPF example. Open Visual Studio 2008 and create a new WPF Window project called Chapter01. Remove the default window1.xaml and window1.xaml.cs files from the project. Add a new WPF Window to the project, and name it StartMenu, which will add two files, StartMenu.xaml and StartMenu.xaml.cs, to the project. This window will be the main menu window, from which you can access all of the examples in this chapter. You can examine the soruce code of these two files and see how to implement them. This file structure will be used for accessing code examples in each chapter throughout the book.

Add another new WPF Window to the project and name it FirstWPFProgram.

Figure 1-1 shows the results of running this example.

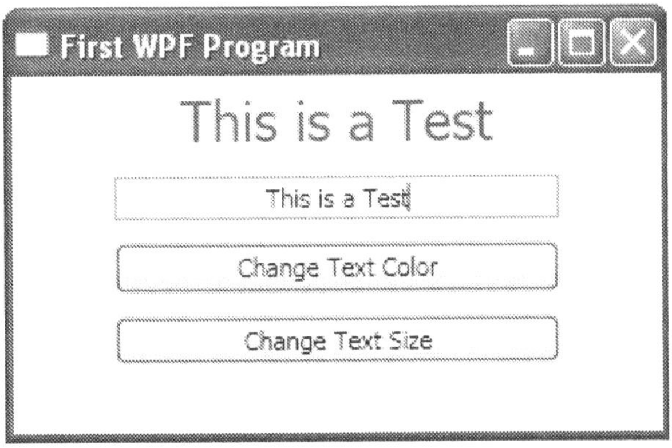

Figure 1-1 Your first WPF program example.

This example includes several controls: a Grid, which is the most common control for arranging layouts in WPF, a StackPanel inside the Grid used to hold other controls, including a TextBlock, a TextBox, and two Button controls. The goal of this example is to change the text in the TextBlock accordingly when the user enters text in the TextBox. At the same time, the text color or font size of the text in the TextBlock control can be also changed when the user clicks the Change Text Color or Change Text Size button.

Properties in XAML

Here is the XAML file of this example:

```
<Window x:Class="Chapter01.FirstWPFProgram"
    xmlns="http://schemas.microsoft.com/winfx
        /2006/xaml/presentation"
    xmlns:x="http://schemas.microsoft.com/winfx/2006/xaml"
    Title="First WPF Program" Height="300" Width="300">
    <Grid>
        <StackPanel>
            <TextBlock Name="textBlock" Margin="5"
                TextAlignment="Center"
                Text="Hello WPF!"/>
            <TextBox Name="textBox" Margin="5" Width="200"
                TextAlignment="Center"
                TextChanged="OnTextChanged"/>
            <Button Margin="5" Width="200"
                Content="Change Text Color"
                Click="btnChangeColor_Click"/>
            <Button Margin="5" Width="200"
                Content="Change Text Size"
                Click="btnChangeSize_Click"/>
        </StackPanel>
    </Grid>
</Window>
```

You can see that the attributes of an element set properties of the corresponding object. For example, the TextBlock control in the above XAML file configures the name, margin, text alignment, and text:

```
<TextBlock Name="textBlock" Margin="5"
        TextAlignment="Center" Text="Hello WPF!"/>
```

In order for this to work, the TextBlock class in WPF must provide corresponding properties. You specify various properties for other controls that affect your layout and UI in a similar fashion.

To achieve the goal of this example, you need to have the ability to manipulate the TextBlock, TextBox and Button controls programmatically in the code-behind file. First, you need to name the TextBlock and TextBox controls in your XAML file. In this example, these controls are named textBlock and textBox. Remember that in a traditional Windows Forms application, every control must have a name. However, in a WPF application, you only need to name the elements that you want to manipulate programmatically. Here, you don't need to name the Grid, StackPanel, and Button controls, for example.

Event Handlers in Code-Behind Files

In the previous section, you learned how to map attributes to corresponding properties. However, to make controls functioning, sometimes you need to attach attributes with event handlers. In the above XAML file, you must attach an OnTextChanged event handler to the TextChanged property of the TextBox. You must also define the Click property of the two buttons using two click event handlers; btnChangeColor_Click and btnChangeSize_Click.

This assumes that there should be methods associated with names OnTextChanged, btnChangeColor_Click, and btnChangeSize_Click in the code-behind file. Here is the corresponding code-behind file of this example:

```
using System;
using System.Windows;
using System.Windows.Controls;
using System.Windows.Media;

namespace Chapter01
{
    public partial class FirstWPFProgram : Window
    {
        public FirstWPFProgram()
        {
            InitializeComponent();
        }

        private void OnTextChanged(object sender,
            TextChangedEventArgs e)
        {
            textBlock.Text = textBox.Text;
        }

        private void btnChangeColor_Click(object sender,
            RoutedEventArgs e)
        {
            if (textBlock.Foreground == Brushes.Black)
                textBlock.Foreground = Brushes.Red;
            else
                textBlock.Foreground = Brushes.Black;
        }

        private void btnChangeSize_Click(object sender,
            RoutedEventArgs e)
        {
            if (textBlock.FontSize == 11)
                textBlock.FontSize = 24;
            else
                textBlock.FontSize = 11;
        }
    }
}
```

Note that event handlers must have the correct signature. The event model in WPF is slightly different than that in earlier versions of .NET. WPF supports a new model based on event routing. The rest of the above code-behind file is very similar to that used in Windows Forms applications, which you should already be familiar with.

Running this example produces the results shown in Figure 1-1. If you type any text in the text box field, the text in the text block will change correspondingly. In addition, the color or font size will be changed depending on which button is clicked.

Code-Only Example

As mentioned previously, XAML isn't a must in order to create a WPF application. WPF fully supports code-only implementation, even though the use of this kind of implementation is less common. There are some pros and cons with the code-only approach. The advantage is that the code-only method gives you full control over customization. For example, when you want to conditionally add or substitute controls depending on the user's input, you can easily implement a condition logic in code. By contrast, this is hard to do with XAML because controls in XAML are embedded in your assembly as fixed unchanging resources. The disadvantage is that since WPF controls don't include parametric constructors, developing a code-only application in WPF is sometimes tedious. Even adding a simple control, such as a button, to your application takes several lines of code.

In the following example, we'll convert the previous example, FirstWPFProgram, into a code-only application. Add a new class to the project Chapter01 and name it CodeOnly. The following code listing will reproduce the results shown in Figure 1-1:

```
using System;
using System.Windows;
using System.Windows.Media;
using System.Windows.Controls;
using System.Windows.Markup;

namespace Chapter01
{
    public class CodeOnly : Window
    {
        private TextBlock textBlock;
        private TextBox textBox;

        public CodeOnly()
        {
            Initialization();
        }

        private void Initialization()
```

```
{
    // Configure the window:
    this.Height = 300;
    this.Width = 300;
    this.Title = "Code Only Example";

    // Create Grid and StackPanel and
    // add them to window:
    Grid grid = new Grid();
    StackPanel stackPanel = new StackPanel();
    grid.Children.Add(stackPanel);
    this.AddChild(grid);

    // Add a text block to stackPanel:
    textBlock = new TextBlock();
    textBlock.Margin = new Thickness(5);
    textBlock.Height = 30;
    textBlock.TextAlignment = TextAlignment.Center;
    textBlock.Text = "Hello WPF!";
    stackPanel.Children.Add(textBlock);

    // Add a text box to stackPanel:
    textBox = new TextBox();
    textBox.Margin = new Thickness(5);
    textBox.Width = 200;
    textBox.TextAlignment = TextAlignment.Center;
    textBox.TextChanged += OnTextChanged;
    stackPanel.Children.Add(textBox);

    // Add button to stackPanel used to
    // chnage text color:
    Button btnColor = new Button();
    btnColor.Margin = new Thickness(5);
    btnColor.Width = 200;
    btnColor.Content = "Change Text Color";
    btnColor.Click += btnChangeColor_Click;
    stackPanel.Children.Add(btnColor);

    // Add button to stackPanel used to
    // change text font size:
    Button btnSize = new Button();
    btnSize.Margin = new Thickness(5);
    btnSize.Width = 200;
    btnSize.Content = "Change Text Color";
    btnSize.Click += btnChangeSize_Click;
    stackPanel.Children.Add(btnSize);
}

private void OnTextChanged(object sender,
    TextChangedEventArgs e)
{
    textBlock.Text = textBox.Text;
}
```

```
private void btnChangeColor_Click(object sender,
    RoutedEventArgs e)
{
    if (textBlock.Foreground == Brushes.Black)
        textBlock.Foreground = Brushes.Red;
    else
        textBlock.Foreground = Brushes.Black;
}

private void btnChangeSize_Click(object sender,
    RoutedEventArgs e)
{
    if (textBlock.FontSize == 11)
        textBlock.FontSize = 24;
    else
        textBlock.FontSize = 11;
}
    }
}
```

You can see that the CodeOnly class is similar to a form class in a traditional Windows Forms application. It derives from the base Window class and adds private member variables for TextBlock and TextBox. Pay close attention to how controls are added to their parents and how event handlers are attached.

XAML-Only Example

In the previous sections, you learned how to create the same WPF application using both the XAML+code and the code-only techniques. The standard approach for developing WPF applications is to use XAML from a code-based application. Namely, you use XAML to lay out your UI, and use code to implement event handlers. For applications with a dynamic UI, you may want to go with the code-only method.

However, for simple applications, it is also possible to use a XAML-only file without writing any C# code. This is called a loose XAML file. At first glance, you may think that a loose XAML file seems useless – what's the point of a UI with no code to drive it? In fact, XAML provides several features that allow you to perform some functions with a loose XAML file. For example, you can develop a XAML-only application using features such as animation, event trigger, and data binding.

Here we'll create a loose XAML application that mimics the FirstWPFProgram example. Even though it can't reproduce exactly the results shown in Figure 1-1, the XAML-only application still generates a much more impressive result than static HTML would.

Add a new WPF window to the project Chapter01 and name it XamlOnly. Here is the markup of this example:

```
<Window x:Class="Chapter01.XamlOnly"
```

```
xmlns="http://schemas.microsoft.com/winfx
    /2006/xaml/presentation"
xmlns:x="http://schemas.microsoft.com/winfx/2006/xaml"
Title="XamlOnly" Height="300" Width="300">
<Grid>
    <StackPanel>
        <TextBlock Name="textBlock" Margin="5"
            TextAlignment="Center" Height="30"
        Text="{Binding ElementName=textBox,Path=Text}"/>
        <TextBox Name="textBox" Margin="5" Width="200"
            TextAlignment="Center" Text="Hello, WPF!"/>
        <Button Margin="5" Width="200"
            Content="Change Text Color">
            <Button.Triggers>
                <EventTrigger RoutedEvent="Button.Click">
                    <BeginStoryboard>
                        <Storyboard>
                            <ColorAnimation
    Storyboard.TargetName="textBlock"
    Storyboard.TargetProperty=
        "(TextBlock.Foreground).(SolidColorBrush.Color)"
    From="Black" To="Red" Duration="0:0:1"/>
                        </Storyboard>
                    </BeginStoryboard>
                </EventTrigger>
            </Button.Triggers>
        </Button>

        <Button Margin="5" Width="200"
            Content="Change Text Size">
            <Button.Triggers>
                <EventTrigger RoutedEvent="Button.Click">
                    <BeginStoryboard>
                        <Storyboard>
                            <DoubleAnimation
    Storyboard.TargetName="textBlock"
    Storyboard.TargetProperty="FontSize"
    From="11" To="24" Duration="0:0:0.2"/>
                        </Storyboard>
                    </BeginStoryboard>
                </EventTrigger>
            </Button.Triggers>
        </Button>
    </StackPanel>
</Grid>
</Window>
```

This XAML file first binds the Text property of the TextBlock to the Text property of the TextBox. This data-binding allows you to change the text of the TextBlock by typing text in the TextBox field. Then two buttons are created, which are used to change text color and font size. This can be done by using the buttons' event triggers, which start the color animation or the double animation, depending on which button is clicked. The detailed procedure of the WPF animation will be described in Chapter 6.

Even though this application lacks the code-behind file, the buttons are still functioning. Of course, this XAML-only example can't reproduce exactly the results of the previous example with a code-behind file. The reason is that although the event triggers in XAML files can start an animation, they can't involve if-statements, for-loops, methods, and any other computation algorithm.

Chapter 2
WPF Graphics Basics in 2D

As mentioned in the previous chapter, WPF provides a unified graphics platform that allows you to easily create a variety of user interfaces and graphics objects in WPF applications. This chapter begins by describing graphics coordinate systems used in WPF, and shows you several different coordinate systems that you can use to make graphics programming easier. Then it shows you how to create basic 2D shapes in WPF applications.

2D Coordinate Systems in WPF

When you create a graphic object in WPF, you must determine where the graphics object or drawing will be displayed. To do this, you need to understand how WPF measures graphics object's coordinates. Each point on a WPF window or page has an X and Y coordinate. In the following sections, we'll discuss various coordinate systems and their relationships.

Default Coordinates

For 2D graphics, the WPF coordinate system locates the origin in the upper-left corner of the rendering area. In the 2D space, the positive X-axis points to the right, and the positive Y-axis points to downward, as shown in Figure 2-1.

All coordinates and sizes in the default WPF system are measured in units of 96 dots per inch (DPI), called device-independent pixels. In this system, you can create adaptive layouts to deal with different resolutions, making sure your controls and graphics objects stretch accordingly when the window is stretched.

The rendering area in WPF can be defined using layout elements deriving from the Panel class, including Canvas, DockPanel, Grid, StackPanel, VirtualizingStatckPanel, WrapPanel, etc. However, it is also possible to use a custom layout component as the rendering area by overriding the default behavior of any of these layout elements.

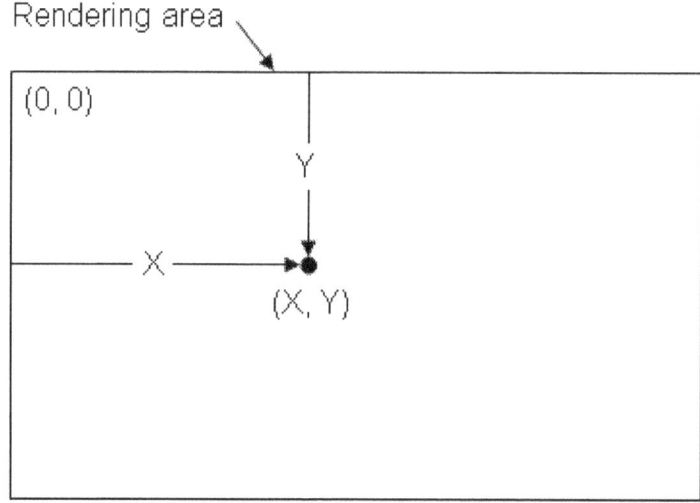

Figure 2-1 Default coordinate system in WPF.

Let's look at an example and see how this can be achieved . Start with Microsoft Visual Studio 2008, create a new WPF Windows project, and name it Chapter02. Add a new WPF Window to the project and name it LineInDefaultSystem. Add a Canvas element to the application. The canvas is particularly useful when you need to place graphics and other drawing elements at absolute positions. What's interesting is that Canvas elements can be nested. Namely, you can prepare part of a drawing in a canvas, and then insert that entire drawing as a single element into another canvas. You can also apply various transformations, such as scaling or rotation, directly to the canvas.

Now you can draw a line from Point (0, 0) to Point (100, 100) on the canvas with the default units of device-independent pixels using the following XAML file:

```
<Window x:Class="Chapter02.LineInDefaultSystem"
    xmlns="http://schemas.microsoft.com/winfx
        /2006/xaml/presentation"
    xmlns:x="http://schemas.microsoft.com/winfx/2006/xaml"
    Title="Line in Default System" Height="300" Width="300">
    <Canvas Height="300" Width="300">
        <Line X1="0" Y1="0"
            X2="100" Y2="100"
            Stroke="Black"
            StrokeThickness="2" />
    </Canvas>
</Window>
```

Figure 2-2 shows the results of running this example.

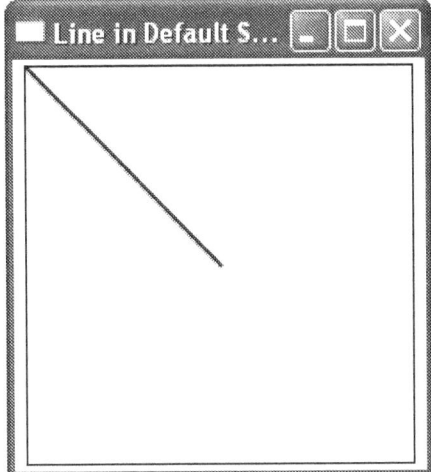

Figure 2-2 Draw a line from (0, 0) to (100, 100) on the canvas.

It is also possible to use other units for creating graphics objects. WPF provides four different units of measures:

- px: is the default device-independent unit (1/96th inch per unit)
- in: is inches; 1in = 96px
- cm: is centimeters; 1cm = (96/2.54) px
- pt: is points; 1pt = (96/72) px

You can create graphics objects and UI using either any unit of measure listed above or mixed units. For example, the coordinates for the starting and ending points of the line can be specified in pixels (px), centimeters (cm), inches (in), or points (pt). If you omit the unit (such as in the StrokeThickness attribute), the default device-independent pixels will be implied.

If you replace the code inside the canvas of the previous example with the following piece of XAML code:

```
<Canvas Height="300" Width="300">
    <Line X1="0.5in" Y1="2.0cm"
          X2="150" Y2="80pt"
          Stroke="Blue"
          StrokeThickness="0.1cm" />
</Canvas>
```

this generates the output of Figure 2-3.

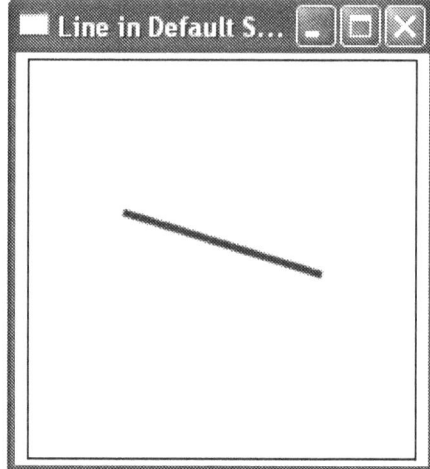

Figure 2-3 Draw a line on the canvas using different units of measures.

Also note the decimal values in the above XAML code: all coordinates in WPF are double precision values. This allows you to easily create device-independent applications by simply using real-world units, and the WPF rendering engine will make sure that everything is rendered in the correct sizes, regardless of whether you are drawing to the screen or printing.

Custom Coordinates

In addition to the default WPF coordinate system discussed in the previous section, a WPF application can define its own coordinate system. For example, 2D charting applications usually use a coordinate system where the Y-axis points from bottom to top, as illustrated in Figure 2-4.

This system can be easily created in WPF by directly performing corresponding transformations to the canvas. Let's consider an example. Add a new WPF Window to the project Chapter02 and name it LineInCustomSystem. Here is the XAML file of this example:

```
<Window x:Class="Chapter02.LineInCustomSystem"
    xmlns="http://schemas.microsoft.com/winfx
        /2006/xaml/presentation"
    xmlns:x="http://schemas.microsoft.com/winfx/2006/xaml"
  Title="Line In Custom System" Height="240" Width="220">
<Border BorderBrush="Black" BorderThickness="1"
    Height="200" Width="200">
        <Canvas Height="200" Width="200">
            <Canvas.RenderTransform>
                <TransformGroup>
                    <ScaleTransform ScaleY="-1" />
                    <TranslateTransform Y="200" />
                </TransformGroup>
            </Canvas.RenderTransform>
```

```
            <Line X1="0" Y1="0"
                  X2="100" Y2="100"
                  Stroke="Black"
                  StrokeThickness="2" />
        </Canvas>
      </Border>
   </Window>
```

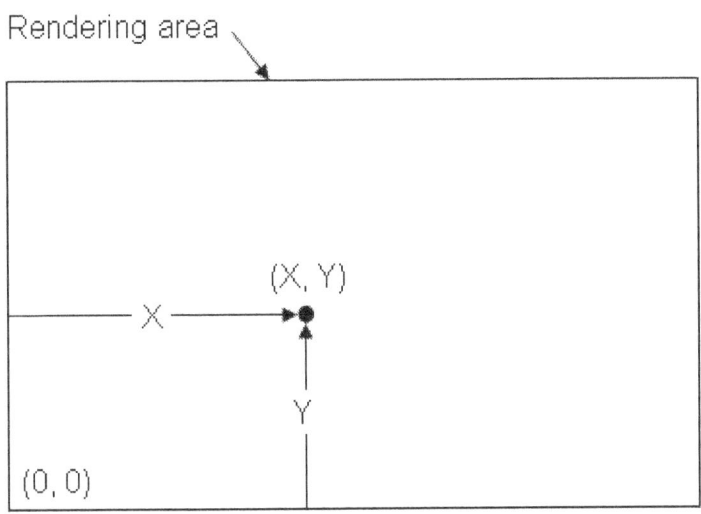

Figure 2-4 A custom coordinate system.

In this example, you perform two successive transforms on the canvas. The scale transform, which reverses the Y axis, and the translation transform, which translates 200px (the height of the canvas) in the Y direction. These transforms move the origin from the top-left corner to the bottom-left corner of the canvas.

Figure 2-5 shows the result of this example. The line from (0, 0) to (100, 100) is now measured relative to the origin of the new custom coordinate system. You can compare this line with that drawn in the default system of Figure 2-2.

You may notice that there is an issue with this custom coordinate system: everything inside the Canvas will be transformed in the same way that the canvas is. For instance, when you add a button control and a text block to the canvas, using the following XAML code:

```
<Button Canvas.Top="50" Canvas.Left="80" FontSize="15"
        Foreground="Red" Name="label1" Content="My Button"/>
<TextBlock Canvas.Top="120" Canvas.Left="20" FontSize="12pt"
           Foreground="Blue"> <Bold>My Text Block</Bold>
</TextBlock>
```

The content of the button and the text block will be up-side down, as shown in Figure 2-6. In order to view the normal text content in this custom coordinate system, you have to perform a reflective transform on the corresponding controls using the following XAML code:

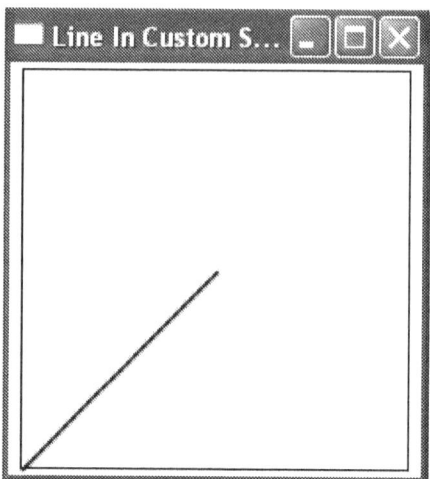

Figure 2-5 Draw a line from (0, 0) to (100, 100) in the custom coordinate system.

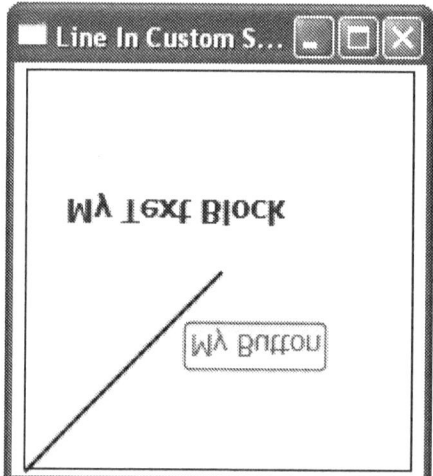

Figure 2-6 The button and text block are up-side down in the custom coordinate system.

```
<Button Canvas.Top="50" Canvas.Left="80" FontSize="15"
        Foreground="Red" Content="My Button">
    <Button.RenderTransform>
        <ScaleTransform ScaleY="-1"/>
    </Button.RenderTransform>
</Button>
```

```
<TextBlock Canvas.Top="120" Canvas.Left="20"
        FontSize="12pt"
        Foreground="Blue">
        <Bold>My Text Block</Bold>
    <TextBlock.RenderTransform>
        <ScaleTransform ScaleY="-1"/>
    </TextBlock.RenderTransform>
</TextBlock>
```

The bold text statements in the above code snippet perform a reflection transform in the Y direction (corresponding to a scale transform with a scaling factor of "-1"). Running this application now produces the result of Figure 2-7.

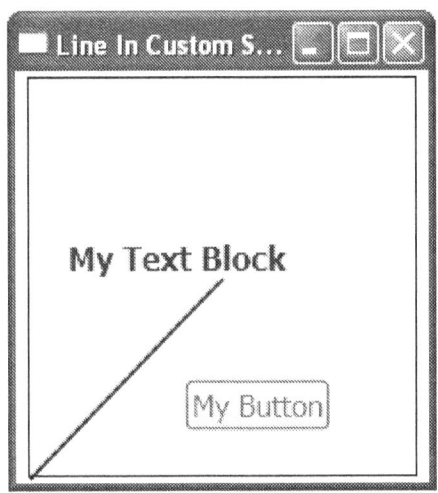

Figure 2-7 The button and text block in the custom coordinate system after the reflection.

You can change the apparent size and location of the graphics objects and user controls on the screen using this custom coordinate system, which is called "Zooming" and "Panning". Zooming and Panning can be achieved using scaling and translation transforms.

Add a new WPF Window to the project Chapter02, and call it ScaleInCustomSystem. Add a StackPanel to the application, add a slider control and a border control to the content of the StackPanel, and add a canvas to the border control. Finally create a line and a rectangle object on the canvas control. The XAML file of this example is listed below:

```
<Window x:Class="Chapter02.ScaleInCustomSystem"
    xmlns="http://schemas.microsoft.com/winfx
        /2006/xaml/presentation"
    xmlns:x="http://schemas.microsoft.com/winfx/2006/xaml"
    Title="Scale In Custom System" Height="310" Width="260">
    <StackPanel Height="280" Width="250">
        <Border BorderBrush="Black" BorderThickness="1"
                Height="200" Width="200" Margin="20">
```

```
<Canvas Height="200" Width="200">
    <Canvas.RenderTransform>
        <TransformGroup>
            <ScaleTransform ScaleY="-1" />
            <TranslateTransform Y="200" />
        </TransformGroup>
    </Canvas.RenderTransform>

    <Line X1="0" Y1="0" X2="80" Y2="80"
      Stroke="Black" StrokeThickness="2">
        <Line.RenderTransform>
            <ScaleTransform
  ScaleX="{Binding ElementName=slider,Path=Value}"
  ScaleY="{Binding ElementName=slider,Path=Value}"/>
        </Line.RenderTransform>
    </Line>

    <Rectangle Canvas.Top="100" Canvas.Left="30"
               Width="80" Height="40"
               Stroke="DarkRed"
               StrokeThickness="3">
        <Rectangle.RenderTransform>
            <ScaleTransform
  ScaleX="{Binding ElementName=slider,Path=Value}"
  ScaleY="{Binding ElementName=slider,Path=Value}"/>
        </Rectangle.RenderTransform>
    </Rectangle>
</Canvas>
</Border>

<Slider Name="slider" Minimum="0" Maximum="3"
        Value="1" TickPlacement="BottomRight"
        TickFrequency="0.2"
        IsSnapToTickEnabled="True"/>
    </StackPanel>
</Window>
```

Here, you bind the scaling factors of ScaleX and ScaleY of the line and rectangle to the value of the slider. The value of the slider varies from 0 to 3, meaning that the scaling factor for both the line and rectangle changes in the range of [0, 3]. When the user moves the slider with the mouse, the dimension of the line and rectangle will change accordingly.

Figure 2-8 shows the results of running this example. You can zoom in or zoom out by moving the slider with your mouse. When you increase the scaling factor further, you might obtain unexpected results, such as those shown in the figure. Namely, the graphics objects are extended outside of the canvas1 control specified by the black border line.

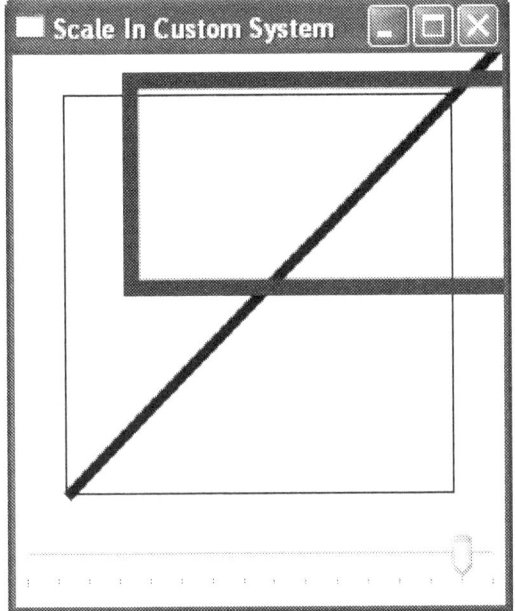

Figure 2-8 The line and rectangle objects are scaled.

This can easily be fixed by specifying the ClipToBounds property of the canvas to true:

```
<Canvas Height="200" Width="200" ClipToBounds="True">
```

This will produce the results shown in Figure 2-9. You can clearly see the difference between Figure 2-8 and Figure 2-9.

There are still issues associated with this custom coordinate system. First, the scaling affects not only the shape of the graphics objects, but also the StrokeThickness, which is undesirable for some applications. For example, for charting applications, we only want the shape of the graphics or the line length to vary with the scaling factor, but not the StrokeThickness itself.

Another issue is the unit of the measure used in the coordinate system, where the default units are used. In real-world applications, sometimes, the real-world units are usually used. For example, it is impossible to draw a line with a length of 100 miles on the screen in the current coordinate system. In the following section, we'll develop a new custom coordinate system that can be used in 2D charting applications.

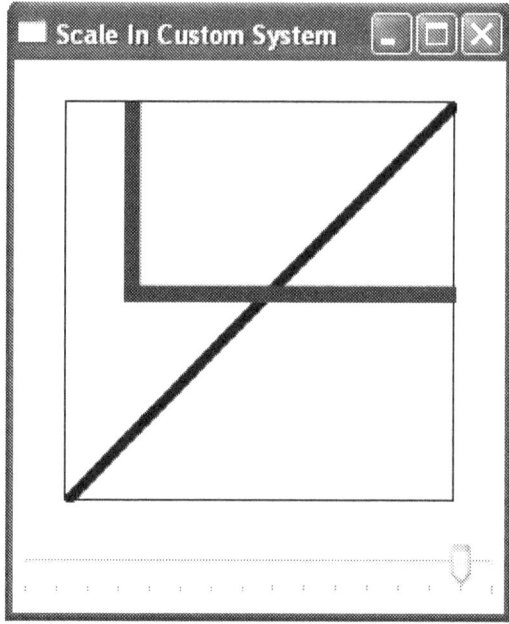

Figure 2-9 The line and rectangle objects are always drawn inside of the canvas control.

Custom Coordinates for 2D Charts

The custom coordinate system used in 2D charting applications must satisfy the following conditions: it must be independent of the unit of your real-world graphics objects, and its Y-axis must point from bottom to top as it does in most charting applications. This custom coordinate system is illustrated in Figure 2-10.

The real-world X-Y coordinate system is defined within the rendering area. You can create such a coordinate system using a custom panel control by overriding the MeasureOverride and ArrangeOverride methods. Each method returns the size data that is needed to position and render child elements. This is a standard method used to create custom coordinate system. Instead of creating a custom panel control, here we'll construct this coordinate system using another approach based on direct coding.

Add a new WPF Window to the project Chapter02 and name it Chart2DSystem. The following is the XAML file of this example:

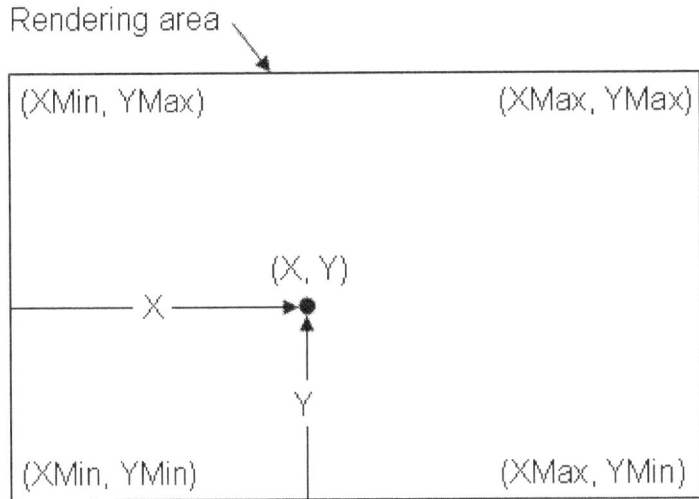

Figure 2-10 Custom Coordinate system for 2D charting applications.

```
<Window x:Class="Chapter02.Chart2DSystem"
    xmlns="http://schemas.microsoft.com/winfx
        /2006/xaml/presentation"
    xmlns:x="http://schemas.microsoft.com/winfx/2006/xaml"
Title="Chart2D Coordinate System"
Height="420"  Width="360">

    <Viewbox Stretch="Uniform">
        <StackPanel Height="420" Width="360">
            <Canvas x:Name="plotCanvas"ClipToBounds="True"
                    Width="300" Height="250"
                    Margin="30,30,30,30">
                <Rectangle x:Name="plotArea"
                        Width="300" Height="250"
                        Stroke="Black"
                        StrokeThickness="1"/>
            </Canvas>
            <Grid Width="340" Height="100"
                    HorizontalAlignment="Left"
                    VerticalAlignment="Top">
                <Grid.ColumnDefinitions>
                    <ColumnDefinition Width="60" />
                    <ColumnDefinition Width="110" />
                    <ColumnDefinition Width="60"/>
                    <ColumnDefinition Width="110" />
                </Grid.ColumnDefinitions>
                <Grid.RowDefinitions>
                    <RowDefinition Height="Auto" />
                    <RowDefinition Height="Auto" />
                    <RowDefinition Height="Auto" />
                </Grid.RowDefinitions>
```

```xml
            <TextBlock Grid.Column="0" Grid.Row="0"
                    Margin="25,5,10,5">XMin</TextBlock>
            <TextBox Name="tbXMin" Grid.Column="1"
                Grid.Row="0"
                TextAlignment="Center">0</TextBox>
            <TextBlock Grid.Column="2" Grid.Row="0"
                    Margin="25,5,10,5">XMax</TextBlock>
            <TextBox Name="tbXMax" Grid.Column="3"
                Grid.Row="0"
                TextAlignment="Center">10</TextBox>
            <TextBlock Grid.Column="0" Grid.Row="1"
                    Margin="25,5,10,5">YMin</TextBlock>
            <TextBox Name="tbYMin" Grid.Column="1"
                Grid.Row="1"
                TextAlignment="Center" >0</TextBox>
            <TextBlock Grid.Column="2" Grid.Row="1"
                    Margin="25,5,10,5">YMax</TextBlock>
            <TextBox Name="tbYMax" Grid.Column="3"
                Grid.Row="1"
                TextAlignment="Center">10</TextBox>
            <Button Click="btnApply_Click"
                    Margin="40,20,20,0"
                    Height="25" Grid.ColumnSpan="2"
                    Grid.Column="0" Grid.Row="2">Apply
            </Button>
            <Button Click="btnClose_Click"
                    Margin="40,20,20,0"
                    Height="25" Grid.ColumnSpan="2"
                    Grid.Column="2" Grid.Row="2">Close
            </Button>
        </Grid>
        </StackPanel>
    </Viewbox>
</Window>
```

This XAML file places a Viewbox as the topmost element and sets its Stretch property to UniForm, which will preserve the aspect ratio of the child elements when the window gets resized. Otherwise, the Stretch property could have been set to Fill, which disregard the aspect ratio. The best thing about the ViewBox is that everything inside is scalable.

The graphics objects or drawings will be created on a canvas control, called plotCanvas. The rectangle, named plotArea, serves as the border of the rendering area. The other UI elements will be used to control the appearance of the graphics.

The corresponding C# code of the code-behind file is listed below:

```csharp
using System;
using System.Collections.Generic;
using System.Windows;
using System.Windows.Controls;
using System.Windows.Media;
using System.Windows.Shapes;
```

```
namespace Chapter02
{
    public partial class Chart2DSystem : Window
    {
        private double xMin = 0.0;
        private double xMax = 10.0;
        private double yMin = 0.0;
        private double yMax = 10.0;
        private Line line1;
        private Polyline polyline1;

        public Window1()
        {
            InitializeComponent();
            AddGraphics();
        }

        private void AddGraphics()
        {
            line1 = new Line();
            line1.X1 = XNormalize(2.0);
            line1.Y1 = YNormalize(4.0);
            line1.X2 = XNormalize(8.0);
            line1.Y2 = YNormalize(10.0);
            line1.Stroke = Brushes.Blue;
            line1.StrokeThickness = 2;
            plotCanvas.Children.Add(line1);

            polyline1 = new Polyline();
            polyline1.Points.Add(new Point(XNormalize(8),
                YNormalize(8)));
            polyline1.Points.Add(new Point(XNormalize(6),
                YNormalize(6)));
            polyline1.Points.Add(new Point(XNormalize(6),
                YNormalize(4)));
            polyline1.Points.Add(new Point(XNormalize(4),
                YNormalize(4)));
            polyline1.Points.Add(new Point(XNormalize(4),
                YNormalize(6)));
            polyline1.Points.Add(new Point(XNormalize(6),
                YNormalize(6)));
            polyline1.Stroke = Brushes.Red;
            polyline1.StrokeThickness = 5;
            plotCanvas.Children.Add(polyline1);
        }

        private double XNormalize(double x)
        {
            double result = (x - xMin) *
                plotCanvas.Width / (xMax - xMin);
            return result;
        }
```

```
private double YNormalize(double y)
{
    double result = plotCanvas.Height - (y - yMin)*
        plotCanvas.Height / (yMax - yMin);
    return result;
}

private void btnClose_Click(object sender,
                            EventArgs e)
{
    this.Close();
}

private void btnApply_Click(object sender,
                            EventArgs e)
{
    xMin = Convert.ToDouble(tbXMin.Text);
    xMax = Convert.ToDouble(tbXMax.Text);
    yMin = Convert.ToDouble(tbXMin.Text);
    yMax = Convert.ToDouble(tbYMax.Text);
    plotCanvas.Children.Remove(line1);
    plotCanvas.Children.Remove(polyline1);
    AddGraphics();
}
    }
}
```

In this code-behind file, we begin by defining private members to hold the minimum and maximum values of the custom coordinate axes. Note that by changing the values of xMin, xMax, yMin, and yMax, you can define any size of the rendering area you like depending on the requirements of your applications. Make sure that the units of these qualtities are in real-world units defined in the real-world coordinate system.

You may notice that there is an issue over how to draw graphics objects inside the rendering area, which should be independent of the units of the world coordinate system. Here we use the XNormalize and YNormalize methods to convert the X and Y coordinates in the real-world coordinate system to the default device-independent coordinate system. After this conversion, the units for all graphics objects are in device-independent pixels. This can be easily done by passing the X and Y coordinates of any unit in the world coordinate system to the XNormalize and YNormalize methods, which will perform the unit conversion automatically and always return the X and Y coordinates in device-independent pixels in the default WPF coordinate system.

Let's examine what we did inside the XNormalize method. We convert the X coordinate in the real-world coordinate system using the following formula:

```
double result = (x - xMin) *
                plotCanvas.Width / (xMax - xMin);
```

Here, we simply perform the scaling operation. Both (x – xMin) and (xMax – xMin) have the same unit in the world coordinate system, which is cancelled out by division. This means that the unit of this scaling term is determined solely by the unit of plotCanvas.Width, whose unit is in device-independent pixels. You can easily examine that the above conversion indeed provides not only the correct unit, but also the correct position in the default WPF coordinate system.

For the Y coordinate conversion, the situation is a bit different. You need to not only perform the scaling operation, but also reverse the Y axis in the default coordinate system. The following formula is used for the Y coordinate conversion:

```
double result = plotCanvas.Height - (y - yMin) *
                plotCanvas.Height / (yMax - yMin);
```

Next, you add a straight line (line1) and a polyline (polyline1) to the plotCanvas using the AddGraphics method. You draw the straight line from point (2, 4) to point (8, 10). The end points of this line are in the unit (which can be any unit!) defined in the world coordinate system. These points aren't directly used in drawing the line, but their converted X and Y coordinates are used instead. The same procedure is used to create the polyline object.

The click event of the "Apply" button allows you to redraw the straight line and polyline using new values for axis limits specified in corresponding TextBox elements. Notice that the statements inside the "Apply" button's event handler

```
plotCanvas.Children.Remove(line1);
plotCanvas.Children.Remove(polyline1);
```

are required. Otherwise, both the original and newly created graphics objects will remain on the screen. The above statements ensure that original objects are removed when new graphics objects are created.

Figure 2-11 shows the result of running this example. From this window, you can change the appearance of the graphics objects by changing the values of xMin, XMax, Ymin, and yMax, and then clicking the "Apply" button.

2D Viewport

A graphics object can be considered to be defined in its own coordinate system, which is some abstract place with boundaries. For example, suppose that you want to create a simple X-Y chart that plots Y-values from 50 to 100 over an X-data range from 0 to 10. You can work in a coordinate system space with $0 \leq X \leq 10$ and $50 \leq Y \leq 100$. This space is called the world coordinate system.

In practice, you usually aren't interested in the entire graphic, but only a portion of it. Thus, you can define the portion of interest as a specific area in the world coordinate system. This area of interest is called the "Window". In order to draw graphics objects on the screen, you need to map this "Window" to the default WPF coordinate system. We call this mapped "Window" in the default coordinate system a 2D viewport. The concept of the window and viewport in 2D space is illustrated in Figure 2-12.

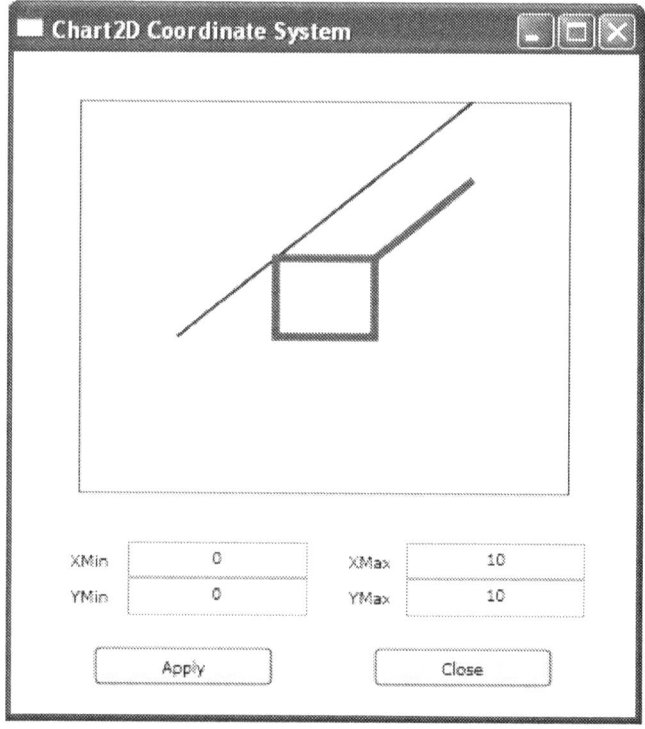

Figure 2-11 Draw a line and a polyline in the custom coordinate system.

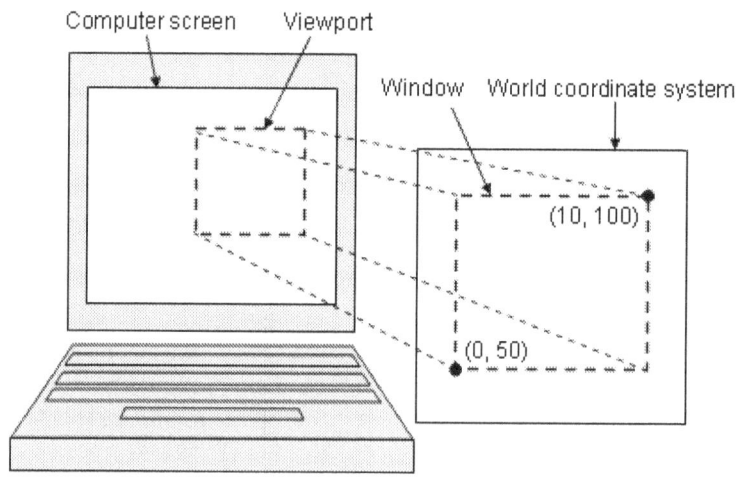

Figure 2-12 Window and viewport in 2D space.

In the previous section, we defined the default limits for the X and Y axes in the custom (world) coordinate system. For example:

```
private double xMin = 0.0;
private double xMax = 10.0;
private double yMin = 0.0;
private double yMax = 10.0;
```

This defines a portion of interest in the custom coordinate system. This area of interest is called the "Window". Once you know what you want to display, you need to decide where on the computer screen to display it. In previous example of Chart2DSystem, we defined a rendering area (plotCanvas) in the default WPF coordinate system, which creates a screen area to display the graphics objects. This rendering area is called the viewport.

You can use this viewport to change the apparent size and location of the graphics objects on the screen. Changing the viewport affects the display of the graphics objects on the screen. These effects are called "Zooming" and "Panning".

Zooming and Panning

The size and position of the "Window" determine which part of the graphics object is drawn. The relative size of the Window and the Viewport determine the scale at which the graphics object is displayed on the screen. For a given viewport or rendering area, a relatively large Window produces a small graphics object, because you are drawing a large piece of the custom coordinate space into a small viewport (rendering area). On the other hand, a relatively small Window produces a large graphics object. Therefore, you can increase the size of the Window (specified by the X and Y axis limits) to see the "zooming out" effect, which can be done by changing the values of the parameters, such as xMin, xMax, yMin, and yMax in the Chart2DSystem example discussed in the previous section. For instance, setting

```
xMin = -10;
xMax = 20;
yMin = 0;
yMax = 20;
```

and clicking the "Apply" button will generate the results shown in Figure 2-13.

On the other hand, if you decrease the Window size, the objects will appear larger on the screen; then you would have a "zoom in" effect. Change the parameters of your axis limits to the following:

```
xMin = 2;
xMax = 7;
yMin = 2;
yMax = 7;
```

You will get the following result by clicking the "Apply" button, as shown in Figure 2-14.

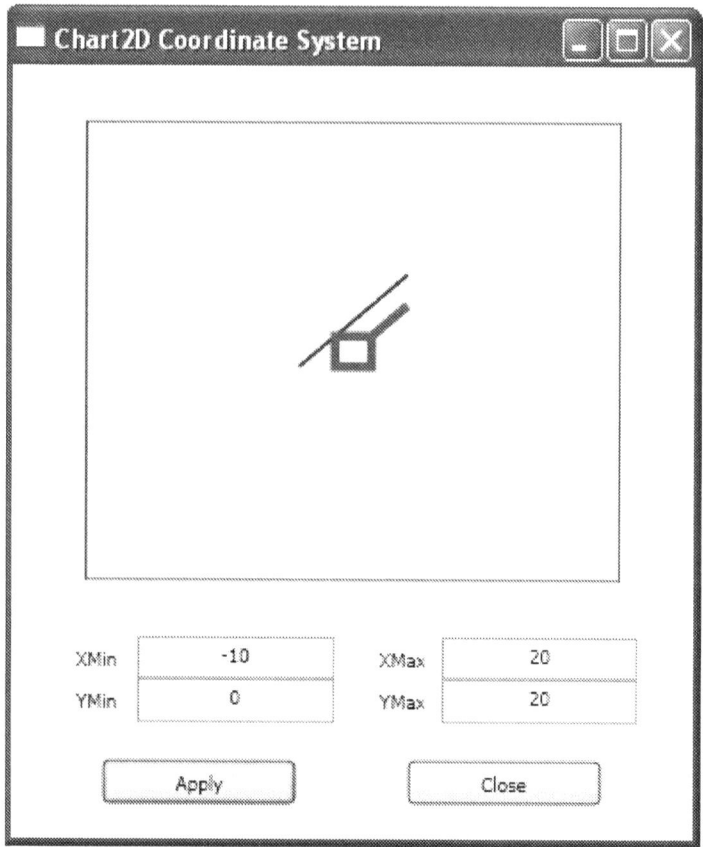

Figure 2-13 Both the size and location of the graphics objects are
changed by increasing the size of the Window: "Zoom out".

Panning is defined as the moving of all graphics objects in the scene by shifting the Window. In a panning process, the Window size is kept unchanged. For example, you can move the Window to the left by changing the following parameters:

```
xMin = -3;
xMax = 7;
yMin = 0;
yMax = 10;
```

This is equivalent to moving graphics objects toward the right side of the rendering area.

Please note that when you increase or decrease the size of graphics objects by zooming in or zooming out, the stroke thickness remains unchanged, which is different from when you directly scale the plotCanvas, where both the shape and stroke thickness change correspondingly with the scaling factor. In 2D charting applications, you usually want to change the size of the graphics only, and keep the stroke thickness unchanged.

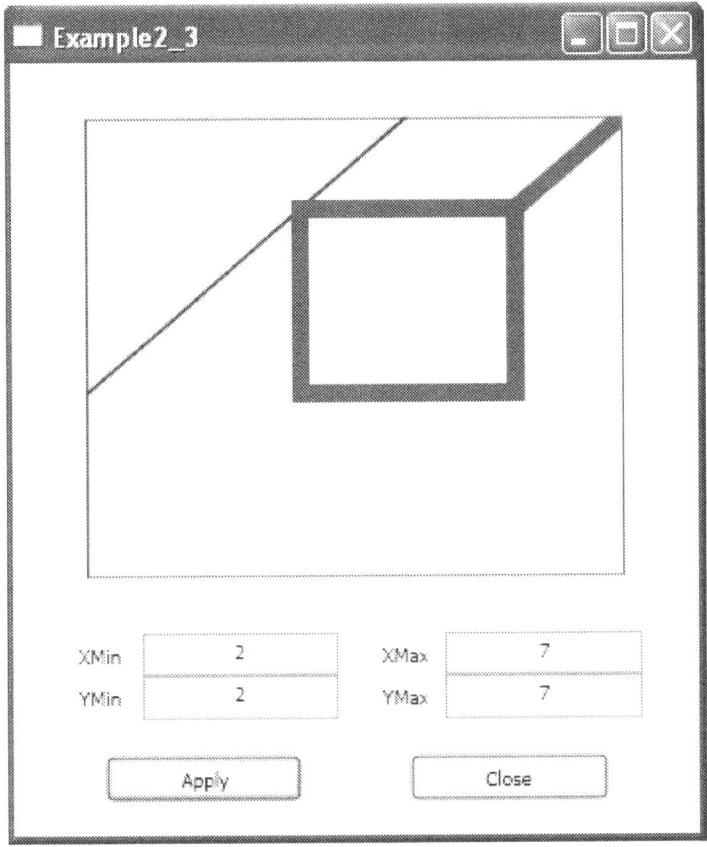

Figure 2-14 Both the size and location of the graphics objects are changed by decreasing the size of the Window: "Zoom in".

Basic 2D Graphics Shapes

The simplest way to create 2D graphics objects in a WPF application is to use the Shape class that represents a number of ready-to-use graphics shape objects. Available shape objects in WPF include Line, Polyline, Path, Rectangle, and Ellipse. These shapes are drawing primitives. You can combine these basic shapes to generate more complex graphics. In the following sections, we'll consider these basic WPF shapes.

Lines

The Line class in WPF is used to create straight lines between two end points. The X1 and Y1 properties specify the start point, and the X2 and Y2 properties represent the end point. The following XAML code snippet creates a blue line from point (30, 30) to point (180, 30):

```
<Line X1="30" Y1="30"
      X2 ="180" Y2="30"
      Stroke="Blue"
      StrokeThickness="2"/>
```

This code snippet produces a solid line. However, lines can have many different styles. For example, you can draw a dash-line with line caps, as shown in Figure 2-15. This means that a line can have three parts: the line body, starting cap, and ending cap.

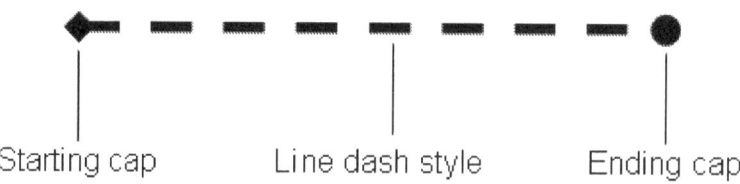

Figure 2-15 A line with starting cap, ending cap, and dash style.

The starting and ending caps can be specified by the StrokeStartLineCap and StrokeEndLineCap properties, respectively. Both the StrokeStartLineCap and StrokeEndLineCap get or set a PenLineCap enumeration value that describes the shape at the ends of a line. Available values in the PenLineCap enumeration include Flat, Round, Square, and Triangle. Unfortunately, the size of the line cap is the same as the StrokeThickness of the line. Thus, these caps aren't very useful in practical applications. If you want to create a line with an end anchor or an arrowhead, you have to create a custom shape, which will be discussed in Chapter 4.

The dash style of a line is specified by the StrokeDashArray property that gets or sets a collection of double variables, which specify the pattern of dashes and gaps of the line. Consider the following code snippet:

```
<Line X1="30" Y1="50" X2 ="250" Y2="50"
      Stroke="Blue" StrokeThickness="2"
      StrokeDashArray="5,3" />
```

The above code creates a dashed line, which is shown in Figure 2-16.

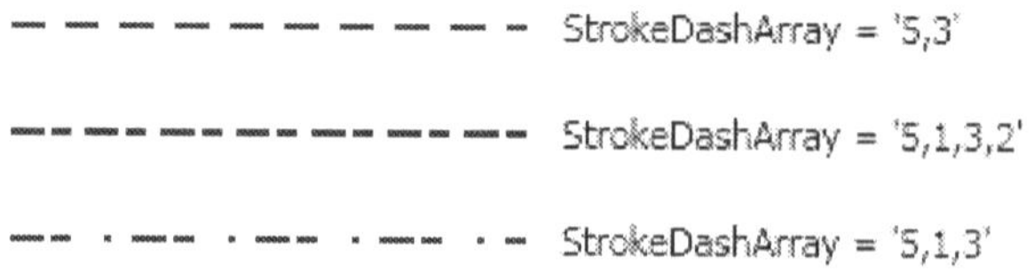

— — — — — — — —   StrokeDashArray = '5,3'

—- —- —- —- —-   StrokeDashArray = '5,1,3,2'

— · —- · —- · —   StrokeDashArray = '5,1,3'

Figure 2-16 Dash Lines with different patterns.

The first line in the figure is a dashed line that is specified by the StrokeDashArray="5,3". These values means that it has a line value of 5 and a gap of 3, interpreted relative to the StrokeThickness of the line. So if your line is 2 units thick (as it is in this example), the solid portion is 5 x 2 = 10 units, followed by a gap portion of 3 x 2 = 6 units. The line then repeats this pattern for its entire length.

You can create a line with more complex dash pattern by varying the values of the StrokeDashArray. For example, you can specify the StrokeDashArray as the following:

```
StrokeDashArray="5,1,3,2"
```

This creates a line with a more complex sequence: a solid portion that is 10 units length, then a 1 x 2 = 2 unit break, followed by a solid portion of 3 x 2 = 6 units, and another gap of 2 x 2 = 4 units. At the end of this sequence, the line repeats the pattern from the beginning.

A funny thing happens if you use an odd number of values for the StrokeDashArray. Take this one, for example:

```
StrokeDashArray="5,1,3"
```

When you draw this line, you begin with a 10 unit solid line, followed by a 2 unit gap, followed by a 6 unit line. But when it repeats the pattern it starts with a gap, indicating you get a 10 units space, followed by a 2 units line, and so on. The dash line simply alternates its pattern between solid portions and gaps, as shown in Figure 2-16.

The second line has a Round starting cap and a Triangle ending cap. If you reduce StrockThickness, it is difficult to see the line caps, making them not very useful in real-world applications

Rectangles and Ellipses

The rectangle and ellipse are the two simplest shapes. To create either one, set the Height and Width properties to define the size of the shape; then set the Fill and Stroke properties to make the shape visible.

The Rectangle class has two extra properties: RadiusX and RadiusY. When setting to nonzero values, these two properties allow you to create rectangles with rounded corners.

Let's consider an example that shows how to create rectangles in WPF. Add a new WPF Window to the project Chapter02 and name it RectangleShape. Here is the XAML file of this example:

```
<Window x:Class="Chapter02.RectangleShape"
    xmlns="http://schemas.microsoft.com/winfx
        /2006/xaml/presentation"
    xmlns:x="http://schemas.microsoft.com/winfx/2006/xaml"
    Title="Rectangles" Height="340" Width="200">
    <Grid>
```

```
<StackPanel>
    <TextBlock Text="RadiusX = 0, RadiusY = 0:"
               Margin="10 10 10 5"/>
    <Rectangle Width="150" Height="70"
               Fill="LightGray" Stroke="Black"/>
    <TextBlock Text="RadiusX = 20, RadiusY = 10:"
               Margin="10 10 10 5"/>
    <Rectangle Width="150" Height="70"
               RadiusX="20" RadiusY="10"
               Fill="LightGray" Stroke="Black"/>
    <TextBlock Text="RadiusX = 75, RadiusY = 35:"
               Margin="10 10 10 5"/>
    <Rectangle Width="150" Height="70"
               RadiusX="75" RadiusY="35"
               Fill="LightGray" Stroke="Black"/>
</StackPanel>
    </Grid>
</Window>
```

Figure 2-17 shows the results of running this example. You can easily create rectangles with rounded corners by specifying RadiusX and RadiusY properties with nonzero values. It can be seen that you can even create an ellipse by setting its RadiusX and RadiusY with large values (larger than the half of the respective side length).

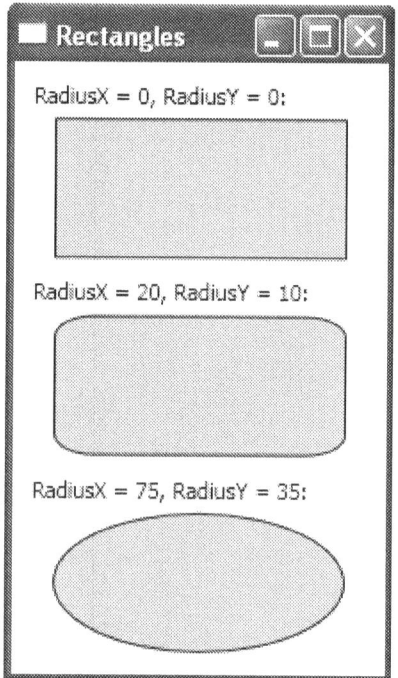

Figure 2-17 Rectangles in WPF.

You can create ellipse shape using properties similar to those used in creating rectangles. You can also create a circle by setting RadiusX = RadiusY.

Add a new WPF Window to the project Chapter02 and name it EllipseShape. Here is the XAML file of this example:

```
<Window x:Class="Chapter02.EllipseShape"
    xmlns="http://schemas.microsoft.com/winfx
        /2006/xaml/presentation"
    xmlns:x="http://schemas.microsoft.com/winfx/2006/xaml"
    Title="Ellipses" Height="280" Width="200">
  <Grid>
    <StackPanel>
        <TextBlock Text="Ellipse:" Margin="10 10 10 5"/>
        <Ellipse Width="150" Height="70"
            Fill="LightGray" Stroke="Black"/>
        <TextBlock Text="Circle:" Margin="10 10 10 5"/>
        <Ellipse Width="100" Height="100"
            Fill="LightGray" Stroke="Black"/>
    </StackPanel>
  </Grid>
</Window>
```

This example produces the results shown in Figure 2-18.

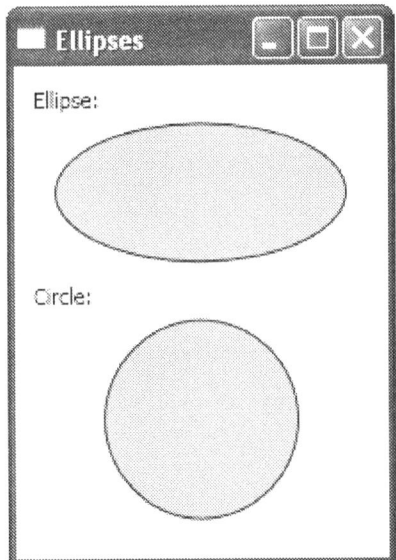

Figure 2-18 Ellipses in WPF.

Both rectangle and ellipse have the ability to resize themselves to fill the available space. If the Height and Width properties aren't specified, the shape is sized based on its container. The sizing behavior of a shape depends on the value of its stretch property. The default value is set to Fill, which stretches a shape to fill its container if an explicit size is not specified.

Let's consider another example that illustrates how to place and size rectangles and ellipses in Grid cells. Add a new WPF Window to the project Chapter02 and name it PlaceShapes. Here is the markup of this example:

```
<Window x:Class="Chapter02.PlaceShapes"
    xmlns="http://schemas.microsoft.com/winfx
        /2006/xaml/presentation"
    xmlns:x="http://schemas.microsoft.com/winfx/2006/xaml"
    Title="Place Shapes" Height="300" Width="360">

    <Grid ShowGridLines="True">
        <Grid.RowDefinitions>
            <RowDefinition Height="Auto"/>
            <RowDefinition/>
            <RowDefinition/>
        </Grid.RowDefinitions>
        <Grid.ColumnDefinitions>
            <ColumnDefinition Width="Auto"/>
            <ColumnDefinition/>
            <ColumnDefinition/>
            <ColumnDefinition/>
        </Grid.ColumnDefinitions>

        <TextBlock Grid.Column="0" Grid.Row="1"
                Text="Rectagle" Margin="5"/>
        <TextBlock Grid.Column="0" Grid.Row="2"
                Text="Ellipse" Margin="5"/>
        <TextBlock Grid.Column="1" Grid.Row="0" Text="Fill"
                TextAlignment="Center" Margin="5"/>
        <TextBlock Grid.Column="2" Grid.Row="0" Text="Uniform"
                TextAlignment="Center" Margin="5"/>
        <TextBlock Grid.Column="3" Grid.Row="0"
                Text="UniformToFill" TextAlignment="Center"
                Margin="5"/>

        <Rectangle Grid.Column="1" Grid.Row="1"
                Fill="LightGray" Stroke="Black"
                Stretch="Fill" Margin="5"/>
        <Rectangle Grid.Column="2" Grid.Row="1"
                Fill="LightGray" Stroke="Black"
                Stretch="Uniform" Margin="5"/>
        <Rectangle Grid.Column="3" Grid.Row="1"
                Fill="LightGray" Stroke="Black"
                Stretch="UniformToFill" Margin="5"/>

        <Ellipse Grid.Column="1" Grid.Row="2" Fill="LightGray"
                Stroke="Black" Stretch="Fill" Margin="5"/>
        <Ellipse Grid.Column="2" Grid.Row="2" Fill="LightGray"
                Stroke="Black" Stretch="Uniform" Margin="5"/>
        <Ellipse Grid.Column="3" Grid.Row="2" Fill="LightGray"
                Stroke="Black" Stretch="UniformToFill"
                Margin="5"/>
    </Grid>
</Window>
```

In this example, you create three rectangles and three ellipses, each shape with different Stretch property. Figure 2-19 shows the result of running this application. You can see how the different Stretch properties affect the appearances of shapes.

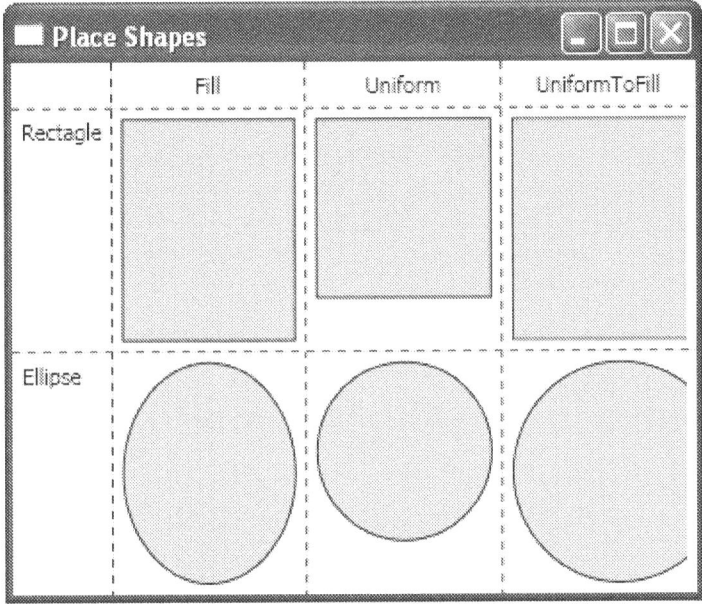

Figure 2-19 Shapes with different Stretch properties.

Polylines

The Polyline class allows you to draw a series connected straight lines. You simply provide a list of points using its Points property. The Points property requires a PointCollection object if you create a polyline using code. However, you can fill this collection in XAML by simply using a lean string-based syntax.

Let's consider an example that shows you how to create a simple polyline, a closed polyline, and a Sine curve in code. Add a new WPF Window to the project Chapter02 and name it Polylines. Here is the XAML file of this example:

```
<Window x:Class="Chapter02.Polylines"
    xmlns="http://schemas.microsoft.com/winfx
        /2006/xaml/presentation"
    xmlns:x="http://schemas.microsoft.com/winfx/2006/xaml"
    Title="Polylines" Height="340" Width="250">
    <Grid>
        <StackPanel Name="stackPanel1" Margin="10">
            <TextBlock Text="Polyline:"/>
            <Polyline Stroke="Black" StrokeThickness="3"
                Points="0 70,60 10,110 60,160 10,210 70"/>
            <TextBlock Text="Closed polyline:"
```

```
                         Margin="0 10 0 0"/>
        <Polyline Stroke="Black" StrokeThickness="3"
           Points="0 70,60 10,110 60,160 10,210 70, 0 70"/>
        <TextBlock Text="Sine curve:" Margin="0 10 0 0"/>
        <Polyline Name="polyline1" Stroke="Red"
                  StrokeThickness="2"/>
      </StackPanel>
    </Grid>
  </Window>
```

Here you create two polylines directly in the XAML file. You also define
another polyline called polyline1 that represents a Sine curve and needs to be
created in code. Here is the code-behind file used to generate the Sine curve:

```
using System;
using System.Windows;
using System.Windows.Media;
using System.Windows.Shapes;

namespace Chapter02
{
    public partial class Polylines : Window
    {
        public Polylines()
        {
            InitializeComponent();

            for (int i = 0; i < 70; i++)
            {
                double x = i * Math.PI;
                double y = 40 + 30 * Math.Sin(x/10);
                polyline1.Points.Add(new Point(x, y));
            }
        }
    }
}
```

Here, you simply add points to polyline1's Points collection using a Sine
function with a for-loop. Running this application produces the results shown in
Figure 2-20.

Polygons

The polygon is very similar to the polyline. Like the Polyline class, the Polygon
class has a Points collection that takes a list of X and Y coordinates. The only
difference is that the Polygon adds a final line segment that connects the final
point to the starting point. You can fill the interior of this shape using the Fill
property.

Add a new WPF Window to the project Chapter02 and name it Polygons. This
example fills the polylines in the previous example with a light gray color. Here
is the XAML file of this example:

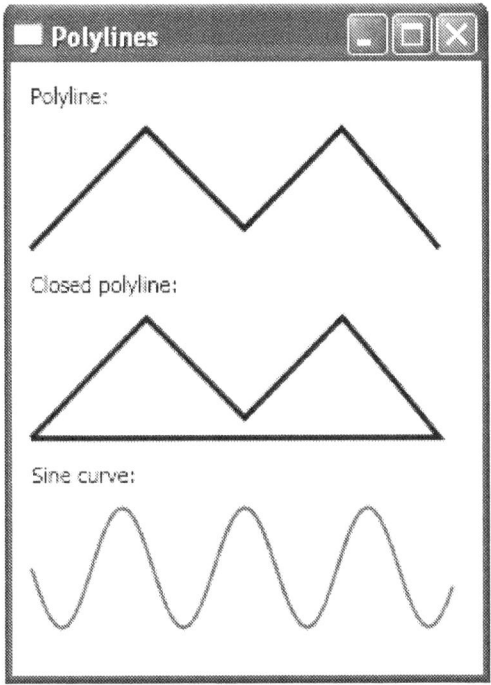

Figure 2-20 Polylines in WPF.

```
<Window x:Class="Chapter02.Polygons"
    xmlns="http://schemas.microsoft.com/winfx
        /2006/xaml/presentation"
    xmlns:x="http://schemas.microsoft.com/winfx/2006/xaml"
    Title="Polygons" Height="300" Width="300">
    <Grid>
        <StackPanel Name="stackPanel1" Margin="10">
            <TextBlock Text="Polygon:"/>
            <Polygon Stroke="Black" StrokeThickness="3"
                    Fill="LightGray"
                    Points="0 70,60 10,110 60,160 10,210 70"/>
            <TextBlock Text="Filled sine curve:"
                    Margin="0 10 0 0"/>
            <Polygon Name="polygon1" Stroke="Red"
                StrokeThickness="2" Fill="LightCoral"/>
        </StackPanel>
    </Grid>
</Window>
```

The polygon1 is created using a Sine function in the code-behind file:

```
using System;
using System.Windows;
using System.Windows.Media;
using System.Windows.Shapes;
```

```
namespace Chapter02
{
    public partial class Polygons : Window
    {
        public Polygons()
        {
            InitializeComponent();
            for (int i = 0; i < 71; i++)
            {
                double x = i * Math.PI;
                double y = 40 + 30 * Math.Sin(x / 10);
                polygon1.Points.Add(new Point(x, y));
            }
        }
    }
}
```

Running this application produces the results shown in Figure 2-21.

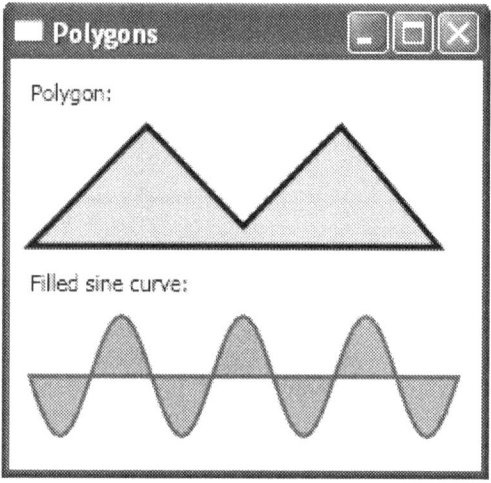

Figure 2-21 Polygons in WPF.

In a simple shape where the lines never cross, it is easy to fill the interior. However, sometimes, you'll have a more complex polygon where it isn't necessarily obvious what portions should be filled and what portions should not.

Let's consider an example, which shows a line that crosses more than one other line, leaving an irregular region at the center that you may or may not want to fill. Add a new WPF Window to the project Chapter02 and name it PolygonFillRule. Here is the XAML file of this example:

```
<Window x:Class="Chapter02.PolygonFillRule"
    xmlns="http://schemas.microsoft.com/winfx
        /2006/xaml/presentation"
    xmlns:x="http://schemas.microsoft.com/winfx/2006/xaml"
    Title="PolygonFillRule" Height="600" Width="300">
```

```
<Grid>
    <StackPanel Margin="10">
        <TextBlock Text="FileRule = EvenOdd:"
                Margin="0 0 0 5"/>
        <Polygon Stroke="Black" Fill="LightGray"
                FillRule="EvenOdd"
                Points="0 0,0 150,100 150,100 50,
                        50 50,50 100,150 100,150 0"/>
        <TextBlock Text="FileRule = NonZero:"
                Margin="0 10 0 5"/>
        <Polygon Stroke="Black" Fill="LightGray"
                FillRule="Nonzero"
                Points="0 0,0 150,100 150,100 50,50 50,
                        50 100,150 100,150 0"/>
        <TextBlock Text="FileRule = NonZero:"
                Margin="0 10 0 5"/>
        <Polygon Stroke="Black" Fill="LightGray"
                FillRule="Nonzero"
                Points="0 0,0 150,100 150,100 100,50 100,
                        50 50,100 50,100 100,150 100,150 0"/>
    </StackPanel>
</Grid>
</Window>
```

Here, you use the FillRule property to control the filled regions. Every polygon has a FillRule property that allows you to choose between two different methods for filling in regions, EvenOdd (the default value) or NonZero. In the EvenOdd case, in order to determine which region will be filled, WPF counts the number of lines that must be crossed to reach the outside of the shape. If this number is odd, the region is filled; if it is even, the region isn't filled, as shown in Figure 2-22.

When FillRule is set to NonZero, determining which region will be filled becomes tricky. In this case, WPF follows the same line-counting process as EvenOdd, but it takes into account the line direction. If the number of lines going in one direction is equal to the number of lines going in the opposite direction, the region isn't filled. If the difference between these two counts isn't zero, the region is filled.

Figure 2-23 shows the results of running this example.

The difference between the two shapes in the figure is that the order of points in the Points collection is different, leading to different line directions. This means that in the NonZero case, whether a region is filled or not depends on how you draw the shape, not what the shape itself looks like. Figure 2-23 clearly demonstrates this conclusion.

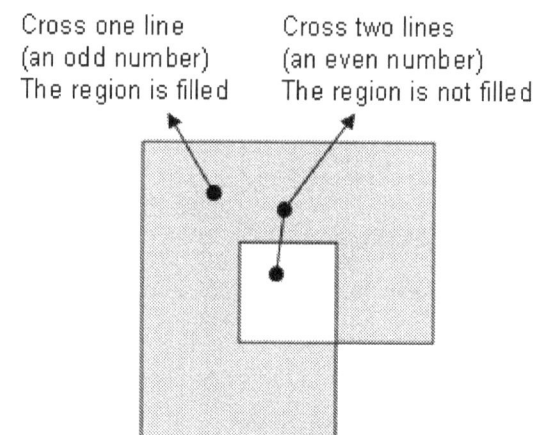

Figure 2-22 Determining filled regions when FillRule is set to EvenOdd.

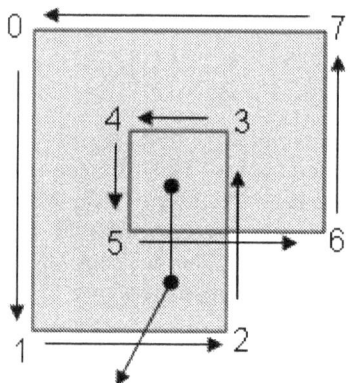

Cross two left-to-right lines
The count difference is not zero
The region is filled

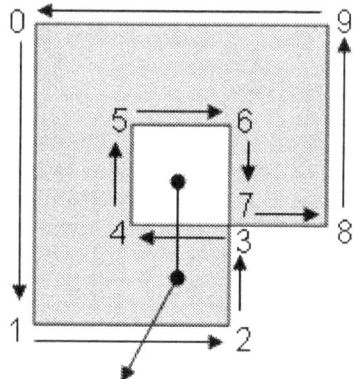

Cross one right-to-left line and
one left-to-right line
The count difference is zero
The region is not filled

Figure 2-23 Determining filled regions when FillRule is set to NonZero.

Chapter 3
2D Transformations

In the previous chapter, you learned about coordinate systems and basic shapes in WPF. To create complex shapes in real-world WPF applications, you need to understand transform operations on graphics objects.

In a graphics application, operations can be performed in different coordinate systems. Moving from one coordinate space to another requires the use of transformation matrices. In this chapter, we review the mathematic basis of vectors, matrices, and transforms in 2D space. Here we acknowledge the importance of matrices and transforms in graphics applications by presenting you with a more formal exposition for their properties. We concern ourselves with linear transformations among different coordinate systems. Such transforms include simple scaling, reflection, translation, and rotations. You'll learn how to perform matrix operations and graphics object transforms in WPF. More complicated transformations in 3D will be the topic of Chapter 9.

Basics of Matrices and Transforms

Vectors and matrices play an important role in the transformation process. WPF uses a row-major definition for both vectors and matrices. Thus, a vector is a row array and a matrix is a multi-dimensional array in WPF. This section explains the basics of 2D matrices and 2D transforms. As we discussed in the previous chapter, by changing the coordinates of a graphics object in the world coordinate system, such as zooming and panning, you can easily move the graphics object to another part of a viewport. However, if the graphic contains more than one object, you may want to move one of the objects without moving the others. In this case, you can't use simple zooming and panning to move the object because these approaches would move the other objects as well.

Instead, you can apply a transform to the object you want to move. Here we'll discuss transforms that scale, rotate, and translate an object.

Vectors and Points

In a row-major representation, a vector is a row array that represents a displacement in a 2D space. On the other hand, a point is defined by its X and Y coordinates at a fixed position, as shown in Figure 3-1.

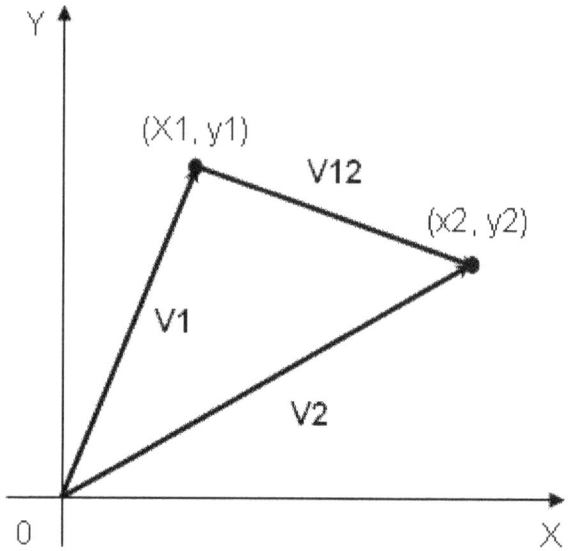

Figure 3-1 Points and Vectors.

The difference between a vector and a point is that a point represents a fixed position, while a vector represents a direction and a magnitude. Thus, the end points (x1, y1) and (x2, y2) of a line segment are points, but their difference V12 is a vector that represents the direction and length of that line segment. In WPF, the following code snippet is a valid statement:

```
Vector v12 = new Point(x2, y2) - new Point(x1, y1);
```

Mathematically, you should keep in mind that V12 = V2 – V1, where V2 and V1 are vectors from the origin to the point (x1, y1) and the point (x2, y2), respectively.

In WPF, you can apply a transform matrix directly to either a vector or a point.

Scaling

To scale or stretch an object in the X direction, you simply need to multiply the X coordinates of each of the object's points by the scaling factor s_x. Similarly, you can also scale an object in the Y direction. The scaling process can be described by the following equation:

$$(x1 \quad y1) = (x \quad y)\begin{pmatrix} s_x & 0 \\ 0 & s_y \end{pmatrix} = (s_x x \quad s_y y) \qquad (3.1)$$

For example, the scaling matrix that shrinks x and y uniformly by a factor of two, as well as a matrix that halves in the y direction and increases by three-halves in the x direction, are given below respectively:

$$\begin{pmatrix} 0.5 & 0 \\ 0 & 0.5 \end{pmatrix} \text{ and } \begin{pmatrix} 1.5 & 0 \\ 0 & 0.5 \end{pmatrix}$$

The above two scaling matrix operations have very different effects on objects, as shown in Figure 3-2.

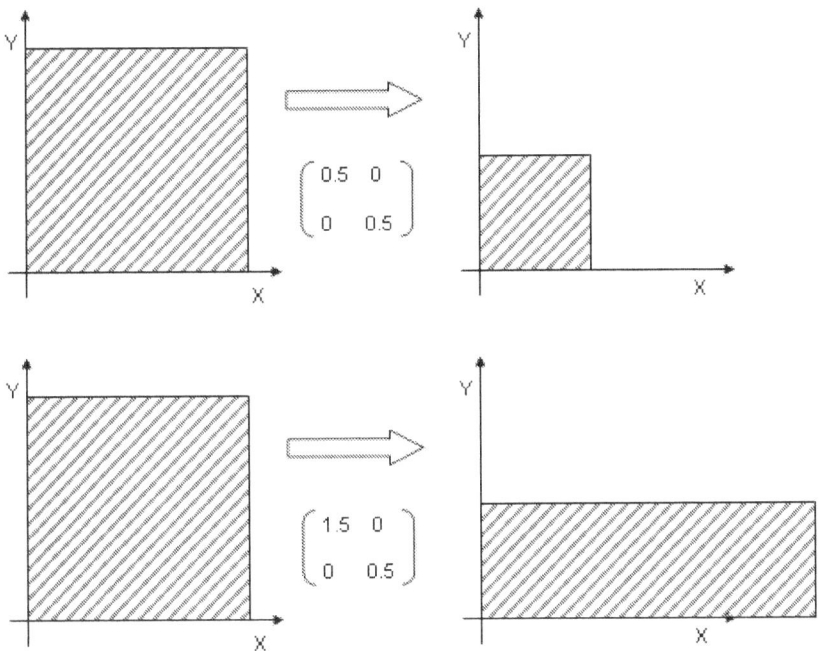

Figure 3-2 Uniform scaling by half in the x and y directions (top) and non-uniform scaling in the x and y directions (bottom).

Reflection

By reflecting an object across the X and Y axis, you can create a mirror image of the object. Reflecting an object across an axis is equivalent to scaling it with a negative scaling factor. The transform matrices across either of the coordinate axes can be written in the following forms:

Reflect across the x axis: $\begin{pmatrix} -1 & 0 \\ 0 & 1 \end{pmatrix}$

Reflect across the y axis: $\begin{pmatrix} 1 & 0 \\ 0 & -1 \end{pmatrix}$

As you might expect, a matrix with -1 in both elements of the diagonal is a reflection that is simply a rotation by 180 degrees.

Rotation

Suppose you want to rotate an object by an angle θ counter-clockwise. First, suppose you have a point (x1, y1) that you want to rotate by an angle θ to get to the point (x2, y2), as shown in Figure 3-3.

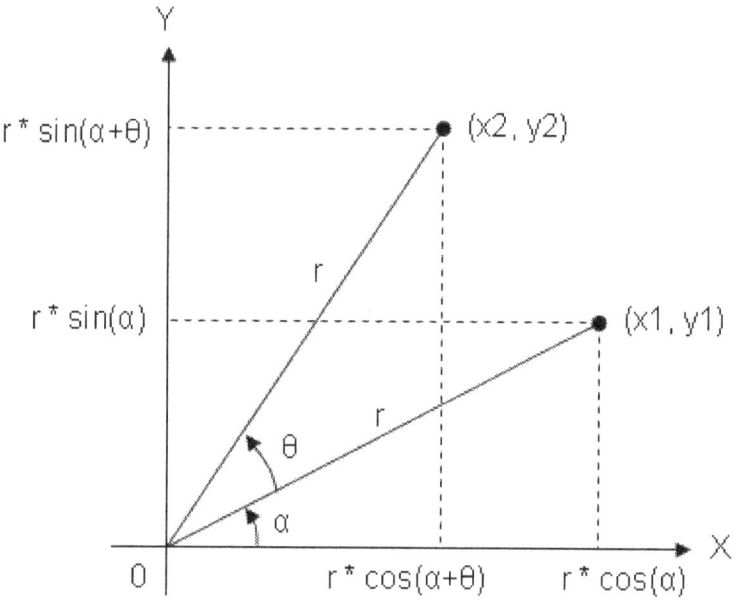

Figure 3-3 Rotation from point (x1, y1) to (x2, y2).

The distance from the point to the origin is assumed to be r. Then, we have the following relations:

$$x1 = r \cos \alpha$$
$$y1 = r \sin \alpha$$

The point (x2, y2) is the same point rotated by an additional angle of θ. Since this point also has a distance r from the origin, its coordinates are given by:

$$x2 = r \cos(\alpha + \theta) = r \cos \alpha \cos \theta - r \sin \alpha \sin \theta$$
$$y2 = r \sin(\alpha + \theta) = r \sin \alpha \cos \theta + r \cos \alpha \sin \theta$$

Substituting the components of x1 = $r\cos\alpha$ and y1 = $r\sin\alpha$ into the above equations gives

$$x2 = x1\cos\theta - y1\sin\theta$$
$$y2 = x1\sin\theta + y1\cos\theta$$

In matrix form, the equivalent rotation transform that takes point (x1, y1) to (x2, y2) is given by the following rotation matrix:

$$R(\theta) = \begin{pmatrix} \cos\theta & \sin\theta \\ -\sin\theta & \cos\theta \end{pmatrix} \tag{3.2}$$

Translation

To translate an object, you simply add an offset to the original X and Y coordinates of the points that make up the object

$$x1 = x + dx$$
$$y1 = y + dy \tag{3.3}$$

Although translations look very simple, they can't be expressed in terms of a transform matrix. It would be feasible to keep track of scales, reflections, and rotations as a matrix, while keeping track of translations separately. However, doing so would involve fairly painful bookkeeping, particularly the application includes many different transforms. Instead, you can use a technique to move the computation into a higher dimension. This technique allows you to treat the different transforms in a uniform or homogeneous way. This approach, called homogeneous coordinates, has become standard in almost every graphiccs program. In the following section, we'll introduce homogeneous coordinates that allow you to manipulate all of these transforms with matrices.

Homogeneous Coordinates

We expect that all transforms in 2D space, including scaling, reflection, rotation, and translation, can be treated equally if points are expressed in homogeneous coordinates. Homogeneous coordinates were first introduced in geometry and have been applied subsequently to graphics.

In homogeneous coordinates, you add a third coordinate to a point. Instead of being represented by a pair of (X, Y) numbers, each point is represented by a triple (X, Y, W). If the W coordinate is nonzero, you can divide through by it: (X, Y, W) represents the same point as (X/W, Y/W, 1). When W is nonzero, you normally perform this division, and the numbers X/W and Y/W are usually called the point coordinates in the homogeneous coordinate system. The points where W = 0 are called points at infinity.

Since vectors and points in 2D space are now three-element row arrays, transform matrices, which multiply a vector to produce another vector, should be 3 x 3.

Translation in Homogeneous Coordinates

In homogeneous coordinates, a translation can be expressed in the form:

$$(x1 \quad y1 \quad 1) = (x \quad y \quad 1) \begin{pmatrix} 1 & 0 & 0 \\ 0 & 1 & 0 \\ dx & dy & 1 \end{pmatrix} \tag{3.4}$$

The above transform can be expressed differently as

$$P_1 = P \cdot T(dx, dy) \tag{3.5}$$

Here P and P_1 represent point (x, y) and point (x1, y1) respectively, and T(dx, dy) is the translation matrix:

$$T(dx, dy) = \begin{pmatrix} 1 & 0 & 0 \\ 0 & 1 & 0 \\ dx & dy & 1 \end{pmatrix} \tag{3.6}$$

What happens if a point P is translated by T(dx1, dy1) to P_1; and then translated by T(dx2, dy2) to P_2? The result, you might intuitively expect, is a net translation of T(dx1 + dx2, dy1+ dy2). This can be confirmed by the definitions:

$$P_1 = P \cdot T(dx1, dy1)$$
$$P_2 = P_1 \cdot T(dx2, dy2)$$

From the above equations we have:

$$P_2 = P \cdot T(dx1, dy1) \cdot T(dx2, dy2)$$

The matrix product T(dx1, dy1) T(dx2, dy2) is

$$\begin{pmatrix} 1 & 0 & 0 \\ 0 & 1 & 0 \\ dx1 & dy1 & 1 \end{pmatrix} \begin{pmatrix} 1 & 0 & 0 \\ 0 & 1 & 0 \\ dx2 & dy2 & 1 \end{pmatrix} = \begin{pmatrix} 1 & 0 & 0 \\ 0 & 1 & 0 \\ dx1+dx2 & dy1+dy2 & 1 \end{pmatrix} \tag{3.7}$$

The net translation is indeed T(dx1 + dx2, dy1 + dy2).

Scaling in Homogeneous Coordinates

Similarly, the scaling equation (3.1) can be represented in matrix form in homogeneous coordinates as:

$$(x1 \quad y1 \quad 1) = (x \quad y \quad 1) \begin{pmatrix} s_x & 0 & 0 \\ 0 & s_y & 0 \\ 0 & 0 & 1 \end{pmatrix}$$

It can also be expressed in the form:

$$P_1 = P \cdot S(s_x, s_y) \tag{3.9}$$

Just as successive translations are additive, we expect that successive scalings should be multiplicative. Given

$$P_1 = P \cdot S(s_{x1}, s_{y1}) \tag{3.10}$$

$$P_2 = P_1 \cdot S(s_{x2}, s_{y2}) \tag{3.11}$$

Substituting Eq.(3.10) into Eq.(3.11) obtains

$$P_2 = (P \cdot S(s_{x1}, s_{y1})) \cdot S(s_{x2}, s_{y2}) = P \cdot (S(s_{x1}, s_{y1}) \cdot S(s_{x2}, s_{y2}))$$

The matrix product in the above equation is

$$\begin{pmatrix} s_{x1} & 0 & 0 \\ 0 & s_{y1} & 0 \\ 0 & 0 & 1 \end{pmatrix} \begin{pmatrix} s_{x2} & 0 & 0 \\ 0 & s_{y2} & 0 \\ 0 & 0 & 1 \end{pmatrix} = \begin{pmatrix} s_{x1}s_{x2} & 0 & 0 \\ 0 & s_{y1}s_{y2} & 0 \\ 0 & 0 & 1 \end{pmatrix}$$

Thus, scalings are indeed multiplicative.

Reflection is a special case of scaling with a scaling factor of -1. You can represent a reflection in the same way as scaling.

Rotation in Homogeneous Coordinates

A rotation in homogeneous coordinates can be represented as

$$(x1 \quad y1 \quad 1) = (x \quad y \quad 1) \begin{pmatrix} \cos\theta & \sin\theta & 0 \\ -\sin\theta & \cos\theta & 0 \\ 0 & 0 & 1 \end{pmatrix} \tag{3.12}$$

It can be also written as

$$P_1 = P \cdot R(\theta)$$

Where $R(\theta)$ is the rotation matrix in homogeneous coordinates. You would expect that two successive rotations should be additive. Given

$$P_1 = P \cdot R(\theta_1) \tag{3.13}$$

$$P_2 = P_1 \cdot R(\theta_2) \tag{3.14}$$

Substituting Eq. (3.13) into Eq. (3.14) gets

$$P_2 = (P \cdot R(\theta_1)) \cdot R(\theta_2) = P \cdot (R(\theta_1) \cdot R(\theta_2))$$

The matrix product $R(\theta_1)\, R(\theta_2)$ is

$$\begin{pmatrix} \cos\theta_1 & \sin\theta_1 & 0 \\ -\sin\theta_1 & \cos\theta_1 & 0 \\ 0 & 0 & 1 \end{pmatrix} \begin{pmatrix} \cos\theta_2 & \sin\theta_2 & 0 \\ -\sin\theta_2 & \cos\theta_2 & 0 \\ 0 & 0 & 1 \end{pmatrix}$$

$$= \begin{pmatrix} \cos\theta_1 \cos\theta_2 - \sin\theta_1 \sin\theta_2 & \cos\theta_1 \sin\theta_2 + \sin\theta_1 \cos\theta_2 & 0 \\ -\sin\theta_1 \cos\theta_2 - \cos\theta_1 \sin\theta_2 & \cos\theta_1 \cos\theta_2 - \sin\theta_1 \sin\theta_2 & 0 \\ 0 & 0 & 1 \end{pmatrix}$$

$$= \begin{pmatrix} \cos(\theta_1 + \theta_2) & \sin(\theta_1 + \theta_2) & 0 \\ -\sin(\theta_1 + \theta_2) & \cos(\theta_1 + \theta_2) & 0 \\ 0 & 0 & 1 \end{pmatrix}$$

Thus, rotations are indeed additive.

Combining Transforms

It is common for graphics applications to apply more than one transform to a graphics object. For example, you might want to first apply a scaling transform S, and then a rotation transform R. You can combine the fundamental S, T, and R matrices to produce desired general transform results. The basic purpose of combining transforms is to gain efficiency by applying a single composed transform to a point, rather than applying a series of transforms, one after another.

Consider the rotation of an object about some arbitrary point P1. Since you only know how to rotate about the origin, you need to convert the original problem into several separate problems. Thus, to rotate about P1, you need to perform a sequence of several fundamental transformations:

- Translate it so that the point is at the origin
- Rotate it to the desired angle
- Translate so that the point at the origin returns back to P1.

This sequence is illustrated in Figure 3-4, in which a rectangle is rotated about P1 (x1, y1). The first translation is by (-x1,-y1), whereas the later translation is by the inverse (x1, y1). The result is quite different from that of applying just the rotation. The net transformation is

$$T(-x1,-y1) \cdot R(\theta) \cdot T(x1,y1) = \begin{pmatrix} 1 & 0 & 0 \\ 0 & 1 & 0 \\ -x1 & -y1 & 1 \end{pmatrix} \begin{pmatrix} \cos\theta & \sin\theta & 0 \\ -\sin\theta & \cos\theta & 0 \\ 0 & 0 & 1 \end{pmatrix} \begin{pmatrix} 1 & 0 & 0 \\ 0 & 1 & 0 \\ x1 & y1 & 1 \end{pmatrix}$$

$$= \begin{pmatrix} \cos\theta & -\sin\theta & 0 \\ \sin\theta & \cos\theta & 0 \\ x1\cdot(1-\cos\theta)+y1\cdot\sin\theta & y1\cdot(1-\cos\theta)-x1\cdot\sin\theta & 1 \end{pmatrix}$$

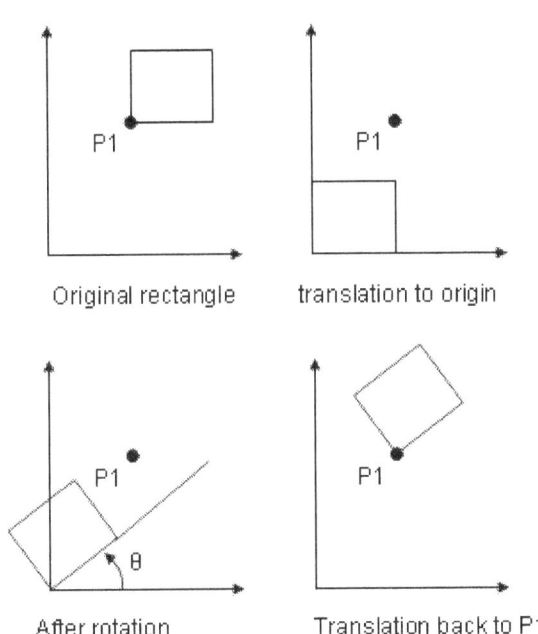

Figure 3-4 Rotation of a rectangle about a point P1.

Vector and Matrix in WPF

WPF implements a Vector and a Matrix structure in homogeneous coordinates in 2D space. It uses a convention of pre-multiplying matrices by row vectors. A point or a vector in homogeneous coordinates is defined using three double values (X, Y, 1). In WPF, they can also be expressed in terms of two doubles (X, Y) since the third double is always equal to one.

Vector Structure

A vector in WPF is defined using structure. A structure is similar in nature to a class. Both the class and structure can contain data members and function members. One major difference between a structure and a class is that a structure is a value type and therefore is stored in the stack. On the other hand, a class is a reference type, and it stores a reference to a dynamically allocated object. Usually, structures have a performance advantage over classes because structures are allocated on the stack and are immediately de-allocated when out of scope. Note that a structure can't inherit from another class or structure; i.e., a structure can't be a base class due to its implicitly sealed nature. Structures are not permitted to have a parameterless constructor. Many simple math functions, including vector and matrix in WPF are defined using structures because of their performance advantage.

A Vector object is a row array with three elements in homogeneous coordinates. Since the last element is always equal to one, only the first two elements need to be specified. For instance:

```
Vector v = new Vector(10, 20);
```

Note that a vector and a point in WPF are two different objects. The following statement is invalid in WPF:

```
Vector v = new Point(10,20);
```

However, you can define a Vector using Points, or vice versa:

```
Vector v1 = new Point(10, 20) - new Point(20, 30);
Vector v2 = (Vector)new Point(10,20);
Point pt1 = (Point)new Vector(10, 20);
```

A Vector has four public properties:

- Length – Gets the length of the vector.

- LengthSquared – Gets the square of the length of the vector.

- X – Gets or sets the X component of the vector.

- Y – Gets or sets the Y component of the vector.

In addition, there are methods assocated with vectors that allow you to perform various mathematical operations on them. The following are some frequently used methods:

- Add – Adds a vector to a point or another vector.

- Subtract – Subtracts a vector from another vector.

- Multiply – Multiplies a vector by a specified double, matrix, or vector, and returns the result as a vector.

- Divide – Divides a vector by a scalar and returns a vector.

- CrossProduct – Calculates the cross product of two vectors.

- AngleBetween – Retrieves the angle, expressed in degrees, between two vectors.

- Normalize – Normalizes the vector.

For example:

```
Vector v1 = new Vector(20, 10);
Vector v2 = new Vector(10, 20);
Vector cross = Vector.CrossProduct(v1, v2);
Vector angle = Vector.AngleBetween(v1, v2);
v1.Normalize();
double length2 = v1.LengthSQuared;
```

This generates the output: cross = 300 with a direction along the Z axis, which can be easily confirmed by the formula

$$result = v1.X \cdot v2.Y - v1.Y \cdot v2.X = 20 \cdot 20 - 10 \cdot 10 = 300,$$

and angle = 36.87 degrees, which can be confirmd by the following formula used to calculate the angle between these two vectors:

$$\theta = \arctan\left(\frac{v2.Y}{v2.X}\right) - \arctan\left(\frac{v1.Y}{v1.X}\right) = \arctan(10/20) - \arctan(20/10) = 36.87 \deg$$

The normalized result of v1 is stored in v1 again; in this case, v1 becomes (0.894, 0.447), which is confirmed by its length squared: length2 = 1.

Matrix Structure

We have demonstrated that the transform matrices in homogeneous coordinates always have a last column of (0 0 1). It can be shown that any combined transform matrix using these fundamental transforms has the same last column. Based on this fact, WPF defines the transform in terms of a 3x2 matrix. Namely, the matrix structure in WPF takes 6 elements arranged in 3 rows by 2 columns. In methods and properties, the Matrix object is usually specified as a vector with six members, as follows: (M11, M12, M21, M22, OffsetX, OffsetY). The OffsetX and OffsetY represent translation values.

For example, the default identity matrix constructed by the default constructor has a value of (1, 0, 0, 1, 0, 0). In matrix representation, this means:

$$\begin{pmatrix} 1 & 0 \\ 0 & 1 \\ 0 & 0 \end{pmatrix}. \text{ This is a simplification of } \begin{pmatrix} 1 & 0 & 0 \\ 0 & 1 & 0 \\ 0 & 0 & 1 \end{pmatrix}. \text{ The last column is always } \begin{pmatrix} 0 \\ 0 \\ 1 \end{pmatrix}.$$

Thus a translation of of 3 units in the X direction and 2 units in the Y direction would be represented as (1, 0, 0, 1, 3, 2). In matrix form, we should have:

$$\begin{pmatrix} 1 & 0 \\ 0 & 1 \\ 3 & 2 \end{pmatrix}. \text{ This is a simplification of } \begin{pmatrix} 1 & 0 & 0 \\ 0 & 1 & 0 \\ 3 & 2 & 1 \end{pmatrix}.$$

You can create a matrix object in WPF by using overloaded constructors, which take an array of double values (which hold the matrix items) as arguments.

Please note that before using the matrix class in your applications, you need to add a reference to the System.Windows.Media namespace. The following code snippet creates three matrix objects for translation, scaling, and rotation in code:

```
double dx = 3;
double dy = 2;
double sx = 0.5;
double sy = 1.5;
double theta = Math.PI / 4;
double sin = Math.Sin(theta);
double cos = Math.Cos(theta);
Matrix tm = new Matrix(1, 0, 0, 1, dx, dy);
Matrix sm = new Matrix(sx, 0, 0, sy, 0, 0);
Matrix rm = new Matrix(cos, sin, -sin, cos, 0, 0);
```

The matrix tm is a translation matrix that moves an object by 3 units in the x direction and by 2 units in the y direction. The scaling matrix sm scales an object by a factor of 0.5 in the x direction and by a factor of 1.5 in the y direction. The other matrix rm is a rotation matrix that rotates an object by 45 degrees about the origin.

In addition to the properties of these six matrix elements, there are four other public properties associated with a matrix, which are:

- Determinant – Gets the determinant of the Matrix structure.

- HasInverse – Gets a value that indicates whether the Matrix structure is invertible.

- Identity – Gets an identity matrix.

- IsIdentity – Gets a value that indicates whether the Matrix structure is an identity matrix.

There are many public methods associated with the Matrix structure which allow you to perform various matrix operations.

Matrix Operations

The Matrix structure in WPF provides methods to perform rotation, scale, and translation. It also implements several methods to perform matrix operations. For example, the Invert method is used to reverse a matrix if it is invertible. This method takes no parameters. The Multiply method multiplies two matrices and returns the result in a new matrix. The following are some of the frequently used methods for matrix operations:

- Scale – Appends the specified scale vector to the Matrix structure.

- ScaleAt – Scale the matrix by the specified amount about the specified point.

- Translate – Appends a translation of the specified offsets to the Matrix structure.

- Rotate – Applies a rotation of the specified angle about the origin of the Matrix structure.

- RotateAt – Rotates the matrix about the specified point.

- Skew – Appends a skew of the specified angles in the X and Y directions to the Matrix structure.

- Invert – Inverts the Matrix structure.

- Multiply – Multiplies a Matrix structure by another Matrix structure.

- Transform – Transforms the specified point, array of points, vector, or array of vectors by the Matrix structure.

There are also corresponding Prepend methods associated with the Scale, Translation, Rotation, and Skew. The default method is Append. Both Append and Prepend determine the matrix order. Append specifies that the new operation is applied after the preceding operation; Prepend specifies that the new operation is applied before the preceding operation during cumulative operations.

Let's consider an example that shows how to perform matrix operations in WPF. Start with a new WPF Windows Application project, and name it Chapter03. Add a new WPF Window called MatrixOperation to the project.

Here is the XAML file of this example:

```
<Window x:Class="Chapter03.MatrixOperations"
    xmlns="http://schemas.microsoft.com/winfx
        /2006/xaml/presentation"
    xmlns:x="http://schemas.microsoft.com/winfx/2006/xaml"
    Title="Matrix Operations" Height="250" Width="250">
    <Grid>
        <StackPanel>
            <TextBlock Margin="10,10,5,5"
                    Text="Original Matrix:"/>
            <TextBlock x:Name="tbOriginal" Margin="20,0,5,5"/>
            <TextBlock Margin="10,0,5,5"
                    Text="Inverted Matrix:"/>
            <TextBlock x:Name="tbInvert" Margin="20,0,5,5"/>
            <TextBlock Margin="10,0,5,5"
                    Text="Original Matrices:"/>
            <TextBlock x:Name="tbM1M2" Margin="20,0,5,5"/>
            <TextBlock Margin="10,0,5,5" Text="M1 x M2:"/>
            <TextBlock x:Name="tbM12" Margin="20,0,5,5"/>
            <TextBlock Margin="10,0,5,5" Text="M2 x M1:"/>
            <TextBlock x:Name="tbM21" Margin="20,0,5,5"/>
        </StackPanel>
    </Grid>
</Window>
```

This markup creates the layout for displaying results using TextBlocks. The matrix operations are performed in the corresponding code-behind file, as listed below:

```
using System;
using System.Windows;
using System.Windows.Media;

namespace Chapter03
{
    public partial class MatrixOperations : Window
    {
        public MatrixOperation()
        {
            InitializeComponent();

            // Invert matrix:
            Matrix m = new Matrix(1, 2, 3, 4, 0, 0);
            tbOriginal.Text = "(" +  m.ToString() +")";
            m.Invert();
            tbInvert.Text = "(" + m.ToString() + ")";

            // Matrix multiplication:
            Matrix m1 = new Matrix(1, 2, 3, 4, 0, 1);
            Matrix m2 = new Matrix(0, 1, 2, 1, 0, 1);
            Matrix m12 = Matrix.Multiply(m1, m2);
            Matrix m21 = Matrix.Multiply(m2, m1);

            tbM1M2.Text = "M1 = (" + m1.ToString() + "), " +
                " M2 = (" + m2.ToString() + ")";
            tbM12.Text = "(" + m12.ToString() + ")";
            tbM21.Text = "(" + m21.ToString() + ")";
        }
    }
}
```

This code-behind file performs matrix inversion and multiplications. In particular, it shows that the results of the matrix multiplication depend on the order of the matrix operations. Executing this example generates the output shown in Figure 3-5.

First, let's examine the matrix invert method which inverts a matrix (1, 2, 3, 4, 0, 0). The Matrix.Invert method gives the result (-2, 1, 1.5, -0.5, 0, 0). This can be easily confirmed by considering the matrix operation: matrix (1, 2, 3, 4, 0, 0) multiplied by (-2, 1, 1.5, -0.5, 0, 0) should be equal to an identity matrix (1, 0, 0, 1, 0, 0). In fact:

$$
\begin{pmatrix} 1 & 2 & 0 \\ 3 & 4 & 0 \\ 0 & 0 & 1 \end{pmatrix}
\begin{pmatrix} -2 & 1 & 0 \\ 1.5 & -0.5 & 0 \\ 0 & 0 & 1 \end{pmatrix}
=
\begin{pmatrix} -2+2\times1.5 & 1-2\times0.5 & 0 \\ -2\times3+4\times1.5 & 3-4\times0.5 & 0 \\ 0 & 0 & 1 \end{pmatrix}
=
\begin{pmatrix} 1 & 0 & 0 \\ 0 & 1 & 0 \\ 0 & 0 & 1 \end{pmatrix}
$$

which is indeed an identity matrix, as expected.

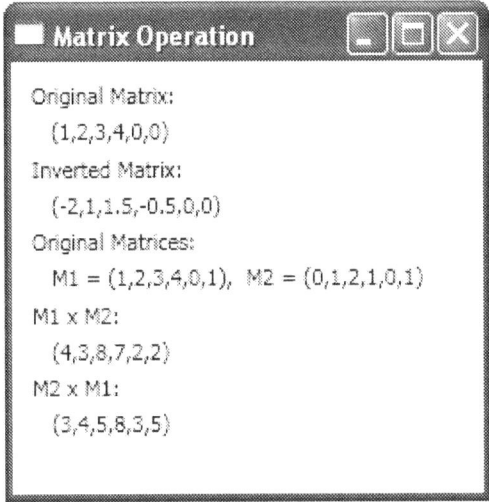

Figure 3-5 Results of matrix operations in WPF.

Next, let's consider the matrix multiplication. In the code, you created two matrices m1 = (1, 2, 3, 4, 0, 1) and m2 = (0, 1, 2, 1, 0, 1). You first multiply m1 by m2 and return the result in m12, then multiply m2 by m1 and store the result in m21. Please note that the result is stored in m1 if the matrix m1 is multiplied by m2. You can see from Figure 3-5 that M12 = (4, 3, 8, 7, 2, 2). In fact:

$$\begin{pmatrix} 1 & 2 & 0 \\ 3 & 4 & 0 \\ 0 & 1 & 1 \end{pmatrix} \begin{pmatrix} 0 & 1 & 0 \\ 2 & 1 & 0 \\ 0 & 1 & 1 \end{pmatrix} = \begin{pmatrix} 4 & 3 & 0 \\ 8 & 7 & 0 \\ 2 & 2 & 1 \end{pmatrix}$$

For M21 = m2 x m1, you would expect the following result:

$$\begin{pmatrix} 0 & 1 & 0 \\ 2 & 1 & 0 \\ 0 & 1 & 1 \end{pmatrix} \begin{pmatrix} 1 & 2 & 0 \\ 3 & 4 & 0 \\ 0 & 1 & 1 \end{pmatrix} = \begin{pmatrix} 3 & 4 & 0 \\ 5 & 8 & 0 \\ 3 & 5 & 1 \end{pmatrix}$$

which is consistent with (3, 4, 5, 8, 3, 5) shown in the figure.

Matrix Transforms

As mentioned in the previous section, the matrix structure in WPF also provides methods to rotate, scale, and translate the matrices.

Both the Rotate and RotateAt methods are used to rotate a matrix. The Rotate method rotates a matrix at a specified angle. This method takes a single argument, a double value, specifying the angle. The RotateAt method is useful when you need to change the center of the rotation. Its first parameter is the angle; and the second and third parameters (of type double) specify the center of rotation.

Let's illustrate the basic matrix transforms (translation, scaling, rotation, and skew) in WPF through an example. Add a new WPF Window to the project Chapter03 and name it MatrixTransforms. The following is the XAML file of this example:

```
<Window x:Class="Chapter03.MatrixTransforms"
    xmlns="http://schemas.microsoft.com/winfx
        /2006/xaml/presentation"
    xmlns:x="http://schemas.microsoft.com/winfx/2006/xaml"
    Title="Matrix Transforms" Height="450" Width="270">
    <StackPanel>
        <TextBlock Margin="10,10,5,5"
                    Text="Original Matrix:"/>
        <TextBlock Name="tbOriginal" Margin="20,0,5,5"/>
        <TextBlock Margin="10,0,5,5" Text="Scale:"/>
        <TextBlock Name="tbScale" Margin="20,0,5,5"/>
        <TextBlock Margin="10,0,5,5" Text="Scale - Prepend:"/>
        <TextBlock Name="tbScalePrepend" Margin="20,0,5,5"/>
        <TextBlock Margin="10,0,5,5" Text="Translation:"/>
        <TextBlock Name="tbTranslate" Margin="20,0,5,5"/>
        <TextBlock Margin="10,0,5,5"
                    Text="Translation - Prepend:"/>
        <TextBlock Name="tbTranslatePrepend"
                    Margin="20,0,5,5"/>
        <TextBlock Margin="10,0,5,5" Text="Rotation:"/>
        <TextBlock Name="tbRotate" Margin="20,0,5,5"
                    TextWrapping="Wrap"/>
        <TextBlock Margin="10,0,5,5"
                    Text="Rotation - Prepend:"/>
        <TextBlock Name="tbRotatePrepend"
                    Margin="20,0,5,5" TextWrapping="Wrap"/>
        <TextBlock Margin="10,0,5,5" Text="RotationAt:"/>
        <TextBlock x:Name="tbRotateAt" Margin="20,0,5,5"
                    TextWrapping="Wrap"/>
        <TextBlock Margin="10,0,5,5"
                    Text="RotationAt - Prepend:"/>
        <TextBlock x:Name="tbRotateAtPrepend"
                    Margin="20,0,5,5" TextWrapping="Wrap"/>
        <TextBlock Margin="10,0,5,5" Text="Skew:"/>
        <TextBlock Name="tbSkew" Margin="20,0,5,5"/>
        <TextBlock Margin="10,0,5,5" Text="Skew - Prepend:"/>
        <TextBlock Name="tbSkewPrepend" Margin="20,0,5,5"/>
    </StackPanel>
</Window>
```

This markup creates the layout for displaying results using TextBlocks, which are embedded into a StackPanel control. The corresponding code-behind file is given by the following code:

```
using System;
using System.Windows;
using System.Windows.Media;

namespace Chapter03
```

```
{
    public partial class MatrixTransform : Window
    {
        public MatrixTransform()
        {
            InitializeComponent();

            // Original matrix:
            Matrix m = new Matrix(1, 2, 3, 4, 0, 1);
            tbOriginal.Text = "(" + m.ToString() + ")";

            //Scale:
            m.Scale(1, 0.5);
            tbScale.Text = "(" + m.ToString() + ")";

            // Scale - Prepend:
            m = new Matrix(1, 2, 3, 4, 0, 1);
            m.ScalePrepend(1, 0.5);
            tbScalePrepend.Text = "(" + m.ToString() + ")";

            //Translation:
            m = new Matrix(1, 2, 3, 4, 0, 1);
            m.Translate(1, 0.5);
            tbTranslate.Text = "(" + m.ToString() + ")";

            // Translation - Prepend:
            m = new Matrix(1, 2, 3, 4, 0, 1);
            m.TranslatePrepend(1, 0.5);
            tbTranslatePrepend.Text =
                    "(" + m.ToString() + ")";

            //Rotation:
            m = new Matrix(1, 2, 3, 4, 0, 1);
            m.Rotate(45);
            tbRotate.Text = "(" + MatrixRound(m).ToString()
                            + ")";

            // Rotation - Prepend:
            m = new Matrix(1, 2, 3, 4, 0, 1);
            m.RotatePrepend(45);
            tbRotatePrepend.Text = "(" +
                MatrixRound(m).ToString() + ")";

            //Rotation at (x = 1, y = 2):
            m = new Matrix(1, 2, 3, 4, 0, 1);
            m.RotateAt(45, 1, 2);
            tbRotateAt.Text = "(" +
                    MatrixRound(m).ToString() + ")";

            // Rotation at (x = 1, y = 2) - Prepend:
            m = new Matrix(1, 2, 3, 4, 0, 1);
            m.RotateAtPrepend(45, 1, 2);
            tbRotateAtPrepend.Text = "(" +
                MatrixRound(m).ToString() + ")";
```

```
// Skew:
m = new Matrix(1, 2, 3, 4, 0, 1);
m.Skew(45, 30);
tbSkew.Text =
    "(" + MatrixRound(m).ToString() + ")";

// Skew - Prepend:
m = new Matrix(1, 2, 3, 4, 0, 1);
m.SkewPrepend(45, 30);
tbSkewPrepend.Text =
    "(" + MatrixRound(m).ToString() + ")";
}

private Matrix MatrixRound(Matrix m)
{
    m.M11 = Math.Round(m.M11, 3);
    m.M12 = Math.Round(m.M12, 3);
    m.M21 = Math.Round(m.M21, 3);
    m.M22 = Math.Round(m.M22, 3);
    m.OffsetX = Math.Round(m.OffsetX, 3);
    m.OffsetY = Math.Round(m.OffsetY, 3);
    return m;
}
}
}
```

Building and running this application generate the output shown in Figure 3-6. The original matrix m = (1, 2, 3, 4, 0, 1) is operated on by various transforms. First, let's examine the scale transform that sets the scaling factor as 1 in the x direction and 0.5 in the y direction. For the Apppend scaling (the default setting), we have:

$$\begin{pmatrix} 1 & 2 & 0 \\ 3 & 4 & 0 \\ 0 & 1 & 1 \end{pmatrix} \begin{pmatrix} 1 & 0 & 0 \\ 0 & 0.5 & 0 \\ 0 & 0 & 1 \end{pmatrix} = \begin{pmatrix} 1 & 1 & 0 \\ 3 & 2 & 0 \\ 0 & 0.5 & 1 \end{pmatrix}$$

This gives the same result (1, 1, 3, 2, 0, 0.5) shown in Figure 3-6. On the other hand, for the Prepend scaling, we have:

$$\begin{pmatrix} 1 & 0 & 0 \\ 0 & 0.5 & 0 \\ 0 & 0 & 1 \end{pmatrix} \begin{pmatrix} 1 & 2 & 0 \\ 3 & 4 & 0 \\ 0 & 1 & 1 \end{pmatrix} = \begin{pmatrix} 1 & 2 & 0 \\ 1.5 & 2 & 0 \\ 0 & 1 & 1 \end{pmatrix}$$

This confirms the result (1, 2, 1.5, 2, 0, 1) shown in Figure 3-6.

Then, we translate the matrix m by one unit in the X direction, and by a half unit in the Y direction. For the Append (the default setting) translation, we have:

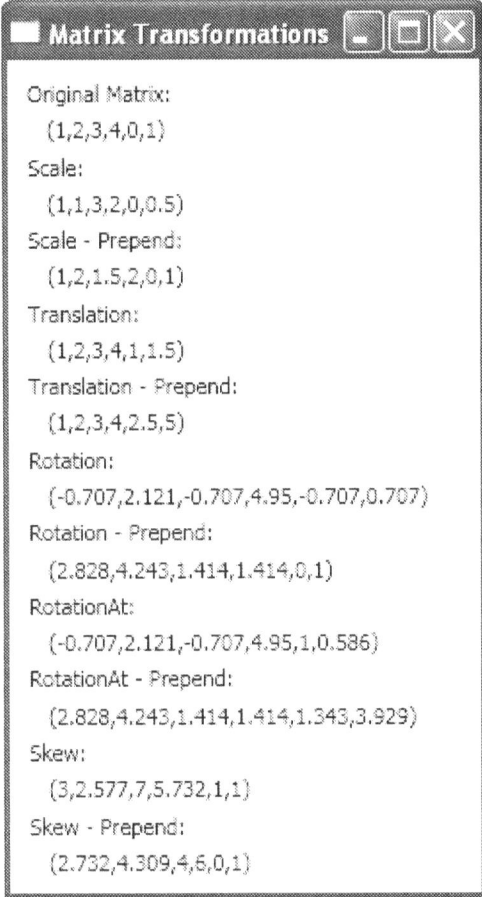

Figure 3-6 The results of matrix transformations.

$$\begin{pmatrix} 1 & 2 & 0 \\ 3 & 4 & 0 \\ 0 & 1 & 1 \end{pmatrix} \begin{pmatrix} 1 & 0 & 0 \\ 0 & 1 & 0 \\ 1 & 0.5 & 1 \end{pmatrix} = \begin{pmatrix} 1 & 2 & 0 \\ 3 & 4 & 0 \\ 1 & 1.5 & 1 \end{pmatrix}$$

This is consistent with the result (1, 2, 3, 4, 1, 1.5) shown in Figure 3-6.

For the Prepend translation, we perform the following transformation:

$$\begin{pmatrix} 1 & 0 & 0 \\ 0 & 1 & 0 \\ 1 & 0.5 & 1 \end{pmatrix} \begin{pmatrix} 1 & 2 & 0 \\ 3 & 4 & 0 \\ 0 & 1 & 1 \end{pmatrix} = \begin{pmatrix} 1 & 2 & 0 \\ 3 & 4 & 0 \\ 2.5 & 5 & 1 \end{pmatrix}$$

This confirms the result (1, 2, 3, 4, 2.5, 5) shown in Figure 3-6.

For the rotation transformation, the original m matrix is rotated by 45 degrees. In the case of the Append rotation, we have:

$$\begin{pmatrix} 1 & 2 & 0 \\ 3 & 4 & 0 \\ 0 & 1 & 1 \end{pmatrix} \begin{pmatrix} \cos(\pi/4) & \sin(\pi/4) & 0 \\ -\sin(\pi/4) & \cos(\pi/4) & 0 \\ 0 & 0 & 1 \end{pmatrix} = \begin{pmatrix} -0.707 & 2.121 & 0 \\ -0.707 & 4.949 & 0 \\ -0.707 & 0.707 & 1 \end{pmatrix}$$

Note that in the above calculation, we have used the fact that $\cos(\pi/4) = \sin(\pi/4)$ = 0.707. This gives the same result (-0.707, 2.121, -0.707, 4.95, -0.707, 0.707) as that given in Figure 3-6.

For the Prepend rotation, we have:

$$\begin{pmatrix} \cos(\pi/4) & \sin(\pi/4) & 0 \\ -\sin(\pi/4) & \cos(\pi/4) & 0 \\ 0 & 0 & 1 \end{pmatrix} \begin{pmatrix} 1 & 2 & 0 \\ 3 & 4 & 0 \\ 0 & 1 & 1 \end{pmatrix} = \begin{pmatrix} 2.828 & 4.243 & 0 \\ 1.414 & 1.414 & 0 \\ 0 & 1 & 1 \end{pmatrix}$$

This result is the same as (2.828, 4.243, 1.414, 1.414, 0, 1) shown in Figure 3-6.

The RotateAt method is designed for cases in which you need to change the center of rotation. In fact, the Rotate method is a special case of RotateAt with the rotation center at (0, 0). In this example, the matrix m is rotated by 45 degrees at the point (1, 2). As discussed previously in this chapter, the rotation of an object about an arbitrary point P1 must be performed according to the following procedures:

• Translate P1 to the origin.

• Rotate it to the desired angle.

• Translate so that the point at the origin returns back to P1.

Considering the matrix transform definition in WPF, the rotation matrix at point (1, 2) should be expressed in the following form:

$T(-dx,-dy) \cdot R(\theta) \cdot T(dx,dy)$

$$= \begin{pmatrix} 1 & 0 & 0 \\ 0 & 1 & 0 \\ -1 & -2 & 1 \end{pmatrix} \begin{pmatrix} \cos(\pi/4) & \sin(\pi/4) & 0 \\ -\sin(\pi/4) & \cos(\pi/4) & 0 \\ 0 & 0 & 1 \end{pmatrix} \begin{pmatrix} 1 & 0 & 0 \\ 0 & 1 & 0 \\ 1 & 2 & 1 \end{pmatrix} = \begin{pmatrix} 0.707 & 0.707 & 0 \\ -0.707 & 0.707 & 0 \\ 1.707 & -0.121 & 1 \end{pmatrix}$$

Thus, the Append rotation of Matrix m by 45 degrees at Point(1,2) becomes:

$$\begin{pmatrix} 1 & 2 & 0 \\ 3 & 4 & 0 \\ 0 & 1 & 1 \end{pmatrix} \begin{pmatrix} 0.707 & 0.707 & 0 \\ -0.707 & 0.707 & 0 \\ 1.707 & -0.121 & 1 \end{pmatrix} = \begin{pmatrix} -0.707 & 2.121 & 0 \\ -0.707 & 4.949 & 0 \\ 1 & 0.586 & 1 \end{pmatrix}$$

This gives the same result of (-0.707, 2.121, -0.707, 4.949, 1, 0.586) shown in Figure 3-6. The minor difference is due to the decimal rounding.

Similarly, for the Prepend rotation of Matrix m by 45 degrees at Point(1, 2) should be:

$$\begin{pmatrix} 0.707 & 0.707 & 0 \\ -0.707 & 0.707 & 0 \\ 1.707 & -0.121 & 1 \end{pmatrix}\begin{pmatrix} 1 & 2 & 0 \\ 3 & 4 & 0 \\ 0 & 0 & 1 \end{pmatrix} = \begin{pmatrix} 2.828 & 4.242 & 0 \\ 1.414 & 1.414 & 0 \\ 1.344 & 3.93 & 1 \end{pmatrix}$$

Again, the result is the same as the one shown in Figure 3-6.

Finally, we'll examine the Skew method, which provides a shearing transform. This method takes two double arguments, AngleX and AngleY, which represent the horizontal and vertical skew factors. The skew transformation in homogeneous coordinates can be expressed in the form:

$$\begin{pmatrix} x1 & y1 & 1 \end{pmatrix} = \begin{pmatrix} x & y & 1 \end{pmatrix}\begin{pmatrix} 1 & \tan(AngleY) & 0 \\ \tan(AngleX) & 1 & 0 \\ 0 & 0 & 1 \end{pmatrix}$$

$$= \begin{pmatrix} x + y\tan(AngleX) & y + x\tan(AngleY) & 1 \end{pmatrix}$$

where tan(AngleX) and tan(AngleY) are the skew transform factors in the X and Y directions, respectively. Return to the Skew transform in this example. The skew angles used in the example are AngleX = 45 degrees and AngleY = 30 degrees. In this case, the Skew matrix is given by

$$\begin{pmatrix} 1 & \tan(30^o) & 0 \\ \tan(45^o) & 1 & 0 \\ 0 & 0 & 1 \end{pmatrix} = \begin{pmatrix} 1 & 0.577 & 0 \\ 1 & 1 & 0 \\ 0 & 0 & 1 \end{pmatrix}$$

Thus, for the Append skew transformation, we have:

$$\begin{pmatrix} 1 & 2 & 0 \\ 3 & 4 & 0 \\ 0 & 1 & 1 \end{pmatrix}\begin{pmatrix} 1 & 0.577 & 0 \\ 1 & 1 & 0 \\ 0 & 0 & 1 \end{pmatrix} = \begin{pmatrix} 3 & 2.577 & 0 \\ 7 & 5.732 & 0 \\ 1 & 1 & 1 \end{pmatrix}$$

This confirms the result shown in Figure 3-6.

For the Prepend Skew transformation, we have:

$$\begin{pmatrix} 1 & 0.577 & 0 \\ 1 & 1 & 0 \\ 0 & 0 & 1 \end{pmatrix}\begin{pmatrix} 1 & 2 & 0 \\ 3 & 4 & 0 \\ 0 & 1 & 1 \end{pmatrix} = \begin{pmatrix} 2.732 & 4.308 & 0 \\ 4 & 6 & 0 \\ 0 & 1 & 1 \end{pmatrix}$$

This result is again the same as the one given in Figure 3-6.

Here, we have presented detailed explanations of the matrix transforms in WPF. This information is useful for understanding the definitions and internal representations of matrices in WPF, and applying matrices to your applications correctly.

Creating Perpendicular Lines

Remember that the matrix transforms discussed in the previous sections can't be directly applied to graphics objects. Instead, they can only be applied to points and vectors. If these transforms aren't related to the objects, you may ask why we need them in the first place. Here, I'll show you that you do need matrix transforms in some real-world applications.

I'll use an example to demonstrate how to use matrix transforms in a WPF application. The example application is very simple. As shown in Figure 3-7, for a given line segment (the solid line) specified by two end points, (x1, y1) and (x2, y2), we want to find a perpendicular line segment (the dashed line) at one end (for example, at Point(x2, y2)) of the original line segment.

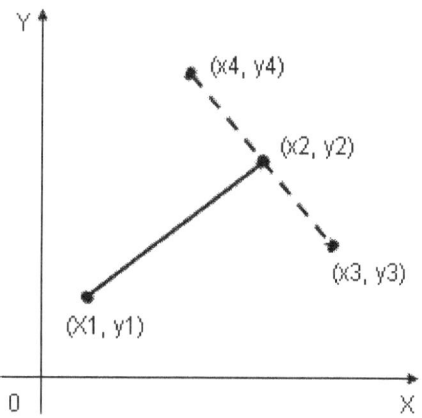

Figure 3-7 Creating a perpendicular line for a given line segment.

Open the project Chapter03 and add a new WPF Window to the project. Name this new Window PerpendicularLine. Create a user interface using the following XAML code:

```
<Window x:Class="Chapter03.PerpendicularLine"
    xmlns="http://schemas.microsoft.com/winfx
        /2006/xaml/presentation"
    xmlns:x="http://schemas.microsoft.com/winfx/2006/xaml"
    Title="Perpendicular Line" Height="300" Width="400">

    <Viewbox Stretch="Uniform">
        <Grid Width="430" Height="300"
            HorizontalAlignment="Left"
            VerticalAlignment="Top">
            <Grid.ColumnDefinitions>
                <ColumnDefinition Width="150" />
                <ColumnDefinition Width="280" />
            </Grid.ColumnDefinitions>
            <Grid Width="140" Height="300" Margin="5,10,5,5">
                <Grid.ColumnDefinitions>
```

```xml
        <ColumnDefinition Width="60" />
        <ColumnDefinition Width="70" />
    </Grid.ColumnDefinitions>
    <Grid.RowDefinitions>
        <RowDefinition Height="Auto" />
        <RowDefinition Height="Auto" />
        <RowDefinition Height="Auto" />
        <RowDefinition Height="Auto" />
        <RowDefinition Height="Auto" />
        <RowDefinition Height="Auto" />
        <RowDefinition Height="Auto" />
    </Grid.RowDefinitions>

    <TextBlock HorizontalAlignment="Right"
            Grid.Column="0" Grid.Row="0"
            Margin="5,5,10,5">X1</TextBlock>
    <TextBox Name="tbX1" Grid.Column="1"
            Grid.Row="0"
            TextAlignment="Center">50</TextBox>
    <TextBlock HorizontalAlignment="Right"
            Grid.Column="0" Grid.Row="1"
            Margin="5,5,10,5">Y1</TextBlock>
    <TextBox Name="tbY1" Grid.Column="1"
            Grid.Row="1"
            TextAlignment="Center">200</TextBox>
    <TextBlock HorizontalAlignment="Right"
            Grid.Column="0" Grid.Row="2"
            Margin="5,5,10,5">X2</TextBlock>
    <TextBox Name="tbX2" Grid.Column="1"
            Grid.Row="2"
            TextAlignment="Center">150</TextBox>
    <TextBlock HorizontalAlignment="Right"
            Grid.Column="0" Grid.Row="3"
            Margin="5,5,10,5">Y2</TextBlock>
    <TextBox Name="tbY2" Grid.Column="1"
            Grid.Row="3"
            TextAlignment="Center">100</TextBox>
    <TextBlock HorizontalAlignment="Right"
            Grid.Column="0" Grid.Row="4"
            Margin="5,5,10,5">Length</TextBlock>
    <TextBox Name="tbLength" Grid.Column="1"
            Grid.Row="4"
            TextAlignment="Center">100</TextBox>
    <Button Click="BtnApply_Click"
            Margin="15,20,15,5"
            Grid.Row="5" Height="25"
            Grid.ColumnSpan="2"
            Grid.Column="0">Apply</Button>
    <Button Click="BtnClose_Click"
            Margin="15,0,15,5"
            Grid.Row="6" Height="25"
            Grid.ColumnSpan="2"
            Grid.Column="0">Close</Button>
</Grid>
```

```
<Canvas Name="canvas1" Grid.Column="1"
        Margin="10" ClipToBounds="True"
        Width="270" Height="280">
    <TextBlock Name="tbPoint1"
        Canvas.Top="10">Point1</TextBlock>
    <TextBlock Name="tbPoint2"
        Canvas.Top="25">Point2</TextBlock>
    <TextBlock Name="tbPoint3"
        Canvas.Top="40">Point3</TextBlock>
    <TextBlock Name="tbPoint4"
        Canvas.Top="55">Point4</TextBlock>
</Canvas>
        </Grid>
    </Viewbox>
</Window>
```

This XAML code creates a user interface that allows you to specify the end points of the line and the length of the perpendicular line segment. The corresponding code-behind file of this example is given below:

```csharp
using System;
using System.Windows;
using System.Windows.Controls;
using System.Windows.Media;
using System.Windows.Shapes;

namespace Chapter03
{
    public partial class PerpendicularLine : Window
    {
        private Line line1;
        private Line line2;
        public PerpendicularLine()
        {
            InitializeComponent();
            Rectangle rect = new Rectangle();
            rect.Stroke = Brushes.Black;
            rect.Width = canvas1.Width;
            rect.Height = canvas1.Height;
            canvas1.Children.Add(rect);
            line1 = new Line();
            line2 = new Line();
            AddLines();
        }

        private void AddLines()
        {
            Point pt1 = new Point();
            Point pt2 = new Point();

            pt1.X = Convert.ToDouble(tbX1.Text);
            pt1.Y = Convert.ToDouble(tbY1.Text);
            pt2.X = Convert.ToDouble(tbX2.Text);
```

```
        pt2.Y = Convert.ToDouble(tbY2.Text);
        double length =
              0.5 * Convert.ToDouble(tbLength.Text);

        line1 = new Line();
        line1.X1 = pt1.X;
        line1.Y1 = pt1.Y;
        line1.X2 = pt2.X;
        line1.Y2 = pt2.Y;
        line1.Stroke = Brushes.Gray;
        line1.StrokeThickness = 4;
        canvas1.Children.Add(line1);
        Canvas.SetLeft(tbPoint1, pt1.X);
        Canvas.SetTop(tbPoint1, pt1.Y);
        Canvas.SetLeft(tbPoint2, pt2.X);
        Canvas.SetTop(tbPoint2, pt2.Y);
        tbPoint1.Text = "Pt1(" + pt1.ToString() + ")";
        tbPoint2.Text = "Pt2(" + pt2.ToString() + ")";

        Vector v1 = pt1 - pt2;
        Matrix m1 = new Matrix();
        Point pt3 = new Point();
        Point pt4 = new Point();
        m1.Rotate(-90);
        v1.Normalize();
        v1 *= length;
        line2 = new Line();
        line2.Stroke = Brushes.Gray;
        line2.StrokeThickness = 4;
        line2.StrokeDashArray =
              DoubleCollection.Parse("3, 1");
        pt3 = pt2 + v1 * m1;
        m1 = new Matrix();
        m1.Rotate(90);
        pt4 = pt2 + v1 * m1;
        line2.X1 = pt3.X;
        line2.Y1 = pt3.Y;
        line2.X2 = pt4.X;
        line2.Y2 = pt4.Y;
        canvas1.Children.Add(line2);
        Canvas.SetLeft(tbPoint3, pt3.X);
        Canvas.SetTop(tbPoint3, pt3.Y);
        Canvas.SetLeft(tbPoint4, pt4.X);
        Canvas.SetTop(tbPoint4, pt4.Y);
        pt3.X = Math.Round(pt3.X, 0);
        pt3.Y = Math.Round(pt3.Y, 0);
        pt4.X = Math.Round(pt4.X, 0);
        pt4.Y = Math.Round(pt4.Y, 0);
        tbPoint3.Text = "Pt3(" + pt3.ToString() + ")";
        tbPoint4.Text = "Pt4(" + pt4.ToString() + ")";
}

public void BtnApply_Click(object sender, EventArgs e)
{
```

```
            if (line1 != null)
                canvas1.Children.Remove(line1);
            if (line2 != null)
                canvas1.Children.Remove(line2);
            AddLines();
        }

        public void BtnClose_Click(object sender, EventArgs e)
        {
            this.Close();
        }
    }
}
```

Here, we first create a Line segment (line1) using two end points specified by the user, then create a vector using these two end points:

```
            Vector v1 = pt1 - pt2;
```

This gives the direction of line1. The perpendicular line you want to create will have a length specified by the user. We want the vector to have the same length as the perpendicular line (line2), so we use the following statements:

```
            v1.Normalize();
            v1 *= length;
```

This vector is first normalized to a unit vector, then multiplied by the length of the perpendicular line. Now, the vector has the proper length and direction along Point(x2, y2) to Point(x1, y1). If we rotate this vector by 90 or -90 degrees at Point(x2, y2), we'll obtain a perpendicular line. This can be achieved using the code snippet:

```
            Matrix m1 = new Matrix();
            m1.Rotate(-90);
            pt3 = pt2 + v1 * m1;
            m1 = new Matrix();
            m1.Rotate(90);
            pt4 = pt2 + v1 * m1;
```

Here a rotation matrix m1 is used to rotate the vector by 90 or -90 degrees to find two end points that define the perpendicular line.

Executing this project produces the results shown in Figure 3-8. The user interface allows the user to specify arbitrary points and length, and the program automatically draws the perpendicular line on the screen.

If you change the rotation angle and make some modifications to the program, you can easily create a line with an arrowhead.

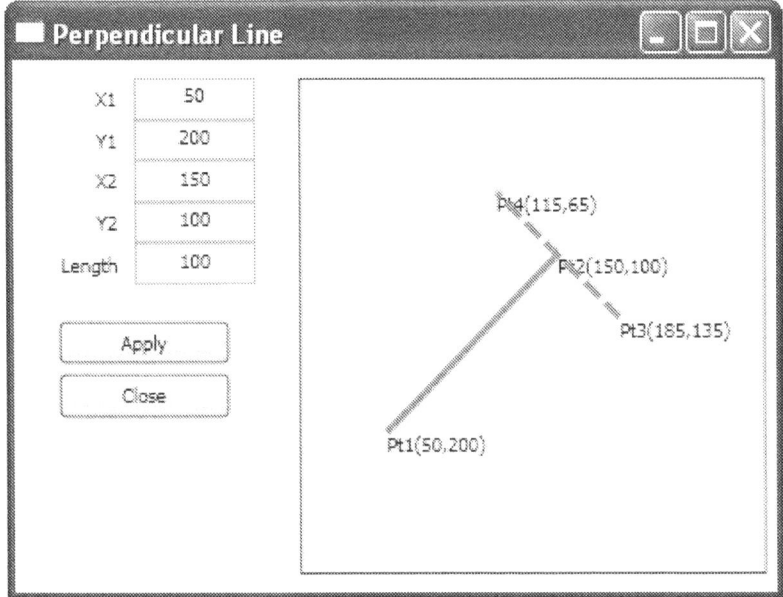

Figure 3-8 A perpendicular line in WPF.

Object Transforms in WPF

In the previous sections, we discussed the Vector and Matrix structures, as well as their operations in WPF. The Matrix structure can be applied to a Point or a Vector object. However, if you want to apply 2D transforms to objects or coordinate systems, you need to use the Transform classes. In WPF, there are five derived classes that can be used to perform specific transforms on objects:

- ScaleTransform – Scales an object in both the X and Y directions. The ScaleX property specifies how much to stretch or shrink an object along the X direction, and the ScaleY property specifies how much to stretch or shrink an object along the Y direction. Scale operations are centered on the point specified by the CenterX and CenterY properties.

- TranslateTransform – Defines a translation along the X and Y directions. The amount the object translated is specified using the X and Y properties.

- RotateTransform – Rotates an object in 2D space by specifying an angle using the Angle property and a center point specified by the CenterX and CenterY properties.

- SkewTransform – Defines a 2D skew that stretches the coordinate space in a non-uniform manner. Use the CenterX and CenterY properties to specify the center point for the transform. Use the AngleX and AngleY properties to specify the skew angle along the X and Y directions.

- MatrixTransform – Creates an affine matrix transform to manipulate an object in 2D space using a custom transform that isn't provided by the other Transform classes. Affine transform matrices can be multiplied to form any number of linear transforms, such as rotation and skew, followed by translation.

The structure of the TransformMatrix is the same as the Matrix structure in WPF. In the homogeneous coordinate system, the TransformMatrix always has a last column of (0, 0, 1). Based on this fact, WPF defines the TransformMatrix in terms of a 3x2 matrix. Namely, the TransformMatrix classes in WPF take 6 elements arranged in 3 rows by 2 columns. In methods and properties, the transform matrix is usually specified as a vector with six members, as follows: (M11, M12, M21, M22, OffsetX, OffsetY). The OffsetX and OffsetY represent translation values.

By directly manipulating matrix values using the MatrixTransform class, you can rotate, scale, skew, and move an object. For example, if you change the value in the first column of the third row (the OffsetX value) to 100, you can use it to move an object 100 units along the X-axis. If you change the value in the second column of the second row to 3, you can use it to stretch an object to three times its current height. If changing both values, you move the object 100 units along the x-axis and stretch its height by a factor of 3. Since WPF only supports affine transforms in 2D, the values in the third column are always (0, 0, 1).

Although WPF allows you to directly manipulate matrix values in the MatrixTransform class, it also provides several Transform classes that enable you to transform an object without knowing how the underlying matrix structure is configured. For example, the ScaleTransform class enables you to scale an object by setting its ScaleX and ScaleY properties, instead of manipulating a transform matrix. Likewise, the RotateTransfrom class enables you to rotate an object simply by setting its Angle property. WPF will use the underlying structure of the TransformMatrix to perform the corresponding operation on the object. For instance, when you specify a RotateTransform by an angle of 45 degrees, the corresponding underlying TransformMatrix takes the following form:

$$
\begin{pmatrix} \cos\theta & \sin\theta & 0 \\ -\sin\theta & \cos\theta & 0 \\ 0 & 0 & 1 \end{pmatrix} = \begin{pmatrix} 1 & 1 & 0 \\ -1 & 1 & 0 \\ 0 & 0 & 1 \end{pmatrix}
$$

One way to transform an object is to declare the appropriate Transform type and apply it to the transform property of the object. Different types of objects have different types of transform properties. The following table lists several commonly used WPF types and their transform properties.

Type	Transform Properties
FrameworkElement	RenderTransform, LayoutTransform
UIElement	RenderTransform
Geometry	Transform
TextEffect	Transform
Brush	Transform, RelativeTransform
ContainerVisual	Transform
DrawingGroup	Transform

When transforming an object, you don't simply transform the object itself, but transform the coordinate space in which that object exists. By default, a transform is centered at the origin of the target object's coordinate system: (0, 0). You can change the transform center by specifying the CenterX and CenterY properties of the transform matrix. The only exception is the TranslateTransform. A TranslateTransform object has no center properties to set, because the translation effect is the same regardless where it is centered.

In the following few sections, you will apply various transforms to a Rectangle shape, a type of FrameworkElement that derives from the UIElement class.

MatrixTransform Class

You can create a custom transform using the MatrixTransform class. The custom transform can be applied to any FrameworkElement or UIElement objects, including graphics shapes, user controls, panels, etc.

Here I'll use an example to show you how to perform transforms on a Rectangle shape using the MatrixTransform class. Open the Chapter03 project, and add a new WPF Window named ObjectMatrixTransforms. This application will allow the user to enter matrix elements for the transform matrix and to view the transformed Rectangle shape on the screen interactively. The XAML file of this example is listed below:

```
<Window x:Class="Chapter03.ObjectMatrixTransforms"
    xmlns="http://schemas.microsoft.com/winfx
        /2006/xaml/presentation"
    xmlns:x="http://schemas.microsoft.com/winfx/2006/xaml"
Title="Object Matrix Transforms" Height="300" Width="400">

    <Viewbox Stretch="Uniform">
        <Grid Width="430" Height="300"
            HorizontalAlignment="Left"
            VerticalAlignment="Top">
            <Grid.ColumnDefinitions>
                <ColumnDefinition Width="150"/>
                <ColumnDefinition Width="280"/>
            </Grid.ColumnDefinitions>
            <Grid Width="140" Height="300" Margin="5,10,5,5">
```

```
<Grid.ColumnDefinitions>
    <ColumnDefinition Width="60"/>
    <ColumnDefinition Width="70"/>
</Grid.ColumnDefinitions>
<Grid.RowDefinitions>
    <RowDefinition Height="Auto"/>
    <RowDefinition Height="Auto"/>
    <RowDefinition Height="Auto"/>
    <RowDefinition Height="Auto"/>
    <RowDefinition Height="Auto"/>
    <RowDefinition Height="Auto"/>
    <RowDefinition Height="Auto"/>
    <RowDefinition Height="Auto"/>
</Grid.RowDefinitions>

<TextBlock HorizontalAlignment="Right"
        Grid.Column="0" Grid.Row="0"
        Margin="5,5,10,5">M11</TextBlock>
<TextBox Name="tbM11" Grid.Column="1"
        Grid.Row="0"
        TextAlignment="Center">1</TextBox>
<TextBlock HorizontalAlignment="Right"
        Grid.Column="0" Grid.Row="1"
        Margin="5,5,10,5">M12</TextBlock>
<TextBox Name="tbM12" Grid.Column="1"
        Grid.Row="1"
        TextAlignment="Center">0</TextBox>
<TextBlock HorizontalAlignment="Right"
        Grid.Column="0" Grid.Row="2"
        Margin="5,5,10,5">M21</TextBlock>
<TextBox Name="tbM21" Grid.Column="1"
        Grid.Row="2"
        TextAlignment="Center">0</TextBox>
<TextBlock HorizontalAlignment="Right"
        Grid.Column="0" Grid.Row="3"
        Margin="5,5,10,5">M22</TextBlock>
<TextBox Name="tbM22" Grid.Column="1"
        Grid.Row="3"
        TextAlignment="Center">1</TextBox>
<TextBlock HorizontalAlignment="Right"
        Grid.Column="0" Grid.Row="4"
        Margin="5,5,10,5">
        OffsetX</TextBlock>
<TextBox Name="tbOffsetX" Grid.Column="1"
        Grid.Row="4"
        TextAlignment="Center">0</TextBox>
<TextBlock HorizontalAlignment="Right"
        Grid.Column="0" Grid.Row="5"
        Margin="5,5,10,5">
        OffsetY</TextBlock>
<TextBox Name="tbOffsetY" Grid.Column="1"
        Grid.Row="5"
        TextAlignment="Center">0</TextBox>
<Button Click="BtnApply_Click"
```

```
                    Margin="15,20,15,5" Grid.Row="6"
                    Height="25" Grid.ColumnSpan="2"
                    Grid.Column="0">Apply</Button>
            <Button Click="BtnClose_Click"
                    Margin="15,0,15,5" Grid.Row="7"
                    Height="25" Grid.ColumnSpan="2"
                    Grid.Column="0">Close</Button>
        </Grid>

        <Border Margin="10" Grid.Column="1"
                BorderBrush="Black"
                BorderThickness="1"
                HorizontalAlignment="Left"
        Background="{StaticResource MyGrayGridBrush}">
            <Canvas Name="canvas1" Grid.Column="1"
                    ClipToBounds="True" Width="270"
                    Height="280">
                <TextBlock Canvas.Top="53"
                           Canvas.Left="90">
                           Original shape</TextBlock>
                <Rectangle Canvas.Top="70"
                           Canvas.Left="100"
                           Width="50" Height="70"
                           Stroke="Black"
                           StrokeThickness="2"
                           StrokeDashArray="3,1"/>
                <Rectangle Name="rect" Canvas.Top="70"
                           Canvas.Left="100"
                           Width="50" Height="70"
                           Fill="LightCoral" Opacity="0.5"
                           Stroke="Black"
                           StrokeThickness="2">
                    <Rectangle.RenderTransform>
                        <MatrixTransform
                            x:Name="matrixTransform"/>
                    </Rectangle.RenderTransform>
                </Rectangle>
            </Canvas>
        </Border>
    </Grid>
  </Viewbox>
</Window>
```

This markup creates a user interface that contains TextBoxes, Buttons, and a Canvas, which allows you to interactively manipulate the elements of the TransformMatrix and dispay the transformed Rectangle shape on your screen. In order to precisely monitor the transformed shape, we also add the gridlines to the Canvas (canvas1). These gridlines, called MyGrayGridBrush, are defined in the Application.Resource of the App.xaml file. The transform on the rectangle is specified with the following XAML snippet:

```
<Rectangle.RenderTransform>
    <MatrixTransform x:Name="matrixTransform"/>
</Rectangle.RenderTransform>
```

From this snippet, you can see that to apply transforms to a FrameworkElement, you need to create a Transform matrix and apply it to one of the two properties that the FrameworkElement class provides:

LayoutTransform – A transform that is applied before the layout pass. After the transform is applied, the layout system processes the transformed size and position of the element.

RenderTransform – A transform that modifies the appearance of the element but is applied after the layout pass is completed. By using the RenderTransform property instead of the LayoutTransform, you can gain some performance benefits.

You may ask which property we should use. Because of the performance benefits that it provides, use the RenderTransform property whenever possible, especially when you use animated Transform objects. Use the LayoutTransform property when you are scaling, rotating, or skewing, and you need the parent of the element to adjust to the transformed size of the element. Note that when they are used with the LayoutTransform property, TranslateTransform objects appear to have no effect on elements. This is because the layout system returns the translated element to its original position as part of its processing.

In this example, the RenderTransform property of the rectangle is used. The following is the corresponding C# code that is responsible for the event handlers:

```csharp
using System;
using System.Windows;
using System.Windows.Controls;
using System.Windows.Media;
using System.Windows.Shapes;
namespace Chapter03
{
public partial class ObjectMatrixTransforms : Window
    {
        public ObjectMatrixTransforms()
        {
            InitializeComponent();
        }

        public void BtnApply_Click(object sender, EventArgs e)
        {
            Matrix m = new Matrix();
            m.M11 = Double.Parse(tbM11.Text);
            m.M12 = Double.Parse(tbM12.Text);
            m.M21 = Double.Parse(tbM21.Text);
            m.M22 = Double.Parse(tbM22.Text);
            m.OffsetX = Double.Parse(tbOffsetX.Text);
            m.OffsetY = Double.Parse(tbOffsetY.Text);
            matrixTransform.Matrix = m;
        }

        public void BtnClose_Click(object sender, EventArgs e)
        {
```

```
                this.Close();
            }
        }
    }
```

The main part of this code-behind file is the Apply button's click event handler. We create a new Matrix instance m, and specify its elements using the text content of the corresponding TextBoxes. Then the matrix m is passed to the transform matrix named matrixTransform, which is defined in the XAML file.

Building and running this project produce the output shown in Figure 3-9. In the left pane, you can change all six elements of a custom transform matrix by entering values of the double type in the TextBoxes. The entered values take effect after you click the Apply button. The original location of the Rectangle is obtained by an identical matrix (1, 0, 0, 1, 0, 0) in homogeneous coordinates. The results shown in Figure 3-9 are obtained by moving the rectangle –50 units in the X direction and 100 units in the Y direction.

By changing the other elements, you can obtain a variety of transforms, including translation, scale, rotation, and skew.

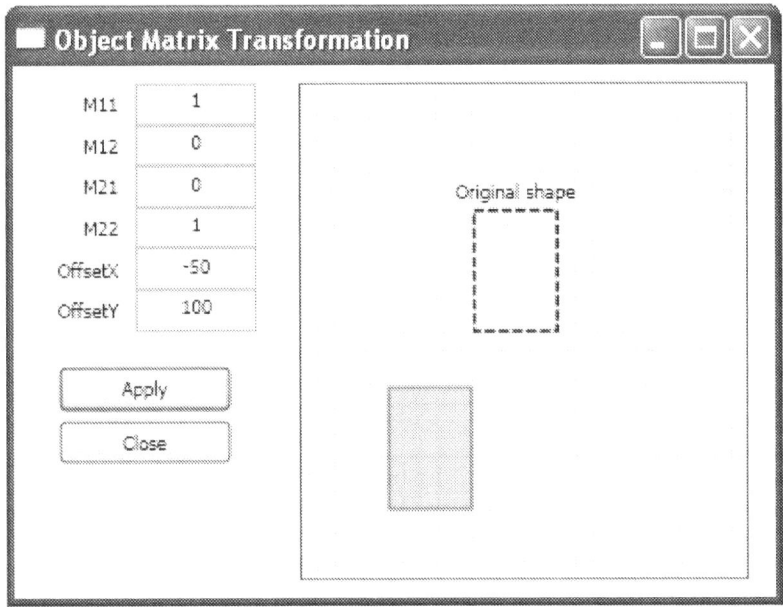

Figure 3-9 Transform on a rectangle using MatrixTransform class.

ScaleTransform Class

In the previous section, we discussed how to perform transforms on UIElement or FrameworkElement objects by directly manipulating transform matrix values. However, WPF also provides several Transform classes that allow you to transform an object without knowing how the underlying matrix structure is configured. For example, the ScaleTransform class enables you to scale an object by setting its ScaleX and ScaleY properties, instead of directly manipulating a transform matrix.

Let's look at an example. Open the Chapter03 project, add a WPF Window, and name it ScaleTransforms. In this example, you create two Canvas panels. The left Canvas is used for animating the scale transform on a rectangle shape, while the right Canvas is used for an interactive transform that allows you to change the ScaleX and ScaleY on the screen. The animation gives you the real feeling of how the scale transform works. I'll discuss the animation process in Chapter 6. The following is the XAML file of this example:

```
<Window x:Class="Chapter03.ScaleTransforms"
    xmlns="http://schemas.microsoft.com/winfx
        /2006/xaml/presentation"
    xmlns:x="http://schemas.microsoft.com/winfx/2006/xaml"
    Title="Scale Transforms" Height="330" Width="480">

    <Viewbox Stretch="Uniform">
        <Grid Width="525" Height="330"
            HorizontalAlignment="Left"
            VerticalAlignment="Top"
            ShowGridLines="True">
            <Grid.ColumnDefinitions>
                <ColumnDefinition Width="260" />
                <ColumnDefinition Width="260" />
            </Grid.ColumnDefinitions>

            <StackPanel Grid.Column="0">
                <TextBlock HorizontalAlignment="Center"
                        Margin="10,10,10,0"
                        TextWrapping="Wrap"
                        FontSize="14" FontWeight="Bold"
                        Text="Scaling Animation"/>
                <TextBlock Margin="10,10,10,0"
                        TextWrapping="Wrap"
                        Text="The scaling parameters ScaleX
                    and ScaleY are animated from 0 to 4."/>
                <Border Margin="10" BorderBrush="Black"
                        BorderThickness="1"
                    Background="{StaticResource MyGrayGridBrush}"
                        HorizontalAlignment="Left">
                    <Canvas ClipToBounds="True" Width="240"
                            Height="250">
                        <Rectangle Canvas.Left="100"
                                Canvas.Top="80"
                                Width="50" Height="70"
                                Fill="LightCoral"
                                Opacity="0.5"
                                Stroke="Black"
                                StrokeThickness="2">
                            <Rectangle.RenderTransform>
                                <ScaleTransform
```

```
                            x:Name="rectScale"
                            CenterX="25"
                            CenterY="35" />
                </Rectangle.RenderTransform>
            </Rectangle>

            <!-- Animate the rectangle: -->
            <Canvas.Triggers>
<EventTrigger RoutedEvent="Canvas.Loaded">
    <BeginStoryboard>
        <Storyboard RepeatBehavior="Forever"
            AutoReverse="True">
            <DoubleAnimation
                Storyboard.TargetName="rectScale"
                Storyboard.TargetProperty="ScaleX"
                From="0" To="4" Duration="0:0:5"/>
            <DoubleAnimation
                Storyboard.TargetName="rectScale"
                Storyboard.TargetProperty="ScaleY"
                From="0" To="4" Duration="0:0:5"/>
        </Storyboard>
    </BeginStoryboard>
</EventTrigger>
                </Canvas.Triggers>
            </Canvas>
        </Border>
    </StackPanel>

    <StackPanel Grid.Column="1">
        <TextBlock  HorizontalAlignment="Center"
                Margin="10,10,10,10"
                TextWrapping="Wrap"
                FontSize="14" FontWeight="Bold"
                Text="Interactive Scaling"/>
        <Grid Width="260" Height="26"
            HorizontalAlignment="Left"
            VerticalAlignment="Top">
            <Grid.ColumnDefinitions>
                <ColumnDefinition Width="70" />
                <ColumnDefinition Width="50" />
                <ColumnDefinition Width="70" />
                <ColumnDefinition Width="50" />
            </Grid.ColumnDefinitions>

            <TextBlock Margin="2,2,10,2"
                    TextAlignment="Right"
                    Text="ScaleX"/>
            <TextBox Name="tbScaleX" Width="50"
                    Height="20" Grid.Column="1"
                    TextAlignment="Center" Text="1"/>
            <TextBlock Margin="2,2,10,2"
                    Grid.Column="2"
                    TextAlignment="Right"
                    Text="ScaleY"/>
```

```
                <TextBox Name="tbScaleY" Width="50"
                    Height="20" Grid.Column="3"
                    TextAlignment="Center" Text="1"/>
            </Grid>

            <Border Margin="10" BorderBrush="Black"
                BorderThickness="1"
              Background="{StaticResource MyGrayGridBrush}"
                HorizontalAlignment="Left">
              <Canvas ClipToBounds="True"
                    Width="240" Height="250">
                <TextBlock Canvas.Left="90"
                        Canvas.Top="63"
                        Text="Original shape"/>
                <Rectangle Canvas.Top="80"
                        Canvas.Left="100"
                        Width="50" Height="70"
                        Stroke="Black"
                        StrokeThickness="1"
                        StrokeDashArray="3,1"/>

                <Rectangle Canvas.Top="80"
                        Canvas.Left="100"
                        Width="50" Height="70"
                        Fill="LightCoral"
                        Opacity="0.5"
                        Stroke="Black"
                        StrokeThickness="2">
          <!-- Set interactive scale: -->
          <Rectangle.RenderTransform>
              <ScaleTransform
                  ScaleX="{Binding ElementName=tbScaleX,Path=Text}"
                  ScaleY="{Binding ElementName=tbScaleY,Path=Text}"
                  CenterX="25" CenterY="35"/>
          </Rectangle.RenderTransform>
                </Rectangle>
              </Canvas>
            </Border>
          </StackPanel>
        </Grid>
      </Viewbox>
  </Window>
```

This XAML file creates a complete WPF application that includes not only the layout and user interface, but also the animation and interactive scale transform on the rectangle shapes.

You start the animation for the rectangle object by varying its ScaleX and ScaleY dependency properties from 0 to 4. The details of WPF animations will be covered in Chapter 6.

For the interactive scale transform on the other rectangle in the right pane, the ScaleX and ScaleY properties of the transform are bound to the Text properties of the corresponding TextBoxes, which can be specified by the user's input.

This allows you to interactively examine the scaling transform directly on the screen. Figure 3-10 shows a snapshot of this example.

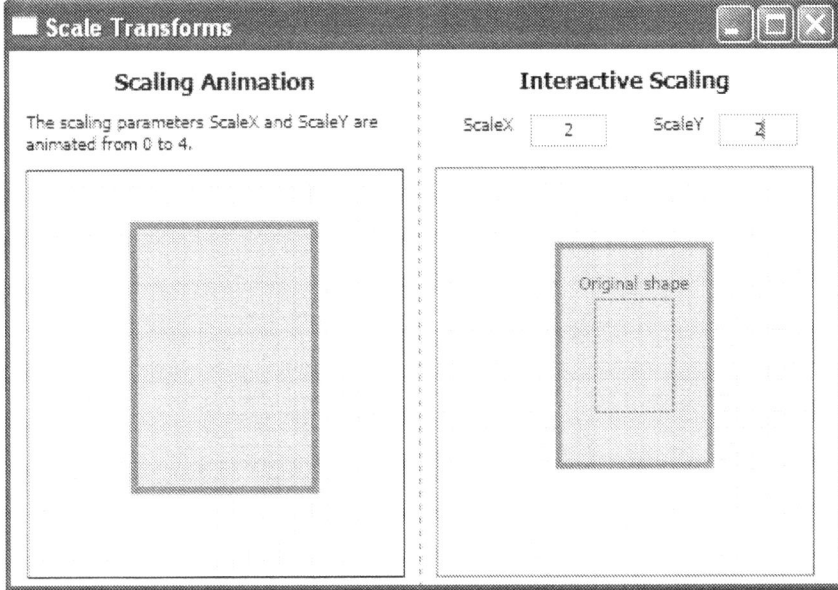

Figure 3-10 Scale transformation on Rectangle objects.

TranslateTransform Class

The TranslateTransform class enables you to move an object by setting its X and Y properties. This transform has no center properties to set because the translation effect is the same regardless of where it is centered.

Let's consider an example of a translation on a Rectangle object using the same layout as that used in the previous example. Add a WPF Window to the project Chapter03 and call it TranslateTransforms. The XAML file is similar to the previous ScaleTransformation example, except for the RenderTransform property of the rectangle. For animating the translation on the rectangle, you use the following XAML snippet:

```
......
<Rectangle.RenderTransform>
  <TranslateTransform x:Name="translate" />
</Rectangle.RenderTransform>
......
<Storyboard RepeatBehavior="Forever" AutoReverse="True">
<DoubleAnimation Storyboard.TargetName="translate"
                 Storyboard.TargetProperty="X"
                 From="-90" To="90" Duration="0:0:5"/>
<DoubleAnimation Storyboard.TargetName="translate"
                 Storyboard.TargetProperty="Y"
```

```
                              From="-90" To="90" Duration="0:0:5"/>
        </Storyboard>
        ......
```

The animation is performed using a storyboard that animates the X and Y properties of the translation. For the interactive translation of the rectangle in the right pane, the following XAML snippet defines its RenderTransform property:

```
<!-- Set interactive translation: -->
<Rectangle.RenderTransform>
    <TranslateTransform
        X="{Binding ElementName=tbX,Path=Text}"
        Y="{Binding ElementName=tbY,Path=Text}"/>
</Rectangle.RenderTransform>
```

Here the X and Y properties of the translation are attached to the text fields of the corresponding TextBoxes with data binding. This allows you to interactively manipulate the translation of the rectangle by changing the text fields of the TextBoxes. Figure 3-11 shows a snapshot of this example.

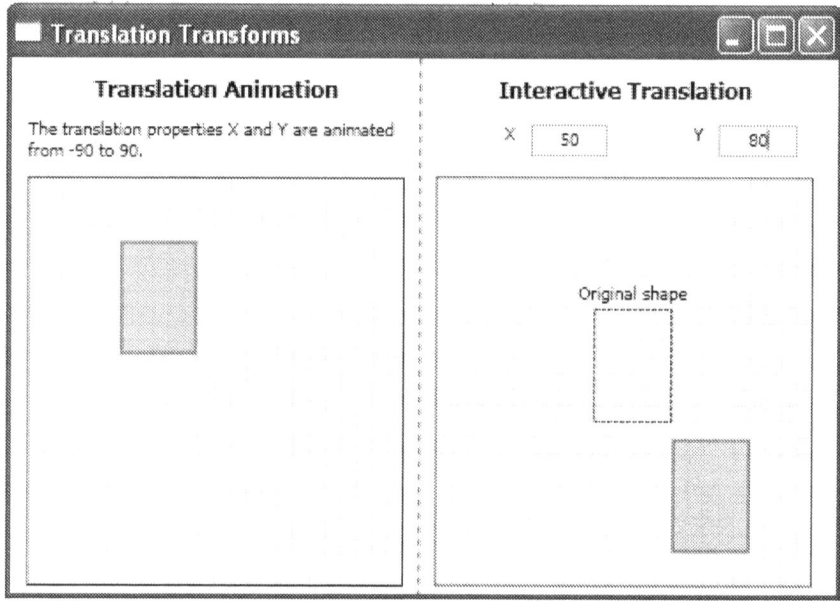

Figure 3-11 Translation transformation on a Rectangle.

RotateTransform Class

The RotateTransform class allows you to rotate an object by setting its Angle, CenterX, and CenterY properties. In the next example, we'll animate the rotation of a Rectangle object about its center. However, the origin of this rectangle will be moved from 0 to 180 units. For the interactive rotation, the Angle, CenterX, and CenterY properties of the transform take values directly from the user's inputs.

Open the Chapter03 project, add a WPF Window, and name it RotateTransforms.
The XAML file is similar to that used in the previous example, except for the
RenderTransform property of the rectangle. To animate the rotation transform
on the rectangle, use the following XAML snippet:

```
.....
<Rectangle.RenderTransform>
    <RotateTransform x:Name="rotate"/>
</Rectangle.RenderTransform>
.....
<Storyboard RepeatBehavior="Forever">
    <DoubleAnimation Storyboard.TargetName="rotate"
                     Storyboard.TargetProperty="Angle"
                     From="0" To="360" Duration="0:0:5"/>
    <DoubleAnimation Storyboard.TargetName="rotate"
                     Storyboard.TargetProperty="CenterX"
                     From="-20" To="120" Duration="0:0:5"/>
    <DoubleAnimation Storyboard.TargetName="rotate"
                     Storyboard.TargetProperty="CenterY"
                     From="-50" To="90" Duration="0:0:5"/>
</Storyboard>
.....
```

The animation is performed using a storyboard that animates the CenterX,
CenterY, and Angle properties of the rotation transform. For the interactive
rotation transform on the rectangle in the right pane, the following XAML
snippet defines its RenderTransform property:

```
<!-- Set interactive rotation: -->
<Rectangle.RenderTransform>
    <RotateTransform
        CenterX="{Binding ElementName=tbCenterX,Path=Text}"
        CenterY="{Binding ElementName=tbCenterY,Path=Text}"
        Angle="{Binding ElementName=tbAngle,Path=Text}"/>
</Rectangle.RenderTransform>
```

Here the Angle, CenterX, and CenterY properties of the rotation transform are
attached to the text fields of the corresponding TextBoxes with data binding.
This allows you to interactively manipulate the rotation transform on the
rectangle by changing the text fields of the TextBoxes.

Figure 3-12 shows the result of running this application.

SkewTransform Class

The SkewTransform class defines a 2D skew that stretches the coordinate space
of a FrameworkElement or an UIElement object in a non-uniform manner. You
can use the CenterX and CenterY properties to specify the center point for the
transform, and use the AngleX and AngleY properties to specify the skew angle
along the X and Y directions.

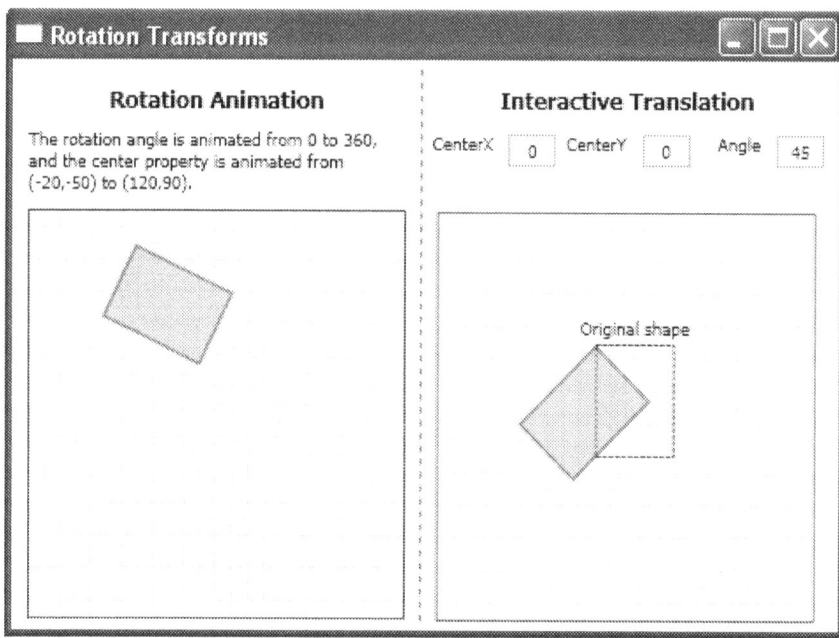

Figure 3-12 Rotation transform on rectangles.

In this example, we'll animate the skew transform of a Rectangle object about its center by varying the AngleX and AngleY properties. For the interactive skew transformation, the AngleX and AngleY properties of the transform take values directly from the user's input.

Open the Chapter03 project, add a WPF Window, and name it SkewTransforms. The XAML file is similar to that of the previous example, except for the RenderTransform property of the rectangle. To animate the skew transform on the rectangle, use the following XAML snippet:

```
.....
<Rectangle.RenderTransform>
    <SkewTransform x:Name="skew" CenterX="25" CenterY="35"/>
</Rectangle.RenderTransform>
.....
<Storyboard RepeatBehavior="Forever">
    <DoubleAnimation Storyboard.TargetName="skew"
                     Storyboard.TargetProperty="AngleX"
                     From="0" To="360" Duration="0:0:10"/>
    <DoubleAnimation Storyboard.TargetName="skew"
                     Storyboard.TargetProperty="AngleY"
                     From="0" To="360" Duration="0:0:10"/>
</Storyboard>
.....
```

The animation is performed using a storyboard that animates the AngleX and AngleY properties of the skew transform. For the interactive skew transform on the rectangle in the right pane, the following XAML snippet defines its RenderTransform property:

```
<!-- Set interactive skew: -->
<Rectangle.RenderTransform>
    <SkewTransform CenterX="25" CenterY="35"
        AngleX="{Binding ElementName=tbAngleX,Path=Text}"
        AngleY="{Binding ElementName=tbAngleY,Path=Text}"/>
</Rectangle.RenderTransform>
```

Here the AngleX and AngleY properties of the skew transform are attached to the text fields of the corresponding TextBoxes with data binding. This allows you to interactively manipulate the skew transform on the rectangle by changing the text fields of the TextBoxes.

Figure 3-13 shows a snapshot of this example.

Composite Transforms

The TransformGroup class, which allows you to combine any of the above transform classes, can be applied to any UIElement or FrameworkElement object. In other words, a composite transform that consists of any number of transforms can be applied to a graphics object. The TransformGroup class derived from the Transform base class represents a combined transform that contains a collection of Transforms.

You can represent various transforms using a simple C# code snippet. For example, to scale a rectangle 2 times in the X direction and 3 times in the Y direction, you can use a ScaleTransform object:

```
Rectangle.RenderTransformation =
        new ScaleTransformation(2, 3);
```

To move the rectangle 100 units in the X direction and -100 units in the Y direction, you can simply write:

```
Rectangle.RenderTransform =
        new TranslateTransform(100, - 100);
```

To rotate the Rectangle 45 degrees, you can create a new RotateTransform object and set the angle to 45.

```
Rectangle.RenderTransform = new RotateTransform(45);
```

To skew an element 30 degrees in the X direction and 45 degrees in the Y direction, you can use a SkewTransform:

```
Rectangle.RenderTransform = new SkewTransform(30, 45);
```

Finally, if you want to apply all of these transforms to this rectangle, you can use a TransformGroup:

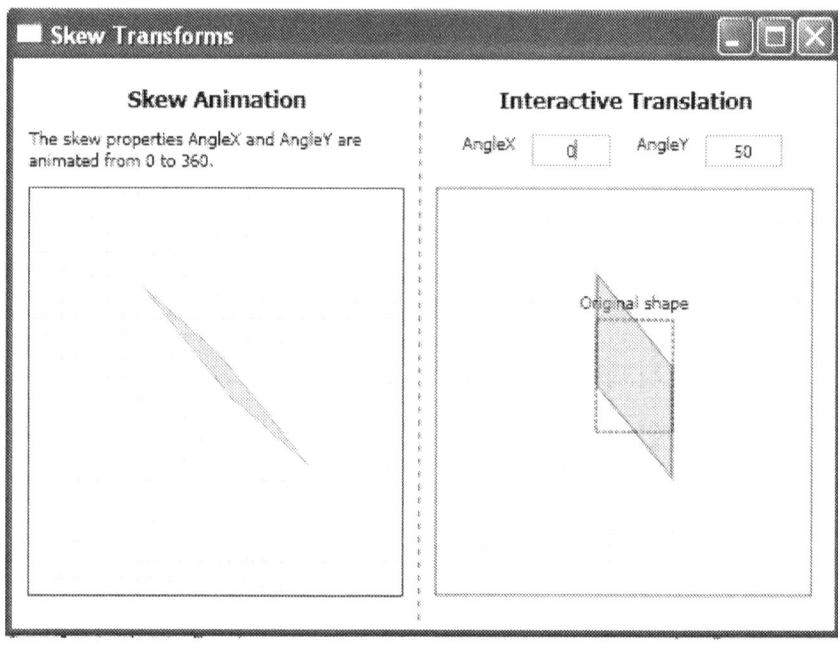

Figure 3-13 Skew transformation on rectangles.

```
TransformGroup tg = new TransformGroup();
tg.Children.Add(ScaleTransform(2, 3));
tg.Children.Add(TranslateTransform(100, -100));
tg.Children.Add(RotateTransform(45));
tg.Children.Add(SkewTransform(30, 45));
Rectangle.RenderTransform = tg;
```

Let's consider an example that illustrates how to use the TransformGroup class in a WPF application. In this example, you'll use a composite transform that contains a scale and a rotation transform. This transform is applied to a rectangle object (a square in this case) about its center. You'll animate the dependency properties for both the scale and rotation transforms.

Open the Chapter03 project, add a WPF Window, and name it CombineTransforms. Here, we'll only consider the animation of the combined transform. The following is the XAML file of this example:

```
<Window x:Class="Chapter03.CombineTransforms"
    xmlns="http://schemas.microsoft.com/winfx
        /2006/xaml/presentation"
    xmlns:x="http://schemas.microsoft.com/winfx/2006/xaml"
    Title="Combining Transforms" Height="330" Width="300">

    <Viewbox Stretch="Uniform">
        <StackPanel>
            <TextBlock HorizontalAlignment="Center"
                    Margin="10,10,10,0" TextWrapping="Wrap"
                    FontSize="14" FontWeight="Bold"
                Text="Animation of Combining Transform"/>
```

```xml
<Border Margin="10" BorderBrush="Black"
        BorderThickness="1"
     Background="{StaticResource MyGrayGridBrush}"
        HorizontalAlignment="Left">
    <Canvas ClipToBounds="True"
           Width="340" Height="320">
        <Ellipse Canvas.Left="165"
                Canvas.Top="145" Width="10"
                Height="10" Fill="Red"/>

        <Rectangle Canvas.Left="120"
                Canvas.Top="100" Width="100"
                Height="100" Fill="LightCoral"
                Opacity="0.5" Stroke="Black"
                StrokeThickness="2">
            <Rectangle.RenderTransform>
                <TransformGroup>
                    <ScaleTransform x:Name="scale"
                                   CenterX="50"
                                   CenterY="50" />
                    <RotateTransform
                        x:Name="rotate"
                        CenterX="50"
                        CenterY="50"/>
                </TransformGroup>
            </Rectangle.RenderTransform>
        </Rectangle>

<!-- Animate the shape: -->
<Canvas.Triggers>
    <EventTrigger RoutedEvent="Canvas.Loaded">
        <BeginStoryboard>
            <Storyboard RepeatBehavior="Forever"
                        AutoReverse="True">
        <DoubleAnimation Storyboard.TargetName="scale"
                        Storyboard.TargetProperty="ScaleX"
                        From="0" To="3" Duration="0:0:5"/>
        <DoubleAnimation Storyboard.TargetName="scale"
                        Storyboard.TargetProperty="ScaleY"
                        From="0" To="3" Duration="0:0:5"/>
        <DoubleAnimation Storyboard.TargetName="rotate"
                        Storyboard.TargetProperty="Angle"
                        From="0" To="360" Duration="0:0:5"/>
                </Storyboard>
            </BeginStoryboard>
        </EventTrigger>
    </Canvas.Triggers>
        </Canvas>
    </Border>
    </StackPanel>
    </Viewbox>
</Window>
```

Here, we specify the rectangle's RenderTransform property using a TransformGroup. Within this TransformGroup, we define two transforms: a ScaleTransform named "scale" and a RotateTransform named "rotate". Both transforms are animated using a StoryBoard. Within the StoryBoard, we first animate the ScaleX and ScaleY dependency properties of the ScaleTransform. Then we perform the rotation animation on the rectangle by animating the Angle property from 0 to 360 degrees.

This example produces the results shown in Figure 3-14.

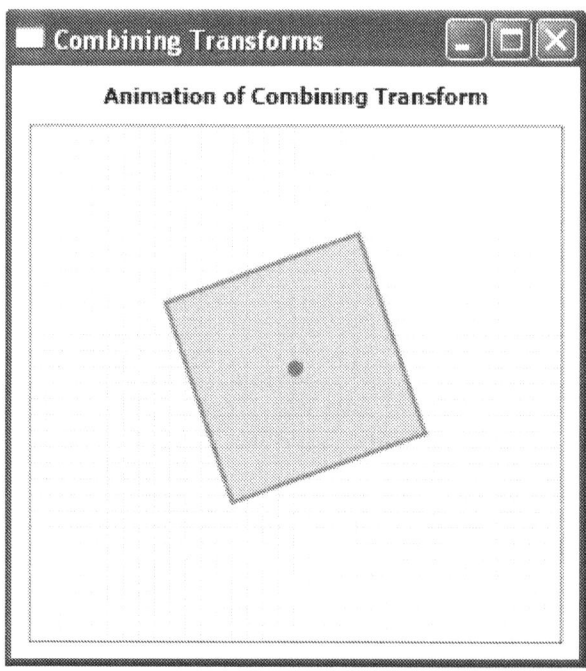

Figure 3-14 Combining transform on a Square.

Chapter 4
Geometry and 2D Drawing

In the previous two chapters, graphics examples were created using simple shapes that derive from the Shape class. The Shape class inherits from FrameworkElement. Because Shape objects from the Shape class are elements, they can render themselves and participate in the layout system. In this sense, Shape objects are readily usable.

This chapter shows you how to create and manipulate more complex 2D graphics objects using the more powerful Path class, which can wrap complex geometry objects derived from the Geometry class. It shows you how to develop an advanced interactive 2D drawing program using the Geometry class, which allows you to add and delete, drag and move, as well as perform logic operations (Union, Intersect, Xor, and Exclude) on the 2D graphics objects. From this chapter, you'll also learn how to create custom shape objects, which can be used in the same way as the WPF built-in shapes.

Path and Geometry Classes

In previous chapters, you learned how to create simple 2D graphics using the simple shapes that derive from the Shape class, including Line, Rectangle, Ellipse, and Polygon. However, you haven't considered a more powerful Shape-derived class, the Path class. The Path class has the ability to draw curves and complex shapes. These curves and shapes are described using the Geometry objects. To use a Path object, you create a Geometry object and use it to set the Path object's Data property. You can't draw a Geometry object directly on your screen because it is an abstract class. Instead, you need to use one of the seven derived classes, as listed below:

- LineGeometry – Represents the geometry of a straight line.
- RectangleGeometry – Represents the geometry of a 2D rectangle.
- EllipseGeometry – Represents the geometry of an ellipse.

- GeometryGroup – Represents a composite geometry, which can be added to a single path.

- CombinedGeometry – Represents a 2D geometry shape defined by the combination of two Geometry objects.

- PathGeometry – Represents a complex geometry shape that may be composed of arcs, curves, ellipses, lines, and rectangles.

- StreamGeometry – Defines a geometric shape described using StreamGeometryContext. This geometry is a read-only light-weight alternative to PathGeometry: it doesn't support data binding, animation, or modification.

The LineGeometry, RectangleGeometry, and EllipseGeometry classes describe relatively simple geometry shapes. To create more complex shapes or curves, you need to use a PathGeometry object.

There is a critical difference between the Shape class and the Geometry class. The Geometry class inherits from the Freezable class, while the Shape class inherits from FrameworkElement. Because Shape objects are elements, they can render themselves and participate in the layout system, while Geometry objects can't.

Although Shape objects are more readily usable than Geometry objects, Geometry objects are more versatile. While a Shape object is used to render 2D graphics, a Geometry object can be used to define the geometric region for 2D graphics, define a region for clipping, or define a region for hit testing, for example. Geometry objects can't render themselves, and must be drawn by another element, such as a Drawing or Path element. The attributes common to shapes, such as the Fill, Stroke, and StrokeThickness properties, are attached to the Path or Drawing, which can be used to draw Geometry objects.

You can see from the above discussion that the Geometry object defines a shape, while a Path object allows you to draw the Geometry shape on your screen. In the following sections, I'll show you how to create shapes using the objects derived from the Geometry class.

Line, Rectangle, and Ellipse Geometries

The LineGeometry, RectangleGeometry, and EllipseGeometry classes correspond directly to the Line, Rectangle, and Ellipse shapes that were used in the previous chapters. For example, you can convert this XAML code, which uses the Line element

```
<Line X1="30" Y1="30" X2 ="180" Y2="30"
      Stroke="Blue" StrokeThickness="2"/>
```

into the following markup, which uses the Path element and LineGeometry:

```
<Path Stroke="Blue" StrokeThickness="2">
    <Path.Data>
        <LineGeometry StartPoint="30 30" EndPoint="180 30"/>
```

```
        </Path.Data>
    </Path>
```

The only difference is that the Line shape takes X1, Y1, X2, and Y2 values, while the LineGeometry object takes StartPoint and EndPoint.

Similarly, you can convert the following code snippet:

```
<Rectangle Fill="Gray" Stroke="Blue" StrokeThickness="2"
           Width="10" Height="20"/>
```

into this RectangleGeometry:

```
<Path Fill="Gray" Stroke="Blue" StrokeThickness="2">
    <Path.Data>
        <RectangleGeometry Rect="0,0,10,20"/>
    </Path.Data>
</Path>
```

It can be seen that the Rectangle shape takes Height and Width values, while the RectangleGeometry element takes four numbers that describe the location and size of the rectangle. The first two numbers represent the X and Y coordinates where the top-left corner will be placed, while the last two numbers define the width and height of the rectangle.

You can also convert an Ellipse shape like this:

```
<Ellipse Fill="Gray" Stroke="Blue" StrokeThickness="2"
         Width="10" Height="20"/>
```

into the EllipseGeometry:

```
<Path Fill="Gray" Stroke="Blue" StrokeThickness="2">
    <Path.Data>
        <EllipseGeometry RadiuX="5" RadiusY="10"
                         Center="5,10"/>
    </Path.Data>
</Path>
```

Notice that the two radius values are simply half of the width and height values. You can also use the Center property to offset the location of the ellipse.

It is clear from the above discussion that these simple geometries work in exactly the same way as the corresponding shapes. Geometry objects allow you to offset rectangles and ellipses, but this isn't necessary if you draw the shapes on a Canvas, which already gives you the ability to position your shapes at a specific position using the Canvas.Top and Canvas.Left properties. The real difference between the Shape and Geometry classes appears when you decide to combine more than one Geometry object in a single path, as described in the next section.

GeometryGroup Class

The simplest way to combine geometries is to use the GeometryGroup object. Here is an example that creates two circles:

```
<Path Fill="LightGray" Stroke="Blue" StrokeThickness="2">
    <Path.Data>
        <GeometryGroup FillRule="Nonzero">
            <EllipseGeometry RadiusX="50" RadiusY="50"
                             Center="120,120"/>
            <EllipseGeometry RadiusX="30" RadiusY="30"
                             Center="120,120"/>
        </GeometryGroup>
    </Path.Data>
</Path>
```

This code snippet creates a similar effect as if you had used two Path elements, each one with an EllipseGeometry object of a different radius. However, there is one advantage to using the GeometryGroup object. Here, you have replaced two elements with one, which means you have reduced the overhead of your user interface. In general, a window that uses a smaller number of elements with more complex geometries will perform faster than a window that uses a large number of elements with simple geometries. This will become significant when you create complicated computer-aided design (CAD) applications.

Another advantage of using the Geometry class is that the same geometry can be reused in separate Path elements. You can simply define the geometry in a Resources collection and refer to it in your path.

Let's start with an example WPF Window project and call it Chapter04. As you did for the previous project Chapter03, add a StartMenu, which will be the interface for accessing all of examples in this chapter. Now, add another WPF Window called GeometryGroupExample to the project. Here is the XAML file of this example:

```
<Window x:Class="Chapter04.GeometryGroupExample"
    xmlns="http://schemas.microsoft.com/winfx
        /2006/xaml/presentation"
    xmlns:x="http://schemas.microsoft.com/winfx/2006/xaml"
    Title="Geometry Group" Height="310" Width="300">

    <Window.Resources>
        <GeometryGroup x:Key="GeometryNonzero"
                       FillRule="Nonzero">
            <EllipseGeometry RadiusX="50" RadiusY="50"
                             Center="65,60"/>
            <EllipseGeometry RadiusX="30" RadiusY="30"
                             Center="65,60"/>
        </GeometryGroup>

        <GeometryGroup x:Key="GeometryEvenOdd"
                       FillRule="EvenOdd">
            <EllipseGeometry RadiusX="50" RadiusY="50"
                             Center="65,60"/>
            <EllipseGeometry RadiusX="30" RadiusY="30"
                             Center="65,60"/>
        </GeometryGroup>
    </Window.Resources>
```

```
<Border Margin="5" BorderBrush="Black" BorderThickness="1"
        Background="{StaticResource MyGrayGridBrush}"
        HorizontalAlignment="Left">
    <Canvas Height="310" Width="300">
        <Grid ShowGridLines="True" Height="265">
            <Grid.ColumnDefinitions>
                <ColumnDefinition Width="140"/>
                <ColumnDefinition Width="140"/>
            </Grid.ColumnDefinitions>

            <StackPanel Margin="5" Grid.Column="0">
                <TextBlock Text="FileRule = Nonzero"
                        Margin="15,5,5,5"/>
                <Path Fill="LightBlue" Stroke="Blue"
                    StrokeThickness="2"
                  Data="{StaticResource GeometryNonzero}"/>
                <Path Fill="LightCoral" Stroke="Red"
                    StrokeThickness="2" Canvas.Left="150"
                  Data="{StaticResource GeometryNonzero}"/>
            </StackPanel>

            <StackPanel Margin="5" Grid.Column="1">
                <TextBlock Text="FileRule = EvenOdd"
                        Margin="15,5,5,5"/>
                <Path Fill="LightBlue" Stroke="Blue"
                    StrokeThickness="2"
                  Data="{StaticResource GeometryEvenOdd}"/>
                <Path Fill="LightCoral" Stroke="Red"
                    StrokeThickness="2"
                    Canvas.Left="150"
                  Data="{StaticResource GeometryEvenOdd}"/>
            </StackPanel>
        </Grid>
    </Canvas>
</Border>
</Window>
```

In the Resources, you define two GeometryGroup objects, GeometryNonzero and GeometryEvenOdd. Each includes two circles with a different radius but the same center location. The main difference lies in their FillRule property: one is set to Nonzero, and the other to EvenOdd. Like the Polygon shape, the GeometryGroup also has a FillRule property that specifies which shapes to fill. You can then use these Resources to create multiple shapes at different locations on a Canvas with different Fill colors and Strokes.

This markup generates the results shown in Figure 4-1. The two solid circles are created at each of different locations. The left images show results when the FillRule of the GeometryGroup is set to Nonzero. Two solid circles with the same center location are created. If you change the FillRule property to EvenOdd, you'll obtain the results shown in the right pane. Here, you create two rings, each made up of a solid circle with a blank hole.

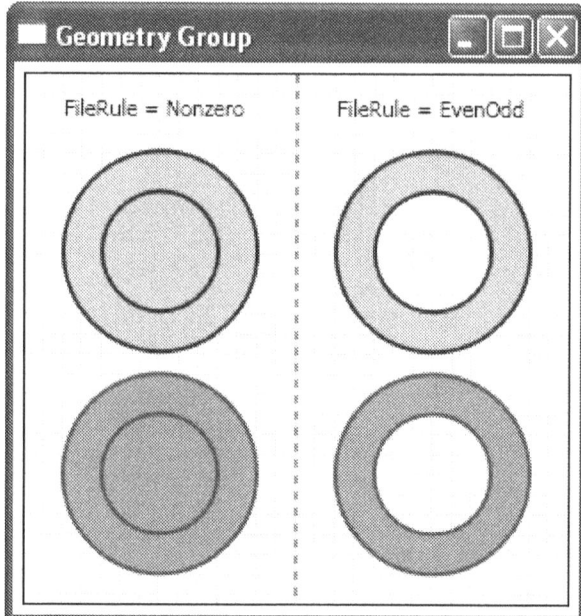

Figure 4-1 2D shapes created using GeometryGroup.

Remember that there are some drawbacks to combining geometries into a single Path element using GeometryGroup: you can't perform event handling on each of the different geometry shapes separately. Instead, the Path object will fire all of the mouse events.

CombinedGeometry Class

The GeometryGroup class has many advantages for creating complex shapes. However, it still has some limitations in developing CAD-like applications. For example, although the GeometryGroup allows you to create a shape by drawing one shape and subtracting out other shapes from inside by changing its FillRule property, it doesn't allow you to perform real logic operations on shapes. To address this issue, WPF implements another class, the CombinedGeometry class, that takes two geometries specified using the Geometry1 and Geometry2 properties.

This class doesn't include the FillRule property, instead, it has a much more powerful GeometryCombineMode property that takes one of four values, as listed below:

- Union – Creates a shape that includes all the areas of the two geometries.
- Intersect – Creates a shape that contains the shared area between the two geometries.
- Xor – Creates a shape that contains the area that isn't shared between the two geometries.

- Exclude – Creates a shape that includes all the area from the first geometry, but doesn't include the area that falls in the second geometry.

Note that CombinedGeometry only combines the Area specified by two geometries, so geometries that don't have area, such as LineGeometry, disappear when combined.

Let's consider an example that demonstrates how you can combine two circles into one shape using CombinedGeometry. Add a new WPF Window to the project Chapter04 and name it CombinedGeometryExample. Here is the XAML file of this example:

```
<Window x:Class="Chapter04.CombinedGeometryExample"
    xmlns="http://schemas.microsoft.com/winfx
        /2006/xaml/presentation"
    xmlns:x="http://schemas.microsoft.com/winfx/2006/xaml"
Title="Combined Geometry" Height="340" Width="300">

  <Border Margin="5" BorderBrush="Black" BorderThickness="1"
        Background="{StaticResource MyGrayGridBrush}"
        HorizontalAlignment="Left">
      <Canvas Width="300" Height="340" Margin="5">
          <Grid>
              <Grid.ColumnDefinitions>
                  <ColumnDefinition Width="140"/>
                  <ColumnDefinition Width="140"/>
              </Grid.ColumnDefinitions>

              <StackPanel Grid.Column="0">
                  <TextBlock FontSize="12pt" Text="Union"
                        Margin="40,5,5,10"/>
                  <Path Fill ="LightBlue" Stroke="Blue">
                      <Path.Data>
                          <CombinedGeometry
                              GeometryCombineMode="Union">
                              <CombinedGeometry.Geometry1>
                                  <EllipseGeometry
                                      Center="50,50"
                                      RadiusX="50"
                                      RadiusY="50"/>
                              </CombinedGeometry.Geometry1>
                              <CombinedGeometry.Geometry2>
                                  <EllipseGeometry
                                      Center="80,50"
                                      RadiusX="50"
                                      RadiusY="50"/>
                              </CombinedGeometry.Geometry2>
                          </CombinedGeometry>
                      </Path.Data>
                  </Path>

                  <TextBlock FontSize="12pt" Text="Xor"
                        Margin="45,15,5,10"/>
                  <Path Fill ="LightBlue" Stroke="Blue">
```

```xml
                    <Path.Data>
                        <CombinedGeometry
                            GeometryCombineMode="Xor">
                            <CombinedGeometry.Geometry1>
                                <EllipseGeometry
                                    Center="50,50"
                                    RadiusX="50"
                                    RadiusY="50"/>
                            </CombinedGeometry.Geometry1>
                            <CombinedGeometry.Geometry2>
                                <EllipseGeometry
                                    Center="80,50"
                                    RadiusX="50"
                                    RadiusY="50"/>
                            </CombinedGeometry.Geometry2>
                        </CombinedGeometry>
                    </Path.Data>
                </Path>
            </StackPanel>

            <StackPanel Grid.Column="1">
                <TextBlock FontSize="12pt"
                    Text="Intersect" Margin="30,5,5,10"/>
                <Path Fill ="LightBlue" Stroke="Blue"
                    Margin="5,0,0,0">
                    <Path.Data>
                        <CombinedGeometry
                            GeometryCombineMode="Intersect">
                            <CombinedGeometry.Geometry1>
                                <EllipseGeometry
                                    Center="50,50"
                                    RadiusX="50"
                                    RadiusY="50"/>
                            </CombinedGeometry.Geometry1>
                            <CombinedGeometry.Geometry2>
                                <EllipseGeometry
                                    Center="80,50"
                                    RadiusX="50"
                                    RadiusY="50"/>
                            </CombinedGeometry.Geometry2>
                        </CombinedGeometry>
                    </Path.Data>
                </Path>

                <TextBlock FontSize="12pt" Text="Exclude"
                    Margin="35,15,5,10"/>
                <Path Fill ="LightBlue" Stroke="Blue"
                    Margin="10,0,0,0">
                    <Path.Data>
                        <CombinedGeometry
                            GeometryCombineMode="Exclude">
                            <CombinedGeometry.Geometry1>
                                <EllipseGeometry
                                    Center="50,50"
```

```
                              RadiusX="50"
                              RadiusY="50"/>
                  </CombinedGeometry.Geometry1>
                  <CombinedGeometry.Geometry2>
                      <EllipseGeometry
                          Center="80,50"
                          RadiusX="50"
                          RadiusY="50"/>
                  </CombinedGeometry.Geometry2>
              </CombinedGeometry>
          </Path.Data>
        </Path>
      </StackPanel>
    </Grid>
  </Canvas>
 </Border>
</Window>
```

Figure 4-2 shows the results of running this example. You can clearly see how the CombinedGeometryMode property affects the combined area.

Although the CombinedGeometry only takes two geometries, you can actually combine any number of shapes by successively using the CombinedGeometry objects.

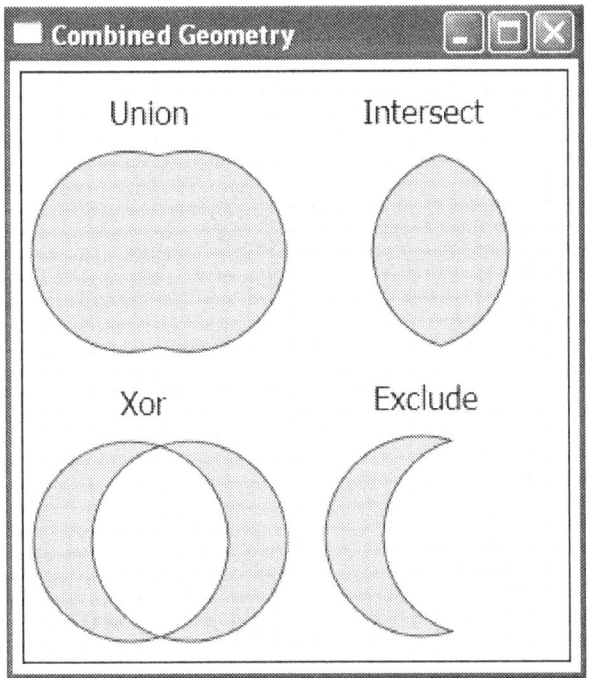

Figure 4-2 Shapes created using CombinedGeometry.

PathGeometry Class

The PathGeometry class is more powerful than the derived geometry classes discussed previously. It can be used to create any of the shapes that the other geometries can and much more. A PathGeometry object is built out of one or more PathFigure objects. Each PathFigure object is a continuous set of connected lines and curves that can be closed or open. The PathFigure object is closed if the end point of the last line in the object connects to the starting point of the first line.

The PathFigure class has four key properties, as listed below:

- StartPoint – A Point that indicates where the line or figure begins

- Segments – A collection of PathSegment objects that are used to draw the figure.

- IsClosed – If true, WPF adds a straight line to connect the starting and end points.

- IsFilled – If true, the area inside the figure is filled using the Path.Fill property.

Note that the PathFigure is a shape that is drawn using an unbroken line consisting of a number of segments. There are several types of segments, all of which derive from the PathSegment class. You can use different types of segments freely to build your figure. The segment classes in WPF are listed below:

- LineSegment – Creates a straight line between two points.

- ArcSegment – Creates an elliptical arc between two points.

- PolyLineSegment – Creates a series of straight lines.

- BezierSegment – Creates a Bezier curve between two points.

- QuadraticBezierSegment – Creates a Bezier curve that has one point instead of two.

- PolyBezierSegment – Creates a series of Bezier curves.

- PolyQuadraticBezierSegment – Creates a series of simpler quadratic Bezier curves.

The Line, Arc, and PolyLine segments may be more familiar to you than the Bezier-related segments. However, Bezier lines are one of the most important mathematical representations of curves and surfaces used in computer graphics and CAD applications. Bezier curves are polynomial curves based on a complicated mathematical representation. Fortunately, no mathematical knowledge is required in order to use the Bezier curves in WPF.

Lines and Polylines

It is easy to create a simple line using the LineSegment and PathGeometry classes. For example, the following XAML snippet begins at (10, 10), draws a straight line to (150, 150), and then draws a line from (150, 150) to (150, 200):

```
<Path Stroke="Black">
    <Path.Data>
        <PathGeometry>
            <PathFigure StartPoint="10,10">
                <LineSegment Point="150,150"/>
                <LineSegment Point="150,200"/>
            </PathFigure>
        </PathGeometry>
    </Path.Data>
</Path>
```

The PolyLineSegment creates a series of straight lines. You can get the same effect using multiple LineSegment objects, but a single PolyLineSegment is simpler. The following code creates a polyline:

```
<Path Stroke="Blue">
    <Path.Data>
        <PathGeometry>
            <PathFigure StartPoint="100,120">
                <PolyLineSegment
                    Points="200,120,200,220,100,170"/>
            </PathFigure>
        </PathGeometry>
    </Path.Data>
</Path>
```

Note that the number of PathFigure objects in a PathGeometry element is unlimited. This means that you can create several separate open or closed figures that are all considered part of the same path.

Arcs

An ArcSegment object is defined by its start and end points; its X- and Y-radii specified by the Size property; its X-axis rotation factor, a value indicating whether the arc should be greater than 180 degrees; and a value describing the direction in which the arc is drawn. Like the LineSegment, the ArcSegment class doesn't contain a property for the starting point of the arc: it only defines the destination point of the arc it represents. The beginning point of the arc is the current point of the PathFigure to which the ArcSegment is added.

The following markup creates an ellipse shape using two ArcSegment objects:

```
<Path Stroke="Blue">
    <Path.Data>
        <PathGeometry>
            <PathFigure StartPoint="100,50">
                <ArcSegment Point="200,50" Size="50,30"
```

```
                            SweepDirection="Counterclockwise"/>
                </PathFigure>
                <PathFigure StartPoint="100,50">
                    <ArcSegment Point="200,50" Size="50,30"
                            SweepDirection="Clockwise"/>
                </PathFigure>
            </PathGeometry>
        </Path.Data>
    </Path>
```

The complete markup file for Lines, PolyLines, and Arcs is given in the LineCurveExample.xaml file in the project Chapter04.

Bezier Curves

It is also easy to create a Bezier curve using the BezierSegment object. Note that a Bezier curve is defined by four points: a start point, an end point, and two control points. The BezierSegment class doesn't contain a property for the starting point of the curve; it only defines the end point. The beginning point of the curve is the current point of the PathFigure to which the BezierSegment is added.

The two control points of a cubic Bezier curve behave like magnets, attracting portions of what would otherwise be a straight line towards themselves and producing a curve. The first control point affects the beginning portion of the curve; while the second control point affects the ending portion of the curve. The curve doesn't necessarily pass through either of the control points; each control point moves its portion of the line toward itself, not through itself.

The following example shows a Bezier curve, whose two control points are animated. The X-coordinate of the first control point and the Y-coordinate of the second control point vary in the range [50, 250]. You can clearly see how the Bezier curve changes shape when the control points are animated.

Add a new WPF Window to the project Chapter04 and name it AnimateBezierCurve. Here is the markup of this example:

```
<Window x:Class="Chapter04.AnimateBezierCurve"
    xmlns="http://schemas.microsoft.com/winfx
        /2006/xaml/presentation"
    xmlns:x="http://schemas.microsoft.com/winfx/2006/xaml"
    Title="Bezier Curve" Height="300" Width="300">

    <Viewbox Stretch="Fill">
        <Border Margin="5" BorderBrush="Black"
                BorderThickness="1"
                Background="{StaticResource MyGrayGridBrush}"
                HorizontalAlignment="Left">
            <Canvas x:Name="canvas1" Width="300" Height="270">
                <Path Stroke="Black" StrokeThickness="5">
                    <Path.Data>
                        <PathGeometry>
```

```
                        <PathFigure StartPoint="20,20">
                            <BezierSegment
        x:Name="bezierSegment" Point1="150,50"
        Point2="60,160" Point3="250,230"/>
                        </PathFigure>
                    </PathGeometry>
                </Path.Data>
            </Path>
            <Path x:Name="path1" Fill="Red" Stroke="Red">
                <Path.Data>
                    <GeometryGroup>
                        <LineGeometry x:Name="line1"
                                      StartPoint="20,20"
                                      EndPoint="150,50"/>
                        <EllipseGeometry x:Name="ellipse1"
                                      Center="150,50"
                                      RadiusX="5"
                                      RadiusY="5" />
                        <LineGeometry x:Name="line2"
                                      StartPoint="60,160"
                                      EndPoint="250,230"/>
                        <EllipseGeometry x:Name="ellipse2"
                                      Center="60,160"
                                      RadiusX="5"
                                      RadiusY="5" />
                    </GeometryGroup>
                </Path.Data>
            </Path>

            <!-- Set animation: -->
            <Canvas.Triggers>
                <EventTrigger RoutedEvent="Canvas.Loaded">
                    <BeginStoryboard>
<Storyboard RepeatBehavior="Forever" AutoReverse="True">
    <PointAnimation Storyboard.TargetName="bezierSegment"
                    Storyboard.TargetProperty="Point1"
                    From="50 20" To="250 20"
                    Duration="0:0:5"/>

    <PointAnimation Storyboard.TargetName="line1"
                    Storyboard.TargetProperty="EndPoint"
                    From="50 20" To="250 20"
                    Duration="0:0:5"/>

    <PointAnimation Storyboard.TargetName="ellipse1"
                    Storyboard.TargetProperty="Center"
                    From="50 20" To="250 20"
                    Duration="0:0:5"/>

    <PointAnimation Storyboard.TargetName="bezierSegment"
                    Storyboard.TargetProperty="Point2"
                    From="60 50" To="60 250"
                    Duration="0:0:5"/>
```

```
<PointAnimation Storyboard.TargetName="line2"
                Storyboard.TargetProperty="StartPoint"
                From="60 50" To="60 250"
                Duration="0:0:5"/>

<PointAnimation Storyboard.TargetName="ellipse2"
                Storyboard.TargetProperty="Center"
                From="60 50" To="60 250"
                Duration="0:0:5"/>

            </Storyboard>
          </BeginStoryboard>
        </EventTrigger>
      </Canvas.Triggers>
    </Canvas>
  </Border>
 </Viewbox>
</Window>
```

This XAML file creates a Bezier curve using BezierSegment. The two control points, Point1 and Point2, of the Bezier curve are marked specifically by two ellipse shapes. At the same time, two line segments are created to guide your eye during the animation. The first line segment connects the starting point and Point1, while the second segment connects the end point and Point2.

The animation is performed within a Storyboard element using PointAnimation. Here, you animate not only the control points of the Bezier curve, but also the red dots (ellipses) and the guide lines.

This example produces the result shown in Figure 4-3, where you can see how the Bezier curve changes when the control points move.

Geometry and Mini-Language

StreamGeometry is a light-weight alternative to the PathGeometry class for creating complex geometric shapes. You can use StreamGeometry when you need to describe a complex geometry but don't want the overhead of supporting data binding, animation, and modification. WPF supports a powerful mini-language that you can use to describe geometric paths.

There are two classes in WPF that provide the mini-language for describing geometric paths: StreamGeometry, and PathFigureCollection. You need to use the StreamGeometry mini-language when you set a property of the Geometry type, such as the Data property of a Path element. On the other hand, you use the PathFigureCollection mini-language when you set the Figures property of a PathGeometry.

To understand the mini-language, you need to realize that it is simply a long string that holds a series of commands. These commands are used by WPF to create corresponding geometries. Each command is a single letter followed by numeric information separated by spaces or commas.

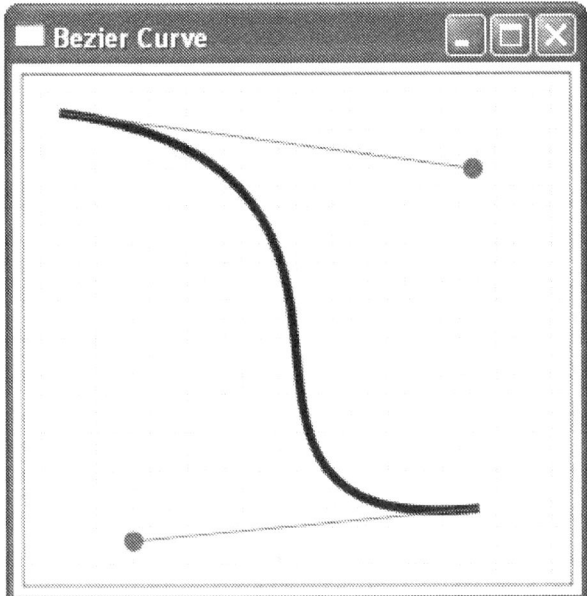

Figure 4-3 A Bezier curve.

For example, in the earlier section, you created a polyline with a PathGeometry using the following XAML snippet:

```
<Path Stroke="Blue">
    <Path.Data>
        <PathGeometry>
            <PathFigure StartPoint="100,120">
                <PolyLineSegment
                    Points="200,120,200,220,100,170"/>
            </PathFigure>
        </PathGeometry>
    </Path.Data>
</Path>
```

You can use the StreamGeometry mini-language to duplicate this polyline:

```
<Path Stroke="Blue"
      Data="M 100 120 L 200 120 L 200 220 L 100 170"/>
```

This path uses a sequence of four commands. The first command, M, creates the PathFigure and sets the starting point to (100, 120). The following three commands (L) create line segments.

When you create a StreamGeometry object using the StreamGeometry mini-language, you can't modify the geometry later on in your code. If this isn't acceptable, you can create a PathGeometry using the PathFigureCollection mini-language. The following example uses a attribute syntax to create a PathFigure collection for a PathGeometry:

```
<Path Stroke="Blue">
    <Path.Data>
        <PathGeometry Figures="M 100 120
                    L 200 120 L 200 220 L 100 170"/>
    </Path.Data>
</Path>
```

As you can see from the above examples, the two mini-languages are very similar. It is always possible to use PathGeometry in any situation where you could use StreamGeometry; so which one should you use? Use StreamGeometry when you don't need to modify the path after creating it; use PathGeometry if you do need to modify the path in your code.

It is easy to use the mini-language to create complex geometry shapes. The mini-language uses a fairly small set of commands. For your reference, the mini-language commands are listed in Table 4-1.

Table 4-1 Commands for the Geometry Mini-Language

Name	Command	Description
Full rule	F0 or F1	Specifies geometry's FillRule property. F0 for EvenOdd, F1 for Nonzero. This command must appear at beginning of the string.
Move	M startPt m startPt	Creates a new PathFigure and sets its start point. This command must be used before any other commands except for F0 or F1.
Line	L endpt l endPt	Creates a LineSegment from the current point to the specified end point.
Horizontal line	H x h x	Creates a horizontal line between the current point and the specified X-coordinate.
Vertical line	V y v y	Creates a vertical line between the current point and the specified Y-coordinate.
Cubic Bezier curve	C pt1, pt2, endPt c pt1, pt2, endPt	Creates a cubic Bezier curve between the current point and the specified end point by using the two specified control points (pt1 and pt2).
Quadratic Bezier curve	Q pt, endpt q pt, endPt	Creates a quadratic Bezier curve between the current point and the specified end point using the specified control point (pt).
Smooth cubic Bezier curve	S pt2, endpt s pt2, endPt	Creates a cubic Bezier curve between the current point and specified end point. The first control point is assumed to be the reflection of the second control point of the previous command relative to the

		current point.
Smooth Quadratic Bezier curve	T pt, endpoint t pt, endPoint	Creates a quadratic Bezier curve between the current point and the specified end point. The control point is assumed to be the reflection of the control point of the previous command relative to the current point.
Elliptical Arc	A size, angle, isLargeArc, Direction, endpoint a size, angle,…	Creates an elliptical arc between the current point and the specified end point. You specify the size of the ellipse, the rotation angle, and Boolean flags that set the IsLargeArc and SweepDirection properties.
Close	Z z	Ends the current figure and creates a line that connects the current point to the starting point of the figure. You don't need to use this command if you don't want to close the path.
Point	X, Y or x y	Describe the X- and Y-coordinates of a point.
Special values	Infinity -Infinity NaN	Instead of a standard numerical value, you can also use these special values. These values are case-sensitive.

The commands with uppercase letters use absolute coordinates while the commands with lowercase letters evaluate parameters relative to the previous point.

Interactive 2D Drawing

In the previous sections, we discussed Geometry and Path, as well as GeometryGroup and CombinedGeometry. Now it is time for you to put all of them together in a real-world WPF application. This application allows you to draw 2D shapes using your mouse, combine shapes, drag and move shapes, and delete shapes interactively. The approach applied in this project will be useful when you develop interactive CAD applications.

First I'll present all of the source code and the corresponding results, which show you what this program can do and how to use it. Next, I'll discuss the functionality of the properties and methods used in the program.

Add a new WPF Window to the project Chapter04 and call it Interactive2DDrawing. The following XAML file creates the interface and layout for the application:

```xml
<Window x:Class="Chapter04.Interactive2DDrawing"
    xmlns="http://schemas.microsoft.com/winfx
        /2006/xaml/presentation"
    xmlns:x="http://schemas.microsoft.com/winfx/2006/xaml"
    Title="Interactive 2D Drawing" Height="400" Width="400">

    <Grid>
        <Grid.RowDefinitions>
            <RowDefinition Height="Auto"/>
            <RowDefinition/>
        </Grid.RowDefinitions>

        <ToolBarTray Grid.Row="0">
            <ToolBar>
                <RadioButton x:Name="rbSquare"
                    IsChecked="True" ToolTip="Add Square">
                    <Rectangle Width="15" Height="15"
                        Stroke="Blue" Fill="LightBlue"/>
                </RadioButton>

                <RadioButton x:Name="rbRectangle"
                    IsChecked="False" ToolTip="Add Rectangle">
                    <Rectangle Width="20" Height="12"
                        Stroke="Blue" Fill="LightBlue"/>
                </RadioButton>

                <RadioButton x:Name="rbCircle"
                    IsChecked="False" ToolTip="Add Circle">
                    <Ellipse Width="18" Height="18"
                            Stroke="Blue" Fill="LightBlue"/>
                </RadioButton>

                <RadioButton x:Name="rbEllipse"
                    IsChecked="False" ToolTip="Add Ellipse">
                    <Ellipse Width="22" Height="15"
                            Stroke="Blue" Fill="LightBlue"/>
                </RadioButton>

                <RadioButton x:Name="rbCombine"
                    IsChecked="False" ToolTip="Combine shapes">
                    <Path Fill="LightBlue" Stroke="Blue">
                        <Path.Data>
                            <CombinedGeometry>
                                <CombinedGeometry.Geometry1>
                                    <EllipseGeometry
                                        RadiusX="8"
                                        RadiusY="8"
                                        Center="8,8"/>
                                </CombinedGeometry.Geometry1>
                                <CombinedGeometry.Geometry2>
                                    <EllipseGeometry
                                        RadiusX="8"
                                        RadiusY="8"
                                        Center="20,8"/>
```

```
                              </CombinedGeometry.Geometry2>
                          </CombinedGeometry>
                      </Path.Data>
                  </Path>
              </RadioButton>

              <RadioButton x:Name="rbSelect"
                  IsChecked="False" ToolTip="Select/Move">
                  <Polygon
                   Points="6 1,10 1,10 10,14 10,8 16,2 10,6 10"
                          Fill="LightBlue" Stroke="Blue">
                          <Polygon.RenderTransform>
                              <RotateTransform CenterX="8"
                                              CenterY="8"
                                              Angle="225"/>
                          </Polygon.RenderTransform>
                  </Polygon>
              </RadioButton>

              <RadioButton x:Name="rbDelete"
                  IsChecked="False" ToolTip="Delete">
                  <Grid>
                      <Line X1="2" Y1="2" X2="14"
                              Y2="14" Stroke="Blue"/>
                      <Line X1="2" Y1="14" X2="14"
                              Y2="2" Stroke="Blue"/>
                  </Grid>
              </RadioButton>
          </ToolBar>
      </ToolBarTray>

      <Viewbox Stretch="Uniform" Grid.Row="1">
          <Border Margin="5" BorderBrush="Black"
                  BorderThickness="1" Grid.Row="1"
                  HorizontalAlignment="Left">
              <Canvas Name="canvas1" Width="400"
                      Height="345" ClipToBounds="True"
          Background="{StaticResource MyGrayGridBrush}"
          MouseLeftButtonDown="OnMouseLeftButtonDown"
          MouseLeftButtonUp="OnMouseLeftButtonUp"
          MouseMove="OnMouseMove"/>
          </Border>
      </Viewbox>
      </Grid>
  </Window>
```

Here, we add a ToolBarTray to the layout, which contains toolbars made of seven radio buttons. These radio buttons have different functionalities and can be used to add a square, rectangle, circle, or ellipse; combine shapes; select/move shapes; and delete shapes, depending on which radio button is selected. Different technologies are used to create these buttons, including CombinedGeometry and rotation transforms.

The drawing area is defined by a Canvas object, canvas1, where several mouse click events are involved. These events include MouseLeftButtonDown, MouseLeftButtonUp, and MouseMove, which allow you to implement interactive applications in code. More about mouse events will be discussed later in this chapter.

The code-behind file of this application is listed below:

```
using System;
using System.Collections.Generic;
using System.Windows;
using System.Windows.Controls;
using System.Windows.Input;
using System.Windows.Media;
using System.Windows.Shapes;

namespace Chapter04
{
    public partial class Interactive2DDrawing : Window
    {
        private List<Path> paths = new List<Path>();
        private Point startPoint = new Point();
        private Shape rubberBand = null;
        Point currentPoint = new Point();
        private bool isDragging = false;
        private bool isDown = false;
        private Path originalElement = new Path();
        private Path movingElement = new Path();
        private Path path1 = new Path();
        private Path path2 = new Path();
        private SolidColorBrush fillColor =
                            new SolidColorBrush();
        private SolidColorBrush borderColor =
                            new SolidColorBrush();
        private SolidColorBrush selectFillColor =
                            new SolidColorBrush();
        private SolidColorBrush selectBorderColor =
                            new SolidColorBrush();

        public Interactive2DDrawing()
        {
            InitializeComponent();
            fillColor.Color = Colors.LightGray;
            fillColor.Opacity = 0.5;
            borderColor.Color = Colors.Gray;
            selectFillColor.Color = Colors.LightCoral;
            selectFillColor.Opacity = 0.5;
            selectBorderColor.Color = Colors.Red;
        }

        private void OnMouseLeftButtonDown(
            object sender, MouseButtonEventArgs e)
        {
            if (!canvas1.IsMouseCaptured)
```

```
    {
        startPoint = e.GetPosition(canvas1);
        canvas1.CaptureMouse();

        if (rbCombine.IsChecked == true)
        {
            SetCombineShapes(e);
        }
        else if (rbSelect.IsChecked == true)
        {
            if (canvas1 == e.Source)
                return;
            isDown = true;
            originalElement = (Path)e.Source;
            e.Handled = true;
        }
        else if (rbDelete.IsChecked == true)
        {
            originalElement = (Path)e.Source;
            DeleteShape(originalElement);
        }
    }
}

private void DeleteShape(Path path)
{
    path.Stroke = selectBorderColor;
    string msg =
        "Do you really want to delete this shape?";
    string title = "Delete Shape?";
    MessageBoxButton buttons = MessageBoxButton.YesNo;
    MessageBoxImage icon = MessageBoxImage.Warning;
    MessageBoxResult result =
        MessageBox.Show(msg, title, buttons, icon);
    if (result == MessageBoxResult.Yes)
        canvas1.Children.Remove(path);
    else
    {
        path.Stroke = borderColor;
        return;
    }
}

private void SetCombineShapes(MouseButtonEventArgs e)
{
    if (path1.Name != "path1Selected")
    {
        path1 = (Path)e.Source;
        path1.Cursor = Cursors.Hand;
        path1.Stroke = selectBorderColor;
        path1.Name = "path1Selected";
    }
    else
    {
```

```
            if (path2 != null)
            {
                path2.Stroke = borderColor;
                path2.Cursor = Cursors.Arrow;
            }
            path2 = (Path)e.Source;
            path2.Cursor = Cursors.Hand;
            path2.Stroke = selectBorderColor;

            ContextMenu cm = new ContextMenu();
            path2.ContextMenu = cm;
            MenuItem mi = new MenuItem();
            mi.Header = "Union";
            mi.Click +=
                new RoutedEventHandler(Union_Click);
            cm.Items.Add(mi);
            mi = new MenuItem();
            mi.Header = "Xor";
            mi.Click +=
                new RoutedEventHandler(Xor_Click);
            cm.Items.Add(mi);
            mi = new MenuItem();
            mi.Header = "Intersect";
            mi.Click +=
                new RoutedEventHandler(Intersect_Click);
            cm.Items.Add(mi);
            mi = new MenuItem();
            mi.Header = "Exclude";
            mi.Click +=
                new RoutedEventHandler(Exclude_Click);
            cm.Items.Add(mi);
        }
    }

    private void Union_Click(
        object sender, RoutedEventArgs e)
    {
        CombineShapes(path1, path2, "Union");
        path1.Name = "";
    }

    private void Xor_Click(object sender,
        RoutedEventArgs e)
    {
        CombineShapes(path1, path2, "Xor");
        path1.Name = "";
    }

    private void Intersect_Click(object sender,
        RoutedEventArgs e)
    {
        CombineShapes(path1, path2, "Intersect");
        path1.Name = "";
    }
```

```
private void Exclude_Click(object sender,
    RoutedEventArgs e)
{
    CombineShapes(path1, path2, "Exclude");
    path1.Name = "";
}

private void CombineShapes(Path p1, Path p2, string s)
{
    Path myPath = new Path();
    myPath.Fill = fillColor;
    myPath.Stroke = borderColor;
    CombinedGeometry cg = new CombinedGeometry();

    if (s == "Union")
        cg.GeometryCombineMode =
            GeometryCombineMode.Union;
    else if (s == "Xor")
        cg.GeometryCombineMode =
            GeometryCombineMode.Xor;
    else if (s == "Intersect")
        cg.GeometryCombineMode =
            GeometryCombineMode.Intersect;
    else if (s == "Exclude")
        cg.GeometryCombineMode =
            GeometryCombineMode.Exclude;
    cg.Geometry1 = p1.Data;
    cg.Geometry2 = p2.Data;
    myPath.Data = cg;
    paths.Add(myPath);
    canvas1.Children.Add(paths[paths.Count - 1]);
    canvas1.Children.Remove(p1);
    canvas1.Children.Remove(p2);
}

private void OnMouseMove(object sender,
    MouseEventArgs e)
{
    if (canvas1.IsMouseCaptured)
    {
        currentPoint = e.GetPosition(canvas1);
        if (rubberBand == null)
        {
            rubberBand = new Rectangle();
            rubberBand.Stroke = Brushes.LightCoral;
            rubberBand.StrokeDashArray =
              new DoubleCollection(new double[]{4,2});
            if (rbSquare.IsChecked == true ||
                rbRectangle.IsChecked == true ||
                rbCircle.IsChecked == true ||
                rbEllipse.IsChecked == true)
            {
                canvas1.Children.Add(rubberBand);
```

```
                                    }
                                }

                    double width = Math.Abs(
                        startPoint.X - currentPoint.X);
                    double height = Math.Abs(
                        startPoint.Y - currentPoint.Y);
                    double left = Math.Min(
                        startPoint.X, currentPoint.X);
                    double top = Math.Min(
                        startPoint.Y, currentPoint.Y);

                    rubberBand.Width = width;
                    rubberBand.Height = height;
                    Canvas.SetLeft(rubberBand, left);
                    Canvas.SetTop(rubberBand, top);

                    if (rbSelect.IsChecked == true)
                    {
                        if (isDown)
                        {
        if (!isDragging && Math.Abs(currentPoint.X - startPoint.X) >
            SystemParameters.MinimumHorizontalDragDistance &&
            Math.Abs(currentPoint.Y - startPoint.Y) >
            SystemParameters.MinimumVerticalDragDistance)
            DragStarting();
                            if (isDragging)
                                DragMoving();
                        }
                    }
                }
            }

        private void OnMouseLeftButtonUp(
            object sender, MouseButtonEventArgs e)
        {
            if (rbSquare.IsChecked == true)
                AddSquare(startPoint, currentPoint);
            else if (rbRectangle.IsChecked == true)
                AddRectangle(startPoint, currentPoint);
            else if (rbCircle.IsChecked == true)
                AddCircle(startPoint, currentPoint);
            else if (rbEllipse.IsChecked == true)
                AddEllipse(startPoint, currentPoint);

            if (rubberBand != null)
            {
                canvas1.Children.Remove(rubberBand);
                rubberBand = null;
                canvas1.ReleaseMouseCapture();
            }

            if (rbSelect.IsChecked == true)
            {
```

```
        if (isDown)
        {
            DragFinishing(false);
            e.Handled = true;
        }
    }
}

private void AddRectangle(Point pt1, Point pt2)
{
    Path path = new Path();
    path.Fill = fillColor;
    path.Stroke = borderColor;
    RectangleGeometry rg = new RectangleGeometry();
    double width = Math.Abs(pt1.X - pt2.X);
    double height = Math.Abs(pt1.Y - pt2.Y);
    double left = Math.Min(pt1.X, pt2.X);
    double top = Math.Min(pt1.Y, pt2.Y);
    rg.Rect = new Rect(left, top, width, height);
    path.Data = rg;
    paths.Add(path);
    canvas1.Children.Add(paths[paths.Count - 1]);
}

private void AddSquare(Point pt1, Point pt2)
{
    Path path = new Path();
    path.Fill = fillColor;
    path.Stroke = borderColor;
    RectangleGeometry rg = new RectangleGeometry();
    double width = Math.Abs(pt1.X - pt2.X);
    double height = Math.Abs(pt1.Y - pt2.Y);
    double left = Math.Min(pt1.X, pt2.X);
    double top = Math.Min(pt1.Y, pt2.Y);
    double side = width;
    if (width > height)
        side = height;
    rg.Rect = new Rect(left, top, side, side);
    path.Data = rg;
    paths.Add(path);
    canvas1.Children.Add(paths[paths.Count - 1]);
}

private void AddCircle(Point pt1, Point pt2)
{
    Path path = new Path();
    path.Fill = fillColor;
    path.Stroke = borderColor;
    EllipseGeometry eg = new EllipseGeometry();
    double width = Math.Abs(pt1.X - pt2.X);
    double height = Math.Abs(pt1.Y - pt2.Y);
    double left = Math.Min(pt1.X, pt2.X);
    double top = Math.Min(pt1.Y, pt2.Y);
    double side = width;
```

```
            if (width > height)
                side = height;
            eg.Center = new Point(left + side / 2,
                top + side / 2);
            eg.RadiusX = side / 2;
            eg.RadiusY = side / 2;
            path.Data = eg;
            paths.Add(path);
            canvas1.Children.Add(paths[paths.Count - 1]);
        }

        private void AddEllipse(Point pt1, Point pt2)
        {
            Path path = new Path();
            path.Fill = fillColor;
            path.Stroke = borderColor;
            EllipseGeometry eg = new EllipseGeometry();
            double width = Math.Abs(pt1.X - pt2.X);
            double height = Math.Abs(pt1.Y - pt2.Y);
            double left = Math.Min(pt1.X, pt2.X);
            double top = Math.Min(pt1.Y, pt2.Y);
            eg.Center = new Point(left + width / 2,
                top + height / 2);
            eg.RadiusX = width / 2;
            eg.RadiusY = height / 2;
            path.Data = eg;
            paths.Add(path);
            canvas1.Children.Add(paths[paths.Count - 1]);
        }

        private void DragStarting()
        {
            isDragging = true;
            movingElement = new Path();
            movingElement.Data = originalElement.Data;
            movingElement.Fill = selectFillColor;
            movingElement.Stroke = selectBorderColor;
            canvas1.Children.Add(movingElement);
        }

        private void DragMoving()
        {
            currentPoint = Mouse.GetPosition(canvas1);
            TranslateTransform tt = new TranslateTransform();
            tt.X = currentPoint.X - startPoint.X;
            tt.Y = currentPoint.Y - startPoint.Y;
            movingElement.RenderTransform = tt;
        }

        private void DragFinishing(bool cancel)
        {
            Mouse.Capture(null);
            if(isDragging)
            {
```

```
if (!cancel)
{
    currentPoint = Mouse.GetPosition(canvas1);
    TranslateTransform tt0 = new TranslateTransform();
    TranslateTransform tt = new TranslateTransform();
    tt.X = currentPoint.X - startPoint.X;
    tt.Y = currentPoint.Y - startPoint.Y;
       Geometry geometry =
                 (RectangleGeometry)new RectangleGeometry();

string s = originalElement.Data.ToString();
if (s == "System.Windows.Media.EllipseGeometry")
    geometry = (EllipseGeometry)originalElement.Data;
else if (s == "System.Windows.Media.RectangleGeometry")
    geometry = (RectangleGeometry)originalElement.Data;
else if (s == System.Windows.Media.CombinedGeometry")
    geometry = CombinedGeometry)originalElement.Data;

if (geometry.Transform.ToString()!= "Identity")
{
    tt0 = (TranslateTransform)geometry.Transform;
    tt.X += tt0.X;
    tt.Y += tt0.Y;
}

                    geometry.Transform = tt;
                    canvas1.Children.Remove(originalElement);
                    originalElement = new Path();
                    originalElement.Fill = fillColor;
                    originalElement.Stroke = borderColor;
                    originalElement.Data = geometry;
                    canvas1.Children.Add(originalElement);
                }
                canvas1.Children.Remove(movingElement);
                movingElement = null;
            }
            isDragging = false;
            isDown = false;
        }
    }
}
```

The above code-behind file involves several techniques, including mouse click events that allow the user to interact with the program, the rubberband for the outline of the shape to be drawn following the mouse cursor, shapes created using Geometry objects, combinations of shapes, transforms on Path and Geometry objects, etc.

In the following sections, I'll explain how this application works. But first I want to show you the results of this project. Figure 4-4 is a snapshot generated from this program. You can see from this figure that the application allows the user to add various shapes, including squares, rectangles, circles, and ellipses, and perform various operations on the shapes, such as combining, dragging, moving, and deleting the shapes.

Figure 4-4 Interactive 2D drawing application in WPF.

Mouse Events

In the above example, several mouse events were used to perform various operations, including LeftMouseButtomDown, LeftMouseButtonUp, and MouseMove. The mouse button events provide a MouseButtonEventArgs object. The MouseButtonEventArgs class derives from the MouseEventArgs base class. Different tasks are performed depending on which radio button is checked when you press the left mouse button down. First, you obtain a position (a Point object) at which the left mouse button is clicked on the canvas1 control. Then you set the mouse's Capture state. Usually, when an object receives a mouse button down event, it will receive a corresponding mouse button up event shortly thereafter. However, in this example, you need to hold down the mouse and move it around. Thus, you want to have a notification of the mouse up event. To do so, you need to capture the mouse by calling the CaptureMouse() method and passing to the canvas1 control.

At the same time, this MouseLeftButtonDown event also controls combining, selecting and moving, or deleting shapes, depending on which radio button is checked.

The MouseMove event performs two main tasks. First it draws various shapes, including squares, rectangles, circles, or ellipses. When it draws a shape, a rubberband is created. This rubberband is a common feature in graphics applications. It provides an outline of a shape to be drawn following the mouse cursor, so you can visualize exactly where the shape will be drawn on your screen.

The other task performed by the MouseMove event is selecting and moving shapes when the Select/Move radio button is clicked. Two Boolean numbers, isDown and isDragging, are used to control the DragStarting and DragMoving.

Sevral actions happen in the MouseLeftButtonUp event. The event adds a shape to the canvas1 if the square, rectangle, circle, or ellipse radio button is checked. It also removes the rubberband after creating the shape. Finally, it is responsible for calling the DragFinishing method, which terminates the moving of the shape when the Select/Move radio button is checked.

In this example, you use three Mouse events. There are more mouse events in WPF that you can use in developing interactive graphics applications. For example, mouse events allow you to react when the mouse pointer moves over a graphics object. These events include MouseEnter and MouseLeave, which provide information about a MouseEventArgs object for your program. The MouseEventArgs object includes properties that show you the state of the mouse button. There are also many other mouse events in WPF that you can use in your applications. If you need more information about mouse events, you can refer to Microsoft online help or tutorial books on the topic.

Creating and Combining Shapes

In this example, the shapes are created using the RectangleGeometry and EllipseGeometry classes. You can also create shapes directly using the Rectangle and Ellipse shapes deriving from the Shape class, but if you do so, you won't be able to perform shape combination.

Let's look at the AddRectangle method. It takes two Point objects as input parameters. One is the start point, pt1, recorded when the MouseLeftButtonDown event fires, and the other is the current point, pt2, recorded when the MouseLeftButtonUp event fires. After some manipulations, these two points are used to set the Rect property of the RectangleGeometry object. You then use a Path object to draw the RectangleGeometry. Notice that a path collection object, named paths, created using List<Path>, is used to hold all the Path objects. This allows you to add any number of rectangles to the canvas1 control. Following the same procedure, you can create square, circle, or ellipse shapes.

The advantage of using Geometry objects is that shapes can be combined using the CombinedGeometry class. The SetCombineShapes method performs the shape combination. You pick up two shapes (both are Path objects) to combine with the different GeometryCombineMode by clicking you rmouse. The GeometryCombineMode includes Union, Xor, Intersect, and Exclude, and are implemented in a Context Menu attached to the second Path object. You can select the GeometryCombineMode by right clicking on the path2 object.

The CombineShapes method performs the shape combination. The code snippet

```
Path myPath = new Path();
CombinedGeometry cg = new CombinedGeometry();
.......
cg.Geometry1 = p1.Data;
cg.Geometry2 = p2.Data;
myPath.Data = cg;
paths.Add(myPath);
canvas1.Children.Add(paths[paths.Count - 1]);
```

shows the detailed combining procedure. First, you create a new Path and a new CombinedGeometry object, named "myPath" and "cg". Then the GeometryCombineMode property of cg is specified (not shown in the above code snippet). Next, you set cg's Geometry1 and Geometry2 properties using Data property of the first Path object, p1, and second Path object, p2, respectively. Finally, you add the combined shape (myPath) to the canvas1 control via the Path collection "paths".

Dragging and Moving Shapes

This application also allows you to select, drag, and move shapes using the mouse when the Select/Move RadioButton is checked.

The dragStarting and DragMoving methods are responsible for dragging and moving the shape. When the user starts dragging, the DragStarting method creates a MovingElement that is simply a copy of the selected shape, but with different Stroke and Fill properties to distinguish it from the other unselected shapes. This MovingElement is added to the canvas1 control.

The DragMoving method is simple:

```
private void DragMoving()
{
    currentPoint = Mouse.GetPosition(canvas1);
    TranslateTransform tt = new TranslateTransform();
    tt.X = currentPoint.X - startPoint.X;
    tt.Y = currentPoint.Y - startPoint.Y;
    movingElement.RenderTransform = tt;
}
```

It simply performs a translation transform using the current point of your mouse cursor relative to the dragging starting point. Thus, the movingElement will move with your mouse pointer.

When the user finishes dragging and moving the shape, you need to delete the MovingElement from the canvas1 and place the original selected shape in the final position. In this step, you need to record all the translation transforms associated with the shape and pass these transforms to the Geometry's Transform property, as you did in the DragFinishing method:

```
........
if (geometry.Transform.ToString() != "Identity")
{
    tt0 = (TranslateTransform)geometry.Transform;
    tt.X += tt0.X;
    tt.Y += tt0.Y;
}
geometry.Transform = tt;
........
```

Notice that the transforms are performed on the underlying Geometry, not directly on the shape (the Path object). This is necessary because WPF performs the RenderTransform of a shape in a local coordinate system associated with the shape. The shape's absolute coordinates don't change after transforms. Thus, if you place the shape using its RenderTransform property, and then drag and move the already dragged and moved shape, you'll start dragging and moving the shape from its original location, instead of its location after you dragged.

Based on this example, you can develop a sophisticated 2D drawing program by adding more features. You could easily add more types of shapes, such as polygons, lines, and polylines. You could also easily add features like copy, paste, undo, edit, save, etc. to the program.

Hit Testing

In the above interactive 2D drawing example, the user's interaction with the shapes is treated directly using mouse event handlers. However, WPF provides powerful hit-testing for visuals through the static VisualTreeHelper.HitTest method. In developing interactive 2D drawing applications, you can perform tasks such as dragging, moving, dropping, and deleting shapes more efficiently using the HitTest method. In particular, when you design a complex application that contains overlapped visuals, this HitTest method allow you to retrieve all the visuals (not just the topmost visual) at a specified point, even the visuals obscured underneath other visuals. You can also find all the visuals that fall within a given geometry.

In order to use this advanced hit-testing feature, you need to create a callback. The VisualTreeHelper will then walk through your visuals from top to bottom. Whenever it finds a match, it calls the callback with the details. You can then choose to stop the search or continue until no more visuals remain.

The following example shows how to use this advanced hit-testing feature. Add a new WPF Window to the project Chapter04 and name it HitTestExample. In this example, you'll create several rectangle shapes on a Canvas, some of which are overlapped each other. The program will tell you how many rectangles are hit when the user clicks a point on the rectangles.

Here is the XAML file of this example:

```
<Window x:Class="Chapter04.HitTestExample"
    xmlns="http://schemas.microsoft.com/winfx
        /2006/xaml/presentation"
    xmlns:x="http://schemas.microsoft.com/winfx/2006/xaml"
    Title="Chapter04" Height="300" Width="300">

<Canvas x:Name="canvas1"
        MouseLeftButtonDown="OnMouseLeftButtonDown">
        <Rectangle Canvas.Left="20" Canvas.Top="20"
                Width="100" Height="60"
                Stroke="Black" Fill="LightBlue"
                Opacity="0.7"/>
        <Rectangle Canvas.Left="70" Canvas.Top="50"
                Width="100" Height="60"
                Stroke="Black" Fill="LightBlue"
                Opacity="0.7"/>
        <Rectangle Canvas.Left="150" Canvas.Top="80"
                Width="100" Height="60"
                Stroke="Black" Fill="LightBlue"
                Opacity="0.7"/>
        <Rectangle Canvas.Left="20" Canvas.Top="100"
                Width="50" Height="50"
                Stroke="Black" Fill="LightBlue"
                Opacity="0.7"/>
        <Rectangle Canvas.Left="40" Canvas.Top="60"
                Width="50" Height="50"
                Stroke="Black" Fill="LightBlue"
                Opacity="0.7"/>
        <Rectangle Canvas.Left="30" Canvas.Top="130"
                Width="50" Height="50"
                Stroke="Black" Fill="LightBlue"
                Opacity="0.7"/>
    </Canvas>
</Window>
```

This XAMl file adds six rectangles to the Canvas. The hit-testing is performed in code:

```
using System;
using System.Collections.Generic;
using System.Windows;
using System.Windows.Controls;
using System.Windows.Input;
using System.Windows.Media;
using System.Windows.Shapes;

namespace Chapter04
{
    public partial class HitTestExample : Window
    {
```

```csharp
private List<Rectangle> hitList =
        new List<Rectangle>();
private EllipseGeometry hitArea =
        new EllipseGeometry();

public HitTestExample()
{
    InitializeComponent();
    Initialize();
}

private void Initialize()
{
    foreach (Rectangle rect in canvas1.Children)
    {
        rect.Fill = Brushes.LightBlue;
    }
}

private void OnMouseLeftButtonDown(
    object sender, MouseButtonEventArgs e)
{
    // Initialization:
    Initialize();

    // Get mouse click point:
    Point pt = e.GetPosition(canvas1);

    // Define hit-testing area:
    hitArea = new EllipseGeometry(pt, 1.0, 1.0);
    hitList.Clear();

    // Call HitTest method:
    VisualTreeHelper.HitTest(canvas1, null,
        new HitTestResultCallback(HitTestCallback),
        new GeometryHitTestParameters(hitArea));

    if (hitList.Count > 0)
    {
        foreach (Rectangle rect in hitList)
        {
        // Change rectangle fill color if it is hit:
            rect.Fill = Brushes.LightCoral;
        }
        MessageBox.Show("You hit " +
            hitList.Count.ToString() + " rectangles.");
    }
}

public HitTestResultBehavior HitTestCallback(
    HitTestResult result)
{
    // Retrieve the results of the hit test.
```

```
            IntersectionDetail intersectionDetail =
((GeometryHitTestResult)result).IntersectionDetail;

            switch (intersectionDetail)
            {
                case IntersectionDetail.FullyContains:
                    // Add the hit test result to the list:
                    hitList.Add((Rectangle)result.VisualHit);
                    return HitTestResultBehavior.Continue;

                case IntersectionDetail.Intersects:
    // Set the behavior to return visuals at all z-order levels:
                    return HitTestResultBehavior.Continue;

                case IntersectionDetail.FullyInside:

    // Set the behavior to return visuals at all z-order levels:
                    return HitTestResultBehavior.Continue;

                default:
                    return HitTestResultBehavior.Stop;
            }
        }
    }
}
```

In this code-behind file, you expand the hit test area using an EllipseGeometry. When the user clicks on the Canvas, the program starts the hit-testing process by calling the HitTestCallback method. If it hits any rectangle, that rectangle will be added to the hitList. When the process is finished, the program gives a collection in the hitList with all of the rectangles that are found.

Note that the HitTestCallback method implements the hit testing behavior. Usually, the HitTestResult object provides just a single property (VisualHit), but you can cast it to one of two derived types depending on the type of hit test you're performing.

If you're hit testing a point, you can cast HitTestResult to PointHitTestResult, which provides a PointHit property that returns the original point you used to perform the hit test. But if you are hit testing a Geometry object (or shape), like you are in this example, you can cast HitTestResult to GeometryHitTestResult and get access to the IntersectionDetail property. This property tells you whether your geometry (hitArea) completely wraps your rectangle (FullyInside), overlaps it (Intersect), or within it (FullyContains). In this example, you implement all these options in the HitTestCallback. You can choose any of these options depending on the requirements of your application. In this example, hits are only counted if the geometry (hitArea) is completely inside the rectangle (FullyContains). Finally, at the end of the callback, you can return one of two values from the HitTestResultBehavior enumeration: Continue to keep looking for hits, or Stop to end the hit-testing process.

Figure 4-5 shows results of running this example.

Figure 4-5 Hit Testing in WPF.

Custom Shapes

Sometimes, you may find that the simple shapes defined in WPF aren't enough for advanced graphics applications. In these cases, you can create custom shapes that derive from the Shape class. The custom shapes you create in this way inherit all of the properties and methods of the Shape class, and they become FrameworkElement objects. Therefore, you can use them in your applications just like standard WPF shapes (Line, Rectangle, Ellipse, and Polygon, for example).

In this section, I'll show you how to create some commonly used custom shapes, including a Star, ArrowLine, and USFlag. Following the procedure presented here, you can easily develop your own custom shape library.

Star Shape

Creating a custom shape is relatively easy. You simply need to inherit the custom shape that you want to create from the abstract Shape class and provide an override for the getter of the DefiningGeometry property. This returns the Geometry object, which defines the geometry of your shape.

Let's consider an example that shows how to create a custom Star shape. Open the project Chapter04 and add a new class, called Star, to the project. I first list the code and then explain how it works.

```
using System;
using System.Windows;
using System.Windows.Media;
using System.Windows.Shapes;

namespace Chapter04
{
    public class Star : Shape
    {
        protected PathGeometry pg;
        PathFigure pf;
        PolyLineSegment pls;

        public Star()
        {
            pg = new PathGeometry();
            pf = new PathFigure();
            pls = new PolyLineSegment();
            pg.Figures.Add(pf);
        }

        // Specify the center of the star
        public static readonly DependencyProperty
            CenterProperty =
            DependencyProperty.Register("Center",
            typeof(Point), typeof(Star),
            new FrameworkPropertyMetadata(
            new Point(20.0, 20.0),
            FrameworkPropertyMetadataOptions.AffectsMeasure));

        public Point Center
        {
            set { SetValue(CenterProperty, value); }
            get { return (Point)GetValue(CenterProperty); }
        }

        // Specify the size of the star:
        public static readonly DependencyProperty
            SizeRProperty =
            DependencyProperty.Register("SizeR",
            typeof(double), typeof(Star),
            new FrameworkPropertyMetadata(10.0,
            FrameworkPropertyMetadataOptions.AffectsMeasure));

        public double SizeR
        {
            set { SetValue(SizeRProperty, value); }
            get { return (double)GetValue(SizeRProperty); }
        }

        protected override Geometry DefiningGeometry
        {
            get
            {
```

```
double r = SizeR;
double x = Center.X;
double y = Center.Y;
double sn36 = Math.Sin(
                36.0 * Math.PI / 180.0);
double sn72 = Math.Sin(
                72.0 * Math.PI / 180.0);
double cs36 = Math.Cos(
                36.0 * Math.PI / 180.0);
double cs72 = Math.Cos(
                72.0 * Math.PI / 180.0);

pf.StartPoint = new Point(x, y - r);
pls.Points.Add(new Point(x + r * sn36,
                         y + r * cs36));
pls.Points.Add(new Point(x - r * sn72,
                         y - r * cs72));
pls.Points.Add(new Point(x + r * sn72,
                         y - r * cs72));
pls.Points.Add(new Point(x - r * sn36,
                         y + r * cs36));
pls.Points.Add(new Point(x, y - r));
pf.Segments.Add(pls);
pf.IsClosed = true;
pg.FillRule = FillRule.Nonzero;
return pg;
        }
    }
  }
}
```

In order to draw a Star shape, you need to have a reference to two parameters. One is the Center (a Point object) of the Star, the other is the size of the Star named SizeR (a double object). However, you need to add two dependency properties in the above code for these two parameters. You may notice that these two properties are passed into the DependencyProperty.Register method. This registration process is necessary in order to expose these properties to the user.

Next, you override the getter of the DefiningGeometry property. Here the Star shape is created using the PolyLineSegment object. First, you need to define the coordinates of the Star. As illustrated in Figure 4-6, we assume that the center coordinates of the star are at (x, y), and r is the radius of the circle around the star shape. In this notation, r is the same as SizeR. The angle α is equal to 72 degrees and β is equal to 36 degrees. From this figure, you can easily determine the coordinates of points 0 to 4, as shown in Table 4-2.

Note that the NonZero fill rule is used here. As discussed in Chapter 2, with Nonzero, WPF follows the same line-counting process as the default EvenOdd fill rule, but it takes into account the direction that each line flows. If the number of lines going in one direction is equal to the number going in the opposite direction, the region is not filled. Otherwise, the region will be filled. You can see from Figure 4-6 that the pentagon at the center will be filled because the difference between these two counts is not zero. If you had set the fill rule to EvenOdd, the pentagon at the center will not be filled because you must across two lines to get out of the pentagon.

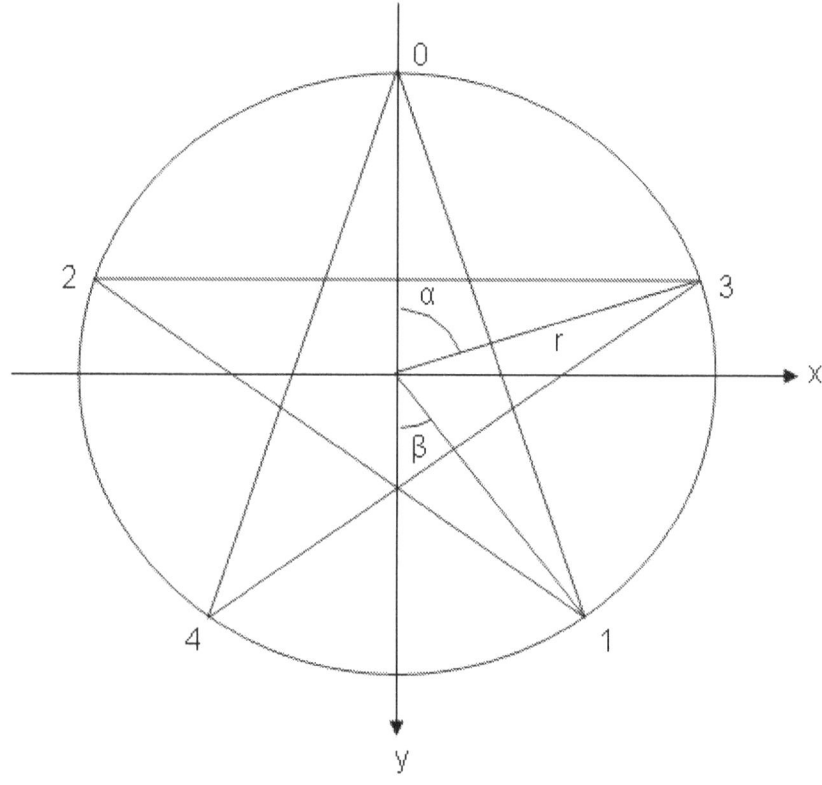

Figure 4-6 Coordinates of a star shape.

Table 4-2 Coordinates of the star

Points	X Coordinate	Y coordinate
0	x	Y - r
1	x + r*sinβ	y + r*cosβ
2	x - r*sinα	y - r*cosα
3	x + r*sinα	y - r*cosα
4	x - r*sinβ	y + r*cosβ

Using this information, you can easily create a custom Star shape.

Arrow Line

In Chapter 2, we mentioned that you can specify the end caps of a line shape through its StrokeStartLineCap and StrokeEndLineCap properties. However, the size of these caps is always the same as the StrokeThickness. Thus, it is impossible to create a line with an arrowhead using these properties.

Instead, you can create such an arrowhead line using a custom shape class. In this class, in addition to the standard line properties such as X1, Y1, X2, and Y2, you need to add four more dependency properties that are used to control the arrowhead: ArrowheadSizeX, ArrowheadSizeY, ArrowheadEnd, and IsArrowheadClosed. The ArrowheadSizeX and ArrowheadSizeY properties are used to specify the size of the arrow head, as defined in Figure 4-7. The ArrowheadEnd property allows you to select whether the arrowhead should be at the start point, end point, both ends, or neither end of the line. The IsArrowheadClosed property lets you set the arrowhead type as open or closed, as illustrated in Figure 4-7.

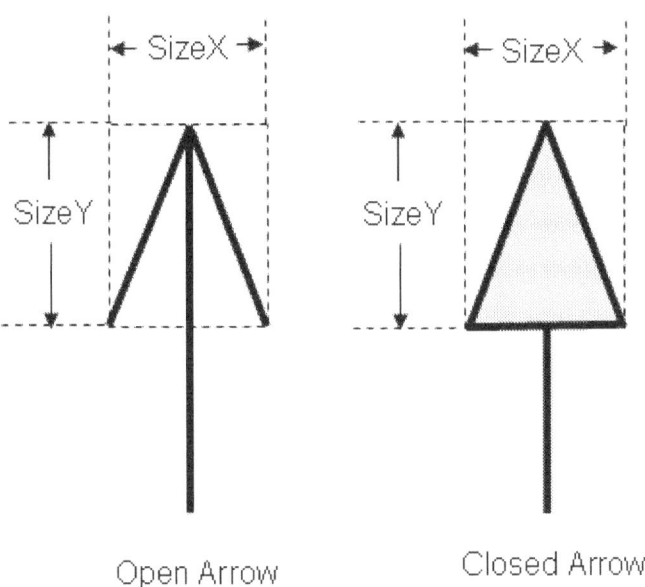

Figure 4-7 Arrowheads to be used in the ArrowLine class.

Open the project Chapter04, and add a class named ArrowLine to the project. This class also inherites from the Shape class. Here is the C# code of this class:

```
using System;
using System.Windows;
using System.Windows.Media;
using System.Windows.Shapes;
```

```
namespace Chapter04
{
    public class ArrowLine : Shape
    {
        protected PathGeometry pg;
        protected PathFigure pf;
        protected PolyLineSegment pls;

        PathFigure pfStartArrow;
        PolyLineSegment plsStartArrow;
        PathFigure pfEndArrow;
        PolyLineSegment plsEndArrow;

        public ArrowLine()
        {
            pg = new PathGeometry();
            pf = new PathFigure();
            pls = new PolyLineSegment();
            pf.Segments.Add(pls);
            pfStartArrow = new PathFigure();
            plsStartArrow = new PolyLineSegment();
            pfStartArrow.Segments.Add(plsStartArrow);
            pfEndArrow = new PathFigure();
            plsEndArrow = new PolyLineSegment();
            pfEndArrow.Segments.Add(plsEndArrow);
        }

        // Specify the X1 dependency property:
        public static readonly DependencyProperty X1Property =
            DependencyProperty.Register("X1",
            typeof(double), typeof(ArrowLine),
            new FrameworkPropertyMetadata(0.0,
            FrameworkPropertyMetadataOptions.AffectsMeasure));

        public double X1
        {
            set { SetValue(X1Property, value); }
            get { return (double)GetValue(X1Property); }
        }

        // Specify the Y1 dependency property:
        public static readonly DependencyProperty Y1Property =
            DependencyProperty.Register("Y1",
            typeof(double), typeof(ArrowLine),
            new FrameworkPropertyMetadata(0.0,
            FrameworkPropertyMetadataOptions.AffectsMeasure));

        public double Y1
        {
            set { SetValue(Y1Property, value); }
            get { return (double)GetValue(Y1Property); }
        }

        // Specify the X2 dependency property:
```

```
public static readonly DependencyProperty X2Property =
    DependencyProperty.Register("X2",
    typeof(double), typeof(ArrowLine),
    new FrameworkPropertyMetadata(0.0,
    FrameworkPropertyMetadataOptions.AffectsMeasure));

public double X2
{
    set { SetValue(X2Property, value); }
    get { return (double)GetValue(X2Property); }
}

// Specify the Y2 dependency property:
public static readonly DependencyProperty Y2Property =
    DependencyProperty.Register("Y2",
    typeof(double), typeof(ArrowLine),
    new FrameworkPropertyMetadata(0.0,
    FrameworkPropertyMetadataOptions.AffectsMeasure));

public double Y2
{
    set { SetValue(Y2Property, value); }
    get { return (double)GetValue(Y2Property); }
}

// Specify the arrowhead size in the x direction:
public static readonly DependencyProperty
    ArrowheadSizeXProperty =
    DependencyProperty.Register("ArrowheadSizeX",
    typeof(double), typeof(ArrowLine),
    new FrameworkPropertyMetadata(10.0,
    FrameworkPropertyMetadataOptions.AffectsMeasure));

public double ArrowheadSizeX
{
    set { SetValue(ArrowheadSizeXProperty, value); }
    get { return
        (double)GetValue(ArrowheadSizeXProperty); }
}

// Specify the arrowhead size in the y direction:
public static readonly DependencyProperty
    ArrowheadSizeYProperty =
    DependencyProperty.Register("ArrowheadSizeY",
    typeof(double), typeof(ArrowLine),
    new FrameworkPropertyMetadata(10.0,
    FrameworkPropertyMetadataOptions.AffectsMeasure));

public double ArrowheadSizeY
{
    set { SetValue(ArrowheadSizeYProperty, value); }
    get { return
        (double)GetValue(ArrowheadSizeYProperty); }
}
```

```
// Specify arrowhead ends:
public static readonly DependencyProperty
    ArrowheadEndProperty =
    DependencyProperty.Register("ArrowheadEnd",
    typeof(ArrowheadEndEnum), typeof(ArrowLine),
   new FrameworkPropertyMetadata(ArrowheadEndEnum.End,
    FrameworkPropertyMetadataOptions.AffectsMeasure));

public ArrowheadEndEnum ArrowheadEnd
{
    set { SetValue(ArrowheadEndProperty, value); }
    get { return
    (ArrowheadEndEnum)GetValue(ArrowheadEndProperty);}
}

// Specify IsArrowheadClosed property
public static readonly DependencyProperty
    IsArrowheadClosedProperty =
    DependencyProperty.Register("IsArrowheadClosed",
    typeof(bool), typeof(ArrowLine),
    new FrameworkPropertyMetadata(false,
    FrameworkPropertyMetadataOptions.AffectsMeasure));

public bool IsArrowheadClosed
{
    set { SetValue(IsArrowheadClosedProperty,
          value); }
    get { return
       (bool)GetValue(IsArrowheadClosedProperty); }
}

protected override Geometry DefiningGeometry
{
    get
    {
        pg.Figures.Clear();
        pf.StartPoint = new Point(X1, Y1);
        pls.Points.Clear();
        pls.Points.Add(new Point(X2, Y2));
        pg.Figures.Add(pf);

        if (pls.Points.Count > 0)
        {
            Point pt1 = new Point();
            Point pt2 = new Point();

            if ((ArrowheadEnd &
                ArrowheadEndEnum.Start)
                == ArrowheadEndEnum.Start)
            {
                pt1 = pf.StartPoint;
                pt2 = pls.Points[0];
                pg.Figures.Add(CreateArrowhead(
```

```
                            pfStartArrow, pt2, pt1));
                }

                if ((ArrowheadEnd & ArrowheadEndEnum.End)
                    == ArrowheadEndEnum.End)
                {
                    pt1 = pls.Points.Count == 1 ?
                        pf.StartPoint :
                        pls.Points[pls.Points.Count - 2];
                    pt2 = pls.Points[
                        pls.Points.Count - 1];
                    pg.Figures.Add(CreateArrowhead(
                        pfEndArrow, pt1, pt2));
                }
            }
            return pg;
        }
    }
}

PathFigure CreateArrowhead(PathFigure pathFigure,
    Point pt1, Point pt2)
{
    Point pt = new Point();
    Vector v = new Vector();

    Matrix m = ArrowheadTransform(pt1, pt2);
    PolyLineSegment pls1 = pathFigure.Segments[0]
        as PolyLineSegment;

    pls1.Points.Clear();
    if (!IsArrowheadClosed)
    {
        v = new Point(0, 0) - new Point(
            ArrowheadSizeX / 2, ArrowheadSizeY);
        pt = pt2 + v * m;
        pathFigure.StartPoint = pt;
        pls1.Points.Add(pt2);
        v = new Point(0, 0) -
            new Point(-ArrowheadSizeX / 2,
            ArrowheadSizeY);
        pt = pt2 + v * m;
        pls1.Points.Add(pt);
    }
    else if (IsArrowheadClosed)
    {
        v = new Point(0, 0) -
            new Point(ArrowheadSizeX / 2, 0);
        pt = pt2 + v * m;
        pathFigure.StartPoint = pt;
        v = new Point(0, 0) -
            new Point(0, -ArrowheadSizeY);
        pt = pt2 + v * m;
        pls1.Points.Add(pt);
        v = new Point(0, 0) -
```

```
                    new Point(-ArrowheadSizeX / 2, 0);
              pt = pt2 + v * m;
              pls1.Points.Add(pt);
          }
          pathFigure.IsClosed = IsArrowheadClosed;
          return pathFigure;
      }

      private Matrix ArrowheadTransform(
          Point pt1, Point pt2)
      {
          Matrix m = new Matrix();
          double theta = 180 * (Math.Atan((pt2.X - pt1.X) /
              (pt2.Y - pt1.Y))) / Math.PI;
          double dx = pt2.X - pt1.X;
          double dy = pt2.Y - pt1.Y;

          if (dx >= 0 && dy >= 0)
              theta = -theta;
          else if (dx < 0 && dy >= 0)
              theta = -theta;
          else if (dx < 0 && dy < 0)
              theta = 180 - theta;
          else if (dx >= 0 && dy < 0)
              theta = 180 - theta;
          m.Rotate(theta);
          return m;
      }
  }

  public enum ArrowheadEndEnum
  {
      None = 0,
      Start = 1,
      End = 2,
      Both = 3
  }
}
```

In this class, you add eight dependency properties and pass them to the DependencyProperty.Register method. This registration process is necessary in order to expose these properties to the user.

Next, you override the getter of the DefiningGeometry property. The arrowhead line is created using PolyLineSegment. The arrowhead is first created in the absolute coordinate system, and then placed at the starting or end point of the line using matrix transforms.

Following the procedures presented here, you can create more custom shapes and build you own custom 2D shape library.

Testing Custom Shapes

The custom shapes Star and ArrowLine created in the preceding sections can be used in the same way as the standard shapes in WPF. They can be used in both XAML and code-behind files. In order to use custom shapes in XAML files, you need to add the project that the custom shape classes reside to the xmlns namespace. In this way the markup code can find the location of your custom classes. In the current case, you need to add the following line:

```
xmlns:local="clr-namespace:Chapter04"
```

Let's consider an example, in which you first create a US flag in code using the custom Star shape. Then you create a Star and two arrowhead lines in the XAML file. Finally you perform various transforms and animations to the star and arrowhead lines.

Add a new WPF Window to the project Chapter04 and name it CustomShape. Here is the markup of this example:

```
<Window x:Class="Chapter04.CustomShape"
    xmlns="http://schemas.microsoft.com/winfx
        /2006/xaml/presentation"
    xmlns:x="http://schemas.microsoft.com/winfx/2006/xaml"
    xmlns:local="clr-namespace:Chapter04"
    Title="Custom Shapes" Height="400" Width="300">

    <Viewbox Stretch="Uniform">
        <Border Margin="5" BorderBrush="Black"
                BorderThickness="1"
                Background="LightCyan"
                HorizontalAlignment="Left">
            <Canvas x:Name="canvas1" Width="300" Height="375"
                    ClipToBounds="True">
                <local:Star x:Name="star1"  Canvas.Top="190"
                        Canvas.Left ="50" Fill="Red"
                        Stroke="Blue" SizeR="30"
                        Center="0,20">
                    <local:Star.RenderTransform>
                        <TransformGroup>
                            <ScaleTransform x:Name="starScale"
                                CenterX="0" CenterY="20" />
                            <TranslateTransform
                                x:Name="starTranslate"/>
                        </TransformGroup>
                    </local:Star.RenderTransform>
                </local:Star>

                <local:ArrowLine x:Name="arrowLine1"
                            Canvas.Top="280" X1="50"
                            Y1="20" X2="100" Y2="20"
                            Stroke="Blue" Fill="Red"
                            IsArrowheadClosed="True"
                            ArrowheadEnd="Both">
                    <local:ArrowLine.RenderTransform>
```

```
                        <ScaleTransform x:Name="line1Scale"/>
                    </local:ArrowLine.RenderTransform>
                </local:ArrowLine>
                <local:ArrowLine x:Name="arrowLine2"
                            Canvas.Top="250" X1="150"
                            Y1="20" X2="230" Y2="20"
                            Stroke="Blue"
                            StrokeThickness="3">
                    <local:ArrowLine.RenderTransform>
                        <RotateTransform x:Name="line2Rotate"
                            CenterX="150" CenterY="20"/>
                    </local:ArrowLine.RenderTransform>
                </local:ArrowLine>
            </Canvas>
        </Border>
    </Viewbox>
</Window>
```

The corresponding C# code is listed below:

```csharp
using System;
using System.Windows;
using System.Windows.Controls;
using System.Windows.Media;
using System.Windows.Media.Animation;
using System.Windows.Shapes;

namespace Chapter04
{
    public partial class CustomShape : Window
    {
        public CustomShape()
        {
            InitializeComponent();
            AddUSFlag(10, 10, 280);
            StartAnimation();
        }

        private void AddUSFlag(double x0,
            double y0, double width)
        {
            SolidColorBrush whiteBrush =
                new SolidColorBrush(Colors.White);
            SolidColorBrush blueBrush =
                new SolidColorBrush(Colors.DarkBlue);
            SolidColorBrush redBrush =
                new SolidColorBrush(Colors.Red);
            Rectangle rect = new Rectangle();
            double height = 10 * width / 19;

            //Draw white rectangle background:
            rect.Fill = whiteBrush;
            rect.Width = width;
            rect.Height = height;
```

```
    Canvas.SetLeft(rect, x0);
    Canvas.SetTop(rect, y0);
    canvas1.Children.Add(rect);

    // Draw seven red stripes:
    for (int i = 0; i < 7; i++)
    {
        rect = new Rectangle();
        rect.Fill = redBrush;
        rect.Width = width;
        rect.Height = height / 13;
        Canvas.SetLeft(rect, x0);
        Canvas.SetTop(rect, y0 + 2 * i * height / 13);
        canvas1.Children.Add(rect);
    }

    // Draw blue box:
    rect = new Rectangle();
    rect.Fill = blueBrush;
    rect.Width = 2 * width / 5;
    rect.Height = 7 * height / 13;
    Canvas.SetLeft(rect, x0);
    Canvas.SetTop(rect, y0);
    canvas1.Children.Add(rect);

    // Draw fifty stars:
    double offset = rect.Width / 40;
    double dx = (rect.Width - 2 * offset) / 11;
    double dy = (rect.Height - 2 * offset) / 9;
    for (int j = 0; j < 9; j++)
    {
        double y = y0 + offset + j * dy + dy / 2;
        for (int i = 0; i < 11; i++)
        {
            double x = x0 + offset + i * dx + dx / 2;
            if ((i + j) % 2 == 0)
            {
                Star star = new Star();
                star.Fill = whiteBrush;
                star.SizeR = width / 55;
                star.Center = new Point(x, y);
                canvas1.Children.Add(star);
            }
        }
    }
}

private void StartAnimation()
{
    // Animating the star:
    AnimationTimeline at = new DoubleAnimation(
        0.1, 1.2, new Duration(new TimeSpan(0, 0, 5)));
    at.RepeatBehavior = RepeatBehavior.Forever;
    at.AutoReverse = true;
```

```
starScale.BeginAnimation(
    ScaleTransform.ScaleXProperty, at);
starScale.BeginAnimation(
    ScaleTransform.ScaleYProperty, at);
at = new DoubleAnimation(0, 200,
    new Duration(new TimeSpan(0, 0, 3)));
at.RepeatBehavior = RepeatBehavior.Forever;
at.AutoReverse = true;
starTranslate.BeginAnimation(
    TranslateTransform.XProperty, at);

// Animating arrowline1:
at = new DoubleAnimation(0, 2.5,
    new Duration(new TimeSpan(0, 0, 4)));
at.RepeatBehavior = RepeatBehavior.Forever;
at.AutoReverse = true;
line1Scale.BeginAnimation(
    ScaleTransform.ScaleXProperty, at);
line1Scale.BeginAnimation(
    ScaleTransform.ScaleYProperty, at);

// Animating arrowline2:
at = new DoubleAnimation(0, 50,
    new Duration(new TimeSpan(0, 0, 5)));
at.RepeatBehavior = RepeatBehavior.Forever;
at.AutoReverse = true;
arrowLine2.BeginAnimation(
    ArrowLine.ArrowheadSizeXProperty, at);
arrowLine2.BeginAnimation(
    ArrowLine.ArrowheadSizeYProperty, at);
at = new DoubleAnimation(0, 360,
    new Duration(new TimeSpan(0, 0, 5)));
at.RepeatBehavior = RepeatBehavior.Forever;
line2Rotate.BeginAnimation(
    RotateTransform.AngleProperty, at);
        }
    }
}
```

In the above code, the AddUSFlag method creates a US flag. You can specify the location and width of the flag. Inside this method, the fifty stars on the US flag are drawn using the custom Star shape class. Next, you perform the animations for a star and arrowlines using various transforms. Note here that the animation is implemented in code instead of the Storyboard approach in XAML, which was used extensively in earlier chapters of this book.

Running this example produces the output shown in Figure 4-8.

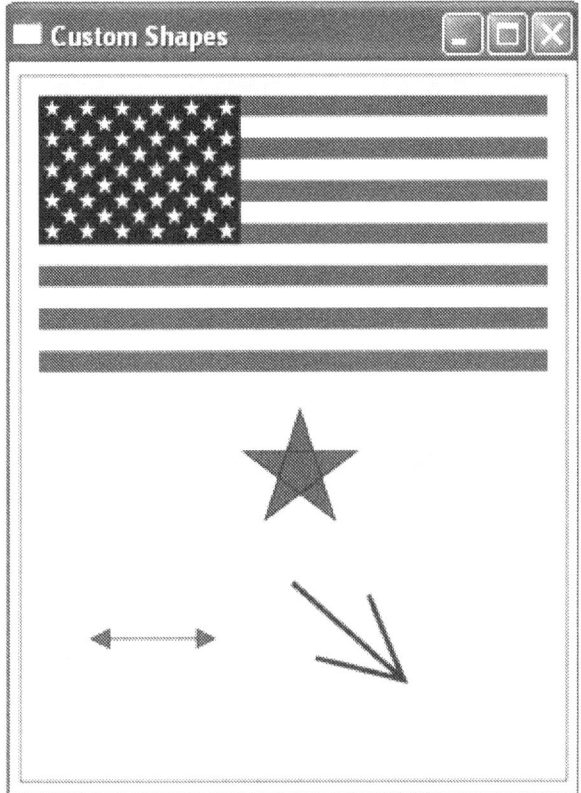

Figure 4-8 Shapes created using custom shape classes.

Chapter 5
Colors and Brushes

Almost everything visible on your computer screen is somehow related to colors and brushes. For example, a brush with a specified color is used to paint the background of a button, the foreground of text, and the fill of a shape. We have used colors and brushes throughout this book, but so far we have done most of the work with the simple SolidColorBrush object. In fact, you can use colors and brushes to paint user interface and graphics objects with anything from simple solid colors to complex sets of patterns and images. This chapter covers the color system used in WPF and a variety of brushes, including gradient, image, tile, and visual brushes, as well as brush transformations.

Colors

In WPF, a color is specified as a Color structure from the System.Windows.Media namespace. This Color structure describes a color in terms of alpha (A), red (R), green (G), and blue (B) channels. WPF uses two color systems, sRGB and ScRGB. You have the option to specify a color using either system.

sRGB is a standard RGB color space created coorperatively by HP and Microsoft for use on monitors, printers, and the Internet. It is designed to match typical home and office viewing conditions. sRGB has found wide applications. Software, LCD displays, digital cameras, printers, and scanners all follow the sRGB standard. For this reason, you can assume that any 8-bit image file or device interface falls in the sRGB color space.

ScRGB system is the latest color space developed by Microsoft. This system offers 64-bit encoding with 16-bits per channel, which allows you to specify over 65,000 steps for each color instead of the 256 steps available with sRGB's 8-bits per channel.

Unlike sRGB, ScRGB allows negative values and values above 1.0, which offers some significant improvements for color processing. In manipulating color information based on sRGB, most applications have to cut off anything below 0 (black) and anything above 1 (white), resulting in the throwing away of some color information.

Microsoft's goal for ScRGB is to give it the same ease of use and simplicity of sRGB. This means that it should require little or no extra work to take advantage of it. However, there is a trade-off: ScRGB will make more demands on performance and bandwidth. It may not work acceptably with low-end systems. Since there are no ScRGB device available yet, it isn't clear how the system will translate into the real-world applications.

WPF allows you to specify a color using both sRGB and ScRGB. There are several ways available in WPF of creating colors, including:

- An ARGB color value. You specify each value as an integer in the range [0, 255].

- A ScRGB value. The current version of the ScRGB system in WPF has a value range of [0, 1].

- A predefined color name. You choose from the correspondingly named property from the System.Windows.Media.Colors class. There are 141 predefined color names in the Colors class.

In addition, you may find the ColorConverter class useful. This class allows you to convert a color from a string or vice versa.

System Colors

In WPF, as mentioned previously, a color is represented by a 32-bit structure made up of four components: A, R, G, and B, referred to as sRGB. Color can also be represented by a 64-bit structure made up of four components: ScA, ScR, ScG, ScB, referred to as ScRGB. In the sRGB system, the components' values range from 0 to 255, while this range becomes [0, 1] in the ScRGB system. The alpha component of the color represents transparency, which determines how such a color is blended with the background. An alpha value of zero represents a fully transparent color, while a value of 255 in sRGB or 1 in ScRGB represents a fully opaque color.

The following code snippet shows several ways of specifying a color:

```
Color color = new Color();

//Create a color from a RGB value:
color = Color.FromRgb(255, 0, 0);

// Create a color from an ARGB value:
color = Color.FromArgb(100, 255, 0, 0);

// Create a color from a ScRGB value:
color = Color.FromScRgb(0.5f, 1.0f, 0.0f, 0.0f);
```

```
// Create a color using predefined color names:
color = Colors.Red;

// Create a color using ColorConverter:
color = (Color)ColorConverter.ConvertFromString("#FFFF0000");
```

Pay attention to the ScRGB value. It requires a Float value rather than a Double value. You can also use a few useful methods on any Color structure to retrieve color information. For example, you can use a predefined color name from the Colors class to obtain corresponding color information, including sRGB and ScRGB values.

Let's look at an example, which puts all of these techniques to work. Start with a new WPF Windows project and name it Chapter05. Add a StartMenu Window like you did the projects presented in the previous chapters. Then add a new WPF Window called ColorExample to the project.

This example allows you to select a color from a ListBox loaded with all of the predefined color names in the Colors class. When you type in the Opacity in a TextBox and select an item from the ListBox, the Fill color of a rectangle is changed accordingly.

Here is the markup of this example:

```
<Window x:Class="Chapter05.ColorExample"
    xmlns="http://schemas.microsoft.com/winfx
        /2006/xaml/presentation"
    xmlns:x="http://schemas.microsoft.com/winfx/2006/xaml"
    Title="Color Example" Height="300" Width="300">
    <Grid>
        <Grid.ColumnDefinitions>
            <ColumnDefinition Width="145"/>
            <ColumnDefinition Width="145"/>
        </Grid.ColumnDefinitions>
        <StackPanel Grid.Column="0" Margin="5">
            <TextBlock Text ="Select Color" Margin="5,5,5,0"/>
            <ListBox Name="listBox1"
                SelectionChanged="listBox1SelectionChanged"
                Height="100" Margin="5"/>
            <TextBlock Text="Show selected color:"
                    Margin="5,5,5,0"/>
            <Rectangle x:Name="rect1" Stroke="Blue"
                    Fill="AliceBlue"
                    Height="100" Width="122" Margin="5"/>
        </StackPanel>

        <StackPanel Grid.Column="1" Margin="5">
            <TextBlock Text="Opacity:" Margin="5,5,5,0"/>
            <TextBox x:Name="textBox"
                    HorizontalAlignment="Left"
                    TextAlignment="Center"
                    Text="1" Width="50" Margin ="5,5,5,8"/>
            <Separator/>
            <TextBlock FontWeight="Bold"
```

```
                              Text="sRGB Information:"
                              Margin="5,5,5,2"/>
                <TextBlock Name="tbAlpha" Text="Alpha ="
                              Margin="5,0,5,2"/>
                <TextBlock Name="tbRed" Text="Red ="
                              Margin="5,0,5,2"/>
                <TextBlock Name="tbGreen" Text="Green ="
                              Margin="5,0,5,2"/>
                <TextBlock Name="tbBlue" Text="Blue ="
                              Margin="5,0,5,2"/>
                <TextBlock Name="tbRGB" Text="ARGB Hex ="
                              Margin="5,0,5,5"/>
                <Separator/>
                <TextBlock FontWeight="Bold"
                              Text="ScRGB Information:"
                              Margin="5,5,5,2"/>
                <TextBlock Name="tbScA" Text="ScA ="
                              Margin="5,0,5,2"/>
                <TextBlock Name="tbScR" Text="ScR ="
                              Margin="5,0,5,2"/>
                <TextBlock Name="tbScG" Text="ScG ="
                              Margin="5,0,5,2" />
                <TextBlock Name="tbScB" Text="ScB ="
                              Margin="5,0,5,2"/>
            </StackPanel>
        </Grid>
    </Window>
```

The corresponding code-behind file of this example is listed below:

```
using System;
using System.Windows;
using System.Windows.Controls;
using System.Windows.Input;
using System.Windows.Media;
using System.Windows.Shapes;
using System.Reflection;
using System.Collections.Generic;

namespace Chapter05
{
    public partial class ColorExample : Window
    {
        private Color color;
        SolidColorBrush colorBrush = new SolidColorBrush();
        public ColorExample()
        {
            InitializeComponent();

            Type colorsType = typeof(Colors);
            foreach (PropertyInfo property in
                colorsType.GetProperties())
            {
                listBox1.Items.Add(property.Name);
```

```
                color = Colors.AliceBlue;
                listBox1.SelectedIndex = 0;
                ColorInfo();
            }
        }

        private void listBox1SelectionChanged(
            object sender, EventArgs e)
        {
            string colorString =
                listBox1.SelectedItem.ToString();
            color = (Color)ColorConverter.ConvertFromString(
                colorString);
            float opacity = Convert.ToSingle(textBox.Text);
            if(opacity > 1.0f)
                opacity = 1.0f;
            else if (opacity < 0.0f)
                opacity = 0.0f;
            color.ScA = opacity;
            ColorInfo();
        }

        private void ColorInfo()
        {
            rect1.Fill = new SolidColorBrush(color);
            // sRGB color info :
            tbAlpha.Text = "Alpha = " + color.A.ToString();
            tbRed.Text = "Red = " + color.R.ToString();
            tbGreen.Text = "Green = " + color.G.ToString();
            tbBlue.Text = "Blue = " + color.B.ToString();
            string rgbHex =
                string.Format("{0:X2}{1:X2}{2:X2}{3:X2}",
                color.A, color.R, color.G,color.B);
            tbRGB.Text = "ARGB = #" + rgbHex;

            // ScRGB color info:
            tbScA.Text = "ScA = " + color.ScA.ToString();
            tbScR.Text = "ScR = " + color.ScR.ToString();
            tbScG.Text = "ScG = " + color.ScG.ToString();
            tbScB.Text = "ScB = " + color.ScB.ToString();
        }
    }
}
```

To put all of the predefined color names from the Colors class into the ListBox, you use the following foreach loop:

```
Type colorsType = typeof(Colors);
foreach (PropertyInfo property in colorsType.GetProperties())
{
    listBox1.Items.Add(property.Name);
    ......
}
```

A using System.Reflection statement is needed to make this loop work. You simply retrieve the PropertyInfo of the Colors class and place its name into the ListBox.

Now, change the Opacity (with the range of 0 to 1) in the TextBox, and select the item from the ListBox. The rectangle's fill color will change correspondingly, and the color information will be also displayed on your screen. Figure 5-1 shows the result of running this example.

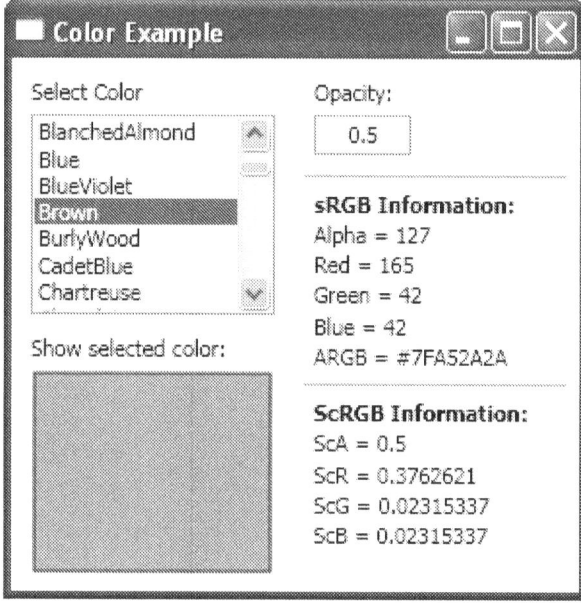

Figure 5-1 Color information in WPF.

Color Picker

You might have noticed that unlike GDI+ and Window Forms, WPF unfortunately doesn't contain some of the standard common dialogs. For example, WPF doesn't implement a ColorDialog. If you want to have a Color Picker-like functionality, you need to create a custom ColorDialog control by yourself.

Fortunately, the WPF team did create several sample custom dialogs, including a ColorPickerDialog. I don't want to re-invent the wheel, so instead, I'll only show you how to use this ColorPickerDialog in your WPF applications.

The ColorDialog control is packed in a ColorPicker.dll. If you want to use it in a WPF application, you can simply add this DLL file to the References of your project. You also need to add a using statement such as this:

```
using Microsoft.Samples.CustomControls;
```

Then you can create an instance of the color dialog:

```
ColorPickerDialog cPicker = new ColorPickerDialog();
```

Here, I'll use an example to show you how to use this color dialog in a simple 2D drawing application. In this application, you can draw the Rectangle and Ellipse shapes with your mouse. You can then change the fill color of the selected shape using the ColorPickerDialog.

Open the project Chapter05 and add a new WPF Window called ColorPickerExample to the project. Here is the markup of this example:

```
<Window x:Class="Chapter05.ColorPickerExample"
    xmlns="http://schemas.microsoft.com/winfx
        /2006/xaml/presentation"
    xmlns:x="http://schemas.microsoft.com/winfx/2006/xaml"
    Title="Example: Color Picker" Height="300" Width="300">

    <DockPanel>
        <ToolBarTray DockPanel.Dock="Left"
                    Orientation="Vertical" IsLocked="True">
            <ToolBar Padding="2">

                <RadioButton x:Name="rbRectangle"
                            IsChecked="True"
                            ToolTip="Add Rectangle"
                            Margin="3">
                    <Rectangle Width="20" Height="12"
                            Stroke="Blue"
                            Fill="LightBlue"/>
                </RadioButton>

                <RadioButton x:Name="rbEllipse"
                            IsChecked="False"
                            ToolTip="Add Ellipse" Margin="3">
                    <Ellipse Width="22" Height="15"
                            Stroke="Blue" Fill="LightBlue"/>
                </RadioButton>

                <RadioButton x:Name="rbSelect"
                            IsChecked="False"
                            ToolTip="Select" Margin="3">
                    <Path Stroke="Blue" Fill="LightBlue"
                        Width="20" Height="20">
                        <Path.Data>
                            <PathGeometry
 Figures="M5,15 L 10,0 15,15 12,15 12,20 8,20 8,15Z">
                                <PathGeometry.Transform>
                                    <RotateTransform
                                        CenterX="10"
                                        CenterY="10"
                                        Angle="45"/>
                                </PathGeometry.Transform>
                            </PathGeometry>
```

```
                                </Path.Data>
                            </Path>
                        </RadioButton>

                        <RadioButton x:Name="rbDelete"
                                    IsChecked="False"
                                    ToolTip="Delete Shape"
                                    Margin="3">
                            <Path Stroke="Blue" Fill="LightBlue"
                                Width="20" Height="20">
                                <Path.Data>
                                    <CombinedGeometry>
                                        <CombinedGeometry.Geometry1>
                                            <PathGeometry
                                    Figures="M0,0 L 15,20 15,15 20,15Z"/>
                                        </CombinedGeometry.Geometry1>
                                        <CombinedGeometry.Geometry2>
                                            <PathGeometry
                                    Figures="M20,0 L 0,15 5,15 5,20Z"/>
                                        </CombinedGeometry.Geometry2>
                                    </CombinedGeometry>
                                </Path.Data>
                            </Path>
                        </RadioButton>

                        <Separator Margin="0,10,0,10"></Separator>

                        <TextBlock Margin="10,3,0,0">Fill</TextBlock>
                        <Button Click="btnFill_Click"
                                Background="Transparent">
                            <Rectangle x:Name="rectFill" Width="20"
                                        Height="20" Stroke="Black"
                                        Fill="LightBlue"/>
                        </Button>

                    </ToolBar>
                </ToolBarTray>

                <Border BorderThickness="2" BorderBrush="LightBlue"
                        Margin="5">
                    <Canvas Name="canvas1" Background="Transparent"
                        MouseLeftButtonDown="OnMouseLeftButtonDown"
                        MouseMove="OnMouseMove"
                        MouseLeftButtonUp="OnMouseLeftButtonUp">
                    </Canvas>
                </Border>
            </DockPanel>
    </Window>
```

The above XAML file creates a user interface and layout for this example. The corresponding code-behind file is listed below:

```
using System;
using System.Windows;
```

```
using System.Windows.Controls;
using System.Windows.Input;
using System.Windows.Media;
using System.Windows.Shapes;
using Microsoft.Samples.CustomControls;

namespace Chapter05
{
    public partial class ColorPickerExample : Window
    {
        private Rectangle rubberBand;
        private Point startPoint;
        private Point currentPoint;
        private Path selectedShape;
        private double selectedStrokeThickness = 5;
        private double originalStrokeThickness = 1;
        private SolidColorBrush strokeBrush =
            new SolidColorBrush(Colors.Blue);
        private SolidColorBrush fillBrush =
            new SolidColorBrush(Colors.LightBlue);

        public ColorPickerExample()
        {
            InitializeComponent();
        }

        private void OnMouseLeftButtonDown(object sender,
            MouseButtonEventArgs e)
        {
            if (!canvas1.IsMouseCaptured)
            {
                startPoint = e.GetPosition(canvas1);
                canvas1.CaptureMouse();

                if (rbSelect.IsChecked == true)
                {
                    if (canvas1 == e.Source)
                        return;

                    foreach (Path path in canvas1.Children)
                        path.StrokeThickness =
                            originalStrokeThickness;

                    selectedShape = (Path)e.Source;
                    selectedShape.StrokeThickness =
                        selectedStrokeThickness;
                    fillBrush =
                        (SolidColorBrush)selectedShape.Fill;
                    e.Handled = true;
                }
                else if (rbDelete.IsChecked == true)
                {
                    if (canvas1 == e.Source)
                        return;
```

```
                    selectedShape = (Path)e.Source;
                    DeleteShape(selectedShape);
                }
            }

    private void DeleteShape(Path path)
    {
        path.StrokeThickness = selectedStrokeThickness;
        string msg =
            "Do you really want to delete this shape?";
        string title = "Delete Shape?";
        MessageBoxButton buttons = MessageBoxButton.YesNo;
        MessageBoxImage icon = MessageBoxImage.Warning;
        MessageBoxResult result =
            MessageBox.Show(msg, title, buttons, icon);
        if (result == MessageBoxResult.Yes)
            canvas1.Children.Remove(path);
        else
        {
            path.StrokeThickness =
                originalStrokeThickness;
            return;
        }
    }

    private void OnMouseMove(object sender,
        MouseEventArgs e)
    {
        if (canvas1.IsMouseCaptured)
        {
            currentPoint = e.GetPosition(canvas1);
            if (rubberBand == null)
            {
                rubberBand = new Rectangle();
                rubberBand.Stroke = Brushes.LightCoral;
                rubberBand.StrokeDashArray =
                  new DoubleCollection(
                     new double[] { 4, 2 });
                if (rbRectangle.IsChecked == true ||
                  rbEllipse.IsChecked == true)
                {
                    canvas1.Children.Add(rubberBand);
                }
            }

            double width = Math.Abs(
                startPoint.X - currentPoint.X);
            double height = Math.Abs(
                startPoint.Y - currentPoint.Y);
            double left = Math.Min(
                startPoint.X, currentPoint.X);
            double top = Math.Min(
                startPoint.Y, currentPoint.Y);
```

```
            rubberBand.Width = width;
            rubberBand.Height = height;
            Canvas.SetLeft(rubberBand, left);
            Canvas.SetTop(rubberBand, top);
        }
    }

    private void OnMouseLeftButtonUp(object sender,
        MouseButtonEventArgs e)
    {
        if (rbRectangle.IsChecked == true)
            AddShape(startPoint, currentPoint,
                "rectangle");
        else if (rbEllipse.IsChecked == true)
            AddShape(startPoint, currentPoint, "ellipse");

        if (rubberBand != null)
        {
            canvas1.Children.Remove(rubberBand);
            rubberBand = null;
            canvas1.ReleaseMouseCapture();
        }
    }

    private void AddShape(Point pt1, Point pt2, string s)
    {
        Path path = new Path();
        path.Fill = fillBrush;
        path.Stroke = strokeBrush;
        path.StrokeThickness = originalStrokeThickness;
        if (s == "rectangle")
        {
            RectangleGeometry geometry =
                new RectangleGeometry();
            double width = Math.Abs(pt1.X - pt2.X);
            double height = Math.Abs(pt1.Y - pt2.Y);
            double left = Math.Min(pt1.X, pt2.X);
            double top = Math.Min(pt1.Y, pt2.Y);
            geometry.Rect = new Rect(left, top,
                width, height);
            path.Data = geometry;
        }
        else if (s == "ellipse")
        {
            EllipseGeometry geometry =
                new EllipseGeometry();
            double width = Math.Abs(pt1.X - pt2.X);
            double height = Math.Abs(pt1.Y - pt2.Y);
            double left = Math.Min(pt1.X, pt2.X);
            double top = Math.Min(pt1.Y, pt2.Y);
            geometry.Center = new Point(
                left + width / 2, top + height / 2);
            geometry.RadiusX = width / 2;
            geometry.RadiusY = height / 2;
```

```
        path.Data = geometry;
    }
    canvas1.Children.Add(path);
}

private void btnFill_Click(object sender,
    RoutedEventArgs e)
{
    ColorPickerDialog cPicker =
        new ColorPickerDialog();
    cPicker.StartingColor = fillBrush.Color;
    cPicker.Owner = this;
    rectFill.Fill = fillBrush;

    bool? dialogResult = cPicker.ShowDialog();
    if (dialogResult != null &&
        (bool)dialogResult == true)
    {
        if (selectedShape != null)
        {
            if (selectedShape.StrokeThickness ==
                selectedStrokeThickness)
            {
                selectedShape.Fill = new
                    SolidColorBrush(
                        cPicker.SelectedColor);
                selectedShape.StrokeThickness =
                        originalStrokeThickness;
            }
        }
        fillBrush = new SolidColorBrush(
                    cPicker.SelectedColor);
        rectFill.Fill = fillBrush;
    }
}
}
}
```

You can see that this example is a simplified version of the interactive 2D drawing program presented in the previous chapter. This application allows you to add Rectangle and Ellipse shapes, but it doesn't implement the dragging/moving functionality because the purpose of this example is to show you how to change the color of a selected shape using the ColorPickerDialog control. The btnFill_Click handler is responsible for the color changes using the color picker control. Figure 5-2 shows a snapshot of this example.

In this application, you draw shapes by selecting the Add Rectangle or Add Ellipse button. You can then change a shape's fill color by clicking on the Select button, then clicking on a shape, which highlights the selected shape by increasing its StrokeThickness (see the figure where the rectangle shape is selected). Then, select the Fill button (the square beneath the word "Fill"), which brings up the ColorPickerDialog, as shown in Figure 5-3.

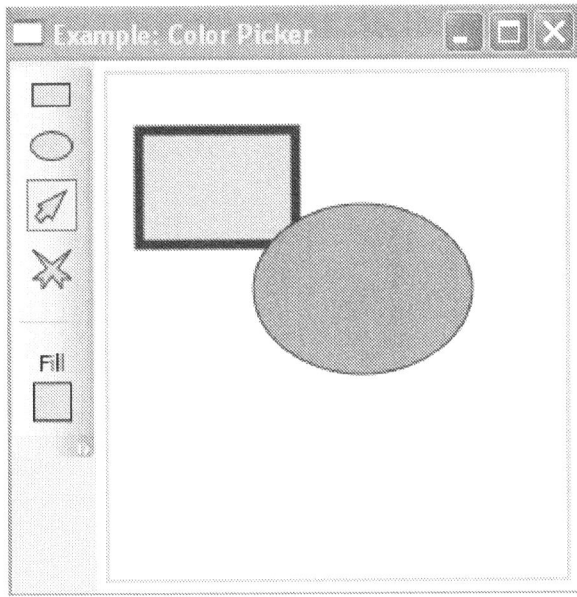

Figure 5-2 Change the fill color of a selected shape using the ColorPickerDialog.

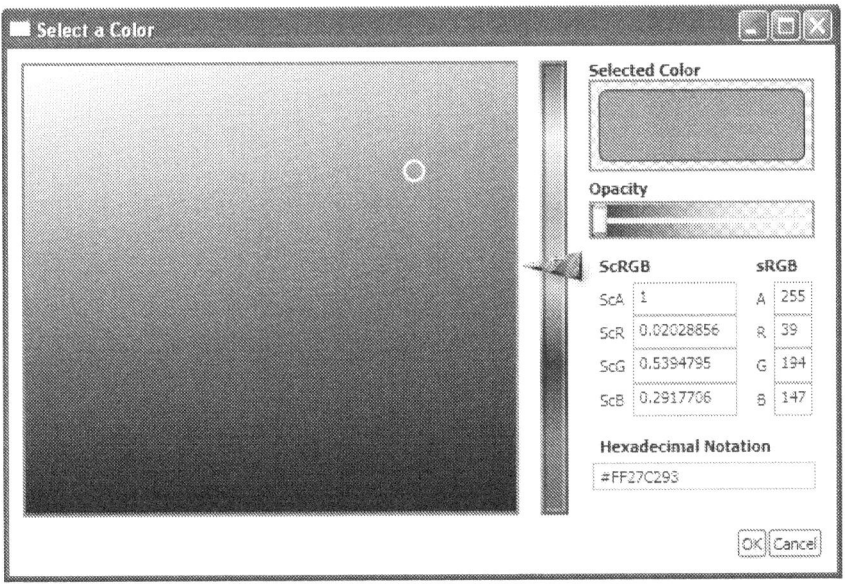

Figure 5-3 The color picker dialog from which you can specify whatever color you like.

To use this color picker, you select a color by clicking on the left color pane with your mouse, then changing the R, G, and B component using the slider. The dialog also allows you to change the opacity of the color. You can preview the selected color in the Selected Color view window. If you're satisfied with the selected color, click the OK button. The fill color of the selected shape will be changed.

The ColorPicker.dll file is located in the ~Chapter05/bin/Debug directory. You can use it in your application by adding it to the References of your project.

Brushes

Brushes aren't new to you. You have used brushes throughout this book, but so far you have done most of your work with the simple SolidColorBrush object. However, WPF provides a variety of brushes that you can use to create graphically rich applications. A brush is much more than a means of applying color to pixels: it also allows you to paint with color, gradients, images, drawings, etc. A brush with gradients gives you a way to create glass effects or the illusion of depth. Painting with an ImageBrush object provides a means to stretch, tile, or fill an area with a specified bitmap. A VisualBrush allows you to fill an area with a visual from another part of the application's visual tree. You can use this brush to create illusions of reflection or magnification in your user interfaces.

In WPF, a brush paints an area with its output. Different brushes have different types of output. The following describes the different types of brushes:

- SolidColorBrush – Paints an area with a solid color. The color can have different opacities.

- LinearGradientBrush – Paints an area with a linear gradient fill, a gradually shaded fill that changes from one color to another.

- RadialGradientBrush – Paints an area with a radial gradient fill, which is similar to a linear gradient except that it radiates out in a circular pattern from a center point.

- ImageBrush – Paints an area with an image that can be stretched, scaled, or tiled.

- DrawingBrush – Paints an area with a Drawing object. This object can include shapes and bitmaps.

- VisualBrush – Paints an area with a Visual object. A VisualBrush enables you to project content from one portion of your application into another area. It is useful for creating reflection effects and magnifying portions of the screen.

From this list, you can see that a brush can indeed provide output other than simple solid colors. By using different brushes available in WPF, you can create interesting effects such as gradient, reflection, and lighting effects, among others.

In the following sections, you will explore each of these brushes and learn how to use them in your WPF applications.

SolidColorBrush

The most common brush, and the simplest to use, is the SolidColorBrush. This brush simply paints an area with a solid color. Please note that a brush is different from a color. A brush is an object that tells the system to paint specific pixels with a specified output defined by the brush. A SolidColorBrush paints a color in a specific area of your screen. The output of a SolidColorBrush is the color.

A SolidColorBrush can be defined by simply providing a value for its Color property. As mentioned previously, there are several ways to specify a color, including declaring sRGB or ScRGB values, using hexadecimal string, using the predefined color names in the Colors class, and even using the ColorPickerDialog, as discussed in the preceding section. You can also specify the opacity of a SolidColorBrush.

Like the Colors class for colors, WPF also provides some handy classes for brushes. The Brushes class, for example, exposes a set of predefined brushes based on solid colors. This provides a shortcut you can use for creating common solid color brushes.

Let's consider an example, SolidColorBrushExample, in which you define a SolidColorBrush using different methods. In this example, you create the interface and layout using XAML, while you fill the color of Rectangle shapes using C# code. Of course, you can obtain the same result using either XAML or C# code only. The following is the XAML and the corresponding C# code of this example:

```
<Window x:Class="Chapter05.SolidColorBrushExample"
    xmlns="http://schemas.microsoft.com/winfx
        /2006/xaml/presentation"
    xmlns:x="http://schemas.microsoft.com/winfx/2006/xaml"
    Title="SolidColorBrush Example" Height="415" Width="270">

    <Canvas Margin="5">
        <StackPanel>
            <TextBlock Margin="0,0,0,5">Predefined Brush in
                    the Brushes class:</TextBlock>
            <Rectangle x:Name="rect1" Width="100"
                    Height="30" Stroke="Blue"/>
            <TextBlock Margin="0,10,0,5">From predefined
                    color name in the Colors
                    class:</TextBlock>
            <Rectangle x:Name="rect2" Width="100"
                    Height="30" Stroke="Blue"/>
            <TextBlock Margin="0,10,0,5">From sRGB value in
                    the Color structure:</TextBlock>
            <Rectangle x:Name="rect3" Width="100"
                    Height="30" Stroke="Blue"/>
            <TextBlock Margin="0,10,0,5">From SsRGB value in
                    the Color structure:</TextBlock>
            <Rectangle x:Name="rect4" Width="100"
```

```
                         Height="30" Stroke="Blue"/>
            <TextBlock Margin="0,10,0,5">From Hex string using
                         ColorConverter:</TextBlock>
            <Rectangle x:Name="rect5" Width="100"
                         Height="30" Stroke="Blue"/>
            <TextBlock Margin="0,10,0,5">From
                         ColorPickerDialog:</TextBlock>
            <Rectangle x:Name="rect6" Width="100" Height="30"
                         Stroke="Blue" Fill="LightBlue"/>
            <Button Click="ChangeColor_Click" Width="100"
                         Height="25" Content="Change Color"/>
        </StackPanel>
    </Canvas>
</Window>

using System;
using System.Windows;
using System.Windows.Controls;
using System.Windows.Input;
using System.Windows.Media;
using System.Windows.Shapes;
using Microsoft.Samples.CustomControls;

namespace Chapter05
{
    public partial class SolidColorBrushExample : Window
    {

        public SolidColorBrushExample()
        {
            InitializeComponent();

            SolidColorBrush brush = new SolidColorBrush();

            // Predefined brush in Brushes Class
            brush = Brushes.Red;
            rect1.Fill = brush;

            // From predefined color name in the Colors class:
            brush = new SolidColorBrush(Colors.Green);
            rect2.Fill = brush;

            // From sRGB values in the Color strutcure:
            brush = new SolidColorBrush(
                Color.FromArgb(100, 0, 0, 255));
            rect3.Fill = brush;

            // From ScRGB values in the Color structure:
            brush = new SolidColorBrush(
                Color.FromScRgb(0.5f, 0.7f, 0.0f, 0.5f));
            rect4.Fill = brush;

            // From a Hex string using ColorConverter:
            brush = new SolidColorBrush(
```

```
            (Color)ColorConverter.
            ConvertFromString("#CBFFFFAA"));
        rect5.Fill = brush;
    }

    // From ColorPickerDialog:
    private void ChangeColor_Click(
        object sender, RoutedEventArgs e)
    {
        ColorPickerDialog cPicker =
            new ColorPickerDialog();
        cPicker.StartingColor = Colors.LightBlue;
        cPicker.Owner = this;
        bool? dialogResult = cPicker.ShowDialog();
        if (dialogResult != null &&
            (bool)dialogResult == true)
        {
            rect6.Fill =
              new SolidColorBrush(cPicker.SelectedColor);
        }
    }
  }
}
```

In this example, you create six Rectangle shapes and specify their Fill property using a different SolidColorBrush for each of them. In particular, for rect6, you use the ColorPickerDialog to specify the color of the brush. You need to click the Change Color button to bring up the Color Picker window, from which you can select any color you like.

Figure 5-4 shows the results of executing this sample application.

LinearGradientBrush

The LinearGradientBrush allows you to paint an area with multiple colors, and create a blended fill effect that changes from one color to another.

The LinearGradientBrush follows a linear gradient axis. You can define the direction of the axis to obtain vertical, horizontal, or diagonal gradient effects. The gradient axis is defined by two points, StartPoint and EndPoint. These point map to a one by one matrix. For example, a StartPoint of (0, 0) and an EndPoint of (0, 1) produces a vertical gradient, while a StartPoint of (0, 0) and an EndPoint of (1, 1) generates a diagonal gradient. The StartPoint and EndPoint properties of a LinearGradientBrush let you choose the point where the first color begins to change and the point where the color change ends with the final color. Remember that the coordinates you use for the StartPoint and EndPoint aren't real coordinates. Instead, the LinearGradientBrush assigns the point (0, 0) to the top-left corner and (1, 1) to the bottom-right corner of the area you want to fill, no matter how high and wide it actually is.

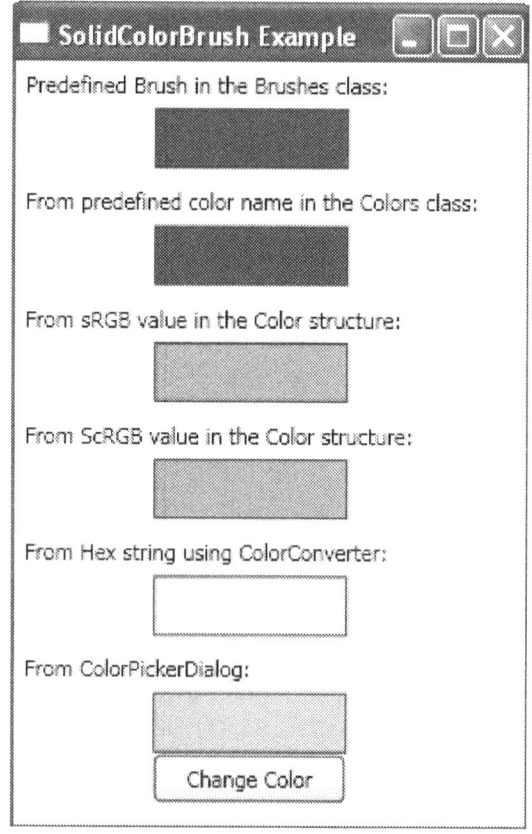

Figure 5-4 Shapes painted using SolidColorBrush.

Along the axis you specify a series of GradientStop objects, which are points on the axis where you want the colors to blend and transition to other colors. You can define as many GradientStop objects as you need. A GradientStop object has two properties of interest, Color and Offset. The Offset property defines a distance, ranging from 0 to 1, from the start point of the axis from which the color specified in the Color property should begin.

Now, let's look at an example using the LinearGradientBrush. Add a new WPF Window, called LinearGradientBrushExample, to the project Chapter05. Here is the markup of this example:

```
<Window x:Class="Chapter05.LinearGradientBrushExample"
    xmlns="http://schemas.microsoft.com/winfx
        /2006/xaml/presentation"
    xmlns:x="http://schemas.microsoft.com/winfx/2006/xaml"
    Title="LinearGradientBrush" Height="375" Width="300">
    <Grid>
        <Grid.ColumnDefinitions>
            <ColumnDefinition/>
            <ColumnDefinition/>
        </Grid.ColumnDefinitions>
```

```
<Grid.RowDefinitions>
    <RowDefinition Height="Auto"/>
    <RowDefinition Height="Auto"/>
    <RowDefinition Height="Auto"/>
</Grid.RowDefinitions>

<StackPanel Grid.Column="0" Grid.Row="0">
    <TextBlock Margin="5"
            Text="Vertical linear gradient:"/>
    <Rectangle Width="100" Height="75" Stroke="Blue">
        <Rectangle.Fill>
            <LinearGradientBrush StartPoint="0,0"
                            EndPoint="1,0">
                <GradientStop Color="Blue"
                            Offset="0"/>
                <GradientStop Color="Yellow"
                            Offset="1"/>
            </LinearGradientBrush>
        </Rectangle.Fill>
    </Rectangle>
</StackPanel>

<StackPanel Grid.Column="1" Grid.Row="0">
    <TextBlock Margin="5"
            Text="Horizontal linear gradient:"/>
    <Rectangle Width="100" Height="75" Stroke="Blue">
        <Rectangle.Fill>
            <LinearGradientBrush StartPoint="0,0"
                            EndPoint="0,1">
                <GradientStop Color="Red" Offset="0"/>
                <GradientStop Color="White"
                            Offset="1"/>
            </LinearGradientBrush>
        </Rectangle.Fill>
    </Rectangle>
</StackPanel>

<StackPanel Grid.Column="0" Grid.Row="1">
    <TextBlock Margin="5,10,5,0"
            Text="Diagonal linear gradient"/>
    <TextBlock Margin="5,0,5,5"
            Text="- with 1 Offset for White"/>
    <Rectangle Width="100" Height="75" Stroke="Blue">
        <Rectangle.Fill>
            <LinearGradientBrush StartPoint="0,0"
                            EndPoint="1,1">
                <GradientStop Color="Green"
                            Offset="0"/>
                <GradientStop Color="White"
                            Offset="1"/>
            </LinearGradientBrush>
        </Rectangle.Fill>
    </Rectangle>
</StackPanel>
```

```
<StackPanel Grid.Column="1" Grid.Row="1">
    <TextBlock Margin="5,10,5,0"
               Text="Diagonal linear gradient"/>
    <TextBlock Margin="5,0,5,5"
               Text="- with 0.5 Offset for White"/>
    <Rectangle Width="100" Height="75" Stroke="Blue">
        <Rectangle.Fill>
            <LinearGradientBrush StartPoint="0,0"
                                 EndPoint="1,1">
                <GradientStop Color="Green"
                              Offset="0"/>
                <GradientStop Color="White"
                              Offset="0.5"/>
            </LinearGradientBrush>
        </Rectangle.Fill>
    </Rectangle>
</StackPanel>

<StackPanel Grid.Column="0" Grid.Row="2">
    <TextBlock Margin="5,10,5,0"
               Text="Vertical linear gradient"/>
    <TextBlock Margin="5,0,5,5"
               Text="- multiple colors"/>
    <Rectangle Width="100" Height="75" Stroke="Blue">
        <Rectangle.Fill>
            <LinearGradientBrush StartPoint="0,0"
                                 EndPoint="1,0">
                <GradientStop Color="Red"
                              Offset="0.3"/>
                <GradientStop Color="Green"
                              Offset="0.5"/>
                <GradientStop Color="Blue"
                              Offset="0.8"/>
            </LinearGradientBrush>
        </Rectangle.Fill>
    </Rectangle>
</StackPanel>

<StackPanel Grid.Column="1" Grid.Row="2">
    <TextBlock Margin="5,10,5,0"
               Text="Diagonal linear gradient"/>
    <TextBlock Margin="5,0,5,5"
               Text="- multiple colors"/>
    <Rectangle Width="100" Height="75" Stroke="Blue">
        <Rectangle.Fill>
            <LinearGradientBrush StartPoint="0,0"
                                 EndPoint="1,1">
                <GradientStop Color="Red"
                              Offset="0.2"/>
                <GradientStop Color="Yellow"
                              Offset="0.3"/>
                <GradientStop Color="Coral"
                              Offset="0.4"/>
```

```
                    <GradientStop Color="Blue"
                                  Offset="0.5"/>
                    <GradientStop Color="White"
                                  Offset="0.6"/>
                    <GradientStop Color="Green"
                                  Offset="0.7"/>
                    <GradientStop Color="Purple"
                                  Offset="0.8"/>
                </LinearGradientBrush>
            </Rectangle.Fill>
          </Rectangle>
       </StackPanel>
    </Grid>
 </Window>
```

Figure 5-5 illustrates the results of this example.

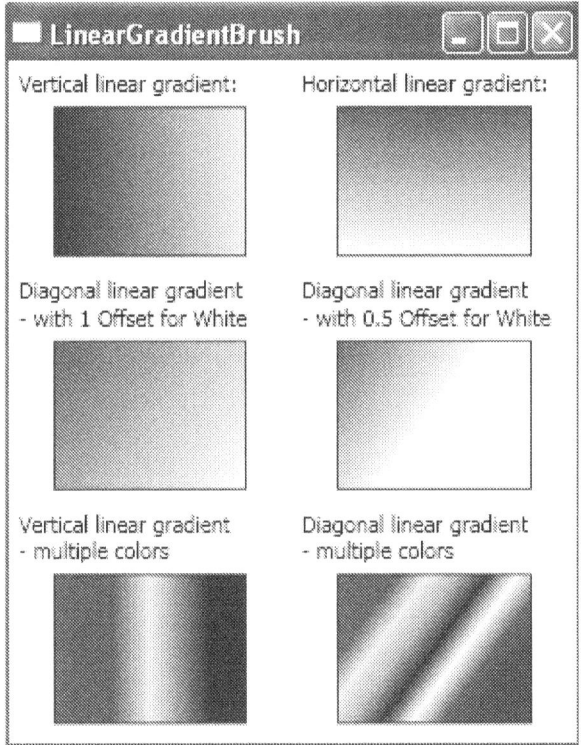

Figure 5-5 Rectangles filled with different linear gradients.

The first rectangle is filled by a LinearGradientBrush with blue and yellow along a vertical gradient axis. The second rectangle is filled by a horizontal gradient brush with red and white colors. Now look at rect3 and rect4. Both rectangles are filled by a diagonal gradient brush with green and white colors. The GradientStop for the green color has an offset of 0, which means that the green color is placed at the very beginning of the gradient. The GradientStop for the white has an offset of 1 for rect3, which places the white color at the end. For rect4, however, the offset of the GradientStop for the white color is set to 0.5, resulting in the much quicker color blend from green (in the top-left corner) to white in the middle (the point between the two corners). It can be seen from Figure 5-5 that the right side of rect4 is almost completely white. The last two rectangles, rect5 and rect6, are filled by a multi-color brush, the first along a vertical gradient axis, and the second along a diagonal gradient axis.

The LinearGradientBrush example presented here is intended to demonstrate the use of the brush's basic features in WPF applications. In real-world applications, you may need to create a custom colormap in order to achieve specific visual effects. In next section, I'll show you how to create custom colormaps using the LinearGradientBrush.

Custom Colormap Brush

In WPF, these is a ColorMap class in the System.Windows.Media.Imaging namespace. This class defines a mapping between existing colors and the new colors to which they are to be converted. When the map is applied, any pixel of the old color is converted to the new color. This class is useful for image prcessing applications.

However, in some graphics applications, you may need custom color maps to achieve specific visual effects. These color maps are simply tables or lists of colors that are organized in some desired fashion. The shape, surface, and image objects can be associated with a custom color map.

In many existing CAD and software development tools, many commonly-used color maps have already been defined. Here, I'll show you how to create these colormaps using the LinearGradientBrush object.

Remember that here you simply create some predefined LinearGradientBrush objects: these objects still belong to the type of LinearGradientBrush. You don't create a new type of brush itself. If you do want to create a new type of custom brush, you need to inherit from the Brush class. In this case, you must override the CreateInstanceCore method. Depending on whether your class should perform additional initialization work or contain non-dependency property data members, you might need to override additional Freezable methods.

Add a ColormapBrush class to the project Chapter05. In this class, you'll implement several custom colormap brushes, each with a special name. These colormaps are commonly used in graphics applications. They can be regarded as predefined LinearGradientBrush objects, which can be directly used in your WPF applications.

The following is the code listing of this class:

```
using System;
using System.Collections.Generic;
using System.Windows;
using System.Windows.Media;
```

```
namespace Chapter05
{
    public class ColormapBrush
    {
        private double opacity = 1;
        private Point startPoint = new Point(0, 0);
        private Point endPoint = new Point(1, 0);
        private LinearGradientBrush brush =
            new LinearGradientBrush();

        public double Opacity
        {
            get { return opacity; }
            set { opacity = value; }
        }

        public Point StartPoint
        {
            get { return startPoint; }
            set { startPoint = value; }
        }

        public Point EndPoint
        {
            get { return endPoint; }
            set { endPoint = value; }
        }

        public LinearGradientBrush Spring()
        {
            brush.GradientStops.Add(new GradientStop(
                Color.FromRgb(255, 0, 255), 0));
            brush.GradientStops.Add(new GradientStop(
                Color.FromRgb(255, 255, 0), 1));
            brush.StartPoint = StartPoint;
            brush.EndPoint = EndPoint;
            brush.Opacity = opacity;
            return brush;
        }

        public LinearGradientBrush Summer()
        {
            brush.GradientStops.Add(new GradientStop(
                Color.FromRgb(0, 128, 90), 0));
            brush.GradientStops.Add(new GradientStop(
                Color.FromRgb(255, 255, 90), 1));
            brush.StartPoint = StartPoint;
            brush.EndPoint = EndPoint;
            brush.Opacity = opacity;
            return brush;
        }

        public LinearGradientBrush Autumn()
```

```
    {
        brush.GradientStops.Add(new GradientStop(
            Color.FromRgb(255, 0, 0), 0));
        brush.GradientStops.Add(new GradientStop(
            Color.FromRgb(255, 255, 0), 1));
        brush.StartPoint = StartPoint;
        brush.EndPoint = EndPoint;
        brush.Opacity = opacity;
        return brush;
    }

    public LinearGradientBrush Winter()
    {
        brush.GradientStops.Add(new GradientStop(
            Color.FromRgb(0, 0, 255), 0));
        brush.GradientStops.Add(new GradientStop(
            Color.FromRgb(0, 255, 128), 1));
        brush.StartPoint = StartPoint;
        brush.EndPoint = EndPoint;
        brush.Opacity = opacity;
        return brush;
    }

    public LinearGradientBrush Hot()
    {
        brush.GradientStops.Add(new GradientStop(
            Color.FromRgb(85, 0, 0), 0));
        brush.GradientStops.Add(new GradientStop(
            Color.FromRgb(255, 0, 0), 0.25));
        brush.GradientStops.Add(new GradientStop(
            Color.FromRgb(255, 85, 0), 0.375));
        brush.GradientStops.Add(new GradientStop(
            Color.FromRgb(255, 255, 0), 0.625));
        brush.GradientStops.Add(new GradientStop(
            Color.FromRgb(255, 255, 128), 0.75));
        brush.GradientStops.Add(new GradientStop(
            Color.FromRgb(255, 255, 255), 1));
        brush.StartPoint = StartPoint;
        brush.EndPoint = EndPoint;
        brush.Opacity = opacity;
        return brush;
    }

    public LinearGradientBrush Cool()
    {
        brush.GradientStops.Add(new GradientStop(
            Color.FromRgb(0, 255, 255), 0));
        brush.GradientStops.Add(new GradientStop(
            Color.FromRgb(255, 0, 255), 1));
        brush.StartPoint = StartPoint;
        brush.EndPoint = EndPoint;
        brush.Opacity = opacity;
        return brush;
    }
```

```
public LinearGradientBrush Gray()
{
    brush.GradientStops.Add(new GradientStop(
        Color.FromRgb(0, 0, 0), 0));
    brush.GradientStops.Add(new GradientStop(
        Color.FromRgb(255, 255, 255), 1));
    brush.StartPoint = StartPoint;
    brush.EndPoint = EndPoint;
    brush.Opacity = opacity;
    return brush;
}

public LinearGradientBrush Jet()
{
    brush.GradientStops.Add(new GradientStop(
        Color.FromRgb(0, 0, 255), 0));
    brush.GradientStops.Add(new GradientStop(
        Color.FromRgb(0, 128, 255), 0.143));
    brush.GradientStops.Add(new GradientStop(
        Color.FromRgb(0, 255, 255), 0.286));
    brush.GradientStops.Add(new GradientStop(
        Color.FromRgb(128, 255, 128), 0.429));
    brush.GradientStops.Add(new GradientStop(
        Color.FromRgb(255, 255, 0), 0.571));
    brush.GradientStops.Add(new GradientStop(
        Color.FromRgb(255, 128, 0), 0.714));
    brush.GradientStops.Add(new GradientStop(
        Color.FromRgb(255, 0, 0), 0.857));
    brush.GradientStops.Add(new GradientStop(
        Color.FromRgb(128, 0, 0), 1));
    brush.StartPoint = StartPoint;
    brush.EndPoint = EndPoint;
    brush.Opacity = opacity;
    return brush;
}
}
```

This class has three public properties: StartPoint, EndPoint, and Opacity. The first two Point objects are used to specify the corresponding properties of the LinerGradientBrush. The default values of StartPoint = (0, 0) and EndPoint = (1, 0), which define a vertical gradient brush. You can change these Point properties if you want to use a different gradient axis.

The Opacity property is used to define the alpha channel of a color. The default value of the Opacity is 1, corresponding to a completely opaque color. In this class, the color is defined using an sRGB value. The custom colormap brushes are created with different colors, each one with a different number of GradientStops and Offsets.

Now, let's use an example to show you how to use these colormap brushes in a WPF application. Add a new WPF Window to the project Chapter05 and name it ColormapBrushExample. In this example, you'll first create several rectangles and fill their color using different ColormapBrush objects. Then, you'll draw some math functions using the ColormapBrush. Here is the markup of this example:

```xml
<Window x:Class="Chapter05.ColormapBrushExample"
    xmlns="http://schemas.microsoft.com/winfx
        /2006/xaml/presentation"
    xmlns:x="http://schemas.microsoft.com/winfx/2006/xaml"
    Title="Custom Colormap" Height="500" Width="300">

  <Canvas>
      <Grid>
          <Grid.RowDefinitions>
              <RowDefinition Height="Auto"/>
              <RowDefinition Height="Auto"/>
          </Grid.RowDefinitions>
          <StackPanel Margin="5" Grid.Row="0">
              <TextBlock Margin="10,5,5,5"
                        Text="Rectangles filled using
                        ColormapBrush objects"/>
              <Rectangle x:Name="rect1" Width="280"
                        Height="30" Stroke="Blue"
                        Margin="0,0,0,5"/>
              <Rectangle x:Name="rect2" Width="280"
                        Height="30" Stroke="Blue"
                        Margin="0,0,0,5"/>
              <Rectangle x:Name="rect3" Width="280"
                        Height="30" Stroke="Blue"
                        Margin="0,0,0,5"/>
              <Rectangle x:Name="rect4" Width="280"
                        Height="30" Stroke="Blue"
                        Margin="0,0,0,5"/>
              <Rectangle x:Name="rect5" Width="280"
                        Height="30" Stroke="Blue"
                        Margin="0,0,0,5"/>
              <Rectangle x:Name="rect6" Width="280"
                        Height="30" Stroke="Blue"
                        Margin="0,0,0,5"/>
              <Rectangle x:Name="rect7" Width="280"
                        Height="30" Stroke="Blue"
                        Margin="0,0,0,5"/>
              <Rectangle x:Name="rect8" Width="280"
                        Height="30" Stroke="Blue"
                        Margin="0,0,0,10"/>
              <TextBlock Margin="10,5,5,-5"
                        Text="Sine and Cosine curve painted
                        using colormap"/>
          </StackPanel>
          <Canvas x:Name="canvas1" Grid.Row="1"/>
      </Grid>
  </Canvas>
</Window>
```

The corresponding C# code is listed below:

```
using System;
using System.Collections.Generic;
using System.Windows;
using System.Windows.Controls;
using System.Windows.Input;
using System.Windows.Media;
using System.Windows.Shapes;

namespace Chapter05
{
    public partial class ColormapBrushExample : Window
    {
        public ColormapBrushExample()
        {
            InitializeComponent();
            FillRectangles();
            AddMathFunction();
        }

        private void FillRectangles()
        {
            // Fill rect1 with "Spring" colormap:
            ColormapBrush brush = new ColormapBrush();
            rect1.Fill = brush.Spring();

            // Fill rect2 with "Summer" colormap:
            brush = new ColormapBrush();
            rect2.Fill = brush.Summer();

            // Fill rect3 with "Autumn" colormap:
            brush = new ColormapBrush();
            rect3.Fill = brush.Autumn();

            // Fill rect4 with "Winter" colormap:
            brush = new ColormapBrush();
            rect4.Fill = brush.Winter();

            // Fill rect5 with "Jet" colormap:
            brush = new ColormapBrush();
            rect5.Fill = brush.Jet();

            // Fill rect6 with "Gray" colormap:
            brush = new ColormapBrush();
            rect6.Fill = brush.Gray();

            // Fill rect7 with "Hot" colormap:
            brush = new ColormapBrush();
            rect7.Fill = brush.Hot();

            // Fill rect8 with "Cool" colormap:
            brush = new ColormapBrush();
            rect8.Fill = brush.Cool();
        }
```

```
private void AddMathFunction()
{
    // Create a cosine curve:
    ColormapBrush brush1 = new ColormapBrush();
    brush1.StartPoint = new Point(0, 0);
    brush1.EndPoint = new Point(0, 1);
    Polyline line1 = new Polyline();
    for (int i = 0; i < 250; i++)
    {
        double x = i;
        double y = 70 +
            50 * Math.Sin(x / 4.0 / Math.PI);
        line1.Points.Add(new Point(x, y));
    }
    line1.Stroke = brush1.Spring();
    line1.StrokeThickness = 5;
    Canvas.SetLeft(line1, 20);
    canvas1.Children.Add(line1);

    // Create a cosine curve:
    brush1 = new ColormapBrush();
    brush1.StartPoint = new Point(0, 1);
    brush1.EndPoint = new Point(0, 0);
    line1 = new Polyline();
    for (int i = 0; i < 250; i++)
    {
        double x = i;
        double y = 70 +
            50 * Math.Cos(x / 4.0 / Math.PI);
        line1.Points.Add(new Point(x, y));
    }
    line1.Stroke = brush1.Jet();
    line1.StrokeThickness = 5;
    Canvas.SetLeft(line1, 20);
    canvas1.Children.Add(line1);
}
}
}
```

This example produces the output shown in Figure 5-6.

Here, the default vertical colormap brush is used to paint the rectangles. You simply create a ColormapBrush instance and set the Fill property of rectangles to the corresponding method. For the Sine and Cosine curves, you specify a horizontal gradient axis by changing the StartPoint and EndPoint properties. You should notice that if you exchange the StartPoint with the EndPoint, you'll reverse the color gradient.

Following the procedure presented here, you can easily add your own colormaps to the ColormapBrush class.

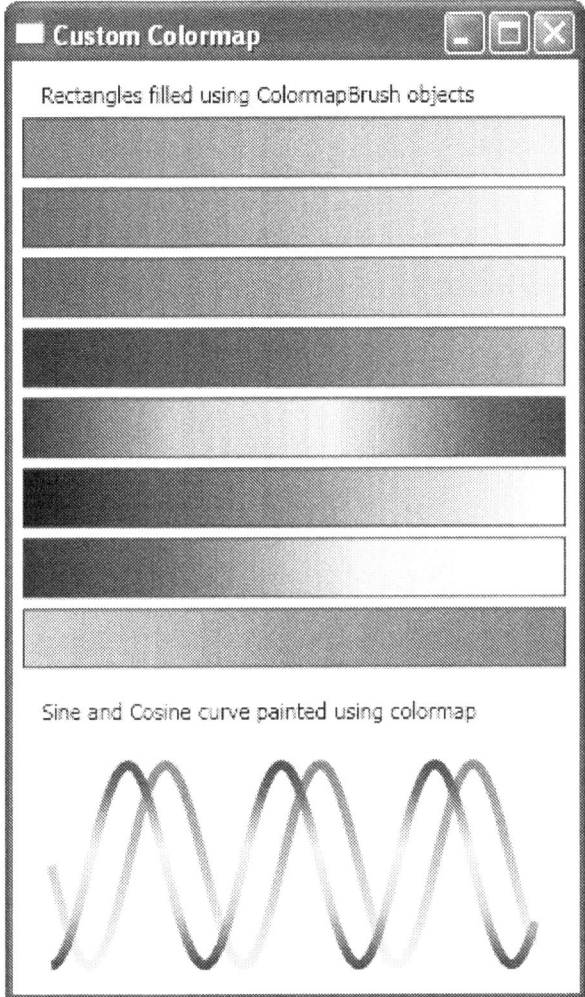

Figure 5-6 Rectangles and curves drawn using ColormapBrush objects.

RadialGradientBrush

RadialGradientBrush works in a similar way to the LinearGradientBrush. It also takes a sequence of colors with different offsets, but blends colors in a radial pattern. A radial gradient is defined as a circle. The axis of RadialGradientBrush starts from the origin, which you specify using its GradientOrigin, and runs to the outer edge of the circle.

You can set the edge of the gradient circle using three properties: Center, RadiusX, and RadiusY. By default, the Center property is at (0.5, 0.5), which places the center of the circle in the middle of your fill region and in the same position as the gradient origin.

Let's take a look at an example to see how the RadialGradientBrush works. Add a new WPF Window to the project Chapter05 and name it RadialGradientBrushExample. Here is the XAML file of this example:

```xml
<Window x:Class="Chapter05.RadialGradientBrushExample"
    xmlns="http://schemas.microsoft.com/winfx
        /2006/xaml/presentation"
    xmlns:x="http://schemas.microsoft.com/winfx/2006/xaml"
    Title="Radial Gradient" Height="320" Width="368">
  <Canvas>
      <Grid>
        <Grid.ColumnDefinitions>
            <ColumnDefinition/>
            <ColumnDefinition/>
            <ColumnDefinition/>
        </Grid.ColumnDefinitions>
        <Grid.RowDefinitions>
            <RowDefinition/>
            <RowDefinition/>
        </Grid.RowDefinitions>

        <StackPanel Grid.Column="0" Grid.Row="0"
                Margin="5">
            <TextBlock Text="ellipse1" Margin="35,5,5,5"/>
            <Ellipse x:Name="ellipse1" Stroke="Blue"
                Width="100" Height="100" Margin="5">
              <Ellipse.Fill>
                <RadialGradientBrush
                    GradientOrigin="0.5,0.5"
                    Center="0.5,0.5"
                    RadiusX="1" RadiusY="1">
                    <GradientStop Color="Red"
                            Offset="0" />
                    <GradientStop Color="Yellow"
                            Offset="0.3" />
                    <GradientStop Color="Green"
                            Offset="0.6" />
                </RadialGradientBrush>
              </Ellipse.Fill>
            </Ellipse>
        </StackPanel>

        <StackPanel Grid.Column="1" Grid.Row="0"
                Margin="5">
            <TextBlock Text="ellipse2" Margin="35,5,5,5"/>
            <Ellipse x:Name="ellipse2" Stroke="Blue"
                Width="100" Height="100" Margin="5">
              <Ellipse.Fill>
                <RadialGradientBrush
                    GradientOrigin="0.5,0.5"
                    Center="0,0"
                    RadiusX="1" RadiusY="1">
                    <GradientStop Color="Red"
                            Offset="0" />
```

```
                <GradientStop Color="Yellow"
                              Offset="0.3" />
                <GradientStop Color="Green"
                              Offset="0.6" />
              </RadialGradientBrush>
            </Ellipse.Fill>
        </Ellipse>
</StackPanel>

<StackPanel Grid.Column="2" Grid.Row="0"
            Margin="5">
    <TextBlock Text="ellipse3" Margin="35,5,5,5"/>
    <Ellipse x:Name="ellipse3" Stroke="Blue"
             Width="100" Height="100" Margin="5">
        <Ellipse.Fill>
            <RadialGradientBrush
                GradientOrigin="0.5,0.5"
                Center="0.5,0.5"
                RadiusX="0.5" RadiusY="0.5">
                <GradientStop Color="Red"
                              Offset="0" />
                <GradientStop Color="Yellow"
                              Offset="0.3" />
                <GradientStop Color="Green"
                              Offset="0.6" />
              </RadialGradientBrush>
            </Ellipse.Fill>
        </Ellipse>
</StackPanel>

<StackPanel Grid.Column="0" Grid.Row="1"
            Margin="5">
    <TextBlock Text="ellipse4" Margin="35,5,5,5"/>
    <Ellipse x:Name="ellipse4" Stroke="Blue"
             Width="100" Height="100" Margin="5">
        <Ellipse.Fill>
            <RadialGradientBrush
                GradientOrigin="0.5,0.5"
                Center="0,0"
                RadiusX="0.5" RadiusY="0.5">
                <GradientStop Color="Red"
                              Offset="0" />
                <GradientStop Color="Yellow"
                              Offset="0.3" />
                <GradientStop Color="Green"
                              Offset="0.6" />
              </RadialGradientBrush>
            </Ellipse.Fill>
        </Ellipse>
</StackPanel>

<StackPanel Grid.Column="1" Grid.Row="1"
            Margin="5">
    <TextBlock Text="ellipse5" Margin="35,5,5,5"/>
```

```xml
          <Ellipse x:Name="ellipse5" Stroke="Blue"
                Width="100" Height="100" Margin="5">
            <Ellipse.Fill>
              <RadialGradientBrush
                  GradientOrigin="0.5,0.5"
                  Center="0.5,0.5"
                  RadiusX="1" RadiusY="0.5">
                <GradientStop Color="Red"
                              Offset="0" />
                <GradientStop Color="Yellow"
                              Offset="0.3" />
                <GradientStop Color="Green"
                              Offset="0.6" />
              </RadialGradientBrush>
            </Ellipse.Fill>
          </Ellipse>
        </StackPanel>

        <StackPanel Grid.Column="2" Grid.Row="1"
                Margin="5">
          <TextBlock Text="ellipse6" Margin="35,5,5,5"/>
          <Ellipse x:Name="ellipse6" Stroke="Blue"
                Width="100" Height="100" Margin="5">
            <Ellipse.Fill>
              <RadialGradientBrush
                  GradientOrigin="0.5,0.5"
                  Center="0.5,0.5"
                  RadiusX="0.5" RadiusY="1">
                <GradientStop Color="Red"
                              Offset="0" />
                <GradientStop Color="Yellow"
                              Offset="0.3" />
                <GradientStop Color="Green"
                              Offset="0.6" />
              </RadialGradientBrush>
            </Ellipse.Fill>
          </Ellipse>
        </StackPanel>
      </Grid>
    </Canvas>
  </Window>
```

This XAML file create six circles using the Ellipse shape class. The first two circles are filled using a RadialGradientBrush with a RadiusX = 1 and RadiusY = 1. The difference is that the brush for the first circle has a Center at (0.5, 0.5), which is the same as its GradientOrigin of (0.5, 0.5), while the brush for the second circle has a Center at (0, 0), which isn't lined up with its GradientOrigin of (0.5, 0.5). Ellipse3 and ellipse4 have fill properties similar to the first two shapes, except that they have smaller RadiusX and RadiusY. The last two circles have different RadiusX and RadiusY properties, which turns the gradient into an ellipse instead of a circle.

Figure 5-7 illustrates the results of running this example.

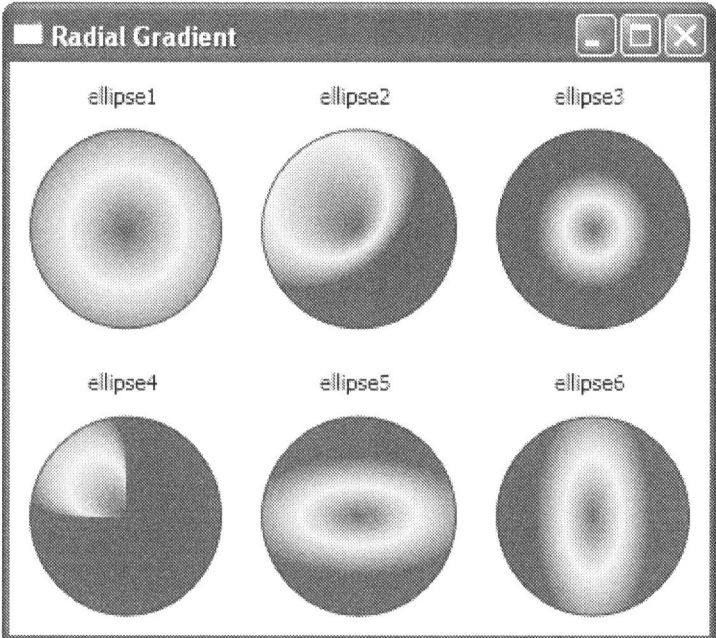

Figure 5-7 Shapes filled using RadialGradientBrush objects.

Custom Radial Colormap Brush

Like ColormapBrush for the custom predefined LinearGradientBrush, you can also create RadialColormapBrush for the predefined RadialGradientBrush. This custom defined radial brush may be useful when you want to create some special radial visual effects.

Add a new class, called RadialColormapBrush, to the project Chapter05. Implement the following C# code for this class:

```
using System;
using System.Collections.Generic;
using System.Windows;
using System.Windows.Media;

namespace Chapter05
{
    public class RadialColormapBrush
    {
        private Point center = new Point(0.5,0.5);
        private Point gradientOrigin = new Point(0.5, 0.5);
        private double radiusX = 0.5;
        private double radiusY = 0.5;
        private double opacity = 1;
        private RadialGradientBrush brush =
            new RadialGradientBrush();
```

```
public Point Center
{
    get { return center; }
    set { center = value; }
}

public Point GradientOrigin
{
    get { return gradientOrigin; }
    set { gradientOrigin = value; }
}

public double RadiusX
{
    get { return radiusX; }
    set { radiusX = value; }
}

public double RadiusY
{
    get { return radiusY; }
    set { radiusY = value; }
}

public double Opacity
{
    get { return opacity; }
    set { opacity = value; }
}

public RadialGradientBrush Spring()
{
    brush.GradientStops.Add(new GradientStop(
        Color.FromRgb(255, 0, 255), 0));
    brush.GradientStops.Add(new GradientStop(
        Color.FromRgb(255, 255, 0), 1));
    brush.Center = Center;
    brush.GradientOrigin = GradientOrigin;
    brush.RadiusX = RadiusX;
    brush.RadiusY = RadiusY;
    brush.Opacity = Opacity;
    return brush;
}

public RadialGradientBrush Summer()
{
    brush.GradientStops.Add(new GradientStop(
        Color.FromRgb(0, 128, 90), 0));
    brush.GradientStops.Add(new GradientStop(
        Color.FromRgb(255, 255, 90), 1));
    brush.Center = Center;
    brush.GradientOrigin = GradientOrigin;
    brush.RadiusX = RadiusX;
    brush.RadiusY = RadiusY;
```

```
        brush.Opacity = Opacity;
        return brush;
    }
    public RadialGradientBrush Autumn()
    {
        brush.GradientStops.Add(new GradientStop(
            Color.FromRgb(255, 0, 0), 0));
        brush.GradientStops.Add(new GradientStop(
            Color.FromRgb(255, 255, 0), 1));
        brush.Center = Center;
        brush.GradientOrigin = GradientOrigin;
        brush.RadiusX = RadiusX;
        brush.RadiusY = RadiusY;
        brush.Opacity = Opacity;
        return brush;
    }
    public RadialGradientBrush Winter()
    {
        brush.GradientStops.Add(new GradientStop(
            Color.FromRgb(0, 0, 255), 0));
        brush.GradientStops.Add(new GradientStop(
            Color.FromRgb(0, 255, 128), 1));
        brush.Center = Center;
        brush.GradientOrigin = GradientOrigin;
        brush.RadiusX = RadiusX;
        brush.RadiusY = RadiusY;
        brush.Opacity = Opacity;
        return brush;
    }

    public RadialGradientBrush Hot()
    {
        brush.GradientStops.Add(new GradientStop(
            Color.FromRgb(85, 0, 0), 0));
        brush.GradientStops.Add(new GradientStop(
            Color.FromRgb(255, 0, 0), 0.25));
        brush.GradientStops.Add(new GradientStop(
            Color.FromRgb(255, 85, 0), 0.375));
        brush.GradientStops.Add(new GradientStop(
            Color.FromRgb(255, 255, 0), 0.625));
        brush.GradientStops.Add(new GradientStop(
            Color.FromRgb(255, 255, 128), 0.75));
        brush.GradientStops.Add(new GradientStop(
            Color.FromRgb(255, 255, 255), 1));
        brush.Center = Center;
        brush.GradientOrigin = GradientOrigin;
        brush.RadiusX = RadiusX;
        brush.RadiusY = RadiusY;
        brush.Opacity = Opacity;
        return brush;
    }

    public RadialGradientBrush Cool()
    {
```

```
            brush.GradientStops.Add(new GradientStop(
                Color.FromRgb(0, 255, 255), 0));
            brush.GradientStops.Add(new GradientStop(
                Color.FromRgb(255, 0, 255), 1));
            brush.Center = Center;
            brush.GradientOrigin = GradientOrigin;
            brush.RadiusX = RadiusX;
            brush.RadiusY = RadiusY;
            brush.Opacity = Opacity;
            return brush;
        }

        public RadialGradientBrush Gray()
        {
            brush.GradientStops.Add(new GradientStop(
                Color.FromRgb(0, 0, 0), 0));
            brush.GradientStops.Add(new GradientStop(
                Color.FromRgb(255, 255, 255), 1));
            brush.Center = Center;
            brush.GradientOrigin = GradientOrigin;
            brush.RadiusX = RadiusX;
            brush.RadiusY = RadiusY;
            brush.Opacity = Opacity;
            return brush;
        }

        public RadialGradientBrush Jet()
        {
            brush.GradientStops.Add(new GradientStop(
                Color.FromRgb(0, 0, 255), 0));
            brush.GradientStops.Add(new GradientStop(
                Color.FromRgb(0, 128, 255), 0.143));
            brush.GradientStops.Add(new GradientStop(
                Color.FromRgb(0, 255, 255), 0.286));
            brush.GradientStops.Add(new GradientStop(
                Color.FromRgb(128, 255, 128), 0.429));
            brush.GradientStops.Add(new GradientStop(
                Color.FromRgb(255, 255, 0), 0.571));
            brush.GradientStops.Add(new GradientStop(
                Color.FromRgb(255, 128, 0), 0.714));
            brush.GradientStops.Add(new GradientStop(
                Color.FromRgb(255, 0, 0), 0.857));
            brush.GradientStops.Add(new GradientStop(
                Color.FromRgb(128, 0, 0), 1));
            brush.Center = Center;
            brush.GradientOrigin = GradientOrigin;
            brush.RadiusX = RadiusX;
            brush.RadiusY = RadiusY;
            brush.Opacity = Opacity;
            return brush;
        }
    }
}
```

This class has five public properties: Center, GradientOrigin, RadiusX, RadiusY, and Opacity. These properties are used to specify the corresponding properties of RadialGradientBrush. The default values of these properties remain the same as those of the RadialGradientBrush. In this class, color is defined using sRGB values. The custom colormap brushes are created with different colors, each one with a different number of GradientStops and Offsets.

Now, let's consider an example that shows you how to use these radial colormap brushes in a WPF application. Add a new WPF Window to the project Chapter05, and name it RadialColormapBrushExample. In this example, you'll create several circles and specify their Fill property using different RadialColormapBrush objects. Here is the XAML file of this example:

```xml
<Window x:Class="Chapter05.RadialColormapBrushExample"
    xmlns="http://schemas.microsoft.com/winfx
        /2006/xaml/presentation"
    xmlns:x="http://schemas.microsoft.com/winfx/2006/xaml"
    Title="Radial Colormap" Height="275" Width="425">
  <Canvas>
      <Grid>
          <Grid.ColumnDefinitions>
              <ColumnDefinition/>
              <ColumnDefinition/>
              <ColumnDefinition/>
              <ColumnDefinition/>
          </Grid.ColumnDefinitions>
          <Grid.RowDefinitions>
              <RowDefinition/>
              <RowDefinition/>
          </Grid.RowDefinitions>

          <StackPanel Margin="2,5,2,2" Grid.Column="0"
                  Grid.Row="0">
              <TextBlock Text="Spring" Margin="33,0,0,0"/>
              <Ellipse x:Name="ellipse1" Stroke="Blue"
                      Width="90" Height="90" Margin="5"/>
          </StackPanel>

          <StackPanel Margin="2,5,2,2" Grid.Column="1"
                  Grid.Row="0">
              <TextBlock Text="Summer" Margin="30,0,0,0"/>
              <Ellipse x:Name="ellipse2" Stroke="Blue"
                      Width="90" Height="90" Margin="5"/>
          </StackPanel>

          <StackPanel Margin="2,5,2,2" Grid.Column="2"
                  Grid.Row="0">
              <TextBlock Text="Autumn" Margin="30,0,0,0"/>
              <Ellipse x:Name="ellipse3" Stroke="Blue"
                      Width="90" Height="90" Margin="5"/>
          </StackPanel>

          <StackPanel Margin="2,5,2,2" Grid.Column="3"
```

```
                              Grid.Row="0">
                <TextBlock Text="Winter" Margin="30,0,0,0"/>
                <Ellipse x:Name="ellipse4" Stroke="Blue"
                        Width="90" Height="90" Margin="5"/>
            </StackPanel>

            <StackPanel Margin="2,5,2,2" Grid.Column="0"
                              Grid.Row="1">
                <TextBlock Text="Jet" Margin="40,0,0,0"/>
                <Ellipse x:Name="ellipse5" Stroke="Blue"
                        Width="90" Height="90" Margin="5"/>
            </StackPanel>

            <StackPanel Margin="2,5,2,2" Grid.Column="1"
                              Grid.Row="1">
                <TextBlock Text="Gray" Margin="38,0,0,0"/>
                <Ellipse x:Name="ellipse6" Stroke="Blue"
                        Width="90" Height="90" Margin="5"/>
            </StackPanel>

            <StackPanel Margin="2,5,2,2" Grid.Column="2"
                              Grid.Row="1">
                <TextBlock Text="Hot" Margin="40,0,0,0"/>
                <Ellipse x:Name="ellipse7" Stroke="Blue"
                        Width="90" Height="90" Margin="5"/>
            </StackPanel>

            <StackPanel Margin="2,5,2,2" Grid.Column="3"
                              Grid.Row="1">
                <TextBlock Text="Cool" Margin="38,0,0,0"/>
                <Ellipse x:Name="ellipse8" Stroke="Blue"
                        Width="90" Height="90" Margin="5"/>
            </StackPanel>
        </Grid>
    </Canvas>
</Window>
```

The corresponding code-behind file of this example is listed below:

```
using System;
using System.Windows;
using System.Windows.Controls;
using System.Windows.Input;
using System.Windows.Media;
using System.Windows.Shapes;

namespace Chapter05
{
    public partial class RadialColormapBrushExample : Window
    {

        public RadialColormapBrushExample()
        {
            InitializeComponent();
```

```
        FillEllipses();
    }

    private void FillEllipses()
    {
        // Fill ellipse1 with "Spring" colormap:
        RadialColormapBrush brush =
            new RadialColormapBrush();
        ellipse1.Fill = brush.Spring();

        // Fill ellipse2 with "Summer" colormap:
        brush = new RadialColormapBrush();
        ellipse2.Fill = brush.Summer();

        // Fill ellipse3 with "Autumn" colormap:
        brush = new RadialColormapBrush();
        ellipse3.Fill = brush.Autumn();

        // Fill ellipse4 with "Winter" colormap:
        brush = new RadialColormapBrush();
        ellipse4.Fill = brush.Winter();

        // Fill ellipse5 with "Jet" colormap:
        brush = new RadialColormapBrush();
        ellipse5.Fill = brush.Jet();

        // Fill ellipse6 with "Gray" colormap:
        brush = new RadialColormapBrush();
        ellipse6.Fill = brush.Gray();

        // Fill ellipse7 with "Hot" colormap:
        brush = new RadialColormapBrush();
        ellipse7.Fill = brush.Hot();

        // Fill ellipse8 with "Cool" colormap:
        brush = new RadialColormapBrush();
        ellipse8.Fill = brush.Cool();
    }
}
}
```

You can see from the above code that the default radial colormap brush is used to fill the circles. You simply create a RadialColormapBrush instance, and set the Fill property of the circles to the corresponding method. Figure 5-8 shows the results of this example.

ImageBrush

ImageBrush is used to paint an area with an ImageSource. The ImageSource contains the most common image file types, including bmp, gif, png, and jpg. You simply specify the image you want to use by setting the ImageSource property.

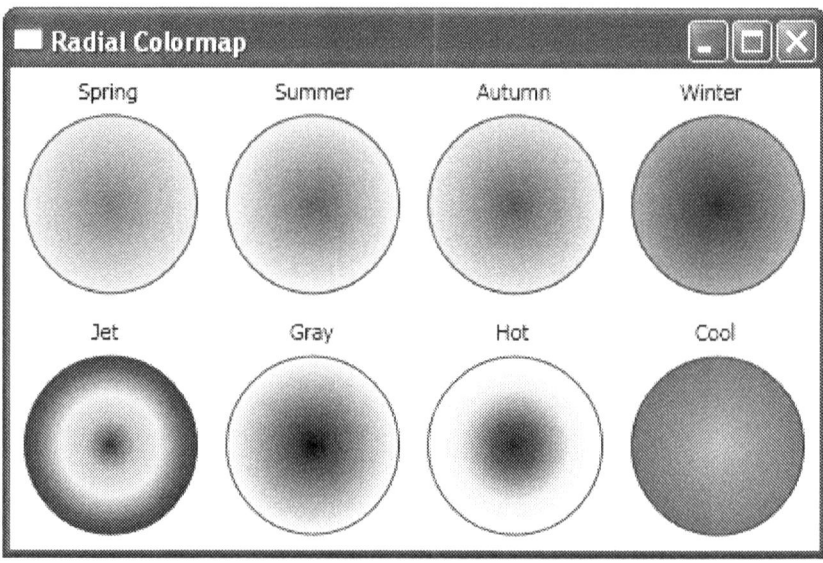

Figure 5-8 Circles painted using RadialColormapBrush objects.

The following example, ImageBrushExample, shows you how to specify an image to be used as the background of a button:

```
<Window x:Class="Chapter05.ImageBrushExample"
    xmlns="http://schemas.microsoft.com/winfx
        /2006/xaml/presentation"
    xmlns:x="http://schemas.microsoft.com/winfx/2006/xaml"
    Title="Chapter05" Height="300" Width="300">

<Canvas>
    <Grid>
        <Grid.ColumnDefinitions>
            <ColumnDefinition/>
            <ColumnDefinition/>
        </Grid.ColumnDefinitions>
        <Grid.RowDefinitions>
            <RowDefinition/>
            <RowDefinition/>
        </Grid.RowDefinitions>

        <StackPanel Margin="5" Grid.Column="0"
                Grid.Row="0">
            <TextBlock Margin="5" Text="Stretch = None"/>
            <Button Width="135" Height="100">
                <Button.Background>
                    <ImageBrush
                        ImageSource="ImageFile.jpg"
                        Stretch="None"/>
                </Button.Background>
            </Button>
        </StackPanel>
```

```
            <StackPanel Margin="5" Grid.Column="1"
                    Grid.Row="0">
                <TextBlock Margin="5" Text="Stretch = Fill"/>
                <Button Width="135" Height="100">
                    <Button.Background>
                        <ImageBrush
                            ImageSource="ImageFile.jpg"
                            Stretch="Fill"/>
                    </Button.Background>
                </Button>
            </StackPanel>

            <StackPanel Margin="5" Grid.Column="0"
                    Grid.Row="1">
                <TextBlock Margin="5"
                        Text="Stretch = Uniform"/>
                <Button Width="135" Height="100">
                    <Button.Background>
                        <ImageBrush
                            ImageSource="ImageFile.jpg"
                            Stretch="Uniform"/>
                    </Button.Background>
                </Button>
            </StackPanel>

            <StackPanel Margin="5" Grid.Column="1"
                    Grid.Row="1">
                <TextBlock Margin="5"
                        Text="Stretch = UniformToFill"/>
                <Button Width="135" Height="100">
                    <Button.Background>
                        <ImageBrush
                            ImageSource="ImageFile.jpg"
                            Stretch="UniformToFill"/>
                    </Button.Background>
                </Button>
            </StackPanel>
        </Grid>
    </Canvas>
</Window>
```

This XAML file defines four buttons. You need to add the image file to the project by right clicking on the Solution Explorer and selecting Add | Existing Item…, and then selecting your image file. For each button, the ImageBrush is used to set the button's Background property. You may notice that the Stretch property of each ImageBrush is set differently to demonstrate its effect.

Figure 5-9 illustrates the results of this example. For the first button, the Stretch property of the ImageBrush is set to None, which preserves the original image size and places the image at the center of the button. For the second button, this property is set to Fill, which is the default setting and forces the image to fill the whole button. For the third button, the stretch property is set to Uniform, which maintains the image aspect ratio, but resizes the image to fit inside the button's content area. For the last button, the Stretch property is set to UniformToFill, which resizes the image to best-fit while preserving the original image aspect ration. In this case, the best-fit is still much larger than the content area of the button, so the image gets clipped.

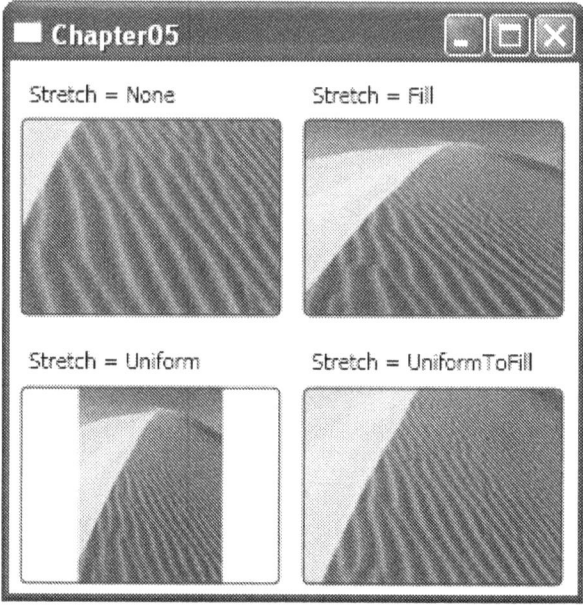

Figure 5-9 Button's background painted using ImageBrush objects.

The ImageBrush derives from the TileBrush class. You can get some special effects using ImageBrush by tiling the image across the surface of the brush. To tile an image, in addition to setting the ImageSource, you must also specify the Viewport and TileMode properties of the ImageBrush object. The latter two properties determine the size of your tile and the way it is arranged.

The Viewport property is used to set the size of each tile. To use proportionately sized tiles, the ViewportUnits must be set to RelativeToBoundingBox, which is the default setting. Then, you define the size of the tile using a proportional coordinate system that stretches from 0 to 1 in both dimensions. Namely, a tile that has a top-left corner at (0, 0) and a bottom-right corner at (1, 1) occupies the entire fill area. To get a tiled pattern, you need to define a Viewport that is smaller than the total size of the fill area, as shown in the following code snippet:

```
<ImageBrush ImageSource="Flower.jpg"
            TileMode="Tile"
            ViewPort="0,0,0.2,0.25"/>
```

This code creates a Viewport box that begins at the top-left corner of the fill area (0, 0) and stretches down to (0.2, 0.25). As a result, the flower image will repeat 5 times in the X direction and 4 times in the Y direction, regardless of how big or small the original image is.

Because the size of the tile in this example is relative to the size of the fill area, a larger fill area will use a larger tile. It is also possible to define the size of your tile in absolute coordinates based on the size of your original image. In this case, you can set the ViewPortUnits to Absolute, as shown here:

```
<ImageBrush ImageSource="Flower.jpg" TileMode="Tile"
            ViewPort="0,0,25,25" ViewPortUnits="Absolute"/>
```

This code snippet defines a size of 25×25 units for each tile and starts tiling from the top-left corner. The drawback of using Absolute units is that the height and width of your fill area must be divisible by 25. Otherwise, you will get a partial tile at the edge.

There are several options in the TileMode:

- Tile – Copies the image across the fill area.

- FlipX – Copies the image, but flips each second column vertically.

- FlipY – Copies the image, but flips each second row horizontally.

- FlipXY – Copies the image, but flips each second column vertically and each second row horizontally.

You can change the TileMode to set how alternating tiles are flipped. The flipping behavior is often useful when you need to make tiles blend more seamlessly.

Now, I'll use an example, called ImageBrushTile, to show you how the image tile works. Here is the XAML file of this example:

```
<Window x:Class="Chapter05.ImageBrushTile"
    xmlns="http://schemas.microsoft.com/winfx
        /2006/xaml/presentation"
    xmlns:x="http://schemas.microsoft.com/winfx/2006/xaml"
    Title="ImageBrush Tiling" Height="300" Width="300">

<Viewbox Stretch="Fill">
    <Grid>
        <Grid.ColumnDefinitions>
            <ColumnDefinition/>
            <ColumnDefinition/>
        </Grid.ColumnDefinitions>
        <Grid.RowDefinitions>
            <RowDefinition/>
            <RowDefinition/>
        </Grid.RowDefinitions>

        <StackPanel Margin="5" Grid.Column="0"
                Grid.Row="0">
            <TextBlock Margin="5,5,5,0"
                    Text="TileMode = Tile"/>
            <TextBlock Margin="5,0,5,5"
                    Text="Unit: Absolute"/>
            <Button Width="135" Height="100">
                <Button.Background>
```

```
                            <ImageBrush ImageSource="Flower.jpg"
                                Viewport="0,0,25,25"
                                TileMode="Tile"
                                ViewportUnits="Absolute"/>
                    </Button.Background>
                </Button>
            </StackPanel>
            <StackPanel Margin="5" Grid.Column="1"
                    Grid.Row="0">
                <TextBlock Margin="5,5,5,0"
                        Text="TileMode = FlipX"/>
                <TextBlock Margin="5,0,5,5"
                        Text="Unit: Absolute"/>
                <Button Width="135" Height="100">
                    <Button.Background>
                        <ImageBrush ImageSource="Flower.jpg"
                            Viewport="0,0,25,25"
                            TileMode="FlipX"
                            ViewportUnits="Absolute"/>
                    </Button.Background>
                </Button>
            </StackPanel>

            <StackPanel Margin="5"
                    Grid.Column="0" Grid.Row="1">
                <TextBlock Margin="5,5,5,0"
                        Text="TileMode = FlipY"/>
                <TextBlock Margin="5,0,5,5"
                        Text="Unit: Reltive"/>
                <Button Width="135" Height="100">
                    <Button.Background>
                        <ImageBrush ImageSource="Flower.jpg"
                            Viewport="0,0,0.2,0.25"
                            TileMode="FlipY"/>
                    </Button.Background>
                </Button>
            </StackPanel>
            <StackPanel Margin="5" Grid.Column="1"
                    Grid.Row="1">
                <TextBlock Margin="5,5,5,0"
                        Text="TileMode = FlipXY"/>
                <TextBlock Margin="5,0,5,5"
                        Text="Unit: Reltive"/>
                <Button Width="135" Height="100">
                    <Button.Background>
                        <ImageBrush ImageSource="Flower.jpg"
                            Viewport="0,0,0.2,0.25"
                            TileMode="FlipXY"/>
                    </Button.Background>
                </Button>
            </StackPanel>
        </Grid>
    </Viewbox>
</Window>
```

Figure 5-10 shows the results of running this application. Here, the backgrounds of four buttons are filled using the ImageBrush object with different TileModes, including Tile, FlipX, FlipY, and FlipXY. The ViewportUnits are set to Absolute for the first two butons and Relative for the last two buttons. The more interesting pattern is obtained when the TileMode property is set to FlipXY. In this case, the pattern appears similar to a mosaic.

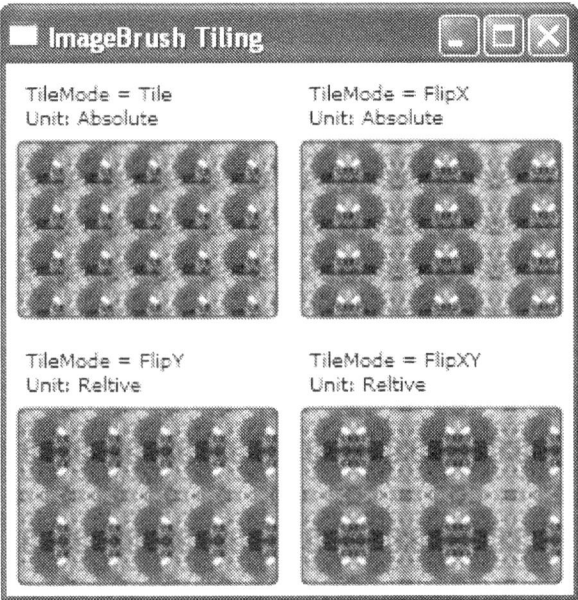

Figure 5-10 Image tiles in WPF.

DrawingBrush

DrawingBrush fills an area using a Drawing object. It can paint shapes, text, images, and video. The Drawing class represents a 2D drawing and is the base class for other drawing objects including GeometryDrawing, GlyphRunDrawing, ImageDrawing, and VideoDrawing. The GeometryDrawing class allows you to define and render shapes using a specified Fill and Stroke. The GlyphRunDrawing provides text operations.

The GeometryDrawing class adds the stroke and fill details that determine how the geometry should be painted. There is another class that derives from Drawing class, the DrawingGroup, which allows you to group multiple Drawing objects together to create a single complex Drawing object.

The following example applies a DrawingBrush and DrawingGroup to draw gridlines as a background of a Grid control. Add a new WPF Window to the project Chapter05 and name it DrawingBrushGridline. Here is the XAML file of this example:

```
<Window x:Class="Chapter05.DrawingBrushGridline"
    xmlns="http://schemas.microsoft.com/winfx
        /2006/xaml/presentation"
    xmlns:x="http://schemas.microsoft.com/winfx/2006/xaml"
Title="Drawing Brush - Gridline" Height="300" Width="300">

    <Grid>
        <Grid.Background>
            <DrawingBrush Viewport="0,0,50,50"
                        ViewportUnits="Absolute"
                        TileMode="Tile">
                <DrawingBrush.Drawing>
                    <DrawingGroup>
                        <DrawingGroup.Children>
                            <GeometryDrawing
                                Geometry="M0,0 L50,0">
                                <GeometryDrawing.Pen>
                                    <Pen Thickness="2"
                                        Brush="LightGreen"/>
                                </GeometryDrawing.Pen>
                            </GeometryDrawing>
                            <GeometryDrawing
                                Geometry="M0,10 L50,10">
                                <GeometryDrawing.Pen>
                                    <Pen Thickness="1"
                                        Brush="LightGreen"/>
                                </GeometryDrawing.Pen>
                            </GeometryDrawing>
                            <GeometryDrawing
                                Geometry="M0,20 L50,20">
                                <GeometryDrawing.Pen>
                                    <Pen Thickness="1"
                                        Brush="LightGreen"/>
                                </GeometryDrawing.Pen>
                            </GeometryDrawing>
                            <GeometryDrawing
                                Geometry="M0,30 L50,30">
                                <GeometryDrawing.Pen>
                                    <Pen Thickness="1"
                                        Brush="LightGreen"/>
                                </GeometryDrawing.Pen>
                            </GeometryDrawing>
                            <GeometryDrawing
                                Geometry="M0,40 L50,40">
                                <GeometryDrawing.Pen>
                                    <Pen Thickness="1"
                                        Brush="LightGreen"/>
                                </GeometryDrawing.Pen>
                            </GeometryDrawing>

                            <GeometryDrawing
                                Geometry="M0,0 L0,50">
                                <GeometryDrawing.Pen>
                                    <Pen Thickness="2"
```

```
                                    Brush="LightGreen"/>
                      </GeometryDrawing.Pen>
                  </GeometryDrawing>
                  <GeometryDrawing
                      Geometry="M10,0 L10,50">
                      <GeometryDrawing.Pen>
                          <Pen Thickness="1"
                              Brush="LightGreen"/>
                      </GeometryDrawing.Pen>
                  </GeometryDrawing>
                  <GeometryDrawing
                      Geometry="M20,0 L20,50">
                      <GeometryDrawing.Pen>
                          <Pen Thickness="1"
                              Brush="LightGreen"/>
                      </GeometryDrawing.Pen>
                  </GeometryDrawing>
                  <GeometryDrawing
                      Geometry="M30,0 L30,50">
                      <GeometryDrawing.Pen>
                          <Pen Thickness="1"
                              Brush="LightGreen"/>
                      </GeometryDrawing.Pen>
                  </GeometryDrawing>
                  <GeometryDrawing
                      Geometry="M40,0 L40,50">
                      <GeometryDrawing.Pen>
                          <Pen Thickness="1"
                              Brush="LightGreen"/>
                      </GeometryDrawing.Pen>
                  </GeometryDrawing>
              </DrawingGroup.Children>
          </DrawingGroup>
      </DrawingBrush.Drawing>
    </DrawingBrush>
  </Grid.Background>
</Grid>
</Window>
```

This example uses DrawingBrush to define the background of a Grid control. The Viewport and TileMode properties of DrawingBrush are specified to have the drawing repeat. Furthermore, the ViewportUnits are set to Absolute to make sure that the gridlines don't change when the Grid control gets resized. Then the Drawing objects are created for the DrawingBrush by using a DrawingGroup object. Next, we create five horizontal and five vertical line segments using GeometryDrawing with the Pen object. Notice that the top-most and left-most line segments use a thick Pen, which gives a better view of the gridlines. The Drawing element created using DrawingGroup is illustrated in Figure 5-11. If this Drawing element is repeated in both the X and Y directions by specifying the TileMode property of DrawingBrush, you'll create gridlines for the entire Grid control, as shown in this figure.

Figure 5-12 shows the results of running this example.

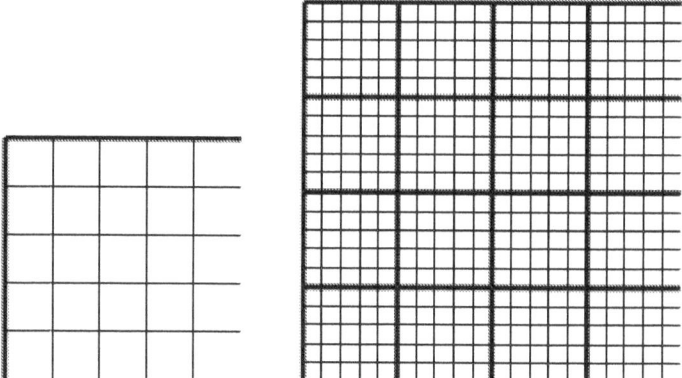

Figure 5-11 Drawing Element (left) used to create gridlines (right).

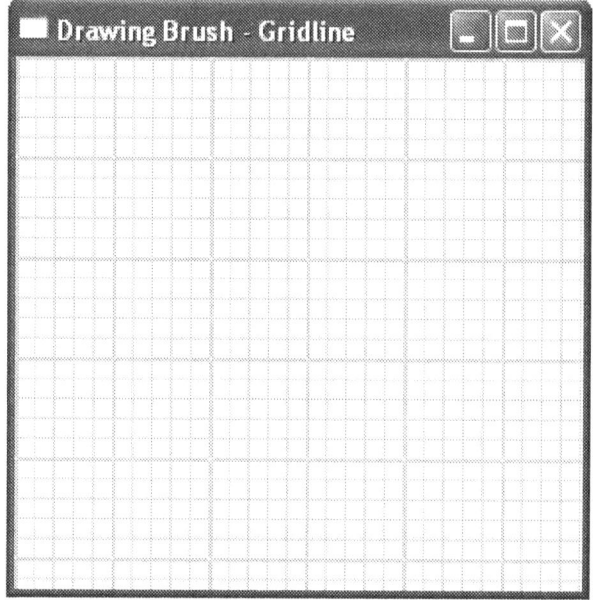

Figure 5-12 Gridlines created using DrawingBrush objects.

Remember that since the Drawing-derived classes aren't elements, they can't be placed in your user interface directly. Instead, to display a drawing object, you need to use DrawingBrush to paint it, as illustrated in the above example. The DrawingBrush allows you to wrap a drawing with a brush, and can be used to paint any surface. You can also use several other ways to display Drawing objects, including DrawingImage and DrawingVisual. The DrawingImage class allows you to host a drawing inside an Image element, while DrawingVisual lets you place a drawing in a lower-level visual object.

If you want to use a piece of vector art to create an icon for a button, you can easily put several Drawing objects into a DrawingGroup and then place the DrawingGroup in a DrawingImage, which can in turn be placed in an Image element.

Here is an example called DrawingImageExample which shows you how to create buttons using DrawingImage objects.

```
<Window x:Class="Chapter05.DrawingImageExample"
    xmlns="http://schemas.microsoft.com/winfx
        /2006/xaml/presentation"
    xmlns:x="http://schemas.microsoft.com/winfx/2006/xaml"
  Title="DrawingImage Example" Height="130" Width="320">

    <Grid>
        <Grid.ColumnDefinitions>
            <ColumnDefinition Width="Auto"/>
            <ColumnDefinition Width="Auto"/>
            <ColumnDefinition Width="Auto"/>
        </Grid.ColumnDefinitions>
        <Grid.RowDefinitions>
            <RowDefinition Height="Auto"/>
        </Grid.RowDefinitions>

        <Button Name="Select" Grid.Column="0"
                ToolTip="Select" Margin="5">
            <Image Width="80" Height="80">
                <Image.Source>
                    <DrawingImage>
                        <DrawingImage.Drawing>
                            <GeometryDrawing
                                Brush="LightGray">
                                <GeometryDrawing.Geometry>
                                    <PathGeometry
  Figures="M25,75 L 50,0 75,75 60,75 60,100 40,100,40,75Z">
                                        <PathGeometry.Transform>
                                            <RotateTransform
                                                CenterX="50"
                                                CenterY="50"
                                                Angle="45"/>
                                        </PathGeometry.Transform>
                                    </PathGeometry>
                                </GeometryDrawing.Geometry>
                                <GeometryDrawing.Pen>
                                    <Pen Brush="Gray"
                                        Thickness="3"/>
                                </GeometryDrawing.Pen>
                            </GeometryDrawing>
                        </DrawingImage.Drawing>
                    </DrawingImage>
                </Image.Source>
            </Image>
        </Button>
```

```xml
<Button Name="DrawRectangle" Grid.Column="1"
        ToolTip="Draw Rectangle" Margin="5">
  <Image Width="80" Height="80">
    <Image.Source>
      <DrawingImage>
        <DrawingImage.Drawing>
          <GeometryDrawing
              Brush="LightGray">
            <GeometryDrawing.Geometry>
              <RectangleGeometry
                  Rect="0,20,100,60"/>
            </GeometryDrawing.Geometry>
            <GeometryDrawing.Pen>
              <Pen Brush="Gray"
                  Thickness="3"/>
            </GeometryDrawing.Pen>
          </GeometryDrawing>
        </DrawingImage.Drawing>
      </DrawingImage>
    </Image.Source>
  </Image>
</Button>

<Button Name="DrawEllipse" Grid.Column="2"
        ToolTip="Draw Ellipse" Margin="5">
  <Image Width="80" Height="80">
    <Image.Source>
      <DrawingImage>
        <DrawingImage.Drawing>
          <GeometryDrawing
              Brush="LightGray">
            <GeometryDrawing.Geometry>
              <EllipseGeometry
                  Center="50,50"
                  RadiusX="50"
                  RadiusY="35"/>
            </GeometryDrawing.Geometry>
            <GeometryDrawing.Pen>
              <Pen Brush="Gray"
                  Thickness="3"/>
            </GeometryDrawing.Pen>
          </GeometryDrawing>
        </DrawingImage.Drawing>
      </DrawingImage>
    </Image.Source>
  </Image>
</Button>
      </Grid>
    </Window>
```

Figure 5-13 illustrates the results of running this example. Here, you create three buttons using DrawingImage objects. You can use the similar approach to create custom buttons that can be used in your own WPF applications.

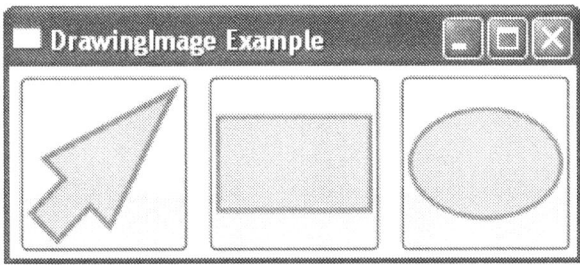

Figure 5-13 Button painted using DrawingImage objects.

DrawingBrush is very flexible and powerful. It allows you to paint many low-level objects from the WPF framework. These objects don't derive from the UIElement or FrameworkElement, so they don't participate in the layout system, which is why they are so lightweight.

VisualBrush

The VisualBrush fills an area with any object that derives from the visual. It allows you to take the visual content of an element and use it to paint any surface. For example, you can use a VisaulBrush to copy the appearance of a button in a window to a region somewhere else in the same window. Note that the VisualBrush is "copying" the button only. This button copied using the VisualBrush would not be clickable or interactive in any way. It is simply a copy of how your element looks.

Here is an example, called VisualBrushExample, that is included in project Chapter05:

```
<Window x:Class="Chapter05.VisualBrushExample"
    xmlns="http://schemas.microsoft.com/winfx
        /2006/xaml/presentation"
    xmlns:x="http://schemas.microsoft.com/winfx/2006/xaml"
    Title="VisualBrush Example" Height="190" Width="250">

<Grid>
    <Grid.ColumnDefinitions>
        <ColumnDefinition Width="Auto"/>
        <ColumnDefinition Width="Auto"/>
    </Grid.ColumnDefinitions>
    <Grid.RowDefinitions>
        <RowDefinition Height="Auto"/>
    </Grid.RowDefinitions>

    <StackPanel Margin="5" Grid.Column="0">
        <TextBlock Text="Original button:" Margin="5"/>
        <Button Name="Select" ToolTip="Select" Margin="5"
                Width="40" Height="40">
            <Image Width="30" Height="30">
                <Image.Source>
                    <DrawingImage>
```

```
                            <DrawingImage.Drawing>
                                <GeometryDrawing
                                    Brush="LightGray">
                                    <GeometryDrawing.Geometry>
                                        <PathGeometry
     Figures="M25,75 L 50,0 75,75 60,75 60,100 40,100,40,75Z">
                                            <PathGeometry.Transform>
                                                RotateTransform
                                                    CenterX="50"
                                                    CenterY="50"
                                                    Angle="45"/>
                                            </PathGeometry.Transform>
                                        </PathGeometry>
                                    </GeometryDrawing.Geometry>
                                    <GeometryDrawing.Pen>
                                        <Pen Brush="Gray"
                                            Thickness="3"/>
                                    </GeometryDrawing.Pen>
                                </GeometryDrawing>
                            </DrawingImage.Drawing>
                        </DrawingImage>
                    </Image.Source>
                </Image>
            </Button>

            <TextBlock Text="Copied button:" Margin="5"/>
            <Button Height="40" Width="40">
                <Button.Background>
    <VisualBrush Visual="{Binding ElementName=Select}"/>
                </Button.Background>
            </Button>
        </StackPanel>

        <StackPanel Margin="10,5,5,5" Grid.Column="1">
            <TextBlock Text="Tiled button:" Margin="5"/>
            <Button Foreground="Blue" Height="120"
                    Width="120">
                <Button.Background>
    <VisualBrush Visual="{Binding ElementName=Select}"
                    Viewport="0,0,40,40"
                    ViewportUnits="Absolute" TileMode="Tile">
                    </VisualBrush>
                </Button.Background>
            </Button>
        </StackPanel>
    </Grid>
</Window>
```

In this example, you draw the original button's background using DrawingBrush like you did in the previous example. Although you could directly define the visual element you want to use in VisualBrush, it is much more common to use a binding expression to refer to an element in the current window, as you do in this example. In addition to the original button, you add two more buttons.

These two new buttons use VisualBrush to paint their background. The second button simply uses VisualBrush to copy the first button and use it as its background. The last button does the same, only this time it uses the TileMode. Figure 5-14 illustrates the results of running this example.

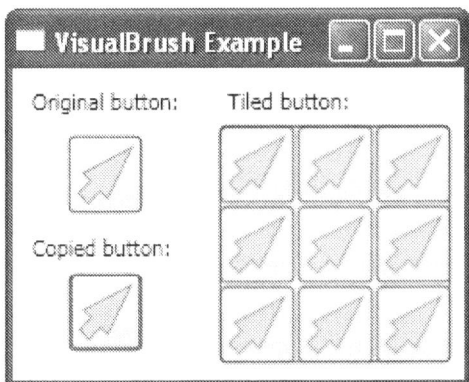

Figure 5-14 Button painted using VisualBrush objects.

The background for the last two buttons is created using VisualBrush. By default, when you mouse over a button, the button is highlighted yellow. Notice that if you mouse over the original button, the background of the other buttons becomes highlighted as well. For the tiled button, each of the tiles of the VisualBrush is highlighted. This is because VisualBrush "copies" the entire visual tree of its source object. Part of the button's visual tree is the border and event trigger associated with it.

Because the content of VisualBrush isn't interactive, you might wonder what purpose the VisualBrush has. In fact, the VisualBrush is powerful and opens the door for creating lots of special effects. For example, you can take an element that contains a significant amount of nested content, shrink it down to a smaller size, and use it for a live preview. VisualBrush is also key for achieving reflection effects.

Bitmap Effects

You can apply Bitmap effects to any WPF element. The purpose of the Bitmap effect is to give you an easy way to enhance the appearance of text, images, buttons, and other controls. This effect allows you to add special effects to your visual elements, such as blurring, drop shadows, and glows. Note that UIElement exposes a BitmapEffect property, while the Visual element exposes a VisualBitmapEffect property. Both of these properties accept the BitmapEffect object as a value.

Bitmap effects have some drawbacks. The first is that bitmap effects in WPF are implemented in unmanaged code, so they require a fully trusted application. As a result, you can't use bitmap effects in an XBAP application. The other drawback is that bitmap effects are rendered in software and don't use the resources of a video card. Therefore, bitmap effects can be expensive for large visual objects.

Bitmap effects are classes deriving from the BitmapEffect base class. These classes are found in the System.Windows.Media.Effects namespace. WPF provides six types of bitmap effects. These are:

- BlurBitmapEffect – Creates a blurring effect on your element.

- BevelBitmapEffect – Adds a raised edge around your content.

- DropShadowBitmapEffect – Creates a shadow behind your element.

- EmbossedBitmapEffect – Gives your content an illusion of depth.

- OuterGlowBitmapEffect – Creates a glowing effect around your content.

- BitmapEffectGroup – Applies a composite of bitmap effects.

Now, let's start with an example in which you create a number of elements, including Buttons, TextBlocks, and images. You then apply various bitmap effects to these elements.

Here is the XAML file of this example:

```
<Window x:Class="Chapter05.BitmapEffectsExample"
    xmlns="http://schemas.microsoft.com/winfx
        /2006/xaml/presentation"
    xmlns:x="http://schemas.microsoft.com/winfx/2006/xaml"
    Title="Bitmap Effects" Height="500" Width="400">

    <Grid ShowGridLines="True">
        <Grid.ColumnDefinitions>
            <ColumnDefinition Width="Auto"/>
            <ColumnDefinition Width="Auto"/>
        </Grid.ColumnDefinitions>
        <Grid.RowDefinitions>
            <RowDefinition Height="Auto"/>
            <RowDefinition Height="Auto"/>
            <RowDefinition Height="Auto"/>
        </Grid.RowDefinitions>

        <!-- Berel Effect: -->
        <StackPanel Margin="5" Grid.Column="0" Grid.Row="0">
            <Button Content="A Beveled Button" Width="175"
                    Height="50" Margin="5">
                <Button.BitmapEffect>
                    <BevelBitmapEffect BevelWidth="10"
                        EdgeProfile="CurvedIn" LightAngle="45"
                        Relief="0.2" Smoothness="0.5" />
                </Button.BitmapEffect>
            </Button>
            <TextBlock Text="Bevel" FontSize="65"
                    FontWeight="Bold" Foreground="DarkRed">
                <TextBlock.BitmapEffect>
```

```
                <BevelBitmapEffect/>
            </TextBlock.BitmapEffect>
        </TextBlock>
</StackPanel>

<!-- Blur Effect: -->
<StackPanel Margin="5" Grid.Column="1" Grid.Row="0">
    <Button Content="A Blur Button"  Width="175"
            Height="50" Margin="5">
        <Button.BitmapEffect>
            <BlurBitmapEffect Radius="1"/>
        </Button.BitmapEffect>
    </Button>
    <Button Content="A Blur Button"  Width="175"
            Height="50" Margin="5">
        <Button.BitmapEffect>
            <BlurBitmapEffect Radius="3"/>
        </Button.BitmapEffect>
    </Button>
</StackPanel>

<!-- Glowing Effect: -->
<StackPanel Margin="5,20,5,5" Grid.Column="0"
            Grid.Row="1">
    <Button Content="A Growing Button" Width="150"
            Height="30" Margin="10">
        <Button.BitmapEffect>
            <OuterGlowBitmapEffect GlowColor="Gray"
                GlowSize="15" Noise="1"/>
        </Button.BitmapEffect>
    </Button>
    <TextBlock Text="Growing" FontSize="40"
               FontWeight="Bold"
               Foreground="White" Margin="5">
        <TextBlock.BitmapEffect>
            <OuterGlowBitmapEffect GlowColor="Gray"
                GlowSize="10" Noise="0.5"/>
        </TextBlock.BitmapEffect>
    </TextBlock>
</StackPanel>

<!-- Shadow Effect: -->
<StackPanel Margin="5,20,5,5" Grid.Column="1"
            Grid.Row="1">
    <Button Content="A Shadow Button" Width="150"
            Height="30" Margin="5">
        <Button.BitmapEffect>
            <DropShadowBitmapEffect ShadowDepth="10"
                Color="DarkRed"/>
        </Button.BitmapEffect>
    </Button>

    <TextBlock Text="Shadow" Margin="3,0,3,13"
               FontSize="40" FontWeight="Bold"
```

```
                           Foreground="LightCoral">
                   <TextBlock.BitmapEffect>
                       <DropShadowBitmapEffect ShadowDepth="20"
                           Color="Gray" Softness="0"/>
                   </TextBlock.BitmapEffect>
               </TextBlock>
           </StackPanel>

           <!-- Embossed Effect: -->
           <StackPanel Margin="5,10,5,5" Grid.Column="0"
                   Grid.Row="2">
               <TextBlock Text="Original Image" Margin="5"/>
               <Image Width="175" Source="Flower.jpg" Margin="5"
                   Grid.Column="0" Grid.Row="2"/>
           </StackPanel>

           <StackPanel Margin="5,10,5,5" Grid.Column="1"
                   Grid.Row="2">
               <TextBlock Text="Embossed Image" Margin="5"/>
               <Image Width="175" Source="Flower.jpg" Margin="5">
                   <Image.BitmapEffect>
                       <EmbossBitmapEffect Relief="0.5"
                                           LightAngle="320" />
                   </Image.BitmapEffect>
               </Image>
           </StackPanel>
       </Grid>
   </Window>
```

Figure 5-15 shows the results of executing this example.

In this example, let's first consider the BevelBitmapEffect, which creates a raised edge around the border of a Button and a TextBlock element. You can see from the figure how the beveling affects the appearance of the elements. The beveling creates a cleanly defined border that wraps the button element, and creates crisp edges on the text. When you set a bevel, you can adjust the effect by changing corresponding properties. BevelWidth property controls the width of the beveled edge (the default value is 5), and the EdgeProfile controls how this edge is shaped. The values for the EdgeProfile include Linear, CurvedIn, CurvedOut, and BulgeUp.

You can also change how the beveled edge is shaded by specifying the Relief, Smoothness, and LightAngle properties. Relief takes a value from 0 to 1, where 1 creates the strongest shadows (0.3 is default). Smoothness also has a value range from 0 to 1, where 1 creates the smoothest shadows (the default value is 0.2). Finally, the LightAngle determines where the shadows appear. It takes a value in degrees, where the default value is 135 degrees, which puts the light source at the top-left corner and creates shadows on the bottom and right edges.

In this example, the LightAngle is set to 45 degrees for the Button element, resulting in a shadow on the bottom and left edges. For the Text element, the default values for all of the properties are used.

Figure 5-15 Bitmap effects.

Next, we'll look at the blur effect. The BlurBitmapEffect includes two properties. The Radius property allows you to control the strength of the blur from 0 (no blur) to a blurring level of your choice. In this example, you apply the blur effect to two buttons. The blur effect for the first button has a Radius of 1, while the second button uses a Radius of 3.

In addition to the Radius property, you can also set the KernelType property to change the style of blurring. The default is Gaussian, which creates a smooth blur. Alternatively, you can use Box, which is less soft and looks a little bit more like a double image.

The OuterGlowBitmapEffect is used to add a diffuse halo of light around a Button and Text elements. You can control the color of the glow by using the GlowColor property, the width of the glow by using the GlowSize property, the sharpness of the glow by using the Noise property, and the transparency of the glow by using the Opacity property.

The DropShadowBitmapEffect has a set of properties similar to those of the OuterGlowBitmapEffect, including Color, Noise, Softness, and Opacity. It also includes a LightAngle property, which allows you to set the light direction, and a ShadowDepth property, which lets you set how far away the shadow appears. In this example, you apply this effect to both a Button and a Text element.

The final effect is the EmbossBitmapEffect, which provides a textured stand-out effect to your content. It exposes two properties, Relief and LightAngle. The Relief property (from 0 to 1 with the default value = 0.44) is used to adjust the amount of embossing, and the LightAngle property is used to set the direction that light falls on the embossed edge. In this example, you apply this effect to a flower image. Both the original and embossed images are displayed in Figure 5-15 for comparison. For the embossed image in the figure, the Relief was set to 0.5 and the LightAngle to 320 degrees.

Opacity Masks

As discussed previously, you can change a color's transparency by specifying its Opacity or changing the color's alpha value. However, all elements in WPF can be modified in many different ways. The OpacityMask property can be used to make specific regions of an element transparent or partially transparent. You can use the opacity mask to create the glass-like surface effects, which make an element look glossy or semitransparent.

Although any type of Brush object can be used as the opacity mask, the gradient brush is typically used. This is because the fact that for a SolidColorBrush object, you can accomplish the same effect more easily with the Opacity property than you can with the OpacityMask. On the other hand, for a gradient brush, OpacityMask becomes more useful. Using a gradient brush that moves from a solid to transparent color, you can create a transparent effect that fades in over the surface of your element.

To create an opacity mask, you apply a brush to the OpacityMask property of an element or visual object. The following example, called OpacityMaskExample, shows you how to apply an opacity mask to an image, and how to create a reflection effect by combining an opacity mask with a VisualBrush and a RenderTransform.

```
<Window x:Class="Chapter05.OpacityMaskExample"
    xmlns="http://schemas.microsoft.com/winfx
        /2006/xaml/presentation"
    xmlns:x="http://schemas.microsoft.com/winfx/2006/xaml"
    Title="Chapter05" Height="430" Width="300">

    <Grid>
        <Grid.RowDefinitions>
            <RowDefinition Height="Auto"/>
```

```
                <RowDefinition Height="Auto"/>
        </Grid.RowDefinitions>

        <Grid Grid.Row="0" Margin="5">
            <Grid.Background>
                <ImageBrush ImageSource="Flower.jpg"/>
            </Grid.Background>
            <Ellipse Width="200" Height="200"
                     StrokeThickness="0" Fill="Yellow"
                     Margin="20">
                <Ellipse.OpacityMask>
                    <RadialGradientBrush
                        GradientOrigin="0.5,0.5"
                        Center="0.5,0.5"
                        RadiusX="1" RadiusY="1">
                        <GradientStop Offset="0"
                                      Color="Transparent" />
                        <GradientStop Offset="1"
                                      Color="Yellow"/>
                    </RadialGradientBrush>
                </Ellipse.OpacityMask>
            </Ellipse>
        </Grid>

        <Grid Grid.Row="1">
            <StackPanel Margin="10">
                <Button Name="Select" ToolTip="Select"
                        Margin="5" Width="60" Height="60"
                    Background="LightCoral">
                    <Image Width="50" Height="50">
                        <Image.Source>
                            <DrawingImage>
                                <DrawingImage.Drawing>
                                    <GeometryDrawing
                                        Brush="Yellow">
                                    <GeometryDrawing.Geometry>
                                        <PathGeometry
Figures="M25,75 L 50,0 75,75 60,75 60,100 40,100,40,75Z">
                                        <PathGeometry.Transform>
                                        <RotateTransform
                                            CenterX="50"
                                            CenterY="50"
                                            Angle="45"/>
                                        </PathGeometry.Transform>
                                            </PathGeometry>
                                    </GeometryDrawing.Geometry>
                                        <GeometryDrawing.Pen>
                                        <Pen Brush="Gray"
                                            Thickness="3"/>
                                        </GeometryDrawing.Pen>
                                    </GeometryDrawing>
                                </DrawingImage.Drawing>
                            </DrawingImage>
                        </Image.Source>
```

```
                    </Image>
                </Button>

            <Button Height="60" Width="60"
                    RenderTransformOrigin="1,0.5">
                <Button.Background>
        <VisualBrush Visual="{Binding ElementName=Select}"/>
                </Button.Background>
                <Button.OpacityMask>
                    <LinearGradientBrush StartPoint="0,0"
                                         EndPoint="0,1">
            <GradientStop Color="Transparent" Offset="0"/>
            <GradientStop Color="#77000000" Offset="1"/>
                    </LinearGradientBrush>
                </Button.OpacityMask>
                <Button.RenderTransform>
                    <ScaleTransform ScaleY="-1"/>
                </Button.RenderTransform>
            </Button>
        </StackPanel>
    </Grid>
  </Grid>
</Window>
```

Figure 5-16 shows the result of running this application. In the top image, you place a circle mask created using a RadialGradientBrush on an image, which gives the effect of a flower inside a yellow glass jar.

In the bottom image, you reflect a Select button using the OpacityMask property in conjunction with VisualBrush. The LinearGradientBrush is used to fade between a completely transparent color and a partially transparent color, which makes the reflected button appear more realistic. A RenderTransform is also applied, which flips the button and makes it upside down.

Brush Transforms

In Chapter 3, we discussed object transformations. However, you can apply similar transforms to brushes. The difference between object and brush transforms is that object transformations transform the object itself, while brush transformations only affect the way the object is painted by the brush. Namely, brush transforms only change the fill pattern of the object.

The Brush class provides two transform properties, Transform and RelativeTransform. These properties allow you to rotate, scale, skew, and translate a brush's contents. When you apply a transform to a brush's Transform property and want to transform the brush contents about the center, you need to know the size of the painted area. Suppose the painted area is 200×100. If you use a RotateTransform to rotate the brush's output 45 degrees about its center, you'd give the RotateTransform a CenterX of 100 and a CenterY of 50.

Figure 5-16 OpacityMask effects.

On the other hand, when you apply a transform to a brush's RelativeTransform property, that transform is applied to the brush before its output is mapped to the painted area. The following list describes the order in which a brush's contents are processed and transformed.

- First the brush's contents are processed. For a GradientBrush, this means determining the gradient area. For a TileBrush, (ImageBrush, DrawingBrush, and VisualBrush derive from the TileBush class), the ViewBox is mapped to the Viewport. This becomes the brush's output.

- Then, the brush's output is projected onto a 1 x 1 transform rectangle.

- The brush's RelativeTransform is applied, if it has one.

- The transformed output is projected onto the area to paint.

- Finally, the brush's Transform is applied, if it has one.

Because the RelativeTransform is applied while the brush's output is mapped to a 1 x 1 rectangle, the transform center and offset values appear to be relative. For example, if you use a RotateTransform to rotate the brush's output 45 degrees about its center, you would give the RotateTransform a CenterX of 0.5 and a CenterY of 0.5.

Remember that there are no effects if you apply transforms to a SolidColorBrush, because this brush always gives the solid color paint no matter if it is transformed or not.

Let's consider an example that applies the rotation transform to various brushes. You can easily apply other transforms to the brushes by following the same procedure presented in this example.

In this section, rather than create a separate code example of rotation transforms for each of the brushes, here we'll present a single example to demonstrate all of them. The coding details will then be explained in the following sections.

Here is the XAML file of the example, named BrushTransformExample:

```
<Window x:Class="Chapter05.BrushTransformExample"
    xmlns="http://schemas.microsoft.com/winfx
        /2006/xaml/presentation"
    xmlns:x="http://schemas.microsoft.com/winfx/2006/xaml"
    Title="Brush Transforms" Height="475" Width="510">

    <Window.Resources>
        <DrawingBrush x:Key="MyDrawingBrush">
            <DrawingBrush.Drawing>
                <DrawingGroup>
                    <DrawingGroup.Children>
                        <GeometryDrawing
Geometry="M0,30 L20,25 20,35Z" Brush="Blue"/>
                        <GeometryDrawing
Geometry="M30,0 L25,20 35,20Z" Brush="Blue"/>
                        <GeometryDrawing
Geometry="M60,30 L40,25 40,35Z" Brush="Blue"/>
                        <GeometryDrawing
Geometry="M30,60 L25,40 35,40Z" Brush="Blue"/>
                        <GeometryDrawing
Geometry="M20,20 L30,20 30,30 20,30Z" Brush="Red"/>
                        <GeometryDrawing
Geometry="M30,20 L40,20 40,30 30,30Z" Brush="Yellow"/>
                        <GeometryDrawing
Geometry="M20,30 L30,30 30,40 20,40Z" Brush="LightGray"/>
                        <GeometryDrawing
Geometry="M30,30 L40,30 40,40 30,40Z" Brush="Black"/>
                        <GeometryDrawing>
                            <GeometryDrawing.Geometry>
                                <EllipseGeometry RadiusX="30"
                                                 RadiusY="30"
                                        Center="30,30"/>
                            </GeometryDrawing.Geometry>
                            <GeometryDrawing.Pen>
                                <Pen Thickness="5"
                                     Brush="Green"/>
                            </GeometryDrawing.Pen>
```

```
                </GeometryDrawing>
            </DrawingGroup.Children>
        </DrawingGroup>
    </DrawingBrush.Drawing>
  </DrawingBrush>
</Window.Resources>

<Grid>
    <Grid.ColumnDefinitions>
        <ColumnDefinition Width="Auto"/>
        <ColumnDefinition Width="Auto"/>
        <ColumnDefinition Width="Auto"/>
        <ColumnDefinition Width="Auto"/>
    </Grid.ColumnDefinitions>
    <Grid.RowDefinitions>
        <RowDefinition Height="Auto"/>
        <RowDefinition Height="Auto"/>
        <RowDefinition Height="Auto"/>
        <RowDefinition Height="Auto"/>
        <RowDefinition Height="Auto"/>
        <RowDefinition Height="Auto"/>
        <RowDefinition Height="Auto"/>
    </Grid.RowDefinitions>

    <TextBlock Text="No Transform" Margin="30,5,5,0"
            Grid.Column="1" Grid.Row="0"/>
    <TextBlock Text="Relative Transform" Margin="18,5,5,0"
            Grid.Column="2" Grid.Row="0"/>
    <TextBlock Text="Transform" Margin="38,5,5,0"
            Grid.Column="3" Grid.Row="0"/>
    <TextBlock Text="LinearGradientBrush"
            Margin="5,25,0,5" Grid.Column="0"
            Grid.Row="1"
            HorizontalAlignment="Right"/>
    <TextBlock Text="RadialGradientBrush"
            Margin="5,25,0,5" Grid.Column="0"
            Grid.Row="2"
            HorizontalAlignment="Right"/>
    <TextBlock Text="ImageBrush" Margin="5,25,0,5"
            Grid.Column="0" Grid.Row="3"
            HorizontalAlignment="Right"/>
    <TextBlock Text="Tiled ImageBrush" Margin="5,25,0,5"
            Grid.Column="0" Grid.Row="4"
            HorizontalAlignment="Right"/>
    <TextBlock Text="Drawing,Visual Brush"
            Margin="5,25,0,5" Grid.Column="0"
            Grid.Row="5"
            HorizontalAlignment="Right"/>
    <TextBlock Text="Titled VisualBrush" Margin="5,25,0,5"
            Grid.Column="0" Grid.Row="6"
            HorizontalAlignment="Right"/>

    <Rectangle Width="120" Height="60" Margin="5"
            Grid.Column="1" Grid.Row="1">
```

```
        <Rectangle.Fill>
            <LinearGradientBrush StartPoint="0,0"
                                 EndPoint="1,0">
                <GradientStop Color="Gray" Offset="0.4"/>
                <GradientStop Color="Yellow"
                              Offset="0.5"/>
                <GradientStop Color="Gray" Offset="0.6"/>
            </LinearGradientBrush>
        </Rectangle.Fill>
    </Rectangle>

    <Rectangle Width="120" Height="60" Margin="5"
               Grid.Column="2" Grid.Row="1">
        <Rectangle.Fill>
            <LinearGradientBrush StartPoint="0,0"
                                 EndPoint="1,0">
                <GradientStop Color="Gray" Offset="0.4"/>
                <GradientStop Color="Yellow"
                              Offset="0.5"/>
                <GradientStop Color="Gray" Offset="0.6"/>
                <LinearGradientBrush.RelativeTransform>
                    <RotateTransform CenterX="0.5"
                                     CenterY="0.5"
                                     Angle="45" />
                </LinearGradientBrush.RelativeTransform>
            </LinearGradientBrush>
        </Rectangle.Fill>
    </Rectangle>

    <Rectangle Width="120" Height="60" Margin="5"
               Grid.Column="3" Grid.Row="1">
        <Rectangle.Fill>
            <LinearGradientBrush StartPoint="0,0"
                                 EndPoint="1,0">
                <GradientStop Color="Gray" Offset="0.4"/>
                <GradientStop Color="Yellow"
                              Offset="0.5"/>
                <GradientStop Color="Gray" Offset="0.6"/>
                <LinearGradientBrush.Transform>
                    <RotateTransform CenterX="60"
                                     CenterY="30"
                                     Angle="45" />
                </LinearGradientBrush.Transform>
            </LinearGradientBrush>
        </Rectangle.Fill>
    </Rectangle>

    <Rectangle Width="120" Height="60" Margin="5"
               Grid.Column="1" Grid.Row="2">
        <Rectangle.Fill>
            <RadialGradientBrush>
                <GradientStop Color="Gray" Offset="0.3"/>
                <GradientStop Color="Yellow"
                              Offset="0.5"/>
```

```
            <GradientStop Color="Gray" Offset="0.7"/>
        </RadialGradientBrush>
    </Rectangle.Fill>
</Rectangle>

<Rectangle Width="120" Height="60" Margin="5"
        Grid.Column="2" Grid.Row="2">
    <Rectangle.Fill>
        <RadialGradientBrush>
            <GradientStop Color="Gray" Offset="0.3"/>
            <GradientStop Color="Yellow"
                        Offset="0.5"/>
            <GradientStop Color="Gray" Offset="0.7"/>
            <RadialGradientBrush.RelativeTransform>
                <RotateTransform CenterX="0.5"
                                CenterY="0.5"
                                Angle="45"/>
            </RadialGradientBrush.RelativeTransform>
        </RadialGradientBrush>
    </Rectangle.Fill>
</Rectangle>

<Rectangle Width="120" Height="60" Margin="5"
        Grid.Column="3" Grid.Row="2">
    <Rectangle.Fill>
        <RadialGradientBrush>
            <GradientStop Color="Gray" Offset="0.3"/>
            <GradientStop Color="Yellow"
                        Offset="0.5"/>
            <GradientStop Color="Gray" Offset="0.7"/>
            <RadialGradientBrush.Transform>
                <RotateTransform CenterX="60"
                                CenterY="30"
                                Angle="45"/>
            </RadialGradientBrush.Transform>
        </RadialGradientBrush>
    </Rectangle.Fill>
</Rectangle>

<Rectangle Width="120" Height="60" Margin="5"
        Grid.Column="1" Grid.Row="3">
    <Rectangle.Fill>
        <ImageBrush ImageSource="Flower.jpg"/>
    </Rectangle.Fill>
</Rectangle>

<Rectangle Width="120" Height="60" Margin="5"
        Grid.Column="2" Grid.Row="3">
    <Rectangle.Fill>
        <ImageBrush ImageSource="Flower.jpg">
            <ImageBrush.RelativeTransform>
                <RotateTransform CenterX="0.5"
                                CenterY="0.5"
                                Angle="45"/>
```

```
                </ImageBrush.RelativeTransform>
            </ImageBrush>
        </Rectangle.Fill>
    </Rectangle>

    <Rectangle Width="120" Height="60" Margin="5"
            Grid.Column="3" Grid.Row="3">
        <Rectangle.Fill>
            <ImageBrush ImageSource="Flower.jpg">
                <ImageBrush.Transform>
                    <RotateTransform CenterX="60"
                                     CenterY="30"
                                     Angle="45"/>
                </ImageBrush.Transform>
            </ImageBrush>
        </Rectangle.Fill>
    </Rectangle>

    <Rectangle Width="120" Height="60" Margin="5"
            Grid.Column="1" Grid.Row="4">
        <Rectangle.Fill>
            <ImageBrush ImageSource="Flower.jpg"
                    TileMode="Tile"
                    Viewport="0,0,0.5,0.5"/>
        </Rectangle.Fill>
    </Rectangle>

    <Rectangle Width="120" Height="60" Margin="5"
            Grid.Column="2" Grid.Row="4">
        <Rectangle.Fill>
            <ImageBrush ImageSource="Flower.jpg"
                    TileMode="Tile"
                    Viewport="0,0,0.5,0.5">
                <ImageBrush.RelativeTransform>
                    <RotateTransform CenterX="0.5"
                                     CenterY="0.5"
                                     Angle="45"/>
                </ImageBrush.RelativeTransform>
            </ImageBrush>
        </Rectangle.Fill>
    </Rectangle>

    <Rectangle Width="120" Height="60" Margin="5"
            Grid.Column="3" Grid.Row="4">
        <Rectangle.Fill>
            <ImageBrush ImageSource="Flower.jpg"
                    TileMode="Tile"
                    Viewport="0,0,0.5,0.5">
                <ImageBrush.Transform>
                    <RotateTransform CenterX="60"
                                     CenterY="30"
                                     Angle="45"/>
                </ImageBrush.Transform>
            </ImageBrush>
```

```
                </Rectangle.Fill>
        </Rectangle>

        <Rectangle x:Name="MyDrawingRectangle" Width="120"
                   Height="60" Margin="5"
                   Grid.Column="1" Grid.Row="5"
Fill="{StaticResource MyDrawingBrush}"/>

        <Rectangle Width="120" Height="60" Margin="5"
                   Grid.Column="2" Grid.Row="5">
            <Rectangle.Fill>
                <VisualBrush
Visual="{Binding ElementName=MyDrawingRectangle}">
                    <VisualBrush.RelativeTransform>
                        <RotateTransform CenterX="0.5"
                                         CenterY="0.5"
                                         Angle="45"/>
                    </VisualBrush.RelativeTransform>
                </VisualBrush>
            </Rectangle.Fill>
        </Rectangle>

        <Rectangle Width="120" Height="60" Margin="5"
                   Grid.Column="3" Grid.Row="5">
            <Rectangle.Fill>
                <VisualBrush
Visual="{Binding ElementName=MyDrawingRectangle}">
                    <VisualBrush.Transform>
                        <RotateTransform CenterX="60"
                                         CenterY="30"
                                         Angle="45"/>
                    </VisualBrush.Transform>
                </VisualBrush>
            </Rectangle.Fill>
        </Rectangle>

        <Rectangle Width="120" Height="60" Margin="5"
                   Grid.Column="1" Grid.Row="6">
            <Rectangle.Fill>
                <VisualBrush TileMode="Tile"
                             Viewport="0,0,0.5,0.5"
Visual="{Binding ElementName=MyDrawingRectangle}"/>
            </Rectangle.Fill>
        </Rectangle>

        <Rectangle Width="120" Height="60" Margin="5"
                   Grid.Column="2" Grid.Row="6">
            <Rectangle.Fill>
                <VisualBrush TileMode="Tile"
                             Viewport="0,0,0.5,0.5"
Visual="{Binding ElementName=MyDrawingRectangle}">
                    <VisualBrush.RelativeTransform>
                        <RotateTransform CenterX="0.5"
                                         CenterY="0.5"
```

```
                                        Angle="45"/>
                    </VisualBrush.RelativeTransform>
                </VisualBrush>
            </Rectangle.Fill>
        </Rectangle>

        <Rectangle Width="120" Height="60" Margin="5"
                Grid.Column="3" Grid.Row="6">
            <Rectangle.Fill>
                <VisualBrush TileMode="Tile"
                            Viewport="0,0,0.5,0.5"
    Visual="{Binding ElementName=MyDrawingRectangle}">
                    <VisualBrush.Transform>
                        <RotateTransform CenterX="60"
                                         CenterY="30"
                                         Angle="45"/>
                    </VisualBrush.Transform>
                </VisualBrush>
            </Rectangle.Fill>
        </Rectangle>
    </Grid>
</Window>
```

In this example, you first create a Window Resource, called MyDrawingBrush, for a DrawingBrush object, which will be used for the DrawingBrush and VisualBrush transforms. Then, you create several rectangle shapes that are filled using various brushes with or without transforms. This example generates the output shown in Figure 5-17.

LinearGradientBrush Transform

In this example, you create three rectangle shapes that are painted using a LinearGradientBrush. The first rectangle is filled using a LinearGradientBrush without a RotateTransform. You can see that a vertical yellow bar is at the center of the rectangle.

The second rectangle is filled using a transformed LinearGradientBrush. A RotateTransform of 45 degrees is applied to the brush's RelativeTransform property. You might wonder how you can obtain the result shown in Figure 5-17 for this relative transform. This can be easily understood using the definition of a brush's RelativeTransform property. Figure 5-18 shows each step of the process.

The third rectangle is painted using LinearGradientBrush with a Transform property specified using a RotateTransform of 45 degrees. The result from this absolute transform is easy to understand: it is simply a direct rotation (45 degrees) of the original (not transformed) brush.

After understanding the difference between the RelativeTransform and Transform properties of a brush, you can easily create various interesting effects by using brushes with different transforms.

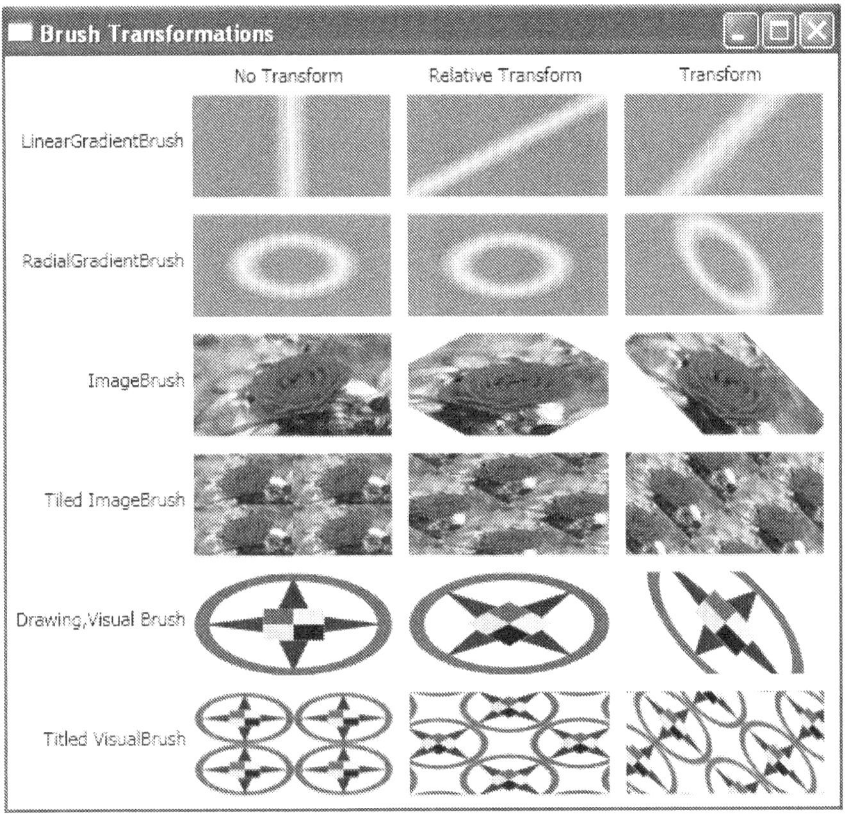

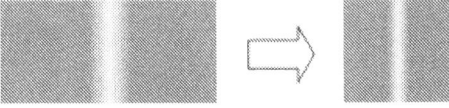

Figure 5-17 Brush Transformations.

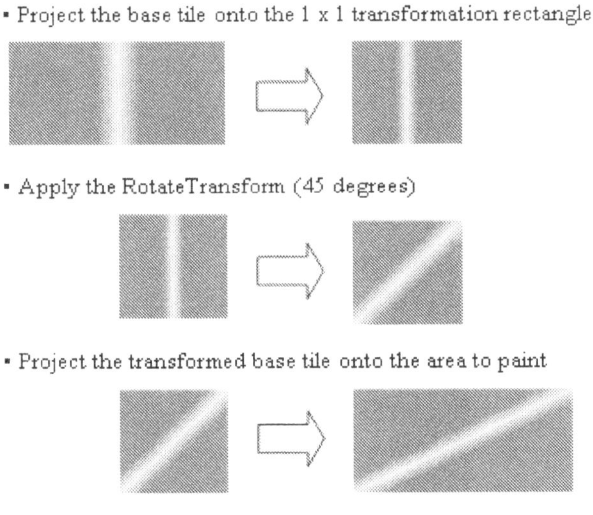

• Project the base tile onto the 1 x 1 transformation rectangle

• Apply the RotateTransform (45 degrees)

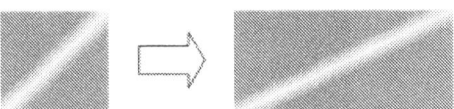

• Project the transformed base tile onto the area to paint

Figure 5-18 Relative rotation of a LinearGradientBrush.

RadialGradientBrush Transform

Like the LinearGradientBrush discussed in the preceding section, RadialGradientBrush also has two different types of transformations – Transform and RelativeTransform. In this example, the second row of rectangles are filled using different RadialGradientBrush objects. The first rectangle is painted using a brush without a rotation. Take a look at the corresponding code segment. You actually define RadialGradientBrush with a yellow circular ring. This circular ring becomes the ellipse pattern seen in Figure 5-17. This is because you are trying to fill and fit a rectangle shape using this brush.

The fill pattern of the third rectangle in this case is obtained by directly rotating the original brush by 45 degrees. However, you might wonder why the paint pattern of the second rectangle is identical to that of the first one. Why is there no effect on the brush after it is rotated by 45 degrees relatively? The answer to this can be understood from the explanation of Figure 5-19.

- Project the base tile onto the 1 x 1 transformation rectangle

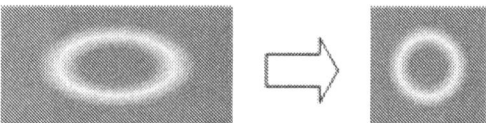

- Apply the RotateTransform (45 degrees)

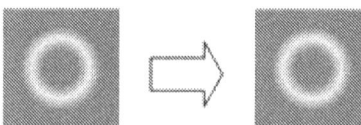

- Project the transformed base tile onto the area to paint

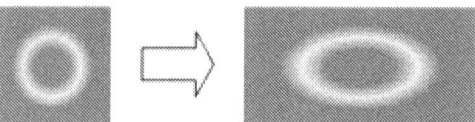

Figure 5-19 Relative rotation of a RadialGradientBrush.

In fact, according to the process of relative transform, the original rectangle needs to be projected onto a 1×1 transform square. In this projected space, the original ellipse pattern becomes a circular ring. The rotation should be applied to the RelativeTransform property of the brush in this projected space. Since the pattern of the brush is a ring shape, there should be no effect on the pattern when you rotate it about its center. This is why you get the same ellipse pattern as you would have using original brush after you project the rotated brush back onto the rectangle paint area.

ImageBrush Transform

In the third row, you fill rectangle shapes using ImageBrush. The fill image pattern using an ImageBrush with a relative rotation is different than that of a pattern using a brush with an absolute rotation. The results can be expained based on the process of the Transform and RelativeTranform properties of an ImageBrush.

In the next row, the rectangle is painted using a tiled ImageBrush. The TileMode and Viewport properties are specified for a transformed brush in the same way as those of the original ImageBrush. Notice that for the untransformed brush, the Viewport(0, 0, 0.5, 0.5) always results in a fill region with four tiles, no matter how big or small the region is. However, this isn't true for the transformed brush. Because of the rotation, the tiles don't line up with the edges of the rectangles, so instead you get partial tiles at the edges.

Drawing and Visual Brush Transform

In this case, you first create a DrawingBrush in Windows Resources, named MyDrawingBrush. You fill the first rectangle with this DrawingBrush by calling the StaticResource name. Then, you create two new rectangle shapes, each of which uses VisualBrush to fill its background. In this example, you copy the first rectangle using VisualBrush, and then use this copy to specify the Fill property of second rectangle. At the same time, VisualBrush is transformed by a relative rotation of 45 degrees about the second rectangle's center. The third rectangle does the same, only this time the VisualBrush is rotated by 45 degrees in an absolute system.

Finally, you use a tiled VisualBrush to paint the last three rectangles. The first rectangle simply uses VisualBrush to copy MyDrawingBrush, then tiles its Fill property. The second rectangle is painted using a tiled VisualBrush that is transformed by a RelativeTransform. The Fill property of the last rectangle is specified using a tiled VisualBrush that is transformed by an absolute rotation. You can see that all three rectangles have different fill patterns.

Chapter 6
Animation

From the previous chapters you learned that WPF provides a powerful set of graphics and layout features that enable you to create attractive user interfaces and appealing graphics objects. Animation can make user interfaces and graphics even more spectacular and usable. Animation allows you to create truly dynamic WPF applications and make your programs more responsive and intuitive. Animation can also draw attention to important objects and guide the user through transitions to new content.

WPF animation is an important part of the Windows Vista, .NET 3.0, and .NET 3.5. It is integrated seamlessly into WPF windows and pages. To create an animation in WPF applications, you don't need to write your own code using timers and event handling; instead, you can directly use corresponding animation classes that WPF provides.

In this chapter, we'll consider the rich set of WPF animation classes and show how to use them in WPF applications. As always, this chapter will also provide a wide range of animation examples.

WPF Animation Basics

Animation is an illusion that is created by quickly cycling through a series of frames, each slightly different from the last. For example, in order to create a real-time stock chart, you might follow the steps listed here:

- Create a timer.

- Check the timer at specified intervals (say, every 30 seconds) to see how much time has elapsed.

- When you check the timer, feed the lastest market stock data into your stock chart program.

- Update the stock chart with the new stock data and redraw it on your screen.

Prior to WPF, Windows-based developers had to create and manage their own timing systems and event handling or use special custom libraries. Although this kind of timer-based animation isn't very difficult to implement, there are some issues associated with integrating it into a window application. For example, the timer-based animation usually assumes a single animation. If you want multiple animations running at the same time, you need to rewrite all of your animation code. Another issue is that the animation frame rate is fixed. If you want to change the timer interval, you might need to change your animation code too.

WPF includes an efficient timing system that is exposed through managed code and XAML, deeply integrated into the WPF framework. WPF animation makes it easy to animate controls and other graphical objects.

WPF handles all the behind-the-scene work of managing a timing system and redrawing the screen efficiently. It provides timing classes that enable you to focus on the effects you want to create, instead of the mechanics of achieving those effects. WPF also makes it easy to create your own animations by exposing animation base classes, from which you can inherit. These custom animations gain many of performance benefits of the standard animation classes.

Property-Based Animation

The WPF animation system uses a different model than the timer-based animation. Basically, a WPF animation directly modifies the value of a dependency property over an interval of time. For example, to make a drawing of a rectangle fade out of view, you can modify its Opacity property in an animation. To make it grow or shrink, you can modify its Width and Height properties. The secret to creating the animation you want becomes determining what properties you need to modify.

For a property to have animation capabilities, it must meet the following requirements:

- It must be a dependency property.
- It must belong to a class that inherits from DependencyObject and implements the IAnimatable interface.
- There must be a compatible animation data type available.

This means that to animate a dependency property, you need to have an animation class that supports its data type. For example, the Width property of a rectangle uses the double data type. To animate it, you use the DoubleAnimation class. However, the Color property of a SolidColorBrush object uses the color structure, so it requires the ColorAnimation class. If WPF doesn't provide the data type you want to use, you can create your own animation class for that data type. In fact, you will find that the System.Windows.Media.Animation namespace contains over 100 animation classes for almost every data type that you'll want to use.

There are three types of animations in WPF: linear interpolation animation, key frame animation, and path-based animation. Linear interpolation animations represent animations that vary properties gradually between starting and ending values. DoubleAnimation and ColorAnimation belong to this category, and they use interpolation to smoothly change their values. On the other hand, key frame animations change property values abruptly at specified times, and are often used when changing certain data types, such as string and reference type of objects. All key frame animation classes in WPF are named in the form, Type Name + AnimationUsingKeyFrames; i.e., StringAnimationUsingKeyFrames and ObjectAnimationUsingKeyFrames.

Every data type supports key frame animations. However, some data types have a key frame animation class but no interpolation animation class. For example, you can animate a string using key frames, but you can't animate a string using interpolation. In other worlds, a data type that has a normal animation class that uses interpolation, such as DoubleAnimation, also has a corresponding animation type for key frame animation, such as DoubleAnimationUsingKeyFrames.

The third type of animation is called path-based animation. Unlike interpolation and key frame-based animations, path-based animations change a value according to a shape described by a PathGeometry object. Path-based animations are useful for moving an element along a path. The classes for path-based animations have names in the form Type Name + AnimationUsingPath; i.e., DoubleAnimationUsingPath and PointAnimationUsingPath.

All three of the above types of animation classes derive from an abstract Type, called Name + AnimationBase (such as DoubleAnimationBase) class. This base animation class provides you a way to create your own animation classes. You can take a look at the members of the System.Windows.Media.Animation namespace from Microsft WPF reference materials, where you will find over 100 animation classes.

A Simple Animation in Code

As you have already learned, the most common animation technique is linear interpolation. You have used this type of animations in previous chapters. Now let's use a simple example to illustrate how an animation works in WPF. Start off with a new WPF Windows project and name it Chapter06. Add a StartMenu window to the project, from which you can access all of the examples in this chapter.

Then, add a new WPF Window, called SimpleAnimation, to the current project. In this example, you'll move a Rectangle shape around a Canvas. To create this effect, you use an animation that modifies the Canvas.Left and Canvas.Top properties of the rectangle. The animation is created in code. Here are the XAML and code-behind files of this example:

```
<Window x:Class="Chapter06.SimpleAnimation"
    xmlns="http://schemas.microsoft.com/winfx
```

```
        /2006/xaml/presentation"
    xmlns:x="http://schemas.microsoft.com/winfx/2006/xaml"
    Title="Simple Animation Example" Height="300" Width="300">
    <Canvas>
        <Rectangle x:Name="rect1" Width="100" Height="50"
                   Fill="Blue"/>
    </Canvas>
</Window>

using System;
using System.Windows;
using System.Windows.Controls;
using System.Windows.Media;
using System.Windows.Shapes;
using System.Windows.Media.Animation;

namespace Chapter06
{
    public partial class SimpleAnimation : Window
    {
        public SimpleAnimation()
        {
            InitializeComponent();

            DoubleAnimation da = new DoubleAnimation();
            da.From = 0;
            da.To = 200;
            da.Duration = TimeSpan.FromSeconds(5);
            da.AutoReverse = true;
            da.RepeatBehavior = RepeatBehavior.Forever;
            rect1.BeginAnimation(Canvas.LeftProperty, da);
            rect1.BeginAnimation(Canvas.TopProperty, da);
        }
    }
}
```

In this example, you define a blue rectangle on a Canvas using XAML and perform the corresponding animations in code. First, you create a DoubleAnimation instance. There are three key properties that are required by any interpolation-based animation: the starting value (From), the ending value (To), and the time that the animation should take (Duration). In this example, you also use two more properties, AutoReverse and RepeatBehavior. These two properties control the playback and repeatability of the animation.

If you execute this sample application, you will obtain a rectangle that moves around inside the Canvas.

Instead of using the To property, you can use the By property. The By property is used to create an animation that changes a value by a set amount, rather than to a specific target. For example, you could create an animation that enlarges the rectangle's width by 50 units more than its current width, as shown here:

```
DoubleAnimation da = new DoubleAnimation();
da.By = 50;
```

```
da.Duration = TimeSpan.FromSeconds(5);
rect1.BeginAnimation(WidthProperty, da);
```

This approach isn't necessary in this rectangle example, because you could achieve the same effect using a simple calculation to set the To property, such as:

```
da.To = rect1.Width + 50;
```

However, the By value makes more sense when you create animations in XAML because the markup code doesn't provide a way to perform any calculations.

The preceding example creates the animation in code using the BeginAnimation method. This approach is called local animation and provides a convenient way to animate the dependency property of any animatable object. You can use this approach when you want to apply an animation to a dependency property and don't need to interactively control the animation after it starts.

Remember that the local animation is a per-instance approach, indicating that the local animation is applied directly to the instance of an object. It can't be defined in style, control templates, or data templates. If you do want more animation features, such as interactive control, you need to use the Storyboard animations.

Animation and Storyboard

WPF animations are represented by a group of animation classes. You create an animation instance and specify the animation properties, such as the From, To, and Duration properties. This makes these animation classes a great fit for XAML files. What's less clear is how to hook an animation up to a particular element and property, and how to trigger it at the right time. To solve these issues, WPF implements two critical components for animations, storyboard and event trigger.

You'll learn how to create an animation using a storyboard and event trigger in the following sections.

Storyboard and Event Trigger

In the earlier chapters of this book, you used Storyboard animation extensively without considering the detailed animation process. Actually, the storyboard in WPF is simply the XAML equivalent of the BeginAnimation() method in code, and can be regarded as a special type of container Timeline, which provides targeting information for animations it contains. It allows you to direct an animation to the right element and property. An event trigger responds to a property change or event, and controls the storyboard. For example, to start an animation, the event trigger must begin the storyboard.

You can use the storyboard to control multiple animations and playback behaviors. However, the most basic feature provided by the Storyboard class is its ability to point to a specific property and specific element using its TargetProperty and TargetName properties. This means that the storyboard fills the gap between your animation and the property you want to animate.

You should use storyboard when you want to define and apply your animations in XAML, interactively control your animations after they start, create a complex tree of animations, or create animations in a Style, ControlTemplate, or DataTemplate. Note that for an object to be animated by storyboard, it must be a UIElement or FrameworkElement.

Here, let's consider an example that shows how to create an animation using the storyboard. You can rewrite the previous example, SimpleAnimation, using XAML and storyboard, like this:

```
<Window x:Class="Chapter06.StoryboardAnimation"
    xmlns="http://schemas.microsoft.com/winfx
        /2006/xaml/presentation"
    xmlns:x="http://schemas.microsoft.com/winfx/2006/xaml"
  Title="Storyboard Animation" Height="300" Width="300">

    <Canvas>
        <Rectangle x:Name="rect1" Width="100" Height="50"
                Fill="Blue">
            <Rectangle.Triggers>
                <EventTrigger RoutedEvent="Rectangle.Loaded">
                    <EventTrigger.Actions>
                        <BeginStoryboard>
                            <Storyboard>
                                <DoubleAnimation
                        Storyboard.TargetName="rect1"
                        Storyboard.TargetProperty="(Canvas.Left)"
                        From="0" To="200" Duration="0:0:5"
                        RepeatBehavior="Forever"
                        AutoReverse="True"/>

                                <DoubleAnimation
                        Storyboard.TargetName="rect1"
                        Storyboard.TargetProperty="(Canvas.Top)"
                        From="0" To="200" Duration="0:0:5"
                        RepeatBehavior="Forever"
                        AutoReverse="True" />
                            </Storyboard>
                        </BeginStoryboard>
                    </EventTrigger.Actions>
                </EventTrigger>
            </Rectangle.Triggers>
        </Rectangle>
    </Canvas>
</Window>
```

Here you create an event trigger, Rectangle.Triggers, which performs an action for an event specified by its RoutedEvent property. Since the EventTrigger object only supports one event, the Loaded event, you set the RoutedEvent property to Rectangle.Loaded, which starts the animation when the Rectangle loads. If you want the animation to start when the window first loads, you can add an event trigger in the Window.Triggers collection that responds to the Window.Loaded event. It is also possible to add an event trigger in the Canvas.Triggers collection which responds to the Canvas.Loaded event. In this case, the animation starts when the Canvas first loads.

Next, you add a storyboard to describe and control two animations, one for the Canvas.Left and the other for the Canvas.Top property of the rectangle; using the DoubleAnimation class. Note how you specify the TargetName and TargetProperty using rect1 and Canvas.Left (or Canvas.Top) respectively. The syntax in this example is more common, because it allows you to put several aniamtions in the same storyboard, but allows each animation to act on a different element and property.

You may notice that there are brackets around the Canvas.Left and Canvas.Top properties. These brackets are necessary because both Canvas.Left and Canvas.Top are attached properties. An attached property is a dependency property and is managed by the WPF property system. The difference is that an attached property applies to a class other than the one where it is defined. The most common examples of attached properties are found in the layout containers. For example, the Canvas defines the attached properties Left, Right, Top, and Bottom. Similarly, the DockPanel defines the attached property Dock, and the Grid class defines the attached properties Row and Column. You need to wrap the entire property in brackets when you set an attached property to the TargetProperty. It doesn't need the brackets if you set the dependency property (such as, the Width property) to the TargetProperty, like this:

```
< … Storyboard.TargetProperty="Width" … />
```

From this example, you can see that an animation in WPF can be created in either XAML or code. Animations in XAML use the Storyboard and event triggers, while animations in code use the BeginAnimation method. This, however, isn't necessary true. You can also use the Storyboard in code to create animations.

Storyboard Animation in Code

Here, I'll use an example, called StoryboardInCode, to demonstrate how to create animations using the Storyboard in code. In this example, you create two Button objects and animate their background colors. Also, you'll set different animation starting times for these two buttons. For instance, you want the second button to start its animation 5 seconds later than the first button.

As usual, you create the layout using an XAML file:

```
<Window x:Class="Chapter06.StoryboardInCode"
    xmlns="http://schemas.microsoft.com/winfx
        /2006/xaml/presentation"
    xmlns:x="http://schemas.microsoft.com/winfx/2006/xaml"
    Title="Storyboard Animation in Code"
```

```
Height="300"  Width="300">

    <Canvas>
        <Button Content="Button1" Width="150" Height="80"
                Canvas.Left="50" Canvas.Top="20">
            <Button.Background>
                <SolidColorBrush x:Name="brush1"/>
            </Button.Background>
        </Button>

        <Button Content="Button2" Width="150" Height="80"
                Canvas.Left="50" Canvas.Top="110">
            <Button.Background>
                <SolidColorBrush x:Name="brush2"/>
            </Button.Background>
        </Button>
    </Canvas>
</Window>
```

This defines two Button objects and exposes their Background properties with a
SolidColorBrush object, which will be animated in code. The code below
demonstrates how to animate the buttons' background using Storyboard in code:

```csharp
using System;
using System.Windows;
using System.Windows.Controls;
using System.Windows.Input;
using System.Windows.Media;
using System.Windows.Shapes;
using System.Windows.Media.Animation;

namespace Chapter06
{
    public partial class StoryboardInCode : Window
    {
        public StoryboardInCode()
        {
            InitializeComponent();

            Storyboard sb = new Storyboard();
            ColorAnimation ca1 =
                new ColorAnimation(
                Colors.Blue, Colors.Yellow,
                new Duration(new TimeSpan(0, 0, 10)));
            ca1.RepeatBehavior = RepeatBehavior.Forever;
            ca1.AutoReverse = true;
            Storyboard.SetTargetName(ca1, "brush1");
            Storyboard.SetTargetProperty(ca1,
            new PropertyPath(SolidColorBrush.ColorProperty));

            ColorAnimation ca2 =
                new ColorAnimation(Colors.Red, Colors.Green,
                new Duration(new TimeSpan(0, 0, 10)));
            ca2.RepeatBehavior = RepeatBehavior.Forever;
```

```
        ca2.AutoReverse = true;
        ca2.BeginTime = new TimeSpan(0, 0, 5);
        Storyboard.SetTargetName(ca2, "brush2");
        Storyboard.SetTargetProperty(ca2,
            new PropertyPath(
            SolidColorBrush.ColorProperty));

        sb.Children.Add(ca1);
        sb.Children.Add(ca2);
        sb.Begin(this);
    }
  }
}
```

Here, you first create a Storyboard object, and then define the ColorAnimation. Next you use the storyboard to hook ColorAnimation up to the buttons' brush properties. Finally, you add animations to the Storyboard and start the simulation using the Storyboard.Begin method. For the second animation ca2, you also specify its BeginTime property by a five second delay. Of course, you don't need to use Storyboard when you're working in code, instead, you can use the BeginAnimation method, like this:

```
Brush1.BeginAnimation(SolidColorBrush.ColorProperty, ca1);
Brush2.BeginAnimation(SolidColorBrush.ColorProperty, ca2);
```

You can see from the above discussion that you have several options for creating animations in WPF. You can use XAML and Storyboard, or simply use the BeginAnimation method or Storyboard in code. However, the most commonly used approach in WPF animations is XAML plus Storyboard.

Animation and Timing Behavior

In WPF, an animation is a type of timeline. A timeline represents a segment of time and provides properties that allow you to specify the length of that segment, when it should start, how many times it will repeat, how fast time progresses in that segment, etc.

Classes that inherit from the Timeline base class provide additional functionality. WPF provides the following Timeline types:

- AnimationTimeline – This is an abstract base class for Timeline objects that generate output values for animating properties. It is used for the property-based animation system.

- MediaTimeline – This class generates output from a media file and is used to play audio or video files.

- ParallelTimeline – This class is a type of TimelineGroup that groups and controls child Timeline objects.

- Storyboard – This class is a type of ParallelTimeline that provides targeting information for the Timeline objects it contains.

- Timeline – This is an abstract base class that defines timing behaviors.

- TimelineGroup – This is an abstract class for Timeline objects that can contain other Timeline objects.

There are some useful members in the Timeline class which define time-related properties used in animation, including Duration, FillBehavior, and etc. Here is a list of some properties that are often used in animations:

- BeginTime – Sets a delay time before the animation starts.

- Duration – Sets the length of time the animation runs, from start to finish, as a Duration object.

- SpeedRatio – Increases or decreases the speed of the animation. The default value is 1.

- AccelerationRatio and DecelerationRatio – Makes an animation nonlinear, so it starts off slow and then speeds up (by increasing AccelerationRatio) or slows down at the end (by increasing the DecelerationRatio). Both values are set from 0 to 1.

- AutoReverse – If this is set to true, the animation will play out in reverse once it is complete, reversing to the original value.

- FillBehavior – Determines what happens when the animation finishes. Usually, it keeps the property fixed at the ending value (FillBehavior.HoldEnd), but you can choose to return it to its original value by setting FillBehavior.Stop.

- RepeatBehavior – Allows you to repeat an animation in a specific number of times.

Since some of the timing behaviors such as Duration, RepeatBehavior, and AutoReverse play an important role in creating animations, the following sections will explain how to use them in your applications.

Duration

As mentioned previously, a timeline represents a segment of time. The length of the segment is determined by the timeline's Duration property. In the case of animations, the Duration specifies how long the animation takes to transition from its starting value to its ending value. Duration and TimeSpan of an animation are very similar. In the previous SimpleAnimation example, Duration is set using TimeSpan. This is because the Duration structure defines an implicit cast, which can convert System.TimeSpan to System.Windows.Duration as needed. That is why all of the following four statement are valid:

```
da.Duration = TimeSpan.FromSeconds(5);
da.Duration = new TimeSpan(0, 0, 5);
da.Duration = new Duration(TimeSpan.FromSeconds(5));
da.Duration = new Duration(new TimeSpan(0, 0, 5));
```

Correspondingly, the line of code in the StoryboardInCode example

```
ColorAnimation ca1 = new ColorAnimation(Colors.Blue,
    Colors.Yellow, new Duration(new TimeSpan(0, 0, 10)));
```

can be rewritten in the form:

```
ColorAnimation ca1 = new ColorAnimation(Colors.Blue,
    Colors.Yellow, TimeSpan.FromSeconds(10));
```

You can also specify a Duration using the special values Automatic or Forever, like this:

```
da.Duration = Duration.Automatic;
da.Duration = Duration.Forever;
```

The value Automatic simply sets the animation to a one-second duration, and Forever makes the animation infinite in length, which prevents the animation from having any effect. These values becomes useful when creating more complex animations.

Storyboard has a default duration of Automatic, which means it automatically ends when its last child animation ends. The following markup shows a storyboard whose Duration resolves in five seconds, the length of time it takes all of its child DoubleAnimation objects to complete:

```
<Storyboard>
    <DoubleAnimation
        Storyboard.TargetName="rect1"
        Storyboard.TargetProperty="Width"
        From="0" To="100" Duration="0:0:5"/>

    <DoubleAnimation
        Storyboard.TargetName="rect2"
        Storyboard.TargetProperty="Width"
        From="0" To="150" Duration="0:0:3"/>
</Storyboard>
```

You can specifically set the Duration of the Storyboard to a TimeSpan value, which forces the animation to play longer or shorter than its child Timeline objects. The following code snippet sets Duration of the storyboard to two seconds. As a result, the first DoubleAnimation stops progressing after two seconds, when it has animated the target rectangle's width to 40. The second DoubleAnimation also stops after two seconds, when it has animated rect2's width to 100.

```
<Storyboard Duration ="0:0:2">
    <DoubleAnimation
        Storyboard.TargetName="rect1"
        Storyboard.TargetProperty="Width"
        From="0" To="100" Duration="0:0:5"/>

    <DoubleAnimation
        Storyboard.TargetName="rect2"
        Storyboard.TargetProperty="Width"
        From="0" To="150" Duration="0:0:3"/>
</Storyboard>
```

RepeatBehavior

The RepeatBehavior property of a timeline controls how many times the animation repeats its duration. Using the RepeatBehavior property, you can specify how many times the timeline plays (an iteration Count) or the total length of time it should play (a repeat Duration). In either case, the animation goes through as many runs as necessary to fill the requested count or duration. By default, timelines have an iteration count of 1, which means they play once and don't repeat at all.

The following markup uses the RepeatBehavior property to make a DoubleAnimation play for 10 times by specifying the iteration count:

```
<DoubleAnimation
    Storyboard.TargetName="rect1"
    Storyboard.TargetProperty="Width"
    From="0" To="100" Duration="0:0:5"
    RepeatBehavior="10x"/>
```

You can also specify a repeat duration using the RepeatBehavior property, like this:

```
<DoubleAnimation
    Storyboard.TargetName="rect1"
    Storyboard.TargetProperty="Width"
    From="0" To="100" Duration="0:0:5"
    RepeatBehavior="0:5:30"/>
```

This makes the DoubleAnimation play for a period of 5 minutes and 30 seconds. If you set the RepeatBehavior property to Forever, the animation repeats until it is stopped interactively or by the timing system.

AutoReverse

The AutoReverse property specifies whether a timeline will play backwards at the end of each forward iteration. The following XAML snippet sets the AutoReverse property of a DoubleAnimation to true. As a result, it animates the Width property of the rectangle from zero to 100, then from 100 to zero. It plays for a total of 5 minutes.

```
<DoubleAnimation
    Storyboard.TargetName="rect1"
    Storyboard.TargetProperty="Width"
    From="0" To="100"
    Duration="0:2:30"
    AutoReverse="True"/>
```

When you use a Count value to specify the RepeatBehavior of a timeline and the AutoReverse property of that timeline is set to true, a single repetition consists of one forward iteration followed by one backward iteration.

Begin Time

The BeginTime property enables you to specify when a timeline starts. A timeline's BeginTime is relative to its parent timeline. A begin time of zero seconds means the timeline starts as soon as its parent starts. A finite value creates an offset between when the parent timeline starts playing and when the child timeline plays. By default, all timelines have a begin time of zero seconds. You may also set a timeline's begin time to null, which prevents the timeline from starting.

Note that the begin time isn't applied each time a timeline repeats due to its RepeatBehavior setting. For example, if you create a animation with a BeginTime of 5 seconds and a RepeatBehavior of Forever, there would be a 5-second delay before the animation played for the first time, but not for each successive repetition. However, if the animation's parent timeline restarts or repeats, the 5-second delay will still occur.

The BeginTime property is useful for staggering timelines. In the StoryboardInCode example, you set the BeginTime property for the second button's background animation to a 5-second delay. The following code snippet creates a storyboard that has two DoubleAnimation objects. The first animation has a Duration of 10 seconds, and the second has a Duration of 5 seconds. The BeginTime of the second DoubleAnimation is set to 10 seconds so that it begins playing after the first DoubleAnimation ends:

```
<Storyboard>
    <DoubleAnimation
        Storyboard.TargetName="rect1"
        Storyboard.TargetProperty="Width"
        From="0" To="100"
        Duration="0:0:10"
        BeginTime="0:0:0"/>

    <DoubleAnimation
        Storyboard.TargetName="rect2"
        Storyboard.TargetProperty="Width"
        From="0" To="100"
        Duration="0:0:5"
        BeginTime="0:0:10"/>
</Storyboard>
```

The other property, FillBehavior, specifies whether an animation stops or holds its last value. An animation with a FillBehavior of HoldEnd holds its output value – the property being animated retains the last value of the animation. A value of Stop causes the animation to return its original value after it ends.

Speed Controls

The Timeline class provides three properties for specifying its speed: SpeedRatio, AccelerationRatio, and DecelerationRatio. The SpeedRatio sets the rate, relative to its parent, at which time progresses for a timeline. Values greater than one increase the speed of the animation; values between zero and one slow it down. A value of one (the default value) indicates that the timeline progresses at the same speed as its parent. The SpeedRatio setting of a container timeline affects all of its child's Timeline objects as well.

The AccelerationRatio and DecelerationRatio properties allow you to compress parts of the timeline so that it progresses faster or slower. The rest of the timeline is stretched to compensate so that the total time is unchanged. Both of these properties represent a percentage value. For example, an AccelerationRatio of 0.5 means that you want to spend the first 50% of the duration of the animation accelerating. Thus, for a ten-second animation, the first five seconds of the animation would be accelerating, and the remaining five seconds would progress at a constant speed. The speed of the last five seconds is faster than the speed of a nonaccelerated animation, because the animation needs to make up for its slow start. The DecelationRatio can be discussed in a similar manner.

Animations with an acceleration and deceleration are often used to give a more natural appearance, such as when you animate a car. Now, let's consider an example that shows you how to control the animation speed. Open the project Chapter06, add a new WPF Window to the project, and name it AnimationSpeed. Here is the XAML file of this example:

```
<Window x:Class="Chapter06.AnimationSpeed"
    xmlns="http://schemas.microsoft.com/winfx
       /2006/xaml/presentation"
    xmlns:x="http://schemas.microsoft.com/winfx/2006/xaml"
    Title="Animation Speed Example" Height="240" Width="410">

    <StackPanel Margin="5">
       <!-- Animation without acceleration or deceleration: -->
          <Rectangle Name="rect1" Fill="Red" Margin="2"
                   Width="20" Height="20"
                   HorizontalAlignment="Left" />

          <!-- Animation with a fast speed: -->
          <Rectangle Name="rect2" Fill="Green" Margin="2"
                   Width="20" Height="20"
                   HorizontalAlignment="Left" />

          <!-- Animation with a slow speed: -->
          <Rectangle Name="rect3" Fill="Blue" Margin="2"
                   Width="20" Height="20"
                   HorizontalAlignment="Left" />

          <!-- Animation that accelerates through 50% of
                   its duration: -->
          <Rectangle Name="rect4" Fill="Gray" Margin="2"
                   Width="20" Height="20"
                   HorizontalAlignment="Left" />

          <!-- Animation that decelerates through 50%
```

```
              of its duration: -->
<Rectangle Name="rect5" Fill="Coral" Margin="2"
           Width="20" Height="20"
           HorizontalAlignment="Left" />

<!-- Animation that accelerates through 50%
     of its duration and decelerates through
     the 50% of its duration: -->
<Rectangle Name="rect6" Fill="Purple" Margin="2"
           Width="20" Height="20"
           HorizontalAlignment="Left" />

<!-- Set animation: -->
<Button Margin="2,20,0,0" HorizontalAlignment="Left"
        Content="Start Animations" Width="100">
    <Button.Triggers>
        <EventTrigger RoutedEvent="Button.Click">
            <EventTrigger.Actions>
                <BeginStoryboard>
                    <Storyboard>
    <DoubleAnimation
        Storyboard.TargetName="rect1"
        Storyboard.TargetProperty="Width"
        From="20" To="400" Duration="0:0:10"/>

    <DoubleAnimation
        Storyboard.TargetName="rect2"
        Storyboard.TargetProperty="Width"
        From="20" To="400" Duration="0:0:10"
        SpeedRatio="1.5"/>

    <DoubleAnimation
        Storyboard.TargetName="rect3"
        Storyboard.TargetProperty="Width"
        From="20" To="400" Duration="0:0:10"
        SpeedRatio="0.5"/>

    <DoubleAnimation
        Storyboard.TargetName="rect4"
        Storyboard.TargetProperty="Width"
        From="20" To="400" Duration="0:0:10"
        AccelerationRatio="0.5"/>

    <DoubleAnimation
        Storyboard.TargetName="rect5"
        Storyboard.TargetProperty="Width"
        From="20" To="400" Duration="0:0:10"
        DecelerationRatio="0.5"/>

    <DoubleAnimation
        Storyboard.TargetName="rect6"
        Storyboard.TargetProperty="Width"
        From="20" To="400" Duration="0:0:10"
        AccelerationRatio="0.5"
```

```
                DecelerationRatio="0.5"/>
                   </Storyboard>
                </BeginStoryboard>
             </EventTrigger.Actions>
          </EventTrigger>
       </Button.Triggers>
    </Button>
 </StackPanel>
</Window>
```

This XAML file creates seven rectangles and a button. The Width property of the rectangles is animated using different animating speeds.

The first rectangle is animated without any speed changes, acceleration or deceleration for comparison. The animations for the rest of rectangles progress with different speeds that are controlled by SpeedRatio, AccelerationRatio, DecelerationRatio, or a combination of them. Figure 6-1 illustrates the results of running this example. Click on the Start Animations button to start the animations and watch how the animations progress with different speeds.

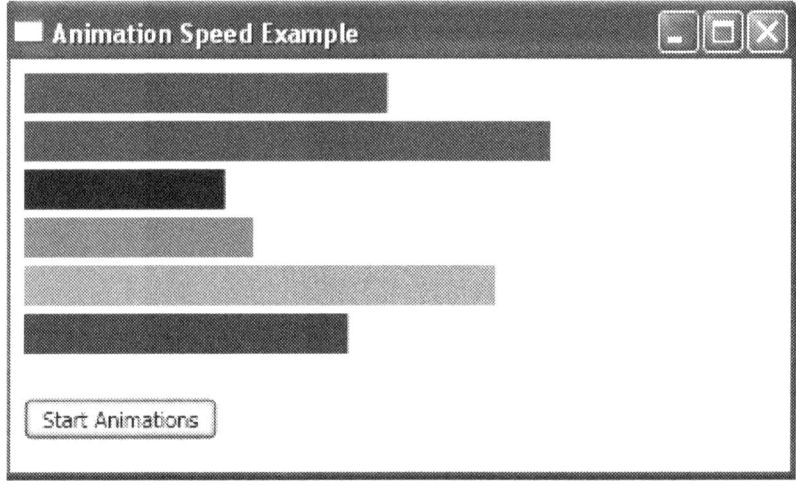

Figure 6-1 Animations with different speeds.

Interactive Control

So far, you have been using only one action of the Storyboard – the BeginStoryboard that launches the animation. If this is only the functionality you need in your animations, you actually don't need the storyboard at all, because you can perform the same action more easily using the BeginAnimation method in code. However, the Storyboard becomes more powerful when you create interactive animations.

If you give the BeginStoryboard a name by specifying its Name property, you'll make it a controllable storyboard. You can then interactively control the storyboard after it is started. Here is a list of controllable storyboard actions available in WPF that you can use with event triggers to control a storyboard:

- PauseStoryboard – Stops an animation and keeps it at its current position.

- ResumeStoryboard – Resumes a paused animation.

- SetStoryboardSpeedRatio – Changes the storyboard's speed.

- SkipStoryboardToFill – Advances a storyboard to the end of its fill period, if it has one.

- StopStoryboard – Stops the storyboard.

- RemoveStoryboard – Removes the storyboard.

Let's consider an example called InteractiveStoryboard, in which you create a circle that is painted using RadialGradientBrush. You'll then animate the brush's RadiusX and RadiusY properties interactively. Here is the XAML file of this example:

```
<Window x:Class="Chapter06.InteractiveStoryboard"
    xmlns="http://schemas.microsoft.com/winfx
        /2006/xaml/presentation"
    xmlns:x="http://schemas.microsoft.com/winfx/2006/xaml"
    Title="Interactive Storyboard" Height="300" Width="300">

    <Window.Resources>
        <Style TargetType="{x:Type Button}">
            <Setter Property="Margin" Value="2"/>
            <Setter Property="Width" Value="75"/>
            <Setter Property="Height" Value="25"/>
        </Style>
    </Window.Resources>

    <StackPanel Margin="10">

        <Ellipse Name="ellipse" Width="150" Height="150">
            <Ellipse.Fill>
                <RadialGradientBrush>
                    <GradientStop Color="White" Offset="0"/>
                    <GradientStop Color="LightCoral"
                            Offset="0.1"/>
                    <GradientStop Color="LightBlue"
                            Offset="0.2"/>
                    <GradientStop Color="Red" Offset="0.3"/>
                    <GradientStop Color="Blue" Offset="0.5"/>
                    <GradientStop Color="Yellow"
                            Offset="0.7"/>
                    <GradientStop Color="Green" Offset="0.8"/>
                    <GradientStop Color="Gold" Offset="0.9"/>
                    <GradientStop Color="Purple" Offset="1"/>
                </RadialGradientBrush>
            </Ellipse.Fill>
        </Ellipse>
```

```xml
<StackPanel Orientation="Horizontal"
            HorizontalAlignment="Center"
            Margin="0,20,0,0">
    <Button Name="btnBegin">Begin</Button>
    <Button Name="btnPause">Pause</Button>
    <Button Name="btnResume">Resume</Button>
</StackPanel>
<StackPanel Orientation="Horizontal"
            HorizontalAlignment="Center">
    <Button Name="btnSkipToFill">Skip To Fill</Button>
    <Button Name="btnStop">Stop</Button>
    <Button Click="btnClose_Click">Close</Button>
</StackPanel>

<StackPanel.Triggers>
    <EventTrigger RoutedEvent="Button.Click"
                  SourceName="btnBegin">
        <EventTrigger.Actions>
            <BeginStoryboard Name="MyBeginStoryboard">
                <Storyboard>
    <DoubleAnimation
        Storyboard.TargetName="ellipse"
        Storyboard.TargetProperty="Fill.RadiusX"
        From="0" To="1" Duration="0:0:2"
        RepeatBehavior="5x"/>

    <DoubleAnimation
        Storyboard.TargetName="ellipse"
        Storyboard.TargetProperty="Fill.RadiusY"
        From="0" To="1" Duration="0:0:2"
        RepeatBehavior="5x"/>

    <ColorAnimation
        Storyboard.TargetName="ellipse"
    Storyboard.TargetProperty="Fill.GradientStops[2].Color"
        To="Black" Duration="0:0:2"
        RepeatBehavior="5x"/>
                </Storyboard>
            </BeginStoryboard>
        </EventTrigger.Actions>
    </EventTrigger>

    <EventTrigger RoutedEvent="Button.Click"
                  SourceName="btnPause">
        <PauseStoryboard
            BeginStoryboardName="MyBeginStoryboard" />
    </EventTrigger>
    <EventTrigger RoutedEvent="Button.Click"
                  SourceName="btnResume">
        <ResumeStoryboard
            BeginStoryboardName="MyBeginStoryboard" />
    </EventTrigger>
    <EventTrigger RoutedEvent="Button.Click"
                  SourceName="btnSkipToFill">
```

```
        <SkipStoryboardToFill
            BeginStoryboardName="MyBeginStoryboard" />
      </EventTrigger>
      <EventTrigger RoutedEvent="Button.Click"
                  SourceName="btnStop">
        <StopStoryboard
            BeginStoryboardName="MyBeginStoryboard" />
      </EventTrigger>
    </StackPanel.Triggers>
  </StackPanel>
</Window>
```

In this example, you should pay close attention to several points. First, the BeginStoryboard is named MyBeginStoryboard, which will be used by the buttons' event triggers. Also notice how to set the Storyboard.TargetProperty to the RadiusX (or RadiusY) property of the ellipse's fill brush using the statement:

```
Storyboard.TargetProperty="Fill.RadiusX"
```

The Color of the GradientStop of the brush is also changed. Since the GradientStop is a collection, the color of the third GradientStop (with a LightBlue color) can be changed using the following XAML snippet:

```
<ColorAnimation Storyboard.TargetName="ellipse"
                Storyboard.TargetProperty=
                    "Fill.GradientStops[2].Color"
                To="Black" Duration="0:0:2"
                RepeatBehavior="5x"/>
```

The RepeatBehavior is set to 5x, indicating that you want to repeat the original animation five times. Remember here that if you set the RepeatBehavior property to Forever, the program will throw an exception when you click the SkipToFill button, because the animation never ends and the final value is never reached.

Another point I should mention here is that for all of the control buttons to work properly, you must define all of the triggers in one Triggers collection – here, the StackPanel.Triggers collection is used. If you place the BeginStoryboard action in a different trigger collection than the buttons' event triggers, all of the buttons' actions, including PauseStoryboard, ResumeStoryboard, and StopStoryboard, would not work.

Finally, the Close button's click event is handled in code because XAML can't call the Close method.

Figure 6-2 illustrates the results of running this example.

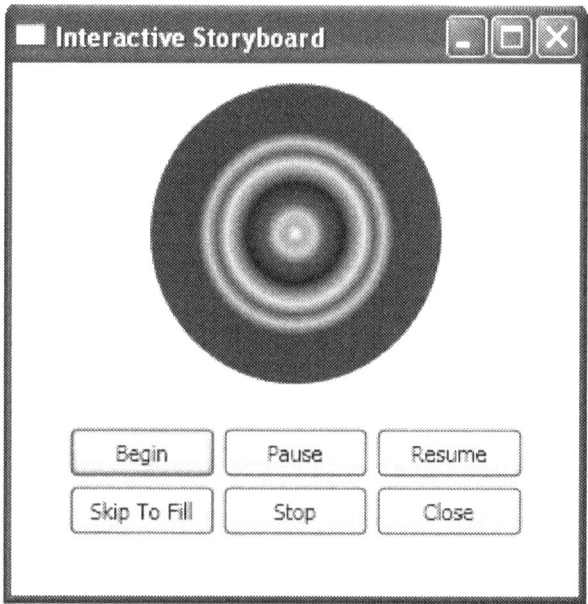

Figure 6-2 Interactive animation.

Animation and Transform

Transformation is a powerful approach for customizing elements. When you apply transforms, you don't just change the bounds of an element. In fact, the entire visual appearance of the element can be moved by translation, enlarged or shrunk by scaling, skewed by skew transforms, or rotated by rotation transforms. For example, if you animate the rotation of a button using RotateTransform, the entire button is rotated, including its border and its inner content.

Animating Translation

As you learned in the previous chapters, you can apply transforms to any element, even brush objects. In order to use a transform in animation, the first step is to define the transform. For example, if you want to perform a translation on a Rectangle shape, you need to specify the rectangle's RenderTransform property using the TranslateTransform:

```
<Rectangle Width="200" Height="35" Fill="Blue">
    <Rectangle.RenderTransform>
        <TranslateTransform/>
    </Rectangle.RenderTransform>
</Rectangle>
```

To animate this transformation, you need an event trigger to make the rectangle translate when the mouse moves over it. For this interactive animation, you can use the storyboard approach. The RenderTransform.X property (corresponding to the translation in the X direction) can be used as the target property. The event trigger reads the rectangle's RenderTransform property and modifies the X property of the TranslateTransform object.

```
<EventTrigger RoutedEvent="Rectangle.MouseEnter">
    <EventTrigger.Actions>
        <BeginStoryboard Name="translateStoryboardBegin">
            <Storyboard>
                <DoubleAnimation
                    Storyboard.TargetProperty
                        ="RenderTransform.X"
                    From ="0" To="70" Duration="0:0:1"
                    RepeatBehavior="1x"/>
            </Storyboard>
        </BeginStoryboard>
    </EventTrigger.Actions>
</EventTrigger>
```

The above XAML snippet create a rectangle that moves 70 units in the X direction in one second and stops when your mouse moves over the rectangle. When your mouse leaves the rectangle, you can use a second trigger that responds to the MouseLeave event. At this point, you could remove the storyboard that performs the translation, but this causes the rectangle to jump back to its original position in one step. A better approach is to start a second animation that replaces the first one. This animation leaves out the From and To properties, which means it seamlessly translates the rectangle back to its original position in a snappy 0.5 seconds.

```
<EventTrigger RoutedEvent="Rectangle.MouseLeave">
    <EventTrigger.Actions>
        <BeginStoryboard>
            <Storyboard>
                <DoubleAnimation
                    Storyboard.TargetProperty
                        ="RenderTransform.X"
                    Duration="0:0:0.5"/>
            </Storyboard>
        </BeginStoryboard>
    </EventTrigger.Actions>
</EventTrigger>
```

To create the translating rectangle, you need to add both triggers to the Rectangle.Triggers collection. However, a better method is to put these triggers and the translation into a style, which you can apply to as many rectangles as you like. You can put all these together into an example, called AnimationTransform, and add it to the Chapter06 project. Here is the markup of this example:

```
<Window x:Class="Chapter06.AnimationTransform"
    xmlns="http://schemas.microsoft.com/winfx
        /2006/xaml/presentation"
    xmlns:x="http://schemas.microsoft.com/winfx/2006/xaml"
    Title="Animating Translation" Height="300" Width="300">
```

```
<Window.Resources>
    <Style TargetType="{x:Type Rectangle}">
        <Setter Property="Width" Value="200"/>
        <Setter Property="Height" Value="35"/>
        <Setter Property="RenderTransform">
            <Setter.Value>
                <TranslateTransform/>
            </Setter.Value>
        </Setter>

        <Style.Triggers>
            <EventTrigger
                RoutedEvent="Rectangle.MouseEnter">
                <EventTrigger.Actions>
                    <BeginStoryboard
                        Name="translateStoryboardBegin">
                        <Storyboard>
<DoubleAnimation
    Storyboard.TargetProperty="RenderTransform.X"
    From ="0" To="70" Duration="0:0:1"
    RepeatBehavior="1x"/>
                        </Storyboard>
                    </BeginStoryboard>
                </EventTrigger.Actions>
            </EventTrigger>
            <EventTrigger
                RoutedEvent="Rectangle.MouseLeave">
                <EventTrigger.Actions>
                    <BeginStoryboard>
                        <Storyboard>
<DoubleAnimation
    Storyboard.TargetProperty="RenderTransform.X"
    Duration="0:0:0.5"/>
                        </Storyboard>
                    </BeginStoryboard>
                </EventTrigger.Actions>
            </EventTrigger>
        </Style.Triggers>
    </Style>
</Window.Resources>

<Canvas Margin="10">
    <Rectangle Fill="Red" Canvas.Top="0"/>
    <Rectangle Fill="Green" Canvas.Top="40"/>
    <Rectangle Fill="Blue" Canvas.Top="80"/>
    <Rectangle Fill="Yellow" Canvas.Top="120"/>
    <Rectangle Fill="Purple" Canvas.Top="160"/>
    <Rectangle Fill="Gray" Canvas.Top="200"/>
</Canvas>
</Window>
```

Figure 6-3 illustrates results of running this example. If your mouse moves over any rectangle, that rectangle will move 70 units toward right. When your mouse leaves, the rectangle will return back to its original position.

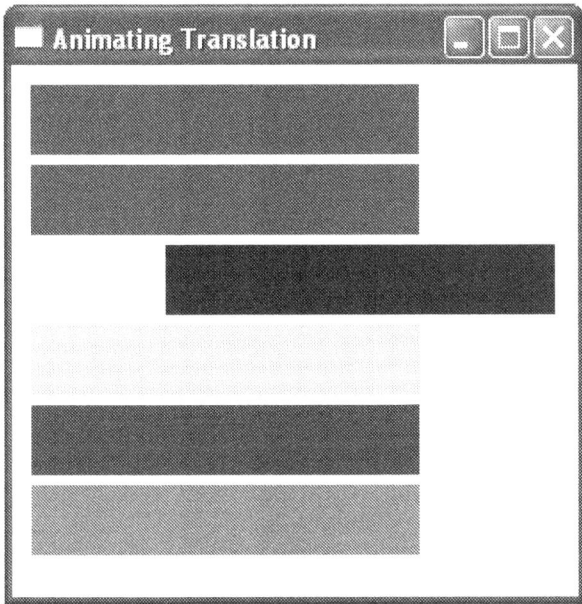

Figure 6-3 Animating Translation.

Rolling Balls

You can use an approach similar to that used in the previous section to animate a rotation. Here I'll present a rolling ball example that shows how to create a rotation animation.

The motion of a rolling ball consists of two motions, translation and rotation. If the ball rolls without slipping, the center of the ball will move a distance of $2\pi r$ for every revolution of the ball, where r is the radius of the ball. Thus, for a rolling ball animation, you need to animate two transforms, translation and rotation. The translation and rotation must satisfy the non-slipping condition.

In this example, named RollingBall, you create four balls. The first ball moves and rotates with a constant speed, the second ball with an acceleration, the third one with a decelation, and the last one with both an acceleration and decelation. For simplicity, you create the layout using XAML and perform the animations in code. Here is the XAML file of this example:

```
<Window x:Class="Chapter06.RollingBall"
    xmlns="http://schemas.microsoft.com/winfx
        /2006/xaml/presentation"
    xmlns:x="http://schemas.microsoft.com/winfx/2006/xaml"
    Title="Rolling Balls" Height="350" Width="518">
```

```
<Border BorderBrush="Gray" BorderThickness="1" Margin="4">
    <Canvas>
        <Rectangle Fill ="Gray" Width="500" Height="5
                Canvas.Top="60"/>
        <Ellipse x:Name="ellipse1" Width="50" Height="50"
                Stroke="Blue" Canvas.Top="10"
                Canvas.Left="0">
            <Ellipse.Fill>
                <LinearGradientBrush>
                    <GradientStop Color="Blue"
                                  Offset="0.5"/>
                    <GradientStop Color="LightBlue"
                                  Offset="0.5"/>
                </LinearGradientBrush>
            </Ellipse.Fill>
            <Ellipse.RenderTransform>
                <RotateTransform x:Name="ellipse1Rotate"
                            CenterX="25" CenterY="25"/>
            </Ellipse.RenderTransform>
        </Ellipse>

        <Rectangle Fill ="Gray" Width="500" Height="5
                Canvas.Top="130"/>
        <Ellipse x:Name="ellipse2" Width="50" Height="50"
                Stroke="Red" Canvas.Top="80"
                Canvas.Left="0">
            <Ellipse.Fill>
                <LinearGradientBrush>
                    <GradientStop Color="Red"
                                  Offset="0.5"/>
                    <GradientStop Color="LightSalmon"
                                  Offset="0.5"/>
                </LinearGradientBrush>
            </Ellipse.Fill>
            <Ellipse.RenderTransform>
                <RotateTransform x:Name="ellipse2Rotate"
                            CenterX="25" CenterY="25"/>
            </Ellipse.RenderTransform>
        </Ellipse>

        <Rectangle Fill="Gray" Width="500" Height="5
                Canvas.Top="200"/>
        <Ellipse x:Name="ellipse3" Width="50" Height="50"
                Stroke="Green" Canvas.Top="150"
                Canvas.Left="0">
            <Ellipse.Fill>
                <LinearGradientBrush>
                    <GradientStop Color="Green"
                                  Offset="0.5"/>
                    <GradientStop Color="LightGreen"
                                  Offset="0.5"/>
                </LinearGradientBrush>
            </Ellipse.Fill>
```

```xml
            <Ellipse.RenderTransform>
                <RotateTransform x:Name="ellipse3Rotate"
                                 CenterX="25" CenterY="25"/>
            </Ellipse.RenderTransform>
        </Ellipse>

        <Rectangle Fill ="Gray" Width="500" Height="5"
                   Canvas.Top="270"/>
        <Ellipse x:Name="ellipse4" Width="50" Height="50"
                 Stroke="Purple" Canvas.Top="220"
                 Canvas.Left="0">
            <Ellipse.Fill>
                <LinearGradientBrush>
                    <GradientStop Color="Purple"
                                  Offset="0.5"/>
                    <GradientStop Color="LightPink"
                                  Offset="0.5"/>
                </LinearGradientBrush>
            </Ellipse.Fill>
            <Ellipse.RenderTransform>
                <RotateTransform x:Name="ellipse4Rotate"
                                 CenterX="25" CenterY="25"/>
            </Ellipse.RenderTransform>
        </Ellipse>
    </Canvas>
  </Border>
</Window>
```

The following is the code-behind file of this example:

```csharp
using System;
using System.Windows;
using System.Windows.Controls;
using System.Windows.Input;
using System.Windows.Media;
using System.Windows.Media.Animation;
using System.Windows.Shapes;

namespace Chapter06
{
    public partial class RollingBall : Window
    {
        public RollingBall()
        {
            InitializeComponent();
            StartRolling();
        }

        private void StartRolling()
        {
            double nRotation = 360 * 450 / 2 / Math.PI / 25;

            // Constant speed:
            DoubleAnimation da = new DoubleAnimation(0, 450,
```

```
        TimeSpan.FromSeconds(5));
da.RepeatBehavior = RepeatBehavior.Forever;
da.AutoReverse = true;
ellipse1.BeginAnimation(Canvas.LeftProperty, da);

da = new DoubleAnimation(0, nRotation,
    TimeSpan.FromSeconds(5));
da.RepeatBehavior = RepeatBehavior.Forever;
da.AutoReverse = true;
ellipse1Rotate.BeginAnimation(
    RotateTransform.AngleProperty, da);

// Acceleration:
da = new DoubleAnimation(0, 450,
    TimeSpan.FromSeconds(5));
da.AccelerationRatio = 0.4;
da.RepeatBehavior = RepeatBehavior.Forever;
da.AutoReverse = true;
ellipse2.BeginAnimation(Canvas.LeftProperty, da);

da = new DoubleAnimation(0, nRotation,
    TimeSpan.FromSeconds(5));
da.AccelerationRatio = 0.4;
da.RepeatBehavior = RepeatBehavior.Forever;
da.AutoReverse = true;
ellipse2Rotate.BeginAnimation(
    RotateTransform.AngleProperty, da);

// Deceleration:
da = new DoubleAnimation(0, 450,
    TimeSpan.FromSeconds(5));
da.DecelerationRatio = 0.6;
da.RepeatBehavior = RepeatBehavior.Forever;
da.AutoReverse = true;
ellipse3.BeginAnimation(Canvas.LeftProperty, da);

da = new DoubleAnimation(0, nRotation,
    TimeSpan.FromSeconds(5));
da.DecelerationRatio = 0.6;
da.RepeatBehavior = RepeatBehavior.Forever;
da.AutoReverse = true;
ellipse3Rotate.BeginAnimation(
    RotateTransform.AngleProperty, da);

// Acceleration + Deceleration:
da = new DoubleAnimation(0, 450,
    TimeSpan.FromSeconds(5));
da.DecelerationRatio = 0.6;
da.AccelerationRatio = 0.4;
da.RepeatBehavior = RepeatBehavior.Forever;
da.AutoReverse = true;
ellipse4.BeginAnimation(Canvas.LeftProperty, da);

da = new DoubleAnimation(0, nRotation,
```

```
                TimeSpan.FromSeconds(5));
        da.DecelerationRatio = 0.6;
        da.AccelerationRatio = 0.4;
        da.RepeatBehavior = RepeatBehavior.Forever;
        da.AutoReverse = true;
        ellipse4Rotate.BeginAnimation(
            RotateTransform.AngleProperty, da);
        }
    }
}
```

Each ball's RotateTransform property is exposed in XAML using its corresponding name, such as ellipse1Rotate, which will be used in the animations in code. The translation is animated using the Canvas.Left property (from 0 to 450 in 5 seconds). For a non-slipping rolling ball, you need to calculate how many revolutions the ball goes through in the translation distance using the formula:

```
double nRotation = 360 * 450 / 2 / Math.PI / 25;
```

This gives the total degrees the ball should rotate in 5 seconds.

Figure 6-4 shows the results of running this example. You can see how the AccelerationRatio and DecelerationRatio affect the balls' motion.

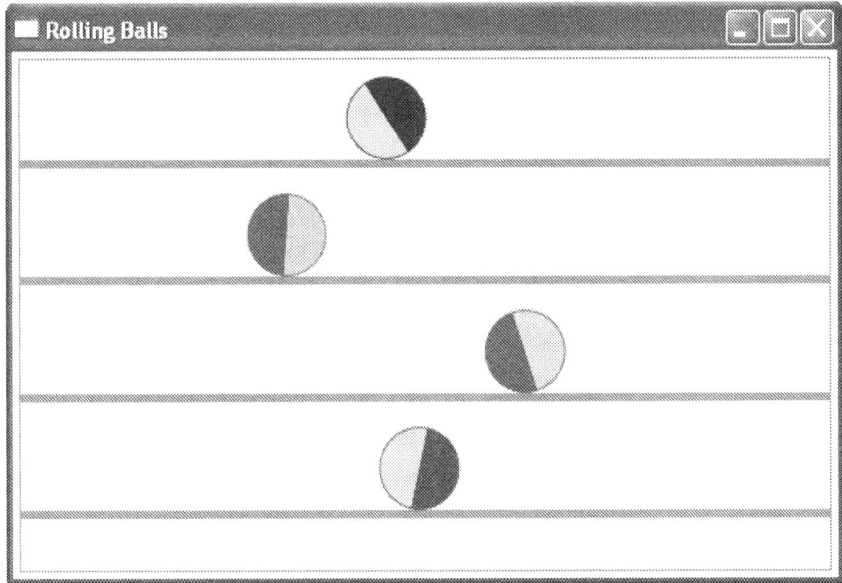

Figure 6-4 Rolling balls.

Combining Transform Animations

In WPF, you can easily perform composite transforms on any element using the TransformGroup, as discussed in Chapter 3. This can be done by simply setting the element's RenderTransform property using the TransformGroup.

Let's use an example, named CombineTransformAnimation, to illustrate how to animate composite transforms. In this example, you want to perform a combining transform, including scale, skew, and rotation, on a buttom:

```
<Button.RenderTransform>
    <TransformGroup>
        <ScaleTransform/>
        <SkewTransform/>
        <RotateTransform/>
    </TransformGroup>
</Button.RenderTransform>
```

To target this RenderTransform collection, you need to use the following path syntax:

```
RenderTransform.Children[CollectionIndex].PropertyName
```

where CollectionIndex is the index of objects in the TransformGroup. For example, if you want to animate the Angle property of the RotateTransform, you need to set the CollectionIndex = 2.

Here we want to create an interactive animation using XAML and the Storyboard. Like you did in the AnimationTransform example, you need to add event triggers and transforms to a style, then apply this style to as many buttons as you like. Here is the XAML file of this example:

```
<Window x:Class="Chapter06.CombineTransformAnimation"
    xmlns="http://schemas.microsoft.com/winfx
        /2006/xaml/presentation"
    xmlns:x="http://schemas.microsoft.com/winfx/2006/xaml"
Title="Animating Combine Transforms"
Height="320" Width="300">

    <Window.Resources>
        <Style TargetType="{x:Type Button}">
            <Setter Property="HorizontalAlignment"
                    Value="Center"/>
            <Setter Property="RenderTransformOrigin"
                    Value="0.5,0.5"/>
            <Setter Property="Margin" Value="10"/>
            <Setter Property="Width" Value="80"/>
            <Setter Property="Height" Value="40"/>
            <Setter Property="RenderTransform">
                <Setter.Value>
                    <TransformGroup>
                        <ScaleTransform/>
                        <SkewTransform/>
                        <RotateTransform/>
```

```
                  </TransformGroup>
              </Setter.Value>
          </Setter>

          <Style.Triggers>
              <EventTrigger RoutedEvent="Button.MouseEnter">
                  <EventTrigger.Actions>
                      <BeginStoryboard
                          Name="StoryboardBegin">
                          <Storyboard>
    <DoubleAnimation
        Storyboard.TargetProperty=
            "RenderTransform.Children[0].ScaleX"
        To="1.5" Duration="0:0:1"
        RepeatBehavior="1x"/>
<DoubleAnimation
    Storyboard.TargetProperty=
        "RenderTransform.Children[0].ScaleY"
        To="1.5" Duration="0:0:1"
        RepeatBehavior="1x"/>
<DoubleAnimation
    Storyboard.TargetProperty=
        "RenderTransform.Children[1].AngleX"
        To="30" Duration="0:0:1"
        RepeatBehavior="1x"/>
<DoubleAnimation
    Storyboard.TargetProperty=
        "RenderTransform.Children[1].AngleY"
        To="30" Duration="0:0:1"
        RepeatBehavior="1x"/>
<DoubleAnimation
    Storyboard.TargetProperty=
        "RenderTransform.Children[2].Angle"
        To="360" Duration="0:0:1"
        RepeatBehavior="1x"/>
                              </Storyboard>
                          </BeginStoryboard>
                      </EventTrigger.Actions>
                  </EventTrigger>
                  <EventTrigger
                      RoutedEvent="Rectangle.MouseLeave">
                      <EventTrigger.Actions>
                          <BeginStoryboard>
                              <Storyboard>
<DoubleAnimation
        Storyboard.TargetProperty=
        "RenderTransform.Children[0].ScaleX"
        Duration="0:0:0.5"/>
<DoubleAnimation
    Storyboard.TargetProperty=
        "RenderTransform.Children[0].ScaleY"
        Duration="0:0:0.5"/>
<DoubleAnimation
    Storyboard.TargetProperty=
```

```
                   "RenderTransform.Children[1].AngleX"
                   Duration="0:0:0.5"/>
            <DoubleAnimation
               Storyboard.TargetProperty=
                   "RenderTransform.Children[1].AngleY"
                   Duration="0:0:0.5"/>
         <DoubleAnimation
            Storyboard.TargetProperty=
                "RenderTransform.Children[2].Angle"
                Duration="0:0:0.5"/>
                              </Storyboard>
                           </BeginStoryboard>
                        </EventTrigger.Actions>
                     </EventTrigger>
                 </Style.Triggers>
              </Style>
         </Window.Resources>

         <StackPanel Margin="20" HorizontalAlignment="Center">
            <Button Click="btn1_Click"
                    x:Name="btn1">Button1</Button>
            <Button Click="btn2_Click"
                    x:Name="btn2">Button2</Button>
            <Button Click="btnClose_Click">Close</Button>
            <TextBlock Name="tb1" Margin="5,40,5,5"/>
         </StackPanel>
      </Window>
```

In this example, the button scales 1.5 times in both the X and Y directions,
skews 30 degrees in both the X and Y axes, and rotates one revolution; all of
these transforms are performed in one seconds whenever your mouse moves
over the button. When the button is being transformed, it is still completely
functioning – for example, you can click it and handle the Click event as normal.

To make sure the button transforms around its center, you set the
RenderTransformOrigin = "0.5, 0.5". Note that the RenderTransformOrigin
property uses relative units from 0 to 1, so the point (0.5, 0.5) represents the
center.

To stop the composite transforms when your mouse leaves, you starts another
animation that replaces the first one. This animation leaves out the To and From
properties, which means that it seamlessly transforms the button back to its
original position in 0.5 seconds.

The C# code handles the button click events:

```
using System;
using System.Windows;
using System.Windows.Controls;
using System.Windows.Input;
using System.Windows.Media;
using System.Windows.Shapes;

namespace Chapter06
```

```
{
    public partial class CombineTransformAnimation : Window
    {
        public CombineTransformAnimation()
        {
            InitializeComponent();
        }

        private void btn1_Click(object sender,
            RoutedEventArgs e)
        {
            tb1.Text = "You are clicking on " + btn1.Content;
        }

        private void btn2_Click(object sender,
            RoutedEventArgs e)
        {
            tb1.Text = "You are clicking on " + btn2.Content;
        }

        private void btnClose_Click(object sender,
            RoutedEventArgs e)
        {
            this.Close();
        }
    }
}
```

Running this project produces the results shown in Figure 6-5.

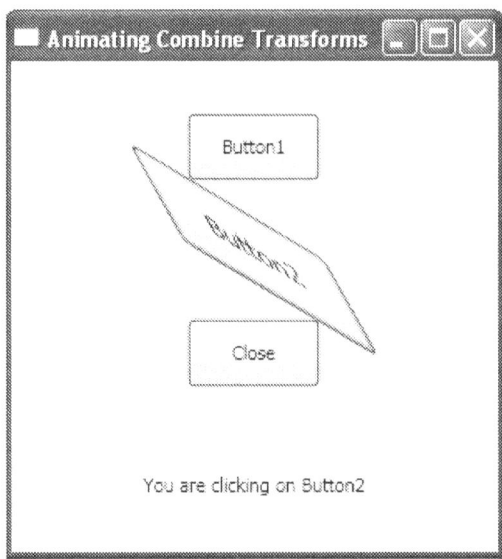

Figure 6-5 Combining transform animations.

Path Animation

A path animation is a type of AnimationTimeline that uses a PathGeometry as its input. Instead of setting a From, To, or By property as you do for a linear interpolation-based animation, you define a geometric path and use it to set the PathGeometry property of the path animation. As the path animation progresses, it reads the X, Y, and angle information from the path and uses this information to generate its output.

You can apply a path animation to a property by using a Storyboard in XAML and code, or by using the BeginAnimation method in code. As you learned in Chapter 4, a PathGeometry can be a complex path object that includes lines, arcs, and curves. Figure 6-6 illustrates the results of a PathAnimationExample, which shows two GeometryPath objects. The first animation path consists of several curve segments that form a closed path. You move an EllipseGeometry object along this path by animating its Center property. Here, the PointAnimationUsingPath class is used to animate the EllipseGeometry object's Center property.

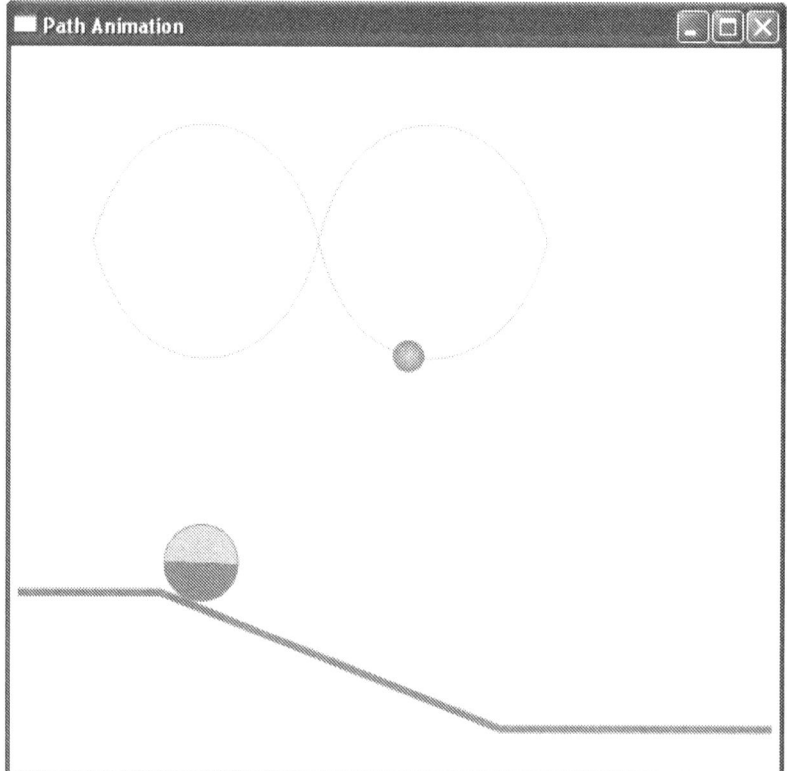

Figure 6-6 Path animations.

The second PathGeometry in this figure consists of three polyline segments. The ellipse shape (a circle) will roll without slipping along this path by combining the path animation with a rotation transform. The AccelerationRatio and DecelerationRatio properties are also specified to create an effect similar to driving a car along a downhill highway.

Creating this example is easy. Add a new WPF Window to the Chapter06 project, and name it PathAnimationExample. Here is the XAML file of this example:

```
<Window x:Class="Chapter06.PathAnimationExample"
    xmlns="http://schemas.microsoft.com/winfx
        /2006/xaml/presentation"
    xmlns:x="http://schemas.microsoft.com/winfx/2006/xaml"
    Title="Path Animation" Height="500" Width="518">

    <Canvas Margin="5">
        <!-- Path1 animation: -->
        <Path Stroke="LightBlue">
            <Path.Data>
                <PathGeometry x:Name="path1"
Figures="M50,120 C75,20 175,20 200,120 220,220 325,220 350,
120 325,20 220,20 200,120 175,220 75,220 50,120"/>
            </Path.Data>
        </Path>


        <Path Stroke="DarkGoldenrod">
            <Path.Fill>
                <RadialGradientBrush>
                    <GradientStop Color="Gold" Offset="0"/>
                    <GradientStop Color="DarkGoldenrod"
                            Offset="1"/>
                </RadialGradientBrush>
            </Path.Fill>
            <Path.Data>
                <EllipseGeometry x:Name="circle1"
                        Center="50,120" RadiusX="10"
                        RadiusY="10"/>
            </Path.Data>
        </Path>

        <!-- Path2 Animation: -->
        <Polyline Points="0,345,96,345,320,432,500,432"
                Stroke="Gray" StrokeThickness="5"/>
        <Path>
            <Path.Data>
                <PathGeometry x:Name="path2"
                    Figures="M0,292 L75,292 300,380,449,380"/>
            </Path.Data>
        </Path>

        <Ellipse Name="circle2" Stroke="DarkGoldenrod"
                Canvas.Left="0" Canvas.Top="293"
```

```
            Width="50" Height="50">
        <Ellipse.Fill>
            <LinearGradientBrush>
                <GradientStop Color="DarkGoldenrod"
                              Offset="0.5"/>
                <GradientStop Color="Gold" Offset="0.5"/>
            </LinearGradientBrush>
        </Ellipse.Fill>
        <Ellipse.RenderTransform>
            <RotateTransform x:Name="circle2Rotate"
                             CenterX="25" CenterY="25"/>
        </Ellipse.RenderTransform>
    </Ellipse>
  </Canvas>
</Window>
```

This XAML file creates the two paths. It also creates two circles using the EllipseGeometry and Ellipse classes, respectively. Note that we also define a RotateTransform for the circle2 which will be used in code to perform the corresponding rotation transform.

The animations are performed in the corresponding code-behind file, which is listed below:

```
using System;
using System.Windows;
using System.Windows.Controls;
using System.Windows.Input;
using System.Windows.Media;
using System.Windows.Media.Animation;
using System.Windows.Shapes;

namespace Chapter06
{
    public partial class PathAnimationExample : Window
    {
        public PathAnimationExample()
        {
            InitializeComponent();
            StartAnimation();
        }

        private void StartAnimation()
        {
            // Path1 animation:
            path1.Freeze(); // For performance benefits.
            PointAnimationUsingPath pa =
                new PointAnimationUsingPath();
            pa.PathGeometry = path1;
            pa.Duration = TimeSpan.FromSeconds(5);
            pa.RepeatBehavior = RepeatBehavior.Forever;
            circle1.BeginAnimation(
                EllipseGeometry.CenterProperty, pa);
```

```
// Path2 animation:
path2.Freeze(); // For performance benefits.
DoubleAnimationUsingPath daPath =
    new DoubleAnimationUsingPath();
daPath.Duration = TimeSpan.FromSeconds(5);
daPath.RepeatBehavior = RepeatBehavior.Forever;
daPath.AccelerationRatio = 0.6;
daPath.DecelerationRatio = 0.4;
daPath.AutoReverse = true;
daPath.PathGeometry = path2;
daPath.Source = PathAnimationSource.X;
circle2.BeginAnimation(
    Canvas.LeftProperty, daPath);

daPath = new DoubleAnimationUsingPath();
daPath.Duration = TimeSpan.FromSeconds(5);
daPath.RepeatBehavior = RepeatBehavior.Forever;
daPath.AccelerationRatio = 0.6;
daPath.DecelerationRatio = 0.4;
daPath.AutoReverse = true;
daPath.PathGeometry = path2;
daPath.Source = PathAnimationSource.Y;
circle2.BeginAnimation(
    Canvas.TopProperty, daPath);

double nRotation = 360 * (224 +
    Math.Sqrt(225 * 225 + 88 * 88))
    / 2 / Math.PI / 25;
DoubleAnimation da = new DoubleAnimation(
    0, nRotation, TimeSpan.FromSeconds(5));
da.RepeatBehavior = RepeatBehavior.Forever;
da.AutoReverse = true;
da.AccelerationRatio = 0.6;
da.DecelerationRatio = 0.4;
circle2Rotate.BeginAnimation(
    RotateTransform.AngleProperty, da);
        }
    }
}
```

The above code creates animations that move the circle objects. To move circle1, its Center property is adjusted using the PointAnimationUsingPath class. The DoubleAnimationUsingPath class is used to animate the circle2 by changing the Canvas.Left and Canvas.Top properties. Here, two animation objects are needed – one for Canvas.Left and the other for Canvas.Top. For circle2, the exact angle rotated during the 5-second time span needs to be calculated. In addition, the same properties for the rotation as for the path animation need to be specified in order to obtain synchronized results, like those shown in Figure 6-6.

As you can see, when you create a path animation, you don't provide starting and ending values. Instead, you specify the PathGeometry that you want to use with the PathGeometry property.

Frame-Based Animation

The animations you have seen so far are based on the linear interpolation approach. In this section, you'll learn other types of animations, including key-frame animation and spline key frame animation.

Like the From-To-By animations based on linear interpolation, key-frame animations animate the value of a target property. A single key-frame animation can create transitions among any number of target values.

WPF also provides a way to create frame-based animation without using target properties. This type of animation is useful when you want to create physics-based animations or are modeling special particle effects such as fire, snow, and bubbles.

Key-Frame Animation

When creating an animation based on linear interpolation, you specify the starting and ending points. However, this approach may not enough in some situations. For example, what if you want to create an animation that has multiple segments and moves less regularly? The easiest way is to use key-frame animation.

A key-frame animation creates a transition among its target values over its Duration and can include any number of segments. Each segment represents an initial, final, or intermediate value in the animation. When you run the animation, it moves smoothly from one target value to another. To specify the animation's target values, you create key frame objects and add them to the animation's KeyFrames collection.

In addition to supporting multiple target values, some key-frame methods also support multiple interpolations. An animation's interpolation method defines how it transitions from one value to the next. There are three types of interpolations: discrete, linear, and splined.

Let's start with an example. Add a new WPF Window to the project Chapter06 and name it KeyFrameAnimation. In this example, a rectangle is painted using the LinearGradientBrush. You'll animate its GradientStop's Color property, which uses the custom color maps defined in Chapter 5. For each key frame, you specify a custom color map with its name, such as Spring, Summer, Autumn, Winter, or Cool. The ColorAnimationUsingKeyFrames class is used to create a smooth transition from one color map to another.

In addition, you also create a string key-frame animation using the StringAnimationUsingKeyFrames class. Note that a string key frame animation's target values are specified by its KeyFrames property, which contains a collection of StringKeyFrame object. Each StringKeyFrame defines a segment of the animation with its own target value and KeyTime. Here you simply want to label the colormap with its name when the colormap is changed.

To achieve this, you need to make sure that both the Color and String key-frame animations are properly synchronized.

Here is the markup of this example:

```
<Window x:Class="Chapter06.KeyFrameAnimation"
    xmlns="http://schemas.microsoft.com/winfx
        /2006/xaml/presentation"
    xmlns:x="http://schemas.microsoft.com/winfx/2006/xaml"
    Title="Key-Frame Animation" Height="200" Width="300">
    <StackPanel Margin="15">

        <TextBlock  Name="label"
                    Block.TextAlignment="Center"
                    Foreground="Blue"/>

        <Rectangle Name="rect" Width="200" Height="100"
                Stroke="Blue" Margin="10">
            <Rectangle.Fill>
                <LinearGradientBrush StartPoint="0,0"
                                        EndPoint="1,0">
                    <GradientStop Offset="0"/>
                    <GradientStop Offset="1"/>
                </LinearGradientBrush>
            </Rectangle.Fill>
        </Rectangle>

        <StackPanel.Triggers>
            <EventTrigger RoutedEvent="StackPanel.Loaded">
                <EventTrigger.Actions>
                    <BeginStoryboard>
                        <Storyboard>

<ColorAnimationUsingKeyFrames
    Storyboard.TargetName="rect"
    Storyboard.TargetProperty= "Fill.GradientStops[0].Color"
    RepeatBehavior="Forever">
    <LinearColorKeyFrame Value="#FF00FF" KeyTime="0:0:0" />
    <LinearColorKeyFrame Value="#00805A" KeyTime="0:0:5" />
    <LinearColorKeyFrame Value="#FF0000" KeyTime="0:0:10" />
    <LinearColorKeyFrame Value="#0000FF" KeyTime="0:0:15" />
    <LinearColorKeyFrame Value="#00FFFF" KeyTime="0:0:20" />
    <LinearColorKeyFrame Value="#FF00FF" KeyTime="0:0:25" />
</ColorAnimationUsingKeyFrames>

<ColorAnimationUsingKeyFrames
    Storyboard.TargetName="rect"
    Storyboard.TargetProperty= "Fill.GradientStops[1].Color"
    RepeatBehavior="Forever">
    <LinearColorKeyFrame Value="#FFFF00" KeyTime="0:0:0" />
    <LinearColorKeyFrame Value="#FFFF5A" KeyTime="0:0:5" />
    <LinearColorKeyFrame Value="#FFFF00" KeyTime="0:0:10" />
    <LinearColorKeyFrame Value="#00FF08" KeyTime="0:0:15" />
    <LinearColorKeyFrame Value="#FF00FF" KeyTime="0:0:20" />
```

```
    <LinearColorKeyFrame Value="#FFFF00" KeyTime="0:0:25" />
</ColorAnimationUsingKeyFrames>

<StringAnimationUsingKeyFrames
    Storyboard.TargetName="label"
    Storyboard.TargetProperty="(TextBlock.Text)"
    RepeatBehavior="Forever">
<DiscreteStringKeyFrame Value="Colormap: Spring"
                        KeyTime="0:0:0" />
<DiscreteStringKeyFrame Value="Colormap: Summer"
                        KeyTime="0:0:5" />
<DiscreteStringKeyFrame Value="Colormap: Autumn"
                        KeyTime="0:0:10" />
<DiscreteStringKeyFrame Value="Colormap: Winter"
                        KeyTime="0:0:15" />
<DiscreteStringKeyFrame Value="Colormap: Cool"
                        KeyTime="0:0:20" />
<DiscreteStringKeyFrame Value="Colormap: Spring"
                        KeyTime="0:0:25" />
</StringAnimationUsingKeyFrames>
                    </Storyboard>
                </BeginStoryboard>
            </EventTrigger.Actions>
        </EventTrigger>
    </StackPanel.Triggers>
  </StackPanel>
</Window>
```

This example includes three key-frame animations, each one with six key frames. The first two key-frame animations are used to animate the color change of LinearGradientBrush by adjusting its GradientStop's Color property. Each pair of GradientStops at a given KeyTime forms a custom colormap.

The third key-frame animation is used to animate the TextBlock's Text property with the StringAnimationUsingKeyFrames class. It includes six discrete string key frames. When the animation progresses, it changes the text property of the TextBlock from one text string to another. Note how the KeyTime properties are specified in these three key-frame animations. You should make sure that the string text change is consistent with the colormap variation.

The animations in this example aren't reversible, but they do repeat. To make sure there is no jump between the final value of one iteration and the starting value of the next iteration, the animations end at the same value as their staring value. That is why you use six key frames to animate five color maps.

Figure 6-7 illustrates the results of running this example.

The above example uses two types of interpolation methods: linear and discrete. There is one more type of key frame: the spline key frame. Every class that supports linear key frames also supports spline key frames.

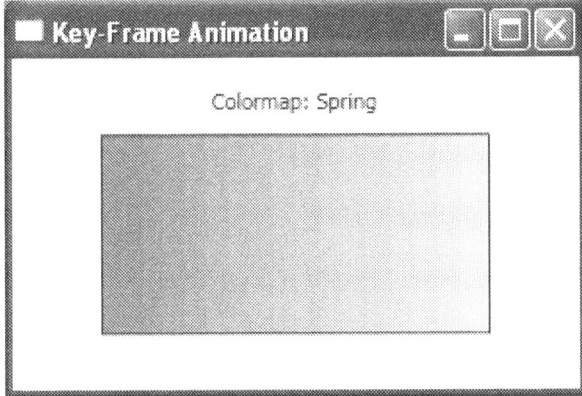

Figure 6-7 Key frame animation.

Spline Key-Frame Animation

Splined interpolation can be used to achieve more realistic timing effects. Spline key frames allow you to animate with splined interpolation. With other key frames, you specify a Value and KeyTime. With a spline key frame, you also need to specify a KeySpline. Using the KeySpline property, you define a cubic Bezier curve that affects the way interpolation is performed. This approach gives you the ability to create more seamless acceleration and deceleration. The following snippet shows a single spline key frame for the DoubleAnimationUsingKeyFrames class:

```
<SplineDoubleKayFrame Value="20" KeyTime="0:0:5"
                      KeySpline="0,1,1,0"/>
```

You may remember from the discussion in Chapter 4 that a cubic Bezier curve is defined by a start point, an end point, and two control points. The KeySpline property of a spline key frame defines two control points of a Bezier curve that extends from (0, 0) to (1, 1). The first control point controls the curve factor of the first half of the Bezier curve, and the second control point controls the curve factor of the second half of the Bezier segment. The resulting curve describes the rate of change for that spine key frame.

Let's consider an example, called SplineKeyFrameAnimation that demonstrates a key spline animation by comparing the motion of two balls across a Canvas. The spline key frame animation simulates the case of a ball moving along a trajectory under a gravity. At the beginning, the ball moves upward with a initial velocity. Its velocity becomes zero when it reaches the highest point. After that, the ball starts free falling with an acceleration of gravity. This process is animated approximately by two spline key frames.

Here is the XAML code of this example:

```
<Window x:Class="Chapter06.SplineKeyFrameAnimation"
    xmlns="http://schemas.microsoft.com/winfx
        /2006/xaml/presentation"
```

```
       xmlns:x="http://schemas.microsoft.com/winfx/2006/xaml"
       Title="Spline Key Frame Animation"
       Height="250" Width="400">

<Canvas Margin="5">
    <TextBlock Canvas.Left="10" Canvas.Top="10">
              Ball moves in a constant speed</TextBlock>
    <Ellipse Name="ball1" Canvas.Left="10" Canvas.Top="50"
           Width="20" Height="20">
        <Ellipse.Fill>
            <RadialGradientBrush>
                <GradientStop Color="Gold" Offset="0"/>
                <GradientStop Color="DarkGoldenrod"
                              Offset="1"/>
            </RadialGradientBrush>
        </Ellipse.Fill>
    </Ellipse>

    <TextBlock Canvas.Left="10" Canvas.Top="120">
        Ball moves following spline key frames</TextBlock>
    <Ellipse Name="ball2" Canvas.Left="10"
           Canvas.Top="160" Width="20" Height="20">
        <Ellipse.Fill>
            <RadialGradientBrush>
                <GradientStop Color="Gold" Offset="0"/>
                <GradientStop Color="DarkGoldenrod"
                              Offset="1"/>
            </RadialGradientBrush>
        </Ellipse.Fill>
    </Ellipse>

    <Canvas.Triggers>
        <EventTrigger RoutedEvent="StackPanel.Loaded">
            <EventTrigger.Actions>
                <BeginStoryboard>
                    <Storyboard>

        <DoubleAnimation
            Storyboard.TargetName="ball1"
            Storyboard.TargetProperty="(Canvas.Left)"
            To="310" Duration="0:0:10"
            RepeatBehavior="Forever"/>

        <DoubleAnimationUsingKeyFrames
            Storyboard.TargetName="ball2"
            Storyboard.TargetProperty="(Canvas.Left)"
            Duration="0:0:10"
            RepeatBehavior="Forever">
            <SplineDoubleKeyFrame
                Value="160" KeyTime="0:0:5"
                KeySpline="0.25,0.5,0.75,1" />
            <SplineDoubleKeyFrame
                Value="310" KeyTime="0:0:10"
                KeySpline="0.25,0.0 0.75,0.5" />
```

```
        </DoubleAnimationUsingKeyFrames>
                </Storyboard>
              </BeginStoryboard>
            </EventTrigger.Actions>
          </EventTrigger>
        </Canvas.Triggers>
      </Canvas>
    </Window>
```

In this example, the first ball moves at a constant speed. The second ball reaches a speed of zero at the end of the first spline frame (the five-second mark), when the second SplineDoubleKeyFrame kicks in. Then the ball falls freely with an acceleration that is described approximately by the second spline key frame.

Figure 6-8 shows the results of running this application.

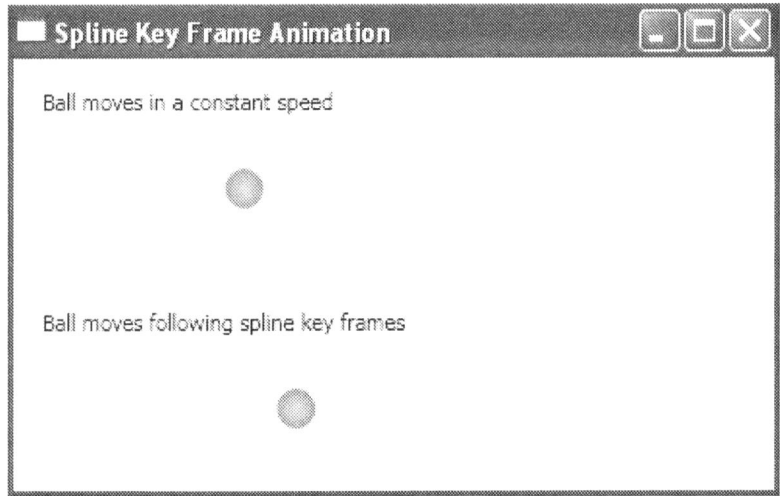

Figure 6-8 Spline key frame animation.

Custom Animation

Although WPF provides powerful animation features, in some cases, you do need to create your own custom animation. For example, if you want to perform a physics-based animation, where each step in the animation requires objects to be recomputed based on the last set of object interactions, you have to create your own animation in code using either per-frame animation or timer-based animation. Both the per-frame and timer based animations completely bypass the WPF animation system.

There are a number of ways to extend the WPF animation system, depending on the level of built-in functionality you want to use. Here are three approaches that I'll use to create custom animations:

- Create a custom animation class by inheriting from AnimationTimeline or one of the <Type>AnimationBase classes.

- Use per-frame callback to generate animations on a per-frame basis. This approach completely bypasses the WPF animation and timing system.

- Create your own timer-based animation using the DispatcherTimer. This approach completely bypasses the WPF animation and timing system.

There is another method that you can use: creating a custom key frame class. You can use this approach when you want to have a different interpolation for a key frame animation. I'll not discuss this approach here.

In the following sections, I'll show you in detail how to create various custom animations.

Custom Animation Class

WPF provides a way that allows you to create your own animation class by inheriting from AnimationTimeline or one of the <Type>AnimationBase classes. Deriving from a <Type>AnimationBase class is the simplest way to create a new custom animation class. Use this method when you want to create a new animation for a type that already has a corresponding <Type>AnimationBase class.

First, you need to derive your animation class from a <Type>AnimationBase class, and then implement the GetCurrentValueCore method. This method returns the current value of the animation. It takes three parameters: a suggested starting value, a suggested ending value, and an AnimationClock, which you use to determine the progress of the animation.

Because the <Type>AnimationBase classes inherit from the Freezable class, you need also to override CreateInstanceCore to return a new instance of your class.

Here, I'll show you how to create a simple custom animation class using an example. In this example, we'll animate the free fall motion of an object. First, add a custom animation class to the project Chapter06, and call it FreefallDoubleAnimation, which derives from the DoubleAnimationBase class. Here is the code listing of this class:

```
using System;
using System.Windows;
using System.Windows.Controls;
using System.Windows.Input;
using System.Windows.Media;
using System.Windows.Media.Animation;
using System.Windows.Shapes;

public class FreefallDoubleAnimation : DoubleAnimationBase
{
public static readonly DependencyProperty
```

```
AccelerationProperty =
    DependencyProperty.Register(
    "Acceleration", typeof(double),
    typeof(FreefallDoubleAnimation),
    new PropertyMetadata(9.8));

public static readonly DependencyProperty FromProperty
    = DependencyProperty.Register("From",
    typeof(double?),
    typeof(FreefallDoubleAnimation),
    new PropertyMetadata(null));

public static readonly DependencyProperty ToProperty =
    DependencyProperty.Register("To",
    typeof(double?),
    typeof(FreefallDoubleAnimation),
    new PropertyMetadata(null));

public double Acceleration
{
    get { return
        (double)GetValue(AccelerationProperty); }
    set { SetValue(AccelerationProperty, value); }
}

public double? From
{
    get { return (double?)GetValue(FromProperty); }
    set { SetValue(FromProperty, value); }
}

public double? To
{
    get { return (double?)GetValue(ToProperty); }
    set { SetValue(ToProperty, value); }
}

protected override double GetCurrentValueCore(
    double defaultOriginValue,
    double defaultDestinationValue,
    AnimationClock clock)
{
    double returnValue;
    double time = clock.CurrentProgress.Value;
    double start = From != null ? (double)From :
        defaultOriginValue;
    double delta = To != null ? (double)To - start :
        defaultOriginValue - start;
    double t0 = Math.Sqrt(2 / Acceleration);
    if (time > t0)
        time = t0;
    returnValue = 0.5 * Acceleration * time * time;
    returnValue *= delta;
    returnValue = returnValue + start;
```

```
        return returnValue;
    }

    protected override Freezable CreateInstanceCore()
    {
        return new FreefallDoubleAnimation();
    }
}
```

In this class, we define several dependency properties, including acceleration (due to gravity), From, and To. Then we override the GetCurrentValueCore method, where we implement the animation according to our specific animation requirements. The method takes three parameters: the defaultOriginValue, defaultDestinationValue, and AnimationClock, which is used to determine the progress of the animation. Finally, we override the CreateInstanceCore method to return a new instance of the class.

Now the custom animation class, FreefallDoubleAnimation, can be used in the same way as the built-in animation classes, such as DoubleAnimation. Add a new WPF Window to the project Chapter06 and name it CustomAnimation. This example shows you how to use the custom animation class in a WPF application. Here is the XAML file of this example:

```
<Window x:Class="Chapter06.CustomAnimation"
    xmlns="http://schemas.microsoft.com/winfx
        /2006/xaml/presentation"
    xmlns:x="http://schemas.microsoft.com/winfx/2006/xaml"
    xmlns:local="clr-namespace:Chapter06"
    Title="Custom Animation" Height="500" Width="300">

    <Canvas>
      <Ellipse Name="ellipse1" Width="50" Height="50"
            Canvas.Left="115" Canvas.Top="20">
        <Ellipse.Fill>
          <RadialGradientBrush GradientOrigin="0.75,0.25">
            <GradientStop Color="LightBlue" Offset="0"/>
            <GradientStop Color="Blue" Offset="1"/>
          </RadialGradientBrush>
        </Ellipse.Fill>
      </Ellipse>

        <Canvas.Triggers>
            <EventTrigger RoutedEvent="Rectangle.Loaded">
                <EventTrigger.Actions>
                    <BeginStoryboard>
                        <Storyboard>
                <local:FreefallDoubleAnimation
                    Storyboard.TargetName="ellipse1"
                    Storyboard.TargetProperty="(Canvas.Top)"
                    From="20" To="400" Acceleration="10"
                    Duration="0:0:10" RepeatBehavior="Forever"/>
                        </Storyboard>
                    </BeginStoryboard>
```

```
            </EventTrigger.Actions>
        </EventTrigger>
    </Canvas.Triggers>
</Canvas>
</Window>
```

In order to use the custom animation class in XAML files, you need to include an XML namespace to associate the custom class:

```
xmlns:local="clr-namespace:Chapter06"
```

If the custom class is in a DLL rather than part of the project, the namespace declaration also needs to indicate the DLL assembly name. You can then use the custom class in your animation. The above XAML file creates an ellipse object in XAML and performs animation on it using the custom FreefallDoubleAnimation class in exactly the same way as you could use the WPF built-in DoubleAnimation class. Figure 6-9 shows the results of running this example.

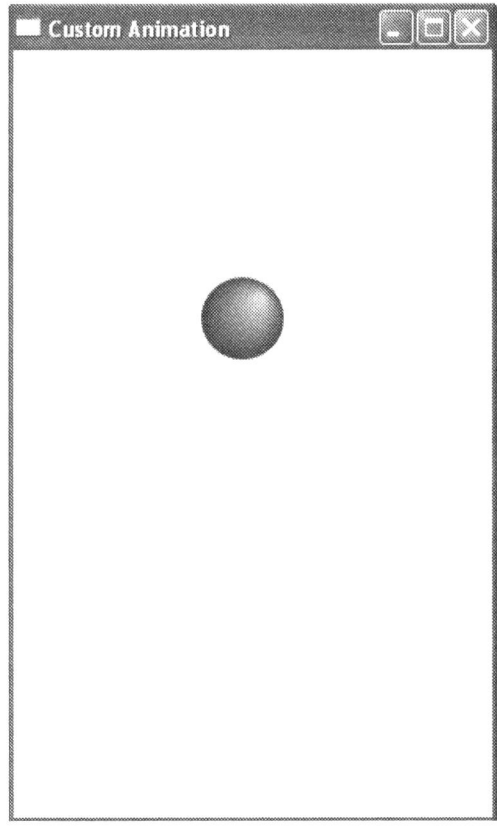

Figure 6-9 Custom animation.

Per-Frame Animation

For physics-based animations, you need to use either per-frame animation or timer-based animation. Both per-frame and timer-based animations completely bypass the WPF animation system. Note that these two kinds of animations must be implemented in code.

To animate frame-by-frame, you simply need to attach an event handler to the static CompositionTarget.Rendering event. This event handler method gets called continuously once per frame. In the rendering event handler, you can perform whatever calculations are necessary for the animation effect you want, and set the properties of objects you want to animate with these values. In other words, you need to manage all the work associated with the animation yourself.

To obtain the presentation time for the current frame, the EventArgs associated with this event can be cast as RenderingEventArgs, which provides a RenderingTime property, which you can use to obtain the current frame's rendering time.

Let's consider an example that shows how to create a per-frame animation. Add a new WPF Window to the project Chapter06 and name it PerFrameAnimation. Here, you'll animate two balls, moving along two ellipse paths. The following is the markup of this example:

```
<Window x:Class="Chapter06.PerFrameAnimation"
    xmlns="http://schemas.microsoft.com/winfx
        /2006/xaml/presentation"
    xmlns:x="http://schemas.microsoft.com/winfx/2006/xaml"
    Title="Per Frame Animation" Height="400" Width="400">

    <Canvas>
        <Path Fill="Blue">
            <Path.Data>
                <EllipseGeometry x:Name="ball1"
                    Center="30,180" RadiusX="5" RadiusY="5"/>
            </Path.Data>
        </Path>

        <Path Fill="Red">
            <Path.Data>
                <EllipseGeometry x:Name="ball2"
                    Center="180,30" RadiusX="5" RadiusY="5"/>
            </Path.Data>
        </Path>

        <Path Stroke="LightBlue">
            <Path.Data>
                <EllipseGeometry Center="180,180"
                    RadiusX="150" RadiusY="75"/>
            </Path.Data>
        </Path>

        <Path Stroke="LightCoral">
```

```
        <Path.Data>
            <EllipseGeometry Center="180,180"
                RadiusX="75" RadiusY="150"/>
        </Path.Data>
    </Path>
  </Canvas>
</Window>
```

Note that the two bigger ellipses in the above XAML aren't the real moving paths of the two balls, but are simply used to guide the viewer's eyes. The corresponding code-behind file is listed below:

```
using System;
using System.Windows;
using System.Windows.Controls;
using System.Windows.Media;
using System.Windows.Media.Animation;
using System.Windows.Shapes;

namespace Chapter06
{
    public partial class PerFrameAnimation : Window
    {
        private TimeSpan lastRender;
        double time = 0;
        double dt = 0;
        public PerFrameAnimation()
        {
            InitializeComponent();
            lastRender = TimeSpan.FromTicks(
                DateTime.Now.Ticks);
            CompositionTarget.Rendering +=
                                StartAnimation;
        }

        private void StartAnimation(
            object sender, EventArgs e)
        {
            RenderingEventArgs renderArgs =
                        (RenderingEventArgs)e;
            dt = (renderArgs.RenderingTime -
                        lastRender).TotalSeconds;
            lastRender = renderArgs.RenderingTime;

            double x = 180 + 150 * Math.Cos(2 * time);
            double y = 180 + 75 * Math.Sin(2 * time);
            ball1.Center = new Point(x, y);
            x = 180 + 75 * Math.Cos(0.5 * time);
            y = 180 + 150 * Math.Sin(0.5 * time);
            ball2.Center = new Point(x, y);
            time += dt;
        }
    }
}
```

You can see that the event handler StartAnimation is attached to the CompositionTarget.Rendering event. Inside the event handler, you obtain the RenderingTime by casting the EventArgs with RenderingEventArgs. You then get the time difference (dt) needed to progress each frame. Next, you specify each ball's Center property using an ellipse function. The argument of this function is related to the time difference dt. Thus, as the animation progresses frame by frame, each ball will move along its respective ellipse path. In this way, your animation speed is independent of the frame rate because dt automatically adjusts according to the frame rate. You can also specify dt as a constant parameter, which will make your animation frame-rate dependent.

Figure 6-10 illustrates the results of running this application.

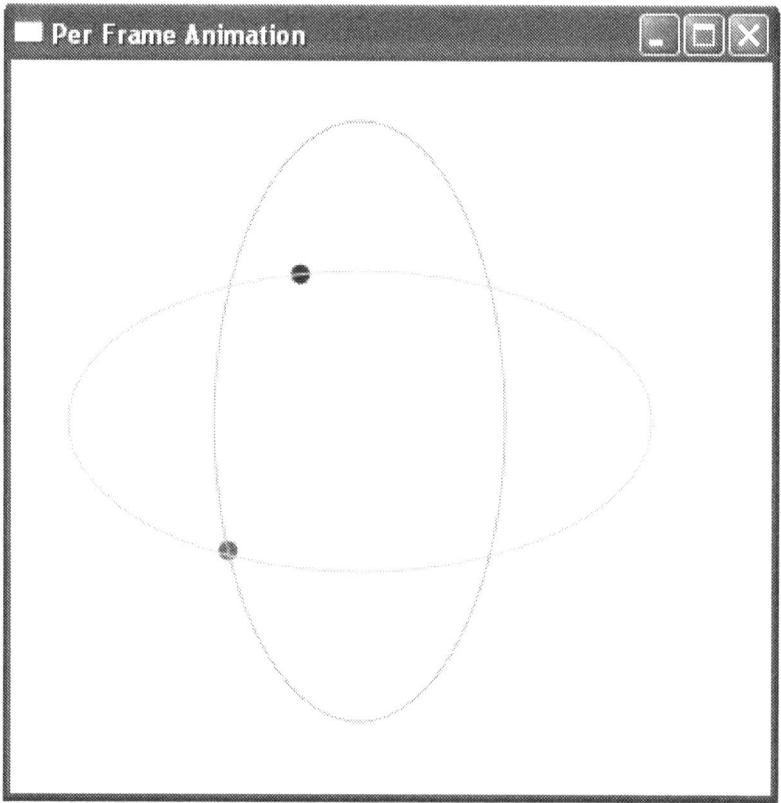

Figure 6-10 Per-frame animation.

Animation Using Timer

Another approach you can use in physics-based animations is to use a timer. This method was commonly used in animation before WPF. Like the per-frame animation, this timer-based animation completely bypasses the WPF animation system. You can use either method to create physics-based animations. My personal preference is to use the per-frame animation over timer-based animation because you don't need to worry about frame rate in the per-frame animation, but you need to manage everything (including the frame rate) yourself in timer-based animation.

There are several timer systems in WPF that you can use in your animations, such as System.Timers.Timer and the DispatcherTimer in the System.Windows.Threading namespace. For timer-based animations, I suggest that you use the DispatcherTimer. This is because the Timer in the System.Timers namespace runs on a different thread than the user interface thread of WPF. In order to access objects on the user interface thread, it is necessary to post the operation onto the Dispatcher of the user interface thread using the Invoke or BeginInvoke method. On the other hand, the DispatcherTimer runs on the same thread as the user interface, and it can directly access objects on the user interface thread.

Using the DispatcherTimer is simple – you first create a DispatcherTimer object, then add the event handler dispatcherTimer_Tick to the Tick event of the DispatcherTimer object. The Interval can be set using a TimeSpan object. Finally, you call the timer's Start() method.

Figure 6-11 shows an example of a projectile, called TimerAnimation.

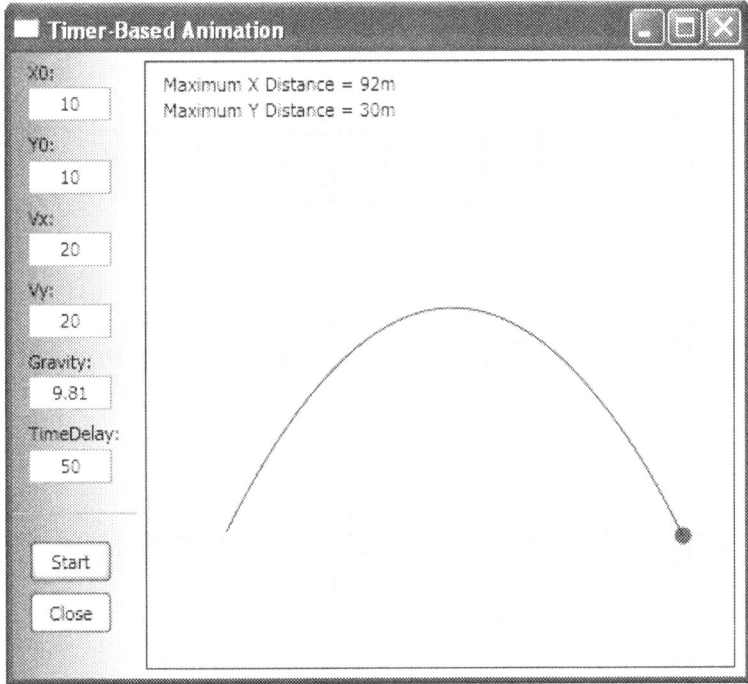

Figure 6-11 Timer-based animation.

Here, an ellipse object with an initial position and velocity moves into the space above a planet (which can be the Moon, the Earth, or any other planet by specifying its acceleration of gravity). The only force acting on the object is the gravity. This physics problem can be animated using a DispatcherTimer.

First, we create a layout for this example using markup:

```
<Window x:Class="Chapter06.TimerAnimation"
    xmlns="http://schemas.microsoft.com/winfx
        /2006/xaml/presentation"
    xmlns:x="http://schemas.microsoft.com/winfx/2006/xaml"
 Title="Timer-Based Animation " Height="400" Width="450">

    <Window.Resources>
        <Style TargetType="{x:Type TextBox}">
            <Setter Property="Width" Value="50"/>
            <Setter Property="Height" Value="20"/>
            <Setter Property="HorizontalAlignment"
                    Value="Left"/>
            <Setter Property="TextAlignment" Value="Center"/>
            <Setter Property="Margin" Value="10,0,2,2"/>
        </Style>
        <Style TargetType="{x:Type TextBlock}">
            <Setter Property="Margin" Value="10,5,0,2"/>
        </Style>
    </Window.Resources>

    <Grid>
        <Grid.ColumnDefinitions>
            <ColumnDefinition Width="75"/>
            <ColumnDefinition Width="Auto"/>
        </Grid.ColumnDefinitions>
        <StackPanel Grid.Column="0">
            <StackPanel.Background>
                <LinearGradientBrush StartPoint="0,0"
                                     EndPoint="1,0">
                    <GradientStop Color="Gray" Offset="0"/>
                    <GradientStop Color="White" Offset="1"/>
                </LinearGradientBrush>
            </StackPanel.Background>
            <TextBlock Text="X0:"/>
            <TextBox Name="tbX0" Text="10"/>
            <TextBlock Text="Y0:"/>
            <TextBox Name="tbY0" Text="10"/>
            <TextBlock Text="Vx:"/>
            <TextBox Name="tbVx" Text="20"/>
            <TextBlock Text="Vy:"/>
            <TextBox Name="tbVy" Text="20"/>
            <TextBlock Text="Gravity:"/>
            <TextBox Name="tbGravity" Text="9.81"/>
            <TextBlock Text="TimeDelay:"/>
            <TextBox Name="tbTimeDelay" Text="50"/>
            <Separator Margin="0,15,0,10"/>
            <Button Click="btnStart_Click" Content="Start"
```

```
                Width="50" Height="25" Margin="10,5,5,5"
                HorizontalAlignment="Left"/>
        <Button Click="btnClose_Click" Content="Close"
                Width="50" Height="25" Margin="10,0,5,5"
                HorizontalAlignment="Left"/>
    </StackPanel>

    <Viewbox Stretch="Fill" Grid.Column="1">
        <Border Margin="5" BorderBrush="Black"
                BorderThickness="1" Grid.Column="1"
                HorizontalAlignment="Left">
            <Canvas x:Name="canvas1" Width="345"
                    Height="345" ClipToBounds="True"
        Background="{StaticResource MyGrayGridBrush}">
                <Ellipse Name="ellipse" Width="10"
                        Height="10" Fill="Red"
                        Canvas.Bottom="20"
                        Canvas.Left="20"/>
                <TextBlock Name="tbXMax"
                        Text="Maximum X distance:" />
                <TextBlock Name="tbYMax"
                        Text="Maximum Y distance:"
                        Canvas.Top="15"/>
            </Canvas>
        </Border>
    </Viewbox>
</Grid>
</Window>
```

This XAML file creates an ellipse object and the user interface that allows the user to type in various input parameters. In particular, the TimeDelay parameter controls the speed of the animation. The following is the code-behind file of this example:

```
using System;
using System.Windows;
using System.Windows.Controls;
using System.Windows.Input;
using System.Windows.Media;
using System.Windows.Shapes;
using System.Windows.Threading;

namespace Chapter06
{
    public partial class TimerAnimation : Window
    {
        double XMin = 0;
        double YMin = 0;
        double XMax = 100;
        double YMax = 50;
        double X0 = 10;
        double Y0 = 10;
        double Vx = 10;
        double Vy = 10;
```

```
double Gravity = 9.81;
double TimeDelay = 50;
double time = 0;
double dt = 0.1;
DispatcherTimer timer = new DispatcherTimer();
Polyline pl = new Polyline();

public TimerAnimation()
{
    InitializeComponent();
    pl.Stroke = Brushes.Blue;
    canvas1.Children.Add(pl);
}

private void btnStart_Click(
    object sender, RoutedEventArgs e)
{
    time = 0;
    dt = 0.1;

    if (canvas1.Children.Count > 3)
        canvas1.Children.Remove(pl);

    pl = new Polyline();
    pl.Stroke = Brushes.Blue;
    canvas1.Children.Add(pl);
    timer = new DispatcherTimer();

    X0 = Double.Parse(tbX0.Text);
    Y0 = Double.Parse(tbY0.Text);
    Vx = Double.Parse(tbVx.Text);
    Vy = Double.Parse(tbVy.Text);
    TimeDelay = Double.Parse(tbTimeDelay.Text);
    Gravity = Double.Parse(tbGravity.Text);

    // Get maximum x and y:
    double xm = 2 * Vx * Vy / Gravity;
    double ym = 0.5 * Vy * Vy / Gravity;
    double x1 = Math.Round(X0 + xm, 0);
    double y1 = Math.Round(Y0 + ym, 0);
    tbXMax.Text = "Maximum X Distance =
        " + x1.ToString() + "m";
    tbYMax.Text = "Maximum Y Distance =
        " + y1.ToString() + "m";

    timer.Interval = TimeSpan.FromMilliseconds(
        TimeDelay);
    timer.Tick += new EventHandler(timer_Tick);
    timer.Start();
}

private void timer_Tick(object sender, EventArgs e)
{
    double x = X0 + Vx * time;
```

```
        double y = Y0 + Vy * time -
            0.5 * Gravity * time * time;

        if (y >= Y0)
        {
            Canvas.SetLeft(ellipse, XNormalize(x));
            Canvas.SetTop(ellipse, YNormalize(y));
            pl.Points.Add(new Point(
                XNormalize(x) + 5, YNormalize(y) + 5));
        }
        else
        {
            timer.Stop();
            return;
        }
        time += dt;
    }

    private double XNormalize(double x)
    {
        double result = (x - XMin) *
            canvas1.Width / (XMax - XMin);
        return result;
    }

    private double YNormalize(double y)
    {
        double result = canvas1.Height - (y - YMin) *
            canvas1.Height / (YMax - YMin);
        return result;
    }

    private void btnClose_Click(
        object sender, RoutedEventArgs e)
    {
        this.Close();
    }
    }
}
```

In the above code, we define several private members that can be changed by
the user's inputs. The animation using timer is straightforward. When you click
the Start button, the program reads in the input parameters and prepares for the
animation. This example also involves the following timer-related statements:

```
timer.Interval = TimeSpan.FromMilliseconds(TimeDelay);
timer.Tick += new EventHandler(timer_Tick);
timer.Start();
```

First, we set the timer interval using the TimeSpan object that takes the input
parameter: TimeDelay. This interval controls the animation speed. Then we add
an event handler, timer_Tick, to the timer.Tick event, and call the timer's Start
method to start the animation.

All the animation-related code is implemented in the timer_Tick event handler. Note how the time variable relates to the timer's tick event. For each tick of the timer, the time adds an additional dt (a constant time increment). The animation progresses with the timer's tick event until the ellipse object touches the ground (corresponding to Y = 0), where the timer stops.

Also note that the calculation uses normalized X and Y coordinates to reflect real-world scales and use a custom coordinate system with a bottom-up Y axis.

In this chapter, we explored a variety of animation techniques in great detail. You learned how to use animations in code and how to construct and control them with XAML. Now that your've matered the basics, you can concentrate on the art of animation – deciding what properties to be animated and how to get the effect you want. This book provides many code examples on animations, including animations of 3D objects, which can be modified and used in your WPF applications.

Chapter 7
Physics and Games in WPF

If you are a game programmer, you know how to render complex game scenes on the screen. You know about game theory and how to make your games interesting and attractive. However, if your games aren't based on a solid physics foundation, they'll look and act fake. Therefore, physics plays a crucial role in game programming, because it can make your games more fun to play and more realistic.

In this chapter, you'll learn how to represent physics events and how to create simple 2D physics-based games in WPF. The chapter begins with ordinary differential equations (ODEs), which form a mathematical foundation for describing many physics phenomena. It then presents a variety of examples that solve different physics models using the ODE solver, including pendulum, coupled spring system, projectile, and collission. The simulators implemented in these examples will be a starting point for developing physics-based games. This chapter also presents a golf game simulator based on the projectile model, and several different kinds of fractals with self-similar behavior.

Ordinary Differiential Equations

Many physics phenomena can be described in terms of a set of ODEs. For example, if a projectile is flying through the air, it will be subject to the force of aerodynamic drag, which is a function of the object's velocity. The force acting on the projectile will vary during its flight, and the resulting equations of motion are a set of ODEs, which can't be solved analytically.

Another example is the spring-mass system. In this system, there are two forces acting on the mass: elastic recovery force, which is proportional to the displacement of the mass, and the damping force, which is proportional to its velocity. The equations of motion describing this system are also a set of ODEs, which can't be directly solved either.

Fortunately, there are a number of techniques that can be used to solve ODEs when an analytically closed-form solution is impossible. In the next section, a technique called the Runge-Kutta method will be presented which can be used to solve the differential equations that you will encounter in your game programming. This technique has been proven to be versatile, reliable, and applicable to a wide range of applications.

Fourth-Order Runge-Kutta Method

Many techniques have been developed over the years for solving ODEs. The one presented and used in this book is called the fourth-order Runge-Kutta method. This method is one of a family of step-wise interpolation methods, indicating that from a set of initial conditions, the differential equation is solved at discrete increments of the independent variable. For the equation of motion, the independent variable is time. The fourth-order Runge-Kutta method isn't the most efficient technique available, but it is simple and reliable, and gives reasonable results as long as extremely high accuracy isn't required.

The Runge-Kutta method is designed to work on first order differential equations. It starts with an initial set of values of t (time variable) and x (position variable) from which subsequent values of x are calculated as a solution for the differential equations

$$\frac{dx}{dt} = f(x,t) \tag{7.1}$$

Here the function of f(x,t) corresponds to the velocity. Suppose that at a given time t_n, the x-position and velocity are known: x_n and f_n. You want to determine the x at a future time t_n+dt, where dt is a certain time increment. Here are the relations involved in the fourth-order Runge-Kutta method:

$$k_1 = dt \cdot f(x_n, t_n) \tag{7.2}$$

$$k_2 = dt \cdot f\left(x_n + \frac{k_1}{2}, t_n + \frac{dt}{2}\right) \tag{7.3}$$

$$k_3 = dt \cdot f\left(x_n + \frac{k_2}{2}, t_n + \frac{dt}{2}\right) \tag{7.4}$$

$$k_4 = dt \cdot f(x_n + k_3, t_n + dt) \tag{7.5}$$

$$x_{n+1} = x_n + \frac{(k_1 + 2k_2 + 2k_3 + k_4)}{6} \tag{7.6}$$

The Runge-Kutta method can be used to solve any first-order ordinary differential equation. As long as a derivative can be expressed as a function of the dependent and independent variables, this method can be used to calculate the value of the dependent variable.

Higher-Order ODEs

As mentioned preiously, the Runge-Kutta method is designed to solve first order ODEs. However, you can also use this technique to solve higher-order differential equations. The trick is to expand higher-order devivatives into a series of first-order ODEs. The Runge-Kutta method is then applied to each first-order ODE. For example, suppose you want to model a spring-mass system with damping, which can be described by the following second-order differential equations:

$$m\frac{d^2x}{dt^2} = -kx - b\frac{dx}{dt} \qquad (7.7)$$

where k is the spring constant and b is the damping coefficient. Since the velocity v = dx/dt, the equation of motion for a spring-mass system in Equation (7.7) can be rewritten in terms of two first-order differential equations:

$$\frac{dv}{dt} = -\frac{k}{m}x - \frac{b}{m}v$$
$$\frac{dx}{dt} = v \qquad (7.8)$$

In the above equation, the derivative of v is a function of v and x, and the derivative of x is a function of v. Since the solution of v as a function of time depends on x and the solution of x as a function of time depends on v, the two equations are coupled and must be solved simultaneously using the Runge-Kutta method.

Most of the ODEs in physics are higher-order ODEs. This means that you must expand them into a series of first-order ODEs before they can be solved using the Runge-Kutta method.

ODE Solver

Now it is time to implement the ODE solver based on the fourth-order Runge-Kutta technique. The solver will be written as generally as possible so that it can be used to solve any number of coupled first-order ODEs.

For a given set of initial values t0 and x0 (here, x0 is an array for multiple coupled ODEs), an increment value dt, and an array x that stores the solution, a function f(x,t) (also an array for multiple coupled ODEs), and a number of differential equations N, you can solve ODEs through the following steps:

- Set t = t0 and x = x0.
- Repeat the subsequent tasks for i = 0, to N-1.
- Set k1 = dt * f(x, t).
- Set k2 = dt * f(x + k1/2, t + dt/2).

- Set k3 = dt * f(x + k2/2, t + dt/2).
- Set k4 = dt * f(x + k3, t + dt);
- Set x = x + (k1 + k2 + k3 + k4)/6.
- Set x0 = x.
- Set t = t + dt.

Note that to solve for multiple coupled differential equations, the Runge-Kutta variables k1 to k4 must also be arrays.

Now, start with a new WPF Windows project and name it Chapter07. Add a new class, ODESolver, to the project. Here is the code listing of this class:

```
using System;
using System.Windows;

namespace Chapter07
{
    public class ODESolver
    {
        public delegate double Function(
            double[] x, double t);

        public static double[] RungeKutta4(
            Function[] f, double[] x0, double t0, double dt)
        {
            int n = x0.Length;
            double[] k1 = new double[n];
            double[] k2 = new double[n];
            double[] k3 = new double[n];
            double[] k4 = new double[n];

            double t = t0;
            double[] x1 = new double[n];
            double[] x = x0;

            for (int i = 0; i < n; i++)
                k1[i] = dt * f[i](x, t);

            for (int i = 0; i < n; i++)
                x1[i] = x[i] + k1[i] / 2;

            for (int i = 0; i < n; i++)
                k2[i] = dt * f[i](x1, t + dt / 2);

            for (int i = 0; i < n; i++)
                x1[i] = x[i] + k2[i] / 2;

            for (int i = 0; i < n; i++)
                k3[i] = dt * f[i](x1, t + dt / 2);

            for (int i = 0; i < n; i++)
                x1[i] = x[i] + k3[i];
```

```
for (int i = 0; i < n; i++)
    k4[i] = dt * f[i](x1, t + dt);

for (int i = 0; i < n; i++)
    x[i] +=
        (k1[i] + 2 * k2[i] + 2 * k3[i] + k4[i]) / 6;

        return x;
    }
}
}
```

Notice that here, you first define a delegate function that takes a double array x and a double time variable t as its input parameters. Then you implement a static method, RungeKutta4, that returns a double array as solutions to the ODEs. This method takes a Function array f, the initial values of the array x0, the initial time t0, and the time increment dt as input parameters. You can see that the delegate function can be used simply like a normal mathematical function, and is very easy to program.

The RungeKutta4 method looks quite simple and only takes a very short code listing. However, it is very powerful in the sense that it can be used to solve first-order ODEs with any number of coupled equations. To apply the ODESolver to a specific physics problem, you simply supply the function array, initial values, and time increment. The following sections will show you how to solve physics problems using this ODE solver.

Pendulum

Let's demonstrate the usefulness of the Runge-Kutta ODE solver by applying it to the problem of a pendulum system. A pendulum is an object that is attached to a pivot point so that it can swing freely. A simple example is the gravity pendulum, which is a mass on the end of a massless string.

Equation of Motion

The equation of motion for this pendulum system can be written in the form:

$$mL\frac{d^2\theta}{dt^2} = -mg\sin\theta - bL\frac{d\theta}{dt} \qquad (7.9)$$

Where m is the mass, L is the length of the string, g is the acceleration of gravity (= 9.81m/s^2), b is the damping coefficient, and θ is the swing angle. If you neglect the damping and have a very small swing angle, this equation of motion has a closed form solution. For a large swing angle and finite damping, you have to solve the equation numerically.

In order to solve this second-order differential equation using the Runge-Kutta method, you need to convert it into a coupled first-order ODEs. Let $d\theta/dt = \alpha$. You can then rewrite Equation (7.9) in the following form:

$$\frac{d\theta}{dt} = \alpha$$

$$\frac{d\alpha}{dt} = -\frac{g}{L}\sin\theta - \frac{b}{m}\alpha$$

$$(7.10)$$

This system consists of two coupled first-order ODEs.

Pendulum Simulator

Let's start with an example that simulates the motion of a pendulum and demonstrates how to solve Equation (7.10) numerically using the Runge-Kutta method. Add a new WPF Window to the project Chapter07 and name it Pendulum. A screen shot of the Pendulum Simulator is shown in Figure 7-1. A string with a mass hanging on one end is displayed in the bottom-left pane. The bottom-right pane shows how the swing angle changes with time. In addition, there are several TextBox fields that allow you to input the mass, string length, damping coefficient, initial angle, and initial angle velocity. A Start button begins the pendulum simulator, a Stop button stops the simulation, and a Reset button stops the simulation and returns the pendulum to its initial position.

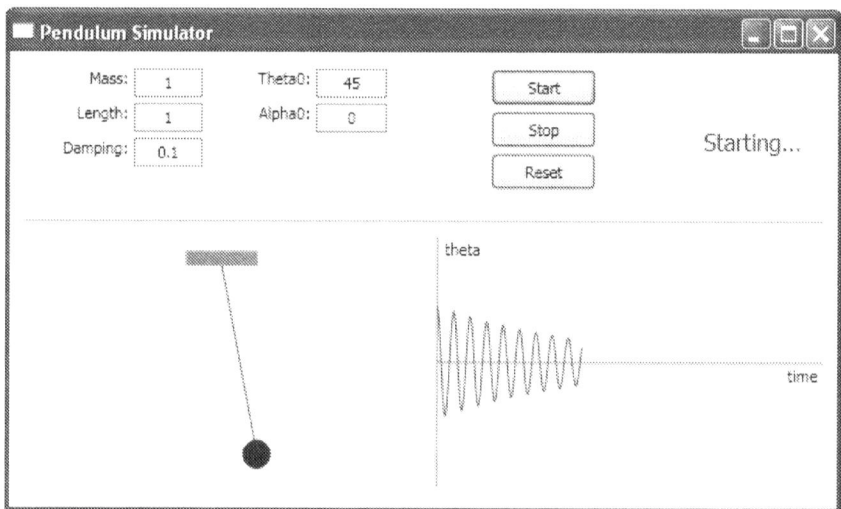

Figure 7-1 Pendulum Simulator.

The layout and user interface are implemented in the following XAML file:

```
<Window x:Class="Chapter07.Pendulum"
    xmlns="http://schemas.microsoft.com/winfx
        /2006/xaml/presentation"
    xmlns:x="http://schemas.microsoft.com/winfx/2006/xaml"
```

```
Title="Pendulum Simulator" Height="350" Width="600">

<Window.Resources>
    <Style TargetType="{x:Type TextBox}">
        <Setter Property="Width" Value="50"/>
        <Setter Property="Height" Value="20"/>
        <Setter Property="HorizontalAlignment"
                Value="Left"/>
        <Setter Property="TextAlignment" Value="Center"/>
        <Setter Property="Margin" Value="2"/>
    </Style>
    <Style TargetType="{x:Type TextBlock}">
        <Setter Property="Margin" Value="5,2,2,5"/>
        <Setter Property="Width" Value="70"/>
        <Setter Property="TextAlignment" Value="Right"/>
    </Style>
    <Style TargetType="{x:Type Button}">
        <Setter Property="Margin" Value="2"/>
        <Setter Property="Width" Value="75"/>
        <Setter Property="Height" Value="25"/>
    </Style>
</Window.Resources>

<StackPanel Margin="10">
    <StackPanel Orientation="Horizontal">
        <StackPanel>
            <StackPanel Orientation="Horizontal">
                <TextBlock>Mass:</TextBlock>
                <TextBox Name="tbMass" Text="1"/>
            </StackPanel>
            <StackPanel Orientation="Horizontal">
                <TextBlock>Length:</TextBlock>
                <TextBox Name="tbLength" Text="1"/>
            </StackPanel>
            <StackPanel Orientation="Horizontal">
                <TextBlock>Damping:</TextBlock>
                <TextBox Name="tbDamping" Text="0.1"/>
            </StackPanel>
        </StackPanel>
        <StackPanel>
            <StackPanel Orientation="Horizontal">
                <TextBlock>Theta0:</TextBlock>
                <TextBox Name="tbTheta0" Text="45"/>
            </StackPanel>
            <StackPanel Orientation="Horizontal">
                <TextBlock>Alpha0:</TextBlock>
                <TextBox Name="tbAlpha0" Text="0"/>
            </StackPanel>
        </StackPanel>
        <StackPanel Margin="70,0,0,10">
            <Button Click="btnStart_Click"
                    Content="Start"/>
            <Button Click="btnStop_Click" Content="Stop"/>
            <Button Click="btnReset_Click"
```

```
                        Content="Reset"/>
            </StackPanel>
            <StackPanel Margin="70,40,0,0">
                <TextBlock Name="tbDisplay" FontSize="16"
                        Foreground="DarkRed">Stopped
                </TextBlock>
            </StackPanel>
        </StackPanel>
        <Separator Margin="0,10,0,10"></Separator>
        <Viewbox Stretch="Fill">
            <Grid>
                <Grid.ColumnDefinitions>
                    <ColumnDefinition/>
                    <ColumnDefinition/>
                </Grid.ColumnDefinitions>

                <Canvas Name="canvasLeft" Grid.Column="0"
                        Width="280" Height="170">
                    <Rectangle Fill="DarkGoldenrod" Width="50"
                            Height="10" Canvas.Left="115"
                            Canvas.Top="10"/>
                    <Line Name="line1" X1 ="140" Y1="20"
                        X2="140" Y2="150" Stroke="Red"/>
                    <Path Fill="Blue">
                        <Path.Data>
                            <EllipseGeometry x:Name="ball"
                                        RadiusX="10"
                                        RadiusY="10"
                                        Center="140,150"/>
                        </Path.Data>
                    </Path>
                </Canvas>

                <Canvas Name="canvasRight" Grid.Column="1"
                        ClipToBounds="True" Width="280"
                        Height="170">
                    <Line X1="10" Y1="0" X2="10" Y2="170"
                        Stroke="Gray" StrokeThickness="1"/>
                    <Line X1="10" Y1="85" X2="280" Y2="85"
                        Stroke="Gray" StrokeThickness="1"/>
                    <TextBlock TextAlignment="Left"
                            Canvas.Left="10">theta
                    </TextBlock>
                    <TextBlock TextAlignment="Left"
                            Canvas.Left="250"
                            Canvas.Top="85">time
                    </TextBlock>
                </Canvas>
            </Grid>
        </Viewbox>
    </StackPanel>
</Window>
```

Here, you need an animation method to display the real-time motion of the pendulum on the screen. As you learned in the previous chapter, there are two techniques available for physics-based animations: per-frame animation and timer-based simulation. Either method works for the pendulum problem. I prefer to use per-frame animation. The following is the code-behind file of this example based on per-frame animation:

```csharp
using System;
using System.Windows;
using System.Windows.Controls;
using System.Windows.Input;
using System.Windows.Media;
using System.Windows.Shapes;

namespace Chapter07
{
    public partial class Pendulum : Window
    {
        private double PendulumMass = 1;
        private double PendulumLength = 1;
        private double DampingCoefficient = 0.5;
        private double Theta0 = 45;
        private double Alpha0 = 0;
        double[] xx = new double[2];

        double time = 0;
        double dt = 0.03;
        Polyline pl = new Polyline();

        double xMin = 0;
        Double yMin = -100;
        double xMax = 50;
        double yMax = 100;

        public Pendulum()
        {
            InitializeComponent();
        }

        private void btnStart_Click(
            object sender, RoutedEventArgs e)
        {
            PendulumMass = Double.Parse(tbMass.Text);
            PendulumLength = Double.Parse(tbLength.Text);
            DampingCoefficient = Double.Parse(tbDamping.Text);
            Theta0 = Double.Parse(tbTheta0.Text);
            Theta0 = Math.PI * Theta0 / 180;
            Alpha0 = Double.Parse(tbAlpha0.Text);
            Alpha0 = Math.PI * Alpha0 / 180;
            tbDisplay.Text = "Starting...";

            if (canvasRight.Children.Count > 4)
                canvasRight.Children.Remove(pl);
```

```
        pl = new Polyline();
        pl.Stroke = Brushes.Red;
        canvasRight.Children.Add(pl);

        time = 0;
        xx = new double[2] { Theta0, Alpha0 };
        CompositionTarget.Rendering += StartAnimation;
    }

    private void StartAnimation(
        object sender, EventArgs e)
    {
        // Invoke ODE solver:
        ODESolver.Function[] f =
            new ODESolver.Function[2] { f1, f2 };
        double[] result = ODESolver.RungeKutta4(
            f, xx, time, dt);

        // Display moving pendulum on screen:
        Point pt = new Point(
            140 + 130 * Math.Sin(result[0]),
            20 + 130 * Math.Cos(result[0]));
        ball.Center = pt;
        line1.X2 = pt.X;
        line1.Y2 = pt.Y;

        // Display theta - time curve on canvasRight:
        if (time < xMax)
            pl.Points.Add(new Point(XNormalize(time) + 10,
                YNormalize(180 * result[0] / Math.PI)));

        // Reset the initial values for next calculation:
        xx = result;
        time += dt;


        if (time > 0 && Math.Abs(result[0]) < 0.01 &&
            Math.Abs(result[1]) < 0.001)
        {
            tbDisplay.Text = "Stopped";
            CompositionTarget.Rendering -= StartAnimation;
        }
    }

    private void btnReset_Click(
        object sender, RoutedEventArgs e)
    {
        PendulumInitialize();
        tbDisplay.Text = "Stopped";
        if (canvasRight.Children.Count > 4)
            canvasRight.Children.Remove(pl);
        CompositionTarget.Rendering -= StartAnimation;
    }
```

```
private void PendulumInitialize()
{
    tbMass.Text = "1";
    tbLength.Text = "1";
    tbDamping.Text = "0.1";
    tbTheta0.Text = "45";
    tbAlpha0.Text = "0";
    line1.X2 = 140;
    line1.Y2 = 150;
    ball.Center = new Point(140, 150);
}

private void btnStop_Click(
    object sender, RoutedEventArgs e)
{
    line1.X2 = 140;
    line1.Y2 = 150;
    ball.Center = new Point(140, 150);
    tbDisplay.Text = "Stopped";
    CompositionTarget.Rendering -= StartAnimation;
}

private double f1(double[]xx, double t)
{
    return xx[1];
}

private double f2(double[] xx, double t)
{
    double m = PendulumMass;
    double L = PendulumLength;
    double g = 9.81;
    double b = DampingCoefficient;
    return -g * Math.Sin(xx[0]) / L - b * xx[1] / m;
}

private double XNormalize(double x)
{
    double result = (x - xMin) *
            canvasRight.Width / (xMax - xMin);
    return result;
}

private double YNormalize(double y)
{
    double result = canvasRight.Height - (y - yMin) *
        canvasRight.Height / (yMax - yMin);
    return result;
}
    }
}
```

Here, you first define several private members that can be changed by the user's inputs. You also define a constant time increment dt for the animation. Thus, the frame rate of the pendulum motion will depend on your computer and how many jobs you are running on your computer. You can control the animation speed by adjusting dt. If you want to have an animation that doesn't depend on the frame rate, you can do so using the approach presented in the PerFrameAnimation example in Chapter 6.

When the Start button is pressed, the input values for the mass, string length, damping coefficient, and initial position and velocity are obtained from the values inside their corresponding TextBox fields. At the same time, the event handler StartAnimation is attached to the static CompositionTarget.Rendering event.

Inside the StartAnimation event handler, you first create a function array, then call the static RungeKutta4 method in the ODESolver class using the statements:

```
ODESolver.Function[] f = new ODESolver.Function[2] { f1, f2 };
double[] result = ODESolver.RungeKutta4(f, xx, time, dt);
```

The methods f1 and f2 represent the functions on the right-hand side of Equation (7.10). The array xx in the RungeKutta4 method represents two dependent variables, θ and α. Namely, $xx[0] = \theta$ and $xx[1] = \alpha$. In this case, the result is also a double array which gives solutions to θ and α. With the animation progressing in a frame-by-frame manner, the RungeKutta4 method gets called continuously to update the string angle and angle velocity of the pendulum.

Once the new values of angle and velocity are obtained, you update the screen that shows the moving pendulum and the swing angle as a function of time on the screen. Next, you set the current solution as the initial values for the next round simulation.

When the swing angle and angle velocity are so small that the pendulum almost doesn't swing, you can stop the animation by detaching the StartAnimation event handler using the statement:

```
CompositionTarget.Rendering -= StartAnimation;
```

As you can see from this example, once the ODESolver class is written, it is a simple process to incorporate a pendulum into a game program. You can play around with the Pendulum Simulator by changing the values of the mass, damping coefficient, initial string angle, and initial angle velocity, and watch their effects on the motion of the pendulum.

Coupled-Spring System

In this section, you'll develop a spring simulator for a coupled spring system with three springs and two masses, as shown in Figure 7-2. This system is fixed at both ends. The parameters m_1 and m_2 represent masses; k_1, k_2, and k_3 are spring constants that define how stiff the springs are; and b_1, b_2, and b_3 are damping coefficients that characterize how quickly the springs' motion will stop.

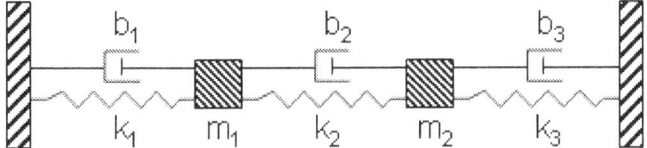

Figure 7-2 A spring-mass system.

Equations of Motion

The equations of motion for this system can be written in terms of two coupled second-order ODEs:

$$m_1 \frac{d^2 x_1}{dt^2} = -(k_1 + k_2)x_1 + k_2 x_2 - (b_1 + b_2)\frac{dx_1}{dt} + b_2 \frac{dx_2}{dt}$$
$$m_2 \frac{d^2 x_2}{dt^2} = -(k_2 + k_3)x_2 + k_2 x_1 - (b_2 + b_3)\frac{dx_2}{dt} + b_2 \frac{dx_1}{dt} \tag{7.11}$$

where x_1 and x_2 are the displacements of m_1 and m_2 respectively. There are no closed-form solutions to this set of coupled differential equations. In order to solve Equation (7.11) numerically using the Runge-Kutta method, you need to first convert it into a series of first-order ODEs. This can be easily done by introducing the velocity variables $v_1 = dx_1/dt$ and $v_2 = dx_2/dt$:

$$\frac{dx_1}{dt} = v_1$$
$$\frac{dx_2}{dt} = v_2$$
$$\frac{dv_1}{dt} = -\frac{1}{m_1}(k_1 + k_2)x_1 + \frac{k_2}{m_1}x_2 - \frac{1}{m_1}(b_1 + b_2)v_1 + \frac{b_2}{m_1}v_2 \tag{7.12}$$
$$\frac{dv_2}{dt} = -\frac{1}{m_2}(k_2 + k_3)x_2 + \frac{k_2}{m_2}x_1 - \frac{1}{m_2}(b_2 + b_3)v_2 + \frac{b_2}{m_2}v_1$$

These coupled first-order ODEs are ready to be solved using the Runge-Kutta method implemented in the ODESolver class.

Coupled Spring Simulator

Now we can develop the simulator for the coupled spring system. Add a new WPF Window to the project Chapter07 and name it CoupledSprings. Again, you'll create the layout and user interface for this example using XAML and perform the computation and animation in code. A sample screen shot of the layout of this example is shown in Figure 7-3.

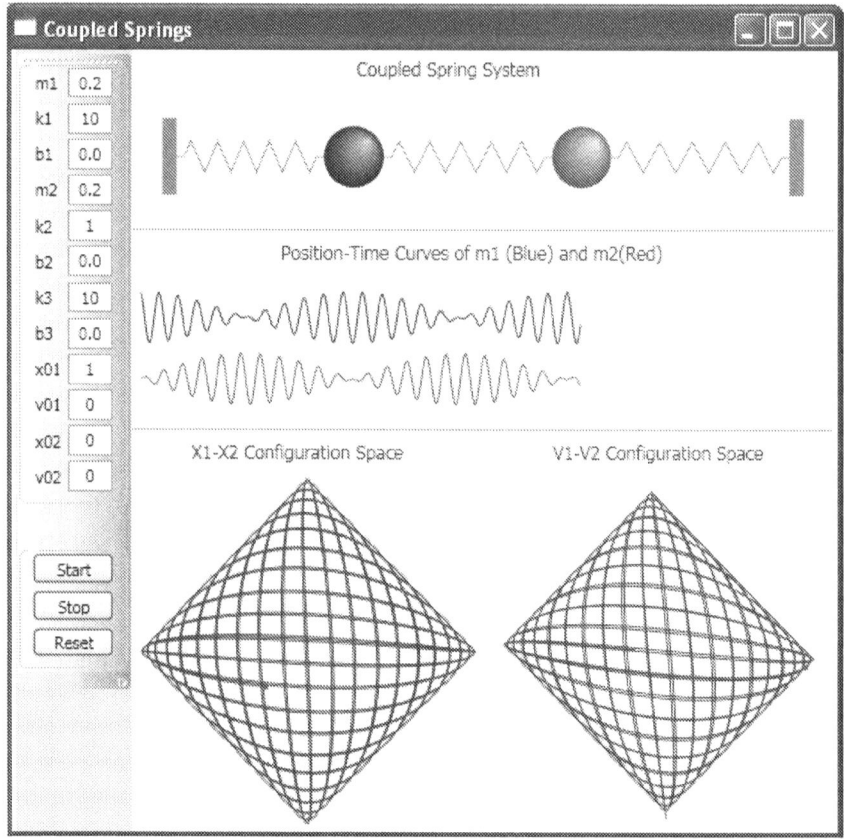

Figure 7-3 A coupled spring system.

You can see from this figure that in addition to the text fields for the masses, spring constants, and damping coefficients, there are also text fields for inputting the initial positions and velocities for m_1 and m_2. All of these parameters can be changed by the user, so this spring system simulator is very general. The right side shows various animation results. On the top shows how the coupled spring system moves during the simulation. The positions for m_1 and m_2 as a function of time are displayed in the middle pane, from which you can clearly see how the positions for these two masses respond differently to time. On the bottom illustrates the position (x_1 vs x_2) and velocity (v_1 vs v_2) phase diagrams. If you have ever played with an oscilloscope, you have probably seen the phase diagrams similar to those displayed here.

A Start button starts the simulation, a Stop buttom stops the simulation, and a Reset button is used to stop the simulation, return all parameters to their default values, and clear up the screen.

This layout is created using the following XAML code:

```
<Window x:Class="Chapter07.CoupledSprings"
    xmlns="http://schemas.microsoft.com/winfx
```

```xml
        /2006/xaml/presentation"
    xmlns:x="http://schemas.microsoft.com/winfx/2006/xaml"
    Title="Coupled Springs" Height="540" Width="560">

    <Window.Resources>
        <Style TargetType="{x:Type TextBox}">
            <Setter Property="Width" Value="30"/>
            <Setter Property="Height" Value="20"/>
            <Setter Property="HorizontalAlignment"
                    Value="Left"/>
            <Setter Property="TextAlignment" Value="Center"/>
            <Setter Property="Margin" Value="0,0,5,0"/>
        </Style>
        <Style TargetType="{x:Type TextBlock}">
            <Setter Property="Margin" Value="5,5,2,5"/>
        </Style>
        <Style TargetType="{x:Type Button}">
            <Setter Property="Margin" Value="2"/>
            <Setter Property="Width" Value="55"/>
            <Setter Property="Height" Value="20"/>
        </Style>
    </Window.Resources>

    <Viewbox Stretch="Uniform">
        <Grid>
            <Grid.ColumnDefinitions>
                <ColumnDefinition Width="Auto"/>
                <ColumnDefinition Width="Auto"/>
            </Grid.ColumnDefinitions>

            <ToolBarTray Orientation="Vertical"
                         Grid.Column="0">
                <ToolBar>
                    <StackPanel>
                        <GroupBox Margin="0">
                            <StackPanel>


                                <StackPanel
Orientation="Horizontal" VerticalAlignment="Top">
        <TextBlock Width="20">m1</TextBlock>
        <TextBox Name="tbm1" Text="0.2"/>
                                </StackPanel>
                                <StackPanel
Orientation="Horizontal" VerticalAlignment="Top">
        <TextBlock Width="20">k1</TextBlock>
        <TextBox Name="tbk1" Text="10"/>
                                </StackPanel>
                                <StackPanel
Orientation="Horizontal" VerticalAlignment="Top">
        <TextBlock Width="20">b1</TextBlock>
        <TextBox Name="tbb1" Text="0.0"/>
                                </StackPanel>
```

```xml
                                <StackPanel
        Orientation="Horizontal" VerticalAlignment="Top">
            <TextBlock Width="20">m2</TextBlock>
            <TextBox Name="tbm2" Text="0.2"/>
                                </StackPanel>
                                <StackPanel
        Orientation="Horizontal" VerticalAlignment="Top">
            <TextBlock Width="20">k2</TextBlock>
            <TextBox Name="tbk2" Text="1"/>
                                </StackPanel>
                                <StackPanel
        Orientation="Horizontal" VerticalAlignment="Top">
            <TextBlock Width="20">b2</TextBlock>
            <TextBox Name="tbb2" Text="0.0"/>
                                </StackPanel>
                                <StackPanel
        Orientation="Horizontal" VerticalAlignment="Top">
            <TextBlock Width="20">k3</TextBlock>
            <TextBox Name="tbk3" Text="10"/>
                                </StackPanel>
                                <StackPanel
        Orientation="Horizontal" VerticalAlignment="Top">
            <TextBlock Width="20">b3</TextBlock>
            <TextBox Name="tbb3" Text="0.0"/>
                                </StackPanel>
                                <StackPanel
        Orientation="Horizontal" VerticalAlignment="Top">
            <TextBlock Width="20">x01</TextBlock>
            <TextBox Name="tbx01" Text="1"/>
                                </StackPanel>
                                <StackPanel
        Orientation="Horizontal" VerticalAlignment="Top">
            <TextBlock Width="20">v01</TextBlock>
            <TextBox Name="tbv01" Text="0"/>
                                </StackPanel>
                                <StackPanel
        Orientation="Horizontal" VerticalAlignment="Top">
            <TextBlock Width="20">x02</TextBlock>
            <TextBox Name="tbx02" Text="0"/>
                                </StackPanel>
                                <StackPanel
        Orientation="Horizontal" VerticalAlignment="Top">
            <TextBlock Width="20">v02</TextBlock>
            <TextBox Name="tbv02" Text="0"/>
                                </StackPanel>
                            </StackPanel>
                        </GroupBox>

                        <GroupBox Margin="0,30,0,0">
                            <StackPanel>
            <Button Name="btnStart" Click="btnStart_Click"
                Content="Start"/>
            <Button Name="btnStop" Click="btnStop_Click"
                Content="Stop"/>
```

```xml
<Button Name="btnReset" Click="btnReset_Click"
        Content="Reset"/>
                    </StackPanel>
                </GroupBox>
            </StackPanel>
        </ToolBar>
    </ToolBarTray>

    <StackPanel Grid.Column="1">
        <TextBlock FontSize="12" Foreground="DarkRed"
                   Margin="150,5,5,5">Coupled Spring
                   System</TextBlock>
        <Canvas Name="canvas1" Width="470"
                Height="90">
            <Rectangle Width="10" Height="50"
                       Fill="DarkGoldenrod"
                       Canvas.Left="20"
                       Canvas.Top="20"/>
            <Rectangle Width="10" Height="50"
                       Fill="DarkGoldenrod"
                       Canvas.Left="440"
                       Canvas.Top="20"/>
<Polyline Name="spring1" Canvas.Left="30"
          Canvas.Top="35" Stroke="Gray"
          Points="0,10 5,10 10,0 20,20 30,0 40,
                  20 50,0 60,20 70,0 80,20 90,
                  0 100,20 105,10 110,10"/>
            <Path>
                <Path.Fill>
<RadialGradientBrush GradientOrigin="0.75,0.25">
    <GradientStop Color="LightBlue" Offset="0"/>
    <GradientStop Color="Blue" Offset="1"/>
</RadialGradientBrush>
                </Path.Fill>
                <Path.Data>
<EllipseGeometry x:Name="mass1" RadiusX="20"
                 RadiusY="20" Center="160,45"/>
                </Path.Data>
            </Path>

<Polyline Name="spring2" Canvas.Left="180"
          Canvas.Top="35" Stroke="Gray"
          Points="0,10 5,10 10,0 20,20 30,0 40,
                  20 50,0 60,20 70,0 80,20 90,
                  0 100,20 105,10 110,10"/>
            <Path>
                <Path.Fill>
<RadialGradientBrush GradientOrigin="0.75,0.25">
    <GradientStop Color="Yellow" Offset="0"/>
    <GradientStop Color="Red" Offset="1"/>
</RadialGradientBrush>
                </Path.Fill>
                <Path.Data>
<EllipseGeometry x:Name="mass2" RadiusX="20"
```

```
                        RadiusY="20" Center="310,45"/>
                    </Path.Data>
                </Path>

        <Polyline Name="spring3" Canvas.Right="30"
                Canvas.Top="35" Stroke="Gray"
                Points="0,10 5,10 10,0 20,20 30,0 40,
                        20 50,0 60,20 70,0 80,20 90,
                        0 100,20 105,10 110,10"/>
            </Canvas>
            <Separator></Separator>
        <TextBlock FontSize="12" Foreground="DarkRed"
            Margin="100,5,5,5">Position-Time Curves of m1
                (Blue) and m2(Red)</TextBlock>
                <Canvas Name="canvas2" ClipToBounds="True"
                        Height="100" Width="460">
                </Canvas>

                <Separator></Separator>
                <StackPanel Orientation="Horizontal">
        <TextBlock FontSize="12" Foreground="DarkRed"
            Margin="40,5,5,5">X1-X2 Configuration
            Space</TextBlock>
        <TextBlock FontSize="12" Foreground="DarkRed"
            Margin="95,5,5,5">V1-V2 Configuration
            Space</TextBlock>
            </StackPanel>
                <StackPanel Orientation="Horizontal">
                    <Canvas Name="canvas3" Height="225"
                            Width="225" Margin="5"
                            ClipToBounds="True">
                        <Path Name="path1">
                            <Path.Data>
        <EllipseGeometry x:Name="redDot1" RadiusX="2"
                    RadiusY="2" Center="10,10"/>
                            </Path.Data>
                        </Path>
                    </Canvas>

                    <Canvas Name="canvas4" Height="225"
                            Width="225" Margin="5"
                            ClipToBounds="True">
                        <Path Name="path2">
                            <Path.Data>
        <EllipseGeometry x:Name="redDot2" RadiusX="2"
                    RadiusY="2" Center="10,10"/>
                            </Path.Data>
                        </Path>
                    </Canvas>
                </StackPanel>
            </StackPanel>
        </Grid>
    </Viewbox>
</Window>
```

Here, you'll also use the per-frame animation approach to display the real-time motion of the spring-mass system. The following is the corresponding C# code of this example based on per-frame animation:

```
using System;
using System.Windows;
using System.Windows.Controls;
using System.Windows.Input;
using System.Windows.Media;
using System.Windows.Shapes;

namespace Chapter07
{
    public partial class CoupledSprings : Window
    {
        private double M1;
        private double K1;
        private double B1;
        private double M2;
        private double K2;
        private double B2;
        private double K3;
        private double B3;
        private double X01;
        private double X02;
        private double V01;
        private double V02;

        private double xb1 = 3.4;
        private double xb2 = 6.6;

        double[] xx = new double[4];
        double[] result = new double[4];
        double time = 0;
        double dt = 0.02;
        Polyline pl1 = new Polyline();
        Polyline pl2 = new Polyline();
        Polyline pl3 = new Polyline();
        Polyline pl4 = new Polyline();

        public CoupledSprings()
        {
            InitializeComponent();
            pl1.Stroke = Brushes.Blue;
            canvas2.Children.Add(pl1);
            pl2.Stroke = Brushes.Blue;
            canvas3.Children.Add(pl2);
            SpringsInitialize();
        }

        private void SpringsInitialize()
        {
            tbm1.Text = "0.2";
            tbk1.Text = "10";
```

```
        tbb1.Text = "0.0";
        tbm2.Text = "0.2";
        tbk2.Text = "1";
        tbb2.Text = "0.0";
        tbk3.Text = "10";
        tbb3.Text = "0.0";
        tbx01.Text = "1";
        tbv01.Text = "0";
        tbx02.Text = "0";
        tbv02.Text = "0";
}

private void btnStart_Click(
    object sender, RoutedEventArgs e)
{
    // Get input parameters:
    M1 = Double.Parse(tbm1.Text);
    K1 = Double.Parse(tbk1.Text);
    B1 = Double.Parse(tbb1.Text);
    M2 = Double.Parse(tbm2.Text);
    K2 = Double.Parse(tbk2.Text);
    B2 = Double.Parse(tbb2.Text);
    K3 = Double.Parse(tbk3.Text);
    B3 = Double.Parse(tbb3.Text);
    X01 = Double.Parse(tbx01.Text);
    X02 = Double.Parse(tbx02.Text);
    V01 = Double.Parse(tbv01.Text);
    V02 = Double.Parse(tbv02.Text);

    // Add polylines for displaying
    // positions of m1 and m2:
    canvas2.Children.Clear();
    pl1 = new Polyline();
    pl1.Stroke = Brushes.Blue;
    canvas2.Children.Add(pl1);
    pl2 = new Polyline();
    pl2.Stroke = Brushes.Red;
    canvas2.Children.Add(pl2);

    // Add polylines for displaying
    // position phase diagram:
    canvas3.Children.Clear();
    path1.Fill = Brushes.Red;
    pl3 = new Polyline();
    pl3.Stroke = Brushes.DarkGreen;
    canvas3.Children.Add(pl3);
    canvas3.Children.Add(path1);

    // Add polylines for displaying
    // velocity phase diagram:
    canvas4.Children.Clear();
    path2.Fill = Brushes.Red;
    pl4 = new Polyline();
    pl4.Stroke = Brushes.DarkGreen;
```

```
    canvas4.Children.Add(pl4);
    canvas4.Children.Add(path2);

    time = 0;
    xx = new double[4] { X01, X02, V01, V02 };
    CompositionTarget.Rendering += StartAnimation;
}

private void StartAnimation(
    object sender, EventArgs e)
{
    // Calculate positions of m1 and m2:
    ODESolver.Function[] f =
        new ODESolver.Function[4] { f1, f2, f3, f4 };
    result = ODESolver.RungeKutta4(f, xx, time, dt);

    AnimatingSprings();
    DisplayPositions();
    PositionPhase();
    VelocityPhase();

    xx = result;
    time += dt;
    if (time > 0 && Math.Abs(result[0]) < 0.01 &&
        Math.Abs(result[1]) < 0.01 &&
        Math.Abs(result[2]) < 0.005 &&
        Math.Abs(result[2]) < 0.005)
    {
        CompositionTarget.Rendering -= StartAnimation;
    }
}

private void AnimatingSprings()
{
    Point pt1 = new Point(XNormalize(canvas1,
        xb1 + result[0], 0, 10), 45);
    Point pt2 = new Point(XNormalize(canvas1,
        xb2 + result[1], 0, 10), 45);
    mass1.Center = pt1;
    mass2.Center = pt2;

    // Animate spring1:
    int n = spring1.Points.Count;
    double delta = (pt1.X - 70) / (n - 5);
    spring1.Points[2] = new Point(
        spring1.Points[1].X + 0.5 * delta,
        spring1.Points[2].Y);
    spring1.Points[n - 1] = new Point(
        pt1.X - 50, spring1.Points[n - 1].Y);
    spring1.Points[n - 2] = new Point(
        pt1.X - 55, spring1.Points[n - 2].Y);
    spring1.Points[n - 3] = new Point(
        spring1.Points[n - 2].X - 0.5 * delta,
        spring1.Points[n - 3].Y);
```

```
for (int i = 3; i < n - 3; i++)
{
    spring1.Points[i] = new Point(
        10 + (i - 2) * delta,
        spring1.Points[i].Y);
}

// Animate spring2:
Canvas.SetLeft(spring2, pt1.X + 20);
delta = (pt2.X - pt1.X - 60) / (n - 5);
spring2.Points[2] = new Point(
    spring2.Points[1].X + 0.5 * delta,
    spring2.Points[2].Y);
for (int i = 3; i < n - 3; i++)
{
    spring2.Points[i] = new Point(
        10 + (i - 2) * delta, spring2.Points[i].Y);
}
spring2.Points[n - 1] = new Point(
    pt2.X - pt1.X - 40, spring2.Points[n - 1].Y);
spring2.Points[n - 2] = new Point(
    pt2.X - pt1.X - 45, spring2.Points[n - 2].Y);
spring2.Points[n - 3] = new Point(
    spring2.Points[n - 2].X - 0.5 * delta,
    spring2.Points[n - 3].Y);

// Animate spring3:
spring3.Points[0] = new Point(
    XNormalize(canvas1, result[1], 0, 10),
    spring3.Points[0].Y);
spring3.Points[1] = new Point(
    spring3.Points[0].X + 5, spring3.Points[1].Y);
delta = (spring3.Points[n - 1].X -
    spring3.Points[0].X - 20) / (n - 5);
spring3.Points[2] = new Point(
    spring3.Points[1].X + 0.5 * delta,
    spring3.Points[2].Y);
spring3.Points[n - 3] = new Point(
    spring3.Points[n - 2].X - 0.5 * delta,
    spring3.Points[n - 3].Y);
for (int i = 3; i < n - 3; i++)
{
    spring3.Points[i] =
        new Point(spring3.Points[2].X +
        (i - 2) * delta, spring3.Points[i].Y);
}
}

private void DisplayPositions()
{
    // Shaw positions of m1 and m2:
    if (time < 30)
    {
        pl1.Points.Add(new Point(
```

```
            XNormalize(canvas2, time, 0, 30),
            YNormalize(canvas2,
            result[0], 0, 6) - 70));
        pl2.Points.Add(new Point(
            XNormalize(canvas2, time, 0, 30),
            YNormalize(canvas2,
            result[1], 0, 6) - 30));
    }
}

private void PositionPhase()
{
    if (time < 30)
    {
        pl3.Points.Add(new Point(
            XNormalize(canvas3, result[0], -1, 1),
            YNormalize(canvas3, result[1], -1, 1)));
        redDot1.Center = new Point(
            XNormalize(canvas3, result[0], -1, 1),
            YNormalize(canvas3, result[1], -1, 1));
    }
}

private void VelocityPhase()
{
    if (time < 30)
    {
        pl4.Points.Add(new Point(
            XNormalize(canvas4, result[2], -8, 8),
            YNormalize(canvas4, result[3], -8, 8)));
        redDot2.Center = new Point(
            XNormalize(canvas4, result[2], -8, 8),
            YNormalize(canvas4, result[3], -8, 8));
    }
}

private double f1(double[] xx, double t)
{
    return xx[2];
}

private double f2(double[] xx, double t)
{
    return xx[3];
}

private double f3(double[] xx, double t)
{
    return -(K1 + K2) * xx[0] / M1 + K2 * xx[1] / M1 -
        (B1 + B2) * xx[2] / M1 + B2 * xx[3] / M1;
}

private double f4(double[] xx, double t)
{
```

```
                    return -(K2 + K3) * xx[1] / M2 + K2 * xx[0] / M2 -
                        (B2 + B3) * xx[3] / M2 + B2 * xx[2] / M2;
            }


            private void btnReset_Click(object sender,
                RoutedEventArgs e)
            {
                SpringsInitialize();
                canvas2.Children.Clear();
                canvas3.Children.Clear();
                canvas4.Children.Clear();
                CompositionTarget.Rendering -= StartAnimation;
            }

            private void btnStop_Click(object sender,
                RoutedEventArgs e)
            {
                CompositionTarget.Rendering -= StartAnimation;
            }

            private double XNormalize(Canvas canvas, double x,
                double min, double max)
            {
                double result = (x - min) *
                        canvas.Width / (max - min);
                return result;
            }

            private double YNormalize(Canvas canvas, double y,
                double min, double max)
            {
                double result = canvas.Height - (y - min) *
                    canvas.Height / (max - min);
                return result;
            }
        }
    }
```

The above code seems to be very involved. However, the basic structure of the implementation is similar to that of the previous example. Most of the code deals with how to correctly display the simulation results on the screen. At the beginning, you define several private members that can be changed by the user's inputs. When the Start button is clicked, the program gets the input parameters and invokes a StartAnimation event handler through the CompositionTarget.Rendering event.

Inside the event handler, you call the RungeKutta4 method to solve the ODEs for this spring system with the statements:

```
    ODESolver.Function[] f =
            new ODESolver.Function[4] { f1, f2, f3, f4 };
    result = ODESolver.RungeKutta4(f, xx, time, dt);
```

Here you define a function array with four components which correspond to the right-hand side of Equation (7.12). The double array xx in the above statement is defined as

```
xx = new double[4] { X01, X02, V01, V02 };
```

Correspondingly, the solution should be x_1 = result[0], x_2 = result[1], v_1 = result[2], and v_2 = result[3]. You then use the solution to update the motion of the spring system and the results displayed on your screen, including the positions as a function of time and position- and velocity-phase diagrams.

When you animate the motion of the spring system, you should remember that you need to consider not only the two masses m_1 and m_2, but also the three springs characterized by the spring constants k_1, k_2, and k_3. The AnimatingSprings method presents the detailed procedure of how to properly animate the spring system. The other animation results shown in Figure 7-3 are produced using the DisplayPosition (used to animate positions vs time), PositionPhase, and VelocityPhase methods.

Projectiles

In this section, you'll learn how to model the flight of a projectile. You have probably worked with projectiles quite a bit in your game programming, including bullets, golf balls, and tennis balls. Simulating projectlite is a straightforward application of Newtonian mechanics and kinetics in physics.

Here, we'll consider two kinds of forces acting on a projectile: gravity and aerodynamic drag force. Effects, such as wind, Laminar and turbulent flows, and spin, will be neglected. We'll also create a golf game based on projectile physics.

Aerodynamic Drag Force

Aerodynamic drag is the resistance force that air exerts on a projectile traveling through it, and directly affects the trajectory of the projectile. This drag force acts in the opposite direction of the velocity of the projectile.

The aerodynamic drag force depends on the geometry of the object, the density of the air, and the square of the velocity. Drag force is usually expressed in the form:

$$F_D = \frac{1}{2} C_D \rho \, A v^2 \qquad (7.13)$$

where F_D stands for the drag force, C_D is the drag coefficient, ρ is the density of the air, v is the velocity, and A is the characteristic body area which depends on the body geometry. For most objects, A is taken to be the frontal area. For a sphere, the frontal area would be the cross-section area; i.e., $A = \pi \, r^2$.

Projectile Equations of Motion

You are now ready to add aerodynamic drag force to the projectile trajectory model. For a projectile that travels in a 2D space, the total drag force in Equation (7.13) needs to be split into directional components. Because the drag force acts in the opposite direction of velocity, the X- and Y-components of the drag force will be in the same proportion relative to each other as the X- and Y-components of velocity, but the signs will be reversed. Thus, the projected drag force on the X- and Y-direction can be written in the following form:

$$F_{Dx} = -F_D \frac{v_x}{v}$$

$$F_{Dy} = -F_D \frac{v_y}{v}$$

(7.14)

where the total magnitude of the velocity $v = \sqrt{v_x^2 + v_y^2}$. The negative signs in the above equation indicate that the drag force acts in the opposite direction of the velocity. The drag force in Equation (7.14) can be easily added to the projectile equation of motion:

$$m \frac{d^2x}{dt^2} = -F_D \frac{v_x}{v}$$

$$m \frac{d^2y}{dt^2} = -mg - F_D \frac{v_y}{v}$$

(7.15)

There are no analytical solutions to this set of coupled differential equations. In order to solve Equation (7.15) numerically using the Runge-Kutta method, you need to first convert it into a series of first-order ODEs. This can be done easily by introducing the velocity variables $v_x = dx/dt$ and $v_y = dy/dt$:

$$\frac{dx}{dt} = v_x$$

$$\frac{dy}{dt} = v_y$$

$$\frac{dv_x}{dt} = -\frac{F_D v_x}{mv}$$

$$\frac{dv_y}{dt} = -g - \frac{F_D v_y}{mv}$$

(7.16)

These coupled first-order ODEs are ready to be solved using the Runge-Kutta method.

Golf Game

Let's create a simple golf game based on the projectile equations of motion described in Equation (7.16). The objective of the game is to hit a golf ball into a hole. A sample screen shot of the GolfGame is shown in Figure 7-4.

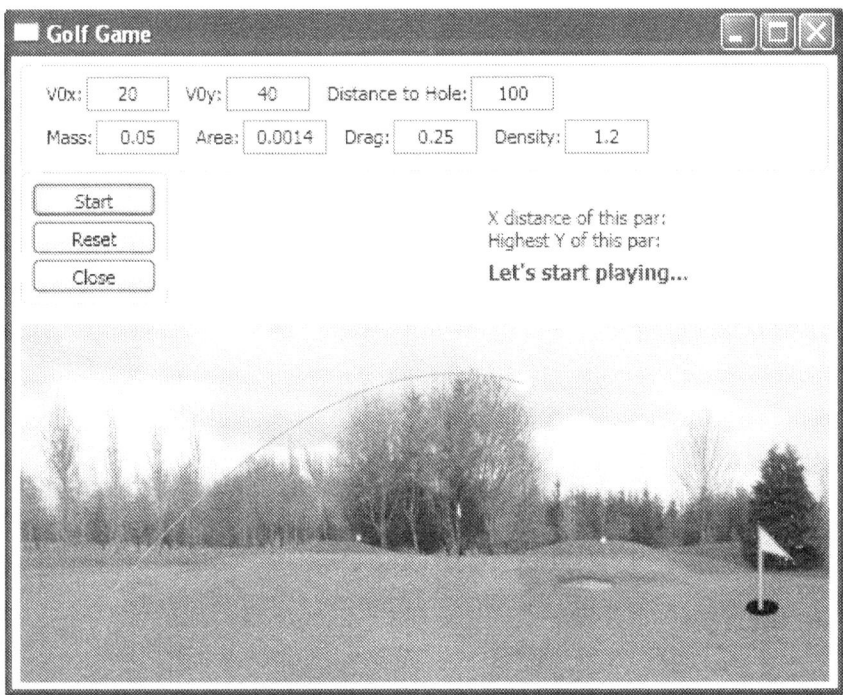

Figure 7-4 Galf game.

The layout and user interface consist of text fields that are used to input the initial velocity components of the golf ball. These values can be changed to adjust the trajectory of the ball. The Distance to Hole field lets you adjust the distance from the tee to the flag. The other text fields allow you to input the mass, area, drag coefficient, and the density of the air. These parameters are used to calculate the drag force acting on the golf ball.

To create such a golf game, you need to add a new WPF Window to the project Chapter07 and name it GolfGame. The layout shown in Figure 7-4 is created using the following XAML file:

```
<Window x:Class="Chapter07.GolfGame"
    xmlns="http://schemas.microsoft.com/winfx
        /2006/xaml/presentation"
    xmlns:x="http://schemas.microsoft.com/winfx/2006/xaml"
    Title="Golf Game" Height="400" Width="500">

    <Window.Resources>
        <Style TargetType="{x:Type TextBox}">
```

```xml
            <Setter Property="Width" Value="50"/>
            <Setter Property="Height" Value="20"/>
            <Setter Property="HorizontalAlignment"
                    Value="Left"/>
            <Setter Property="TextAlignment" Value="Center"/>
            <Setter Property="Margin" Value="0,0,5,0"/>
        </Style>
        <Style TargetType="{x:Type TextBlock}">
            <Setter Property="Margin" Value="5,5,2,5"/>
        </Style>
        <Style TargetType="{x:Type Button}">
            <Setter Property="Margin" Value="1"/>
            <Setter Property="Width" Value="75"/>
            <Setter Property="Height" Value="20"/>
        </Style>
    </Window.Resources>

    <Grid>
        <Grid.RowDefinitions>
            <RowDefinition Height="150"/>
            <RowDefinition Height="Auto"/>
        </Grid.RowDefinitions>

        <StackPanel Margin="5" Grid.Row="0">
            <GroupBox>
                <StackPanel>
                    <StackPanel Orientation="Horizontal"
                            Margin="5,5,5,0">
                        <TextBlock>V0x:</TextBlock>
                        <TextBox Name="tbV0x" Text="20"/>
                        <TextBlock>V0y:</TextBlock>
                        <TextBox Name="tbV0y" Text="40"/>
                        <TextBlock Text="Distance to Hole:"/>
                        <TextBox Name="tbDistance"
                                Text="100"/>
                    </StackPanel>
                    <StackPanel Orientation="Horizontal"
                            Margin="5,2,5,2">
                        <TextBlock>Mass:</TextBlock>
                        <TextBox Name="tbMass" Text="0.05"/>
                        <TextBlock>Area:</TextBlock>
                        <TextBox Name="tbArea" Text="0.0014"/>
                        <TextBlock>Drag:</TextBlock>
                        <TextBox Name="tbDrag" Text="0.25"/>
                        <TextBlock>Density:</TextBlock>
                        <TextBox Name="tbDensity" Text="1.2"/>
                    </StackPanel>
                </StackPanel>
            </GroupBox>
            <StackPanel Orientation="Horizontal">
                <GroupBox Margin="0">
                    <StackPanel Margin="0,5,0,0"
                            HorizontalAlignment="Left">
                        <Button Name="btnStart"
```

```xml
                                Click="btnStart_Click"
                                Content="Start"/>
                    <Button Name="btnReset"
                                Click="btnReset_Click"
                                Content="Reset"/>
                    <Button Name="btnClose"
                                Click="btnClose_Click"
                                Content="Close"/>
                </StackPanel>
            </GroupBox>
            <StackPanel Margin="190,0,0,0"
                            HorizontalAlignment="Left">
                <TextBlock Name="tbXMax"
                                Foreground="DarkRed"
                                Margin="0,20,0,0"
                                Text="X distance of this par:"/>
                <TextBlock Name="tbYMax"
                                Foreground="DarkRed"
                                Margin="0"
                                Text="Highest Y of this par:"/>
                <TextBlock Name="tbResult"
                                Foreground="DarkRed"
                                FontSize="12" FontWeight="Bold"
                                Margin="0,5,0,0"
                                Text="Let's start playing..."/>
            </StackPanel>
        </StackPanel>
    </StackPanel>

    <Viewbox Stretch="Fill" Grid.Row="1">
        <Canvas Name="canvas1" Width="500" Height="215"
                Margin="5">
            <Canvas.Background>
                <ImageBrush ImageSource="golf01.gif"
                            Stretch="Fill"/>
            </Canvas.Background>

            <Ellipse Name="golfBall" Fill="White"
                        Width="10" Height="10"
                        Canvas.Top="170" Canvas.Left="30"/>
            <Ellipse Name="golfHole" Fill="Black"
                        Width="20" Height="10"
                        Canvas.Top="170" Canvas.Left="450"/>
            <Polygon Name="golfFlag" Canvas.Top="175"
                        Canvas.Left="459"
                        Stroke="DarkGoldenrod"
                        Fill="LightGray"
                        Points="0,0 0,-50 20,-30 2,-35 2,0"/>
        </Canvas>
    </Viewbox>
  </Grid>
</Window>
```

Note that the background of the golf court is created from an image file called golf01.gif. The simulation and animation are performed in the corresponding code-behind file using the Runge-Kutta method and per-frame animation respectively. The following is the code-behind file of this example:

```
using System;
using System.Windows;
using System.Windows.Controls;
using System.Windows.Input;
using System.Windows.Media;
using System.Windows.Shapes;

namespace Chapter07
{
    public partial class GolfGame : Window
    {
        double xMin = 0;
        double yMin = 0;
        double xMax = 100;
        double yMax = 100;

        double X0 = 20;
        double Y0 = 20;
        double V0x = 10;
        double V0y = 10;
        double BallMass = 0.05;
        double BallArea = 0.0014;
        double DragCoefficient = 0.25;
        double AirDensity = 1.2;
        double DistanceToHole = 100;

        double[] xx = new double[4];

        double time = 0;
        double dt = 0.1;
        double gravity = 9.81;
        double ym = 0;
        Polyline pl = new Polyline();

        public GolfGame()
        {
            InitializeComponent();
            pl.Stroke = Brushes.Blue;
            canvas1.Children.Add(pl);
            GolfGameInitialize();
        }

        private void GolfGameInitialize()
        {
            tbV0x.Text = "20";
            tbV0y.Text = "40";
            tbDistance.Text = "100";
            tbMass.Text = "0.05";
```

```
    tbArea.Text = "0.0014";
    tbDrag.Text = "0.25";
    tbDensity.Text = "1.2";

    tbXMax.Text = "X distance of this par:";
    tbYMax.Text = "Highest Y of this par:";
    tbResult.Text = "Let's start playing...";
    xMin = X0 - 0.1 * DistanceToHole;
    yMin = X0 - 0.2 * DistanceToHole;
    xMax = X0 + 1.1 * DistanceToHole;
    yMax = X0 + 0.7 * DistanceToHole;
    Canvas.SetLeft(golfBall, XNormalize(X0));
    Canvas.SetTop(golfBall, YNormalize(Y0));
    Canvas.SetLeft(golfHole,
            XNormalize(X0 + DistanceToHole) - 10);
    Canvas.SetTop(golfHole, YNormalize(Y0) - 2);
    Canvas.SetLeft(golfFlag,
            XNormalize(X0 + DistanceToHole) - 2);
    Canvas.SetTop(golfFlag, YNormalize(Y0) + 4);
}

private void btnStart_Click(object sender,
        RoutedEventArgs e)
{
    time = 0;
    dt = 0.1;

    // Add trace curve:
    if (canvas1.Children.Count > 3)
        canvas1.Children.Remove(pl);
    pl = new Polyline();
    pl.Stroke = Brushes.LightCoral;
    canvas1.Children.Add(pl);

    // Get input parameters:
    V0x = Double.Parse(tbV0x.Text);
    V0y = Double.Parse(tbV0y.Text);
    DistanceToHole = Double.Parse(tbDistance.Text);
    BallMass = Double.Parse(tbMass.Text);
    BallArea = Double.Parse(tbArea.Text);
    DragCoefficient = Double.Parse(tbDrag.Text);
    AirDensity = Double.Parse(tbDensity.Text);

    // Set the axis limits:
    xMin = X0 - 0.1 * DistanceToHole;
    yMin = X0 - 0.2 * DistanceToHole;
    xMax = X0 + 1.1 * DistanceToHole;
    yMax = X0 + 0.7 * DistanceToHole;

    // Set the golf court:
    Canvas.SetLeft(golfHole,
            XNormalize(X0 + DistanceToHole) - 10);
    Canvas.SetTop(golfHole, YNormalize(Y0) - 2);
    Canvas.SetLeft(golfFlag,
```

```
            XNormalize(X0 + DistanceToHole) - 2);
        Canvas.SetTop(golfFlag, YNormalize(Y0) + 4);
        tbXMax.Text = "X distance of this par:";
        tbYMax.Text = "Highest Y of this par:";
        tbResult.Text = "Let's start playing...";

        xx = new double[4] { X0, Y0, V0x, V0y };
        CompositionTarget.Rendering += StartAnimation;
    }

    private void StartAnimation(object sender,
            EventArgs e)
    {
        // Calculate the golf ball position:
        ODESolver.Function[] f =
            new ODESolver.Function[4] { f1, f2, f3, f4 };
        double[] result =
            ODESolver.RungeKutta4(f, xx, time, dt);
        xx = result;

        double x = result[0];
        double y = result[1];

        if (y > ym)
            ym = y;

        if (y >= Y0)
        {
            Canvas.SetLeft(golfBall, XNormalize(x));
            Canvas.SetTop(golfBall, YNormalize(y));
            pl.Points.Add(new Point(XNormalize(x) + 5,
                        YNormalize(y) + 5));
        }
        if (x > X0 && y <= Y0)
        {
            double xm = Math.Round(x-X0);
            ym = Math.Round(ym-Y0);
            tbXMax.Text = "X distance of this par: " +
                        xm.ToString() + " m";
            tbYMax.Text = "Highest Y of this par: " +
                        ym.ToString() + " m";
            if (xm > DistanceToHole - 10 &&
                xm < DistanceToHole + 10)
                tbResult.Text =
                        "Congratulations! You win.";
            else
                tbResult.Text = "You missed. Try again.";
            CompositionTarget.Rendering -= StartAnimation;
        }
        time += dt;
    }

    private double f1(double[] xx, double t)
    {
```

```
        return xx[2];
}

private double f2(double[] xx, double t)
{
        return xx[3];
}

private double f3(double[] xx, double t)
{
        double A = BallArea;
        double rho = AirDensity;
        double cd = DragCoefficient;
        double m = BallMass;
        double fd = 0.5 * rho * A * cd * (xx[2] * xx[2] +
                xx[3] * xx[3]);
        return -fd * xx[2] / m / Math.Sqrt(xx[2] * xx[2] +
                xx[3] * xx[3] + 1.0e-10);
}

private double f4(double[] xx, double t)
{
        double A = BallArea;
        double rho = AirDensity;
        double cd = DragCoefficient;
        double m = BallMass;
        double fd = 0.5 * rho * A * cd * (xx[2] * xx[2] +
                xx[3] * xx[3]);
        return -gravity - fd * xx[3] / m / Math.Sqrt(xx[2]
                * xx[2] + xx[3] * xx[3] + 1.0e-10);
}

private double XNormalize(double x)
{
        double result = (x - xMin) *
                canvas1.Width / (xMax - xMin);
        return result;
}

private double YNormalize(double y)
{
        double result = canvas1.Height - (y - yMin) *
                canvas1.Height / (yMax - yMin);
        return result;
}

private void btnReset_Click(object sender,
        RoutedEventArgs e)
{
        GolfGameInitialize();
        if (canvas1.Children.Count > 3)
                canvas1.Children.Remove(pl);
}
```

```
private void btnClose_Click(object sender,
        RoutedEventArgs e)
{
    this.Close();
}
}
}
```

Like the spring system discussed previously, you first define several private members that can be changed by the user's inputs. When the Start button is clicked, the values from the TextBox fields are obtained, and these values are used to initialize the ODESolver. To start the animation, the StartAnimation event handler is attached to the static CompositionTarget.Rendering event.

Inside the event handler, you call the RungeKutta4 method to solve the ODEs for the golf ball described by Equation (7.16). Here you define a function array with four components, which correspond to the right-hand side of Equation (7.16). The double array xx in the above statement is defined as

```
xx = new double[4] { x0, y0, V0x, V0y };
```

Correspondingly, the solution should be x = result[0], y = result[1], v_x = result[2], and v_y = result[3]. You then use the solution to update the motion of the golf ball and the display of the results on your screen.

You can play around with the GolfGame by adjusting the variables that affect the drag force. You can see that drag effects make a big difference when it comes to the flight of a golf ball, as the GolfGame can demonstrate. Figure 7-4 shows the trajectory of the ball with a drag coefficient of 0.25, which is a typical value for a golf ball. In this case the golf ball travels about 100 m. If you turn off the drag effect by setting the drag coefficient to zero while using the same set of initial values, the golf ball will travel 164 m. Clearly, when it comes to projectiles such as golf balls, the drag effect must be included in the model.

Also, you may notice that when the drag effect is included, the shape of the trajectory isn't a perfect parabola. Instead, the downward part of the trajectory is sleeper because the drag force is slowing the golf ball down.

Collision

An important aspect of physics modeling for games is what happens when two objects collide. Do they bounce off each other or stick to each other and travel together? If the objects do bounce off each other, which direction do they travel after the collision and at what speed do they travel? In this section, we'll consider what happens when a ball hits a wall or a flat ground.

In most ball bouncing animations, a linear collision approximation is usually used. Namely, only the vertical component of the velocity changes signs when the ball hits a wall or surface. This isn't a realistic situation. In reality, when a ball is incident obliquely on a flat surface, the ball's rebound spin, speed, and angle will generally differ from the corresponding incident values. This is much more complicated than a linear collision approximation. In this section, we'll investigate physics of a general bouncing ball and create a general bouncing ball simulator.

Bouncing Ball Physics

The physics of a bouncing ball is characterized by the coefficient of restitution (COR) of a ball for a vertical bounce. The COR for a vertical bounce off a flat surface that remains at rest is defined as the ratio of the rebound speed to the incident speed. The horizontal COR can be defined for an oblique impact in terms of the horizontal components of the incident and rebound speeds of the contact point on the ball.

Here, our analysis of a bouncing ball is based on Garwin's model (R. Garwin, "Kinematics of an Ultraelastic rough ball", American Journal of Physics, Vol. 37, pages 88-92 (1969)). Consider a ball of mass m and radius R incident at speed V_1, angular velocity ω_1, and at an angle θ_1 on a flat surface, as shown in Figure 7-5.

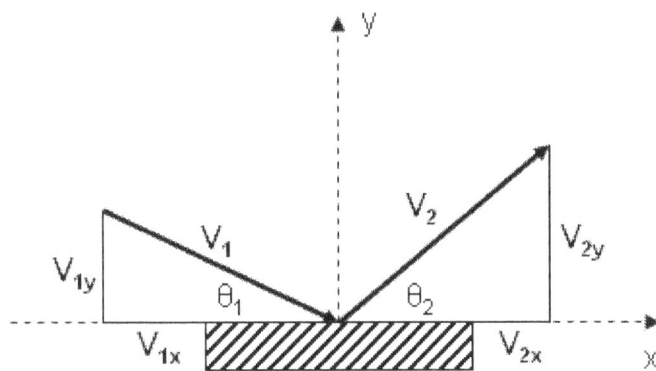

Figure 7-5 A ball is incident at velocity V_1 and angle θ_1 and rebounds at velocity V_2 and angle θ_2.

For simplicity, it is assumed that the mass of the surface is infinite and that the impact force is much larger than the gravity force during collision . In Garwin's model, the equations of motion are not needed explicitly, because the collision can be described in terms of the vertical (CORy) and horizontal (CORx) values of the COR, together with the conservation of angular momentum about the contact point. Referring to Figure 7-5, we can define

$$CORy = -\frac{V_{y2}}{V_{y1}} \qquad (7.17)$$

Here, the subscripts 1 and 2 denote conditions before and after the collision, respectively. Similarly, CORx can be defined by the relation:

$$CORx = -\frac{V_{x2} - R\omega_2}{V_{x1} - R\omega_1} \tag{7.18}$$

where $V_x - R\omega$ is the net horizontal speed of a point at the bottom of the ball. Unlike CORy, CORx can be either positive or negative. If a ball is incident at a sufficiently small angle and without spin, it can slide throughout the impact without rolling and will bounce with $R\omega_2 < V_{x2}$, in which case CORx < 0. A value of CORx = -1 corresponds to a bounce on a frictionless surface, where $V_{x2} = V_{x1}$ and $\omega_2 = \omega_1$.

The horizontal friction force F exerts a torque $FR = I d\omega/dt$, where I is the moment of inertia about an axis through the center of the ball, so that

$$I\frac{d\omega}{dt} + mR\frac{dV_x}{dt} = 0 \tag{7.19}$$

The conservation of angular momentum about a point at the bottom of the ball is therefore described by the relation

$$I\omega_1 + mRV_{x1} = I\omega_2 + mRV_{x2} \tag{7.20}$$

The moment of inertia of a spherical ball is given by $I = 2mR^2/5$. Equations (7.17)-(20) can be solved to show that

$$V_{x2} = \frac{[1-(2/5)CORx)]V_{x1} + (2/5)(1+CORx)R\omega_1}{1+(2/5)}$$

$$V_{y2} = -CORy V_{y1} \tag{7.21}$$

$$\omega_2 = \frac{(1+CORx)V_{x1} + [(2/5)-CORx]R\omega_1}{R[1+(2/5)]}$$

The above results are very interesting. If $\omega_1 = 0$ and CORx = 1, then $V_{x2} = 0.43V_{x1}$ and the corresponding spin value is $R\omega_2/V_{x2} = 10/3$. This means that the ball spins much faster than you would expect from the rolling condition $R\omega_2/V_{x2} = 1$. At the end of the collision, the ball with CORx = 1 will therefore slide backward on the surface due to the recovery of elastic energy stored in the horizontal direction. Alternatively, if $\omega_1 = 0$ and CORx = 0, then $V_{x2} = 0.71V_{x1}$ and $R\omega_2/V_{x2} = 1$, indicating that the ball rolls at the end of the duration of the impact and there is no energy recorvery or no energy stored elastically in the horizontal direction.

Because CORx is close to 1 for a superball and close to zero for a tennis ball, a superball will bounce with a smaller V_{x2} component than a tennis ball when $\omega_1 = 0$ and V_{x1} are the same for both balls. Since V_{y2} is larger for a superball (for the same V_{y1}), a superball will bounce at a steeper angle than a tennis ball. It is also easy to show that a superball with the same radius and same value of Vx1 as a tennis ball will bounce with a greater spin, by a factor of 2.38 if $\omega_1 = 0$.

Bouncing Ball Simulator

With Garwin's bouncing ball model, you can develop a realistic bouncing ball simulator that incorporates the inelastic collision, the change of horizontal speed, and the spin of the ball. The simulator is called BounceBall, and a sample screen shot is shown in Figure 7-6. The simulator consists of a ball inside a 2D 100m×100m box. The collision of the ball with the wall is described in Equation (7.21). When it travels inside the box (without collision), only gravity acts on the ball. If only the initial position of the ball (say x0 = 50m and y0 = 95 m) is specified and the initial velocity is set to zero (V0x = V0y = 0), the ball will drop as a free-fall object. The text fields allow you to change the mass, radius, gravity, and coefficients of restitution, as well as the initial position, velocity, and angle velocity. A Start button starts the simulation, a Stop button stops the simulation, and a Reset button stops the simulation and resets the ball and the parameters to their original position and values.

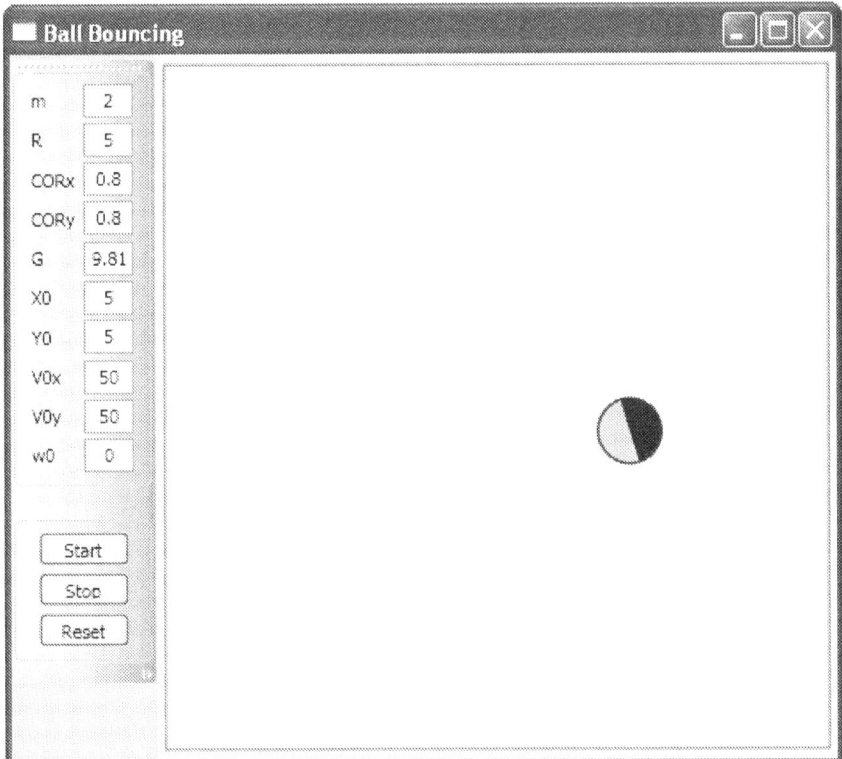

Figure 7-6 Bouncing ball simulator.

The layout of this example is created using the following XAML file:

```
<Window x:Class="Chapter07.BounceBall"
    xmlns="http://schemas.microsoft.com/winfx
        /2006/xaml/presentation"
    xmlns:x="http://schemas.microsoft.com/winfx/2006/xaml"
```

```
        Title="Ball Bouncing" Height="450" Width="510">

    <Window.Resources>
        <Style TargetType="{x:Type TextBox}">
            <Setter Property="Width" Value="30"/>
            <Setter Property="Height" Value="20"/>
            <Setter Property="HorizontalAlignment"
                    Value="Left"/>
            <Setter Property="TextAlignment" Value="Center"/>
            <Setter Property="Margin" Value="0,0,5,0"/>
        </Style>
        <Style TargetType="{x:Type TextBlock}">
            <Setter Property="Margin" Value="5,5,2,5"/>
        </Style>
        <Style TargetType="{x:Type Button}">
            <Setter Property="Margin" Value="2"/>
            <Setter Property="Width" Value="55"/>
            <Setter Property="Height" Value="20"/>
        </Style>
    </Window.Resources>

    <DockPanel>
        <ToolBarTray Orientation="Vertical"
                     DockPanel.Dock="Left">
            <ToolBar>
                <StackPanel>
                    <GroupBox>
                        <StackPanel Margin="0,5,0,0">
                            <StackPanel
                                Orientation="Horizontal"
                                VerticalAlignment="Top">
                                <TextBlock Width="30"
                                        Text="m"/>
                                <TextBox Name="tbM" Text="2"/>
                            </StackPanel>
                            <StackPanel
                                Orientation="Horizontal"
                                VerticalAlignment="Top">
                                <TextBlock Width="30"
                                        Text="R"/>
                                <TextBox Name="tbR" Text="5"/>
                            </StackPanel>
                            <StackPanel
                                Orientation="Horizontal"
                                VerticalAlignment="Top">
                                <TextBlock Width="30"
                                        Text="CORx"/>
                                <TextBox Name="tbCORx"
                                        Text="0.8"/>
                            </StackPanel>
                            <StackPanel
                                Orientation="Horizontal"
                                VerticalAlignment="Top">
                                <TextBlock Width="30"
```

```
                            Text="CORy"/>
            <TextBox Name="tbCORy"
                            Text="0.8"/>
        </StackPanel>
        <StackPanel
            Orientation="Horizontal"
            VerticalAlignment="Top">
            <TextBlock Width="30"
                            Text="G"/>
            <TextBox Name="tbG"
                            Text="9.81"/>
        </StackPanel>
        <StackPanel
            Orientation="Horizontal"
            VerticalAlignment="Top">
            <TextBlock Width="30"
                            Text="X0"/>
            <TextBox Name="tbX0"
                            Text="5"/>
        </StackPanel>
        <StackPanel
            Orientation="Horizontal"
            VerticalAlignment="Top">
            <TextBlock Width="30"
                            Text="Y0"/>
            <TextBox Name="tbY0"
                            Text="5"/>
        </StackPanel>
        <StackPanel
            Orientation="Horizontal"
            VerticalAlignment="Top">
            <TextBlock Width="30"
                            Text="V0x"/>
            <TextBox Name="tbV0x"
                            Text="50"/>
        </StackPanel>
        <StackPanel
            Orientation="Horizontal"
            VerticalAlignment="Top">
            <TextBlock Width="30"
                            Text="V0y"/>
            <TextBox Name="tbV0y"
                            Text="50"/>
        </StackPanel>
        <StackPanel
            Orientation="Horizontal"
            VerticalAlignment="Top">
            <TextBlock Width="30"
                            Text="w0"/>
            <TextBox Name="tbW0"
                            Text="0"/>
        </StackPanel>
    </StackPanel>
</GroupBox>
```

```xml
                    <GroupBox Margin="0,20,0,0">
                        <StackPanel Margin="0,5,0,0">
            <Button Name="btnStart" Click="btnStart_Click"
                    Content="Start"/>
            <Button Name="btnStop" Click="btnStop_Click"
                    Content="Stop"/>
            <Button Name="btnReset" Click="btnReset_Click"
                    Content="Reset"/>
                        </StackPanel>
                    </GroupBox>
                </StackPanel>
            </ToolBar>
        </ToolBarTray>

        <Viewbox Stretch="Uniform">
            <Border BorderBrush="Gray" BorderThickness="2"
                    Margin="5">
                <Canvas Name="canvas1" DockPanel.Dock="Right"
                        Width="500" Height="500"
                        ClipToBounds="True">
                    <Ellipse Name="ball" Canvas.Left="0"
                             Canvas.Bottom="0" Width="50"
                             Height="50" Stroke="Blue"
                             StrokeThickness="2">
                        <Ellipse.Fill>
    <LinearGradientBrush StartPoint="0,0" EndPoint="0,1">
        <GradientStop Color="DarkBlue" Offset="0.5"/>
        <GradientStop Color="LightBlue" Offset="0.5"/>
    </LinearGradientBrush>
                        </Ellipse.Fill>
                        <Ellipse.RenderTransform>
                            <RotateTransform
                                x:Name="ballRotate"
                                CenterX="25" CenterY="25"
                                Angle="0"/>
                        </Ellipse.RenderTransform>
                    </Ellipse>
                </Canvas>
            </Border>
        </Viewbox>
    </DockPanel>
</Window>
```

You may notice that the ball's RenderTransform property is specified by a RotateTransform, which is responsible for the spin of the ball when it is bouncing. The simulation and animation are performed using the following code-behind file:

```csharp
using System;
using System.Windows;
using System.Windows.Controls;
using System.Windows.Input;
using System.Windows.Media;
```

```
using System.Windows.Shapes;

namespace Chapter07
{
    public partial class BounceBall : Window
    {
        private double Mass;
        private double Radius;
        private double CORx;
        private double CORy;
        private double Gravity;
        private double X0;
        private double Y0;
        private double V0x;
        private double V0y;
        private double W0;

        double time = 0;
        double dt = 0.05;
        double x = 0;
        double y = 0;
        double vx = 0;
        double vy = 0;
        double w = 0;
        double theta0 = 0;
        double theta = 0;
        double max = 100;

        public BounceBall()
        {
            InitializeComponent();
            BallInitialize();
        }

        private void BallInitialize()
        {
            tbM.Text = "2";
            tbR.Text = "5";
            tbCORx.Text = "0.8";
            tbCORy.Text = "0.8";
            tbG.Text = "9.81";
            tbX0.Text = "5";
            tbY0.Text = "5";
            tbV0x.Text = "50";
            tbV0y.Text = "50";
            tbW0.Text = "0";

            Canvas.SetLeft(ball, 0);
            Canvas.SetBottom(ball, 0);
            ball.Width = Utility.XNormalize(
                canvas1, 10, 0, max);
            ball.Height = canvas1.Height -
                Utility.YNormalize(canvas1, 10, 0, max);
        }
```

```
private void SetInputParameters()
{
    Mass = Double.Parse(tbM.Text);
    Radius = Double.Parse(tbR.Text);
    CORx = Double.Parse(tbCORx.Text);
    CORy = Double.Parse(tbCORy.Text);
    Gravity = Double.Parse(tbG.Text);
    X0 = Double.Parse(tbX0.Text);
    if (X0 < Radius)
        X0 = Radius;
    Y0 = Double.Parse(tbY0.Text);
    if (Y0 < Radius)
        Y0 = Radius;
    V0x = Double.Parse(tbV0x.Text);
    V0y = Double.Parse(tbV0y.Text);
    W0 = Double.Parse(tbW0.Text);
    ball.Width = Utility.XNormalize(
        canvas1, 2*Radius, 0, max);
    ball.Height = canvas1.Height -
        Utility.YNormalize(canvas1, 2*Radius, 0, max);
    Canvas.SetBottom(ball, 0);
    Canvas.SetLeft(ball, 0);
}

private void btnStart_Click(object sender,
    RoutedEventArgs e)
{
    SetInputParameters();

    x = 0;
    y = 0;
    vx = 0;
    vy = 0;
    theta0 = 0;
    theta = 0;
    time = 0;
    CompositionTarget.Rendering += StartAnimation;
}

private void StartAnimation(object sender,
    EventArgs e)
{
    // Calculate positions and velocities of the ball
    // for the case without collision:
    x = X0 + V0x * dt;
    y = Y0 + V0y * dt - 0.5 * Gravity * dt * dt;
    theta = theta0 + 180 * W0 * dt / Math.PI;
    vx = V0x;
    if (Y0 > Radius)
    {
        vy = V0y - Gravity * dt;
    }
    else
```

```
{
    vy = V0y;
}
w = W0;

// Reset the ball's position:
Canvas.SetLeft(ball, Utility.XNormalize(
    canvas1, X0 - Radius, 0, max));
Canvas.SetBottom(ball, canvas1.Height -
    Utility.YNormalize(canvas1,
    Y0 - Radius, 0, max));
ballRotate.Angle = theta0;

// Determine if the ball hits left or right wall:
if ((V0x < 0 && X0 <= Radius) || (V0x > 0 &&
    X0 >= max - Radius))
{
    vx = -CORy * V0x;
    vy = ((1 - 2 * CORx / 5) * V0y + (2 / 5) *
        (1 + CORx) * Radius * W0) / (1 + 2 / 5);
    w = ((1 + CORx) * V0y + (2 / 5 - CORx) *
        Radius * W0) / Radius / (1 + 2 / 5);
}

// Determine if the ball hits the top or
// bottom wall:
if ((V0y < 0 && Y0 <= Radius) || (V0y > 0 &&
    Y0 >= max - Radius))
{
    vy = -CORy * V0y;
    vx = ((1 - 2 * CORx / 5) * V0x + (2 / 5) *
        (1 + CORx) * Radius * W0) / (1 + 2 / 5);
    w = ((1 + CORx) * V0x + (2 / 5 - CORx) *
        Radius * W0) / Radius / (1 + 2 / 5);
}

// Reset the initial condition for next round
// simulation:
X0 = x;
Y0 = y;
theta0 = theta;
V0x = vx;
V0y = vy;
W0 = w;
time += dt;

// Make sure to keep the ball inside the box:
if (time > 0 && Y0 < Radius)
    Canvas.SetBottom(ball, 0);

// Condition for stoping simulation:
if (time > 100)
{
    CompositionTarget.Rendering -= StartAnimation;
```

```
            }
        }

        private void btnStop_Click(object sender,
            RoutedEventArgs e)
        {
            CompositionTarget.Rendering -= StartAnimation;
        }

        private void btnReset_Click(object sender,
            RoutedEventArgs e)
        {
            BallInitialize();
            CompositionTarget.Rendering -= StartAnimation;
        }
    }
}
```

The code begins with the definition of private members that can be specified by the user. When the Start button is clicked, the values from the TextBox fields are obtained, and these values are used to initialize the simulation. To start the animation, the StartAnimation event handler is attached to the static CompositionTarget.Rendering event.

Inside the event handler, you calculate the position and velocity for the ball under the influence of gravity when the ball doesn't hit to the wall. When the ball collides with the wall, its motion is determined by Equation (7.21).

Now, you can play around with the bouncing ball simulator. Select a different set of input parameters and see what happens. The most interesting thing that may surprise you is that the ball will rotate (spin) at a high angular speed after collision, even its initial angular velocity is zero.

Also, you can see the difference between a superball and a tennis ball using this simulator. Experimental data show that the coefficients of restitution are very different for superballs and tennis balls. For the superball, CORx = 0.76 and CORy = 0.86, while for the tennis ball, CORx = 0.24 and CORy = 0.79. You can perform the simulation with these two sets of parameters to examine the results. You'll find that the superball will bounce with a faster spin speed than the tennis ball.

Fractals

A fractal is a very unusual object with fractional dimension. Fractals are currently a hot topic in mathematical theory and physics. You have probably seen fractals at some point or another: they are those usually colorful pictures seen in math and chaos physics books, where you zoom in on a region of the picture and see something similar to the larger picture. No matter how much you zoom in on a part of the picture, you'll still see the similar pattern repeating over and over again. This is an interesting property of fractals, called self-similar.

This section will concentrate more on how to create interesting fractal graphics than on explaining the mathematical theory and physics implications behind fractals. If you are interested in the theory and physics of fractals, you can read books specifically about fractal or chaos theory.

Binary Tree

You can define a binary tree recursively as a trunk attached to branches. The branches are attached to smaller branches that are attached to still smaller branches, and so on, until you reach some point in the tree where there are no more branches. For example, you could write a program that continues drawing smaller and smaller branches until the new branches are less than one pixel long. At this point, the program would stop.

Let's start with an example called BinaryTree. This example creates a simple binary tree using the recursion approach. In C#, a typical recursion method can be implemented using the following formula:

```
ReturnValue RecursiveFunction(Arguments)
{
    Optionl Action...
    RecursiveFunction(Modified Arguments);
    Optional Action...
}
```

This method starts with a return value. If it doesn't return a value, you can define it as void. After its name, the method can take one or more arguments. Most of the time, a recursive method takes at least one argument that it can then modify. In the body of the method, you can take the necessary actions. There are no particular steps to follow when implementing a recursive method, but there are two main rules you should observe:

- In its body, the method must call itself.

- Before or after calling itself, the method must check a condition that would allow it to stop; otherwise, it might run infinitely.

A sample screen shot of the BinaryTree example is shown in Figure 7-7. When you click the Start button, the program starts drawing the binary tree animately until the depth = 10.

The simple layout is created using the following XAML file:

```
<Window x:Class="Chapter07.BinaryTree"
    xmlns="http://schemas.microsoft.com/winfx
        /2006/xaml/presentation"
    xmlns:x="http://schemas.microsoft.com/winfx/2006/xaml"
    Title="Binary Tree" Height="345" Width="300">

    <Viewbox Stretch="Uniform">
        <StackPanel>
            <StackPanel Orientation="Horizontal"
                    Margin="5,5,5,0">
```

```
                    <Button Name="btnStart" Click="btnStart_Click"
                            Width="50" Content="Start"/>
                    <TextBlock Name="tbLabel" Margin="20,5,0,0"/>
                </StackPanel>
                <Canvas Name="canvas1" Width="300" Height="300"
                        Margin="5"/>
            </StackPanel>
        </Viewbox>
    </Window>
```

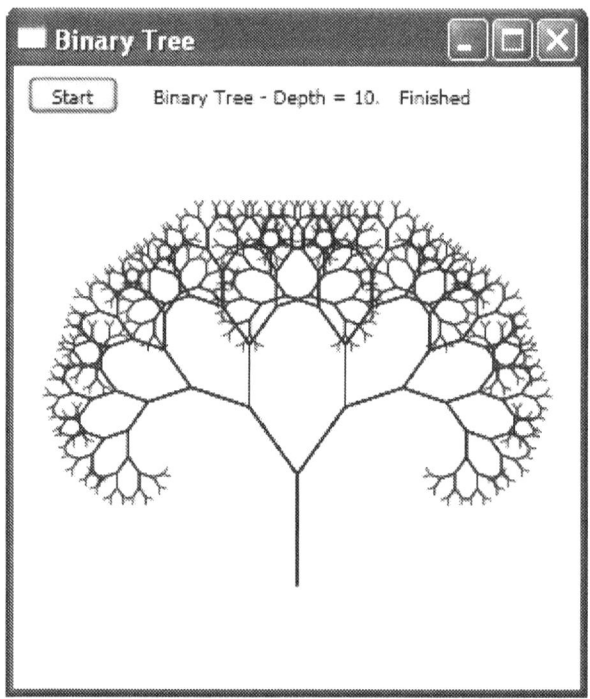

Figure 7-7 A binary tree.

The corresponding code-behind file of this example is listed below:

```
using System;
using System.Windows;
using System.Windows.Controls;
using System.Windows.Input;
using System.Windows.Media;
using System.Windows.Shapes;

namespace Chapter07
{
    public partial class BinaryTree : Window
    {
        private int II = 0;
        private int i = 0;
```

```
public BinaryTree()
{
    InitializeComponent();
}

private void btnStart_Click(object sender,
    RoutedEventArgs e)
{
    canvas1.Children.Clear();
    tbLabel.Text = "";
    i = 0;
    II = 1;
    CompositionTarget.Rendering += StartAnimation;
}

private void StartAnimation(object sender,
    EventArgs e)
{
    i += 1;
    if (i % 60 == 0)
    {
        DrawBinaryTree(canvas1, II,
            new Point(canvas1.Width / 2,
            0.83 * canvas1.Height),
            0.2 * canvas1.Width, -Math.PI / 2);
        string str = "Binary Tree - Depth = " +
            II.ToString();
        tbLabel.Text = str;
        II += 1;
        if (II > 10)
        {
            tbLabel.Text = "Binary Tree - Depth =
                10.    Finished";
            CompositionTarget.Rendering -=
                StartAnimation;
        }
    }
}

private double lengthScale = 0.75;
private double deltaTheta = Math.PI / 5;

private void DrawBinaryTree(Canvas canvas,
    int depth, Point pt, double length, double theta)
{
    double x1 = pt.X + length * Math.Cos(theta);
    double y1 = pt.Y + length * Math.Sin(theta);
    Line line = new Line();
    line.Stroke = Brushes.Blue;
    line.X1 = pt.X;
    line.Y1 = pt.Y;
    line.X2 = x1;
    line.Y2 = y1;
    canvas.Children.Add(line);
```

```
if (depth > 1)
{
    DrawBinaryTree(canvas, depth - 1,
        new Point(x1, y1),
        length * lengthScale, theta + deltaTheta);
    DrawBinaryTree(canvas, depth - 1,
        new Point(x1, y1),
        length * lengthScale, theta - deltaTheta);
}
else
    return;
}
}
}
```

The DrawBinaryTree method in the above code first calculates where its main branch should end, then draws the branch. Its length parameter determines the branch's length. The parameter theta gives the branch's direction.

If the current depth is greater than one, the method recursively calls itself to draw two new branches. These branches are shorter than the main branches by a factor of lengthScale and are drawn in the directions theta + deltaTheta and theta − deltaTheta.

This example also uses per-frame based animation to animate the drawing process. If you press the Start button, the program starts to draw the binary tree. There are several modifications that you can make to this example. For instance, you can modify the parameters lengthScale and deltaTheta to change the binary tree's appearance.

Snowflake

You can also use the recursive method to create a snowflake. Figure 7-8 shows the basic unit used to replace a straight line. This unit is created by the following steps. Start with a straight line and trisect this line into three equal segments. Form an equilateral triangle rising out of the middle segment.

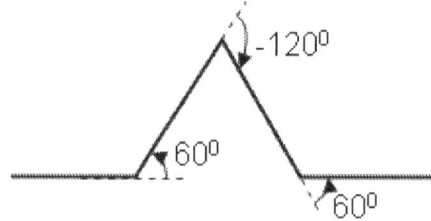

Figure 7-8 A basic unit to replace a straight line.

The snowflake begins with an equilateral triangle. The program replaces each of the triangle's sides with a properly scaled and rotated version of the basic unit shown in Figure 7-8. The program then replaces each of the straight segments in the new figure with a smaller version of the basic unit. It replaces the newer straight segments with smaller and smaller version of the basic unit, until the snowflake reaches the desired depth.

Let's look at an example that demonstrates how to create a snowflake. Add a new WPF Window to the project Chapter07 and name it SnowFlake. A sample screen shot of this example is shown in Figure 7-9. When you click the Start button, the program starts drawing the snowflake animately until the depth = 5.

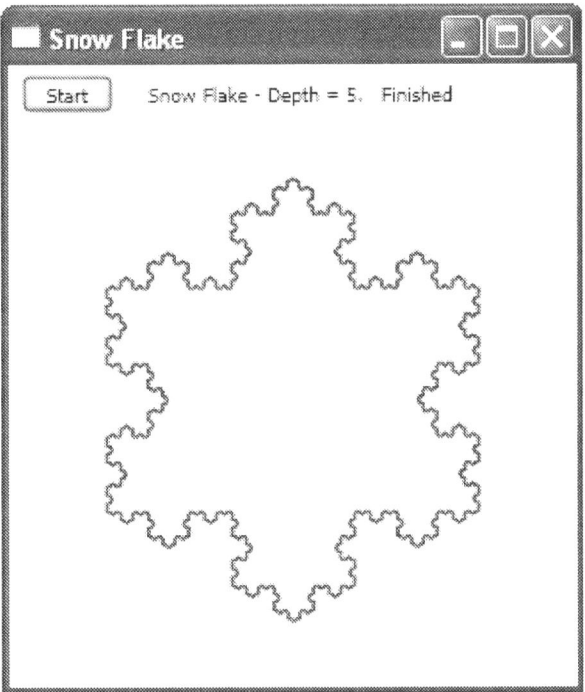

Figure 7-9 Snowflake created using the recursion method.

The layout of this example is created using the following XAML:

```xml
<Window x:Class="Chapter07.SnowFlake"
    xmlns="http://schemas.microsoft.com/winfx
        /2006/xaml/presentation"
    xmlns:x="http://schemas.microsoft.com/winfx/2006/xaml"
        Title="Snow flake" Height="345" Width="300">

    <Viewbox Stretch="Uniform">
        <StackPanel>
            <StackPanel Orientation="Horizontal"
                    Margin="5,5,5,0">
                <Button Name="btnStart" Click="btnStart_Click"
                    Width="50" Content="Start"/>
                <TextBlock Name="tbLabel" Margin="20,5,0,0"/>
```

```
            </StackPanel>
            <Canvas Name="canvas1" Width="300" Height="300"
                    Margin="5">
            </Canvas>
          </StackPanel>
      </Viewbox>
  </Window>
```

The C# code that creates the snowflake using the recursion method is listed below:

```csharp
using System;
using System.Windows;
using System.Windows.Controls;
using System.Windows.Input;
using System.Windows.Media;
using System.Windows.Shapes;

namespace Chapter07
{
    public partial class SnowFlake : Window
    {
        private double distanceScale = 1.0 / 3;
        double[] dTheta = new double[4] { 0, Math.PI / 3,
            -2 * Math.PI / 3, Math.PI / 3 };
        Polyline pl = new Polyline();
        private Point SnowflakePoint = new Point();
        private double SnowflakeSize;
        private int II = 0;
        private int i = 0;

        public SnowFlake()
        {
            InitializeComponent();

            // determine the size of the snowflake:
            double ysize = 0.8 * canvas1.Height /
                (Math.Sqrt(3) * 4 / 3);
            double xsize = 0.8 * canvas1.Width / 2;
            double size = 0;
            if (ysize < xsize)
                size = ysize;
            else
                size = xsize;
            SnowflakeSize = 2 * size;

            pl.Stroke = Brushes.Blue;
        }

        private void btnStart_Click(object sender,
            RoutedEventArgs e)
        {
            canvas1.Children.Clear();
```

```
    tbLabel.Text = "";
    i = 0;
    II = 0;
    canvas1.Children.Add(pl);

    CompositionTarget.Rendering += StartAnimation;
}

private void StartAnimation(object sender,
    EventArgs e)
{
    i += 1;
    if (i % 60 == 0)
    {
        pl.Points.Clear();
        DrawSnowFlake(canvas1, SnowflakeSize, II);
        string str = "Snow Flake - Depth = " +
            II.ToString();
        tbLabel.Text = str;
        II += 1;

        if (II > 5)
        {
            tbLabel.Text = "Snow Flake - Depth =
                5.    Finished";
            CompositionTarget.Rendering -=
                StartAnimation;
        }
    }
}

private void SnowFlakeEdge(Canvas canvas,
    int depth, double theta, double distance)
{
    Point pt = new Point();
    if (depth <= 0)
    {
        pt.X = SnowflakePoint.X +
            distance * Math.Cos(theta);
        pt.Y = SnowflakePoint.Y +
            distance * Math.Sin(theta);
        pl.Points.Add(pt);
        SnowflakePoint = pt;
        return;
    }

    distance *= distanceScale;
    for (int j = 0; j < 4; j++)
    {
        theta += dTheta[j];
        SnowFlakeEdge(canvas, depth - 1,
            theta, distance);
    }
}
```

```
private void DrawSnowFlake(Canvas canvas,
    double length, int depth)
{
    double xmid = canvas.Width / 2;
    double ymid = canvas.Height / 2;
    Point[] pta = new Point[4];
    pta[0] = new Point(xmid, ymid + length / 2 *
        Math.Sqrt(3) * 2 / 3);
    pta[1] = new Point(xmid + length / 2,
        ymid - length / 2 * Math.Sqrt(3) / 3);
    pta[2] = new Point(xmid - length / 2,
        ymid - length / 2 * Math.Sqrt(3) / 3);
    pta[3] = pta[0];
    pl.Points.Add(pta[0]);

    for (int j = 1; j < pta.Length; j++)
    {
        double x1 = pta[j - 1].X;
        double y1 = pta[j - 1].Y;
        double x2 = pta[j].X;
        double y2 = pta[j].Y;
        double dx = x2 - x1;
        double dy = y2 - y1;
        double theta = Math.Atan2(dy, dx);
        SnowflakePoint = new Point(x1, y1);
        SnowFlakeEdge(canvas, depth, theta, length);
    }
}
```

The code defines a double array dTheta that stores the angles, which control the directions of the segments as shown in Figure 7-8. When the program recursively draws a line segment, it begins by drawing a third of the length of the segment in its current direction. It then turns 60 degrees and draws another third of length of the segment. Next, it turns -120 degrees and draws another third. Finally, it turns 60 degrees again and draws yet another third of the length of the original segment. This is why you define the dTheta in the form:

```
double[] dTheta = new double[4] { 0, Math.PI / 3,
                    -2 * Math.PI / 3, Math.PI / 3 };
```

With this dTheta array and the value of the distanceScale factor, you can write a method to draw a segment in the SnowFlake.xaml.cs class. The SnowFlakeEdge method recursively draws a segment (by adding the point to the polyline's point collection) that starts at snowflakePoint and moves in the direction theta by a length of distance. When it is finished, it leaves the value of the snowflakePoint to indicate the endpoint of the segment. This makes it easier to perform all of the necessary recursive calls one after another.

The DrawSnowFlake method calls the SnowFlakeEndge method to draw each of the sides of the initial triangle. Inside this method, the Atan2 function takes the parameters dy and dx, which are the changes in a line segment's Y and X coordinates. It returns the angle with the tangent of dy/dx.

Now, if the Start button is pressed, the program starts drawing the snowflake. There are several modifications you can make to this example. For example, you can modify the parameter dTheta array to create a snowflake with a different appearance.

Using this basic snowflake unit, you can create a realistic snow falling effect by animatedly drawing multiple snowflakes in random positions and falling down in random paths.

You can easily expand the recursive method to create other types of fractals, such as Hilbert, Sierpinski, and Peano curves.

Mandelbrot Set

The Mandelbrot set is probably the most widely recognized fractal. It has become popular both for its aesthetic appeal and for being a complicated structure arising from a simple definition.

The Mandelbrot set is a set of points in the complex plane that forms a fractal. It is based on a very simple equation

$$z_{n+1} = z_n^2 + c$$

where z and c are complex numbers. The easiest approach for modeling the Mandelbrot set is to use a complex class or structure that allows you to perform operations directly on complex variables. Unfortunately, WPF doesn't provide the complex class or structure. However, you can easily implement a complex structure yourself. Here, you can get around without using a complex class or structure. Recall that complex numbers have a real part and an imaginary part. z and c in the above equation can be written as z = x + i y and c = cr + i ci, here i^2 = -1. Thus, you can rewrite the above equation as

$$z_{n+1} = (x_n^2 - y_n^2 + cr) + i \cdot (2x_n y_n + ci)$$

Which can further be rewritten in terms of two separate equations for the real and imaginary parts:

$$x_{n+1} = x_n^2 - y_n^2 + cr$$
$$y_{n+1} = 2x_n y_n + ci$$

Using these equations, you can compute the real and imaginary parts of z_{n+1} for different values of n, x_0, y_0, cr, and ci. It can be shown that after several iterations, if the magnitude of z_n ever exceeds 2, the magnitude of z_n will eventually head towards infinity.

The Mandelbrot set is a map showing how quickly the magnitude of z_n goes towards infinity for different values of c. displaying the Mandelbrot set on your computer screen in a pixel by pixel manner can pose problems. Before WPF, you needed to draw graphics objects in the .NET framework using GDI+. One of the restrictions you often run into with GDI+ was that it becmes extremely slow when you had to work with large raw pixel data using the GetPixel and SetPixel methods, because you needed to call these methods for every single pixel.

WPF allows you to pass in a big array of pixel data to create a new BitmapSource. It also provides the CopyPixel method to copy pixel data out of the bitmap into an array. Thus, WPF can process large raw pixel data vey efficiently. Here, we'll use the WPF pixel-based process to display the Mandelbrot set.

Now we can create a Mandelbrot set program. Add a new WPF Window to the project Chapter07 and name it MandelbrotSet. A sample screen shot of this example is shown in Figure 7-10.

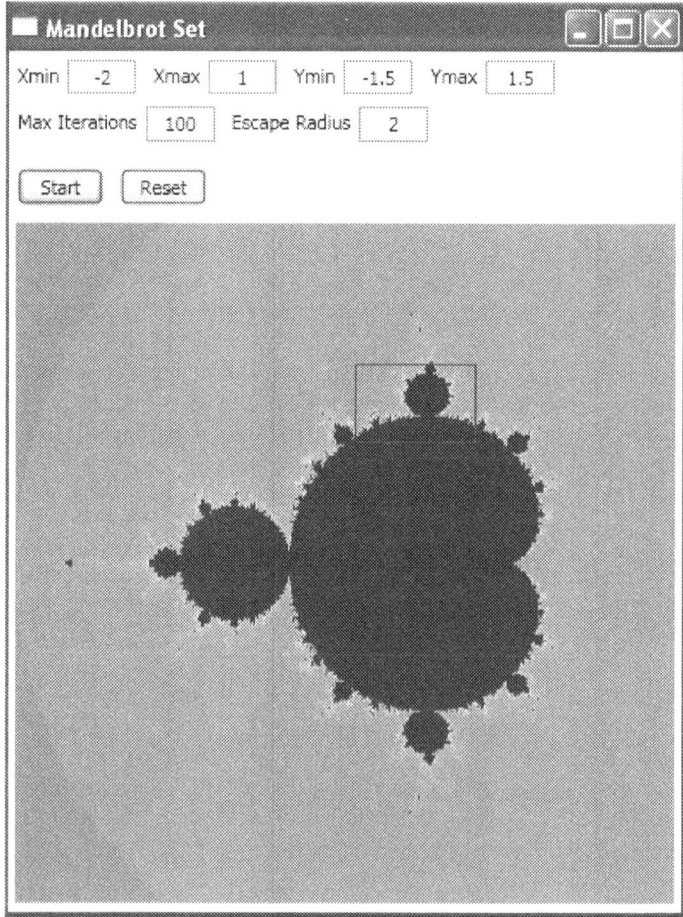

Figure 7-10 Mandelbrot Set.

It can be seen from the figure that there are text fields to input the axis limits, the maximum number of iterations, and the escape radius. A Start button starts the simulation and a Reset button resets the input parameters to their default values.

You can also zoom in to the plot by following these steps. Press your left mouse button, and leaving it pressed, drag the mouse to create a red zoom rectangle. Then release the left mouse button to start the computation of the image within the zoom area defined by the red zoom rectangle. Click the Reset button to restore the original non-zoomed image generated using the default parameters.

The GUI and layout of this example are created using the following markup:

```
<Window x:Class="Chapter07.MandelbrotSet"
    xmlns="http://schemas.microsoft.com/winfx
        /2006/xaml/presentation"
    xmlns:x="http://schemas.microsoft.com/winfx/2006/xaml"
    Title="Mandelbrot Set" Height="520" Width="400">

<StackPanel>
    <StackPanel>
        <StackPanel Orientation="Horizontal"
                Margin="5,5,5,0">
            <TextBlock Margin="0,2,0,0">Xmin</TextBlock>
            <TextBox Name="tbXmin" Text="-2"
                    TextAlignment="Center" Width="40"
                    Margin="5,0,10,5"/>
            <TextBlock Margin="0,2,0,0">Xmax</TextBlock>
            <TextBox Name="tbXmax" Text="1"
                    TextAlignment="Center" Width="40"
                    Margin="5,0,10,5"/>
            <TextBlock Margin="0,2,0,0">Ymin</TextBlock>
            <TextBox Name="tbYmin" Text="-1.5"
                    TextAlignment="Center" Width="40"
                    Margin="5,0,10,5"/>
            <TextBlock Margin="0,2,0,0">Ymax</TextBlock>
            <TextBox Name="tbYmax" Text="1.5"
                    TextAlignment="Center" Width="40"
                    Margin="5,0,10,5"/>
        </StackPanel>

        <StackPanel Orientation="Horizontal"
                Margin="5,2,5,5">
            <TextBlock Margin="0,2,0,0">Max
                    Iterations</TextBlock>
            <TextBox Name="tbIterations" Text="100"
                    TextAlignment="Center" Width="40"
                    Margin="5,0,10,5"/>
            <TextBlock Margin="0,2,0,0">Escape
                    Radius</TextBlock>
            <TextBox Name="tbRadius" Text="2"
                    TextAlignment="Center" Width="40"
                    Margin="5,0,10,5"/>
        </StackPanel>
```

```xml
                <StackPanel Orientation="Horizontal"
                            Margin="5,5,5,10">
                    <Button Name="btnStart" Click="btnStart_Click"
                            Content="Start" Width="50"
                            Margin="0,0,10,0"/>
                    <Button Name="btnReset" Click="btnReset_Click"
                            Content="Reset" Width="50"/>
                </StackPanel>
            </StackPanel>

            <Canvas Name="canvas" Width="384" Height="384"
                    MouseLeftButtonDown="OnMouseLeftButtonDown"
                    MouseLeftButtonUp="OnMouseLeftButtonUp"
                    MouseMove="OnMouseMove">
                <Image Name="showImage" />
            </Canvas>
        </StackPanel>
    </Window>
```

The corresponding code-behind file is listed below:

```csharp
using System;
using System.Windows;
using System.Collections.Generic;
using System.Windows.Controls;
using System.Windows.Input;
using System.Windows.Media;
using System.Windows.Media.Imaging;
using System.Windows.Shapes;

namespace Chapter07
{
    public partial class MandelbrotSet : Window
    {
        private double Xmin = -2;
        private double Xmax = 1;
        private double Ymin = -1.5;
        private double Ymax = 1.5;
        private int NIterations = 200;
        private double MaxRadius = 2;

        private int width  =  3*128;
        private int height = 3*128;
        private double zmax = 0;
        private Shape rubberBand = null;
        private Point startPoint = new Point();
        Point endPoint = new Point();

        public MandelbrotSet()
        {
            InitializeComponent();
            InitializeMandelbrot();
        }
```

```
private void InitializeMandelbrot()
{
    tbIterations.Text = "100";
    tbRadius.Text = "2";
    tbXmin.Text = "-2";
    tbXmax.Text = "1";
    tbYmin.Text = "-1.5";
    tbYmax.Text = "1.5";
    NIterations = 100;
    MaxRadius = 2;
    Xmin = -2;
    Xmax = 1;
    Ymin = -1;
    Ymax = 1;
}

private void btnStart_Click(object sender,
    RoutedEventArgs e)
{
    AddMandelbrotSet();
}

private void btnReset_Click(object sender,
    RoutedEventArgs e)
{
    InitializeMandelbrot();
    AddMandelbrotSet();
}

private void OnMouseLeftButtonDown(object sender,
    MouseButtonEventArgs e)
{
    if (!canvas.IsMouseCaptured)
    {
        startPoint = e.GetPosition(canvas);
        canvas.CaptureMouse();
    }
}

private void OnMouseMove(object sender,
    MouseEventArgs e)
{
    if (canvas.IsMouseCaptured)
    {
        endPoint = e.GetPosition(canvas);
        if (rubberBand == null)
        {
            rubberBand = new Rectangle();
            rubberBand.Stroke = Brushes.Red;
            canvas.Children.Add(rubberBand);
        }

        double width1 = Math.Abs(
            startPoint.X - endPoint.X);
```

```
            double height1 = Math.Abs(
                startPoint.Y - endPoint.Y);
            double left1 = Math.Min(
                startPoint.X, endPoint.X);
            double top1 = Math.Min(
                startPoint.Y, endPoint.Y);
            rubberBand.Width = width1;
            rubberBand.Height = height1;
            Canvas.SetLeft(rubberBand, left1);
            Canvas.SetTop(rubberBand, top1);
        }
    }

    private void OnMouseLeftButtonUp(object sender,
        MouseButtonEventArgs e)
    {
        endPoint = e.GetPosition(canvas);
        if (endPoint.X > startPoint.X)
        {
            Xmin = Xmin + (Xmax - Xmin) *
                startPoint.X / width;
            Xmax = Xmin + (Xmax - Xmin) *
                endPoint.X / width;
        }
        else if (endPoint.X < startPoint.X)
        {
            Xmax = Xmin + (Xmax - Xmin) *
                startPoint.X / width;
            Xmin = Xmin + (Xmax - Xmin) *
                endPoint.X / width;
        }

        if (endPoint.Y > startPoint.Y)
        {
            Ymin = Ymin + (Ymax - Ymin) *
                startPoint.Y / height;
            Ymax = Ymin + (Ymax - Ymin) *
                endPoint.Y / height;

        }
        else if (endPoint.Y < startPoint.Y)
        {
            Ymax = Ymin + (Ymax - Ymin) *
                startPoint.Y / height;
            Ymin = Ymin + (Ymax - Ymin) *
                endPoint.Y / height;
        }

        tbXmin.Text = Xmin.ToString();
        tbXmax.Text = Xmax.ToString();
        tbYmin.Text = Ymin.ToString();
        tbYmax.Text = Ymax.ToString();

        byte[] pixelData = DrawMandelbrotSet();
```

```
    BitmapSource bmpSource = BitmapSource.Create(
        width, height, 96, 96, PixelFormats.Gray8,
        null, pixelData, width);
    showImage.Source = bmpSource;

    if (rubberBand != null)
    {
        canvas.Children.Remove(rubberBand);
        rubberBand = null;
        canvas.ReleaseMouseCapture();
    }
}

private void AddMandelbrotSet()
{
    Xmin = Double.Parse(tbXmin.Text);
    Xmax = Double.Parse(tbXmax.Text);
    Ymin = Double.Parse(tbYmin.Text);
    Ymax = Double.Parse(tbYmax.Text);
    NIterations = Int32.Parse(tbIterations.Text);
    MaxRadius = Double.Parse(tbRadius.Text);

    byte[] pixelData = DrawMandelbrotSet();
    BitmapSource bmpSource =
        BitmapSource.Create(width, height, 96, 96,
        PixelFormats.Gray8, null, pixelData, width);
    showImage.Source = bmpSource;
}

private byte[] DrawMandelbrotSet()
{
    int looper;
    double cx, cy, dcx, dcy, x, y, x2, y2;

    dcx = (Xmax - Xmin) / (width - 1);
    dcy = (Ymax - Ymin) / (height - 1);
    byte[] pixelData =
            new byte[width * height];

    cy = Ymin;
    for (int i = 0; i < height; i++)
    {
        int iIndex = i * height;
        cx = Xmin;
        for (int j = 0; j < height; j++)
        {
            x = 0;
            y = 0;
            x2 = 0;
            y2 = 0;
            looper = 1;

            while (looper < NIterations &&
                x2 + y2 < MaxRadius * MaxRadius)
```

```
                    {
                        x2 = x * x;
                        y2 = y * y;
                        y = 2 * y * x + cy;
                        x = x2 - y2 + cx;
                        looper += 1;
                    }

                    int cindex;
                    if (looper < NIterations)
                    {
                        cindex = 150 + looper % 256;
                        if (cindex < 0)
                            cindex = 0;
                        if (cindex > 255)
                            cindex = 255;
                    }
                    else
                        cindex = 50;
                    pixelData[j + iIndex] =
                                  (byte)cindex;

                    cx += dcx;
                    if (zmax < Math.Sqrt(x2 + y2))
                        zmax = Math.Sqrt(x2 + y2);
                }
                cy += dcy;
            }
            return pixelData;
        }
    }
}
```

The code implements several mouse event handlers for the canvas, including MouseLeftButtonDown, MouseMove, and MouseLeftButtonUp. These event handlers are used to create a zoom area in the Mandelbrot set image with your mouse. In order to display the image on the screen, you create the pixel data directly using the following statements:

```
int cindex;
if (looper < NIterations)
{
    cindex = 150 + looper % 256;
    if (cindex < 0)
        cindex = 0;
    if (cindex > 255)
        cindex = 255;
}
else
    cindex = 50;
pixelData[j + iIndex] = (byte)cindex;
```

If you use a full color map instead of the grayscale that is used in the example, you'll obtain an even better image with full colors.

As long as the pixel data are prepared, you simply create a BitmapSource object using the BitmapSource.Create method, and then define the showImage.Source property using this BitmapSource object:

```
BitmapSource bmpSource =
    BitmapSource.Create(width, height, 96, 96,
                PixelFormats.Gray8, null, pixelData, width);
showImage.Source = bmpSource;
```

Creating an image on your screen using this method is reasonably fast even though it is a pixel-by-pixel based drawing method. In this example, the PixelFormat used is Gray8, which displays an eight bits-per-pixel grayscale channel, allowing 256 shades of gray. You can easily create a full color image by using a different PixelFormat. For example, you could use PixelFormats.Pbgra32, which displays a full color image with Blue, Green, Red, and Alpha channels. Remember that you need to scale up the dimension of the pixel data by 4 in order to use the Pbgra32 PixelFormat.

Play around with different numbers of iterations. This number determines how many values of z_n the program calculates before it decides that the magnitude of z_n is probably not heading toward infinity. Smaller values make the program to run more quickly. You might want to set this value to something small, like 50, or even 20 when you are exploring the Mandelbrot set. Once you have found an interesting area, you can increase this value to 200 or 500 to see more detail.

Julia Set

The Julia set uses the same set of equations as the Mandelbrot set. There are two differences between drawing the Mandelbrot set and drawing Julia set, however. The first difference is in how you select z_0 and c. To draw the Julia set, you pick a constant value of c, then use the coordinates of the pixels in the image to get the value z_0.

The other difference is in selecting colors for the pixels. The Mandelbrot program sets a pixel's color based on how quickly the magnitude of z_n exceeds 2. A Julia set program sets a pixel's color based on how large its magnitude is if it doesn't exceed 2 after a certain number of iterations. If the magnitude does exceed 2, the pixel is given a default background color.

Add a new WPF Window to the project Chapter07 and name it JuliaSet. The layout of this example is similar to the one used in the previous example for the Mandelbrot set. A sample screen shot is shown in Figure 7-11. In addition to the parameters for the axis limits, the maximum number of iterations, and the escape radius, you can also specify the complex constant c. In this sample screen shot, this constant is set to 0.745 + 0.113i. The default value of 1.1 + 0i will give a very different Julia set image.

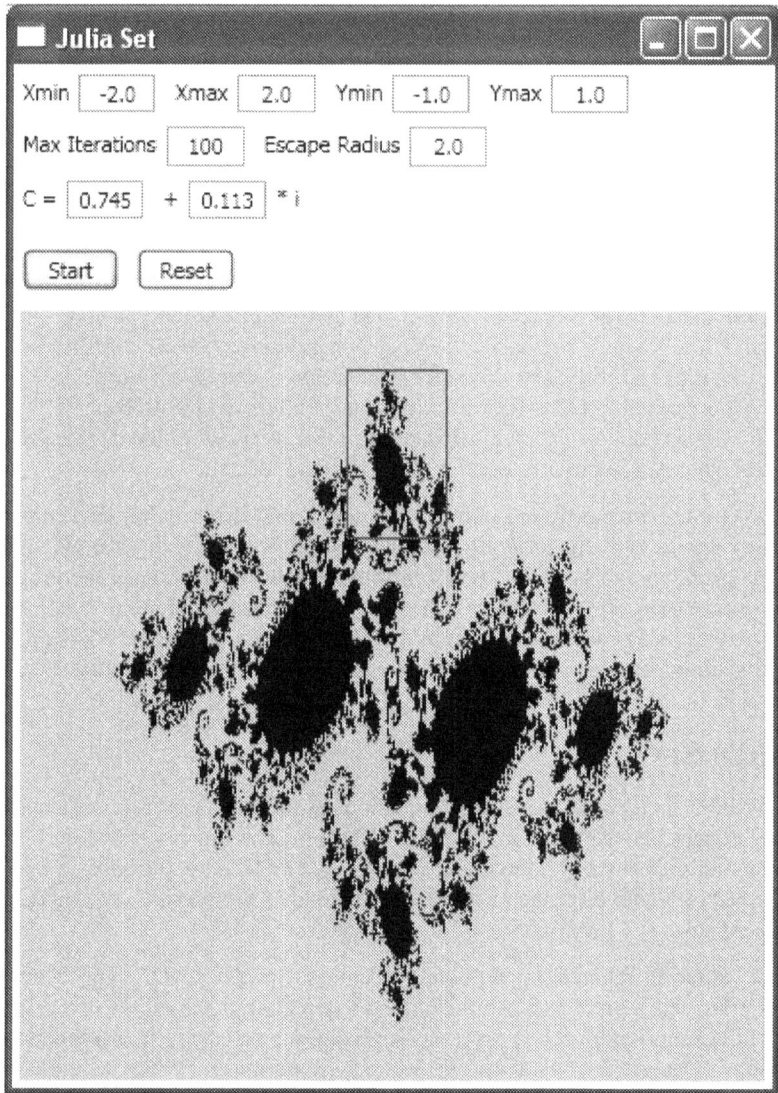

Figure 7-11 A Julia set with c = 0.745 + 0.113i.

The Julia set can also be classified as a fractal and exhibits self-similarity. You can zoom in by selecting a fragment using your mouse. You will find that the selected fragment in a smaller scale on various other locations of the image appears to be minimized copies of the image as a whole.

The layout of the example is created using the following XAML:

```
<Window x:Class="Chapter07.JuliaSet"
    xmlns="http://schemas.microsoft.com/winfx
        /2006/xaml/presentation"
    xmlns:x="http://schemas.microsoft.com/winfx/2006/xaml"
    Title="Julia Set" Height="545" Width="400">
```

```
<StackPanel>
    <StackPanel>
        <StackPanel Orientation="Horizontal"
                    Margin="5,5,5,0">
            <TextBlock Margin="0,2,0,0">Xmin</TextBlock>
            <TextBox Name="tbXmin" Text="-2"
                     TextAlignment="Center" Width="40"
                     Margin="5,0,10,5"/>
            <TextBlock Margin="0,2,0,0">Xmax</TextBlock>
            <TextBox Name="tbXmax" Text="1"
                     TextAlignment="Center" Width="40"
                     Margin="5,0,10,5"/>
            <TextBlock Margin="0,2,0,0">Ymin</TextBlock>
            <TextBox Name="tbYmin" Text="-1.5"
                     TextAlignment="Center" Width="40"
                     Margin="5,0,10,5"/>
            <TextBlock Margin="0,2,0,0">Ymax</TextBlock>
            <TextBox Name="tbYmax" Text="1.5"
                     TextAlignment="Center" Width="40"
                     Margin="5,0,10,5"/>
        </StackPanel>

        <StackPanel Orientation="Horizontal"
                    Margin="5,2,5,2">
            <TextBlock Margin="0,2,0,0">Max
                       Iterations</TextBlock>
            <TextBox Name="tbIterations" Text="50"
                     TextAlignment="Center" Width="40"
                     Margin="5,0,10,5"/>
            <TextBlock Margin="0,2,0,0">Escape
                       Radius</TextBlock>
            <TextBox Name="tbRadius" Text="2"
                     TextAlignment="Center" Width="40"
                     Margin="5,0,10,5"/>
        </StackPanel>
        <StackPanel Orientation="Horizontal"
                    Margin="5,0,5,5">
            <TextBlock Margin="0,2,0,0">C =</TextBlock>
            <TextBox Name="tbCReal" Text="1.1"
                     TextAlignment="Center" Width="40"
                     Margin="5,0,10,5"/>
            <TextBlock Margin="0,2,0,0">+</TextBlock>
            <TextBox Name="tbCImag" Text="0"
                     TextAlignment="Center" Width="40"
                     Margin="5,0,5,5"/>
            <TextBlock Margin="0,2,0,0">* i</TextBlock>
        </StackPanel>

        <StackPanel Orientation="Horizontal"
                    Margin="5,5,5,10">
            <Button Name="btnStart" Click="btnStart_Click"
                    Content="Start" Width="50"
                    Margin="0,0,10,0"/>
```

```
                    <Button Name="btnReset" Click="btnReset_Click"
                            Content="Reset" Width="50"/>
            </StackPanel>
        </StackPanel>

        <Canvas Name="canvas" Width="384" Height="384"
                MouseLeftButtonDown="canvasMouseLeftButtonDown"
                MouseLeftButtonUp="canvasMouseLeftButtonUp"
                MouseMove="canvasMouseMove">
            <Image Name="showImage" />
        </Canvas>
    </StackPanel>
</Window>
```

The following is the corresponding code-behind file:

```
using System;
using System.Windows;
using System.Windows.Controls;
using System.Windows.Input;
using System.Windows.Media;
using System.Windows.Media.Imaging;
using System.Windows.Shapes;

namespace Chapter07
{
    public partial class JuliaSet : Window
    {
        private double Xmin = -2;
        private double Xmax = 2;
        private double Ymin = -1;
        private double Ymax = 1;

        private int NIterations = 50;
        private double MaxRadius2 = 4;
        private double Cx0 = 1.1;
        private double Cy0 = 0;

        private int width = 3*128;
        private int height = 3* 128;
        private Shape rubberBand = null;
        private Point startPoint = new Point();
        Point endPoint = new Point();

        public JuliaSet()
        {
            InitializeComponent();
            InitializeJulia();
        }

        private void InitializeJulia()
        {
            tbCReal.Text = "1.1";
            tbCImag.Text = "0";
```

```
    tbIterations.Text = "50";
    tbRadius.Text = "2.0";
    tbXmin.Text = "-2.0";
    tbXmax.Text = "2.0";
    tbYmin.Text = "-1.0";
    tbYmax.Text = "1.0";

    MaxRadius2 = 4.0;
    Cx0 = 1.1;
    Cy0 = 0;
    NIterations = 50;
    Xmin = -2.0;
    Xmax = 2.0;
    Ymin = -1.0;
    Ymax = 1.0;
}

private void btnStart_Click(object sender,
    RoutedEventArgs e)
{
    AddJuliaSet();
}

private void btnReset_Click(object sender,
    RoutedEventArgs e)
{
    InitializeJulia();
    AddJuliaSet();
}

private void canvasMouseLeftButtonDown(object sender,
    MouseButtonEventArgs e)
{
    if (!canvas.IsMouseCaptured)
    {
        startPoint = e.GetPosition(canvas);
        canvas.CaptureMouse();
    }
}

private void canvasMouseMove(object sender,
    MouseEventArgs e)
{
    if (canvas.IsMouseCaptured)
    {
        endPoint = e.GetPosition(canvas);
        if (rubberBand == null)
        {
            rubberBand = new Rectangle();
            rubberBand.Stroke = Brushes.Red;
            canvas.Children.Add(rubberBand);
        }

        double width1 = Math.Abs(
```

```
                    startPoint.X - endPoint.X);
            double height1 = Math.Abs(
                startPoint.Y - endPoint.Y);
            double left1 = Math.Min(
                startPoint.X, endPoint.X);
            double top1 = Math.Min(
                startPoint.Y, endPoint.Y);
            rubberBand.Width = width1;
            rubberBand.Height = height1;
            Canvas.SetLeft(rubberBand, left1);
            Canvas.SetTop(rubberBand, top1);
        }
    }

    private void canvasMouseLeftButtonUp(object sender,
        MouseButtonEventArgs e)
    {
        endPoint = e.GetPosition(canvas);
        if (endPoint.X > startPoint.X)
        {
            Xmin = Xmin + (Xmax - Xmin) *
                startPoint.X / width;
            Xmax = Xmin + (Xmax - Xmin) *
                endPoint.X / width;
        }
        else if (endPoint.X < startPoint.X)
        {
            Xmax = Xmin + (Xmax - Xmin) *
                startPoint.X / width;
            Xmin = Xmin + (Xmax - Xmin) *
                endPoint.X / width;
        }

        if (endPoint.Y > startPoint.Y)
        {
            Ymin = Ymin + (Ymax - Ymin) *
                startPoint.Y / height;
            Ymax = Ymin + (Ymax - Ymin) *
                endPoint.Y / height;

        }
        else if (endPoint.Y < startPoint.Y)
        {
            Ymax = Ymin + (Ymax - Ymin) *
                startPoint.Y / height;
            Ymin = Ymin + (Ymax - Ymin) *
                endPoint.Y / height;
        }

        tbXmin.Text = Xmin.ToString();
        tbXmax.Text = Xmax.ToString();
        tbYmin.Text = Ymin.ToString();
        tbYmax.Text = Ymax.ToString();
```

```
        byte[] pixelData = DrawJuliaSet();
        BitmapSource bmpSource = BitmapSource.Create(
            width, height, 96, 96,
            PixelFormats.Gray8, null, pixelData, width);
        showImage.Source = bmpSource;

        if (rubberBand != null)
        {
            canvas.Children.Remove(rubberBand);
            rubberBand = null;
            canvas.ReleaseMouseCapture();
        }
    }
}

private void AddJuliaSet()
{
    Xmin = Double.Parse(tbXmin.Text);
    Xmax = Double.Parse(tbXmax.Text);
    Ymin = Double.Parse(tbYmin.Text);
    Ymax = Double.Parse(tbYmax.Text);
    Cx0 = Double.Parse(tbCReal.Text);
    Cy0 = Double.Parse(tbCImag.Text);
    NIterations = Int32.Parse(tbIterations.Text);
    MaxRadius2 = 2.0 * Double.Parse(tbRadius.Text);
    byte[] pixelData = DrawJuliaSet();
    BitmapSource bmpSource = BitmapSource.Create(
        width, height, 96, 96,
        PixelFormats.Gray8, null, pixelData, width);
    showImage.Source = bmpSource;
}

private byte[] DrawJuliaSet()
{
    int looper;
    int cindex = 0;

    double cx, cy, dcx, dcy, x, y, x2, y2;

    dcx = (Xmax - Xmin) / (width - 1);
    dcy = (Ymax - Ymin) / (height - 1);
    byte[] pixelData = new byte[width * height];

    cy = Ymin;
    for (int i = 0; i < height; i++)
    {
        int iIndex = i * height;
        cx = Xmin;
        for (int j = 0; j < width; j++)
        {
            x = cx;
            y = cy;
            x2 = x * x;
            y2 = y * y;
            looper = 1;
```

```
while (looper < NIterations &&
    x2 + y2 < MaxRadius2)
{
    x2 = x * x;
    y2 = y * y;
    y = 2 * y * x - Cy0;
    x = x2 - y2 - Cx0;
    looper += 1;
}
if (looper >= NIterations)
{
    cindex = 1 +
        (255 * (int)(x2 + y2)) % 255;
}
else
    cindex = 200;
pixelData[j + iIndex] = (byte)cindex;

cx += dcx;
        }
        cy += dcy;
    }
    return pixelData;
    }
  }
}
```

The example program JuliaSet is similar to the previous example of the MandelbrotSet. Play around with the Julia set image and zoom in to areas you are interested in. You can also alter the appearance of the image by changing the maximum number of iterations, which the program uses to calculate for each pixel. If you increase the number of iterations, the magnitude of z_n exceeds 2 for more of the pixels. The program gives these pixels the default background color, so that the resulting image contains fewer non-background pixels.

Sometimes, you need to adjust the number of iterations for a particular Julia set to generate the best result. If the number is too small, the program makes many pixels colorful, but the image may not have much detail. On the other hand, if the number is too large, the program will set most or all of the pixels to the background color, and there may be very little to see.

Chapter 8
Charts in WPF

Creating charts (or plots) for data visualization plays a very important role in every Windows application. Charts can make data easier to understand and can make reports more interesting to read. They have found wide applications in our daily life. For example, in the scientific, engineering, and mathematics communities, data and results always need to be represented graphically. You also see the stock charts in almost every news media, including internet, newspaper, and television.

This chapter will show you how to create real-world 2D line charts, the most basic and useful type of charts, in WPF. It'll also explain how to implement a custom chart control and how to reuse it in different WPF applications. If you want to create other specialized types of charts, such as bar, stair-step, error bars, pie, area, polar, stock, 3D surface, mesh, contour charts, and etc., you should refer to my other book *Practcal C# Charts and Graphics*, which provides details on how to create a variety of 2D and 3D chart applications.

Simple Line Charts

The most basic and useful type of chart that you can create with WPF is a simple 2D line chart of numerical data. WPF provides a set of commands and methods that can be used to create these charts. Even the most elementary 2D chart consists of several basic elements, including lines, symbols, axes, tick markers, labels, title, and legend. The following list gives a quick overview of the most basic chart elements without getting into details. These elements will often be referred to in this chapter.

- Axes – a graphics object that defines a region of the chart in which the chart is drawn.
- Line – a graphics object that represents the data you have plotted.
- Text – a graphics object that is comprised of a string of characters.

- Title – the text string object that is located directly above an axis object.

- Label – the text string object associated with the axis object (X- or Y- axis).

- Legend – the text string array object that represents the color and values of the lines.

The X-Y line chart uses two values to represent each data point. It is very useful for describing relationships between data, and is often used in the statistical analysis of data. This type of chart has wide applications in the scientific, mathmatics, engineering, and finance communities, as well as in daily life.

Creating Simple Line Charts

It is easy to create a 2D X-Y line chart in WPF. Let's use an example to illustrate the procedure. Start with a new WPF Windows project and name it Chapter08. Add a new WPF Window to the project and name it SimpleLineChart. You'll create the user interface and layout using XAML and perform the computation and generate the data in code. The XAML file of this example is very simple:

```
<Window x:Class="Chapter08.SimpleLineChart"
    xmlns="http://schemas.microsoft.com/winfx
        /2006/xaml/presentation"
    xmlns:x="http://schemas.microsoft.com/winfx/2006/xaml"
    Title="Simple Line Chart" Height="300" Width="300">

    <Viewbox Stretch="Fill">
        <Border BorderBrush="Black" BorderThickness="1"
                Margin="5">
            <Canvas Name="chartCanvas" Width="250"
                    Height="200" ClipToBounds="True"/>
        </Border>
    </Viewbox>
</Window>
```

Here you want to create the chart on a Canvas named chartCanvas. The corresponding code-behind file that creates the line chart of this example is listed below:

```
using System;
using System.Collections.Generic;
using System.Windows;
using System.Windows.Controls;
using System.Windows.Input;
using System.Windows.Media;
using System.Windows.Shapes;

namespace Chapter08
{
    public partial class SimpleLineChart : Window
    {
        private double xmin = 0;
```

```
private double xmax = 6.5;
private double ymin = -1.1;
private double ymax = 1.1;
private Polyline pl;

public SimpleLineChart()
{
    InitializeComponent();
    AddChart();
}

private void AddChart()
{
    // Draw sine curve:
    pl = new Polyline();
    pl.Stroke = Brushes.Black;
    for (int i = 0; i < 70; i++)
    {
        double x = i/5.0;
        double y = Math.Sin(x);
        pl.Points.Add(NormalizePoint(
            new Point(x, y)));
    }
    chartCanvas.Children.Add(pl);

    // Draw cosine curve:
    pl = new Polyline();
    pl.Stroke = Brushes.Black;
    pl.StrokeDashArray = new DoubleCollection(
        new double[] { 4, 3 });

    for (int i = 0; i < 70; i++)
    {
        double x = i / 5.0;
        double y = Math.Cos(x);
        pl.Points.Add(NormalizePoint(
            new Point(x, y)));
    }
    chartCanvas.Children.Add(pl);
}

private Point NormalizePoint(Point pt)
{
    Point result = new Point();
    result.X = (pt.X - xmin) *
        chartCanvas.Width / (xmax - xmin);
    result.Y = chartCanvas.Height - (pt.Y - ymin) *
        chartCanvas.Height / (ymax - ymin);
    return result;
}
```

Figure 8-1 shows the result of running this example.

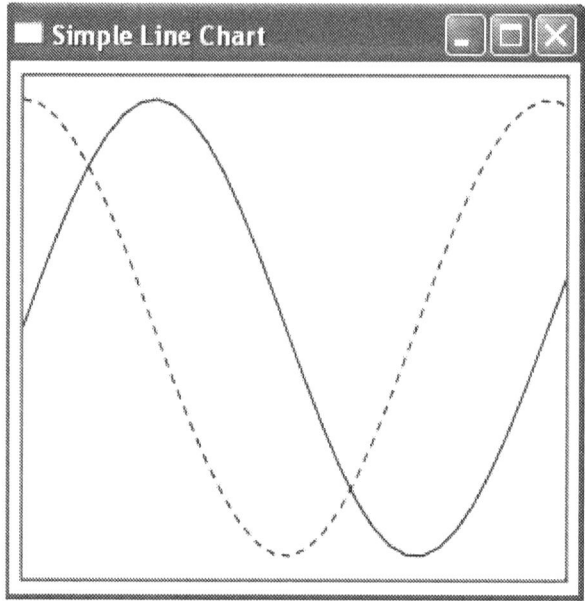

Figure 8-1 Line chart for Sine and Cosine functions.

How It Works

Note that the axis limits xmin, xmax, ymin, and ymax are defined in the real-world coordinate system. The Sine and Cosine functions are represented using the Polyline objects that are added to the chartCanvas's children collection.

A key step to creating this line chart is that the original data points in the world coordinate system need to be transformed into points in the units of device-independent pixels using the NormalizePoint method. The NormalizePoint method converts points with any unit in the world coordinate system into points with a unit of device-independent pixel in the device coordinate system.

Line Charts with Data Collection

The above example demonstrates how easy it is to create a simple 2D line chart in WPF, but doesn't pay much attention to the program structure. In order for the chart program to be more object-oriented and easily extand to add new features, you need to define three new classes: ChartStyle, DataCollection, and DataSeries. The ChartStyle class defines all chart layout related information. The DataCollection class holds the DataSeries objects, with each DataSeries object representing one curve on the chart. The DataSeries class holds the chart data and line styles, including the line color, thickness, dash style, etc.

Chart Style

Now, add a public class, ChartStyle, to the project Chapter08. The following is the code listing of this class:

```csharp
using System;
using System.Windows.Controls;
using System.Windows;

namespace Chapter08
{
    public class ChartStyle
    {
        private double xmin = 0;
        private double xmax = 1;
        private double ymin = 0;
        private double ymax = 1;

        private Canvas chartCanvas;

        public ChartStyle()
        {
        }

        public Canvas ChartCanvas
        {
            get { return chartCanvas; }
            set { chartCanvas = value; }
        }

        public double Xmin
        {
            get { return xmin; }
            set { xmin = value; }
        }

        public double Xmax
        {
            get { return xmax; }
            set { xmax = value; }
        }

        public double Ymin
        {
            get { return ymin; }
            set { ymin = value; }
        }

        public double Ymax
        {
            get { return ymax; }
            set { ymax = value; }
        }
```

```
public void ResizeCanvas(double width, double height)
{
    ChartCanvas.Width = width;
    ChartCanvas.Height = height;
}

public Point NormalizePoint(Point pt)
{
    if (ChartCanvas.Width.ToString() == "NaN")
        ChartCanvas.Width = 270;
    if (ChartCanvas.Height.ToString() == "NaN")
        ChartCanvas.Height = 250;
    Point result = new Point();
    result.X = (pt.X - Xmin) *
        ChartCanvas.Width / (Xmax - Xmin);
    result.Y = ChartCanvas.Height - (pt.Y - Ymin) *
        ChartCanvas.Height / (Ymax - Ymin);
    return result;
}
    }
}
```

In this class, you first pass a Canvas control to this class because it is needed to define the chart area and obtain the point conversion from the real-world coordinate system to the device independent pixels. Then you create various member fields and corresponding public properties, which are used to manipulate the chart layout, including the axis limits. The default values of these properties can be overridded according to your application requirements. You also define a ResizeCanvas method that allows the user to resize the chart canvas directly in the device coordinate system using units of device-independent pixels. Finally, you put the NormalizePoint method in this class, making the code clearer and more readable.

Data Collection

Add another public class, DataCollection, to the current project. The following is the code listing of this class:

```
using System;
using System.Collections.Generic;
using System.Windows.Controls;

namespace Chapter08
{
    public class DataCollection
    {
        private List<DataSeries> dataList;

        public DataCollection()
        {
            dataList = new List<DataSeries>();
        }
```

```
public List<DataSeries> DataList
{
    get { return dataList; }
    set { dataList = value; }
}

public void AddLines(Canvas canvas, ChartStyle cs)
{
    int j = 0;
    foreach (DataSeries ds in DataList)
    {
        if (ds.SeriesName == "Default Name")
        {
            ds.SeriesName = "DataSeries" +
                j.ToString();
        }
        ds.AddLinePattern();
        for (int i = 0; i <
            ds.LineSeries.Points.Count; i++)
        {
            ds.LineSeries.Points[i] =
                cs.NormalizePoint(
                ds.LineSeries.Points[i]);
        }
        canvas.Children.Add(ds.LineSeries);
        j++;
    }
}
```

This class is used to hold the DataSeries objects. You begin with a member field DataSeries list and its corresponding public property DataList. The DataList property holds the DataSeries. Then you implement an AddLines method, which draws lines using the DataSeries objects in the DataCollection class. For each DataSeries, you add a line to the chart canvas using the specified line style for that DataSeries. Notice how to transform all data points from the world coordinate system to the device coordinate system using the NormalizePoint method defined in the ChartStyle class.

Data Series

Finally, you need to add the DataSeries class to the current project. The following is the code listing of this class:

```
using System;
using System.Windows;
using System.Windows.Media;
using System.Windows.Shapes;

namespace Chapter08
```

```csharp
{
    public class DataSeries
    {
        private Polyline lineSeries = new Polyline();
        private Brush lineColor;
        private double lineThickness = 1;
        private LinePatternEnum linePattern;
        private string seriesName = "Default Name";

        public DataSeries()
        {
            LineColor = Brushes.Black;
        }

        public Brush LineColor
        {
            get { return lineColor; }
            set { lineColor = value; }
        }

        public Polyline LineSeries
        {
            get { return lineSeries; }
            set { lineSeries = value; }
        }

        public double LineThickness
        {
            get { return lineThickness; }
            set { lineThickness = value; }
        }

        public LinePatternEnum LinePattern
        {
            get { return linePattern; }
            set { linePattern = value; }
        }

        public string SeriesName
        {
            get { return seriesName; }
            set { seriesName = value; }
        }

        public void AddLinePattern()
        {
            LineSeries.Stroke = LineColor;
            LineSeries.StrokeThickness = LineThickness;

            switch (LinePattern)
            {
                case LinePatternEnum.Dash:
                    LineSeries.StrokeDashArray =
                        new DoubleCollection(
```

```
                            new double[2] { 4, 3 });
                        break;
                    case LinePatternEnum.Dot:
                        LineSeries.StrokeDashArray =
                            new DoubleCollection(
                            new double[2] { 1, 2 });
                        break;
                    case LinePatternEnum.DashDot:
                        LineSeries.StrokeDashArray =
                            new DoubleCollection(
                            new double[4] { 4, 2, 1, 2 });
                        break;
                    case LinePatternEnum.None:
                        LineSeries.Stroke = Brushes.Transparent;
                        break;
                }
            }
        }

        public enum LinePatternEnum
        {
            Solid = 1,
            Dash = 2,
            Dot = 3,
            DashDot = 4,
            None = 5
        }
    }
}
```

This class defines the Polyline object for a given DataSeries. It then defines the
line style for this line object, including line color, thickness, line pattern, and the
series name. The SeriesName property will be used in creating the legend for the
chart. The line pattern is defined by a public enumeration called
LinePatternEnum where five line patterns are defined, including Solid (default),
Dash, Dot, DashDot, and None. The None enumeration means there will be no
line drawn on the chart canvas.

The line pattern is created using the AddLinePattern method. There is no need to
create the solid line pattern because it is the default setting for the Polyline
object. The dash or dot line pattern is created using the StrokeDashArray
property of the Polyline. The invisible line (corresponding to the None type of
the line pattern) is defined by setting the stroke's color to transparent.

Creating Charts

Now, you can create line charts using the ChartStyle, DataCollection, and
DataSeries classes. Again I'll use an example to illustrate how to create a line
chart using these classes. Let's add a new WPF Window, named
LineChartExample, to the project Chapter08. The layout of this example is
created using the following XAML file:

```
<Window x:Class="Chapter08.LineChartExample"
    xmlns="http://schemas.microsoft.com/winfx
        /2006/xaml/presentation"
    xmlns:x="http://schemas.microsoft.com/winfx/2006/xaml"
    Title="Line Chart Example" Height="300" Width="300">

    <Viewbox Stretch="Fill">
        <Border BorderBrush="Gray" BorderThickness="1"
                Margin="10">
            <Canvas Name="chartCanvas" ClipToBounds="True"
                    Width="270" Height="250"/>
        </Border>
    </Viewbox>
</Window>
```

This markup defines a Canvas named chartCanvas, which will then be used to hold the line chart.

The corresponding code-behind file of this example is listed below:

```
using System;
using System.Windows;
using System.Windows.Controls;
using System.Windows.Input;
using System.Windows.Media;
using System.Windows.Shapes;

namespace Chapter08
{
    public partial class LineChartExample : Window
    {
        private ChartStyle cs;
        private DataCollection dc = new DataCollection();
        private DataSeries ds = new DataSeries();

        public LineChartExample()
        {
            InitializeComponent();
            AddChart();
        }

        private void AddChart()
        {
            cs = new ChartStyle(chartCanvas);
            cs.Xmin = 0;
            cs.Xmax = 7;
            cs.Ymin = -1.1;
            cs.Ymax = 1.1;

            // Draw Sine curve:
            ds = new DataSeries();
            ds.LineColor = Brushes.Blue;
            ds.LineThickness = 3;
            for (int i = 0; i < 70; i++)
```

```
        {
            double x = i / 5.0;
            double y = Math.Sin(x);
            ds.LineSeries.Points.Add(new Point(x, y));
        }
        dc.DataList.Add(ds);

        // Draw cosine curve:
        ds = new DataSeries();
        ds.LineColor = Brushes.Red;
        ds.LinePattern =
            DataSeries.LinePatternEnum.DashDot;
        ds.LineThickness = 3;

        for (int i = 0; i < 70; i++)
        {
            double x = i / 5.0;
            double y = Math.Cos(x);
            ds.LineSeries.Points.Add(new Point(x, y));
        }
        dc.DataList.Add(ds);
        dc.AddLines(chartCanvas, cs);
      }
    }
}
```

In this class, you begin by defining instances for the ChartStyle, DataCollection, and DataSeries classes. Inside the AddChart method, you override the axis limit properties which have been originally defined in the ChartStyle class, to meet the requirements of the current application.

Pay attention to how the DataSeries objects are added to the DataCollection class:

```
// Draw Sine curve:
ds = new DataSeries();
ds.LineColor = Brushes.Blue;
ds.LineThickness = 3;
for (int i = 0; i < 70; i++)
{
    double x = i / 5.0;
    double y = Math.Sin(x);
    ds.LineSeries.Points.Add(new Point(x, y));
}
dc.DataList.Add(ds);
```

Here you first create a new DataSeries object and define its line style, including the line color and thickness. Notice that you didn't specify the line pattern, so the default line pattern, Solid, is used. You then add the data points to the ds.LineSeries object's point collection. Finally, you add the data series "ds" to the DataCollection using the dc.DataList.Add method. In this way, you can add any number of DataSeries objects to the DataCollection. The AddLines method in the DataCollection class draws curves on the chart for all the DataSeries objects contained in the DataCollection.

Figure 8-2 illustrates the results of running this example.

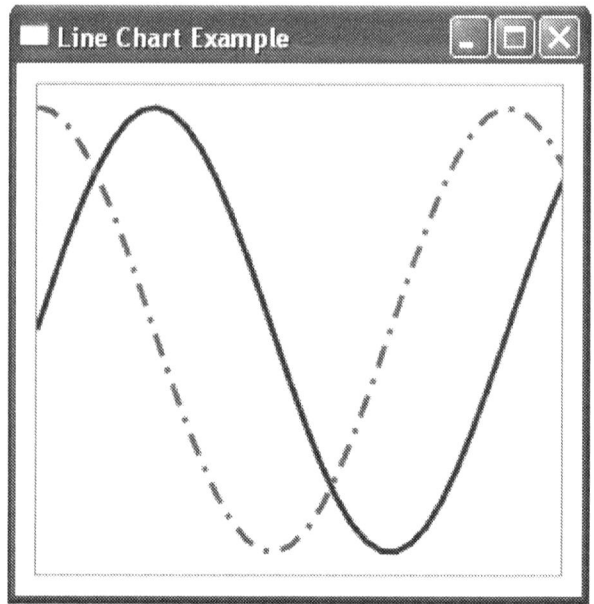

Figure 8-2 Chart for Sine and Cosine functions created using DataCollection class.

Gridlines and Labels

In the previous sections, only the lines for the Sine and Cosine functions were drawn on the chart. In this section, you will add more features to the 2D line chart, including gridlines, title, tick markers, and labels for axes.

XAML Layout

You can create the chart layout using XAML, and put the title and labels for the X- and Y-axes into different cells of a Grid control. Add a new WPF Window to the project Chapter08 and name it LineChartWithGridlines. The following is the XAML file of this example:

```
<Window x:Class="Chapter08.LineChartWithGridlines"
    xmlns="http://schemas.microsoft.com/winfx
    /2006/xaml/presentation"
    xmlns:x="http://schemas.microsoft.com/winfx/2006/xaml"
    Title="Line Chart with Gridlines and Labels" Height="400"
Width="400">
```

```
<Viewbox Stretch="Fill">
    <Grid Name="grid1" Margin="10">
        <Grid.ColumnDefinitions>
            <ColumnDefinition Width="Auto"/>
            <ColumnDefinition Name="column1" Width="*"/>
        </Grid.ColumnDefinitions>
        <Grid.RowDefinitions>
            <RowDefinition Height="Auto"/>
            <RowDefinition Name="row1" Height="*"/>
            <RowDefinition Height="Auto"/>
        </Grid.RowDefinitions>
        <TextBlock Margin="2" x:Name="tbTitle"
            Grid.Column="1" Grid.Row="0"
            RenderTransformOrigin="0.5,0.5" FontSize="14"
            FontWeight="Bold"
            HorizontalAlignment="Stretch"
            VerticalAlignment="Stretch"
            TextAlignment="Center"
            Text="Title"/>

        <TextBlock Margin="2" x:Name="tbXLabel"
            Grid.Column="1" Grid.Row="2"
            RenderTransformOrigin="0.5,0.5"
            TextAlignment="Center"
            Text="X Axis"/>

        <TextBlock Margin="2" Name="tbYLabel"
            Grid.Column="0" Grid.Row="1"
            RenderTransformOrigin="0.5,0.5"
            TextAlignment="Center"
            Text="Y Axis">
            <TextBlock.LayoutTransform>
                <RotateTransform Angle="-90"/>
            </TextBlock.LayoutTransform>
        </TextBlock>

        <Canvas Margin="2" Name="textCanvas" Width="300"
            Height="305" Grid.Column="1" Grid.Row="1"
            ClipToBounds="True">
            <Canvas Name="chartCanvas"
                ClipToBounds="True"/>
        </Canvas>
    </Grid>
</Viewbox>
</Window>
```

Here you also create two canvas controls, textCanvas and chartCanvas. The textCanvas control is used to hold the tick mark labels, and the chartCanvas control is used to hold the chart itself. The DataCollection, DataSeries, and ChartStyle classes, which were used in the previous example, can still be used here. You can add the gridlines and labels to a new class, ChartStyleGridlines, which is inherited from the ChartStyle class.

ChartStyleGridlines Class

As mentioned previously, this class derives from the ChartStyle class. Here is the code listing of this class:

```
using System;
using System.Windows.Controls;
using System.Windows;
using System.Windows.Media;
using System.Windows.Shapes;

namespace Chapter08
{
    public class ChartStyleGridlines : ChartStyle
    {
    private Canvas textCanvas;
        private bool isXGrid = true;
        private bool isYGrid = true;
        private Brush gridlineColor = Brushes.LightGray;
        private GridlinePatternEnum gridlinePattern;
        private string title;
        private string xLabel;
        private string yLabel;
        private double xTick = 1;
        private double yTick = 0.5;
        private double leftOffset = 20;
        private double bottomOffset = 15;
        private double rightOffset = 10;
        private Line gridline = new Line();

        public ChartStyleGridlines()
        {
            title = "Title";
            xLabel = "X Axis";
            yLabel = "Y Axis";
        }

        public string Title
        {
            get { return title; }
            set { title = value; }
        }

        public string XLabel
        {
            get { return xLabel; }
            set { xLabel = value; }
        }

        public string YLabel
        {
            get { return yLabel; }
            set { yLabel = value; }
        }
```

```
public GridlinePatternEnum GridlinePattern
{
    get { return gridlinePattern; }
    set { gridlinePattern = value; }
}

public double XTick
{
    get { return xTick; }
    set { xTick = value; }
}

public double YTick
{
    get { return yTick; }
    set { yTick = value; }
}

public Brush GridlineColor
{
    get { return gridlineColor; }
    set { gridlineColor = value; }
}

public Canvas TextCanvas
{
    get { return textCanvas; }
    set { textCanvas = value; }
}

public bool IsXGrid
{
    get { return isXGrid; }
    set { isXGrid = value; }
}

public bool IsYGrid
{
    get { return isYGrid; }
    set { isYGrid = value; }
}

public void AddChartStyle(TextBlock tbTitle,
    TextBlock tbXLabel, TextBlock tbYLabel)
{
    Point pt = new Point();
    Line tick = new Line();
    double offset = 0;
    double dx, dy;
    TextBlock tb = new TextBlock();

    //  determine right offset:
    tb.Text = Xmax.ToString();
```

```
tb.Measure(new Size(Double.PositiveInfinity,
    Double.PositiveInfinity));
Size size = tb.DesiredSize;
rightOffset = size.Width / 2 + 2;

// Determine left offset:
for (dy = Ymin; dy <= Ymax; dy += YTick)
{
    pt = NormalizePoint(new Point(Xmin, dy));
    tb = new TextBlock();
    tb.Text = dy.ToString();
    tb.TextAlignment = TextAlignment.Right;
    tb.Measure(new Size(Double.PositiveInfinity,
        Double.PositiveInfinity));
    size = tb.DesiredSize;
    if (offset < size.Width)
        offset = size.Width;
}
leftOffset = offset + 5;

Canvas.SetLeft(ChartCanvas, leftOffset);
Canvas.SetBottom(ChartCanvas, bottomOffset);
ChartCanvas.Width = TextCanvas.Width - leftOffset
    - rightOffset;
ChartCanvas.Height = TextCanvas.Height -
    bottomOffset - size.Height / 2;
Rectangle chartRect = new Rectangle();
chartRect.Stroke = Brushes.Black;
chartRect.Width = ChartCanvas.Width;
chartRect.Height = ChartCanvas.Height;
ChartCanvas.Children.Add(chartRect);

// Create vertical gridlines:
if (IsYGrid == true)
{
    for (dx = Xmin + XTick; dx < Xmax;
        dx += XTick)
    {
        gridline = new Line();
        AddLinePattern();
        gridline.X1 = NormalizePoint(
            new Point(dx, Ymin)).X;
        gridline.Y1 = NormalizePoint(
            new Point(dx, Ymin)).Y;
        gridline.X2 = NormalizePoint(
            new Point(dx, Ymax)).X;
        gridline.Y2 = NormalizePoint(
            new Point(dx, Ymax)).Y;
        ChartCanvas.Children.Add(gridline);
    }
}

// Create horizontal gridlines:
if (IsXGrid == true)
```

```
{
    for (dy = Ymin + YTick; dy < Ymax;
        dy += YTick)
    {
        gridline = new Line();
        AddLinePattern();
        gridline.X1 = NormalizePoint(
            new Point(Xmin, dy)).X;
        gridline.Y1 = NormalizePoint(
            new Point(Xmin, dy)).Y;
        gridline.X2 = NormalizePoint(
            new Point(Xmax, dy)).X;
        gridline.Y2 = NormalizePoint(
            new Point(Xmax, dy)).Y;
        ChartCanvas.Children.Add(gridline);
    }
}

// Create x-axis tick marks:
for (dx = Xmin; dx <= Xmax; dx += xTick)
{
    pt = NormalizePoint(new Point(dx, Ymin));
    tick = new Line();
    tick.Stroke = Brushes.Black;
    tick.X1 = pt.X;
    tick.Y1 = pt.Y;
    tick.X2 = pt.X;
    tick.Y2 = pt.Y - 5;
    ChartCanvas.Children.Add(tick);

    tb = new TextBlock();
    tb.Text = dx.ToString();
    tb.Measure(new Size(Double.PositiveInfinity,
        Double.PositiveInfinity));
    size = tb.DesiredSize;
    TextCanvas.Children.Add(tb);
    Canvas.SetLeft(tb, leftOffset +
        pt.X - size.Width / 2);
    Canvas.SetTop(tb, pt.Y + 2 + size.Height / 2);
}

// Create y-axis tick marks:
for (dy = Ymin; dy <= Ymax; dy += YTick)
{
    pt = NormalizePoint(new Point(Xmin, dy));
    tick = new Line();
    tick.Stroke = Brushes.Black;
    tick.X1 = pt.X;
    tick.Y1 = pt.Y;
    tick.X2 = pt.X + 5;
    tick.Y2 = pt.Y;
    ChartCanvas.Children.Add(tick);

    tb = new TextBlock();
```

```
                tb.Text = dy.ToString();
                tb.Measure(new Size(Double.PositiveInfinity,
                    Double.PositiveInfinity));
                size = tb.DesiredSize;
                TextCanvas.Children.Add(tb);
                Canvas.SetRight(tb, ChartCanvas.Width + 10);
                Canvas.SetTop(tb, pt.Y);
            }

            // Add title and labels:
            tbTitle.Text = Title;
            tbXLabel.Text = XLabel;
            tbYLabel.Text = YLabel;
        }

        public void AddLinePattern()
        {
            gridline.Stroke = GridlineColor;
            gridline.StrokeThickness = 1;

            switch (GridlinePattern)
            {
                case GridlinePatternEnum.Dash:
                    gridline.StrokeDashArray =
                        new DoubleCollection(
                        new double[2] { 4, 3 });
                    break;
                case GridlinePatternEnum.Dot:
                    gridline.StrokeDashArray =
                        new DoubleCollection(
                        new double[2] { 1, 2 });
                    break;
                case GridlinePatternEnum.DashDot:
                    gridline.StrokeDashArray =
                        new DoubleCollection(
                        new double[4] { 4, 2, 1, 2 });
                    break;
            }
        }

        public enum GridlinePatternEnum
        {
            Solid = 1,
            Dash = 2,
            Dot = 3,
            DashDot = 4
        }
    }
}
```

To this class, you add more member fields and corresponding properties, which are used to manipulate the chart's layout and appearance. The meaning of each field and property can be easily understood from its name. In addition, the following member fields are added to define gridlines for your chart:

```
private bool isXGrid = true;
private bool isYGrid = true;
private Brush gridlineColor = Brushes.LightGray;
private GridlinePatternEnum gridlinePattern;
```

These fields and corresponding properties provide a great deal of flexibility in customizing the appearance of the gridlines. The gridlinePattern field allows you to choose various line dash styles, including solid, dash, dot, and dash-dot, etc. You can change the gridlines' color using the gridlineColor field. In addition, two bool fields, isXGrid and isYGrid, are defined, which allow you to turn horizontal or vertical gridlines on or off.

You then define member fields and corresponding properties for the X- and Y-labels, title, and the ticks in order to change the labels, title, and tick marks. You can easily add more member fields to change, for example, the fonts and text color for the labels and title.

The AddChartStyle method seems quite complicated in this class; however, it is actually reasonably easy to follow. First, you define the size of the chartCanvas by considering the suitable offset relative to the textCanvas. Next, you draw gridlines with a specified color and line pattern. Please note that all of the end points of the gridlines have been transformed from the world coordinate system to the device-independent pixels using the NormalizePoint method.

You then draw the tick marks for the X- and Y-axes of the chart. For each tick mark, you find the points in the device coordinate system where the tick mark joins the axes and draw a black line, 5 pixels long, from this point toward inside the chartCanvas.

The title and labels for the X- and Y-axes are attached to the corresponding TextBlock names in code. You can also create data bindings that bind the Title, Label, and YLabel properties to the corresponding TextBlock directly in the XAML file.

Testing Project

Open the code-behind file of the LineChartWithGridlines, and add the following code to it:

```
using System;
using System.Windows;
using System.Windows.Controls;
using System.Windows.Media;
using System.Windows.Shapes;

namespace Chapter08
{
    public partial class LineChartWithGridlines : Window
    {
```

```
private ChartStyleGridlines cs;
private DataCollection dc = new DataCollection();
private DataSeries ds = new DataSeries();

public LineChartWithGridlines()
{
    InitializeComponent();
    AddChart();
}


private void AddChart()
{
    cs = new ChartStyleGridlines();
    cs.ChartCanvas = chartCanvas;
    cs.TextCanvas = textCanvas;
    cs.Title = "Sine and Cosine Chart";
    cs.Xmin = 0;
    cs.Xmax = 7;
    cs.Ymin = -1.5;
    cs.Ymax = 1.5;
    cs.YTick = 0.5;
    cs.GridlinePattern =
        ChartStyleGridlines.GridlinePatternEnum.Dot;
    cs.GridlineColor = Brushes.Black;
    cs.AddChartStyle(tbTitle, tbXLabel, tbYLabel);

    // Draw Sine curve:
    ds.LineColor = Brushes.Blue;
    ds.LineThickness = 3;
    for (int i = 0; i < 70; i++)
    {
        double x = i / 5.0;
        double y = Math.Sin(x);
        ds.LineSeries.Points.Add(new Point(x, y));
    }
    dc.DataList.Add(ds);

    // Draw cosine curve:
    ds = new DataSeries();
    ds.LineColor = Brushes.Red;
    ds.LinePattern =
        DataSeries.LinePatternEnum.DashDot;
    ds.LineThickness = 3;

    for (int i = 0; i < 70; i++)
    {
        double x = i / 5.0;
        double y = Math.Cos(x);
        ds.LineSeries.Points.Add(new Point(x, y));
    }
    dc.DataList.Add(ds);
    dc.AddLines(chartCanvas, cs);
}
```

```
        }
    }
```

This code is similar to the code used in the previous example, except that you specify the gridlines' properties. Figure 8-3 illustrates the results of running this application. You can see that the chart has a title, labels, gridlines, and tick marks. Obviously, there is still no chart legend yet. I'll show you how to add a legend in the next section.

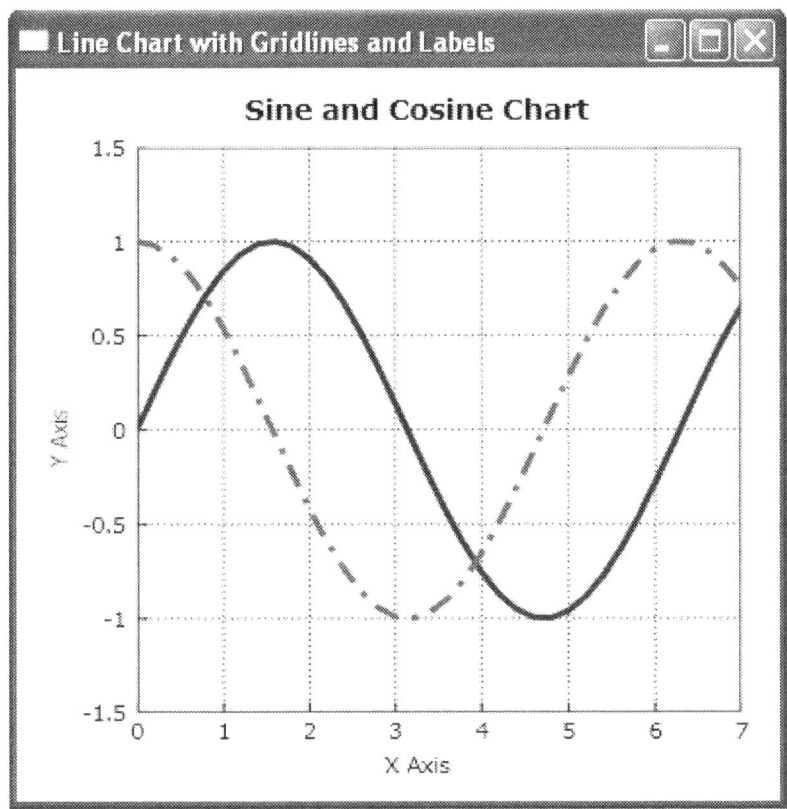

Figure 8-3 Sine and Cosine chart with gridlines and labels.

Legend

For a 2D line chart with multiple curves, you may want to use a legend to identify each curve plotted on your chart. The legend shows a sample of the curve type, marker symbol, color, and text label you specify.

Legend Class

Add a new Legend class to the project Chapter08. The following is its code listing:

```
using System;
using System.Windows.Controls;
using System.Windows;
using System.Windows.Media;
using System.Windows.Shapes;

namespace Chapter08
{
    public class Legend
    {
        private bool isLegend;
        private bool isBorder;
        private Canvas legendCanvas;

        public Legend()
        {
            isLegend = false;
            isBorder = true;
        }

        public Canvas LegendCanvas
        {
            get { return legendCanvas; }
            set { legendCanvas = value; }
        }

        public bool IsLegend
        {
            get { return isLegend; }
            set { isLegend = value; }
        }

        public bool IsBorder
        {
            get { return isBorder; }
            set { isBorder = value; }
        }

        public void AddLegend(ChartStyleGridlines cs,
            DataCollection dc)
        {
            TextBlock tb = new TextBlock();
            if (dc.DataList.Count < 1 || !IsLegend)
                return;
            int n = 0;
            string[] legendLabels =
                new string[dc.DataList.Count];
            foreach (DataSeries ds in dc.DataList)
            {
```

```
        legendLabels[n] = ds.SeriesName;
        n++;
    }

    double legendWidth = 0;
    Size size = new Size(0, 0);
    for (int i = 0; i < legendLabels.Length; i++)
    {
        tb = new TextBlock();
        tb.Text = legendLabels[i];
        tb.Measure(new Size(Double.PositiveInfinity,
            Double.PositiveInfinity));
        size = tb.DesiredSize;
        if (legendWidth < size.Width)
            legendWidth = size.Width;
    }

    legendWidth += 50;
    legendCanvas.Width = legendWidth + 5;
    double legendHeight = 17 * dc.DataList.Count;
    double sx = 6;
    double sy = 2;
    double textHeight = size.Height;
    double lineLength = 34;
    Rectangle legendRect = new Rectangle();
    legendRect.Stroke = Brushes.Black;
    legendRect.Width = legendWidth;
    legendRect.Height = legendHeight;

    if (IsLegend && IsBorder)
        LegendCanvas.Children.Add(legendRect);

    n = 1;
    foreach (DataSeries ds in dc.DataList)
    {
        double xSymbol = sx + lineLength / 2;
        double xText = 2 * sx + lineLength;
        double yText = n * sy +
            (2 * n - 1) * textHeight / 2;
        Line line = new Line();
        AddLinePattern(line, ds);
        line.X1 = sx;
        line.Y1 = yText;
        line.X2 = sx + lineLength;
        line.Y2 = yText;
        LegendCanvas.Children.Add(line);

        tb = new TextBlock();
        tb.Text = ds.SeriesName;
        LegendCanvas.Children.Add(tb);
        Canvas.SetTop(tb, yText - size.Height / 2);
        Canvas.SetLeft(tb, xText);
        n++;
    }
```

```
        }

        private void AddLinePattern(Line line, DataSeries ds)
        {
            line.Stroke = ds.LineColor;
            line.StrokeThickness = ds.LineThickness;

            switch (ds.LinePattern)
            {
                case DataSeries.LinePatternEnum.Dash:
                    line.StrokeDashArray =
                        new DoubleCollection(
                        new double[2] { 4, 3 });
                    break;
                case DataSeries.LinePatternEnum.Dot:
                    line.StrokeDashArray =
                        new DoubleCollection(
                        new double[2] { 1, 2 });
                    break;
                case DataSeries.LinePatternEnum.DashDot:
                    line.StrokeDashArray =
                        new DoubleCollection(
                        new double[4] { 4, 2, 1, 2 });
                    break;
                case DataSeries.LinePatternEnum.None:
                    line.Stroke = Brushes.Transparent;
                    break;
            }
        }
    }
}
```

This class begins with the member fields that describe the legend behavior:

```
            private bool isLegend;
            private bool isBorder;
            private Canvas legendCanvas;
```

The isLegend allows you to turn the legend on or off. The default setting of this field is false. Therefore, you'll need to change this default value to true if you want to display the legend on your chart. The isBorder field allows you to add (or not add) a border to the legend. The legendCanvas is used to hold the legend. You can add more member fields if you want more control over the legend. For example, you can add corresponding field members and properties to change the legend's text color, font, and background color, etc. Here I simply want to show you the basic steps of creating the legend without adding these extra features.

In this class, you place the legend on the right-hand side of the chart. You can easily move the legend to other positions in code. The AddLegend method is used to create the legend with line style, color, and text labels.

Testing Project

Add a new WPF Window to the project Chapter08 and name it LineChartWithLegend. The layout of this example is very similar to the previous example's, except that you add a legendCanvas. Here is the XAML file of this example:

```xml
<Window x:Class="Chapter08.LineChartWithLegend"
    xmlns="http://schemas.microsoft.com/winfx
        /2006/xaml/presentation"
    xmlns:x="http://schemas.microsoft.com/winfx/2006/xaml"
    Title="Line Chart with Legend" Height="400" Width="500">

    <Viewbox Stretch="Fill">
        <Grid Name="grid1" Margin="10">
            <Grid.ColumnDefinitions>
                <ColumnDefinition Width="Auto"/>
                <ColumnDefinition Name="column1" Width="*"/>
                <ColumnDefinition Width="Auto"/>
            </Grid.ColumnDefinitions>
            <Grid.RowDefinitions>
                <RowDefinition Height="Auto"/>
                <RowDefinition Name="row1" Height="*"/>
                <RowDefinition Height="Auto"/>
            </Grid.RowDefinitions>
            <TextBlock Margin="2" x:Name="tbTitle"
                Grid.Column="1" Grid.Row="0"
                RenderTransformOrigin="0.5,0.5" FontSize="14"
                FontWeight="Bold"
                HorizontalAlignment="Stretch"
                VerticalAlignment="Stretch"
                TextAlignment="Center"
                Text="Title"/>

            <TextBlock Margin="2" x:Name="tbXLabel"
                Grid.Column="1" Grid.Row="2"
                RenderTransformOrigin="0.5,0.5"
                TextAlignment="Center"
                Text="X Axis"/>

            <TextBlock Margin="2" Name="tbYLabel"
                Grid.Column="0" Grid.Row="1"
                RenderTransformOrigin="0.5,0.5"
                TextAlignment="Center"
                Text="Y Axis">
                <TextBlock.LayoutTransform>
                    <RotateTransform Angle="-90"/>
                </TextBlock.LayoutTransform>
            </TextBlock>

            <Canvas Name="legendCanvas" Margin="0,10,0,10"
                Grid.Column="2" Grid.Row="1" Width="40"/>
```

```
                <Canvas Margin="2" Name="textCanvas" Width="300"
                    Height="305" Grid.Column="1" Grid.Row="1"
                    ClipToBounds="True">
                    <Canvas Name="chartCanvas"
                        ClipToBounds="True"/>
                </Canvas>
            </Grid>
        </Viewbox>
    </Window>
```

The corresponding code-behind file of this example is listed below:

```
using System;
using System.Windows;
using System.Windows.Controls;
using System.Windows.Media;
using System.Windows.Shapes;

namespace Chapter08
{
    public partial class LineChartWithLegend : Window
    {
        private ChartStyleGridlines cs;
        private Legend lg = new Legend();
        private DataCollection dc = new DataCollection();
        private DataSeries ds = new DataSeries();

        public LineChartWithLegend()
        {
            InitializeComponent();
            AddChart();
            lg.LegendCanvas = legendCanvas;
            lg.IsLegend = true;
            lg.IsBorder = true;
            lg.AddLegend(cs, dc);
        }

        private void AddChart()
        {
            cs = new ChartStyleGridlines();
            cs.ChartCanvas = chartCanvas;
            cs.TextCanvas = textCanvas;
            cs.Title = "Sine and Cosine Chart";
            cs.Xmin = 0;
            cs.Xmax = 7;
            cs.Ymin = -1.5;
            cs.Ymax = 1.5;
            cs.YTick = 0.5;
            cs.GridlinePattern =
                ChartStyleGridlines.GridlinePatternEnum.Dot;
            cs.GridlineColor = Brushes.Black;
            cs.AddChartStyle(tbTitle, tbXLabel, tbYLabel);

            // Draw Sine curve:
```

```
    ds.LineColor = Brushes.Blue;
    ds.LineThickness = 1;
    ds.SeriesName = "Sine";
    for (int i = 0; i < 70; i++)
    {
        double x = i / 5.0;
        double y = Math.Sin(x);
        ds.LineSeries.Points.Add(new Point(x, y));
    }
    dc.DataList.Add(ds);

    // Draw cosine curve:
    ds = new DataSeries();
    ds.LineColor = Brushes.Red;
    ds.SeriesName = "Cosine";
    ds.LinePattern =
        DataSeries.LinePatternEnum.DashDot;
    ds.LineThickness = 2;
    for (int i = 0; i < 70; i++)
    {
        double x = i / 5.0;
        double y = Math.Cos(x);
        ds.LineSeries.Points.Add(new Point(x, y));
    }
    dc.DataList.Add(ds);

    // Draw sine^2 curve:
    ds = new DataSeries();
    ds.LineColor = Brushes.DarkGreen;
    ds.SeriesName = "Sine^2";
    ds.LinePattern = DataSeries.LinePatternEnum.Dot;
    ds.LineThickness = 2;
    for (int i = 0; i < 70; i++)
    {
        double x = i / 5.0;
        double y = Math.Sin(x) * Math.Sin(x);
        ds.LineSeries.Points.Add(new Point(x, y));
    }
    dc.DataList.Add(ds);

    dc.AddLines(chartCanvas, cs);
        }
    }
}
```

Here you add one more curve to the chart for demonstration purpose. Notice that you need to specify the SeriesName property for each DataSeries because the legend uses the SeriesName as the legend labels. Otherwise, the legend will use the default SeriesName (DataSeries0, DataSeries1, DataSeries2,...) as the legend labels.

In order to have the legend on your chart, you need to call the AddLegend method. First, add a new member field to this class:

```
private Legend lg = new Legend();
```

and set the legend's IsLegend property to true. Please note that you must place the AddLegend method after the AddChart, because the legend needs to know how many curves are on your chart.

Figure 8-4 shows the results of running this example.

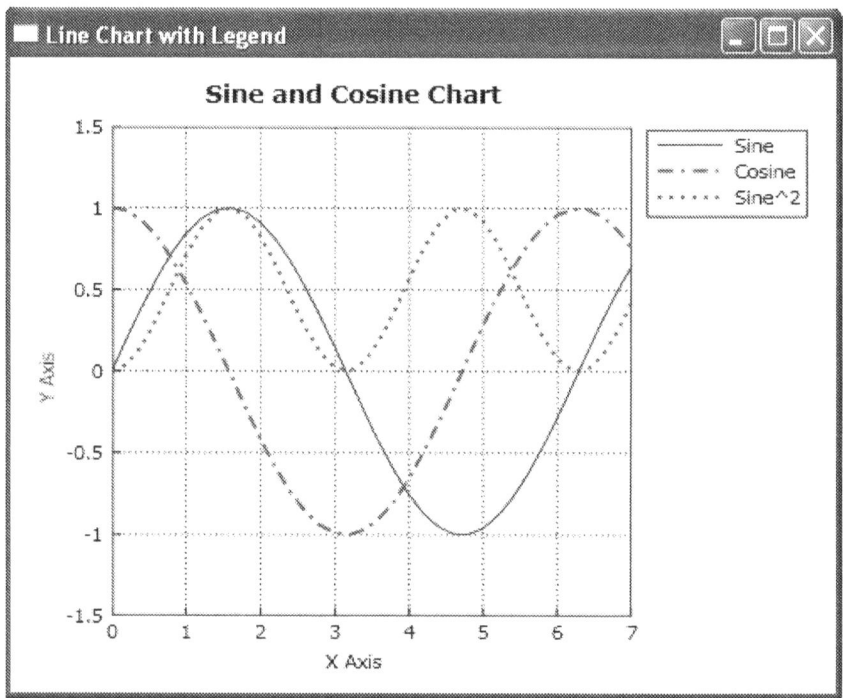

Figure 8-4 Chart with legend.

Chart User Control

In the previous sections, you directly implemented the source code for all of the classes in your line chart program. For simple applications, this approach works well. However, if you want to resue the same code in multiple-window applications, this method should be avoided. WPF provides a powerful means, the user control, to solve this problem.

The custom user controls in WPF are just like the simple buttons or text boxes already provided in WPF. Typically, the controls you design are to be used in multiple windows or modularize your code. These custom controls can reduce the amount of code you have to type, as well as make it easier for you to change the implementation of your program. There is no reason to duplicate code in your applications because this leaves a lot of room for bugs. Therefore, it is a good programming practice to create functionality specific to the user control in the control's source code, which can reduce code duplication and modularize your code.

Custom user controls are a key theme in WPF and .NET development. They can greatly enhance your programming style by improving encapsulation, simplifying a programming model, and making the user interface more pluggable. Of course, custom controls can also have the other benefits, including the ability to transform a generic window into a state-of-art modern interface.

In this section, you'll learn how to put the simple line chart application you developed in the previous sections into a custom user control, and how to use such a control in your WPF applications. You'll also learn how to make the chart control into a first-class WPF citizen and make it available in XAML. This means that you'll need to define dependency properties and routed events for the chart control in order to get support for essential WPF services, such as data binding, styles, and animation.

Creating Chart Control

A UserControl in WPF is a content control that can be configured using a design-time surface. Although a user control is basically similar to an ordinary content control, it is typically used when you want to quickly reuse an unchanging block of user interface in more than one window.

Creating a basic chart control based on the line chart examples developed in previous sections is easy. For simplicity's sake, you will build a line chart control without the legend (adding a legend to this control is trivial). The layout of the control is the same as shown in Figure 8-3. The development model for the chart user control is very similar to the model used for application development in WPF.

Instead of adding a new WPF Window, you add a new WPF UserControl to the project Chapter08 and call it LineChartControl. When you do this, Microsoft Visual Studio creates a XAML markup file and a corresponding custom class to hold your initialization and event handling code. This is the same experience as when you create a new WPF Window or Page application – the only difference is that the top-level container is the UserControl class. Here is the XAML file of the control:

```
<UserControl x:Class="Chapter08.LineChartControl"
    xmlns="http://schemas.microsoft.com/winfx
        /2006/xaml/presentation"
xmlns:x=http://schemas.microsoft.com/winfx/2006/xaml
Height="300" Width="400">

    <Viewbox Stretch="Fill">
        <Grid Name="grid1" Margin="10">
            <Grid.ColumnDefinitions>
                <ColumnDefinition Width="Auto"/>
                <ColumnDefinition Name="column1" Width="*"/>
                <ColumnDefinition Width="Auto"/>
```

```
            </Grid.ColumnDefinitions>
            <Grid.RowDefinitions>
                <RowDefinition Height="Auto"/>
                <RowDefinition Name="row1" Height="*"/>
                <RowDefinition Height="Auto"/>
            </Grid.RowDefinitions>
            <TextBlock Margin="2" Grid.Column="1" Grid.Row="0"
                RenderTransformOrigin="0.5,0.5" FontSize="14"
                FontWeight="Bold" HorizontalAlignment=
                "Stretch" VerticalAlignment="Stretch"
                TextAlignment="Center"
                Text="{Binding Path=Title}"/>

            <TextBlock Margin="2" Grid.Column="1" Grid.Row="2"
                RenderTransformOrigin="0.5,0.5"
                TextAlignment="Center"
                Text="{Binding Path=XLabel}"/>

            <TextBlock Margin="2" Grid.Column="0" Grid.Row="1"
                RenderTransformOrigin="0.5,0.5"
                TextAlignment="Center"
                Text="{Binding Path=YLabel}">
                <TextBlock.LayoutTransform>
                    <RotateTransform Angle="-90"/>
                </TextBlock.LayoutTransform>
            </TextBlock>

            <Canvas Name="legendCanvas" Margin="0,10,0,10"
                Grid.Column="2" Grid.Row="1" Width="40"/>

            <Canvas Margin="2" Name="textCanvas" Width="300"
                Height="305" Grid.Column="1" Grid.Row="1"
                ClipToBounds="True">
                <Canvas Name="chartCanvas"
                    ClipToBounds="True"/>
            </Canvas>
        </Grid>
    </Viewbox>
</UserControl>
```

This markup is basically the same as that used in previous examples, except that the TextBlocks for Title, XLabel, and YLabel are now bound to corresponding dependency properties, which are to be defined in the code-behind file. Data binding in WPF provides a way of extracting information from a source object and using it to set a property in a target object. The simplest data binding scenario occurs when the source object is a WPF element and the source property is a dependency property, because dependency properties have a built-in support for change notification. As a result, when you change the value of the dependency property in the source object, the bound property in the target object is updated immediately. That is exactly what you want – and it happens without requiring you to build any additional infrastructure, such as an INotifyPropertyChanged interface.

Defining Dependency Properties

Next, you need to design the public interface that the chart control exposes to the outside world. In other words, it is time to create the properties, methods, and events that the control consumer (the application that uses the control) will rely on to interact with your chart control.

You may want to expose most of the properties in the ChartStyleGridlines class in the previous example, such as axis limits, title, labels, etc., to the outside world, In order to support WPF features such as data binding, styles, and animation, writable control properties are almost always dependency properties.

The first step in creating a dependency property is to define a static field for it, with the word Property added to the end of the property name. Add the following dependency properties to the code-behind file:

```
using System;
using System.Windows;
using System.Collections.Generic;
using System.Windows.Controls;
using System.Windows.Input;
using System.Windows.Media;
using System.Windows.Shapes;

namespace Chapter08
{
    public partial class LineChartControl : UserControl
    {
        private ChartStyleLineChartControl controlChartStyle;
        private DataCollectionLineChartControl
            controlDataCollection;
        private DataSeriesLineChartControl controlDataSeries;

        public LineChartControl()
        {
            InitializeComponent();
            this.DataContext = this;
            this.controlChartStyle =
                new ChartStyleLineChartControl(this);
            this.controlDataCollection =
                new DataCollectionLineChartControl(this);
            this.controlDataSeries =
                new DataSeriesLineChartControl();
        }

        public ChartStyleLineChartControl ControlChartStyle
        {
            get { return controlChartStyle; }
            set { controlChartStyle = value; }
        }

        public DataCollectionLineChartControl
            ControlDataCollection
```

```
    {
        get { return controlDataCollection; }
        set { controlDataCollection = value; }
    }

    public DataSeriesLineChartControl ControlDataSeries
    {
        get { return controlDataSeries; }
        set { controlDataSeries = value; }
    }

    public static DependencyProperty XminProperty =
        DependencyProperty.Register(
        "Xmin", typeof(double), typeof(LineChartControl),
        new FrameworkPropertyMetadata(0.0,
        new PropertyChangedCallback(OnDoubleChanged)));

    public double Xmin
    {
        get { return (double)GetValue(XminProperty); }
        set { SetValue(XminProperty, value); }
    }

    public static DependencyProperty XmaxProperty =
        DependencyProperty.Register(
        "Xmax", typeof(double), typeof(LineChartControl),
        new FrameworkPropertyMetadata(1.0,
        new PropertyChangedCallback(OnDoubleChanged)));

    public double Xmax
    {
        get { return (double)GetValue(XmaxProperty); }
        set { SetValue(XmaxProperty, value); }
    }

    public static DependencyProperty YminProperty =
        DependencyProperty.Register(
        "Ymin", typeof(double), typeof(LineChartControl),
        new FrameworkPropertyMetadata(0.0,
        new PropertyChangedCallback(OnDoubleChanged)));

    public double Ymin
    {
        get { return (double)GetValue(YminProperty); }
        set { SetValue(YminProperty, value); }
    }

    public static DependencyProperty YmaxProperty =
        DependencyProperty.Register(
        "Ymax", typeof(double), typeof(LineChartControl),
        new FrameworkPropertyMetadata(1.0,
        new PropertyChangedCallback(OnDoubleChanged)));

    public double Ymax
```

```
{
    get { return (double)GetValue(YmaxProperty); }
    set { SetValue(YmaxProperty, value); }
}

public static DependencyProperty XTickProperty =
    DependencyProperty.Register(
    "XTick", typeof(double), typeof(LineChartControl),
    new FrameworkPropertyMetadata(0.5,
    new PropertyChangedCallback(OnDoubleChanged)));

public double XTick
{
    get { return (double)GetValue(XTickProperty); }
    set { SetValue(XTickProperty, value); }
}

public static DependencyProperty YTickProperty =
    DependencyProperty.Register(
    "YTick", typeof(double), typeof(LineChartControl),
    new FrameworkPropertyMetadata(0.5,
    new PropertyChangedCallback(OnDoubleChanged)));

public double YTick
{
    get { return (double)GetValue(YTickProperty); }
    set { SetValue(YTickProperty, value); }
}

public static DependencyProperty TitleProperty =
    DependencyProperty.Register(
    "Title", typeof(string), typeof(LineChartControl),
    new FrameworkPropertyMetadata("My Chart",
    new PropertyChangedCallback(OnStringChanged)));

public string Title
{
    get { return (string)GetValue(TitleProperty); }
    set { SetValue(TitleProperty, value); }
}

public static DependencyProperty XLabelProperty =
    DependencyProperty.Register(
    "XLabel", typeof(string), typeof(LineChartControl),
    new FrameworkPropertyMetadata("X Axis",
    new PropertyChangedCallback(OnStringChanged)));

public string XLabel
{
    get { return (string)GetValue(XLabelProperty); }
    set { SetValue(XLabelProperty, value); }
}

public static DependencyProperty YLabelProperty =
```

```
    DependencyProperty.Register(
    "YLabel", typeof(string), typeof(LineChartControl),
    new FrameworkPropertyMetadata("Y Axis",
    new PropertyChangedCallback(OnStringChanged)));

public string YLabel
{
    get { return (string)GetValue(YLabelProperty); }
    set { SetValue(YLabelProperty, value); }
}

public static DependencyProperty IsXGridProperty =
    DependencyProperty.Register(
    "IsXGrid", typeof(bool), typeof(LineChartControl),
    new FrameworkPropertyMetadata(true,
    new PropertyChangedCallback(OnBoolChanged)));

public bool IsXGrid
{
    get { return (bool)GetValue(IsXGridProperty); }
    set { SetValue(IsXGridProperty, value); }
}

public static DependencyProperty IsYGridProperty =
    DependencyProperty.Register(
    "IsYGrid", typeof(bool), typeof(LineChartControl),
    new FrameworkPropertyMetadata(true,
    new PropertyChangedCallback(OnBoolChanged)));

public bool IsYGrid
{
    get { return (bool)GetValue(IsYGridProperty); }
    set { SetValue(IsYGridProperty, value); }
}

public static DependencyProperty GridlineColorProperty
    = DependencyProperty.Register(
    "GridlineColor", typeof(Brush),
    typeof(LineChartControl),
    new FrameworkPropertyMetadata(Brushes.Gray,
    new PropertyChangedCallback(OnColorChanged)));

public Brush GridlineColor
{
    get { return (Brush)GetValue(
        GridlineColorProperty); }
    set { SetValue(GridlineColorProperty, value); }
}

public static DependencyProperty
    GridlinePatternProperty =
    DependencyProperty.Register(
    "GridLinePattern", typeof(
    ChartStyleLineChartControl.GridlinePatternEnum),
```

```
    typeof(LineChartControl),
    new FrameworkPropertyMetadata(
 ChartStyleLineChartControl.GridlinePatternEnum.Solid,
    new PropertyChangedCallback(
    OnGridlinePatternChanged)));

public ChartStyleLineChartControl.GridlinePatternEnum
    GridlinePattern
{
    get { return (ChartStyleLineChartControl.
        GridlinePatternEnum)GetValue(
        GridlinePatternProperty); }
    set { SetValue(GridlinePatternProperty, value); }
}

private static void OnGridlinePatternChanged(
    DependencyObject sender,
    DependencyPropertyChangedEventArgs e)
{
    LineChartControl lcc = (LineChartControl)sender;
    lcc.GridlinePattern = (ChartStyleLineChartControl.
        GridlinePatternEnum)e.NewValue;
}

private static void OnColorChanged(DependencyObject
    sender, DependencyPropertyChangedEventArgs e)
{
    LineChartControl lcc = (LineChartControl)sender;
    lcc.GridlineColor = (Brush)e.NewValue;
}

private static void OnDoubleChanged(DependencyObject
    sender, DependencyPropertyChangedEventArgs e)
{

    LineChartControl lcc = (LineChartControl)sender;
    if (e.Property == XminProperty)
        lcc.Xmin = (double)e.NewValue;
    else if (e.Property == XmaxProperty)
        lcc.Xmax = (double)e.NewValue;
    else if (e.Property == YminProperty)
        lcc.Ymin = (double)e.NewValue;
    else if (e.Property == YmaxProperty)
        lcc.Ymax = (double)e.NewValue;
    else if (e.Property == XTickProperty)
        lcc.XTick = (double)e.NewValue;
    else if (e.Property == YTickProperty)
        lcc.YTick = (double)e.NewValue;
}

private static void OnStringChanged(DependencyObject
    sender, DependencyPropertyChangedEventArgs e)
{
    LineChartControl lcc = (LineChartControl)sender;
```

```
            if (e.Property == TitleProperty)
            {
                lcc.Title = (string)e.NewValue;
            }
            else if (e.Property == XLabelProperty)
            {
                lcc.XLabel = (string)e.NewValue;
            }
            else if (e.Property == YLabelProperty)
            {
                lcc.YLabel = (string)e.NewValue;
            }
        }

        private static void OnBoolChanged(DependencyObject
            sender, DependencyPropertyChangedEventArgs e)
        {
            LineChartControl lcc = (LineChartControl)sender;
            if (e.Property == IsXGridProperty)
                lcc.IsXGrid = (bool)e.NewValue;
            else if (e.Property == IsYGridProperty)
                lcc.IsYGrid = (bool)e.NewValue;
        }
    }
}
```

After defining dependency properties, you add standard property wrappers of the properties that make them easier to access, and usable in XAML. Note that the property wrappers should not contain any logic, because properties may be set and retrieved directly using the SetValue and GetValue methods of the base DependencyObject class. For example, the property synchronization logic in this control is implemented using callbacks that fire when the property changes through the property wrapper or a direct SetValue call.

The property change callbacks are responsible for keeping the property values consistent with corresponding dependency properties. Whenever the property values are changed, the corresponding dependency properties are adjusted accordingly. There are several kinds of property change callbacks, including callbacks for changes in color, string, double, bool, and line pattern.

The following statement is also required for data binding:

```
        this.DataContext = this;
```

This is a quicker approach that doesn't require any additional code. You simply set a binding expression for the control's DataContext property, as shown in the above statement.

Chart Style for Chart Control

You need to modify the original chart style used in previous examples because most of the public properties in this class have been replaced by dependency properties already defined in the LineChartControl class. Now open the code-behind file of the LineChartControl and add a new chart style class, called ChartStyleLineChartControl, to the file:

```
public class ChartStyleLineChartControl
{
    private double Xmin;
    private double Xmax;
    private double Ymin;
    private double Ymax;
    private string Title;
    private string XLabel;
    private string YLabel;
    private double XTick;
    private double YTick;
    private bool IsXGrid;
    private bool IsYGrid;
    private Brush GridlineColor;
    private GridlinePatternEnum GridlinePattern;

    private double leftOffset = 20;
    private double bottomOffset = 15;
    private double rightOffset = 10;
    private Line gridline = new Line();
    private LineChartControl lcc;
    private Canvas TextCanvas;
    private Canvas ChartCanvas;

    public ChartStyleLineChartControl(
        LineChartControl lcc)
    {
        this.lcc = lcc;
        TextCanvas = lcc.textCanvas;
        ChartCanvas = lcc.chartCanvas;
        UpdateChartStyle();
    }

    public void UpdateChartStyle()
    {
        Xmin = lcc.Xmin;
        Xmax = lcc.Xmax;
        Ymin = lcc.Ymin;
        Ymax = lcc.Ymax;
        XTick = lcc.XTick;
        YTick = lcc.YTick;
        Title = lcc.Title;
        XLabel = lcc.XLabel;
        YLabel = lcc.YLabel;
        IsXGrid = lcc.IsXGrid;
        IsYGrid = lcc.IsYGrid;
        GridlineColor = lcc.GridlineColor;
        GridlinePattern = lcc.GridlinePattern;
    }

    public void AddChartStyle()
```

```
{
    UpdateChartStyle();

    Point pt = new Point();
    Line tick = new Line();
    double offset = 0;
    double dx, dy;
    TextBlock tb = new TextBlock();

    //  determine right offset:
    tb.Text = Xmax.ToString();
    tb.Measure(new Size(Double.PositiveInfinity,
        Double.PositiveInfinity));
    Size size = tb.DesiredSize;
    rightOffset = size.Width / 2 + 2;

    // Determine left offset:
    for (dy = Ymin; dy <= Ymax; dy += YTick)
    {
        pt = NormalizePoint(new Point(Xmin, dy));
        tb = new TextBlock();
        tb.Text = dy.ToString();
        tb.TextAlignment = TextAlignment.Right;
        tb.Measure(new Size(Double.PositiveInfinity,
            Double.PositiveInfinity));
        size = tb.DesiredSize;
        if (offset < size.Width)
            offset = size.Width;
    }
    leftOffset = offset + 5;

    Canvas.SetLeft(ChartCanvas, leftOffset);
    Canvas.SetBottom(ChartCanvas, bottomOffset);
    ChartCanvas.Width = TextCanvas.Width -
        leftOffset - rightOffset;
    ChartCanvas.Height = TextCanvas.Height -
        bottomOffset - size.Height / 2;
    Rectangle chartRect = new Rectangle();
    chartRect.Stroke = Brushes.Black;
    chartRect.Width = ChartCanvas.Width;
    chartRect.Height = ChartCanvas.Height;
    ChartCanvas.Children.Add(chartRect);

    // Create vertical gridlines:
    if (IsYGrid == true)
    {
        for (dx = Xmin + XTick; dx < Xmax;
            dx += XTick)
        {
            gridline = new Line();
            AddLinePattern();
            gridline.X1 = NormalizePoint(
                new Point(dx, Ymin)).X;
            gridline.Y1 = NormalizePoint(
```

```
                new Point(dx, Ymin)).Y;
            gridline.X2 = NormalizePoint(
                new Point(dx, Ymax)).X;
            gridline.Y2 = NormalizePoint(
                new Point(dx, Ymax)).Y;
            ChartCanvas.Children.Add(gridline);
        }
    }

    // Create horizontal gridlines:
    if (IsXGrid == true)
    {
        for (dy = Ymin + YTick; dy < Ymax;
            dy += YTick)
        {
            gridline = new Line();
            AddLinePattern();
            gridline.X1 = NormalizePoint(
                new Point(Xmin, dy)).X;
            gridline.Y1 = NormalizePoint(
                new Point(Xmin, dy)).Y;
            gridline.X2 = NormalizePoint(
                new Point(Xmax, dy)).X;
            gridline.Y2 = NormalizePoint(
                new Point(Xmax, dy)).Y;
            ChartCanvas.Children.Add(gridline);
        }
    }

    // Create x-axis tick marks:
    for (dx = Xmin; dx <= Xmax; dx += XTick)
    {
        pt = NormalizePoint(new Point(dx, Ymin));
        tick = new Line();
        tick.Stroke = Brushes.Black;
        tick.X1 = pt.X;
        tick.Y1 = pt.Y;
        tick.X2 = pt.X;
        tick.Y2 = pt.Y - 5;
        ChartCanvas.Children.Add(tick);

        tb = new TextBlock();
        tb.Text = dx.ToString();
        tb.Measure(new Size(Double.PositiveInfinity,
            Double.PositiveInfinity));
        size = tb.DesiredSize;
        TextCanvas.Children.Add(tb);
        Canvas.SetLeft(tb, leftOffset + pt.X -
            size.Width / 2);
        Canvas.SetTop(tb, pt.Y + 2 + size.Height / 2);
    }

    // Create y-axis tick marks:
    for (dy = Ymin; dy <= Ymax; dy += YTick)
```

```
        {
            pt = NormalizePoint(new Point(Xmin, dy));
            tick = new Line();
            tick.Stroke = Brushes.Black;
            tick.X1 = pt.X;
            tick.Y1 = pt.Y;
            tick.X2 = pt.X + 5;
            tick.Y2 = pt.Y;
            ChartCanvas.Children.Add(tick);

            tb = new TextBlock();
            tb.Text = dy.ToString();
            tb.Measure(new Size(Double.PositiveInfinity,
                Double.PositiveInfinity));
            size = tb.DesiredSize;
            TextCanvas.Children.Add(tb);
            Canvas.SetRight(tb, ChartCanvas.Width + 10);
            Canvas.SetTop(tb, pt.Y);
        }
    }

    public void AddLinePattern()
    {
        gridline.Stroke = GridlineColor;
        gridline.StrokeThickness = 1;

        switch (GridlinePattern)
        {
            case GridlinePatternEnum.Dash:
                gridline.StrokeDashArray =
                    new DoubleCollection(
                    new double[2] { 4, 3 });
                break;
            case GridlinePatternEnum.Dot:
                gridline.StrokeDashArray =
                    new DoubleCollection(
                    new double[2] { 1, 2 });
                break;
            case GridlinePatternEnum.DashDot:
                gridline.StrokeDashArray =
                    new DoubleCollection(
                    new double[4] { 4, 2, 1, 2 });
                break;
        }
    }

    public Point NormalizePoint(Point pt)
    {
        if (ChartCanvas.Width.ToString() == "NaN")
            ChartCanvas.Width = 270;
        if (ChartCanvas.Height.ToString() == "NaN")
            ChartCanvas.Height = 250;
        Point result = new Point();
        result.X = (pt.X - Xmin) *
```

```
            ChartCanvas.Width / (Xmax - Xmin);
        result.Y = ChartCanvas.Height - (pt.Y - Ymin) *
            ChartCanvas.Height / (Ymax - Ymin);
        return result;
    }

    public enum GridlinePatternEnum
    {
        Solid = 1,
        Dash = 2,
        Dot = 3,
        DashDot = 4
    }
}
```

Notice that all of the field members in this class are attached to the corresponding dependency properties in the LineChartControl class, as shown in the UpdateChartStyle method. The original public properties have been removed from this class, which were used in previous examples. The rest of the code is basically the same as the ChartStyleGridlines class used in previous examples.

Data Collection and Data Series

The DataSeries class is almost identical to the class used in previous example. To make the chart control self-contained, you need to copy it, rename it DataSeriesLineChartControl, and add it to the code-behind file. I'll not list the code of this class here. You can look at the complete source code by opening the code-behind file of the control.

Some modifications have been made to the data collection class in order to reflect its relation to the chart control. Add the DataCollectionLineChartControl class to the code-behind file:

```
public class DataCollectionLineChartControl
{
    private List<DataSeriesLineChartControl> dataList;
    private LineChartControl lcc;
    private ChartStyleLineChartControl cs;

    public DataCollectionLineChartControl(
        LineChartControl lcc)
    {
        dataList = new List<DataSeriesLineChartControl>();
        this.lcc = lcc;
        this.cs = lcc.ControlChartStyle;
    }

    public List<DataSeriesLineChartControl> DataList
    {
        get { return dataList; }
        set { dataList = value; }
    }
```

```
public void AddLines()
{
    lcc.ControlChartStyle.AddChartStyle();
    int j = 0;
    foreach (DataSeriesLineChartControl ds
        in DataList)
    {
        if (ds.SeriesName == "Default Name")
        {
            ds.SeriesName = "DataSeries" +
                j.ToString();
        }
        ds.AddLinePattern();
        for (int i = 0; i <
            ds.LineSeries.Points.Count; i++)
        {
            ds.LineSeries.Points[i] =
                cs.NormalizePoint(
                ds.LineSeries.Points[i]);
        }
        lcc.chartCanvas.Children.Add(ds.LineSeries);
        j++;
    }
}
}
```

Using Chart Control

Now that the 2D line chart control has been completed, you can easily use it in your WPF applications. To use the control in another WPF window, you need to begin by mapping the .NET namespace to an XML namespace, as shown here:

```
xmlns:local="clr-namespace:Chapter08"
```

If your control is located in a different assembly than your application, you need to map the assembly too. Using the XML namespace and the user control class name, you can add the user control exactly like you add any other type of object to the XAML file. You can also set its properties and attach event handlers directly in the control tag, as shown here:

```
<local:LineChartControl x:Name="myLineChart"
    Xmin="0" Xmax="7" Ymin="-1.5" Ymax="1.5" Width="350"
    Height="300" Background="LightBlue" Title=" My Chart"
    GridlinePattern="DashDot"/>
```

Notice how you specify the GridlinePattern property – you simply use the Solid, Dash, Dot, or DashDot that are defined in the GridlinePatternEnum of the chart style class. This is much simpler than using code, where you need to type the full path in order to define the gridlines' line pattern, as shown here:

```
myLineChart.GridlinePattern =
```

```
ChartStyleLineChartControl.GridlinePatternEnum.DashDot;
```

You can also specify other properties for the chart control, standard to WPF elements, such as Width, Height, Canvas.Left, Canvas.Top, Background, etc. These standard properties allow you to position the control, set the size of the control, or set the background color of the control.

Creating Simple Chart

Here, you'll learn how to use the line chart control to plot simple Sine and Cosine functions. Add a new WPF Window to the project Chapter08 and name it TestLineChartControl. Figure 8-5 shows a screen shot of this example.

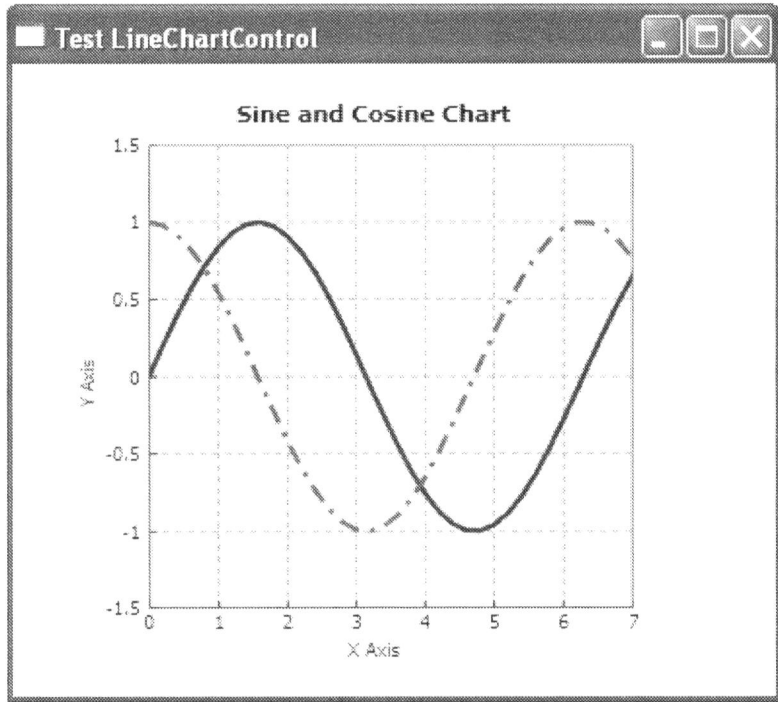

Figure 8-5 Chart created using the line chart control.

The layout of this example is very simple and is created using the following XAML file:

```
<Window x:Class="Chapter08.TestLineChartControl"
    xmlns="http://schemas.microsoft.com/winfx
        /2006/xaml/presentation"
    xmlns:x="http://schemas.microsoft.com/winfx/2006/xaml"
    xmlns:local="clr-namespace:Chapter08"
    Title="Test LineChartControl" Height="350" Width="400">

    <Grid>
```

```
        <local:LineChartControl x:Name="myLineChart"
            Xmin="0" Xmax="7" Ymin="-1.5" Ymax="1.5"
            XTick="1" YTick="0.5"
            Width="350" Height="300"
            Title="Sine and Cosine Chart"
            GridlinePattern="Dash"/>
    </Grid>
</Window>
```

Here, you simply create the line chart control called myLineChart exactly as you create any other type of WPF element. The following is the corresponding code-behind file:

```
using System;
using System.Collections.Generic;
using System.Windows;
using System.Windows.Controls;
using System.Windows.Media;
using System.Windows.Shapes;

namespace Chapter08
{
    public partial class TestLineChartControl : Window
    {
        private DataSeriesLineChartControl ds;
        public TestLineChartControl()
        {
            InitializeComponent();
            AddChart();
        }

        private void AddChart()
        {
            // Draw Sine curve:
            ds = new DataSeriesLineChartControl();
            ds.LineColor = Brushes.Blue;
            ds.LineThickness = 3;
            for (int i = 0; i < 70; i++)
            {
                double x = i / 5.0;
                double y = Math.Sin(x);
                ds.LineSeries.Points.Add(new Point(x, y));
            }
            myLineChart.ControlDataCollection.
                DataList.Add(ds);

            // Draw cosine curve:
            ds = new DataSeriesLineChartControl();
            ds.LineColor = Brushes.Red;
            ds.LinePattern = DataSeriesLineChartControl.
                LinePatternEnum.DashDot;
            ds.LineThickness = 3;

            for (int i = 0; i < 70; i++)
```

```
        {
            double x = i / 5.0;
            double y = Math.Cos(x);
            ds.LineSeries.Points.Add(new Point(x, y));
        }
        myLineChart.ControlDataCollection.
            DataList.Add(ds);

        myLineChart.ControlDataCollection.AddLines();
    }
  }
}
```

Just like in the previous examples, you need to first create the data series and then add them to the ControlDataCollection of your chart control. It is a good programming practice to specify all chart style related properties in XAML and create the data series in code. Of course, if you like, you can use a code-only approach to create your chart using the chart control.

Creating Multiple Charts

With the line chart control, you can easily create multiple charts in a single WPF window. Let's add a new WPF Window to the project Chapter08 and name it MultipleCharts. Create a 2x2 Grid control and add a line chart control to each of the four cells of the Grid, which can be done using the following XAML file:

```
<Window x:Class="Chapter08.MultipleCharts"
    xmlns="http://schemas.microsoft.com/winfx
        /2006/xaml/presentation"
    xmlns:x="http://schemas.microsoft.com/winfx/2006/xaml"
    xmlns:local="clr-namespace:Chapter08"
    Title="MultipleCharts" Height="500" Width="600">

    <Viewbox Stretch="Fill">
        <Grid Margin="5">
            <Grid.ColumnDefinitions>
                <ColumnDefinition/>
                <ColumnDefinition/>
            </Grid.ColumnDefinitions>
            <Grid.RowDefinitions>
                <RowDefinition/>
                <RowDefinition/>
            </Grid.RowDefinitions>

            <local:LineChartControl x:Name="chart1" Xmin="0"
                Xmax="7" Ymin="-1.5" Ymax="1.5" XTick="1"
                YTick="0.5" Title="Sin(x)"
                GridlinePattern="Dash" Grid.Column="0"
                Grid.Row="0"/>

            <local:LineChartControl x:Name="chart2" Xmin="0"
                Xmax="7" Ymin="-1.5" Ymax="1.5" XTick="1"
                YTick="0.5" Title="Cos(x)" IsXGrid="False"
```

```
                    GridlinePattern="Dash" Grid.Column="1"
                    Grid.Row="0"/>

            <local:LineChartControl x:Name="chart3" Xmin="0"
                    Xmax="7" Ymin="-0.5" Ymax="1.5" XTick="1"
                    YTick="0.5" Title="Sin(x)^2" IsYGrid="False"
                    GridlinePattern="DashDot" Grid.Column="0"
                    Grid.Row="1"/>

            <local:LineChartControl x:Name="chart4" Xmin="0"
                    Xmax="7" Ymin="-1.5" Ymax="1.5" XTick="1"
                    YTick="0.5" Title="Cos(x)^3" IsXGrid="False"
                    IsYGrid="False" Grid.Column="1" Grid.Row="1"/>
        </Grid>
    </Viewbox>
</Window>
```

Here, you create four line chart controls, chart1, chart2, chart3, and chart4. For each chart, you plot a different math function specified in its title. You also set different a gridline property for each chart. The corresponding code-behind file that creates curves on each chart is listed below:

```
using System;
using System.Collections.Generic;
using System.Windows;
using System.Windows.Controls;
using System.Windows.Media;
using System.Windows.Shapes;

namespace Chapter08
{
    public partial class MultipleCharts : Window
    {

        public MultipleCharts()
        {
            InitializeComponent();
            AddChart();
        }

        private void AddChart()
        {
            DataSeriesLineChartControl ds;
            double x, y;

            // Create chart1:
            ds = new DataSeriesLineChartControl();
            ds.LineColor = Brushes.Blue;
            ds.LineThickness = 2;
            for (int i = 0; i < 70; i++)
            {
                x = i / 5.0;
                y = Math.Sin(x);
                ds.LineSeries.Points.Add(new Point(x, y));
```

```
        }
        chart1.ControlDataCollection.DataList.Add(ds);
        chart1.ControlDataCollection.AddLines();

        // Create chart2:
        ds = new DataSeriesLineChartControl();
        ds.LineColor = Brushes.Red;
        ds.LinePattern =
            DataSeriesLineChartControl.
            LinePatternEnum.Dash;
        ds.LineThickness = 2;

        for (int i = 0; i < 70; i++)
        {
            x = i / 5.0;
            y = Math.Cos(x);
            ds.LineSeries.Points.Add(new Point(x, y));
        }
        chart2.ControlDataCollection.DataList.Add(ds);
        chart2.ControlDataCollection.AddLines();

        // Create chart3:
        ds = new DataSeriesLineChartControl();
        ds.LineColor = Brushes.Black;
        ds.LineThickness = 2;

        for (int i = 0; i < 70; i++)
        {
            x = i / 5.0;
            y = Math.Sin(x) * Math.Sin(x);
            ds.LineSeries.Points.Add(new Point(x, y));
        }
        chart3.ControlDataCollection.DataList.Add(ds);
        chart3.ControlDataCollection.AddLines();

        // Create chart4:
        ds = new DataSeriesLineChartControl();
        ds.LineColor = Brushes.DarkGreen;
        ds.LineThickness = 2;

        for (int i = 0; i < 70; i++)
        {
            x = i / 5.0;
            y = Math.Cos(x) * Math.Cos(x) * Math.Cos(x);
            ds.LineSeries.Points.Add(new Point(x, y));
        }
        chart4.ControlDataCollection.DataList.Add(ds);
        chart4.ControlDataCollection.AddLines();
    }
  }
}
```

This class creates four charts that give the 2x2 sub-charts. Like any other WPF built-in element, you can place as many line chart controls as you need in a single WPF window.

Figure 8-6 Shows the results of running this example.

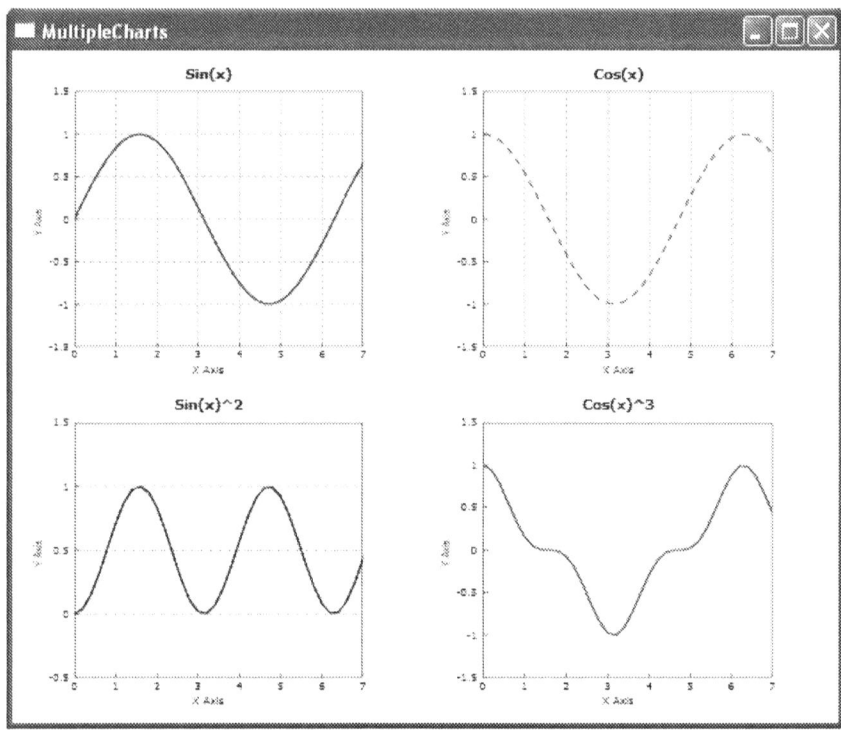

Figure 8-6 Sub-charts created using line chart controls.

In this chapter, you learned how to create 2D line charts and line chart controls in WPF. Following the procedures presented in this chapter, you can easily create a variety of specialized charts according to your application requirements. If you need to create various charts in C# and GDI+ rather than in WPF, you can refer to my other book "Practical C# Charts and Graphics".

Chapter 9
3D Transformations

In the previous chapters, we discussed 2D graphics, transforms, geometry, and drawing. This chapter will explain the mathematical basics of 3D transforms, which will be used to perform operations on 3D graphics objects. Most 3D transformations are analogous to the 2D transformations described in Chapter 3. Using homogeneous coordinates and matrix representations similar to the ones used in 2D, I'll show you how to perform basic transforms, including translation, scaling, and rotation in 3D. This chapter will also describe various projection matrices, which allow you to view 3D graphics objects on a 2D screen. As is the case with 2D, you can combine 3D basic transform matrices to represent a complicated transform with a single transform matrix. This chapter will also show you how WPF defines the transform matrices in 3D an how to perform a variety of transformations on 3D objects.

3D Matrices in WPF

Matrix representations play an important role in transformations and operations on graphics objects. A matrix is a multi-dimensional array. This section explains the basics of 3D matrices and transformations. General 3D transforms are quite complicated. As in the case of 2D, however, you can build more useful transforms with combinations of simple basic transforms, including translation, scaling, rotation, and projection. The following sections describe these fundamental transformations. Once you understand how to use these basic 3D transformations, you can always combine them to create more general 3D transformations.

3D Points and Vectors

WPF defines two 3D Point structures, Point3D and Point4D. The Point3D structure defines the X, Y, and Z coordinates of a point in 3D space. Point4D defines the X, Y, Z, and W coordinates of a point in a 3D homogeneous coordinate system, which is used to perform transforms with non-affine 3D matrices. The Vector3D structure defines a displacement with components X, Y, and Z in 3D space.

A vector in 3D is represented by a row array with three elements X, Y, and Z. For instance, you can create a 3D Vector object using the following code snippet:

```
Vector3D v = new Vector3D(1, 2, 3);
```

Note that a Vector3D object and a Point3D object in WPF are two different objects. The following statement is invalid:

```
Vector3D v = new Point3D(1, 2, 3);
```

However, you can define a Vector3D object using Point3D, or vice versa. The following are valid statements:

```
Vector3D v1 = new Point3D(2, 3, 4) - new Point3D(1, 2, 3);
Vector3D v2 = (Vector3D)new Point3D(1, 2, 3);
Point3D pt = (Point3D)new Vector3D(1, 2, 3);
```

A Vector3D object has five public properties:

- Length – Gets the length of the Vector3D.

- LengthSquared – Gets the square of the length of the Vector3D.

- X – Gets or sets the X component of the Vector3D.

- Y – Gets or sets the Y component of the Vector3D.

- Z – Gets or sets the Z component of the Vector3D.

In addition, there are methods associated with Vector3D, which allow you to perform various mathematical operations for the Vector3D objects. Here are some frequently used methods:

- Add – Adds a Vector3D strcuture to a Point3D or to another Vector3D.

- Subtract – Subtracts a Vector3D structure or a Point3D structure from a Vector3D structure.

- Multiply – Multiplies a Vector3D structure by the specified double or Matrix3D, and returns the result as a Vector3D.

- Divide – Divides a Vector3D structure by a scalar and returns as a Vector3D.

- CrossProduct – Calculates the cross product of two Vector3D structures.

- AngleBetween – Retrieves the angle required to rotate the first Vector3D structure into the second Vector3D structure.

- Normalize – Normalizes the specified Vector3D structure.

For example:

```
Vector3D v1 = new Vector3D(20, 10, 0);
Vector3D v2 = new Vector3D(0, 10, 20);
Vector3D cross = Vector3D.CrossProduct(v1, v2);
```

```
double angle = Vector3D.AngleBetween(v1, v2);
v1.Normalize();
double length2 = v1.LengthSQuared;
```

This generates the output: cross = (100, -200, 100) and angle = 44.42 degrees. The normalized result of v1 is stored in v1 again, in this case, v1 becomes (0.802, 0.535, 0.267), which is confirmed by its length square: length2 = 1.

A Point3D structure has three public properties:

- X – Gets or sets the X coordinate of the Point3D structure.

- Y – Gets or sets the Y cooridinate of the Point3D structure.

- Z – Gets or sets the Z coordinate of the Point3D structure.

In addition, there are methods associated with Point3D that allow you to perform various mathematical operations for the Point3D objects. Here are some frequently used methods:

- Add – Adds a Point3D structure to a Vector3D and returns the results as a Point3D structure.

- Subtract – Subtracts a Point3D structure or a Vector3D structure from a Point3D structure.

- Multiply – Transforms the specified Point3D structure by a specified Matrix3D structure.

- Offset – Change the X, Y, and Z values of the Point3D structure by a specified amount.

The Point4D structure represents a 3D Point in a homogeneous coordinate system. This structure is specifically designed to perform transforms with non-affine 3D matrices.

A Point4D structure has four public properties:

- X – Gets or sets the X component of the Point4D structure.

- Y – Gets or sets the Y component of the Point4D structure.

- Z – Gets or sets the Z component of the Point4D structure.

- W – Gets or sets the W component of the Point4D structure.

In addition, there are methods associated with Point4D that allow you to perform various mathematical operations on the Point4D objects. The following are some frequently used methods:

- Add – Adds a Point4D structure to another Point4D structrue.

- Subtract – Subtracts a Point4D structure from another Point4D structure.

- Multiply – Transforms the specified Point4D structure by the specified Matrix3D structure.

- Offset – Change the X, Y, Z, and W values of the Point4D structure by a specified amount.

It is possible to cast a Point3D object to a Point4D object, as shown in the following statement:

```
Point4D pt4 = (Point4D)new Point3D(10, 15, 20);
```

The following code snippet is also valid:

```
Point4D pt4 = (Point4D)(Point3D)new Vector3D(10, 15, 20);
```

where the Vector3D object is first cast to a Point3D object, which is then cast to a Point4D object. In the above casting process, the Point4D object has the values: pt4 = (10, 15, 20, 1). It simply adds the W component with a value of 1.

Matrix3D Structure

WPF defines a 3D matrix structure, Matrix3D. It is a 4 x 4 matrix in the 3D homogeneous coordinate system and has the following row-vector syntax:

$$
\begin{pmatrix}
M_{11} & M_{12} & M_{13} & M_{14} \\
M_{21} & M_{22} & M_{23} & M_{24} \\
M_{31} & M_{32} & M_{33} & M_{34} \\
OffsetX & OffsetY & OffsetZ & M_{44}
\end{pmatrix}
$$

Unlike in 2D matrices, here the last column is also defined and accessible. The Matrix3D structure allows you to represent affine as well as non-affine 3D transforms. The non-affine transforms with non-zero M14, M24, or M34 value often represent perspective projection transformations.

All of these sixteen elements are public properties of a Matrix3D structure. In particular, the elements of OffsetX, OffsetY, and OffsetZ get and set values of translation in the X, Y, and Z directions, respecitively. In addition to the element properties, there are the other public properties associated with Matrix3D structure that are also useful in performing matrix operations:

- Determinant – Retrieves the determinant of the Matrix3D structure.

- HasInverse – Gets a value that indicates whether the Matrix3D is invertible.

- Identity – Changes a Matrix3D structure into an identity Matrix3D.

- IsAffine – Gets a value that indicates whether the Matrix3D structure is affine.

- IsIdentity – Determines whether the Matrix3D structure is an identity Matrix3D.

You can create a Matrix3D object in WPF by using its overloaded constructors, which take an array of double values as arguments. Please note that before using the Matrix3D structure in the applications, you need to add a reference to the System.Windows.Media.Media3D namespace. The following code snippet creates three Matrix3D objects for translation, scaling, and rotation around the Z axis by directly specifying corresponding matrix elements:

```
double dx = 3;
double dy = 2;
double dz = 1.5;
double sx = 0.5;
double sy = 1.5;
double sz = 2.5;
double theta = Math.PI / 4;
double sin = Math.Sin(theta);
double cos = Math.Cos(theta);
Matrix3D tm = new Matrix3D( 1,   0,   0, 0,
                            0,   1,   0, 0,
                            0,   0,   1, 0,
                           dx,  dy,  dz, 1);
Matrix3D sm = new Matrix3D(sx,   0,   0, 0,
                            0,  sy,   0, 0,
                            0,   0,  sz, 0,
                            0,   0,   0, 1);
Matrix3D rm = new Matrix3D(cos, sin, 0, 0,
                          -sin, cos, 0, 0,
                             0,   0, 1, 0,
                             0,   0, 0, 1);
```

The matrix tm is a translation matrix that translates an object by 3 units in the X direction, by 2 units in the Y direction, and by 1.5 units in the Z direction. The scaling matrix sm scales an object by a factor of 0.5 in the X direction, by a factor of 1.5 in the Y direction, and by a factor of 2.5 in the Z direction. Finally, the matrix rm is a rotation matrix that rotates an object about the Z axis by 45 degrees.

Matrix3D Operations

The Matrix3D structure in WPF provides methods to rotate, scale, and translate. It also uses several methods to perform matrix operations. For example, The Invert method is used to invert a Matrix3D object if it is invertible. This method takes no parameters. The Multiply method multiplies two matrices and returns the result in a new matrix.

Care must be taken when you apply Matrix3D to Point3D, Point4D, and Vector3D objects. For standard scaling and rotation, Matrix3D takes the form such that both the last row and last column have the elements (0, 0, 0, 1). In this case, there will be no surprising results. For example:

```
Matrix3D m3 = new Matrix3D(   1, 0.5, 0, 0,
                           -0.5,   1, 0, 0,
                              0,   0, 1, 0,
                              0,   0, 0, 1);
Point3D pt3 = new Point3D(2, 3, 4);
Vector3D v3 = new Vector3D(2, 3, 4);
Point4D pt4 = new Point4D(2, 3, 4, 1);

Point3D pt3t = pt3 * m3;
Vector3D v3t = v3 * m3;
```

```
Point4D pt4t = pt4 * m3;
```

This generates the expected results of pt3t = (0.5, 4, 4), v3t = (0.5, 4, 4), and pt4t = (0.5, 4, 4, 1), after the transform. However, if you add a translation in the X direction to Matrix3D by changing the m3 to the following form:

```
Matrix3D m3 = new Matrix3D(    1, 0.5, 0, 0,
                            -0.5,   1, 0, 0,
                               0,   0, 1, 0,
                             100,   0, 0, 1);
```

and recalculating the transformation produces the output: pt3t = (100.5, 4, 4), vt3 = (0.5, 4, 4), and pt4t = (100.5, 4, 4, 1). You can see that translating 100 units in the X direction has no effect on the Vector3D object at all. This is because the Vector3D object is defined in a real 3D space, but not in a homogeneous coordinate system. The Vector3D object has no W component. When you transform a Vector3D object using Matrix3D, WPF simply uses the first 3 x 3 sub-matrix of the Matrix3D, and neglects the last column and the last row.

For a Point3D object, even though it is defined using three components, X, Y, and Z, WPF implicitly adds a W = 1 component to the Point3D object. That is why both pt3t and pt4t give the correct results.

Now, let's change the m3 to a non-affine matrix by adding a non-zero element of $M_{34} = 2$:

```
Matrix3D m3 = new Matrix3D(    1, 0.5, 0, 0,
                            -0.5,   1, 0, 0,
                               0,   0, 1, 2,
                             100,   0, 0, 1);
```

This corresponds to a transform matrix with a perspective projection. After this transformation, you will obtain the following "strange" results:

```
pt3t = (11.167, 0.444, 0.444)
v3t = (0.5, 4, 4)
pt4t = (100.5, 4, 4, 9)
```

What happened here? It is easy to understand the result of v3t because it always neglects both the last column and the last row of Matrix3D. It remains the same results even when you change the elements of the last row or last column. The result of pt4t is also expected because it is simply a direct multiplication of pt4*m3.

Let's take a look at pt3t. In fact, it is obtained by two steps. First, you simply use the direct multiplication of Matrix3D and Point3D object with an additional W = 1 component, which gives the result of pt4t. Then, you can obtain the pt3t by normalizing the X, Y, and Z components of the pt4t with its W component:

```
pt3  = (100.9/9, 4/9, 4/9) = (11.167, 0.444, 0.444)
```

In general, for an arbitrary Point4D = (x, y, z, w) in the homogeneous coordinates, the plane at infinity is usually identified with a set of points with w = 0. When points are away from the plane at infinity, you can always use (x/w, y/w, z/w) to define the Point3D's X, Y, Z components. WPF automatically performs the transform on the Point3D objects and gives you the normalized results. The discussion presented here simply shows you the mathematical basis, which is used by WPF to perform transforms on Point3D objects.

Let's use an example to show you how to perform 3D matrix operations in WPF. Start with a new WPF Windows Application project, and call it Chapter09. Add a new WPF Window and name it StartMenu. This window will be the main menu window, from which you can access all the examples in this chapter.

Next, add another WPF Window, called Matrix3DOperation, to the project. Here is the XAML file of this example:

```xml
<Window x:Class="Chapter09.Matrix3DOperation"
    xmlns="http://schemas.microsoft.com/winfx
        /2006/xaml/presentation"
    xmlns:x="http://schemas.microsoft.com/winfx/2006/xaml"
 Title="Matrix3D Operation" Height="320" Width="260">

    <StackPanel>
        <TextBlock Margin="10,10,5,5"
                Text="Original Matrix:"/>
        <TextBlock Name="tbOriginal" Margin="20,0,5,5"/>
        <TextBlock Name="tbOriginal1" Margin="20,0,5,5"/>
        <TextBlock Margin="10,0,5,5" Text="Inverted Matrix:"/>
        <TextBlock TextWrapping="Wrap" x:Name="tbInvert"
                Margin="20,0,5,5"/>
        <TextBlock Margin="10,0,5,5" Text="M * M_Invert:"/>
        <TextBlock TextWrapping="Wrap" x:Name="tbInvert1"
                Margin="20,0,5,5"/>
        <TextBlock Margin="10,0,5,5"
                Text="Original Matrices:"/>
        <TextBlock Name="tbM1" Margin="20,0,5,5"/>
        <TextBlock Name="tbM2" Margin="20,0,5,5"/>
        <TextBlock Margin="10,0,5,5" Text="M1 x M2:"/>
        <TextBlock Name="tbM12" Margin="20,0,5,5"/>
        <TextBlock Margin="10,0,5,5" Text="M2 x M1:"/>
        <TextBlock Name="tbM21" Margin="20,0,5,5"/>
    </StackPanel>
</Window>
```

The above code creates the layout for displaying results using TextBlocks. The corresponding code-behind file of this example is listed below:

```csharp
using System;
using System.Windows;
using System.Windows.Media;
using System.Windows.Media.Media3D;

namespace Chapter09
{
public partial class Matrix3DOperation : Window
    {
        public Matrix3DOperation()
```

```
    {
        InitializeComponent();

        Matrix3D M =   new Matrix3D(1, 2, 3, 4,
                                    2, 1, 0, 0,
                                    0, 0, 1, 0,
                                    1, 2, 3, 1);
        Matrix3D M1 = M;
        Matrix3D M2 = new Matrix3D(1, 2, 0, 0,
                                   2, 1, 0, 3,
                                   0, 0, 1, 2,
                                   1, 2, 3, 1);

        tbOriginal.Text = "M = (" + M.ToString() + ")";
        tbOriginal1.Text = "M1 = M";

        // Invert matrix:
        M.Invert();
        tbInvert.Text = "(" +
            Utility.Matrix3DRound(M, 3).ToString() + ")";
        tbInvert1.Text = "(" + (M1 * M).ToString() + ")";

        // Matrix multiplication:
        Matrix3D M12 = M1 * M2;
        Matrix3D M21 = M2 * M1;
        tbM1.Text = "M1 = (" + M1.ToString() + ")";
        tbM2.Text = "M2 = (" + M2.ToString() + ")";
        tbM12.Text = "(" + M12.ToString() + ")";
        tbM21.Text = "(" + M21.ToString() + ")";
    }
  }
}
```

Here, you perform matrix inversions and multiplications. Note that the example uses a static method, Matrix3DRound, which is implemented in the Utility class, to display the results of Matrix3D inversion. This method allows you to round the decimal of matrix elements for a Matrix3D object. You can see that the results of the matrix multiplications depend on the order of the matrices. By executing the project and selecting the Matrix3DOperation from the Start Menu, you will obtain the output shown in Figure 9-1.

First, we examine the matrix Invert method that inverts a matrix (1, 2, 3, 4, 2, 1, 0, 0, 0, 0, 1, 0, 1, 2, 3, 1). The Matrix3D.Invert() method gives the result shown in the figure. This result is confirmed by direct multiplying M and its inverted matrix, which indeed gives an identity matrix.

For matrix multiplications, as expected, the result depends on the order of the matrices. The results in Figure 9-1 demonstrate that M1 * M2 ≠ M2 * M1.

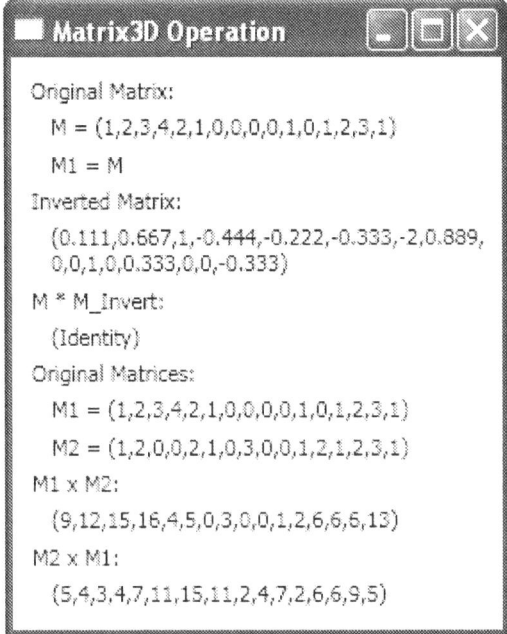

Figure 9-1 Results of Matrix3D operations in WPF.

Matrix3D Transforms

The Matrix3D structure in WPF also provides methods to rotate, scale, and translate the matrices. Here are some of the most frequently used methods for Matrix3D operations:

- Scale – Appends the specified scale Vector3D to the Matrix3D structure.
- ScaleAt – Scale the Matrix3D by the specified Vector3D about the specified Point3D.
- Translate – Appends a translation of the specified offsets to the current Matrix3D structure.
- Rotate – Appends a rotation transformation to the current Matrix3D.
- RotateAt – Rotates the Matrix3D about the specified Point3D.
- Invert – Inverts the Matrix3D structure.
- Multiply – Multiplies the specified matrices.
- Transform – Transforms the specified Point3D, array of Point3D objects, Point4D, array of Point4D objects, Vector3D, or array of Vector3D objects by the Matrix3D.

Please note that there is no Skew transform in the Matrix3D structure. To perform the Skew transformation in 3D, you need to directly manipulate the elements of the Matrix3D object. There are corresponding Prepend methods associated with the Scale, Translation, and Rotation. The default methods are Append. Both Append and Prepend determine the matrix operation order. Append specifies that the new operation is applied after the preceding operation; Prepend specifies that the new operation is applied before the preceding operation during cumulative operations.

Let's illustrate the basic Matrix3D transforms (translation, scaling, and rotation) in WPF using an example. Add a new WPF Window to the project Chapter09, and call it Matrix3DTransforms. The following is the XAML file of this example:

```xml
<Window x:Class="Chapter09.Matrix3DTransforms"
    xmlns="http://schemas.microsoft.com/winfx
        /2006/xaml/presentation"
    xmlns:x="http://schemas.microsoft.com/winfx/2006/xaml"
  Title="Matrix3D Transformations" Height="450" Width="300">

    <StackPanel>
        <TextBlock Margin="10,10,5,5"
                   Text="Original Matrix:"/>
        <TextBlock Name="tbOriginal" Margin="20,0,5,5"/>
        <TextBlock Margin="10,0,5,5" Text="Scale:"/>
        <TextBlock Name="tbScale" Margin="20,0,5,5"/>
        <TextBlock Margin="10,0,5,5" Text="Scale - Prepend:"/>
        <TextBlock Name="tbScalePrepend" Margin="20,0,5,5"/>
        <TextBlock Margin="10,0,5,5" Text="Translation:"/>
        <TextBlock Name="tbTranslate" Margin="20,0,5,5"/>
        <TextBlock Margin="10,0,5,5"
                   Text="Translation - Prepend:"/>
        <TextBlock Name="tbTranslatePrepend"
                   Margin="20,0,5,5"/>
        <TextBlock Margin="10,0,5,5" Text="Rotation:"/>
        <TextBlock Name="tbRotate" Margin="20,0,5,5"
                   TextWrapping="Wrap"/>
        <TextBlock Margin="10,0,5,5"
                   Text="Rotation - Prepend:"/>
        <TextBlock Name="tbRotatePrepend" Margin="20,0,5,5"
                   TextWrapping="Wrap"/>
        <TextBlock Margin="10,0,5,5" Text="RotationAt:"/>
        <TextBlock Name="tbRotateAt" Margin="20,0,5,5"
                   TextWrapping="Wrap"/>
        <TextBlock Margin="10,0,5,5"
                   Text="RotationAt - Prepend:"/>
        <TextBlock Name="tbRotateAtPrepend"
                   Margin="20,0,5,5" TextWrapping="Wrap"/>
    </StackPanel>
</Window>
```

The above code creates the layout for displaying results using TextBlocks, which are embedded in a StackPanel control. The corresponding code-behind file is given by the following code:

```
using System;
using System.Windows;
```

```csharp
    using System.Windows.Media;
using System.Windows.Media.Media3D;

namespace Chapter09
{
public partial class Matrix3DTransforms: Window
    {

        public Matrix3DTransforms()
        {
            InitializeComponent();

            // Original matrix:
            Matrix3D M = new Matrix3D(1, 2, 3, 4,
                                      2, 1, 0, 0,
                                      0, 0, 1, 0,
                                      1, 2, 3, 1);
            Matrix3D M1 = M;
            tbOriginal.Text = "(" + M.ToString() + ")";

            //Scale:
            M.Scale(new Vector3D(0.5, 1.5, 2.5));
            tbScale.Text = "(" + M.ToString() + ")";

            M = M1; // Reset M to the original matrix.
            M.ScalePrepend(new Vector3D(0.5, 1.5, 2.5));
            tbScalePrepend.Text = "(" + M.ToString() + ")";

            //Translation:
            M = M1; // Reset M to the original matrix.
            M.Translate(new Vector3D(100, 150, 200));
            tbTranslate.Text = "(" + M.ToString() + ")";

            // Translation - Prepend:
            M = M1; // Reset M to the original matrix.
            M.TranslatePrepend(new Vector3D(100, 150, 200));
            tbTranslatePrepend.Text =
                "(" + M.ToString() + ")";

            // Rotation:
            M = M1; // Reset M to the original matrix.
            M.Rotate(new Quaternion(
                new Vector3D(1, 2, 3), 45));
            tbRotate.Text = "(" +
                Utility.Matrix3DRound(M, 3).ToString() + ")";

            // Rotation - Prepend:
            M = M1; // Reset M to the original matrix.
            M.RotatePrepend(new Quaternion(
                new Vector3D(1, 2, 3), 45));
            tbRotatePrepend.Text = "(" +
                Utility.Matrix3DRound(M, 3).ToString() + ")";

            //Rotation at (x = 10, y = 20, z = 30):
```

```
M = M1; // Reset M to the original matrix.
M.RotateAt(new Quaternion(
    new Vector3D(1, 2, 3), 45),
    new Point3D(10, 20, 30)));
tbRotateAt.Text = "(" +
    Utility.Matrix3DRound(M, 3).ToString() + ")";

// Rotation at (x = 10, y = 20, z = 30) - Prepend:
M = M1; // Reset M to the original matrix.
M.RotateAtPrepend(new Quaternion(
    new Vector3D(1, 2, 3), 45),
    new Point3D(10, 20, 30)));
tbRotateAtPrepend.Text = "(" +
    Utility.Matrix3DRound(M, 3).ToString() + ")";
        }
    }
}
```

Building and running this example generate the output shown in Figure 9-2. The original Matrix3D object M is operated on by various transforms. In the following, we'll examine the WPF results by direct matrix computations. First, let's examine the scale transform that sets the scaling factor of 0.5 in the X direction, 1.5 in the Y direction, and 2.5 in the Z direction. These scale parameters must be specified using a Vector3D object. For the Append scaling (the default setting), we have:

$$\begin{pmatrix} 1 & 2 & 3 & 4 \\ 2 & 1 & 0 & 0 \\ 0 & 0 & 1 & 0 \\ 1 & 2 & 3 & 1 \end{pmatrix} \begin{pmatrix} 0.5 & 0 & 0 & 0 \\ 0 & 1.5 & 0 & 0 \\ 0 & 0 & 2.5 & 0 \\ 0 & 0 & 0 & 1 \end{pmatrix} = \begin{pmatrix} 0.5 & 3 & 7.5 & 4 \\ 1 & 1.5 & 0 & 0 \\ 0 & 0 & 2.5 & 0 \\ 0.5 & 3 & 7.5 & 1 \end{pmatrix}$$

This gives the same result as seen in Figure 9-2. On the other hand, for the Prepend scaling, we have:

$$\begin{pmatrix} 0.5 & 0 & 0 & 0 \\ 0 & 1.5 & 0 & 0 \\ 0 & 0 & 2.5 & 0 \\ 0 & 0 & 0 & 1 \end{pmatrix} \begin{pmatrix} 1 & 2 & 3 & 4 \\ 2 & 1 & 0 & 0 \\ 0 & 0 & 1 & 0 \\ 1 & 2 & 3 & 1 \end{pmatrix} = \begin{pmatrix} 0.5 & 1 & 1.5 & 2 \\ 3 & 1.5 & 0 & 0 \\ 0 & 0 & 2.5 & 0 \\ 1 & 2 & 3 & 1 \end{pmatrix}$$

This confirms the output result of Figure 9-2.

Then, you translate the matrix M by 100 units in the X direction, 150 units in the Y direction, and 200 units in the Z direction. For the default Append translation, you have:

$$\begin{pmatrix} 1 & 2 & 3 & 4 \\ 2 & 1 & 0 & 0 \\ 0 & 0 & 1 & 0 \\ 1 & 2 & 3 & 1 \end{pmatrix} \begin{pmatrix} 1 & 0 & 0 & 0 \\ 0 & 1 & 0 & 0 \\ 0 & 0 & 1 & 0 \\ 100 & 150 & 200 & 1 \end{pmatrix} = \begin{pmatrix} 401 & 602 & 803 & 4 \\ 2 & 1 & 0 & 0 \\ 0 & 0 & 1 & 0 \\ 101 & 152 & 203 & 1 \end{pmatrix}$$

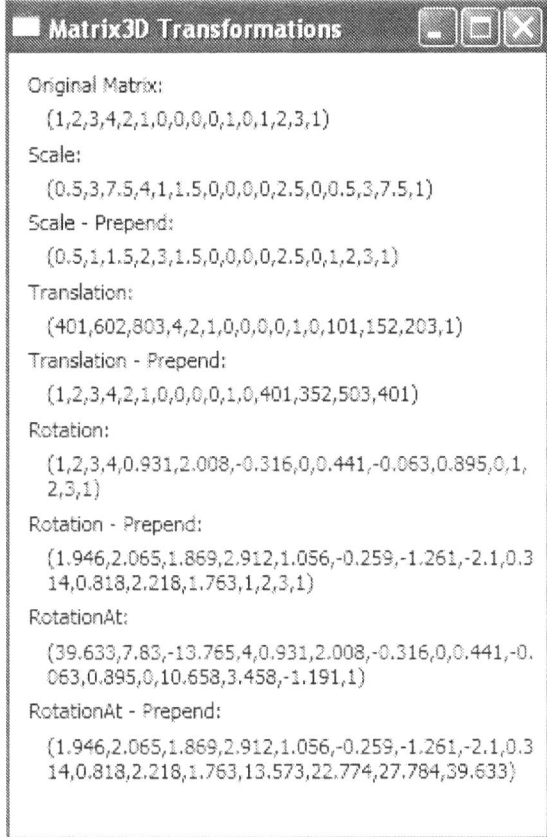

Figure 9-2 The results of Matrix3D transformations.

This is all consistent with the results shown in Figure 9-2. For the Prepend translation, this means the following transformation:

$$
\begin{pmatrix} 1 & 0 & 0 & 0 \\ 0 & 1 & 0 & 0 \\ 0 & 0 & 1 & 0 \\ 100 & 150 & 200 & 1 \end{pmatrix}
\begin{pmatrix} 1 & 2 & 3 & 4 \\ 2 & 1 & 0 & 0 \\ 0 & 0 & 1 & 0 \\ 1 & 2 & 3 & 1 \end{pmatrix}
=
\begin{pmatrix} 1 & 2 & 3 & 4 \\ 2 & 1 & 0 & 0 \\ 0 & 0 & 1 & 0 \\ 401 & 352 & 503 & 401 \end{pmatrix}
$$

This is also confirmed by the result shown in Figure 9-2.

Rotation and Quaternion

Rotation is one of the most commonly used transforms in 3D. The 3D rotation about an arbitrary axis is also one of the most complex 3D transforms. WPF uses the quaternion notation, which can be specified either by a position Vector3D object and a rotation angle or by four quaternion components in the form of (x, y, z, w).

Remember that in order to calculate the quaternion from the rotation axis vector and the rotation angle, the axis vector must be normalized. You can calculate the quaternion components from a unit rotation axis and rotation angle. Suppose that the rotation axis for a 3D rotation is denoted by a unit Vector3D object (ax, ay, az) and the rotation angle is θ. You can find the quaternion (x, y, z, w) by using the following formula:

$$
\begin{aligned}
x &= ax \cdot \sin(\theta/2) \\
y &= ay \cdot \sin(\theta/2) \\
z &= az \cdot \sin(\theta/2) \\
w &= \cos(\theta/2)
\end{aligned}
\tag{9.1}
$$

For the rotation transform in the Matrix3DTransforms example, you rotate the original M matrix by 45 degrees along the axis specified by a Vector3D object (1, 2, 3). The unit rotation axis can be obtained by normalizing this Vector3D object:

$$(ax,\ ay\ az) = (1, 2, 3)/\sqrt{14} = (0.267, 0.535, 0.802)$$

and θ = 45 degrees. You can then easily calculate its quaternion using Eq.(9.1):

$$(x,\ y,\ z,\ w) = (0.102, 0.205, 0.307, 0.924)$$

It can be shown that the above quaternion (x, y, z, w) is also normalized to unity. Using this quaternion, you can construct the rotation matrix:

$$
\begin{pmatrix}
w^2 + x^2 - y^2 - z^2 & 2xy + 2zw & 2xz - 2yw & 0 \\
2xy - 2zw & w^2 - x^2 + y^2 - z^2 & 2yz + 2xw & 0 \\
2xz + 2yw & 2yz - 2xw & w^2 - x^2 - y^2 + z^2 & 0 \\
0 & 0 & 0 & w^2 + x^2 + y^2 + z^2
\end{pmatrix}
$$

$$
=
\begin{pmatrix}
0.728 & 0.609 & -0.315 & 0 \\
-0.525 & 0.791 & 0.315 & 0 \\
0.441 & -0.063 & 0.895 & 0 \\
0 & 0 & 0 & 1
\end{pmatrix}
$$

With this rotation matrix, you can examine the effect of the rotation on the original Matrix3D object M. In the case of the Append rotation, we have:

$$
\begin{pmatrix}
1 & 2 & 3 & 4 \\
2 & 1 & 0 & 0 \\
0 & 0 & 1 & 0 \\
1 & 2 & 3 & 1
\end{pmatrix}
\begin{pmatrix}
0.728 & 0.609 & -0.315 & 0 \\
-0.525 & 0.791 & 0.315 & 0 \\
0.441 & -0.063 & 0.895 & 0 \\
0 & 0 & 0 & 1
\end{pmatrix}
$$

$$= \begin{pmatrix} 1 & 2 & 3 & 4 \\ 0.913 & 2 & -0.316 & 0 \\ 0.441 & -0.063 & 0.895 & 0 \\ 1 & 2 & 3 & 1 \end{pmatrix}$$

This result is the same as that given in Figure 9-2. For the Prepend rotation, we have:

$$\begin{pmatrix} 0.728 & 0.609 & -0.315 & 0 \\ -0.525 & 0.791 & 0.315 & 0 \\ 0.441 & -0.063 & 0.895 & 0 \\ 0 & 0 & 0 & 1 \end{pmatrix} \begin{pmatrix} 1 & 2 & 3 & 4 \\ 2 & 1 & 0 & 0 \\ 0 & 0 & 1 & 0 \\ 1 & 2 & 3 & 1 \end{pmatrix}$$

$$= \begin{pmatrix} 1.946 & 2.065 & 1.869 & 2.912 \\ 1.056 & -0.259 & -0.1.261 & -2.1 \\ 0.314 & 0.818 & 2.218 & 1.763 \\ 1 & 2 & 3 & 1 \end{pmatrix}$$

This result is also consistent with that given in Figure 9-2.

The RotateAt method in 3D is designed for cases, in which you need to change the center of rotation. In fact, the Rotate method is a special case of RotateAt with the rotation center at (0, 0, 0). The rotation center in 3D is specified by a Point3D object. In this example, the matrix is rotated at the point (10, 20, 30). As we've discussed previously, the rotation of an object about an arbitrary point P1 must be performed according to the following procedures:

- Translate P1 to the origin.
- Rotate it to the desired angle.
- Translate so that the point at the origin returns back to P1.

Considering the matrix transform definition in WPF, the rotation matrix at the Point (10, 30, 20) should be expressed in the following form:

$$T(-dx,-dy,-dz) \cdot R(\theta) \cdot T(dx,dy,dz)$$

$$= \begin{pmatrix} 1 & 0 & 0 & 0 \\ 0 & 1 & 0 & 0 \\ 0 & 0 & 1 & 0 \\ -10 & -30 & -20 & 1 \end{pmatrix} \begin{pmatrix} 0.728 & 0.609 & -0.315 & 0 \\ -0.525 & 0.791 & 0.315 & 0 \\ 0.441 & -0.063 & 0.895 & 0 \\ 0 & 0 & 0 & 1 \end{pmatrix} \begin{pmatrix} 1 & 0 & 0 & 0 \\ 0 & 1 & 0 & 0 \\ 0 & 0 & 1 & 0 \\ 10 & 30 & 20 & 1 \end{pmatrix}$$

$$= \begin{pmatrix} 0.728 & 0.609 & -0.315 & 0 \\ -0.525 & 0.791 & 0.315 & 0 \\ 0.441 & -0.063 & 0.895 & 0 \\ 9.658 & 1.458 & -4.191 & 1 \end{pmatrix}$$

Thus, the Append rotation of Matrix M at Point (10, 30, 20) becomes:

$$\begin{pmatrix} 1 & 2 & 3 & 4 \\ 2 & 1 & 0 & 0 \\ 0 & 0 & 1 & 0 \\ 1 & 2 & 3 & 1 \end{pmatrix} \begin{pmatrix} 0.728 & 0.609 & -0.315 & 0 \\ -0.525 & 0.791 & 0.315 & 0 \\ 0.441 & -0.063 & 0.895 & 0 \\ 9.658 & 1.458 & -4.191 & 1 \end{pmatrix} = \begin{pmatrix} 39.633 & 7.83 & -13.765 & 4 \\ 0.931 & 2.008 & -0.316 & 0 \\ 0.441 & -0.063 & 0.895 & 0 \\ 10.658 & 3.458 & -1.191 & 1 \end{pmatrix}$$

This again confirms the result of Figure 9-2.

Similarly, the Prepend rotation of Matrix3D object M at Point (10, 30, 20) should be:

$$\begin{pmatrix} 0.728 & 0.609 & -0.315 & 0 \\ -0.525 & 0.791 & 0.315 & 0 \\ 0.441 & -0.063 & 0.895 & 0 \\ 9.658 & 1.458 & -4.191 & 1 \end{pmatrix} \begin{pmatrix} 1 & 2 & 3 & 4 \\ 2 & 1 & 0 & 0 \\ 0 & 0 & 1 & 0 \\ 1 & 2 & 3 & 1 \end{pmatrix}$$

$$= \begin{pmatrix} 1.946 & 2.065 & 1.869 & 2.912 \\ 1.056 & -0.259 & -1.261 & -2.1 \\ 0.314 & 0.818 & 2.218 & 1.763 \\ 13.573 & 22.774 & 27.784 & 39.633 \end{pmatrix}$$

This result is also the same as the one given in Figure 9-2.

Here, I have presented detailed explanations of 3D matrix transforms in WPF. This information is useful in understanding the definitions and internal representations of Matrix3D in WPF. It is also important when applying matrix tramsforms to 3D objects in your applications correctly.

Projections

Since the computer screen is two dimensional, it can't directly display 3D objects. In order to view 3D objects on a 2D screen, you have to project the objects from 3D to 2D.

The most common types of projections are called planar geometric projections. These are a distinct class of projections that maintain straight lines when mapping an object onto a viewing surface. In a planar geometric projection, a ray or projector is passed from a center of projection through the points being projected onto a planar viewing surface, called the view plane. Figure 9-3 shows the projection of a square object onto a 2D view plane.

WPF implements two kinds of projections, Orthographic and Perspective. I'll discuss these two kinds of projections in the following subsections.

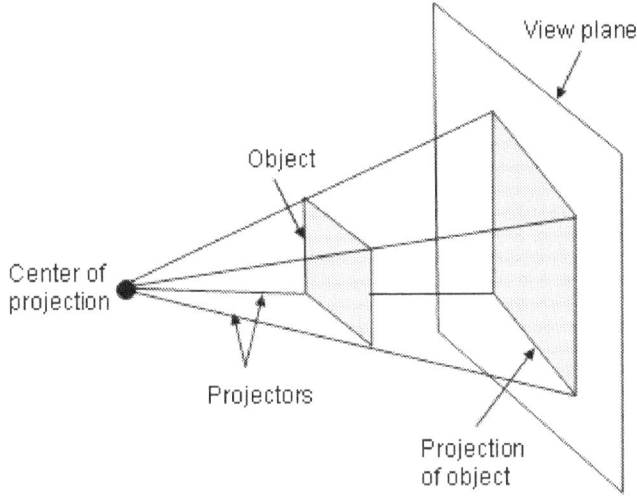

Figure 9-3 Projection of a square object from 3D to a 2D view plane.

Orthographic Projections

Orthographic projection is kind of parallel projection, meaning that the center of projection is located at an infinite distance from the view plane. By placing the center of projection at an infinite distance from the view plane, the projectors become parallel to the view plane. For a parallel projection, instead of specifying a center of projection, you need to specify a direction of projection. Figure 9-4 shows a parallel projection of a square object onto the view plane.

In addition to being parallel, projectors in an orthographic projection are also perpendicular to the view plane. Orthographic projections are often used in architectural and mechanical drawings. They are further categorized as either multi-view or axonometric projections, which are described below.

Multi-View Projections

A multi-view projection shows a single face of a 3D object. Common choices for viewing an object in 2D include front, side, and top view. Figure 9-5 shows a house object as well as its front, side, and top views.

These projections are very simple. To project a point, simply ignore the point's unneeded third coordinate. In top view, the normal of the view plane is parallel to the positive Y axis in a right-handed system, as shown in Figure 9-5. To project the top view of a 3D object, the Y coordinates are discarded and the X and Z coordinates for each point are mapped onto the view plane. By repositioning the normal of the view plane to the positive Z axis and selecting the X and Y coordinates for each point, a front view is projected onto the view plane.

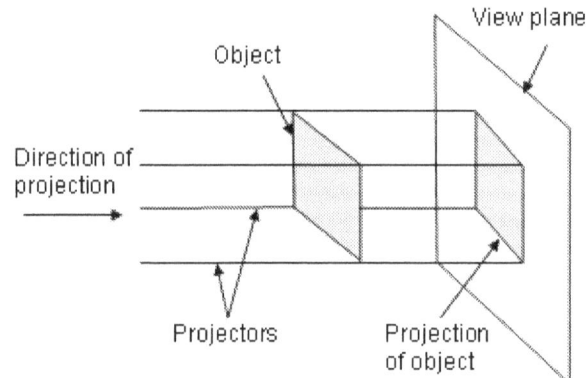

Figure 9-4 A parallel projection of a square object.

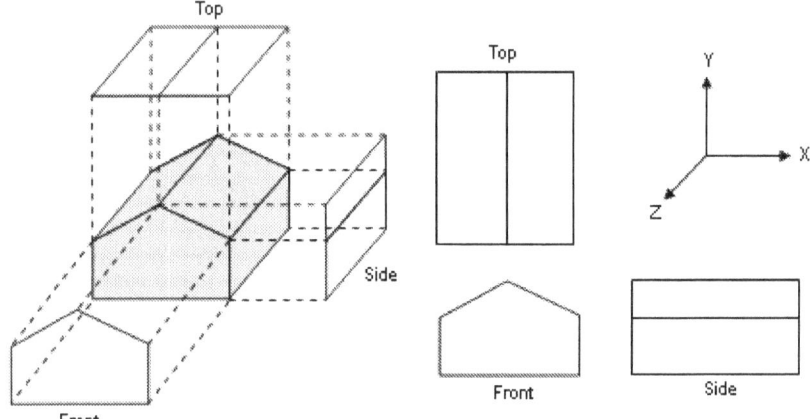

Figure 9-5 Front, side, and top views of orthographic projections.

Likewise, a side view can be achieved when the normal of the view plane is directed along the positive X axis, while the Y and Z coordinates of a 3D object are projected onto the view plane. These projections are often used in engineering and architectural drawings. Although they don't show the 3D aspects of an object, multi-view projections are useful because the angles and dimensions of the object are maintained.

Axonometric Projections

Multi-view projections preserve distances and angles, in other words, you can measure distances and angles directly from the projection of an object. However, it is often difficult to understand the 3D structure of an object by examining only its multi-view projections.

To make the 3D nature of an object more apparent, you can use projections that aren't parallel to the X, Y, or Z axes. This type of projection is called an axonometric orthographic projection. Unlike multi-view projections, axonometric projection allows you to place the normal of the view plane in any direction so that three adjacent faces of a "cube-like" object are visible. To avoid duplication of the views displayed by multi-view projections, the normal of the view plane is usually not placed parallel to a major axis for an axonometric view. The increased versatility in the direction of the normal of the view plane should position the view plane so that it intersects at least two of the major axes. Lines on a 3D object that are parallel in the world coordinate system are likewise projected to the view plane as parallel lines. In addition, the length of a line, or line preservation, is maintained for lines parallel to the view plane. Other receding lines maintain only their proportion and are foreshortened equally with lines along the same axes.

Axonometric projections can be further divided into three types that depend upon the number of major axes foreshortened equally. These axonometric views are defined as isometric, dimetric, or trimetric projections.

Isometric Projections:

An isometric projection is a commonly used type of axonometric projection. In this projection, all three of the major axes are foreshortened equally since the normal of the view plane makes equal angles with all three coordinate axes.

Figure 9-6 shows the isometric projections of a cube object. Isometric projection scales lines equally along each axis, which is often useful since lines along the coordinate axes can be measured and converted using the same scale.

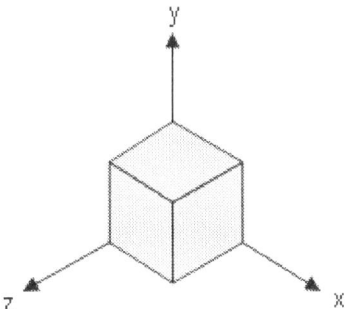

Figure 9-6 Isometric projection of a cube object.

Dimetric Projections:

Dimetric projections differ from isometric projections in the direction of the normal of the view plane. In this case, the view plane is set so that it makes equal angles with two of the coordinate axes.

Figure 9-7 shows a dimetric projection of a cube object. When the normal of the view plane is set so that the view plane is parallel to a major axis, line measurements are maintained in the projection for lines that are parallel to the chosen axis.

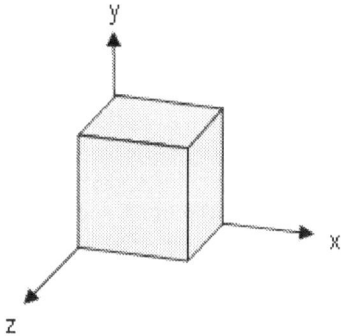

Figure 9-7 Dimetric projection of a cube object.

Trimetric Projections:

In trimetric projection, the normal of the view plane makes different angles with each coordinate axis since no two components have the same value. As with a dimetric view, a trimetric view can display different orientations when differing amounts of emphasis are placed on the faces. A potential disadvantage of the trimetric projections is that measuring lines along the axes is difficult due to the difference in scaling factors.

Figure 9-8 shows a trimetric projection of a cube object. You can see how the unequal-foreshortening characteristic of these projections affects line measurements along the different axes. While disadvantageous in maintaining measurements, a trimetric projection, with the correct orientation, can offer a realistic and natural view of an object.

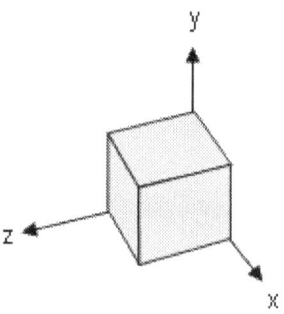

Figure 9-8 Trimetric projection of a cube object.

In addition to orthographic projections, parallel projections also include oblique projections. Oblique projections are useful because they combine the advantageous qualities of both multi-view and axonometric projections. Like axonometric projections, this type of projection emphasizes the 3D features of an object. At the same time, like multi-view projections, oblique views display the exact shape of one face. Oblique view uses parallel projectors, but the angle between the projectors and the view plane is no longer orthogonal. Because of these properties, more than one face of the object is visible in an oblique projection. We'll not discuss oblique projections further in this book. For more information about these projections and their projection matrices, please refer to my another book "Practical C# Charts and Graphics".

Perspective Projections

In a perspective projection, objects of equal size at different distances from the view plane will be projected at different sizes, so that nearer objects will appear closer. The projectors pass from a center of projection through each point in the object to the view plane.

Figure 9-9 shows a perspective projection of two identical square objects. The square that is farther from the center of projection is projected as a smaller image on the view plane.

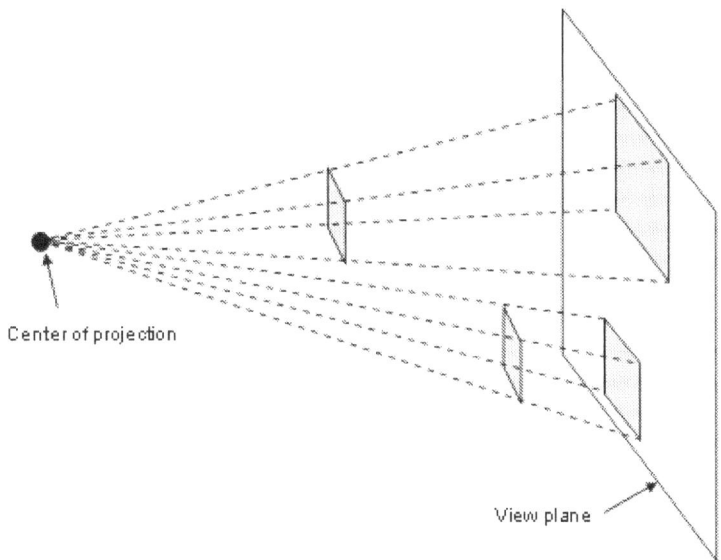

Center of projection

View plane

Figure 9-9 Perspective projections: objects farther from the center of projection appear smaller than closer objects.

In comparison to parallel projections, perspective projections often provide a more natural and realistic view of a 3D object. By comparing the view plane of a perspective projection with the view as seen from the lens of a camera, the underlying principle of perspective projection is easily understood. Like the view from a camera, lines in a perspective projection not parallel to the view plane converge at a distant point (called the vanishing point) in the background. When the eye or camera is positioned close to the object, perspective foreshortening occurs, with distant objects appearing smaller in the view plane than closer objects of the same size, as shown in Figure 9-9.

Perspective projections can be classified by the number of vanishing points they contain. There are three types of perspective projections: one-point, two-point, and three-point perspective projections. Each type differs in the orientation of the view plane and the number of vanishing points.

One-Point Perspective Projections

In one-point perspective, lines of a 3D object along a coordinate axis converge at a single vanishing point while lines parallel to the other axes remain horizontal or vertical in the view plane. To create a one-point perspective view, the view plane is set parallel to one of the principal planes in the world coordinate system. Figure 9-10 shows a one-point perspective view of a cube. In this projection, the view plane is positioned in front of the cube and parallel to the X-Y plane.

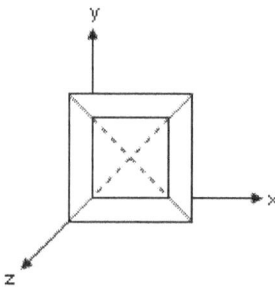

Figure 9-10 One-point perspective projection.

Two-Point Perspective Projections

Two-point perspective projects an object onto the view plane so that lines parallel to two of the major axes converge at two separate vanishing points. To create a two-point perspective projection, the view plane is set parallel to a coordinate axis rather than a plane. To satisfy this condition, the normal of the view plane should be set perpendicular to one of the major world coordinate system axes. Figure 9-11 shows a two-point perspective view of a cube. In this figure, lines parallel to the x-axis converge at a vanishing point while lines parallel to the z-axis converge at another vanishing point. Two-point perspective views often provide additional realism in comparison to other projection types; for this reason, they are commonly used in architectural, engineering, and industrial designs.

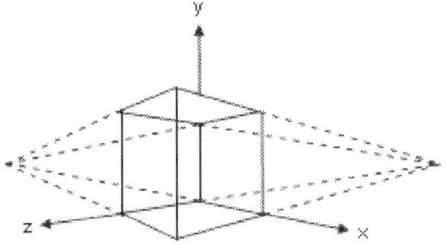

Figure 9-11 Two-point perspective projection.

Three-Point Perspective Projections

A three-point perspective projection has three vanishing points. In this case, the view plane is not parallel to any of the major axes. To position the view plane, each component of the view plane's normal is set to a non-zero value so that the view plane intersects three major axes. Three-vanishing point projection is often used by artists for highlighting features or increasing dramatic effect. Figure 9-12 shows a three-point perspective projection of a cube.

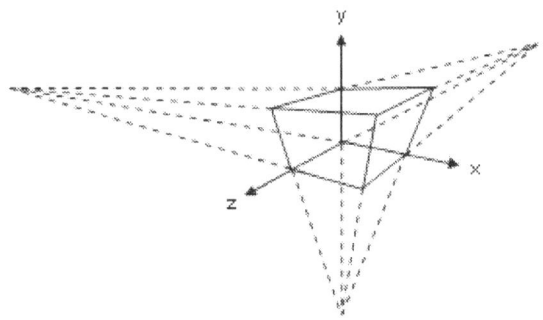

Figure 9-12 Three-point perspective projection.

Perspective Projection Matrix

Constructing a general perspective projection matrix is quite complicated. Here, we only discuss a simple case of perspective projection. This simple perspective view projects onto the X-Y plane when the center of projection lies on the Z axis. Figure 9-13 shows a point $P = (x, y, z)$ being projected onto the point $P1 = (x1, y1, z1)$ in the X-Y plane. The center of projection is located at $(0, 0, d)$, where d is the distance along the Z axis. On the right of Figure 9-13 is a side view of the projection showing the Y and Z axes. The point A is the center of projection, and the point B is the point on the Z axis that has the same Z coordinates as point P.

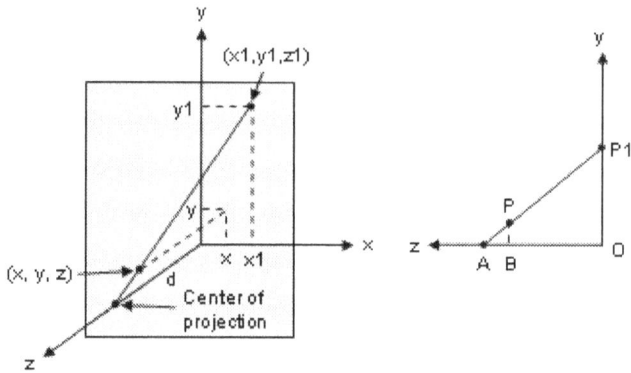

Figure 9-13 Perspective projection of a point P = (x, y, z).

From this figure, you note that AO = d, OP1 = y1, BP = y, and AB = d-z. When you solve for y1, you get y1 = d*y/(d-z). This gives the Y coordinate of the projected point P1. By examining a similar top view that shows the X and Z axes, you can find that x1 = d*x/(d-z). For the projected point on the X-Y plane, z1 should equal 0. From this information, you can construct a transform matrix for this perspective projection:

$$\begin{pmatrix} x1 & y1 & z1 & w1 \end{pmatrix} = \begin{pmatrix} x & y & z & 1 \end{pmatrix} \begin{pmatrix} 1 & 0 & 0 & 0 \\ 0 & 1 & 0 & 0 \\ 0 & 0 & 0 & -1/d \\ 0 & 0 & 0 & 1 \end{pmatrix} = \begin{pmatrix} x & y & 0 & 1-z/d \end{pmatrix}$$

Remember that in homogeneous coordinates, the w-component of a point represents a scaling factor. Normalizing the projected point P1 by w1, you have

$$\begin{pmatrix} x1/w1 & y1/w1 & z1/w1 & 1 \end{pmatrix} = \begin{pmatrix} x/(1-z/d) & y/(1-z/d) & 0 & 1 \end{pmatrix}$$

This agrees with the information deduced from Figure 9-13.

Views and Projections in WPF

In order to dispay 3D objects on a 2D screen, a series of transforms must be performed on the 3D objects. WPF uses several transforms to change the 3D model coordinates into device-independent pixels. These transforms include View transform, Projection transform, and World transform. Remember that the perspective projection in WPF is based on the one-point perspective projection.

The world transform controls how model coordinates are transformed into world coordinates. The world transform can include translation, scaling, and rotation. The view transform controls the transition from world coordinates into camera space. It determines the camera position in the world coordinate system. The projection transform changes the geometry of 3D objects from the camera space into the clipping space and applies perspective distortion to the objects. The clipping space refers to how the geometry is clipped to the view volume during this transformation. Finally, the geometry in the clipping space is transformed into the device-independent pixels (the screen space), This transform is controlled by the Viewport settings.

WPF provides a variety of classes that allow you to perform various transformations on 3D objects. It also constructs transform matrices for View and Projection, and performs the corresponding transforms behind the scene. On your part, you simply specify the Camera and Viewport settings. Technically, in order to create 3D objects in WPF, you don't need to know the matrices of the View and Projection transforms. However, understanding the mathematical basics of these transform matrices, and knowing how to construct them from Camera and Viewport settings, is still very important in developing professional 3D graphics applications. For example, if you want to customize the Camera and Viewport settings provided by WPF, you'll have to construct your own View and Projection transform matrices.

In following sections, you'll learn how to construct the View and Projection transform matrices that are used in WPF.

View Transform

In order to display 3D objects on a 2D computer screen, you must first decide how you want to position the objects in the scene, and you must choose a vantage point from which to view the scene. In these processes, you need to think in 3D coordinates while making many of the decisions that determine what is drawn on the screen.

The transformation process used to create the scene for viewing is analogous to taking a photograph with a camera. Using the view transform is analogous to positioning and aligning a camera. It changes the position and orientation of the viewport.

The view transform locates the viewer in world space and transforms 3D objects into camera space. In camera space, the camera, or viewer, is at the origin, looking in the negative Z direction. Recall that WPF uses a right-handed coordinate system, so Z is negative in a scene. The view matrix relocates the objects in the world coordinate system around a camera's position - the origin of orientation of the camera.

There are many ways to construct a view matrix. In every case, the camera has a logical position and orientation in world space used as a starting point to create a view matrix. This view matrix will be applied to the models in a scene. The view matrix translates and rotates objects in order to place them in camera space, where the camera is at the origin. One way to construct a view matrix is to combine a translation matrix with rotation matrices for each axis. Here are steps to obtain the view transform:

- For a given camera position, translate it to the origin.

- Rotate about the Y axis in the world space to bring the camera coordinate's Z axis into the YZ plane of world coordinates

- Rotate about the world coordinate X axis until the Z axis of both the world and camera systems is aligned.

- Rotate about the world coordinate Z axis to align the Y axis in both the world and camera spaces.

Then, the view transform can be written in the form:

$$V = T \cdot R(y) \cdot R(x) \cdot R(z)$$

In this formula, V is the view matrix, T is a translation matrix that repositions objects (or the camera) in the world space, and R(x), R(y) and R(z) are rotation matrices that rotate objects along the X, Y, and Z axes. The translation and rotation matrices are based on the camera's logical position and orientation in world space. So, if the camera's logical position in the world is (10, 20, 30), the purpose of the translation matrix is to move objects -10 units along the X-axis, -20 units along the Y-axis, and -30 units along the Z-axis. The rotation matrices in the formula are based on the camera's orientation, in terms of how much the axes of camera space are rotated out of alignment with world space.

In practice, the relationship between the camera and the object is specified by three sets of arguments: the camera position P(x, y, z), the look at vector N that defines the camera look at direction, and the up vector U that indicates which direction is the up direction of the camera. Choose the camera postion to yield the desired view of the scene, typically somewhere in the middle of the scene. WPF uses these three quanlities to set the camera. Here, I'll show you how to construct the view transform matrix using these three parameters.

- Create three vectors in 3D space, XScale, YScale, and ZScale.

- Normalize N and U, i.e., let both N and U be unit vectors.

- Let ZScale = N, i.e., set ZScale to the look at direction.

- Compute the YScale using the formula: $YScale = \dfrac{\vec{U} - (\vec{U} \cdot \vec{N})\vec{N}}{\sqrt{1 - (\vec{U} \cdot \vec{N})^2}}$.

- Computer the XScale using the formula: $XScale = \dfrac{\vec{N} \times \vec{U}}{\sqrt{1 - (\vec{U} \cdot \vec{N})^2}}$.

- Construct an M matrix in the 3D homogeneous coordinate system:

$$M = \begin{pmatrix} XScale.X & YScale.X & ZScale.X & 0 \\ XScale.Y & YScale.Y & ZScale.Y & 0 \\ XScale.Z & YScale.Z & ZScale.Z & 0 \\ 0 & 0 & 0 & 1 \end{pmatrix}.$$

- Tanslate the camera position to the origin and reflect it about the Z axis. Thus the view transform matrix V is given by:

$V = T(-x, -y, -z) \cdot M \cdot S(1,1,-1)$, where T is a translation matrix and S is a scaling matrix with a scaling factor of sz = -1, which corresponds to the reflection about the Z axis.

Then, you can easily construct the view transform matrix following the above steps. Open the Chapter09 project, and add a public static method, SetViewMatrix, to the Utility class:

```
public static Matrix3D SetViewMatrix(Point3D cameraPosition,
       Vector3D lookDirection, Vector3D upDirection)
{
    // Normalize vectors:
    lookDirection.Normalize();
    upDirection.Normalize();

    // Define vectors, XScale, YScale, and ZScale:
    double denom = Math.Sqrt(1 -
        Math.Pow(Vector3D.DotProduct(lookDirection,
        upDirection), 2));
    Vector3D XScale = Vector3D.CrossProduct(
        lookDirection, upDirection) / denom;
    Vector3D YScale = (upDirection -
        (Vector3D.DotProduct(upDirection,
        lookDirection)) * lookDirection) / denom;
    Vector3D ZScale = lookDirection;
    // Construct M matrix:
    Matrix3D M = new Matrix3D();
    M.M11 = XScale.X;
    M.M21 = XScale.Y;
    M.M31 = XScale.Z;
    M.M12 = YScale.X;
    M.M22 = YScale.Y;
    M.M32 = YScale.Z;
    M.M13 = ZScale.X;
    M.M23 = ZScale.Y;
    M.M33 = ZScale.Z;

    // Translate the camera position to the origin:
    Matrix3D translateMatrix = new Matrix3D();
    translateMatrix.Translate(new Vector3D(-cameraPosition.X,
        -cameraPosition.Y, -cameraPosition.Z));

    // Define reflect matrix about the Z axis:
    Matrix3D reflectMatrix = new Matrix3D();
    reflectMatrix.M33 = -1;

    // Construct the View matrix:
    Matrix3D viewMatrix =
        translateMatrix * M * reflectMatrix;
    return viewMatrix;
}
```

Perspective Projection

The preceding section described how to compose the view transform matrix so that the correct modeling and viewing transform can be applied. In this section, I'll explain how to define the desired perspective projection matrix in WPF, which is needed to transform the vertices in your scene.

View Frustum

In earlier sections in this chapter, we discussed the projections in a general way, and didn't consider the effect of the camera and viewport settings on the projections. Here, we need to consider these factors in order to apply projections in a real-world WPF graphics application.

The purpose of the projection transformation is to define a view volume, called View Frustum, which is used in two ways. The frustum determines how an object is projected onto the screen. It also defines which objects or portions of objects are clipped out of the final image.

The key feature of perspective projection is foreshortening: the farther an object is from the camera, the smaller it appears on the screen. This occurs because the frustum for a perspective projection is a pyramid, a truncated pyramid whose top has been cut off by a plane parallel to its base. Objects falling within the frustum are projected toward the apex of the pyramid, where the camera is located. Objects that are closer to the camera appear larger because they occupy a proportionally larger amount of the viewing volume than those that are farther away. This method of projection is commonly used in 3D computer graphics and visual simulation, because it is similar to how a camera works.

Remember that the viewing volume is used to clip objects that lie outside of it; the four sides of the frustum, its top and its base correspond to the six clipping planes of the viewing volume, as shown in Figure 9-14. Objects or parts of objects outside these planes are clipped from the final image.

Perspective Transform Matrix

Now, our task is to construct the perspective transform matrix used in WPF. A perspective projection maps the X- and Y-coordinates onto the projection plane while maintaining the depth information, which can be achieved by mapping the View Frustum onto a cube. This cube is the projection into 3D space of what is called the clip space, which is centered at the origin and extends from -1 to 1 on each of the X-, Y-, and Z-axes.

Let $P = (x, y, z, 1)$ be a point in the camera space that lies inside the view frustum. We try to construct the projection matrix using parameters of this view frustum, including the left edge at $x = l$, the right edge at $x = r$, the bottom edge at $y = b$, and the top edge at $y = t$ of the rectangle carved out of the near plane by the four side planes of the view frustum.

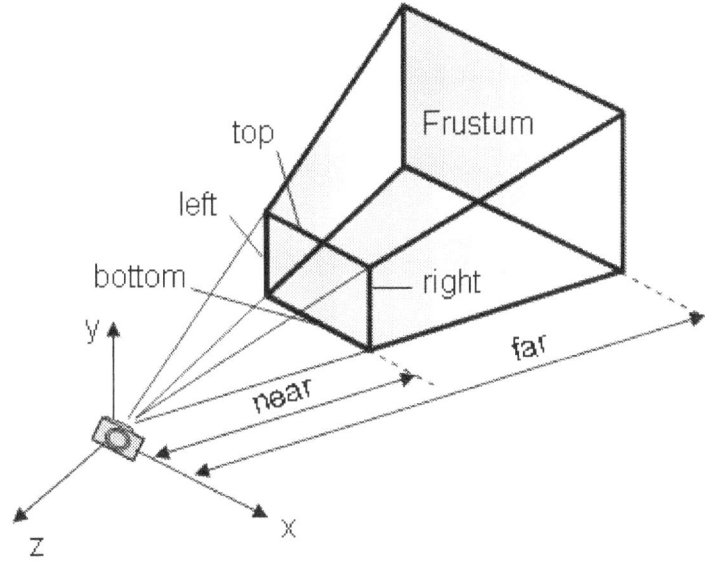

Figure 9-14 Projective view frustum.

The near plane and far plane are located at z = - zn and zf in the right-hand coordinate system. So, you can calculate the projected x1 and y1 coordinates of the point P on the near plane:

$$x1 = -\frac{zn}{z}x, \qquad y1 = -\frac{zn}{z}y \qquad (9.2)$$

Note that z < 0 because the camera points in the negative Z direction. You want to map these coordinates into the [-1, 1] range, which is needed to fit the view frustum into the clip space. This can be done using the following relations:

$$x2 = (x1-l)\frac{2}{r-l}-1, \qquad y2 = (y1-b)\frac{2}{t-b}-1 \qquad (9.3)$$

Substituting x1 and y1 in the above equation using (9.1) yields the results:

$$x2 = \left(-\frac{x}{z}\right)\frac{2\cdot zn}{r-l}-\frac{r+l}{r-l}, \qquad y2 = \left(-\frac{y}{z}\right)\frac{2\cdot zn}{t-b}-\frac{t+b}{t-b} \qquad (9.4)$$

I should point out here that the range used to map the projected Z-component is different for different technologies. In the OpenGL platform, this mapping range is from -1 to +1. However, a mapping range, [0, 1], is used by Microsoft for their Direct3D and WPF frameworks. These two mapping ranges do give a slightly different projection matrix, however, it doesn't affect final image displayed on your screen.

Here, we'll use Microsoft convention. Namely, the range of [0, 1] will be used for mapping the projected Z-component. This mapping involves a somewhat more complex computation. Since the point P lies inside the view frustum, its z-component must be in the range $[-zf, -zn]$. We need to find a function that maps $-zn \rightarrow 0$, $-zf \rightarrow 1$. Assume that the mapping function has the following form:

$$z2 = \frac{C1}{z} + C2 \tag{9.5}$$

You can solve for the coefficients C1 and C2 by plugging in the known mappings $-zn \rightarrow 0$ and $-zf \rightarrow 1$ to obtain

$$0 = \frac{C1}{-zn} + C2 \quad \text{and} \quad 1 = \frac{C1}{-zf} + C2$$

Solving the above equations yields the results:

$$C1 = \frac{zn \cdot zf}{zf - zn}, \quad C2 = \frac{zf}{zf - zn}$$

Substituting the above equations into (9.5), we have

$$z2 = \left(\frac{1}{z}\right)\left(\frac{zn \cdot zf}{zf - zn}\right) + \frac{zf}{zf - zn} \tag{9.6}$$

You can see from Eqs.(9.4) and (9.6) that x2, y2, and z2 all contain a division by $-z$, so the 3D point P2 = (x2, y2, z2) is equivalent to a 4D point in the homogeneous coordinate system:

$$P2 = (-x2 \cdot z, -y2 \cdot z, -z2 \cdot z, -z)$$

From (9.4) and (9.6) we obtain the values of $-x2\ z$, $-y2\ z$, and $-z2\ z$ by equations:

$$-x2 \cdot z = \frac{2 \cdot zn}{r - l}x + \frac{r + l}{r - l}z$$

$$-y2 \cdot z = \frac{2 \cdot zn}{t - b}y + \frac{t + b}{t - b}z$$

$$-z2 \cdot z = -\frac{zf}{zf - zn}z - \frac{zn \cdot zf}{zf - zn}$$

$$w = -z$$

The above equations can be rewritten in a matrix form:

$$P2 = P \cdot M_{perpective} = \begin{pmatrix} x & y & z & 1 \end{pmatrix} \begin{pmatrix} \dfrac{2 \cdot zn}{r - l} & 0 & 0 & 0 \\[2ex] 0 & \dfrac{2 \cdot zn}{t - b} & 0 & 0 \\[2ex] \dfrac{r + l}{r - l} & \dfrac{t + b}{t - b} & \dfrac{zf}{zn - zf} & -1 \\[2ex] 0 & 0 & \dfrac{zn \cdot zf}{zn - zf} & 0 \end{pmatrix} \tag{9.7}$$

The $M_{perspective}$ in the above equation is the perspective projection matrix. This matrix is in a general form and applies to the case if the view frustum is symmetric or not.

For a symmetric view frustum, you can specify the width (w) and height (h) of the near plane, and use the following relations:

$$l = -w/2, \quad r = w/2, \quad b = -h/2, \quad t = h/2$$

Then the perspective matrix in Equation (9.7) reduces to

$$M_{perspective} = \begin{pmatrix} \dfrac{2 \cdot zn}{w} & 0 & 0 & 0 \\ 0 & \dfrac{2 \cdot zn}{h} & 0 & 0 \\ 0 & 0 & \dfrac{zf}{zn - zf} & -1 \\ 0 & 0 & \dfrac{zn \cdot zf}{zn - zf} & 0 \end{pmatrix} \tag{9.8}$$

Sometimes, it is convenient to specify the view frustum using the field of view (fov) in the Y direction and the aspect ratio, instead of the width and height. In this case, we have the relations:

$$yscale = \frac{zn}{h/2} = \frac{1}{\tan(fov/2)}, \quad xscale = \frac{yscale}{aspectRatio}$$

Here aspectRatio = w/h. Thus you can express the perspective matrix in terms of the field of the view angle:

$$M_{perspective} = \begin{pmatrix} xscale & 0 & 0 & 0 \\ 0 & yscale & 0 & 0 \\ 0 & 0 & \dfrac{zf}{zn - zf} & -1 \\ 0 & 0 & \dfrac{zn \cdot zf}{zn - zf} & 0 \end{pmatrix} \tag{9.9}$$

Implementing Perspective Transforms

WPF has implemented a PerspectiveCamera class, which requires a symmetric view frustum with a square near plane and far plane. It uses the field of view and distances to the near plane and the far plane as input parameters. Although it is convenient, it does have many limitations. If you want to customize the perspective transformation, you need to implement your own perspective transform matrix and pass it to the MatrixCamera class.

Now you are ready to implement the customized perspective matrices described in Equations (9.7) - (9.9). Open the project Chapter09, and add the following three public static methods to the Utility class:

```
public static Matrix3D SetPerspectiveOffCenter(
    double left, double right, double bottom,
    double top, double near, double far)
{
    Matrix3D perspectiveMatrix = new Matrix3D();
    perspectiveMatrix.M11 = 2 * near / (right - left);
    perspectiveMatrix.M22 = 2 * near / (top - bottom);
    perspectiveMatrix.M31 = (right + left) / (right - left);
    perspectiveMatrix.M32 = (top + bottom) / (top - bottom);
    perspectiveMatrix.M33 = far / (near - far);
    perspectiveMatrix.M34 = -1.0;
    perspectiveMatrix.OffsetZ = near * far / (near - far);
    perspectiveMatrix.M44 = 0;
    return perspectiveMatrix;
}

public static Matrix3D SetPerspective(
    double width, double height,
    double near, double far)
{
    Matrix3D perspectiveMatrix = new Matrix3D();
    perspectiveMatrix.M11 = 2 * near / width;
    perspectiveMatrix.M22 = 2 * near / height;
    perspectiveMatrix.M33 = far / (near - far);
    perspectiveMatrix.M34 = -1.0;
    perspectiveMatrix.OffsetZ = near * far / (near - far);
    perspectiveMatrix.M44 = 0;
    return perspectiveMatrix;
}

public static Matrix3D SetPerspectiveFov(double fov,
    double aspectRatio, double near, double far)
{
    Matrix3D perspectiveMatrix = new Matrix3D();
    double yscale = 1.0 / Math.Tan(fov * Math.PI / 180 / 2);
    double xscale = yscale / aspectRatio;
    perspectiveMatrix.M11 = xscale;
    perspectiveMatrix.M22 = yscale;
    perspectiveMatrix.M33 = far / (near - far);
    perspectiveMatrix.M34 = -1.0;
    perspectiveMatrix.OffsetZ = near * far / (near - far);
    perspectiveMatrix.M44 = 0;
    return perspectiveMatrix;
}
```

The SetPerspectiveOffCenter method returns a general perspective matrix for an asymmetric frustum, which takes four sides of the near plane, as well as the distances to the near plane and far plane as input parameters.

The method SetPerspetive is designed for a symmetric view frustum with four input parameters, width and height of the near plane, as well as the distances to the near and far planes.

The method SetPerspectiveFov is also for the symmetric view frustum, but with the field of view and aspect ratio as parameters, instead of width and height. By setting the aspect ratio to one, you can compare the result from our perspective matrix method with that obtained directly using the PerspectiveCamera class.

Testing Perspective Projections

With the View transform and Perspective projection matrices that have been implemented in the Utility class, you can test the perspective projection for a 3D graphics object. To test the effect of perspective projections, you need to create a 3D object. I'll discuss the detailed steps on how to create various 3D objects in later chapters. Here we'll simply create a 3D cube for the purpose of testing the perspective effect without getting into the detailed procedure on how to create such a cube.

Let's consider an example that demonstrates the persperctive projection on a 3D cube object. Add a new WPF Window to the project Chapter09 and name it PerspectiveProjection. Here is the XAML file of this example:

```
<Window x:Class="Chapter09.PerspectiveProjection"
    xmlns="http://schemas.microsoft.com/winfx
        /2006/xaml/presentation"
    xmlns:x="http://schemas.microsoft.com/winfx/2006/xaml"
    Title="Perspective Projection" Height="310" Width="400">

    <Window.Resources>
        <MeshGeometry3D x:Key="geometry"
            Positions="-1  1  1, 1  1  1, 1  1 -1,-1  1 -1,
                       -1 -1  1,-1 -1 -1, 1 -1 -1, 1 -1  1,
                       -1  1  1,-1 -1  1, 1 -1  1, 1  1  1,
                        1  1  1, 1 -1  1, 1 -1 -1, 1  1 -1,
                        1  1 -1, 1 -1 -1,-1 -1 -1,-1  1 -1,
                       -1  1 -1,-1 -1 -1,-1 -1  1,-1  1  1"
            TriangleIndices=" 0  1  2, 2  3  0,
                              4  5  6, 6  7  4,
                              8  9 10,10 11  8,
                             12 13 14,14 15 12,
                             16 17 18,18 19 16,
                             20 21 22,22 23 20"/>

        <DiffuseMaterial x:Key="material" Brush="SteelBlue"/>
    </Window.Resources>

    <Viewbox Stretch="Uniform">
        <Grid Width="430" Height="300"
            HorizontalAlignment="Left"
          VerticalAlignment="Top" ShowGridLines="False">
            <Grid.ColumnDefinitions>
                <ColumnDefinition Width="100" />
                <ColumnDefinition Width="330" />
            </Grid.ColumnDefinitions>
```

```xml
<StackPanel Margin="5" Grid.Column="0">
    <TextBlock Text="Camera Position" Margin="2"/>
    <TextBox Name="tbCameraPosition" Margin="2"
            HorizontalAlignment="Left"
            Text="3,4,5"/>
    <TextBlock Text="Look Direction" Margin="2"/>
    <TextBox Name="tbLookDirection" Margin="2"
            HorizontalAlignment="Left"
            Text="-3,-4,-5"/>
    <TextBlock Text="Up Direction" Margin="2"/>
    <TextBox Name="tbUpDirection" Margin="2"
            HorizontalAlignment="Left"
            Text="0,1,0"/>
    <TextBlock Text="Near Plane" Margin="2"/>
    <TextBox Name="tbNearPlane" Margin="2"
            HorizontalAlignment="Left" Text="1"/>
    <TextBlock Text="Far Plane" Margin="2"/>
    <TextBox Name="tbFarPlane" Margin="2"
            HorizontalAlignment="Left"
            Text="100"/>
    <TextBlock Text="Field of View" Margin="2"/>
    <TextBox Name="tbFieldOfView" Margin="2"
            HorizontalAlignment="Left"
            Text="60"/>

    <Button Name="btnApply" Margin="2,5,2,2"
            Click="btnApply_Click">Apply</Button>
</StackPanel>

<Border Margin="5" BorderBrush="Black"
        BorderThickness="1"
        HorizontalAlignment="Left" Width="320"
        Height="290" Grid.Column="1">
    <Viewport3D ClipToBounds="True">
        <!-- Set camera: -->
        <Viewport3D.Camera>
            <MatrixCamera x:Name="myCameraMatrix"/>
        </Viewport3D.Camera>

        <ContainerUIElement3D>
            <ModelUIElement3D>
                <Model3DGroup>

                    <!-- Create a cube: -->
                    <GeometryModel3D
  Geometry="{StaticResource geometry}"
  Material="{StaticResource material}">
                        <!-- Set translation: -->
    <GeometryModel3D.Transform>
        <TranslateTransform3D OffsetZ="1"/>
    </GeometryModel3D.Transform>
                    </GeometryModel3D>

                    <!-- Create another cube: -->
```

```xml
                         <GeometryModel3D
        Geometry="{StaticResource geometry}"
        Material="{StaticResource material}">
                              <!-- Set translation: -->
        <GeometryModel3D.Transform>
            <TranslateTransform3D OffsetZ="-2"/>
        </GeometryModel3D.Transform>
                              </GeometryModel3D>

                         <!-- Create another cube: -->
                         <GeometryModel3D
        Geometry="{StaticResource geometry}"
        Material="{StaticResource material}">
                              <!-- Set translation: -->
        <GeometryModel3D.Transform>
            <TranslateTransform3D OffsetZ="-5"/>
        </GeometryModel3D.Transform>
                              </GeometryModel3D>

                         <!-- Set light source: -->
                         <AmbientLight Color="Gray"/>
                         <DirectionalLight Color="Gray"
                              Direction="-1 -2 -3"/>
                    </Model3DGroup>
                </ModelUIElement3D>
            </ContainerUIElement3D>
        </Viewport3D>
      </Border>
    </Grid>
  </Viewbox>
</Window>
```

Here, we first create a Window Resource that defines the mesh geometry and material for a 3D cube object. You can easily create multiple cube objects by using this resource. In the XAML file, three cube objects are created at different locations by performing different translation transforms on the original cube geometry defined in Window.Resources. This XAML file also creates a layout and user interface, which allow you to interactively examine the perspective projection effect on these three cube objects by entering different values into the TextBoxes. These values include camera position, camera look at direction, up vector, as well as near plane, far plane, and field of view. Notice that the camera is set for the Viewport3D using the MatrixCamera, indicating that the custom camera setting will be used. This camera setting includes both the view transformation and perspective projection. Both transforms will be specified using the transform matrices created in the Utility class.

The corresponding code-behind file of this example is listed below:

```csharp
using System;
using System.Windows;
using System.Windows.Media;
using System.Windows.Media.Media3D;
```

```
namespace Chapter09
{
    public partial class PerspectiveProjection : Window
    {

        public PerspectiveProjection()
        {
            InitializeComponent();
            SetMatrixCamera();
        }

        private void btnApply_Click(object sender,
                RoutedEventArgs e)
        {
            SetMatrixCamera();
        }

        private void SetMatrixCamera()
        {
            Point3D cameraPosition =
                Point3D.Parse(tbCameraPosition.Text);
            Vector3D lookDirection =
                Vector3D.Parse(tbLookDirection.Text);
            Vector3D upDirection =
                Vector3D.Parse(tbUpDirection.Text);
            double fov = Double.Parse(tbFieldOfView.Text);
            double zn = Double.Parse(tbNearPlane.Text);
            double zf = Double.Parse(tbFarPlane.Text);
            double aspectRatio = 1.0;

            myCameraMatrix.ViewMatrix =
                Utility.SetViewMatrix(cameraPosition,
                lookDirection, upDirection);
            myCameraMatrix.ProjectionMatrix =
                Utility.SetPerspectiveFov(fov,
                aspectRatio, zn, zf);
        }
    }
}
```

This class implements the SetMatrixCamera method, in which the parameters are specified by the user's inputs. Then, these parameters are passed to the custom view and perspective projection matrices that you have implemented in the Utility class. Finally, you attach these custom matrices to the ViewMatrix and ProjectionMatrix properties of the MatrixCamera, named myCameraMatrix.

Building and running this project, and selecting PerspectiveProjection from the Start Menu, produce the output shown in Figure 9-15. Note that the physical dimensions of these three cubes are the same. From the figure you can clearly see the foreshortening effect of the perspective projection: the farther the cube is from the camera, the smaller it appears on the screen.

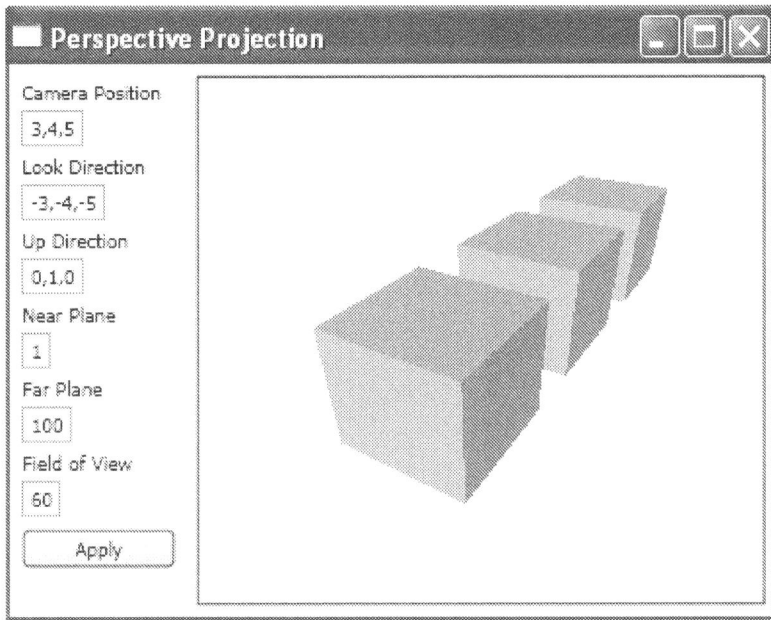

Figure 9-15 Perspective projection of cube objects.

Of course, you can also use the built-in PerspectiveCamera class in WPF directly to perform the similar perspective projection. When you use the PerspectiveCamera class, WPF will create corresponding View and Projection transform matrices internally and use them to create the 3D objects on the screen. The purpose of using a custom MatrixCamera is to demonstrate how the view transform and perspective projection matrices are constructed and how they work mathematically.

Orthographic Projection

In WPF, the viewing volume for an orthographic projection is a rectangular parallelepiped, or a box, as shown in Figure 9-16. Unlike with perspective projection, the size of the viewing volume doesn't change from one end to the other, so the distance from the camera doesn't affect how large an object appears. Namely, no perspective distortion occurs in orthographic projections. The points in the camera space are always mapped to the projection plane by casting rays that are parallel to the camera's viewing direction. As mentioned previously, this type of projection is usually used in applications for architecture and computer-aided design (CAD), where it is important to maintain the actual sizes of objects and the angles between them as they are projected.

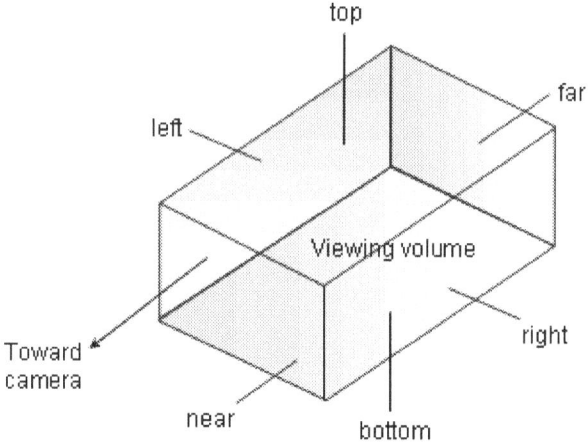

Figure 9-16 Orthographic viewing volume.

Orthographic Transform Matrix

The orthographic projection corresponds to transform the viewing volume shown in Figure 9-16 to a box with $-1 \le x \le 1$, $-1 \le y \le 1$, and $0 \le z \le 1$. Again, Microsoft's conventions are used here. In other technologies, including OpenGL, the range $[-1, 1]$ is used for the mapping in the Z direction.

Since there is no perspective distortion, the orthographic projection must be a linear transformation. Therefore, the transform can be written in the following form:

$$x1 = Cx1 \cdot x + Cx2$$
$$y1 = Cy1 \cdot y + Cy2$$
$$z1 = Cz1 \cdot z + Cz2$$

The mapping relations lead to the results:

$$-1 = Cx1 \cdot l + Cx2, \quad +1 = Cx1 \cdot r + Cx2$$
$$-1 = Cy1 \cdot b + Cy2, \quad +1 = Cy1 \cdot t + Cy2$$
$$0 = Cz1 \cdot zn + Cz2, \quad +1 = Cz2 \cdot zf + Cz2$$

You can obtain the orthographic transform by solving the above equations:

$$x1 = \frac{2}{r-l} x - \frac{r+l}{r-l}$$
$$y1 = \frac{2}{t-b} y - \frac{t+b}{t-b}$$
$$z1 = \frac{1}{zf-zn} z - \frac{zn}{zf-zn}$$

You can then get the orthographic projection matrix by rewriting the above equations in matrix form:

$$Pl = P \cdot M_{orthographic} = (x, y, z, 1) \begin{pmatrix} \dfrac{2}{r-l} & 0 & 0 & 0 \\ 0 & \dfrac{2}{t-b} & 0 & 0 \\ 0 & 0 & \dfrac{1}{zf-zn} & 0 \\ \dfrac{l+r}{l-r} & \dfrac{b+t}{b-t} & \dfrac{zn}{zn-zf} & 1 \end{pmatrix} \qquad (9.10)$$

The matrix $M_{orthographic}$ is the orthographic projection matrix, which is valid for general cases, including for asymmetric viewing volume, or off center cases.

For symmetric cases, you can specify the width (w) and height (h) of the near plane, and use the following relations:

$$l = -w/2, \quad r = w/2, \quad b = -h/2, \quad t = h/2$$

The orthographic projection matrix becomes

$$M_{orthographic} = \begin{pmatrix} 2/w & 0 & 0 & 0 \\ 0 & 2/h & 0 & 0 \\ 0 & 0 & \dfrac{1}{zn-zf} & 0 \\ 0 & 0 & \dfrac{zn}{zn-zf} & 1 \end{pmatrix} \qquad (9.11)$$

Implementing Orthographic Transforms

WPF has implemented an OrthographicCamera class, which requires a symmetric viewing volume with a square near plane and far plane. This class takes the width and the distances to the near plane and far plane as input parameters. Although this class is convenient, it does have many limitations. If you want to customize the orthographic transform, you have to implement your own orthographic transform matrix and pass it to the MatrixCamera class.

Now you can implement the customized orthographic matrices given in Equations (9.10) and (9.11). Open the project Chapter09 and add two public static methods to the Utility class:

```
public static Matrix3D SetOrthographicOffCenter(
double left, double right, double bottom,
double top, double near, double far)
{
    Matrix3D orthographicMatrix = new Matrix3D();
    orthographicMatrix.M11 = 2 / (right - left);
    orthographicMatrix.M22 = 2 / (top - bottom);
    orthographicMatrix.M33 = 1 / (near - far);
```

```
            orthographicMatrix.OffsetX =
                (left + right) / (left - right);
            orthographicMatrix.OffsetY =
                (bottom + top) / (bottom - top);
            orthographicMatrix.OffsetZ = near / (near - far);
            return orthographicMatrix;
    }

    public static Matrix3D SetOrthographic(double width,
        double height, double near, double far)
    {
        Matrix3D orthographicMatrix = new Matrix3D();
        orthographicMatrix.M11 = 2 / width;
        orthographicMatrix.M22 = 2 / height;
        orthographicMatrix.M33 = 1 / (near - far);
        orthographicMatrix.OffsetZ = near / (near - far);
        return orthographicMatrix;
    }
```

The method SetOrthographicOffCenter returns a general orthographic matrix for asymmetric viewing volume, which takes the four sides of the near plane, as well as the distances to the near and the far planes as input parameters.

The method SetOrthographic is designed for a symmetric view frustum with four input parameters: the width and height of the near plane and the distances to the near and far planes. The WPF has implemented an OrthographicCamera class, which uses the squared near and far planes. This means that it only take three parameters: the side length (width) of the near plane and the distances to the near and far planes. If you set height = width in the SetOrthographic method, you can compare the result of the custom matrix method with that obtained by directly using the OrthographicCamera class.

Testing Orthographic Projections

Now, you can perform an orthographic projection on a 3D object using the view transform and orthographic projection matrices that have been implemented in the Utility class.

Add a new WPF Window to the project Chapter09 and name it OrthographicProjection. You can use the XAML file similar to that used in the previous example of testing perspective projection. The only parameter that needs to be changed is the field of view. Simply change the parameter fov to the width.

The code-behind file is also similar to the one used in testing perspective projections. The only change occurs in the SetMatrixCamera method:

```
    private void SetMatrixCamera()
    {
        Point3D cameraPosition =
            Point3D.Parse(tbCameraPosition.Text);
        Vector3D lookDirection =
```

```
      Vector3D.Parse(tbLookDrection.Text);
   Vector3D upDirection =
      Vector3D.Parse(tbUpDirection.Text);
   double w = Double.Parse(tbWidth.Text);
   double zn = Double.Parse(tbNearPlane.Text);
   double zf = Double.Parse(tbFarPlane.Text);

   myCameraMatrix.ViewMatrix =
      Utility.SetViewMatrix(cameraPosition,
      lookDirection, upDirection);
   myCameraMatrix.ProjectionMatrix =
      Utility.SetOrthographic(w, w, zn, zf);
}
```

Here, you set the ProjectionMatrix property of the MatrixCamera to the orthographic matrix defined using the SetOrthographic method in the Utility class.

Executing this project generates the result shown in Figure 9-17. It can be seen that three cubes have the same view size on your screen regardless of where they are located. This means that there is no foreshortening effect in the orthographic projection. For comparison, you can also perform a similar orthographic projection using the built-in OrthographicCamera class in WPF.

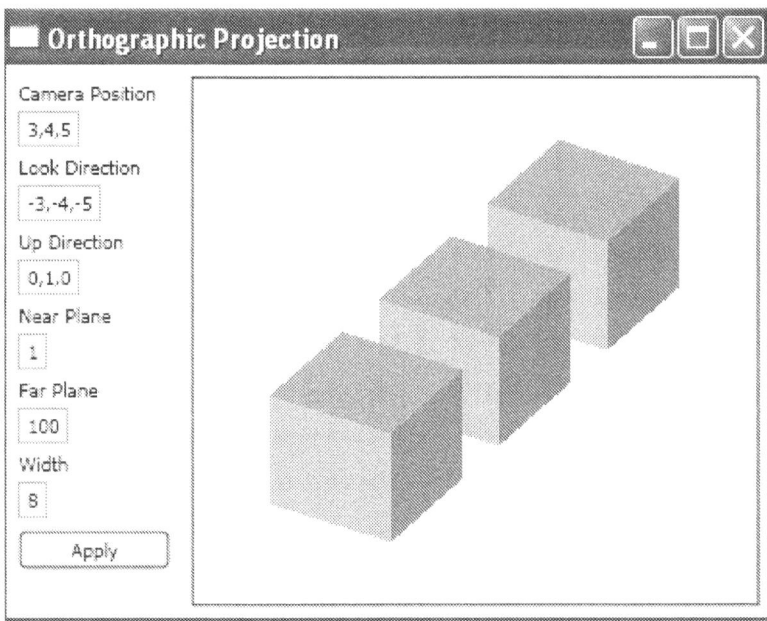

Figure 9-17 Orthographic projection of cube objects.

Object Transforms in WPF

Previously, we discussed Vector3D and Matrix3D structures, as well as their operations in WPF. The Matrix3D structure can be applied to a Point3D or a Vector3D object. However, if you want to apply 3D transforms to objects or coordinate systems, you need to use the Transform3D class. Unlike 2D objects, in order to display the transformed 3D object on your computer screen, you also need to perform projection transforms, as discussed in the last two sections. In WPF, there are several derived classes from the Transform3D class that can be used to perform specific transforms on 3D objects:

- ScaleTransform3D – Scales a 3D object in the X-Y-Z directions, starting from a defined center. Scale factors ScaleX, ScaleY, and ScaleZ are defined in the X-, Y-, and Z-directions from this center point.

- TranslateTransform3D – Defines a translation along the X, Y, and Z directions.The amount an object is translated is specified using the OffsetX, OffsetY, and OffsetZ properties.

- RotateTransform3D – Rotates an object in 3D space by specifying a 3D rotation using the Rotation property and a center point specified by the CenterX, CenterY and CenterZ properties. The Rotation property can be specified by a Rotation3D object. If you want to represent a 3D rotation using a specified angle about a specified rotation axis, you can use the AxisAngleRotation3D object to specify the Rotation property.

- MatrixTransform3D – Creates a 3D transform, specified by a Matrix3D object, used to manipulate objects or coordinate systems in 3D world space. It usually provides a custom transform that isn't provided by the other Transform3D classes. The custom transform matrices can be multiplied to form any number of linear transforms, such as rotation and scale, followed by translation.

The structure of the 3D Transform Matrix is the same as that of the Matrix3D in WPF. In the homogeneous coordinate system, the 3D Transform Matrix has 16 elements defined by M_{ij} (with i, j = 1, 2, 3, 4) except for M_{4j} (with j = 1, 2, 3), where they are replaced by OffsetX, OffsetY, and OffsetZ. These three elements represent the translation in 3D space.

By directly manipulating matrix values via the MatrixTransform3D class, you can rotate, scale, move, and even skew a 3D object. For example, if you change the value of the OffsetX to 10, you can use it to move an object 10 units along the x-axis in the world space. If you change the value in the second column of the second row to 3, you can use it to stretch an object to three times its current size in the Y direction. If you change both values at the same time, you move the object 10 units along the X-axis and stretch its dimension by a factor of 3 in the Y direction.

Although WPF enables you to directly manipulate matrix values in the MatrixTransform3D class, it also provides several transform classes that enable you to transform an object without knowing how the underlying matrix structure is configured. For example, the ScaleTransform3D class enables you to scale an object by setting its ScaleX, ScaleY and ScaleZ properties, instead of manipulating an underlying transform matrix. Likewise, the RotateTransfrom3D class enables you to rotate an object by simply specifying the angle about a rotation axis through its Rotation property. WPF will use the underlying structure of the transform matrix to perform the corresponding operation on objects.

In the following sections, you'll apply various transforms to the 3D cube we used when we discussed projections.

ScaleTransform3D Class

The ScaleTransform3D class in WPF enables you to scale a 3D object by setting its ScaleX, ScaleY, and ScaleZ properties.

Let's look at an example. Open the Chapter09 project, add a new WPF Window, and name it ScaleTransformation. The following is the XAML file of this example:

```
<Window x:Class="Chapter09.ScaleTransformation"
    xmlns="http://schemas.microsoft.com/winfx
        /2006/xaml/presentation"
    xmlns:x="http://schemas.microsoft.com/winfx/2006/xaml"
    Title="Scale Transformation" Height="310" Width="400">

    <Window.Resources>
        <MeshGeometry3D x:Key="geometry"
            Positions="-1  1  1, 1  1  1, 1  1 -1,-1  1 -1,
                       -1 -1  1,-1 -1 -1, 1 -1 -1, 1 -1  1,
                       -1  1  1,-1 -1  1, 1 -1  1, 1  1  1,
                        1  1  1, 1 -1  1, 1 -1 -1, 1  1 -1,
                        1  1 -1, 1 -1 -1,-1 -1 -1,-1  1 -1,
                       -1  1 -1,-1 -1 -1,-1 -1  1,-1  1  1"
            TriangleIndices=" 0  1  2, 2  3  0,
                              4  5  6, 6  7  4,
                              8  9 10,10 11  8,
                             12 13 14,14 15 12,
                             16 17 18,18 19 16,
                             20 21 22,22 23 20"/>

        <DiffuseMaterial x:Key="material" Brush="SteelBlue"/>
    </Window.Resources>

    <Viewbox Stretch="Uniform">
        <Grid Width="430" Height="300"
            HorizontalAlignment="Left"
          VerticalAlignment="Top" ShowGridLines="False">
            <Grid.ColumnDefinitions>
                <ColumnDefinition Width="100" />
                <ColumnDefinition Width="330" />
            </Grid.ColumnDefinitions>
```

```xml
<StackPanel Margin="5" Grid.Column="0">
    <RadioButton x:Name="rbOrthographic"
                 Margin="2"
                 Content="Orthorgriphic"
                 IsChecked="True"/>
    <RadioButton x:Name="rbPerspective" Margin="2"
                 Content="Perspective"
                 IsChecked="False"/>
    <TextBlock Text="ScaleX" Margin="2"/>
    <TextBox Name="tbScaleX" Margin="2"
             HorizontalAlignment="Left" Text="1"/>
    <TextBlock Text="ScaleY" Margin="2"/>
    <TextBox Name="tbScaleY" Margin="2"
             HorizontalAlignment="Left" Text="1"/>
    <TextBlock Text="ScaleZ" Margin="2"/>
    <TextBox Name="tbScaleZ" Margin="2"
             HorizontalAlignment="Left" Text="1"/>
    <TextBlock Text="Scale Center" Margin="2"/>
    <TextBox Name="tbScaleCenter" Margin="2"
             HorizontalAlignment="Left"
             Text="0,0,0"/>
    <Button Name="btnApply" Margin="2,5,2,2"
            Click="btnApply_Click">Apply</Button>
</StackPanel>

<Border Margin="5" BorderBrush="Black"
        BorderThickness="1"
        HorizontalAlignment="Left" Width="320"
        Height="290" Grid.Column="1">
    <Viewport3D Name="myViewport"
                ClipToBounds="True">
        <Viewport3D.Camera>
            <MatrixCamera
                x:Name="myCameraMatrix"/>
        </Viewport3D.Camera>

        <ContainerUIElement3D>
            <ModelUIElement3D>
                <Model3DGroup>
                    <!-- Create a cube: -->
                    <GeometryModel3D
  Geometry="{StaticResource geometry}"
  Material="{StaticResource material}">
                        <!-- Set transform: -->
    <GeometryModel3D.Transform>
        <ScaleTransform3D x:Name="myTransform"/>
    </GeometryModel3D.Transform>
                    </GeometryModel3D>

                    <!-- Set light source: -->
                    <AmbientLight Color="Gray"/>
                    <DirectionalLight Color="Gray"
                        Direction="-1 -2 -3"/>
```

```
            </Model3DGroup>
          </ModelUIElement3D>
        </ContainerUIElement3D>
      </Viewport3D>
    </Border>
  </Grid>
</Viewbox>
</Window>
```

Here, you use the same Window.Resources that you used in the previous example to define the cube geometry and material. This XAML file also creates a user interface that allows you to interactively change the input parameters. Here, the MatrixCamera class is used to set the camera by using the customized View and Projection matrices defined in the Utility class. Of course, you could also use the WPF built-in PerspectiveCamera or OrthographicCamera class to set the camera instead. The user interface also allows you to choose between the perspective or orthographic projection. The input parameters you can specify include the scale factors ScaleX, ScaleY, and ScaleZ, as well as the scaling center.

The corresponding code-behind file is used to handle the MatrixCamera and scale transform:

```
using System;
using System.Windows;
using System.Windows.Media;
using System.Windows.Media.Media3D;

namespace Chapter09
{
    public partial class ScaleTransformation : Window
    {
        public ScaleTransformation()
        {
            InitializeComponent();
            SetMatrixCamera();
            SetScaleTransform();
        }

        private void btnApply_Click(object sender,
                RoutedEventArgs e)
        {
            SetMatrixCamera();
            SetTransform();
        }

        private void SetTransform()
        {
            Point3D center =
                    Point3D.Parse(tbScaleCenter.Text);
            myTransform.CenterX = center.X;
            myTransform.CenterY = center.Y;
            myTransform.CenterZ = center.Z;
```

```
                    myTransform.ScaleX =
                              Double.Parse(tbScaleX.Text);
                    myTransform.ScaleY =
                              Double.Parse(tbScaleY.Text);
                    myTransform.ScaleZ =
                              Double.Parse(tbScaleZ.Text);
        }

        private void SetMatrixCamera()
        {
            Point3D cameraPosition = new Point3D(3, 3, 3);
            Vector3D lookDirection = new Vector3D(-3, -3, -3);
            Vector3D upDirection = new Vector3D(0, 1, 0);
            double w = 6;
            double zn = 1;
            double zf = 100;
            double fov = 60;
            double aspectRatio = 1.0;
            myCameraMatrix.ViewMatrix =
                    Utility.SetViewMatrix(cameraPosition,
                lookDirection, upDirection);

            if (rbOrthographic.IsChecked == true)
            {
                myCameraMatrix.ProjectionMatrix =
                    Utility.SetOrthographic(w, w, zn, zf);
            }
            else if (rbPerspective.IsChecked == true)
            {
                myCameraMatrix.ProjectionMatrix =
                    Utility.SetPerspectiveFov(
                    fov,aspectRatio,zn,zf);
            }
        }
    }
}
```

The SetMatrixCamera method sets the camera using either the perspective or orthographic projection. You can change the parameters used to set the camera as you like.

The SetTransform method in this class performs the scale transform on the cube. You first pass the input parameters to a Point3D object, then attach this Point3D object and the ScaleX, ScaleY, and ScaleZ from the user's inputs to the corresponding properties of the myTransform defined in the XAML file.

Executing this project generates the result shown in Figure 9-18. You can change any parameter in the user interface and click the Apply button to examine the scale effect on the cube.

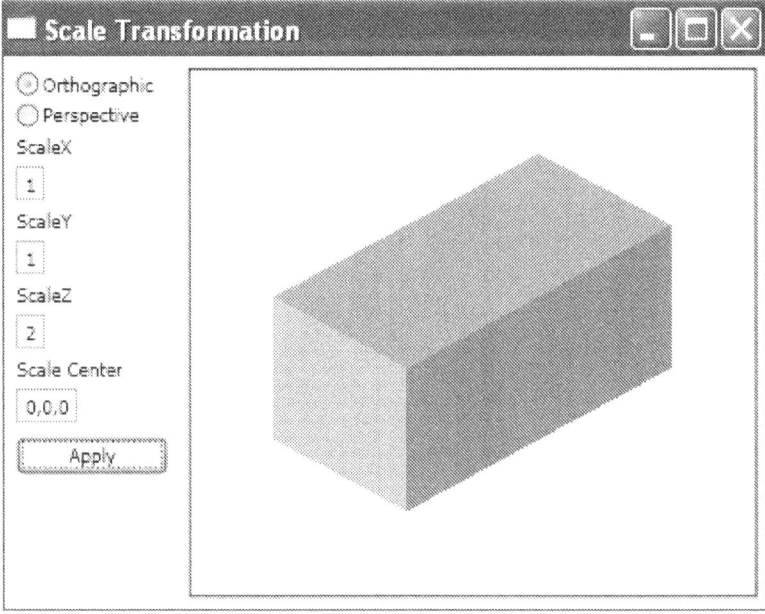

Figure 9-18 Scale transform on a cube.

TranslateTransform3D class

The TranslateTransform3D class enables you to move a 3D object by setting its OffsetX, OffsetY and OffsetZ properties. This transformation has no center property to set because the translation effect is the same regardless of where it is centered.

Here, let's consider an example that demonstrates a translation on a cube object using a similar layout and user interface as the previous example. Open the Chapter09 project, add a WPF Window, and call it TranslateTransformation. The XAML code is similar to the previous ScaleTransformation example, except that you need to change the scale transform to a translation transform. Replace the bold part of the XAML file with the following snippet:

```
<GeometryModel3D.Transform>
    <TranslateTransform3D x:Name="myTransform"/>
</GeometryModel3D.Transform>
```

The corresponding code-behind file is also similar to that of the previous example, except that you need to rewrite the SetTransform method:

```
private void SetTransform()
{
    myTransform.OffsetX = Double.Parse(tbOffsetX.Text);
    myTransform.OffsetY = Double.Parse(tbOffsetY.Text);
    myTransform.OffsetZ = Double.Parse(tbOffsetZ.Text);
}
```

Here, you attach the corresponding input parameters to the OffsetX, OffsetY, and OffsetZ properties of the myTransform defined in the XAML file.

Executing this project produces the result shown in Figure 9-19. You can move the cube around your screen by playing with different parameters for OffsetX, OffsetY, and OffsetZ.

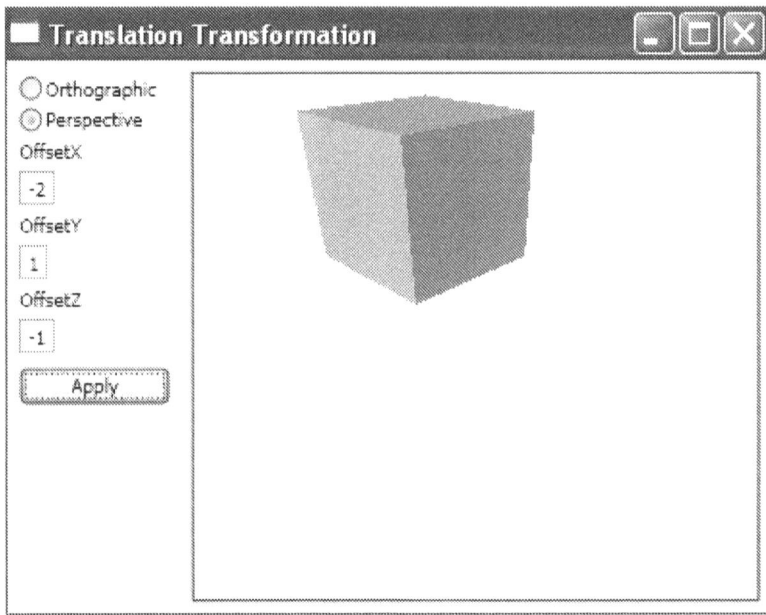

Figure 9-19 Translation transformation on a cube.

RotateTransform3D Class

In an earlier section of this chapter, Rotation and Quaternion, we discussed how to perform a 3D rotation using a quaternion matrix. You can use this matrix to construct your own custom 3D rotation class. However, there is no need to do so. WPF already provides a 3D rotation class called RotateTransform3D. This class defines a Rotation property that you set to an object of type Rotation3D. The Rotation3D class is an abstract class. WPF implements two useful classes that derive from Rotation3D: AxisAngleRotation3D and QuaternionRotation3D. You can use either one to perform a 3D rotation. In fact, these two classes use the same mathematical model: both are based on the quaternion technique.

When considering a 3D object rotated a finite angle about a specified axis, you can directly use AxisAngleRotation3D to perform such a rotation. On the other hand, you can also calculate the quaternion of the rotation using Equation (9.1), then use QuaternionRotation3D to perform the same rotation. For example, if you want to rotate an object about the Y axis 90 degrees, you can use the following XAML snippet to do so:

```
<RotateTransform3D>
<RotateTransform3D.Rotation>
    <AxisAngleRotation3D Axis="0 1 0" Angle="90"/>
</RotateTransform3D.Rotation>
</RotateTransform3D>
```

This rotation can also be performed using QuaternionRotation3D:

```
<RotateTransform3D>
<RotateTransform3D.Rotation>
    <QuaternionRotation3D Quaternion="0 0.707 0 0.707"/>
</RotateTransform3D.Rotation>
</RotateTransform3D>
```

The Quaternion in the above XAML snippet has beed calculated using Equation (9.1). This quaternion describes a rotation of 90 degrees about the Y axis. The number 0.707 (the Y component) is the Sine of half the angle (or 45 degrees), and the other number 0.707 (the W component) is the Cosine of 45 degrees. You can choose either class to perform 3D rotations. The AxisAngleRotation3D class is more straightforward, and will be used extensively in this book.

Here, let's consider an example that performs a rotation transform on a cube object using the same layout as the previous example. Open the Chapter09 project, add a WPF Window, and call it RotateTransformation. You can open the project to look at the complete source code of this example. The XAML file is similar to that of the previous ScaleTransformation example, except that you need to change the transform to a rotation. Replace the bold part of the XAML file with the following snippet:

```
<GeometryModel3D.Transform>
    <RotateTransform3D x:Name="myTransform"/>
</GeometryModel3D.Transform>
```

The corresponding code-behind file is also similar to that of the ScaleTransformation example, except that you need to rewrite the SetTransform method:

```
private void SetTransform()
{
    Point3D rotateCenter = Point3D.Parse(tbCenter.Text);
    Vector3D rotateAxis = Vector3D.Parse(tbAxis.Text);
    double rotateAngle = Double.Parse(tbAngle.Text);
    myTransform.CenterX = rotateCenter.X;
    myTransform.CenterY = rotateCenter.Y;
    myTransform.CenterZ = rotateCenter.Z;
    myTransform.Rotation =
        new AxisAngleRotation3D(rotateAxis, rotateAngle);
}
```

Here, you define the rotateCenter, rotateAxis, and rotateAngle using the user's input parameters. Then you attach the rotateCenter to the CenterX, CenterY, and CenterZ properties of the RotateTransform3D object, myTransform, which is defined in XAML file. Then you create a new AxsAngleRotation3D object using the rotateAxis and rotateAngle properties, and attach it to the Rotation property of myTransform.

Executing this project produces the result shown in Figure 9-20. You can play around with this example by changing the rotation center, angle, and axis, then clicking the Apply button to see the effect on the cube. You can also select the Perspective or Orthographic radio button to examine the different projection effects.

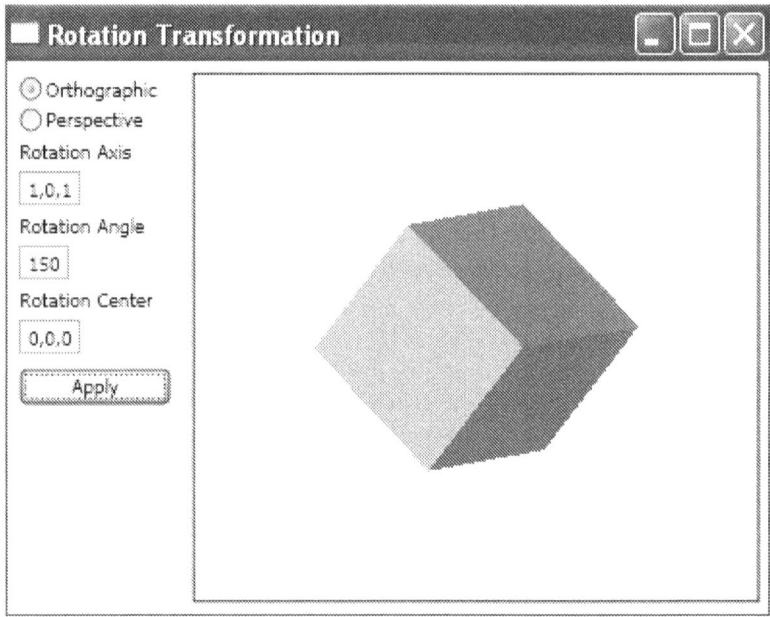

Figure 9-20 Rotation transformation on a cube.

MatrixTransform3D Class

In the previous sections, we discussed the basic 3D transforms on graphics objects. These transforms include scale, translation, and rotation. However, if you want to perform a 3D transform that isn't provided by the basic Transform3D classes (for example, a 3D skew transform), you can create a custom 3D transform using the MatrixTransform3D class.

Here I'll use an example to illustrate how to perform 3D custom transforms on a cube object directly using the MatrixTransform3D class. Add a new WPF Window to the project Chapter09 and name it MatrixTransformation. The XAML file of the MatrixTransformation and its layout are similar to the previous ScaleTransformaion example. The interface allows you to change all sixteen elements of the transform matrix and to view the transformed cube on the screen interactively. In the XAML file, you need to make the following change to the 3D transform:

```
<GeometryModel3D.Transform>
    <MatrixTransform3D x:Name="myTransform"/>
</GeometryModel3D.Transform>
```

Here, the name myTransform represents the MatrixTransform3D object. The corresponding code-behind file is also similar to that of the ScaleTransformation example, except that you need to rewrite the SetTransform method:

```
private void SetTransform()
{
    Matrix3D m3 = new Matrix3D();
    m3.M11 = Double.Parse(tbM11.Text);
    m3.M21 = Double.Parse(tbM21.Text);
    m3.M31 = Double.Parse(tbM31.Text);
    m3.OffsetX = Double.Parse(tbM41.Text);
    m3.M12 = Double.Parse(tbM12.Text);
    m3.M22 = Double.Parse(tbM22.Text);
    m3.M32 = Double.Parse(tbM32.Text);
    m3.OffsetY = Double.Parse(tbM42.Text);
    m3.M13 = Double.Parse(tbM13.Text);
    m3.M23 = Double.Parse(tbM23.Text);
    m3.M33 = Double.Parse(tbM33.Text);
    m3.OffsetZ = Double.Parse(tbM43.Text);
    m3.M14 = Double.Parse(tbM14.Text);
    m3.M24 = Double.Parse(tbM24.Text);
    m3.M34 = Double.Parse(tbM34.Text);
    m3.M44 = Double.Parse(tbM44.Text);

    myTransform.Matrix = m3;
}
```

You can see that the SetTransform method creates a custom transform matrix m3 by taking the input parameters as its elements. This matrix is then attached to the Matrix property of the MatrixTransform3D object called myTransform defined in the XAML file.

Executing this project produces the output shown in Figure 9-21. The result shown in the figure is obtained by setting the elements M13 and M23 to 2, resulting in a shearing effect on the cube. This 3D shearing effect has to be created using a custom transform matrix because WPF doesn't provide a SkewTransform3D class. You can use the MatrixTransform3D class to create any 3D transform by directly manipulating its corresponding elements.

Combining Transforms

The Transform3DGroup class is useful when you want to create a combining transformation that consists of any number of Transform3D children in its Transform3D collection.

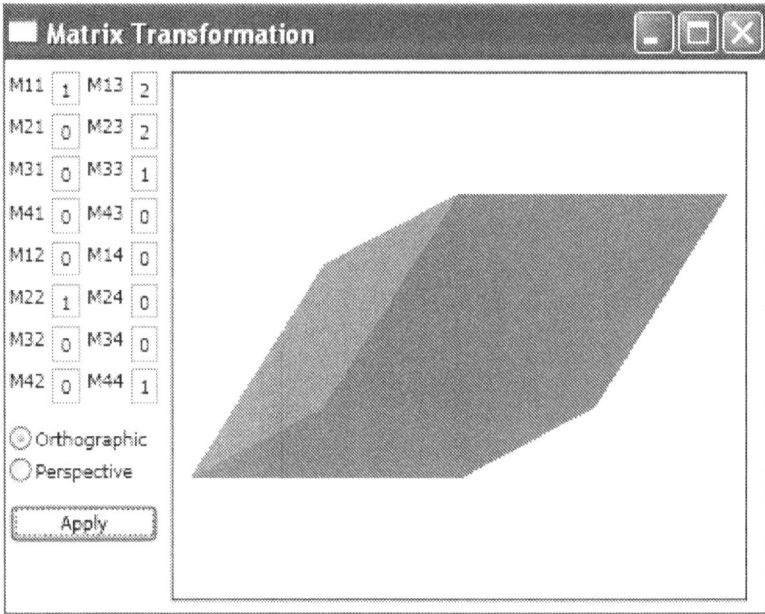

Figure 9-21 Custom transformation on a cube.

Here, I'll use an example to illustrate how to use the Transform3DGroup class in a WPF application. In this example, we'll consider a combining transformation that contains a scale and a rotation transform. This combining transformation is applied to a cube object.

Open the Chapter09 project, add a new WPF Window, and name it CombineTransformation. The layout for this example is also similar to that of the previous ScaleTransformation example. Here I'll only show you the key steps how to perform the composite transform. You can view the complete source code of this example by opening its XAML and code-behind files using Visual Studio. In the XAML file of this example, you need to make the following changes to the 3D transform definition:

```
<GeometryModel3D.Transform>
    <Transform3DGroup>
        <ScaleTransform3D x:Name="scaleTransform"/>
        <RotateTransform3D x:Name="rotateTransform"/>
    </Transform3DGroup>
</GeometryModel3D.Transform>
```

Here, you create a Transform3DGroup object that includes two transforms: a ScaleTransform3D called scaleTransform, and a RotateTransform3D called rotateTransform. A Transform3DGroup object can contain any number of Transform3D objects. Thus, you can easily create complex 3D composite transforms using the Transform3DGroup.

You also need to change the SetTransform method in the corresponding code-behind file:

```
private void SetTransform()
{
    // Scale transformation:
    scaleTransform.ScaleX = Double.Parse(tbScaleX.Text);
    scaleTransform.ScaleY = Double.Parse(tbScaleY.Text);
    scaleTransform.ScaleZ = Double.Parse(tbScaleZ.Text);

    // Rotation Transformation:
    Vector3D rotateAxis = Vector3D.Parse(tbAxis.Text);
    double rotateAngle = Double.Parse(tbAngle.Text);
rotateTransform.Rotation =
    new AxisAngleRotation3D(rotateAxis, rotateAngle);

}
```

Here, you first perform a scale transform, followed by a rotation transform. These transforms specified by attaching the user's input parameters to the corresponding properties of the 3D transform, scaleTransform and rotateTransform.

Executing this project produces the results shown in Figure 9-22.

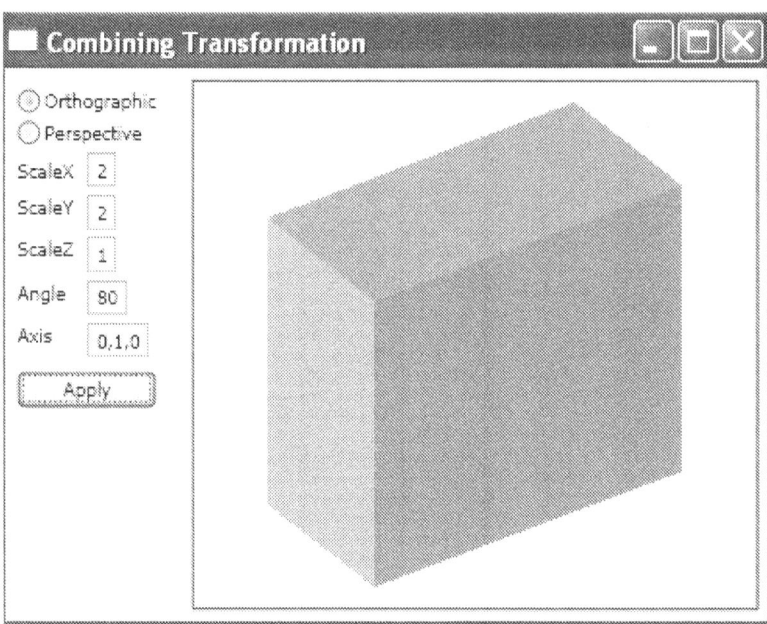

Figure 9-22 Composite transformation on a cube.

Chapter 10
WPF Graphics Basics in 3D

In the previous chapter, you learned the mathematical basics of 3D transformations and how these transformations are implemented in WPF. In this chapter, you'll learn how to create basic 3D shapes in WPF.

WPF introduces a new extensive 3D model that allows you to draw, transform, and animate 3D graphics objects in both markup and code-behind files, using the same capabilities by the platform offered to 2D graphics objects. This makes WPF 3D graphics suitable for everything from eye-catching effects in simple games to 3D charts and data visualization in a business applications.

Please remember that 3D support in WPF isn't designed to provide a full-featured real-time game development platform. If you are planning to build a complex real-time game application, you will be much better off using the raw power of DirectX or OpenGL.

Even though WPF's 3D model is similar to its 2D countpart, implementing rich 3D graphics is still difficult. Creating any meaningful 3D graphics but a trivial 3D scene with XAML or code-behind files is far more involved than the 2D equivalent of creating a XAML or C# code vector image. This chapter covers 3D graphics basics in WPF, including Viewport3D, geometry and mesh, light source, camera setting, and creating basic 3D shapes.

3D Graphics Basics

Even creating the simplest 3D graphics object in WPF, such as a triangle, involves several basic steps, including

- Specifying a Viewport3D object that hosts the 3D content.
- Defining the 3D object, which derives from either ModelVisual3D or ModelUIElement3D.
- Specifying a light source that illuminates part or all of the 3D scene.

- Applying materials to the 3D model that determine the appearance characteristics of the 3D model's surface.

- Setting a camera that projects the 3D object onto a 2D representation, from which you can view the 3D scene.

The above list includes only the basic steps for creating a 3D object in WPF. In a practical 3D WPF application, you may also require other procedures, such as transforms and animation. A practical application may also contain multiple graphics objects, multiple light sources, and different materials. These basic ingredients, however, provide a good starting point.

Compared to 2D graphics, some of the basic steps listed above may seem unnecessary to a new WPF 3D programmer. You might assume that WPF 3D classes are just a simple way to create an object that has a 3D appearance. In some situations, for simple 3D applications, you can construct a graphics object using 2D drawing classes, shapes, and transformation, that appears to be 3D. In fact, this approach is usually easier than working with the WPF 3D classes.

However, there are some advantages to using the 3D support in WPF. First, you can create effects that would be extremely complex to calculate using a simulated 3D model. For instance, the lighting effect for an application with multiple light sources and different materials becomes very involved if you try to construct it based on 2D graphics and ray tracing. The other advantage to using the WPF 3D model is that it allows you to interact with your graphics as a set of 3D objects. This greatly extends what you can do programmatically. For example, once you build the 3D scene you want, it becomes almost trivially easy to rotate your object or rotate the camera around your object. Doing the same work with 2D programming would require an avalanche of code and math.

In the following sections, you'll learn some basic concepts of the 3D graphics in WPF.

Viewport3D

3D graphics content in WPF is encapsulated in the Viewport3D class. The graphics object treats Viewport3D as a 2D visual element like many others in WPF, so it can be placed anywhere you would place a normal element. Viewport3D functions as a window – a viewport – into a 3D scene. More accurately, it is a surface on which a 3D scene is projected.

The Viewport3D class has only two properties, Camera and Children. The Camera property defines your lookout onto the 3D scene, while the Children property holds all the 3D objects you want to place in the scene. The light source that illuminates your 3D scene is itself an object in the viewport.

3D Objects in WPF

The Viewport3D element can host any 3D object that derives from the Visual3D class. However, you need to perform a bit more work than you might expect to create a 3D graphics object. In .NET 3.0 and 3.5, the WPF library lacks a collection of 3D shape primitives. If you want a 3D shape such as a cube to be displayed on your screen, you need to build it yourself.

Model3D is an abstract base class that represents a generic 3D object. To build a 3D scene, you need some objects to view, and the objects that make up the scene derive from Model3D. WPF supports modeling Geometries with GeometryModel3D. The Geometry property of this model takes a mesh primitive.

In .NET 3.0, Visual3D is the base class for all 3D objects. Like the Visual class in the 2D world, you could use the Visual3D class to derive 3D shapes or to create more complex 3D controls that provide a richer set of events and framework services. WPF includes only one class that derives from Visual3D – the all-purpose ModelVisual3D.

.NET 3.5 adds some new features to the WPF 3D model. One of the features is the addition of the UIElement3D class. As you already know, in the 2D world, UIElement adds layout, input, focus, and events to the Visual class. UIElement3D brings these same things to the Visual3D class. This means that the standard events and means of adding event handlers you are used to with 2D UIElement now apply to the 3D world with UIElement3D.

UIElement3D itself is an abstract class that derives from the Visual3D class. To make it easier so that you don't have to derive from UIElement3D yourself, WPF provides two new classes, ModelUIElement3D and ContainerUIElement3D. The latter is a container for other Visual3D objects. It has one main property, Children, which is used to add and remove 3D objects. The ContainerUIElement3D class doesn't have a visual representation itself; rather, it is just a collection of other 3D objects. The ModelUIElement3D class has one property, Model, which is the Model3D that should be displayed to represent the UIElement3D objects. It has no children itself, and in some ways you can think of ModelUIElement3D like a Shape object in the 2D world.

If you are familiar with the ModelVisual3D class that is often used in .NET 3.0, then ContainerUIElement3D and ModelUIElement3D should look very familiar too. The difference is that WPF splits the functionality of ModelVisual3D (i.e. a model and children) into two separate classes, one with a model and the other with children.

In this way, making use of layout, focus, and eventing is very easy. For instance, if you want to create a 3D object that responds to mouse events, you can simply do so using the following statement:

```
<ModelUIElement3D MouseDown="OnMouseDown"/>
```

Then you can implement the OnMouseDown event handler in the code-behind file. This is exactly the same as adding event handlers in the 2D world. Thus, with the addition of UIElement3D, you can get all of the great functionality that UIElement provided to 2D, but now in the 3D world.

From the above discussion, you understand that building a 3D graphics object involves a two-step process. First you need to define the shapes (deriving either from ModelVisual3D or UIElement3D) you want to use, and then fuse them with a visual. This is an optional approach for 2D drawing. However, it is mandatory for 3D drawing because there are no built-in 3D shape classes in WPF.

The two-step process is also important because 3D models are much more complex than 2D models. For instance, when you create a Geometry3D object, you specify not only the vertices of the shape, but also the material out of which it is composed. Different materials have different properties for reflecting and absorbing light.

Geometry and Mesh

To build a 3D object, you begin by building a shape primitive, or mesh. A 3D primitive is a collection of vertices that form a single 3D entity. Most 3D systems provide primitives modeled on the simplest closed figure: a triangle defined by three vertices. Since the three points of a triangle are coplanar, you can continue adding triangles to model more complex shapes, called meshes.

Currently, WPF's 3D model provides the MeshGeometry3D class, which allows you to specify any geometry. If you have ever dealt with 3D drawings or 3D finite-element CAD packages before, you may already know the concept of the Mesh. Understanding how a mesh is defined is one of the first keys to 3D programming. If you examine the MeshGeometry3D class carefully, you'll find that it adds four properties, as listed below:

- Positions – Contains a collection of all the points that define the mesh. Each vertex is specified as a Point3D object. Depending on its geometry, the mesh might be composed of many triangles, some of which share the same corners (vertices), which means that one point will become the vertex of several triangles. You may choose to define the same shared vertex multiple times so that you can better control how separated triangles are shaded with the Normal property.

- TriangleIndices – Defines the triangles. Each entry in this collection represents a single triangle by referring to three points from the Positions collection. It specifies the order in which the points specified in the Positions list will determine a triangle.

- Normals – Provides a vector for each vertex. To render the surface of the model, the graphics system needs information about which direction the surface is facing at any given triangle. It uses this Normals property to make lighting calculations for the model: surfaces that face directly toward a light source appear brighter than those angled away from the light. WPF can determine default normal vectors by using the position coordinates, and you can also specify different normal vectors to approximate the appearance of curved surfaces.

- TexttureCoordinates – Specifies a points collection that tells the graphics system how to map the coordinates, which will determine how a texture is drawn to vertices of the mesh. TextureCoordinates are specified as a value between zero and one. Like in the Normals property, WPF can calculate default texture coordinates, but you might choose to set different texture coordinates to control the mapping of a texture that includes part of a repeating pattern, for example.

Let's look at the simplest possible mesh, which consists of a single triangle. The units you use to create the 3D model aren't important because you can always move the camera closer or farther away, and you can change the size or location of individual 3D objects using transformations. What's important is the coordinate system, which is shown in Figure 10-1. As you can see, the X and Y axes have the same orientation as they do in 2D drawing. What's new is the Z axis. As the Z axis value decreases, the point moves farther away. As it increases, the point moves closer.

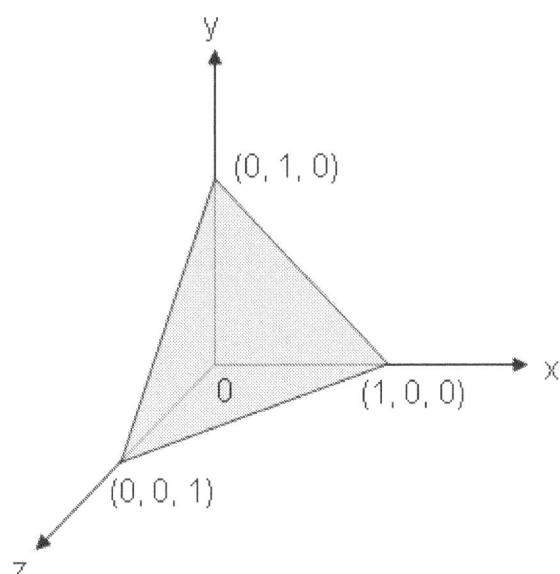

Figure 10-1 A triangle in 3D space.

You can use MeshGeometry3D to define this mesh shape inside a 3D visual. The MeshGeometry3D object in this example doesn't use the Normals property or the TextureCoordinates property (the default values will be used for these two properties) because the shape is simple and will be painted with a SolidColorBrush:

```
<MeshGeometry3D Positions="1,0,0 0,1,0 0,0,1"
                TriangleIndices="0,1,2"/>
```

Here, there are just three points, which are listed one after another in the Positions property. The order you put points in the Positions property is also important because a position's index value in a mesh's position collection is used when adding the triangle indices. For example, let's say you have a surface composed of four positions {p0, p1, p2, p3}. If you want to define a triangle from p0, p2, and p3, you would add triangle indices with index values 0, 2, and 3. If the positions were added in a different order, for instance, {p3, p1, p0, p2} and you want to create a triangle made of the same positions, you would add triangle indices values 2, 3, 0.

The mesh positions alone can't describe the mesh triangles. After the Positions have been added, you need to define what positions make up which triangles. The order in which you add triangle indices is also important. When you define a triangle, you are basically defining the points in either a clockwise or counter-clockwise direction depending on which side of the triangle you are on. The reason this is important is because it affects which side of the triangle is visible.

In this example, the TriangleIndices property states that there is a single triangle made of points #0, #1, and #2. In other words, the TriangleIndices property tells WPF to draw the triangle by drawing a line from (1, 0, 0) to (0, 1, 0), and then to (0, 0, 1).

WPF's 3D model uses a right-hand coordinate system. When defining a shape, you must list the points in a counter-clockwise order around the Z axis. This example follows that rule. However, you could easily violate it if you changed the TriangleIndices to 0, 2, 1. In this case, you would still define the same triangle, but that triangle would be backward – in other words, if you look at it down the Z axis, you will actually be looking at the back of the triangle.

The difference between the back of a 3D shape and the front is not a trivial one. In some cases, you may paint both sides with a different brushes. Or you may choose not to paint the back at all in order to avoid using any resources for a part of the scene that you will never see.

GeometryModel3D and Surfaces

Once you have a properly configured MeshGeometry3D, you need to wrap it in a GeometryModel3D. The GeometryModel3D class has three properties, including Geometry, Material, and BackMaterial. The Geometry property takes the MeshGeometry3D object that defines the shape of your 3D object. The Material and BackMaterial properties define the surface out of which your shape is composed.

For a mesh to look like a 3D object, it must have an applied texture to cover the surface defined by its vertices and triangles so that it can be lit and projected by the camera. In 2D, you use the Brush class to apply colors, patterns, gradients, or other visual content to areas of the screen. The appearance of 3D objects, however, is a function of the lighting model, not just of the color or pattern applied to them. Real-world objects reflect light differently depending on the quality of their surfaces. The surface defines the color of the object and how that material responds to light.

To define the characteristics of a 3D model's surface, WPF uses the Material abstract class. The concrete subclasses of Material determine some of the appearance characteristics of the model's surface, and each subclass provides a Brush property to which you can pass a SolidColorBrush, TitleBrush, or VisualBrush.

WPF includes four subclasses of Material, all of which derive from the abstract Material class, as listed below:

- DiffuseMaterial – Specifies that the brush will be applied to the model as though that model were lit diffusely. Using DiffuseMaterial resembles using brushes directly on 2D models. Model surfaces don't reflect light as if they were shiny.

- SpecularMaterial – Specifies that the brush will be applied to the model as though the model's surface were hard or shiny, capable of reflecting highlights. It can be used to create glossy and hightlighted effects. It reflects light back directly, like a mirror.

- EmissiveMaterial – Specifies that texture will be applied so that the model looks like it is emitting light equal to the color of the brush. It creates a glowing look.

- MaterialGroup – Allows you to combine more than one material. To achieve some surface qualities, like glowing or reflective effects, you might want to apply several different brushes to a model in succession.

Further details about material and how to use different materials in 3D applications will be discussed in Chapter 14. Let's look at a sample XAML code snippet that shows us how to paint a triangle surface with a solid color brush:

```
<GeometryModel3D>
    // Create geometry:
    <GoemetryModel3D.Goemetry>
        <MeshGeometry3D Positions="1,0,0 0,1,0 0,0,1"
                        TriangleIndices="0,1,2"/>
     </GeometryModel3D.Geometry>

    // Set materials:
    <GeometryModel3D.Material>
        <DiffuseMaterial Brush="LightBlue"/>
    </GeometryModel3D.Material>
    <GoemtryModel3D.BackMaterial>
        <DiffuseMaterial Brush = "LightCoral"/>
    </GeometryModel3D.BackMaterial>
</GeometryModel3D>
```

In this example, the BackMaterial property is also specified, so that the triangle can be seen with a different color if viewed from behind.

Our next step is to use this GeometryModel3D to set the Content property of a ModelVisual3D or ModelUIElement3D inside a ContainerUIElement3D, and place that ModelVisual3D or ContainerUIElement3D in a viewport. However, in order to see your object, you will also need to specify a light source and set a camera.

Illuminating the Scene

In order to create real-world shaded 3D graphics objects, WPF uses a lighting model that adds one or more light sources to your 3D scene. Your objects are then illuminated based on the type of light you specify, its position, direction, and power. Lights determine what part of a scene will be included in the projection. Light objects in WPF create a variety of light and shadow effects and are modeled after the behavior of various real-world lights. You must specify at least one light source in your 3D scene, or no objects will be visible.

WPF provides four light classes that derive from the base class, Light, as listed below:

- AmbientLight – Provides ambient lighting that illuminates all objects uniformly regardless of their location or orientation.

- DirectionalLight – Illuminates like a distant light source with parallel rays of light. Directional lights have a direction specified as a Vector3D, but no specified location.

- PointLight – Illuminates like a nearby light source that radiates light in all directions from a single point in 3D space. PointLight has a position and casts light from that position. Objects in the scene are illuminated depending on their position and distance with respect to the light. PointLightBase exposes a Range property, which determines a distance beyond which models will not be illuminated by light. PointLight also exposes attenuation properties which determine how the light's intensity diminishes with distance. You can specify constant, linear, or quadratic interpolations for the light's attenuation.

- SpotLight – Inherits from PointLight. It illuminates like PointLight and has both position and direction. It projects light in a cone-shaped area set by the InnerConeAngle and OuterConeAngle properties, specified in degrees.

More information about light sources and their applications will be discussed in Chapter 14. Here, you can easily define a white DirectionalLight to illuminate the triangle you just created in the previous section using the following statement:

```
<DirectionalLight Color="White" Direction="-1,-1,-1"/>
```

where the vector that determines the path of the light starts at the origin (0, 0, 0) and goes to (-1, -1, -1). This means that each ray of light is a straight line that travels from the top-right front toward the bottom-left back. This makes sense in this example because the front surface of the triangle shown in Figure 10-1 lines up exactly with the direction of the light.

Camera Position

In Chapter 9, you learned how to construct a projection matrix and set up a camera using the MatrixCamera class. When you create a 3D scene, it is important to remember that you are really creating a 2D representation of 3D objects through projection. Since a 3D scene looks different depending on the point of view, you must specify that point of view. The Camera class in WPF allows you to specify this point of view for a 3D scene. This means that in order to see a 3D object, you must set a camera at the correct position and orient it in the correct direction. This is achieved by specifying the Viewport3D.Camera property with a Camera object.

Basically, as discussed in Chapter 9, the camera determines how a 3D scene is represented on the 2D viewing surface of a viewport. WPF introduces three camera classes: PerspectiveCamera, OrthographicCamera, and MatrixCamera. All of these camera classes and their corresponding matrices have been discussed in great detail in Chapter 9. The PerspectiveCamera specifies a projection that foreshortens the scene. In other words, the PerspectiveCamera renders the scene so that objects that are farther away appear smaller; i.e., it provides a vanishing-point perspective projection. You can specify the position of the camera in the coordinate space of the scene, the direction, and the field of view for the camera, and a vector that defines the direction of "up" in the scene.

As you learned in Chapter 9 when we discussed the view frustum, the NearPlaneDistance and FarPlaneDistance properties of the ProjectionCamera limit the range of the camera's projection. Because cameras can be located anywhere in the scene, it is possible for the camera to be actually positioned inside a model or very near a model, making it hard to distinguish objects properly. NearPlaneDistance allows you to specify a minimum distance from the camera beyond which objects will not be drawn. Conversely, FarPlaneDistance lets you specify a distance from the camera beyond which objects will not be drawn, which ensures that objects too far away to be recognizable would not be included in the scene.

The OrthographicCamera flattens 3D objects so that the exact scale is preserved, no matter where a shape is positioned, which is useful for some types of visualization tools, such as 3D chart and technical drawing applications. Like other cameras, it specifies a position, viewing direction, and "upward" direction.

Finally, the MatrixCamera allows you to specify a matrix that is used to transform the 3D scene to a 2D view. This is an advanced tool that is intended for highly specialized effects and for porting code from other frameworks (such as DirectX or OpenGL) that use this type of camera. In Chapter 9, you used the MatrixCamera extensively for viewing a simple cube object.

Selecting the right camera is relatively easy, but placing and configuring it are a bit trickier. First you need to specify a point in 2D space where the camera will be positioned by setting its Position property. The second step is to set a Vector3D object for the LookDirection property, which indicates how the camera is oriented. To make sure the camera is correctly oriented, pick a point - the center point of interest - that you want to see from your camera. You can then calculate the look direction using this formula:

```
CameraLookDirection = CenterPointOfInterest - CameraPosition
```

In the triangle example, you can place the camera at a position of (2, 2, 2); i.e., right on top of the front surface of the triangle. Assuming you want to focus on the origin point at (0, 0, 0), you would use this look direction:

```
CameraLookDirection = (0, 0, 0) - (2, 2, 2) = (-2, -2, -2)
```

This is equivalent to the normalized vector (-1, -1, -1) because the direction it describes is the same. Once you have set the Position and LookDirection properties, you also need to set the UpDirection property. The UpDirection determines how the camera is tiled. Generally, the UpDirection is set to (0, 1, 0), which means the up direction is lined up with the positive Y axis.

With these details in mind, you can define the PerspectiveCamera for this simple triangle example:

```
<Viewport3D.Camera>
    <PerspectiveCamera Position="2,2,2"
                       LookDirection="-2,-2,-2"
                       UpDirection="0,1,0"/>
</Viewport3D.Camera>
```

Simple Triangle in 3D

Now it is time to put all pieces together to create the triangle example. Start a new WPF project and name it Chapter10. Add a new WPF Window to the project and name it SimpleTriangle. The following is the complete XAML file for this example:

```
<Window x:Class="Chapter10.SimpleTriangle"
    xmlns="http://schemas.microsoft.com/winfx
        /2006/xaml/presentation"
    xmlns:x="http://schemas.microsoft.com/winfx/2006/xaml"
    Title="Simple Triangle Example" Height="300" Width="300">

    <Grid Margin="5">
        <Grid.RowDefinitions>
            <RowDefinition/>
            <RowDefinition Height="Auto"/>
        </Grid.RowDefinitions>

        <Border BorderBrush="Gray" BorderThickness="1"
                Grid.Row="0">
            <Viewport3D>
```

```xml
<Viewport3D.Camera>
    <PerspectiveCamera Position="2,2,2"
        LookDirection="-2,-2,-2"
        UpDirection="0,1,0"/>
</Viewport3D.Camera>

<ContainerUIElement3D>
    <ModelUIElement3D>
        <Model3DGroup>

            <!-- Set light source: -->
            <DirectionalLight Color="White"
                Direction="-1,-1,-1" />

            <!-- Add triangle: -->
            <GeometryModel3D>
                <GeometryModel3D.Geometry>
                    <MeshGeometry3D
             Positions="1,0,0 0,1,0 0,0,1"
             TriangleIndices="0,1,2" />
                </GeometryModel3D.Geometry>

                <!-- Set material: -->
                <GeometryModel3D.Material>
                    <DiffuseMaterial
                        Brush="Blue" />
                </GeometryModel3D.Material>
                <GeometryModel3D.BackMaterial>
                    <DiffuseMaterial
                        Brush="Red" />
                </GeometryModel3D.BackMaterial>

                <!-- Set rotation: -->
                <GeometryModel3D.Transform>
                    <RotateTransform3D>
<RotateTransform3D.Rotation>
    <AxisAngleRotation3D x:Name="myRotate"
                    Axis="-0.707,1,-0.707"/>
</RotateTransform3D.Rotation>
                    </RotateTransform3D>
                </GeometryModel3D.Transform>
            </GeometryModel3D>
        </Model3DGroup>
    </ModelUIElement3D>
</ContainerUIElement3D>
        </Viewport3D>
    </Border>

    <Slider Margin="10,20,10,10" Grid.Row="1"
        Minimum="0" Maximum="360"
        Orientation="Horizontal"
        Value="{Binding ElementName=myRotate,
                Path=Angle}"/>
</Grid>
```

```
</Window>
```

Here we add the light source and the Model3DGroup contained inside the ModelUIElement3D. If you are working on the .NET 3.0 framework, you could replace ModelUIElement3D and ContainerUIElement3D with ModelVisual3D.Content and ModelVisual3D, respectively.

We also add a rotation transform to the triangle, which allows you to examine the front and back surfaces of the triangle because they are painted with brushes of different colors. Using this rotation, called myRotate, you create a databound Slider that allows you to rotate the triangle interactively around the axis you specify by using your mouse.

Figure 10-2 shows the result of running this example. You can move the slider with your mouse to see how the color changes when the triangle is rotating.

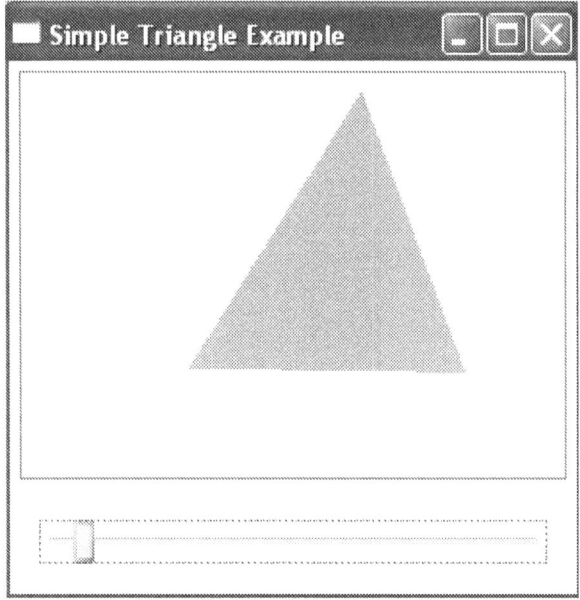

Figure 10-2 A triangle created using WPF 3D model.

Basic 3D Shapes

In this section, you'll learn how to create some basic 3D shapes in WPF, including coordinate axes, simple wireframe, cube, cylinder, cone, sphere, and torus.

Coordinate Axes and Wireframe

In WPF, everything in 3D is considered as a triangle. If you want to draw a 3D line, you have to somehow create it using triangles. It surprises me that WPF doesn't contain a 3D line class, because a 3D line object is so fundamental.

Fortunately, the WPF 3D team at Microsoft has created a 3D tools library that contains several classes designed to make WPF 3D programming easier. One of these classes is the ScreenSpaceLines3D class. You can download the 3DTools library from http://www.codeplex.com/3DTools. The DLL library is original built for the .NET 3.0 framework. I have rebuilt it for the .NET 3.5 and Visual Studio 2008 platform. This newly built DLL library is included in the References of project Chapter10.

If you look at the source code of the ScreenSpaceLines3D class carefully, you'll find that this class inherits from the ModelVisual3D base class. The line event handler is attached to CompositionTarget.Rendering, just like it is for a Per-Frame animation. This handy feature of WPF allows you to register a callback function which gets called whenever something is being rendered. However, this callback may get called too often – in fact, it gets called every frame, about 60 times per second! – which may lead to a serious memory leak problem for a complex 3D wireframe produced using ScreenSpaceLines3D objects.

Here, I still want to use the original 3DTools library because it has already become popular in the WPF 3D community. The ScreenSpaceLines3D class allows you to draw straight lines with an invariant width in 3D space. In other words, these lines have the fixed thickness that you specify no matter where you place the camera. This makes these lines useful for creating coordinate axes and wireframes.

Because the ScreenSpaceLines3D object is a ModelVisual3D object, so you can directly add this object to the Viewport3D, as shown in the following XAML snippet:

```
...
xmlns:tool3d="clr-namespace:_3DTools;assembly=3DTools"
...
<Viewport3D>
    <tool3d:ScreenSpaceLines3D Points="0,0,0 0,2,0"
                               Color="Black" Thickness="2"/>
</Viewport3D>
...
```

Here, to use this class, you first need to register the namespace and assembly in XAML. Then you can create a 3D line object by specifying its points, color, and thickness properties. You can draw multiple line segments by adding a points collection. Please note that the points in the collection must be paired, with each pair of points determining one line segment. For instance, if you have a point collection {p0, p1, p2, p3}, the ScreenSpaceLines3D class will draw two line segments, one from p0 to p1 and the other from p2 to p3. Notice there is no line

segment drawn from p1 to p2. If you want to draw a continuous line, you need
to set the point collection in the form {p0, p1, p1, p2, p2, p3}.

Let's create a simple triangle wireframe with coordinate axes. Add a new WPF
Window to the Chapter10 project and name it Wireframe. The following is the
XAML code for this example:

```
<Window x:Class="Chapter10.Wireframe"
    xmlns="http://schemas.microsoft.com/winfx
        /2006/xaml/presentation"
    xmlns:x="http://schemas.microsoft.com/winfx/2006/xaml"
    xmlns:tool3d="clr-namespace:_3DTools;assembly=3DTools"
    Title="Simple Triangle Example" Height="350" Width="300">

    <Window.Resources>
        <RotateTransform3D x:Key="rotate">
            <RotateTransform3D.Rotation>
                <AxisAngleRotation3D Axis="0,1,0"
                    Angle="{Binding ElementName=slider,
                            Path=Value, Mode=TwoWay}" />
            </RotateTransform3D.Rotation>
        </RotateTransform3D>
    </Window.Resources>

    <Grid Margin="5">
        <Grid.RowDefinitions>
            <RowDefinition/>
            <RowDefinition Height="Auto"/>
        </Grid.RowDefinitions>

        <Border BorderBrush="Gray" BorderThickness="1"
            Grid.Row="0">
            <Viewport3D>
                <Viewport3D.Camera>
                    <PerspectiveCamera Position="1,3,3"
                        LookDirection="-1,-3,-3"
                        UpDirection="0,1,0"/>
                </Viewport3D.Camera>

                <!-- Add coordinate axes: -->
                <tool3d:ScreenSpaceLines3D
                    Points="0,0,0 1.5,0,0" Color="Red"
                    Transform="{StaticResource rotate}"/>

                <tool3d:ScreenSpaceLines3D
                    Points="0,0,0 0,1.5,0" Color="Green"
                    Transform="{StaticResource rotate}"/>

                <tool3d:ScreenSpaceLines3D
                    Points="0,0,0 0,0,1.5" Color="Blue"
                    Transform="{StaticResource rotate}"/>

                <!-- Add triangle wireframe -->
```

```
        <tool3d:ScreenSpaceLines3D
          Points="1,0,0 0,1,0 0,1,0 0,0,1 0,0,1 1,0,0"
            Thickness="3" Color="Black"
            Transform="{StaticResource rotate}"/>
      </Viewport3D>
    </Border>

    <Slider Name="slider" Margin="10,20,10,10"
          Grid.Row="1" Minimum="0" Maximum="360"
          Orientation="Horizontal"/>
  </Grid>
</Window>
```

Here, the code first creates a Window resource that defines a RotateTransform3D object. The Angle property of this rotation is controlled by a slider's Value property. It then draws three lines for coordinate axes with different colors: red (for the X axis), green (for the Y axis), and blue (for the Z axis). Next, you also create a triangular wireframe using ScreenSpaceLines3D. We also perform a rotation transform on the coordinate axes and triangle wireframe by attaching a RotateTransform3D object, called "rotate", defined in the Window.Resources, to the Transform property of the ScreenSpaceLines3D objects. Notice that we only need to define a camera to view the line objects. There is no need to specify the light source and material if you only want to display line objects on your screen.

Figure 10-3 illustrates the results of running this example. If you move the slider with your mouse, the coordinate axes and triangular wireframe will rotate together accordingly.

Creating Cube

In this section, you will create a cube shape in WPF. In the previous chapter, we already created such a cube in the XAML file by directly using Window.Resources. Here, we'll add more features to the cube object, including painting different faces with different colors and adding a wireframe, from which you can clearly see how the triangular meshes are generated. To add these new features, we'll create the cube object in a code-behind file. A cube object is simply an extension of creating a triangle. The cube consists of six faces, and each face can be constructed with two triangles. Remember to follow the right-hand rule with a counter-clockwise direction when you create the triangles.

Let's consider an example of creating a cube in code. Add a new class to the project Chapter10 and name it Utility. Add a CreateTriangleFace method to the Utility class. Here is the code of this class:

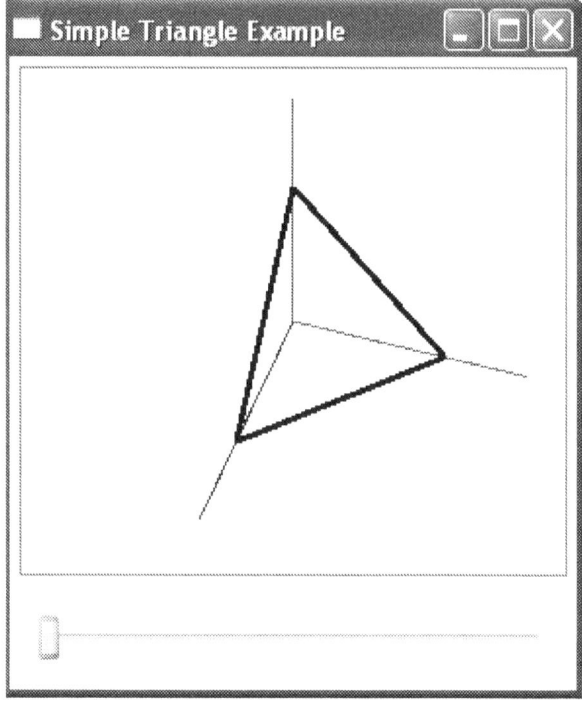

Figure 10-3 Triangle wireframe and coordinate axes.

```
using System;
using System.Windows;
using System.Windows.Media;
using System.Windows.Media.Media3D;
using System.Windows.Controls;
using _3DTools;

namespace Chapter10
{
    public class Utility
    {
        public static void CreateTriangleFace(
            Point3D p0, Point3D p1, Point3D p2,
            Color color, bool isWireframe,
            Viewport3D viewport)
        {
            MeshGeometry3D mesh = new MeshGeometry3D();
            mesh.Positions.Add(p0);
            mesh.Positions.Add(p1);
            mesh.Positions.Add(p2);
            mesh.TriangleIndices.Add(0);
            mesh.TriangleIndices.Add(1);
            mesh.TriangleIndices.Add(2);
            SolidColorBrush brush = new SolidColorBrush();
            brush.Color = color;
            Material material = new DiffuseMaterial(brush);
```

```
GeometryModel3D geometry =
        new GeometryModel3D(mesh, material);
ModelUIElement3D model = new ModelUIElement3D();
model.Model = geometry;
viewport.Children.Add(model);

if (isWireframe == true)
{
    ScreenSpaceLines3D ssl =
        new ScreenSpaceLines3D();
    ssl.Points.Add(p0);
    ssl.Points.Add(p1);
    ssl.Points.Add(p1);
    ssl.Points.Add(p2);
    ssl.Points.Add(p2);
    ssl.Points.Add(p0);
    ssl.Color = Colors.Black;
    ssl.Thickness = 2;
    viewport.Children.Add(ssl);
}
    }
  }
}
```

Note that a using statement

```
using _3DTools;
```

is added to this class to directly use the ScreenSpaceLines3D object. The CreateTriangleFace method is used to create a single triangle model that includes a triangle face and a wireframe if the isWireframe field is set to true. The triangle face is created as a UIElement3D object that defines the geometry mesh and the material. You then add both the triangle face and wireframe directly to the Viewport3D. Thus, each triangle is treated as an individual 3D model. From a programmer's point of view, this approach doesn't seem very efficient. You may want to use another method, such as putting all of the triangles into a Model3DGroup collection, then adding this Model3DGroup to the Viewport3D. However, the approach based on the individual triangle model does provide some advantages. For example, it is easier to implement, and it provides the flexibility to paint each triangle face with a different material. In addition, since the ScreenSpaceLines3D class derives from ModelVisual3D, you can't put the wireframe for each triangle into a Model3DGroup collection, and you need to add it directly to Viewport3D. So for illustration purposes, here we'll create the cube object with a wireframe using the individual triangle model.

Now, add a new WPF Window to the project Chapter10 and name it Cube. In the layout, you'll set the camera and light source, and add the coordinate axes using the ScreenSpaceLines3D objects. Here is the XAML file of this example:

```
<Window x:Class="Chapter10.Cube"
    xmlns="http://schemas.microsoft.com/winfx
        /2006/xaml/presentation"
    xmlns:x="http://schemas.microsoft.com/winfx/2006/xaml"
```

```
        xmlns:tool3d="clr-namespace:_3DTools;assembly=3DTools"
        Title="Cube" Height="350" Width="300">

    <Grid Margin="5">
        <Border BorderBrush="Gray" BorderThickness="1">
            <Viewport3D Name="myViewport">
                <Viewport3D.Camera>
                    <PerspectiveCamera Position="4,5,6"
                        LookDirection="-4,-5,-6"
                        UpDirection="0,1,0"/>
                </Viewport3D.Camera>

                <!-- Set light source: -->
                <ModelUIElement3D>
                    <DirectionalLight Color="White"
                                      Direction="-1,-1,-1" />
                </ModelUIElement3D>

                <!-- Add coordinate axes: -->
                <tool3d:ScreenSpaceLines3D
                    Points="-4,0,0 3,0,0" Color="Red"/>
                <tool3d:ScreenSpaceLines3D
                    Points="0,-5,0 0,3,0" Color="Green"/>
                <tool3d:ScreenSpaceLines3D
                    Points="0,0,-10 0,0,3" Color="Blue"/>
            </Viewport3D>
        </Border>
    </Grid>
</Window>
```

The corresponding code-behind file shows the detailed procedure of creating the cube shapes in WPF:

```
using System;
using System.Windows;
using System.Windows.Controls;
using System.Windows.Media;
using System.Windows.Media.Media3D;

namespace Chapter10
{
    public partial class Cube : Window
    {
        public Cube()
        {
            InitializeComponent();

            // Create a cube:
            CreateCube(new Point3D(0, 0, 0), 2, true);

            // Create another cube:
            CreateCube(new Point3D(0, 0, -4), 2, false);
        }
```

```
public void CreateCube(Point3D center, double side,
                       bool isWireframe)
{
    double a = side / 2.0;
    Point3D[] p = new Point3D[8];
    p[0] = new Point3D(-a,  a,  a);
    p[1] = new Point3D( a,  a,  a);
    p[2] = new Point3D( a,  a, -a);
    p[3] = new Point3D(-a,  a, -a);
    p[4] = new Point3D(-a, -a,  a);
    p[5] = new Point3D( a, -a,  a);
    p[6] = new Point3D( a, -a, -a);
    p[7] = new Point3D(-a, -a, -a);

    // Redefine the center of the cube:
    for (int i = 0; i < 8; i++)
        p[i] += (Vector3D)center;

    // Surface 1 (0,1,2,3):
    Utility.CreateTriangleFace(p[0], p[1], p[2],
        Colors.LightGray, isWireframe, myViewport);
    Utility.CreateTriangleFace(p[2], p[3], p[0],
        Colors.LightGray, isWireframe, myViewport);

    // Surface 2 (4,7,6,5):
    Utility.CreateTriangleFace(p[4], p[7], p[6],
        Colors.Black, isWireframe, myViewport);
    Utility.CreateTriangleFace(p[6], p[5], p[4],
        Colors.Black, isWireframe, myViewport);

    // Surface 3 (0,4,5,1):
    Utility.CreateTriangleFace(p[0], p[4], p[5],
        Colors.Red, isWireframe, myViewport);
    Utility.CreateTriangleFace(p[5], p[1], p[0],
        Colors.Red, isWireframe, myViewport);

    // Surface 4 (1,5,6,2):
    Utility.CreateTriangleFace(p[1], p[5], p[6],
        Colors.Green, isWireframe, myViewport);
    Utility.CreateTriangleFace(p[6], p[2], p[1],
        Colors.Green, isWireframe, myViewport);

    // Surface 5 (2,6,7,3):
    Utility.CreateTriangleFace(p[2], p[6], p[7],
        Colors.Blue, isWireframe, myViewport);
    Utility.CreateTriangleFace(p[7], p[3], p[2],
        Colors.Blue, isWireframe, myViewport);

    // Surface 2 (0,3,7,4):
    Utility.CreateTriangleFace(p[0], p[3], p[7],
        Colors.Black, isWireframe, myViewport);
    Utility.CreateTriangleFace(p[7], p[4], p[0],
        Colors.Black, isWireframe, myViewport);
}
```

```
        }
    }
```

The CreateCube method in this class is used to create the cube object. It first defines a point array object that contains eight vertices, used to specify the coordinates of the cube in the 3D space. Then we create the trangle models for the different surfaces of the cube using different colors by calling the static CreateTriangleFace method in the Utility class. This way, you have the flexibility to specify a different material and wireframe for each individual triangle.

Finally, we create two cube objects at different locations using the CreateCube method, one cube with and the other without the wireframe.

Figure 10-4 illustrates the results of running this application.

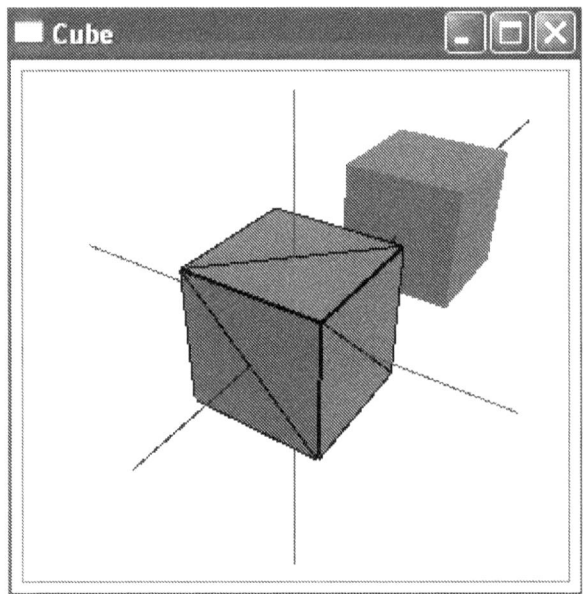

Figure 10-4 Cubes in WPF.

You can add more features to this example, such as normals and texture coordinates. For example, it is easy to create normals inside the CreateTriangleFace method in the Utility class by adding the few lines of code shown below:

```
Vector3D v1 = new Vector3D(
    p1.X - p0.X, p1.Y - p0.Y, p1.Z - p0.Z);
Vector3D v2 = new Vector3D(
    p2.X - p1.X, p2.Y - p1.Y, p2.Z - p1.Z);
Vector3D normal = Vector3D.CrossProduct(v1, v2);
mesh.Normals.Add(normal);
```

Creating Sphere

In this section, you'll create a shere shape in WPF. To do this, you need to be familiar with the spherical coordinate system. A point in the spherical coordinate system is specified by r, θ, and φ. Here, r is the distance from the point to the origin, θ is the polar angle, and φ is the azimuthal angle in the X-Z plane from the X axis. In this notation, you also alternate the conventional Y and Z axes so that the coordinate system is consistent with that used in WPF. Figure 10-5 shows a point in this coordinate system.

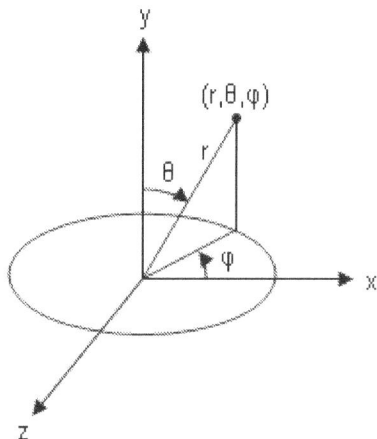

Figure 10-5 Spherical coordinate system.

From this figure, you can easily obtain the following relationships;

$$x = r \sin \theta \cos \varphi$$
$$y = r \cos \theta$$
$$z = -r \sin \theta \sin \varphi$$

In order to create a sphere shape in WPF using these relations, you can start with the familiar concept of longitude and latitude (sometimes, also called the UV-sphere method). The standard UV-sphere method is made out of u segments and v rings, as shown in Figure 10-6. It can be seen that the u and v lines form grids on the surface of the sphere. In order to create triangles for this surface, it is enough to consider just one unit grid, as shown on the right of Figure 10-6. This unit grid can be divided into two triangles. If you run over all of the grids, you can triangulate the entire surface of the sphere.

Now let's start off with the example of creating a sphere. Add a new WPF Window to the project Chapter10 and name it Sphere. The XAML code is the same as that used in the previous example. The XAML file creates the layout, sets the camera and light source, and adds the coordinate axes using the ScreenSpaceLines3D class. The corresponding code-behind file, which creates the sphere, is listed below:

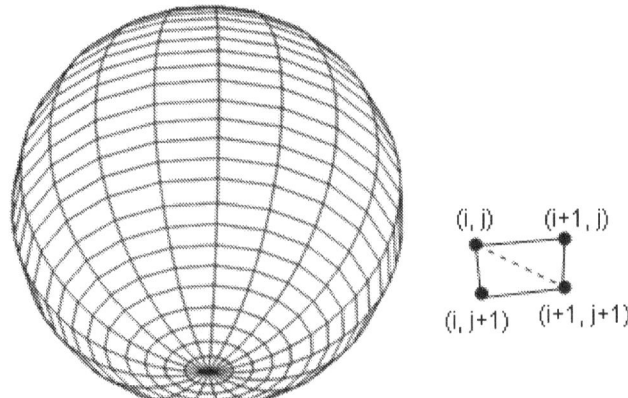

Figure 10-6 A UV-sphere model and a unit grid used to create triangles.

```
using System;
using System.Windows;
using System.Windows.Controls;
using System.Windows.Media;
using System.Windows.Media.Media3D;

namespace Chapter10
{
    public partial class Sphere : Window
    {
        public Sphere()
        {
            InitializeComponent();

            // Add a sphere:
            CreateSphere(new Point3D(0, 0, 0), 1.5, 20, 15,
                        Colors.LightBlue, true);

            // Add another sphere:
            CreateSphere(new Point3D(0, 0, -4), 1.5, 20, 15,
                        Colors.LightCoral, false);
        }

        private Point3D GetPosition(double radius,
            double theta, double phi)
        {
            Point3D pt = new Point3D();
            double snt = Math.Sin(theta * Math.PI / 180);
            double cnt = Math.Cos(theta * Math.PI / 180);
            double snp = Math.Sin(phi * Math.PI / 180);
            double cnp = Math.Cos(phi * Math.PI / 180);

            pt.X = radius * snt * cnp;
```

```
            pt.Y = radius * cnt;
            pt.Z = -radius * snt * snp;
            return pt;
        }

        private void CreateSphere(Point3D center,
            double radius, int u, int v, Color color,
            bool isWireframe)
        {
            if (u < 2 || v < 2)
                return;

            Point3D[,] pts = new Point3D[u, v];
            for (int i = 0; i < u; i++)
            {
                for (int j = 0; j < v; j++)
                {
                    pts[i, j] = GetPosition(radius,
                        i * 180 / (u - 1), j * 360 / (v - 1));
                    pts[i, j] += (Vector3D)center;
                }
            }

            Point3D[] p = new Point3D[4];
            for (int i = 0; i < u - 1; i++)
            {
                for (int j = 0; j < v - 1; j++)
                {
                    p[0] = pts[i, j];
                    p[1] = pts[i + 1, j];
                    p[2] = pts[i + 1, j + 1];
                    p[3] = pts[i, j + 1];
                    Utility.CreateTriangleFace(p[0], p[1],
                        p[2], color, isWireframe, myViewport);
                    Utility.CreateTriangleFace(p[2], p[3],
                        p[0], color, isWireframe, myViewport);
                }
            }
        }
    }
}
```

Here, you construct triangle meshes by dividing the sphere surface into segments and rings. The number of segments and rings can be specified using two integers, u and v. This application also allows you to specify the radius and position (the center location) of the sphere. The GetPosition method returns the points on a sphere surface by specifying their radius, longitude, and latitude.

Notice how you perform the triangulation for the unit grid inside the CreateSphere method, where the four vertex points that define the unit grid are specified, and two triangles are defined using these four vertices within two for-loops. The triangle is created by calling the CreateTriangleFace method in the Utility class, which is the same as that used in the previous example.

Finally, you create two sphere objects using the CreateSphere method at different locations, one with the wieframe and the other without it.

Figure 10-7 shows the results of running this example.

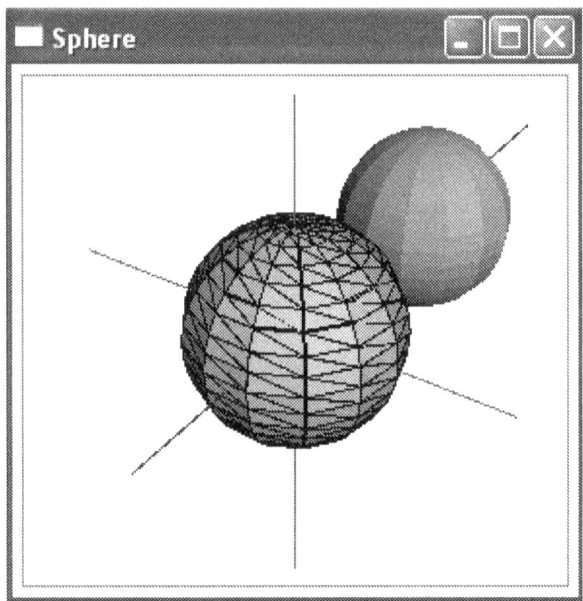

Figure 10-7 Spheres created in WPF.

Creating Cylinder

In this section, I'll show you how to create a cylinder shape in WPF. Here, we'll create a more general cylinder shape that will allow you to specify its inner and outer radii. By setting a non-zero inner radius, you can create a cylindrical tube shape.

As you probably know, in a cylindrical coordinate system, a point is specified by three parameters, r, θ, and y, which are a bit different from the conventional definition of the system using r, θ, and z. The notation we use here is only for convenience because the computer screen can always be described using the X-Y plane. Here r is the distance of a projected point on the X-Z plane from the origin, and θ is the azimuthal angle.

Figure 10-8 shows a point in the cylindrical coordinate system. From this figure you have:

$$x = r\cos\theta$$
$$z = -r\sin\theta$$
$$y = y$$

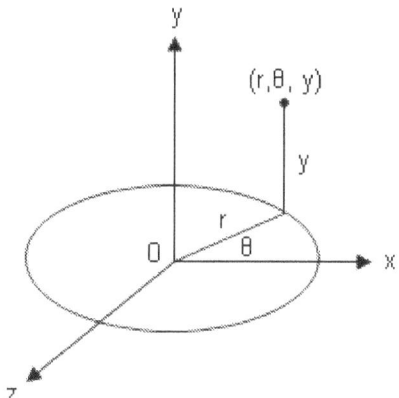

Figure 10-8 Cylindrical coordinate system.

By using the cylindrical coordinate system, you can easily create cylindrical objects in WPF.

First, we need to make slices on the surface of the cylinder. As shown in Figure 10-9, the cylinder surface is divided into n slices, and a unit cell is formed by the i-th and i+1-th slice lines. You can see that each unit contains eight vertices and four surfaces, which need to be triangulated. Furthermore, each surface can be represented using two triangles.

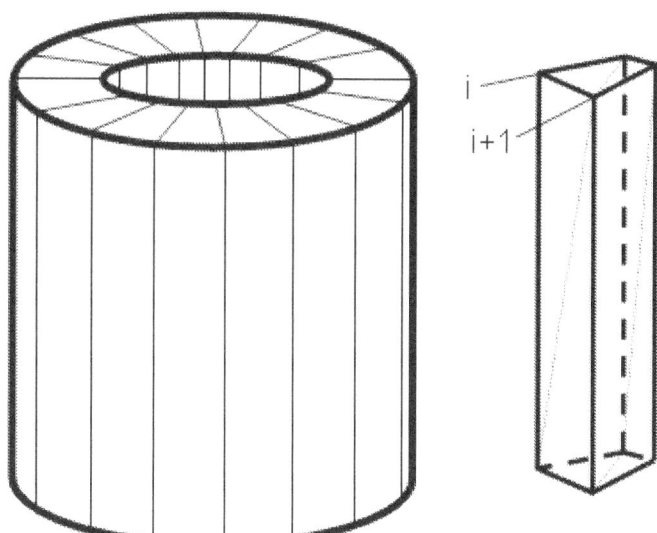

Figure 10-9 A cylinder and a unit cell.

With this background information, now it is time to consider an example in which we create a cylinder shape in WPF. Add a new WPF Window to the project Chapter10 and name it Cylinder. The XAML code is the same as that used in the previous example. The following is the code listing of the code-behind file for this example:

```
using System;
using System.Windows;
using System.Windows.Media;
using System.Windows.Media.Media3D;

namespace Chapter10
{
    public partial class Cylinder : Window
    {
        public Cylinder()
        {
            InitializeComponent();
            //AddCylinder();

            // Create a cylinder:
            CreateCylinder(new Point3D(0, 0, 0),
                0, 1.2, 2, 20, Colors.LightBlue, true);

            // Create another cylinder:
            CreateCylinder(new Point3D(0, 0, -4),
                0.8, 1.2, 0.5, 20, Colors.LightCoral, true);

            // Create another cylinder:
            CreateCylinder(new Point3D(-3, 0, 0),
                1, 1.2, 0.5, 40, Colors.Red, false);
        }

        private Point3D GetPosition(double radius,
            double theta, double y)
        {
            Point3D pt = new Point3D();
            double sn = Math.Sin(theta * Math.PI / 180);
            double cn = Math.Cos(theta * Math.PI / 180);

            pt.X = radius * cn;
            pt.Y = y;
            pt.Z = -radius * sn;
            return pt;
        }

        private void CreateCylinder(Point3D center,
            double rin, double rout, double height, int n,
            Color color, bool isWireframe)
        {
            if (n < 2 || rin == rout)
                return;

            double radius = rin;
            if (rin > rout)
            {
                rin = rout;
```

```
            rout = radius;
    }

    double h = height / 2;
    Model3DGroup cylinder = new Model3DGroup();
    Point3D[,] pts = new Point3D[n, 4];


    for (int i = 0; i < n; i++)
    {
pts[i, 0] = GetPosition(rout, i * 360 / (n - 1), h);
pts[i, 1] = GetPosition(rout, i * 360 / (n - 1), -h);
pts[i, 2] = GetPosition(rin, i * 360 / (n - 1), -h);
pts[i, 3] = GetPosition(rin, i * 360 / (n - 1), h);
    }
    for (int i = 0; i < n; i++)
    {
        for (int j = 0; j < 4; j++)
            pts[i, j] += (Vector3D)center;
    }

    Point3D[] p = new Point3D[8];
    for (int i = 0; i < n - 1; i++)
    {
        p[0] = pts[i, 0];
        p[1] = pts[i, 1];
        p[2] = pts[i, 2];
        p[3] = pts[i, 3];
        p[4] = pts[i + 1, 0];
        p[5] = pts[i + 1, 1];
        p[6] = pts[i + 1, 2];
        p[7] = pts[i + 1, 3];

        // Top surface:
        Utility.CreateTriangleFace(p[0], p[4], p[3],
                color, isWireframe, myViewport);
        Utility.CreateTriangleFace(p[4], p[7], p[3],
                color, isWireframe, myViewport);

        // Bottom surface:
        Utility.CreateTriangleFace(p[1], p[5], p[2],
                color, isWireframe, myViewport);
        Utility.CreateTriangleFace(p[5], p[6], p[2],
                color, isWireframe, myViewport);

        // Outer surface:
        Utility.CreateTriangleFace(p[0], p[1], p[4],
                color, isWireframe, myViewport);
        Utility.CreateTriangleFace(p[1], p[5], p[4],
                color, isWireframe, myViewport);

        // Outer surface:
        Utility.CreateTriangleFace(p[2], p[7], p[6],
                color, isWireframe, myViewport);
```

```
                    Utility.CreateTriangleFace(p[2], p[3], p[7],
                        color, isWireframe, myViewport);
                }
            }
        }
    }
```

This code-behind file enables you to specify the inner and outer radii, the height, the azimuthal angle, and position of the cylinder. The GetPosition method create a point on the cylinder surface using the cylindrical coordinates.

Inside the CreateCylinder method, we construct eight vertices for a unit cell (see Figure 10-9), and then perform the triangulation for the four surfaces of this unit cell, including the top, bottom, inner, and outer surfaces. We need to create two triangles for each surface separately by calling the static CreateTriangleFace method defined in the Utility class, which is identical to that used in the previous examples.

Finally, we create three different cylindrical objects at different locations by calling the CreateCylinder method. The parameter n, the number of slices, affects the surface smoothness of the cylindrical objects.

Figure 10-10 shows the results of running this application. You can see from this figure that this program can generate not only cylinders, but ring objects as well.

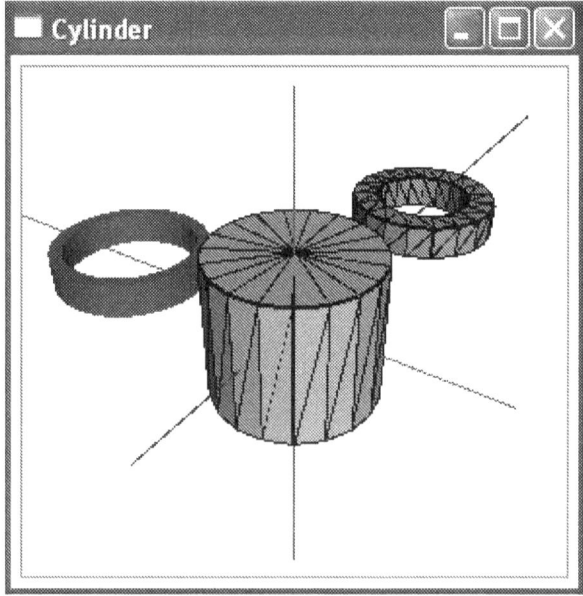

Figure 10-10 Cylinder and rings created in WPF.

Creating Cone

You can also create cone shapes using the cylindrical coordinate system. Here we want to create a more general cone shape that can be specified with a top radius and a bottom radius, as well as a height parameter. Figure 10-11 illustrates how to make slices on the surface of the cone and how to choose a unit cell. This unit cell has three surfaces, which need to be triangulated, including a top, bottom, and outer surface. The top and bottom surfaces are already triangular shapes, while the outer surface can be represented with two triangles.

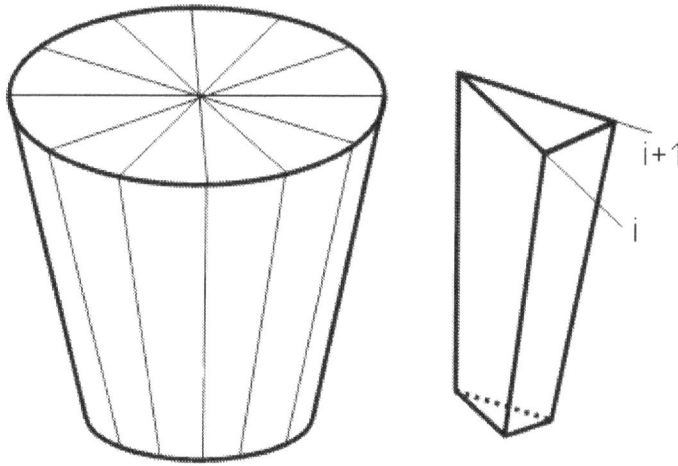

Figure 10-11 A cone shape and a unit cell.

With this background knowledge, we can now create a cone shape in WPF. Let's consider an example. Add a new PWF Window application to the project Chapter10 and name it Cone. Again, we can use the same XAML code as we did in the previous example. The C# code that generates the cone shape is listed below:

```
using System;
using System.Windows;
using System.Windows.Media;
using System.Windows.Media.Media3D;

namespace Chapter10
{
    public partial class Cone : Window
    {
        public Cone()
        {
            InitializeComponent();

            // Create a cone:
            CreateCone(new Point3D(0, 0, 0),
```

```
                              0, 1.2, 2, 20, Colors.LightBlue, true);

               // Create another cone:
               CreateCone(new Point3D(0, 0, -3),
                   0.6, 1.2, 1, 20, Colors.LightCoral, false);

               // Create another cone:
               CreateCone(new Point3D(0, 0, -6),
                   1.2, 0.4, 2, 20, Colors.LightGreen, false);

               // Create another cone:
               CreateCone(new Point3D(0, 0, 3),
                   0.5, 1.2, 1.2, 4, Colors.Goldenrod, false);

               // Create another cone:
               CreateCone(new Point3D(-3, 0, 0),
                   0.8, 0.8, 1.5, 20, Colors.Red, true);

               // Create another cone:
               CreateCone(new Point3D(3, 0, 0),
                   0, 0.8, 1.5, 5, Colors.SteelBlue, false);
          }

          private Point3D GetPosition(double radius,
              double theta, double y)
          {
              Point3D pt = new Point3D();
              double sn = Math.Sin(theta * Math.PI / 180);
              double cn = Math.Cos(theta * Math.PI / 180);

              pt.X = radius * cn;
              pt.Y = y;
              pt.Z = -radius * sn;
              return pt;
          }

          private void CreateCone(Point3D center, double rtop,
              double rbottom, double height, int n,
              Color color, bool isWireframe)
          {
              if (n < 2)
                  return;

              double h = height / 2;
              Model3DGroup cone = new Model3DGroup();
              Point3D[,] pts = new Point3D[n + 1, 4];

              for (int i = 0; i < n + 1; i++)
              {
        pts[i, 0] = GetPosition(rtop, i * 360 / (n - 1), h);
        pts[i, 1] = GetPosition(rbottom, i * 360 / (n - 1), -h);
        pts[i, 2] = GetPosition(0, i * 360 / (n - 1), -h);
        pts[i, 3] = GetPosition(0, i * 360 / (n - 1), h);
```

```
    }
    for (int i = 0; i < n + 1; i++)
    {
        for (int j = 0; j < 4; j++)
            pts[i, j] += (Vector3D)center;
    }

    Point3D[] p = new Point3D[6];
    for (int i = 0; i < n; i++)
    {
        p[0] = pts[i, 0];
        p[1] = pts[i, 1];
        p[2] = pts[i, 2];
        p[3] = pts[i, 3];
        p[4] = pts[i + 1, 0];
        p[5] = pts[i + 1, 1];

        // Top surface:
        Utility.CreateTriangleFace(p[0], p[4], p[3],
                color, isWireframe, myViewport);

        // Bottom surface:
        Utility.CreateTriangleFace(p[1], p[5], p[2],
                color, isWireframe, myViewport);

        // Side surface:
        Utility.CreateTriangleFace(p[0], p[1], p[5],
                color, isWireframe, myViewport);
        Utility.CreateTriangleFace(p[0], p[5], p[4],
                color, isWireframe, myViewport);
    }
}
}
}
```

Note that the CreateCone methods still use the GetPosition method, which returns a point represented in the cylindrical coordinate system, to specify the positions of vertices of the unit cell. Within a for-loop, the corresponding triangles are constructed using these vertices for each of three surfaces by calling the CreateTriangleFace method in the Utility class. Finally, we create several different cone objects using the CreateCone method by specifying the top and bottom radii, the height, and the number of slices.

Figure 10-12 shows the results of running this example. You can see that this application can create various cone shapes including a cylinder (by setting the top and bottom radii equal), cone (by setting one of the radii to zero), a truncated cone (by setting both radii to be finite), and even a pyramid (by setting the number of slices to a small integer).

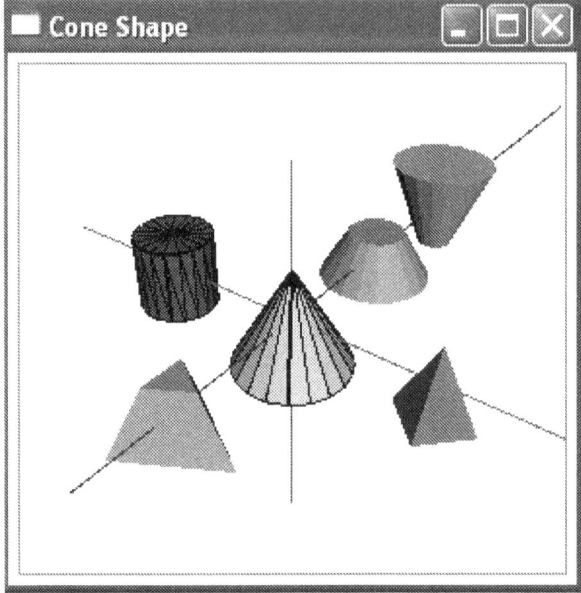

Figure 10-12 Various cone shapes in WPF.

Creating Torus

Another popular 3D shape is the torus. A torus is a surface of revolution generated by revolving a circle in 3D space about an axis. It can be defined using the following parameterized equations:

$$x = (R + r \cos v) \cos u$$
$$y = r \sin v$$
$$z = -(R + r \cos v) \sin u$$

where u and v are angles defined in the range of [0, 2π], R is the distance from the center of the tube to the center of the torus, and r is the radius of the torus.

In order to perform the triangulation for the torus, you need to divide its surface using tube rings and torus rings, as shown in Figure 10-13, which forms grids similar to those used to create a sphere shape (see Figure 10-6). You can use a unit cell (or unit grid) like the one shown to the right of the figure, which contains four vertices. This unit cell can be represented with two triangles. When you run over all of the grids using two for-loops, you'll complete the triangulization for the entire surface of the torus.

Let's create the torus shape in WPF using an example. Add a new WPF Window to the project Chapter10 and name it Torus. Again, you can use the same XAML code as you did in the previous examples. The following is the corresponding code-behind file:

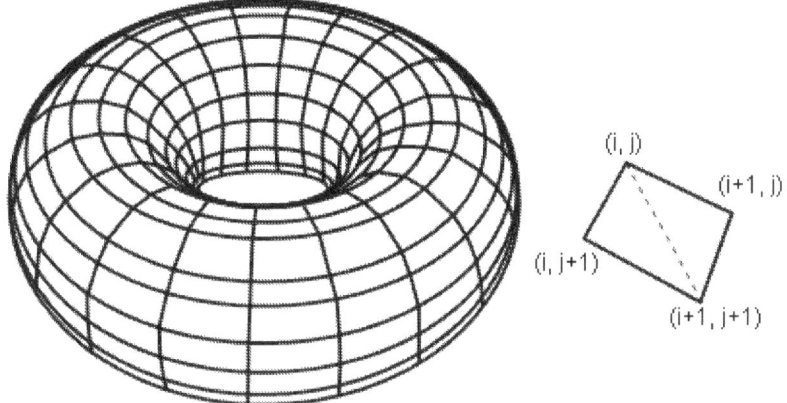

Figure 10-13 A torus and a unit cell.

```
using System;
using System.Windows;
using System.Windows.Media;
using System.Windows.Media.Media3D;

namespace Chapter10
{
    public partial class Torus : Window
    {
        public Torus()
        {
            InitializeComponent();

            // Create a torus:
            CreateTorus(new Point3D(0, 0, 0),
                1, 0.3, 20, 15, Colors.LightBlue, true);

            // Create another torus:
            CreateTorus(new Point3D(0, 0, -3),
                0.5, 0.5, 20, 15, Colors.LightCoral, false);

            // Create another torus:
            CreateTorus(new Point3D(0, 0, -6),
                0.3, 0.5, 20, 15, Colors.LightGreen, true);

            // Create another torus:
            CreateTorus(new Point3D(-3, 0, 0),
                0.0, 0.8, 20, 25, Colors.SteelBlue, false);

            // Create another torus:
            CreateTorus(new Point3D(3, 0, 0),
                0.0, 0.8, 20, 25, Colors.Goldenrod, false);
        }

        private Point3D GetPosition(double R, double r,
```

```
            double u, double v)
    {
        Point3D pt = new Point3D();
        double snu = Math.Sin(u * Math.PI / 180);
        double cnu = Math.Cos(u * Math.PI / 180);
        double snv = Math.Sin(v * Math.PI / 180);
        double cnv = Math.Cos(v * Math.PI / 180);

        pt.X = (R + r * cnv) * cnu;
        pt.Y = r * snv;
        pt.Z = -(R + r * cnv) * snu;
        return pt;
    }

    private void CreateTorus(Point3D center, double R,
        double r, int N, int n, Color color,
        bool isWireframe)
    {
        if (n < 2 || N < 2)
            return;

        Model3DGroup torus = new Model3DGroup();
        Point3D[,] pts = new Point3D[N, n];

        for (int i = 0; i < N; i++)
        {
            for (int j = 0; j < n; j++)
            {
                pts[i, j] = GetPosition(R, r,
                    i * 360 / (N - 1), j * 360 / (n - 1));
                pts[i, j] += (Vector3D)center;
            }
        }

        Point3D[] p = new Point3D[4];
        for (int i = 0; i < N - 1; i++)
        {
            for (int j = 0; j < n - 1; j++)
            {
                p[0] = pts[i, j];
                p[1] = pts[i + 1, j];
                p[2] = pts[i + 1, j + 1];
                p[3] = pts[i, j + 1];
                Utility.CreateTriangleFace(p[0], p[1],
                    p[2], color, isWireframe, myViewport);
                Utility.CreateTriangleFace(p[2], p[3],
                    p[0], color, isWireframe, myViewport);
            }
        }
    }
}
```

The GetPosition method in the above code returns the point on the torus surface. The CreateTorus method uses the GetPosition method to define the four vertices of the unit cell. The two triangles are constructed with these four vertices within two for-loops by calling the static CreateTriangleFace method in the Utility class. Finally, we use the CreateTorus method to create several different torus shapes at different locations with different sets of parameters.

Figure 10-14 shows the results of running this application.

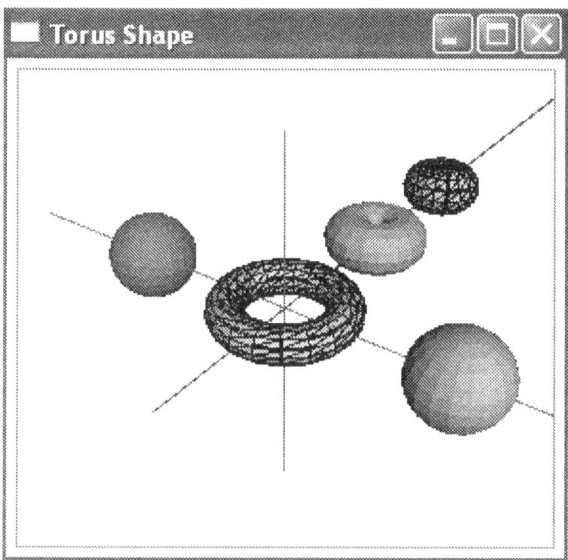

Figure 10-14 Torus shapes in WPF.

You can see that as the distance to the axis of revolution decreases, the ring torus becomes a spindle torus, and finally degenerates into a sphere when the distance goes to zero.

In this chapter, you learned how to create various shapes directly in WPF. This approach is easy to follow and gives you the flexibility to specify a different material for each individual triangle. This approach is usually adequate for creating a one-time WPF application. However, you would like to have the option of creating 3D shape libraries that can be reused in multiple WPF projects.

In following two chapters, I'll show you how to create geometry meshes for different 3D shapes in C# code and how to reference these geometry meshes in XAML files. Furthermore, you will also learn how to create 3D custom shapes that can be used simply like 2D shapes such as Line, Rectangle, Ellipse, etc.

Chapter 11
Custom 3D Geometries

In Chapter 10, you learned how to create basic 3D shapes directly in WPF. Although this direct approach is very convenient for developing one-time 3D WPF applications, in general, you want the option of implementing 3D geometry libraries that can be referred to in XAML files and reused in multiple WPF applications.

In this chapter, you'll learn how to create custom geometry classes for various 3D basic shapes. At the beginning, you might think that a custom geometry class can derive from the MeshGeometry3D class. However, the MeshGeometry3D class is a sealed class in WPF, meaning that you can't inherit custom geometry classes from it.

Although you can't derive a custom class from MeshGeometry3D directly, you can get around this issue by defining your own geometry class that can be used as a resource in XAML files. You can then refer to that resource in your markup with a data binding.

The following sections will show you how to create custom geometry classes for various 3D shapes, and how these classes can be used as resources in WPF.

Cube Geometry

In Chapter 10, you already learned how to create a cube directly in WPF. Here you'll learn how to create a custom geometry class for this simple 3D shape.

CubeGeometry Class

Let's start with a new WPF project and name it Chapter11. Add a new class to the project and name it CubeGeometry. Change its namespace from Chapter11 to Geometries. Here is the code listing of this class:

```csharp
using System;
using System.Windows;
using System.Windows.Media;
using System.Windows.Media.Media3D;

namespace Geometries
{
    public class CubeGeometry
    {
        // Define private fields:
        private double length = 1.0;
        private double width = 1.0;
        private double height = 1.0;
        private Point3D center = new Point3D();

        // Define public properties:
        public double Length
        {
            get { return length; }
            set { length = value; }
        }

        public double Width
        {
            get { return width; }
            set { width = value; }
        }

        public double Height
        {
            get { return height; }
            set { height = value; }
        }

        public Point3D Center
        {
            get { return center; }
            set { center = value; }
        }

        // Get-only property generates MeshGeometry3D object:
        public MeshGeometry3D Mesh3D
        {
            get { return GetMesh3D(); }
        }

        private MeshGeometry3D GetMesh3D()
        {
            MeshGeometry3D mesh = new MeshGeometry3D();
            Point3D[] pts = new Point3D[8];

            double hl = 0.5 * Length;
            double hw = 0.5 * Width;
            double hh = 0.5 * Height;
```

```
pts[0] = new Point3D(hl, hh, hw);
pts[1] = new Point3D(hl, hh, -hw);
pts[2] = new Point3D(-hl, hh, -hw);
pts[3] = new Point3D(-hl, hh, hw);
pts[4] = new Point3D(-hl, -hh, hw);
pts[5] = new Point3D(-hl, -hh, -hw);
pts[6] = new Point3D(hl, -hh, -hw);
pts[7] = new Point3D(hl, -hh, hw);

for (int i = 0; i < 8; i++)
{
    pts[i] += (Vector3D)Center;
}

// Top surface (0-3):
for (int i = 0; i < 4; i++)
    mesh.Positions.Add(pts[i]);

mesh.TriangleIndices.Add(0);
mesh.TriangleIndices.Add(1);
mesh.TriangleIndices.Add(2);

mesh.TriangleIndices.Add(2);
mesh.TriangleIndices.Add(3);
mesh.TriangleIndices.Add(0);

//Bottom surface (4-7):
for (int i = 4; i < 8; i++)
    mesh.Positions.Add(pts[i]);

mesh.TriangleIndices.Add(4);
mesh.TriangleIndices.Add(5);
mesh.TriangleIndices.Add(6);

mesh.TriangleIndices.Add(6);
mesh.TriangleIndices.Add(7);
mesh.TriangleIndices.Add(4);

// Front surface (8-11):
mesh.Positions.Add(pts[0]);
mesh.Positions.Add(pts[3]);
mesh.Positions.Add(pts[4]);
mesh.Positions.Add(pts[7]);

mesh.TriangleIndices.Add(8);
mesh.TriangleIndices.Add(9);
mesh.TriangleIndices.Add(10);

mesh.TriangleIndices.Add(10);
mesh.TriangleIndices.Add(11);
mesh.TriangleIndices.Add(8);

// Back surface (12-15):
```

```
mesh.Positions.Add(pts[1]);
mesh.Positions.Add(pts[2]);
mesh.Positions.Add(pts[5]);
mesh.Positions.Add(pts[6]);

mesh.TriangleIndices.Add(12);
mesh.TriangleIndices.Add(15);
mesh.TriangleIndices.Add(14);

mesh.TriangleIndices.Add(14);
mesh.TriangleIndices.Add(13);
mesh.TriangleIndices.Add(12);

// Left surface (16-19):
mesh.Positions.Add(pts[2]);
mesh.Positions.Add(pts[3]);
mesh.Positions.Add(pts[4]);
mesh.Positions.Add(pts[5]);

mesh.TriangleIndices.Add(16);
mesh.TriangleIndices.Add(19);
mesh.TriangleIndices.Add(18);

mesh.TriangleIndices.Add(18);
mesh.TriangleIndices.Add(17);
mesh.TriangleIndices.Add(16);

// Right surface (20-23):
mesh.Positions.Add(pts[0]);
mesh.Positions.Add(pts[1]);
mesh.Positions.Add(pts[6]);
mesh.Positions.Add(pts[7]);

mesh.TriangleIndices.Add(20);
mesh.TriangleIndices.Add(23);
mesh.TriangleIndices.Add(22);

mesh.TriangleIndices.Add(22);
mesh.TriangleIndices.Add(21);
mesh.TriangleIndices.Add(20);

mesh.Freeze();
return mesh;
        }
    }
}
```

Here you define the CubeGeometry class that doesn't explicitly inherit from any base class. You then define several fields and corresponding properties for the cube, including Length, Width, Height, and Center. The cube object defined in the above class is very general, which allows you to change the length for each side. The GetMesh3D method implements the more detailed steps of creating the geometry mesh for the cube.

One interesting point that you may notice is that you redefine the vertices for each surface of the cube and don't share the vertices with other surfaces. This results in a Positions collection, which has 24 vertices rather than just eight points that define the cube. So why not just use eight vertices in the Positions collection and share the vertices among the surfaces?

There is one issue if the Positions collection uses the shared vertices, resulting from the way that WPF calculates lighting. In order to simplify the calculation process, WPF computes the amount of light that reaches each vertex in a shape, meaning that WPF only pays attention to the corners of your triangles. It then blends the lighting over the surface of the triangle. While this ensures that every triangle is shaded, it may cause other artifacts. For example, if the shared vertices are used in the Positions collection, WPF may prevent the adjacent triangles that share a cube side from being shaded evenly. If you try to use the shared vertices to construct your cube geometry, you may obtain undesirable results where the surfaces of the cube don't look flat and distinct. The simple rule is this, don't share vertices of triangles if the triangles aren't on the same surface.

At the end of this method, you use the Freeze method to freeze your geometry for a small performance gain. You can also add more features inside the GetMesh3D method, such as adding normals and texture coordinates to the mesh. I'll leave them for you to execise on your own.

One key step to creating a custom geometry class is to use the get-only property of the MeshGeomery3D type named Mesh3D. This get-accessor of the Mesh3D property creates a new MeshGeometry3D object by calling the GetMesh3D method, and returns that object.

Tesing CubeGeometry

So how do you use the CubeGeometry class in XAML? In a XAML file, this class can't be used directly within a ModelUIElement3D or a ModelVisual3D element. Instead you must define a CubeGeometry object in the Resources section of an XAML file.

Let's use an example to illustrate how to use the CubeGeometry class in XAML. Add a new WPF Window to the project Chapter11 and name it CubeGeometryTest. Here is the XAML file of this example:

```
<Window x:Class="Chapter11.CubeGeometryTest"
    xmlns="http://schemas.microsoft.com/winfx
        /2006/xaml/presentation"
    xmlns:x="http://schemas.microsoft.com/winfx/2006/xaml"
    xmlns:local="clr-namespace:Geometries"
    Title="Cube Geometry Test" Height="300" Width="300">

    <Window.Resources>
        <local:CubeGeometry x:Key="cube"
                            Center="0,0,0"
                            Length="0.5"
```

```xml
                            Width="0.5"
                            Height="1"/>
    </Window.Resources>

    <Viewport3D>
        <ContainerUIElement3D>
            <ModelUIElement3D>
                <Model3DGroup>

                    <!-- Create first cube: -->
                    <GeometryModel3D Geometry="
                        {Binding Source=
                            {StaticResource cube},
                            Path=Mesh3D}">

                        <!-- Set material: -->
                        <GeometryModel3D.Material>
                            <DiffuseMaterial
                                Brush="LightBlue"/>
                        </GeometryModel3D.Material>

                        <!-- Set rotation: -->
                        <GeometryModel3D.Transform>
                            <RotateTransform3D>
                                <RotateTransform3D.Rotation>
                                    <AxisAngleRotation3D
                                        x:Name="rotate1"
                                        Axis="0,1,0"/>
                                </RotateTransform3D.Rotation>
                            </RotateTransform3D>
                        </GeometryModel3D.Transform>
                    </GeometryModel3D>

                    <!-- Create another cube: -->
                    <GeometryModel3D Geometry="{Binding
                        Source={StaticResource cube},
                            Path=Mesh3D}">

                        <!-- Set material: -->
                        <GeometryModel3D.Material>
                            <DiffuseMaterial
                                Brush="Goldenrod"/>
                        </GeometryModel3D.Material>

                        <!-- Set rotation: -->

                        <GeometryModel3D.Transform>
                            <Transform3DGroup>
                                <TranslateTransform3D
                                    OffsetZ="-1"/>
                                <ScaleTransform3D
                                    ScaleY="0.5"/>
                                <RotateTransform3D>
                                <RotateTransform3D.Rotation>
```

```
                        <AxisAngleRotation3D
                            x:Name="rotate2"
                            Axis="0,1,0"/>
                    </RotateTransform3D.Rotation>
                </RotateTransform3D>
            </Transform3DGroup>
        </GeometryModel3D.Transform>
    </GeometryModel3D>

    <!-- Set light source: -->
    <DirectionalLight Color="Gray"
                    Direction="-1,-2,-1.5" />
    <AmbientLight Color="Gray"/>
  </Model3DGroup>
 </ModelUIElement3D>
</ContainerUIElement3D>

<!-- Set camera: -->
<Viewport3D.Camera>
    <PerspectiveCamera Position="2,2,2"
                LookDirection="-2,-2,-2"
                UpDirection="0,1,0"/>
</Viewport3D.Camera>
</Viewport3D>

<Window.Triggers>
    <EventTrigger RoutedEvent="Window.Loaded">
        <BeginStoryboard>
            <Storyboard>
                <DoubleAnimation
                    Storyboard.TargetName="rotate1"
                    Storyboard.TargetProperty="Angle"
                    From="0" To="360" Duration="0:0:5"
                    RepeatBehavior="Forever"/>

                <DoubleAnimation
                    Storyboard.TargetName="rotate2"
                    Storyboard.TargetProperty="Angle"
                    From="0" To="360" Duration="0:0:5"
                    RepeatBehavior="Forever"/>
            </Storyboard>
        </BeginStoryboard>
    </EventTrigger>
</Window.Triggers>
</Window>
```

In this XAML file, you first include an XML namespace declaration to associate with an XML namespace of your Geometries:

```
xmlns:local="clr-namespace:Geometries"
```

If you prefer to use a DLL for your CubeGeometry rather than part of the project, then the namespace declaration also needs to include the DLL assembly name:

```
xmlns:local="clr-namespace:Geometries;assembly=CubeGeometry"
```

In the Window Resources section, you define a cube geometry, cube. Within the GeometryModel3D element you can then reference that resource with a data binding:

```
<GeometryModel3D Geometry="{Binding Source=
                  {StaticResource cube},Path=Mesh3D}">
```

Notice that the binding references the static reaource named cube and the Geometry property, which is of the MeshGeometry3D type. In this way, the geometry you have defined in the CubeGeometry is assigned to the Geometry property of the GeometryModel3D element in your XAML file.

Here you create a resource, cube, using your custom CubeGeometry class. Then you use this single resouce to provide a MeshGeometry3D for two cubes. Each of these cubes can have different materials and you can apply transforms to the GeometryModel3D (or ModelUIElement3D) to change the size, location, or orientation of the cube.

The XAML file also applies an animation when these two cube objects are rotated, which spins around the (0, 1, 0) axis. Figure 11-1 shows the results of running this application.

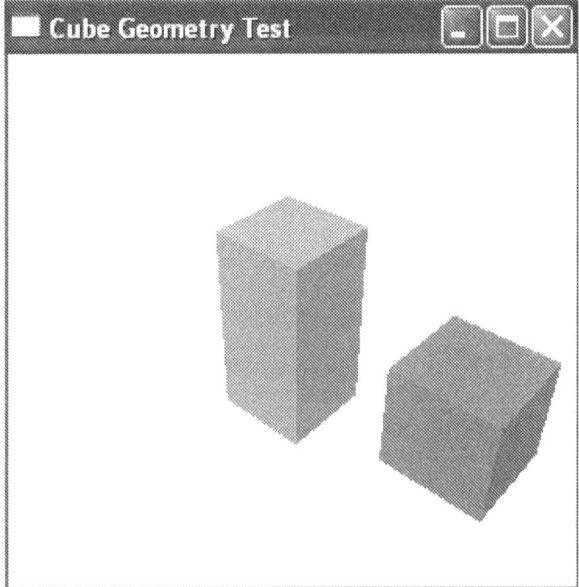

Figure 11-1 Cubes created using custom geometry.

Ellipsoid Geometry

In this section, you will learn how to create a more general sphere - the ellipsoid geometry. The equation of an ellipsoid in 3D can be written in the form:

$$\frac{x^2}{a^2} + \frac{y^2}{b^2} + \frac{z^2}{c^2} = 1 \qquad (11\text{-}1)$$

It can also be represented in terms of the parametric latitude angle θ and longitude angle φ:

$$x = a\cos\theta\cos\varphi$$
$$y = b\sin\theta \qquad (11\text{-}2)$$
$$z = -c\cos\theta\sin\varphi$$

As you did in Chapter 10 for the sphere, here you also need to make segments and slices on the surface of the ellipsoid in order to perform the triangulation.

EllipsoidGeometry Class

Add a new class called EllipsoidGeometry to the project Chapter11, and change its namespace from Chapter11 to Geometries. The procedure used to create your custom EllipsoidGeometry class is the same as for the cube in the previous section. The difference is in the algorithm used to create the mesh geometry. Here is the code listing of this class:

```
using System;
using System.Windows;
using System.Windows.Media;
using System.Windows.Media.Media3D;

namespace Geometries
{
    class EllipsoidGeometry
    {
        // Define private fields:
        private double xLength = 1.0;
        private double yLength = 1.0;
        private double zLength = 1.0;
        private int thetaDiv = 30;
        private int phiDiv = 20;
        private Point3D center = new Point3D();

        // Define public properties:
        public double XLength
        {
            get { return xLength; }
            set { xLength = value; }
        }
    }
```

```csharp
public double YLength
{
    get { return yLength; }
    set { yLength = value; }
}

public double ZLength
{
    get { return zLength; }
    set { zLength = value; }
}

public int ThetaDiv
{
    get { return thetaDiv; }
    set { thetaDiv = value; }
}
public int PhiDiv
{
    get { return phiDiv; }
    set { phiDiv = value; }
}

public Point3D Center
{
    get { return center; }
    set { center = value; }
}

// Get-only property generates MeshGeometry3D object:
public MeshGeometry3D Mesh3D
{
    get { return GetMesh3D(); }
}

private MeshGeometry3D GetMesh3D()
{
    double dt = 360.0 / ThetaDiv;
    double dp = 180.0 / PhiDiv;

    MeshGeometry3D mesh = new MeshGeometry3D();

    for (int i = 0; i <= PhiDiv; i++)
    {
        double phi = i * dp;

        for (int j = 0; j <= ThetaDiv; j++)
        {
            double theta = j * dt;
            mesh.Positions.Add(
                GetPosition(theta, phi));
        }
    }
```

```
for (int i = 0; i < PhiDiv; i++)
{
    for (int j = 0; j < ThetaDiv; j++)
    {
        int x0 = j;
        int x1 = (j + 1);
        int y0 = i * (ThetaDiv + 1);
        int y1 = (i + 1) * (ThetaDiv + 1);

        mesh.TriangleIndices.Add(x0 + y0);
        mesh.TriangleIndices.Add(x0 + y1);
        mesh.TriangleIndices.Add(x1 + y0);

        mesh.TriangleIndices.Add(x1 + y0);
        mesh.TriangleIndices.Add(x0 + y1);
        mesh.TriangleIndices.Add(x1 + y1);
    }
}

mesh.Freeze();
return mesh;
}

private Point3D GetPosition(double theta, double phi)
{
    theta *= Math.PI / 180.0;
    phi *= Math.PI / 180.0;

    double x = XLength * Math.Sin(theta) *
        Math.Sin(phi);
    double y = YLength * Math.Cos(phi);
    double z = -ZLength * Math.Cos(theta) *
        Math.Sin(phi);

    Point3D pt = new Point3D(x, y, z);
    pt += (Vector3D)Center;

    return pt;
}
}
}
```

Here you define the six field members, xLength, yLength, zLength, thetaDiv, phiDiv, and center, as well as their corresponding public properties. The length in the X, Y, and Z directions corresponds to the parameters a, b, and c in Equations (11-1) and (11-2). The thetaDiv and phiDiv are the number of segments and slices along the latitude and longitude directions.

Inside the GetMesh3D method, we only need to consider one unit cell with vertices (i, j), (i+1, j), (i+1, j+1), and (i, j+1). Each unit cell can be represented using two triangles. In Chapter 10, we created mesh for each individual triangle model. However, here we want to put all of the vertices and triangle indices into a single MeshGeometry3D object. Thus, we need to specify the correct triangle indices using the Positions collection. Notice that the Positions collection is constructed by calling the GetPostion method that returns the Point3D object on the surface of the ellipsoid.

Finally, we use the get-only property of the MeshGeomery3D type named Mesh3D to create a new MeshGeometry3D object by calling the GetMesh3D method, and return that object. Every time the Mesh3D property in your EllipsoidGeometry class is accessed, it returns a new MeshGeometry3D object by calling the GetMesh3D method based on the current settings of the other six properties, including XLength, YLength, ZLength, ThetaDiv, PhiDiv, and Center.

Testing EllipsoidGeometry

You can use the EllipsoidGeomtry class in your XAML files by definining an EllipsoidGeometry object in the Resources section of a XAML file. Of course, you can also use the custom geometry class drectly in code, where you can simply create an instance of your custom class and assign the Geometry property of a GeometryModel3D object using the Mesh3D property of the custom geometry class.

Let's use an example to illustrate how to use the EllipsoidGeometry class in XAML. The procedure is similar to that used in the previous example. Add a new WPF Window to the project Chapter11 and name it EllipsoidGeometryTest. Here is the XAML file of this example:

```
<Window x:Class="Chapter11.EllipsoidGeometryTest"
    xmlns="http://schemas.microsoft.com/winfx
        /2006/xaml/presentation"
    xmlns:x="http://schemas.microsoft.com/winfx/2006/xaml"
    xmlns:local="clr-namespace:Geometries"
    Title="Ellipsoid Geometry Test" Height="300" Width="300">

    <Window.Resources>
        <local:EllipsoidGeometry x:Key="ellipsoid1"
            Center="0,0,0" XLength="0.5" YLength="1.0"
            ZLength="0.7" />
        <local:EllipsoidGeometry x:Key="ellipsoid2"
            Center="0,0,-2" XLength="0.6" YLength="0.6"
            ZLength="0.6"/>
    </Window.Resources>

    <Viewport3D>
        <ContainerUIElement3D>
            <ModelUIElement3D>
                <Model3DGroup>

                    <!-- Create cube1: -->
                    <GeometryModel3D Geometry="{Binding
Source={StaticResource ellipsoid1},Path=Mesh3D}">
```

```
<!-- Set material: -->
<GeometryModel3D.Material>
    <MaterialGroup>
<DiffuseMaterial Brush="SteelBlue"/>
<SpecularMaterial Brush="LightBlue" SpecularPower="60"/>
    </MaterialGroup>
</GeometryModel3D.Material>

<!-- Set rotation: -->
<GeometryModel3D.Transform>
    <RotateTransform3D>
        <RotateTransform3D.Rotation>
            <AxisAngleRotation3D
                x:Name="rotate1"
                Axis="0,1,0"/>
        </RotateTransform3D.Rotation>
    </RotateTransform3D>
</GeometryModel3D.Transform>
</GeometryModel3D>

<!-- Create cube2: -->
<GeometryModel3D Geometry="{Binding
Source={StaticResource ellipsoid2},Path=Mesh3D}">

<!-- Set material: -->
<GeometryModel3D.Material>
    <MaterialGroup>
<DiffuseMaterial Brush="Goldenrod"/>
<SpecularMaterial Brush="Yellow" SpecularPower="60"/>
    </MaterialGroup>
</GeometryModel3D.Material>

<!-- Set rotation: -->
<GeometryModel3D.Transform>
    <RotateTransform3D>
        <RotateTransform3D.Rotation>
            <AxisAngleRotation3D
                x:Name="rotate2"
                Axis="0,1,0"/>
        </RotateTransform3D.Rotation>
    </RotateTransform3D>
</GeometryModel3D.Transform>
</GeometryModel3D>

<!-- Set light source: -->
<DirectionalLight Color="Gray"
    Direction="-1,-2,-1.5" />
<AmbientLight Color="Gray"/>
</Model3DGroup>
</ModelUIElement3D>
</ContainerUIElement3D>

<!-- Set camera: -->
<Viewport3D.Camera>
```

```
        <PerspectiveCamera Position="3,4,5"
                    LookDirection="-3,-4,-5"
                    UpDirection="0,1,0"/>
    </Viewport3D.Camera>
</Viewport3D>

<Window.Triggers>
    <EventTrigger RoutedEvent="Window.Loaded">
        <BeginStoryboard>
            <Storyboard>
                <DoubleAnimation
                    Storyboard.TargetName="rotate1"
                    Storyboard.TargetProperty="Angle"
                    From="0" To="360" Duration="0:0:5"
                    RepeatBehavior="Forever"/>

                <DoubleAnimation
                    Storyboard.TargetName="rotate2"
                    Storyboard.TargetProperty="Angle"
                    From="0" To="360" Duration="0:0:5"
                    RepeatBehavior="Forever"/>
            </Storyboard>
        </BeginStoryboard>
    </EventTrigger>
</Window.Triggers>
</Window>
```

In the Window Resources section, you define two ellipsoid geometries, ellipsoid1 and ellipsoid2. The ellipsoid2 is simply a sphere geometry. Within the GeometryModel3D element you can then reference these resources with data binding. In this way, the geometry you have defined in the EllipsoidGeometry class is assigned to the Geometry property of the GeometryModel3D element in your XAML file.

The XAML file also applies an animation to the rotation transform of these two ellipsoid objects, which spins around the (0, 1, 0) axis. Figure 11-2 shows the results of running this application.

Cylindrical Geometry

In this section, I'll show you how to create a custom cylinder geometry in WPF. As you did in Chapter 10, here you'll create a more general cylinder geometry that allows you to specify its inner and outer radii. By setting a non-zero inner radius, you can create a cylindrical tube shape.

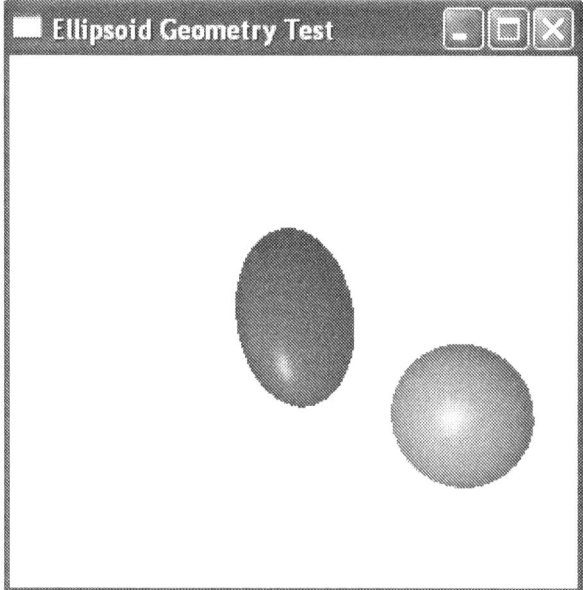

Figure 11-2 Ellipsoids created using custom Geometry.

CylinderGeometry Class

In order to create triangular meshes for the cylinder, you need to make slices on its surface as you did in Chapter 10. Add a new class called CylinderGeometry to the project Chapter11, and change its namespace from Chapter11 to Geometries. The procedure used to create the custom class is the same as that used in the previous examples. The difference is in the algorithm used to create the mesh geometry. Here is the code listing of this class:

```
using System;
using System.Windows;
using System.Windows.Media;
using System.Windows.Media.Media3D;

namespace Geometries
{
    public class CylinderGeometry
    {
        // Define private fields:
        private double rin = 1.0;
        private double rout = 1.0;
        private double height = 1.0;
        private int thetaDiv = 20;
        private Point3D center = new Point3D();

        // Define public properties:
        public double Rin
        {
```

```
            get { return rin; }
            set { rin = value; }
        }

        public double Rout
        {
            get { return rout; }
            set { rout = value; }
        }

        public double Height
        {
            get { return height; }
            set { height = value; }
        }

        public int ThetaDiv
        {
            get { return thetaDiv; }
            set { thetaDiv = value; }
        }

        public Point3D Center
        {
            get { return center; }
            set { center = value; }
        }

        // Get-only property generates MeshGeometry3D object:
        public MeshGeometry3D Mesh3D
        {
            get { return GetMesh3D(); }
        }

        private MeshGeometry3D GetMesh3D()
        {
            MeshGeometry3D mesh = new MeshGeometry3D();

            if (ThetaDiv < 2 || Rin == Rout)
                return null;

            double radius = Rin;
            if (Rin > Rout)
            {
                Rin = rout;
                Rout = radius;
            }

            double h = Height / 2;
            Point3D[,] pts = new Point3D[ThetaDiv, 4];


            for (int i = 0; i < ThetaDiv; i++)
            {
```

```
        pts[i, 0] = GetPosition(rout,
            i * 360 / (ThetaDiv - 1), h);
        pts[i, 1] = GetPosition(rout,
            i * 360 / (ThetaDiv - 1), -h);
        pts[i, 2] = GetPosition(rin,
            i * 360 / (ThetaDiv - 1), -h);
        pts[i, 3] = GetPosition(rin,
            i * 360 / (ThetaDiv - 1), h);
}

for (int i = 0; i < ThetaDiv - 1; i++)
{
    // Top surface:
    mesh.Positions.Add(pts[i, 0]);
    mesh.Positions.Add(pts[i + 1, 0]);
    mesh.Positions.Add(pts[i + 1, 3]);
    mesh.Positions.Add(pts[i, 3]);
    mesh.TriangleIndices.Add(16 * i);
    mesh.TriangleIndices.Add(16 * i + 1);
    mesh.TriangleIndices.Add(16 * i + 2);
  mesh.TriangleIndices.Add(16 * i + 2);
  mesh.TriangleIndices.Add(16 * i + 3);
  mesh.TriangleIndices.Add(16 * i);

    // Bottom surface:
    mesh.Positions.Add(pts[i, 1]);
    mesh.Positions.Add(pts[i, 2]);
    mesh.Positions.Add(pts[i + 1, 2]);
    mesh.Positions.Add(pts[i + 1, 1]);
    mesh.TriangleIndices.Add(16 * i + 4);
    mesh.TriangleIndices.Add(16 * i + 5);
    mesh.TriangleIndices.Add(16 * i + 6);
    mesh.TriangleIndices.Add(16 * i + 6);
    mesh.TriangleIndices.Add(16 * i + 7);
    mesh.TriangleIndices.Add(16 * i + 4);

    // Outer surface:
    mesh.Positions.Add(pts[i, 1]);
    mesh.Positions.Add(pts[i + 1, 1]);
    mesh.Positions.Add(pts[i + 1, 0]);
    mesh.Positions.Add(pts[i, 0]);
    mesh.TriangleIndices.Add(16 * i + 8);
    mesh.TriangleIndices.Add(16 * i + 9);
    mesh.TriangleIndices.Add(16 * i + 10);
    mesh.TriangleIndices.Add(16 * i + 10);
    mesh.TriangleIndices.Add(16 * i + 11);
    mesh.TriangleIndices.Add(16 * i + 8);

    // Inner surface:
    mesh.Positions.Add(pts[i, 3]);
    mesh.Positions.Add(pts[i + 1, 3]);
    mesh.Positions.Add(pts[i + 1, 2]);
    mesh.Positions.Add(pts[i, 2]);
    mesh.TriangleIndices.Add(16 * i + 12);
```

```
                    mesh.TriangleIndices.Add(16 * i + 13);
                    mesh.TriangleIndices.Add(16 * i + 14);
                    mesh.TriangleIndices.Add(16 * i + 14);
                    mesh.TriangleIndices.Add(16 * i + 15);
                    mesh.TriangleIndices.Add(16 * i + 12);
                }
                mesh.Freeze();
                return mesh;
            }

            private Point3D GetPosition(double radius,
                double theta, double y)
            {
                Point3D pt = new Point3D();
                double sn = Math.Sin(theta * Math.PI / 180);
                double cn = Math.Cos(theta * Math.PI / 180);

                pt.X = radius * cn;
                pt.Y = y;
                pt.Z = -radius * sn;
                pt += (Vector3D)Center;
                return pt;
            }
        }
    }
```

In this class, you define five field members, the inner and outer radii, height, center, and the number of slices on the surface, as well as their coresponding public properties. The unit cell you use in this class is the same as that shown in Figure 10-9. It contains four surfaces, including the top, bottom, inner, and outer surfaces. Each of these four surfaces is formed by four vertices. That is why you need to add a factor of 16 * i to each triangle indices in order to take into account 16 vertices added to the Positions collection for each unit cell. Notice that the postions are added to the collection by calling the GetPosition method, which returns the point on the surface of the cylinder.

Finally, you use the get-only property of the MeshGeomery3D type named Mesh3D to create a new MeshGeometry3D object by calling the GetMesh3D method, and return that object. Every time the Mesh3D property in your CylinderGeometry class is accessed, it returns a new MeshGeometry3D object based on the current settings of the other five properties defined in this class.

Testing CylinderGeometry

You can use the CylinderGeomtry class in XAML files by definining a CylinderGeometry object in the Resources section of a XAML file. If you want to use it in code, you can simply create an instance of the custom class and assign the Geometry property of a GeometryModel3D object using its Mesh3D property.

Let's use an example to illustrate how to use the CylinderGeometry class in XAML. This procedure is similar to that used in the previous examples. Add a new WPF Window to the project Chapter11 and name it CylinderGeometryTest. Here is the XAML file of this example:

```
<Window x:Class="Chapter11.CylinderGeometryTest"
    xmlns="http://schemas.microsoft.com/winfx
        /2006/xaml/presentation"
    xmlns:x="http://schemas.microsoft.com/winfx/2006/xaml"
    xmlns:local="clr-namespace:Geometries"
    Title="Cylinder Geometry Test" Height="300" Width="300">

    <Window.Resources>
        <local:CylinderGeometry x:Key="cylinder1"
                Center="0,0,0" Rin="0"
                Rout="0.5" Height="1"/>
        <local:CylinderGeometry x:Key="cylinder2"
                Center="0,0,-2" Rin="0.4"
                Rout="0.5" Height="0.4"/>
    </Window.Resources>

    <Viewport3D>
        <ContainerUIElement3D>
            <ModelUIElement3D>
                <Model3DGroup>

                    <!-- Create cube1: -->
                    <GeometryModel3D Geometry="
                        {Binding Source={StaticResource
                            cylinder1},Path=Mesh3D}">

                        <!-- Set material: -->
                        <GeometryModel3D.Material>
                            <DiffuseMaterial
                                Brush="SteelBlue">
                            </DiffuseMaterial>
                        </GeometryModel3D.Material>

                        <!-- Set rotation: -->
                        <GeometryModel3D.Transform>
                            <RotateTransform3D>
                                <RotateTransform3D.Rotation>
                                    <AxisAngleRotation3D
                                        x:Name="rotate1"
                                        Axis="1,0,0"/>
                                </RotateTransform3D.Rotation>
                            </RotateTransform3D>
                        </GeometryModel3D.Transform>
                    </GeometryModel3D>

                    <!-- Create cube2: -->
                    <GeometryModel3D Geometry=
                        "{Binding Source={StaticResource
```

```
                         cylinder2},Path=Mesh3D}">

                    <!-- Set material: -->
                    <GeometryModel3D.Material>
                        <DiffuseMaterial
                            Brush="Goldenrod">
                        </DiffuseMaterial>
                    </GeometryModel3D.Material>

                    <!-- Set rotation: -->
                    <GeometryModel3D.Transform>
                        <RotateTransform3D>
                            <RotateTransform3D.Rotation>
                                <AxisAngleRotation3D
                                    x:Name="rotate2"
                                    Axis="1,0,0"/>
                            </RotateTransform3D.Rotation>
                        </RotateTransform3D>
                    </GeometryModel3D.Transform>
                </GeometryModel3D>

                <!-- Set light source: -->
                <DirectionalLight Color="Gray"
                    Direction="-1,-2,-1.5" />
                <AmbientLight Color="Gray"/>
            </Model3DGroup>
        </ModelUIElement3D>
    </ContainerUIElement3D>

    <!-- Set camera: -->
    <Viewport3D.Camera>
        <PerspectiveCamera Position="3,4,5"
                        LookDirection="-3,-4,-5"
                        UpDirection="0,1,0"/>
    </Viewport3D.Camera>
</Viewport3D>

<Window.Triggers>
    <EventTrigger RoutedEvent="Window.Loaded">
        <BeginStoryboard>
            <Storyboard>
                <DoubleAnimation
                    Storyboard.TargetName="rotate1"
                    Storyboard.TargetProperty="Angle"
                    From="0" To="360"
                    Duration="0:0:5"
                    RepeatBehavior="Forever"/>

                <DoubleAnimation
                    Storyboard.TargetName="rotate2"
                    Storyboard.TargetProperty="Angle"
                    From="0" To="360"
                    Duration="0:0:5"
                    RepeatBehavior="Forever"/>
```

```
          </Storyboard>
        </BeginStoryboard>
      </EventTrigger>
    </Window.Triggers>
  </Window>
```

In the Window Resources section, you define two cylinder geometries, cylinder1 and cylinder2. cylinder1 is simply a simple cylinder with an inner radius of zero, while cylinder2 has a cylinder ring with a finite inner radius. Within the GeometryModel3D element you can then reference those resources with data binding. In this way, the geometry you have defined in the CylinderGeometry class is assigned to the Geometry property of the GeometryModel3D element in your XAML file.

The XAML file also applies an animation to the rotation transform of these two cylinder objects, which spins around the (1, 0, 0) axis. Figure 11-3 shows the results of running this application.

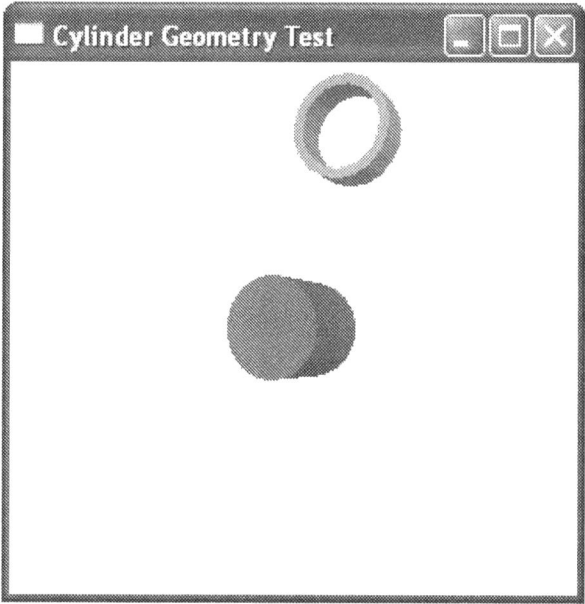

Figure 11-3 Cylinders created using custom geometry.

Cone Geometry

You can also create a custom cone geometry using the cylindrical coordinate system. Here we want to create a more general cone geometry which can be specified with a top radius and a bottom radius, as well as a height parameter, as shown in Figure 10-11.

ConeGeometry Class

In order to create a custom cone geometry, you need to perform triangulations for its surfaces. The unit cell (see Figure 10-11) has three surfaces that needs to be triangulated, including the top, bottom, and outer surfaces. The top and bottom surfaces are already triangular shapes, while the outer surface can be represented with two triangles.

Again, the procedure of creating the custom cone geometry class is the same as that used in the previous examples. The difference is in the algorithm used to create the mesh geometry. Here is the code listing of the ConeGeometry class:

```csharp
using System;
using System.Windows;
using System.Windows.Media;
using System.Windows.Media.Media3D;

namespace Geometries
{
    public class ConeGeometry
    {
        // Define private fields:
        private double rtop = 1.0;
        private double rbottom = 1.0;
        private double height = 1.0;
        private int thetaDiv = 20;
        private Point3D center = new Point3D();

        // Define public properties:
        public double Rtop
        {
            get { return rtop; }
            set { rtop = value; }
        }

        public double Rbottom
        {
            get { return rbottom; }
            set { rbottom = value; }
        }

        public double Height
        {
            get { return height; }
            set { height = value; }
        }

        public int ThetaDiv
        {
            get { return thetaDiv; }
            set { thetaDiv = value; }
        }
```

```
public Point3D Center
{
    get { return center; }
    set { center = value; }
}

// Get-only property generates MeshGeometry3D object:
public MeshGeometry3D Mesh3D
{
    get { return GetMesh3D(); }
}

private MeshGeometry3D GetMesh3D()
{
    MeshGeometry3D mesh = new MeshGeometry3D();

    if (ThetaDiv < 2)
        return null;

    double h = Height / 2;

    Point3D pt = new Point3D(0, h, 0);
    pt += (Vector3D)Center;
    Point3D pb = new Point3D(0, -h, 0);
    pb += (Vector3D)Center;
    Point3D[] pts = new Point3D[ThetaDiv];
    Point3D[] pbs = new Point3D[ThetaDiv];

    for (int i = 0; i < ThetaDiv; i++)
    {
        pts[i] = GetPosition(Rtop,
            i * 360 / (ThetaDiv - 1), h);
        pbs[i] = GetPosition(Rbottom,
            i * 360 / (ThetaDiv - 1), -h);
    }

    for (int i = 0; i < ThetaDiv - 1; i++)
    {
        // Top surface:
        mesh.Positions.Add(pt);
        mesh.Positions.Add(pts[i]);
        mesh.Positions.Add(pts[i + 1]);

        mesh.TriangleIndices.Add(10 * i);
        mesh.TriangleIndices.Add(10 * i + 1);
        mesh.TriangleIndices.Add(10 * i + 2);

        // Bottom surface:
        mesh.Positions.Add(pb);
        mesh.Positions.Add(pbs[i + 1]);
        mesh.Positions.Add(pbs[i]);

        mesh.TriangleIndices.Add(10 * i + 3);
        mesh.TriangleIndices.Add(10 * i + 4);
```

```
                mesh.TriangleIndices.Add(10 * i + 5);

                // Outer surface:
                mesh.Positions.Add(pts[i]);
                mesh.Positions.Add(pbs[i]);
                mesh.Positions.Add(pbs[i + 1]);
                mesh.Positions.Add(pts[i + 1]);

                mesh.TriangleIndices.Add(10 * i + 6);
                mesh.TriangleIndices.Add(10 * i + 7);
                mesh.TriangleIndices.Add(10 * i + 8);
                mesh.TriangleIndices.Add(10 * i + 8);
                mesh.TriangleIndices.Add(10 * i + 9);
                mesh.TriangleIndices.Add(10 * i + 6);
            }

            mesh.Freeze();
            return mesh;
        }

        private Point3D GetPosition(double radius,
            double theta, double y)
        {
            Point3D pt = new Point3D();
            double sn = Math.Sin(theta * Math.PI / 180);
            double cn = Math.Cos(theta * Math.PI / 180);

            pt.X = radius * cn;
            pt.Y = y;
            pt.Z = -radius * sn;

            pt += (Vector3D)Center;
            return pt;
        }
    }
}
```

In this class, you define the five field members, including the top and bottom radii, the height, the center, and thetaDiv, and their corresponding public properties as well. The thetaDiv represents the number of slices you make on the surface of the cone object.

Inside the GetMesh3D method, we consider one unit cell between slice lines i and i+1. Each unit cell contains three surfaces, the top, bottom, and outer surfaces (see Figure 10-11). The top or bottom surface is already a triangle shape, while the outer surface can be represented using two triangles. In Chapter 10, you performed the triangulation for each individual triangle model. However, here you want to put all of the vertices and triangle indices into a single MeshGeometry3D object. Thus, you must specify the correct triangle indices using the Positions collection. A factor of 10*i has been added to the triangle indices because there are ten vertices added to the Positions collection for each unit cell. Notice that the postions are added to the collection by calling the GetPosition method, which returns the point on the surface of the cone.

Finally, you use the get-only property of the MeshGeomery3D type named Mesh3D to create a new MeshGeometry3D object by calling the GetMesh3D method, and return that object. Every time the Mesh3D property in your ConeGeometry class is accessed, it returns a new MeshGeometry3D object by calling the GetMesh3D method based on the current settings of the properties defined in your custom class.

Testing ConeGeometry

You can use the ConeGeomtry class in a XAML file by defining a ConeGeometry object in the Resources section of the XAML file. If you want to use it in code, you can simply create an instance of your custom class and assign the Geometry property of a GeometryModel3D object, using the Mesh3D property of your custom geometry class.

Let's use an example to illustrate how to use the ConeGeometry class in XAML. This procedure is similar to that used in the previous examples. Add a new WPF Window to the project Chapter11 and name it ConeGeometryTest. Here is the XAML file of this example:

```
<Window x:Class="Chapter11.ConeGeometryTest"
    xmlns="http://schemas.microsoft.com/winfx
        /2006/xaml/presentation"
    xmlns:x="http://schemas.microsoft.com/winfx/2006/xaml"
    xmlns:local="clr-namespace:Geometries"
    Title="Cone Geometry Test" Height="300" Width="300">

    <Window.Resources>
        <local:ConeGeometry x:Key="cone1"
                            Center="0,0,0" Rtop="0"
                            Rbottom="0.5" Height="1"/>
        <local:ConeGeometry x:Key="cone2"
                            Center="0,0,-1.5" Rtop="0.3"
                            Rbottom="0.5" Height="0.5"/>
        <local:ConeGeometry x:Key="cone3"
                            Center="0,0,1.5" Rtop="0.5"
                            Rbottom="0.3" Height="0.5"/>
        <local:ConeGeometry x:Key="cone4" Center="1.5,0,0"
                            Rtop="0" Rbottom="0.5"
                            Height="1" ThetaDiv="4"/>
        <local:ConeGeometry x:Key="cone5" Center="-1.5,0,0"
                            Rtop="0.5" Rbottom="0"
                            Height="1" ThetaDiv="6"/>
    </Window.Resources>

    <Viewport3D>
        <ContainerUIElement3D>
            <ModelUIElement3D>
                <Model3DGroup>
```

```xml
<!-- Create cone1: -->
<GeometryModel3D Geometry=
    "{Binding Source={StaticResource
        cone1},Path=Mesh3D}">

    <!-- Set material: -->
    <GeometryModel3D.Material>
        <DiffuseMaterial
            Brush="SteelBlue">
        </DiffuseMaterial>
    </GeometryModel3D.Material>

    <!-- Set rotation: -->
    <GeometryModel3D.Transform>
        <RotateTransform3D>
            <RotateTransform3D.Rotation>
                <AxisAngleRotation3D
                    x:Name="rotate1"
                    Axis="1,0,0"/>
            </RotateTransform3D.Rotation>
        </RotateTransform3D>
    </GeometryModel3D.Transform>
</GeometryModel3D>

<!-- Create cone2: -->
<GeometryModel3D Geometry=
    "{Binding Source={StaticResource
        cone2},Path=Mesh3D}">

    <!-- Set material: -->
    <GeometryModel3D.Material>
        <DiffuseMaterial
            Brush="Goldenrod">
        </DiffuseMaterial>
    </GeometryModel3D.Material>

    <!-- Set rotation: -->
    <GeometryModel3D.Transform>
        <RotateTransform3D>
            <RotateTransform3D.Rotation>
                <AxisAngleRotation3D
                    x:Name="rotate2"
                    Axis="1,0,0"/>
            </RotateTransform3D.Rotation>
        </RotateTransform3D>
    </GeometryModel3D.Transform>
</GeometryModel3D>

<!-- Create cone3: -->
<GeometryModel3D Geometry=
    "{Binding Source={StaticResource
        cone3},Path=Mesh3D}">
```

```xml
    <!-- Set material: -->
    <GeometryModel3D.Material>
        <DiffuseMaterial
            Brush="LightGreen">
        </DiffuseMaterial>
    </GeometryModel3D.Material>

    <!-- Set rotation: -->
    <GeometryModel3D.Transform>
        <RotateTransform3D>
            <RotateTransform3D.Rotation>
                <AxisAngleRotation3D
                    x:Name="rotate3"
                    Axis="1,0,0"/>
            </RotateTransform3D.Rotation>
        </RotateTransform3D>
    </GeometryModel3D.Transform>
</GeometryModel3D>

<!-- Create cone4: -->
<GeometryModel3D Geometry=
    "{Binding Source={StaticResource
        cone4},Path=Mesh3D}">

    <!-- Set material: -->
    <GeometryModel3D.Material>
        <DiffuseMaterial Brush="Red">
        </DiffuseMaterial>
    </GeometryModel3D.Material>

    <!-- Set rotation: -->
    <GeometryModel3D.Transform>
        <RotateTransform3D>
            <RotateTransform3D.Rotation>
                <AxisAngleRotation3D
                    x:Name="rotate4"
                    Axis="1,0,0"/>
            </RotateTransform3D.Rotation>
        </RotateTransform3D>
    </GeometryModel3D.Transform>
</GeometryModel3D>

<!-- Create cone5: -->
<GeometryModel3D Geometry=
    "{Binding Source={StaticResource
        cone5},Path=Mesh3D}">

    <!-- Set material: -->
    <GeometryModel3D.Material>
        <DiffuseMaterial
            Brush="LightCoral">
        </DiffuseMaterial>
    </GeometryModel3D.Material>
```

```
                            <!-- Set rotation: -->
                            <GeometryModel3D.Transform>
                                <RotateTransform3D>
                                    <RotateTransform3D.Rotation>
                                        <AxisAngleRotation3D
                                            x:Name="rotate5"
                                            Axis="1,0,0"/>
                                    </RotateTransform3D.Rotation>
                                </RotateTransform3D>
                            </GeometryModel3D.Transform>
                        </GeometryModel3D>

                        <!-- Set light source: -->
                        <DirectionalLight Color="Gray"
                            Direction="-1,-2,-1.5" />
                        <AmbientLight Color="Gray"/>
                    </Model3DGroup>
                </ModelUIElement3D>
            </ContainerUIElement3D>

        <!-- Set camera: -->
        <Viewport3D.Camera>
            <PerspectiveCamera Position="3,3,4"
                        LookDirection="-3,-3,-4"
                        UpDirection="0,1,0"/>
        </Viewport3D.Camera>
    </Viewport3D>

    <Window.Triggers>
        <EventTrigger RoutedEvent="Window.Loaded">
            <BeginStoryboard>
                <Storyboard>
                    <DoubleAnimation
                        Storyboard.TargetName="rotate1"
                        Storyboard.TargetProperty="Angle"
                        From="0" To="360" Duration="0:0:5"
                        RepeatBehavior="Forever"/>

                    <DoubleAnimation
                        Storyboard.TargetName="rotate2"
                        Storyboard.TargetProperty="Angle"
                        From="0" To="360" Duration="0:0:5"
                        RepeatBehavior="Forever"/>

                    <DoubleAnimation
                        Storyboard.TargetName="rotate3"
                        Storyboard.TargetProperty="Angle"
                        From="0" To="360" Duration="0:0:5"
                        RepeatBehavior="Forever"/>

                    <DoubleAnimation
                        Storyboard.TargetName="rotate4"
                        Storyboard.TargetProperty="Angle"
                        From="0" To="360" Duration="0:0:5"
```

```
                RepeatBehavior="Forever"/>

          <DoubleAnimation
               Storyboard.TargetName="rotate5"
               Storyboard.TargetProperty="Angle"
               From="0" To="360" Duration="0:0:5"
               RepeatBehavior="Forever"/>
        </Storyboard>
      </BeginStoryboard>
    </EventTrigger>
  </Window.Triggers>
</Window>
```

In the Window Resources section, you define five cone geometries using different sets of parameters that generate very different cone-like shapes. Within the GeometryModel3D element you can then reference those resources with data binding. In this way, the geometry that you have defined in the ConeGeometry class is assigned to the Geometry property of the GeometryModel3D element in your XAML file.

The XAML file also applies an animation for the rotation transform of these cone objects, which again spins around the (1, 0, 0) axis. Figure 11-4 shows the results of running this application. You can see that this application can create various cone shapes, including cylinders (by setting the top and bottom radii to be equal), cones (by setting one of the radii to zero), truncated cone shapes (by setting both radii to be finite), and even pyramids (by setting the number of slices as a small integer).

Torus Geometry

Another popular 3D shape is the torus. A torus is a surface of revolution generated by revolving a circle in 3D space about an axis (see Figure 10-13). In order to write a custom torus geometry class, you need perform the triangulation for the torus by dividing its surface using tube rings and torus rings, as shown in Figure 10-13, which form grids similar to those used in creating an ellipsoid geometry.

TorusGeometry Class

Add a new class called TorusGeometry to the project Chapter11, and change its namespace from Chapter11 to Geometries. The procedure to create the custom TorusGeometry class is the same as that for the Ellipsoid in the earlier section. The difference is in the algorithm used to create the mesh geometry. Here is the code listing of this class:

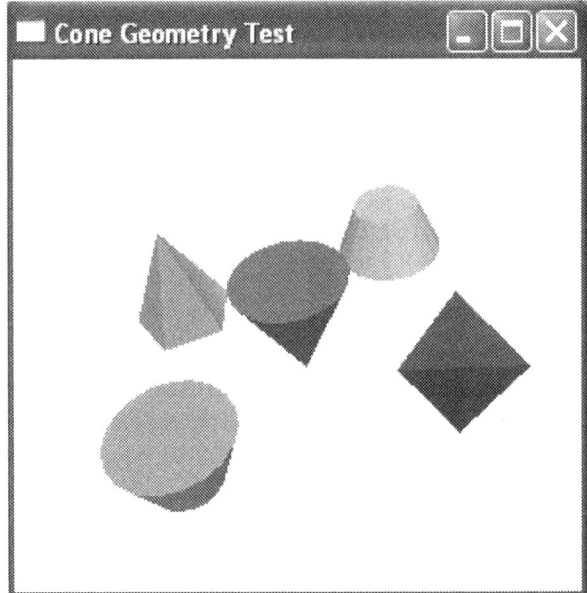

Figure 11-4 Various cone shapes created using custom geometry.

```
using System;
using System.Windows;
using System.Windows.Media;
using System.Windows.Media.Media3D;

namespace Geometries
{
    public class TorusGeometry
    {
        // Define private fields:
        private double r1 = 1.0;
        private double r2 = 0.3;
        private int uDiv = 20;
        private int vDiv = 20;
        private Point3D center = new Point3D();

        // Define public properties:
        public double R1
        {
            get { return r1; }
            set { r1 = value; }
        }

        public double R2
        {
            get { return r2; }
            set { r2 = value; }
        }
```

```
public int UDiv
{
    get { return uDiv; }
    set { uDiv = value; }
}

public int VDiv
{
    get { return vDiv; }
    set { vDiv = value; }
}

public Point3D Center
{
    get { return center; }
    set { center = value; }
}

// Get-only property generates MeshGeometry3D object:
public MeshGeometry3D Mesh3D
{
    get { return GetMesh3D(); }
}

private MeshGeometry3D GetMesh3D()
{
    if (UDiv < 2 || VDiv < 2)
        return null;

    MeshGeometry3D mesh = new MeshGeometry3D();
    Point3D[,] pts = new Point3D[UDiv, VDiv];

    for (int i = 0; i <= UDiv; i++)
    {
        for (int j = 0; j <= VDiv; j++)
        {
            mesh.Positions.Add(
                GetPosition(i * 360 / (UDiv - 1),
                            j * 360 / (VDiv - 1)));
        }
    }

    for (int i = 0; i < UDiv; i++)
    {
        for (int j = 0; j < VDiv; j++)
        {
            int y0 = j;
            int y1 = j + 1;
            int x0 = i * (VDiv + 1);
            int x1 = (i + 1) * (VDiv + 1);

            mesh.TriangleIndices.Add(x0 + y0);
            mesh.TriangleIndices.Add(x0 + y1);
            mesh.TriangleIndices.Add(x1 + y0);
```

```
                    mesh.TriangleIndices.Add(x1 + y0);
                    mesh.TriangleIndices.Add(x0 + y1);
                    mesh.TriangleIndices.Add(x1 + y1);
                }
            }

            mesh.Freeze();
            return mesh;
        }

        private Point3D GetPosition(double u, double v)
        {
            Point3D pt = new Point3D();
            double snu = Math.Sin(u * Math.PI / 180);
            double cnu = Math.Cos(u * Math.PI / 180);
            double snv = Math.Sin(v * Math.PI / 180);
            double cnv = Math.Cos(v * Math.PI / 180);

            pt.X = (R1 + R2 * cnv) * cnu;
            pt.Y = R2 * snv;
            pt.Z = (R1 + R2 * cnv) * snu;

            pt += (Vector3D)Center;
            return pt;
        }
    }
}
```

In this class you define five field members, including r1, r2, uDiv, vDiv, and center, as well as their corresponding public properties. The r1 and r2 respesent the tube radius and torus radius respectively. The uDiv and vDiv are the number of tube rings and torus rings.

Inside the GetMesh3D method, you consider one unit cell with vertices (i, j), (i+1, j), (i+1, j+1), and (i, j+1). Each unit cell can be represented using two triangles. In Chapter 10, you achieved this for each individual triangle model. However, here you want to put all of the vertices and triangle indices into a single MeshGeometry3D object. Thus, you must specify the correct triangle indices using the Positions collection. Notice that the Positions collection is contructed by calling the GetPostion method that returns the Point3D object on the surface of the torus.

You finally use the get-only property of the MeshGeomery3D type named Mesh3D to create a new MeshGeometry3D object by calling the GetMesh3D method, and return that object. Every time the Mesh3D property in your TorusGeometry class is accessed, it returns a new MeshGeometry3D object by calling the GetMesh3D method based on the current settings of the properties defined in the custom class.

Testing TorusGeometry

You can use the TorusGeomtry class in your XAML file by definining a TorusGeometry object in the Resources section of the XAML file. If you want to use it in code, you can simply create an instance of your custom class and assign the Geometry property of a GeometryModel3D object using the Mesh3D property of your custom geometry class.

Let's use an example to illustrate how to use the TorusGeometry class in XAML. This procedure is similar to that used in the previous example. Add a new WPF Window to the project Chapter11 and name it TorusGeometryTest. Here is the XAML file of this example:

```
<Window x:Class="Chapter11.TorusGeometryTest"
    xmlns="http://schemas.microsoft.com/winfx
        /2006/xaml/presentation"
    xmlns:x="http://schemas.microsoft.com/winfx/2006/xaml"
    xmlns:local="clr-namespace:Geometries"
    Title="Torus Geometry Test" Height="300" Width="300">

    <Window.Resources>
        <local:TorusGeometry x:Key="torus1" Center="0,0,0"
            R1="1.5" R2="0.2" VDiv="50"/>
        <local:TorusGeometry x:Key="torus2" Center="0,0,-1.5"
            R1="0.5" R2="0.4"/>
        <local:TorusGeometry x:Key="torus3" Center="0,0,1.5"
            R1="0.3" R2="0.5"/>
        <local:TorusGeometry x:Key="torus4" Center="1.5,0,0"
            R1="0" R2="0.7"/>
        <local:TorusGeometry x:Key="torus5" Center="-1.5,0,0"
            R1="0.5" R2="0.5"/>
    </Window.Resources>

    <Viewport3D>
        <ContainerUIElement3D>
            <ModelUIElement3D>
                <Model3DGroup>

                    <!-- Create torus1: -->
                    <GeometryModel3D Geometry=
"{Binding Source={StaticResource torus1},Path=Mesh3D}">
                        <!-- Set material: -->
                        <GeometryModel3D.Material>
                            <MaterialGroup>
<DiffuseMaterial Brush="SteelBlue"/>
<SpecularMaterial Brush="LightBlue" SpecularPower="60"/>
                            </MaterialGroup>
                        </GeometryModel3D.Material>
                    </GeometryModel3D>

                    <!-- Create torus2: -->
                    <GeometryModel3D Geometry="
{Binding Source={StaticResource torus2},Path=Mesh3D}">
```

```xml
                            <!-- Set material: -->
                            <GeometryModel3D.Material>
                                <MaterialGroup>
        <DiffuseMaterial Brush="Goldenrod"/>
        <SpecularMaterial Brush="Yellow" SpecularPower="60"/>
                                </MaterialGroup>
                            </GeometryModel3D.Material>

                            <!-- Set rotation: -->
                            <GeometryModel3D.Transform>
                                <RotateTransform3D CenterX="0"
                                    CenterY="0" CenterZ="-1.5">
                                    <RotateTransform3D.Rotation>
                                        <AxisAngleRotation3D
                                            x:Name="rotate2"
                                            Axis="1,0,0"/>
                                    </RotateTransform3D.Rotation>
                                </RotateTransform3D>
                            </GeometryModel3D.Transform>
                        </GeometryModel3D>

                        <!-- Create torus3: -->
                        <GeometryModel3D Geometry="
        {Binding Source={StaticResource torus3},Path=Mesh3D}">
                            <!-- Set material: -->
                            <GeometryModel3D.Material>
                                <MaterialGroup>
        <DiffuseMaterial Brush="Green"/>
        <SpecularMaterial Brush="LightGreen" SpecularPower="60"/>
                                </MaterialGroup>
                            </GeometryModel3D.Material>

                            <!-- Set rotation: -->
                            <GeometryModel3D.Transform>
                                <RotateTransform3D CenterX="0"
                                    CenterY="0" CenterZ="1.5">
                                    <RotateTransform3D.Rotation>
                                        <AxisAngleRotation3D
                                            x:Name="rotate3"
                                            Axis="1,0,0"/>
                                    </RotateTransform3D.Rotation>
                                </RotateTransform3D>
                            </GeometryModel3D.Transform>
                        </GeometryModel3D>

                        <!-- Create torus4: -->
                        <GeometryModel3D Geometry="
        {Binding Source={StaticResource torus4},Path=Mesh3D}">
                            <!-- Set material: -->
                            <GeometryModel3D.Material>
                                <MaterialGroup>
        <DiffuseMaterial Brush="Red"/>
        <SpecularMaterial Brush="Yellow" SpecularPower="60"/>
                                </MaterialGroup>
```

```
        </GeometryModel3D.Material>

        <!-- Set rotation: -->
        <GeometryModel3D.Transform>
            <RotateTransform3D CenterX="1.5"
                CenterY="0" CenterZ="0">
                <RotateTransform3D.Rotation>
                    <AxisAngleRotation3D
                        x:Name="rotate4"
                        Axis="0,0,1"/>
                </RotateTransform3D.Rotation>
            </RotateTransform3D>
        </GeometryModel3D.Transform>
    </GeometryModel3D>

    <!-- Create torus5: -->
    <GeometryModel3D Geometry=
"{Binding Source={StaticResource torus5},Path=Mesh3D}">

        <!-- Set material: -->
        <GeometryModel3D.Material>
            <MaterialGroup>
<DiffuseMaterial Brush="Coral"/>
<SpecularMaterial Brush="LightCoral" SpecularPower="60"/>
            </MaterialGroup>
        </GeometryModel3D.Material>

        <!-- Set rotation: -->
        <GeometryModel3D.Transform>
            <RotateTransform3D CenterX="-1.5"
                CenterY="0" CenterZ="0">
                <RotateTransform3D.Rotation>
                    <AxisAngleRotation3D
                        x:Name="rotate5"
                        Axis="0,0,1"/>
                </RotateTransform3D.Rotation>
            </RotateTransform3D>
        </GeometryModel3D.Transform>
    </GeometryModel3D>

    <!-- Set light source: -->
    <DirectionalLight Color="Gray"
                Direction="-1,-1,-1" />
    <AmbientLight Color="Gray"/>

    <!-- Set rotation for Model3DGroup -->
    <Model3DGroup.Transform>
        <RotateTransform3D>
            <RotateTransform3D.Rotation>
                <AxisAngleRotation3D
                    x:Name="rotate"
                    Axis="0,1,0"/>
            </RotateTransform3D.Rotation>
        </RotateTransform3D>
```

```
                    </Model3DGroup.Transform>
                </Model3DGroup>
            </ModelUIElement3D>
        </ContainerUIElement3D>

        <!-- Set camera: -->
        <Viewport3D.Camera>
            <PerspectiveCamera Position="4,5,6"
                        LookDirection="-4,-5,-6"
                        UpDirection="0,1,0"/>
        </Viewport3D.Camera>
    </Viewport3D>

    <Window.Triggers>
        <EventTrigger RoutedEvent="Window.Loaded">
            <BeginStoryboard>
                <Storyboard>
                    <DoubleAnimation
                        Storyboard.TargetName="rotate"
                        Storyboard.TargetProperty="Angle"
                        From="0" To="360" Duration="0:0:5"
                        RepeatBehavior="Forever"/>

                    <DoubleAnimation
                        Storyboard.TargetName="rotate2"
                        Storyboard.TargetProperty="Angle"
                        From="0" To="360" Duration="0:0:1"
                        RepeatBehavior="Forever"/>

                    <DoubleAnimation
                        Storyboard.TargetName="rotate3"
                        Storyboard.TargetProperty="Angle"
                        From="0" To="360" Duration="0:0:1"
                        RepeatBehavior="Forever"/>

                    <DoubleAnimation
                        Storyboard.TargetName="rotate4"
                        Storyboard.TargetProperty="Angle"
                        From="0" To="360" Duration="0:0:1"
                        RepeatBehavior="Forever"/>

                    <DoubleAnimation
                        Storyboard.TargetName="rotate5"
                        Storyboard.TargetProperty="Angle"
                        From="0" To="360" Duration="0:0:1"
                        RepeatBehavior="Forever"/>
                </Storyboard>
            </BeginStoryboard>
        </EventTrigger>
    </Window.Triggers>
</Window>
```

In the Window Resources section, you define five torus geometries using different sets of parameters that generate different torus-like shapes. You can even create a sphere by setting R1 = 0. Within the GeometryModel3D element you can then reference those resources with data binding. In this way, the geometry you have defined in the TorusGeometry class is assigned to the Geometry property of the GeometryModel3D element in your XAML file.

The XAML file also applies several rotation animations for the rotation transform of these torus objects. Here you specify a rotation transform for a Model3DGroup that contains five torus objects. This transform rotates all the objects as a single group. You can also specify rotations for an individual torus that generates spin around the torus1 object.

Figure 11-4 shows the results of running this application.

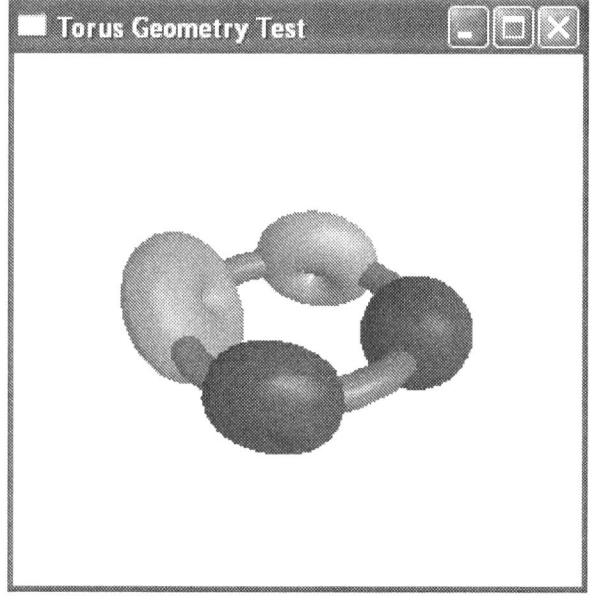

Figure 11-5 Torus objects created using custom geometry.

Icosahedron Geometry

A regular icosahedron is a polyhedron that has 20 equilateral triangular faces, with five meeting at each vertex. It also has 30 edges and 12 vertices. In a Cartesian coordinate system, the coordinates of the vertices of an icosahedrom with a edge length of 2, centered at the origin, are described by

$$(0, \pm 1, \pm \varphi)$$
$$(\pm 1, \pm \varphi, 0)$$
$$(\pm \varphi, 0, \pm 1)$$

where $\varphi = (1+\sqrt{5})/2$ is the golden ratio.

IcosahedronGeometry Class

Add a new class called IcosahedronGeometry to the Chapter11 project, and change its namespace from Chapter11 to Geometries. The procedure to create the custom IcosahedronGeometry class is the same as that for the torus in the previous section. The difference is in the algorithm used to create the mesh geometry. Here is the code listing of this class:

```
using System;
using System.Windows;
using System.Windows.Media;
using System.Windows.Media.Media3D;

namespace Geometries
{
    public class IcosahedronGeometry
    {
        // Define private fields:
        private double sideLength = 1.0;
        private Point3D center = new Point3D();

        // Define public properties:
        public double SideLength
        {
            get { return sideLength; }
            set { sideLength = value; }
        }

        public Point3D Center
        {
            get { return center; }
            set { center = value; }
        }

        // Get-only property generates MeshGeometry3D object:
        public MeshGeometry3D Mesh3D
        {
            get { return GetMesh3D(); }
        }

        private MeshGeometry3D GetMesh3D()
        {
            MeshGeometry3D mesh = new MeshGeometry3D();
            Point3D[] pts = new Point3D[12];

            double phi = 0.5 * SideLength *
                             (1 + Math.Sqrt(5.0));

            pts[0] = new Point3D(SideLength, 0, phi);
            pts[1] = new Point3D(-SideLength, 0, phi);
```

```
pts[2] = new Point3D(0, phi, SideLength);
pts[3] = new Point3D(0, -phi, SideLength);
pts[4] = new Point3D(phi, SideLength, 0);
pts[5] = new Point3D(-phi, SideLength, 0);
pts[6] = new Point3D(-phi, -SideLength, 0);
pts[7] = new Point3D(phi, -SideLength, 0);
pts[8] = new Point3D(0, phi, -SideLength);
pts[9] = new Point3D(0, -phi, -SideLength);
pts[10] = new Point3D(SideLength, 0, -phi);
pts[11] = new Point3D(-SideLength, 0, -phi);

for (int i = 0; i < 12; i++)
    pts[i] += (Vector3D)Center;

// Face1:
mesh.Positions.Add(pts[0]);
mesh.Positions.Add(pts[1]);
mesh.Positions.Add(pts[3]);

// Face2:
mesh.Positions.Add(pts[0]);
mesh.Positions.Add(pts[2]);
mesh.Positions.Add(pts[1]);

// Face3:
mesh.Positions.Add(pts[0]);
mesh.Positions.Add(pts[3]);
mesh.Positions.Add(pts[7]);

// Face4:
mesh.Positions.Add(pts[0]);
mesh.Positions.Add(pts[7]);
mesh.Positions.Add(pts[4]);

// Face5:
mesh.Positions.Add(pts[0]);
mesh.Positions.Add(pts[4]);
mesh.Positions.Add(pts[2]);

// Face6:
mesh.Positions.Add(pts[7]);
mesh.Positions.Add(pts[10]);
mesh.Positions.Add(pts[4]);

// Face7:
mesh.Positions.Add(pts[4]);
mesh.Positions.Add(pts[10]);
mesh.Positions.Add(pts[8]);

// Face8:
mesh.Positions.Add(pts[4]);
mesh.Positions.Add(pts[8]);
mesh.Positions.Add(pts[2]);
```

```
// Face9:
mesh.Positions.Add(pts[2]);
mesh.Positions.Add(pts[8]);
mesh.Positions.Add(pts[5]);

// Face10:
mesh.Positions.Add(pts[2]);
mesh.Positions.Add(pts[5]);
mesh.Positions.Add(pts[1]);

// Face11:
mesh.Positions.Add(pts[1]);
mesh.Positions.Add(pts[5]);
mesh.Positions.Add(pts[6]);

// Face12:
mesh.Positions.Add(pts[1]);
mesh.Positions.Add(pts[6]);
mesh.Positions.Add(pts[3]);

// Face13:
mesh.Positions.Add(pts[3]);
mesh.Positions.Add(pts[6]);
mesh.Positions.Add(pts[9]);

// Face14:
mesh.Positions.Add(pts[3]);
mesh.Positions.Add(pts[9]);
mesh.Positions.Add(pts[7]);

// Face15:
mesh.Positions.Add(pts[7]);
mesh.Positions.Add(pts[9]);
mesh.Positions.Add(pts[10]);

// Face16:
mesh.Positions.Add(pts[11]);
mesh.Positions.Add(pts[10]);
mesh.Positions.Add(pts[9]);

// Face17:
mesh.Positions.Add(pts[11]);
mesh.Positions.Add(pts[8]);
mesh.Positions.Add(pts[10]);

// Face18:
mesh.Positions.Add(pts[11]);
mesh.Positions.Add(pts[5]);
mesh.Positions.Add(pts[8]);

// Face19:
mesh.Positions.Add(pts[11]);
mesh.Positions.Add(pts[6]);
mesh.Positions.Add(pts[5]);
```

```
            // Face20:
            mesh.Positions.Add(pts[11]);
            mesh.Positions.Add(pts[9]);
            mesh.Positions.Add(pts[6]);

            for (int i = 0; i < 60; i++)
                mesh.TriangleIndices.Add(i);

            mesh.Freeze();
            return mesh;
        }
    }
}
```

In this class, you define two field members, including the sideLength and center, as well as their corresponding public properties. The SideLength property can be considered as a scaling factor for the edge length of the icosahedron. You can use this property to control the size of the icosahedron object.

Since each face of the icosahedron is already a triangle, it doesn't need any further triangulation. You first define the coordinates of 12 vertices with the scaling factor of the SideLength, and then add the three vertices for each triangular face to the Positions collection by proper configurations using the right-hand rule. The order of the Positions automatically determines the TriangleIndices:

```
        for (int i = 0; i < 60; i++)
          mesh.TriangleIndices.Add(i);
```

You can see that even though the icosahedron object has only 12 vertices, you need to add 60 vertices to the Postions collection to avoid using shared vertices for different surfaces.

Finally, you use the get-only property of the MeshGeomery3D type named Mesh3D to create a new MeshGeometry3D object by calling the GetMesh3D method, and return that object. Every time the Mesh3D property in your IcosahedronGeometry class is accessed, it returns a new MeshGeometry3D object by calling the GetMesh3D method based on the current settings of the properties defined in your class.

Testing IcosahedronGeometry

You can use the IcosahedromGeomtry class in a XAML file by defining an IcosahedronGeometry object in the Resources section of the XAML file. If you want to use it in code, you can simply create an instance of the custom class and assign the Geometry property of a GeometryModel3D object using the Mesh3D property of the custom geometry class.

Let's use an example to illustrate how to use the IcosahedronGeometry class in XAML. This procedure is similar to that used in the previous examples. Add a new WPF Window to the project Chapter11 and call it IcosahedronGeometryTest. Here is the XAML file of this example:

```
<Window x:Class="Chapter11.IcosahedronGeometryTest"
    xmlns="http://schemas.microsoft.com/winfx
        /2006/xaml/presentation"
    xmlns:x="http://schemas.microsoft.com/winfx/2006/xaml"
    xmlns:local="clr-namespace:Geometries"
    Title="Icosahedron Geometry Test" Height="300"
    Width="300">

    <Window.Resources>
        <local:IcosahedronGeometry x:Key="icosahedron1"
            Center="0,0,0" SideLength="0.4"/>
        <local:IcosahedronGeometry x:Key="icosahedron2"
            Center="0,0,-1.5" SideLength="0.3"/>
    </Window.Resources>

    <Viewport3D>
        <ContainerUIElement3D>
            <ModelUIElement3D>
                <Model3DGroup>

                    <!-- Create icosahedron1: -->
                    <GeometryModel3D Geometry="
                        {Binding Source={StaticResource
                            icosahedron1},Path=Mesh3D}">

                        <!-- Set material: -->
                        <GeometryModel3D.Material>
                            <DiffuseMaterial
                                Brush="SteelBlue">
                            </DiffuseMaterial>
                        </GeometryModel3D.Material>
                    </GeometryModel3D>

                    <!-- Create icosahedron2: -->
                    <GeometryModel3D Geometry=
                        "{Binding Source={StaticResource
                            icosahedron2},Path=Mesh3D}">

                        <!-- Set material: -->
                        <GeometryModel3D.Material>
                            <DiffuseMaterial
                                Brush="Goldenrod">
                            </DiffuseMaterial>
                        </GeometryModel3D.Material>

                        <!-- Set rotation: -->
                        <GeometryModel3D.Transform>
                            <RotateTransform3D CenterX="0"
                                CenterY="0" CenterZ="-1.5">
                                <RotateTransform3D.Rotation>
                                    <AxisAngleRotation3D
```

```
                                    x:Name="rotate2"
                                    Axis="0,0,1"/>
                        </RotateTransform3D.Rotation>
                    </RotateTransform3D>
                </GeometryModel3D.Transform>
            </GeometryModel3D>

            <!-- Set light source: -->
            <DirectionalLight Color="Gray"
                            Direction="-1,-1,-1" />
            <AmbientLight Color="Gray"/>

            <!-- Set rotation for Model3DGroup: -->
            <Model3DGroup.Transform>
                <RotateTransform3D>
                    <RotateTransform3D.Rotation>
                        <AxisAngleRotation3D
                                x:Name="rotate"
                                Axis="0,1,0"/>
                    </RotateTransform3D.Rotation>
                </RotateTransform3D>
            </Model3DGroup.Transform>
        </Model3DGroup>
      </ModelUIElement3D>
    </ContainerUIElement3D>

    <!-- Set camera: -->
    <Viewport3D.Camera>
        <PerspectiveCamera Position="2,3,3"
                        LookDirection="-2,-3,-3"
                        UpDirection="0,1,0"/>
    </Viewport3D.Camera>
  </Viewport3D>

  <Window.Triggers>
    <EventTrigger RoutedEvent="Window.Loaded">
        <BeginStoryboard>
            <Storyboard>
                <DoubleAnimation
                    Storyboard.TargetName="rotate"
                    Storyboard.TargetProperty="Angle"
                    From="0" To="360" Duration="0:0:5"
                    RepeatBehavior="Forever"/>

                <DoubleAnimation
                    Storyboard.TargetName="rotate2"
                    Storyboard.TargetProperty="Angle"
                    From="0" To="360" Duration="0:0:2"
                    RepeatBehavior="Forever"/>
            </Storyboard>
        </BeginStoryboard>
    </EventTrigger>
  </Window.Triggers>
</Window>
```

In the Window Resources section, you define two icosahedron geometries using different sets of parameters that generate icosahedron shapes with different size and location. Within the GeometryModel3D element you can then reference those resources with data binding. In this way, the geometry you have defined in the IcosahedronGeometry class is assigned to the Geometry property of the GeometryModel3D element in your XAML file.

The XAML file also applies two animations for the rotation transform on these icosahedron objects. One rotation transform is applied to the Model3DGroup, which contains both icosahedron objects. This transform rotates both objects as a single group. You also spply another rotation to icosahedron2, which spins around its own (0, 0, 1) axis.

Figure 11-6 shows the results of running this application.

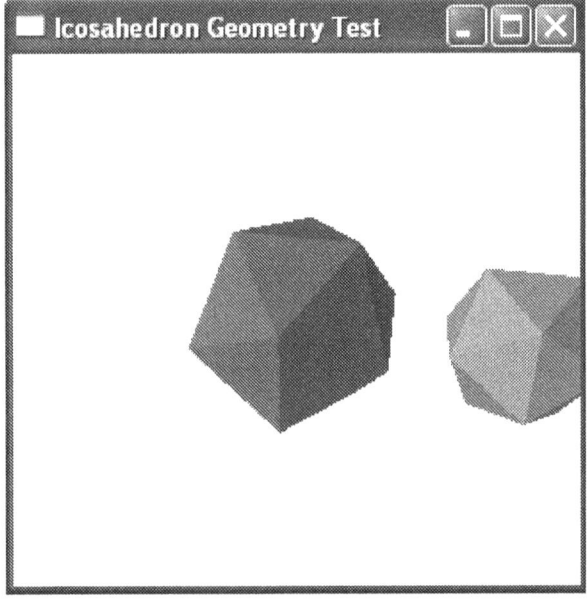

Figure 11-6 Icohedra created using custom geometry.

Dodecahedron Geometry

A regular dodecahedron consists of 12 pentagonal faces, with three meeting at each vertex. It has 20 vertices and 30 edges. The coordinates of these 20 vertices can be expressed in terms of the golden ratio $\varphi = (1 + \sqrt{5})/2$ for a dodecahedron with a side length of $2/\varphi = -1 + \sqrt{5}$:

$$(\pm 1, \pm 1, \pm 1)$$
$$(0, \pm 1/\varphi, \pm \varphi)$$
$$(\pm 1/\varphi, \pm \varphi, 0)$$
$$(\pm \varphi, 0, \pm 1/\varphi)$$

DodecahedronGeometry Class

Add a new class called DodecahedronGeometry to the project Chapter11, and change its namespace from Chapter11 to Geometries. The procedure to create your custom DodecahedronGeometry class is the same as you did for the Icosahedron in the previous section. The difference is in the algorithm used to create the mesh geometry. Here is the code listing of this class:

```
using System;
using System.Windows;
using System.Windows.Media;
using System.Windows.Media.Media3D;

namespace Geometries
{
    public class DodecahedronGeometry
    {
        // Define private fields:
        private double sideLength = 1.0;
        private Point3D center = new Point3D();

        // Define public properties:
        public double SideLength
        {
            get { return sideLength; }
            set { sideLength = value; }
        }

        public Point3D Center
        {
            get { return center; }
            set { center = value; }
        }

        // Get-only property generates MeshGeometry3D object:
        public MeshGeometry3D Mesh3D
        {
            get { return GetMesh3D(); }
        }

        private MeshGeometry3D GetMesh3D()
        {
            MeshGeometry3D mesh = new MeshGeometry3D();

            Point3D[] pts = new Point3D[20];
            double phi = 0.5 * (1 + Math.Sqrt(5.0));
```

```
double phi1 = 1.0 / phi;
phi *= SideLength;
phi1 *= SideLength;

pts[0] = new Point3D(0, phi1, phi);
pts[1] = new Point3D(0, -phi1, phi);
pts[2] = new Point3D(SideLength,
                     SideLength, SideLength);
pts[3] = new Point3D(-SideLength,
                      SideLength, SideLength);
pts[4] = new Point3D(-SideLength,
                      -SideLength, SideLength);
pts[5] = new Point3D(SideLength,
                     -SideLength, SideLength);
pts[6] = new Point3D(phi, 0, phi1);
pts[7] = new Point3D(-phi, 0, phi1);
pts[8] = new Point3D(phi1, phi, 0);
pts[9] = new Point3D(-phi1, phi, 0);
pts[10] = new Point3D(-phi1, -phi, 0);
pts[11] = new Point3D(phi1, -phi, 0);
pts[12] = new Point3D(phi, 0, -phi1);
pts[13] = new Point3D(-phi, 0, -phi1);
pts[14] = new Point3D(SideLength,
                      SideLength, -SideLength);
pts[15] = new Point3D(-SideLength,
                       SideLength, -SideLength);
pts[16] = new Point3D(-SideLength,
                       -SideLength, -SideLength);
pts[17] = new Point3D(SideLength,
                      -SideLength, -SideLength);
pts[18] = new Point3D(0, phi1, -phi);
pts[19] = new Point3D(0, -phi1, -phi);

for (int i = 0; i < 20; i++)
    pts[i] += (Vector3D)Center;

// Face1 (0,1,5,6,2):
mesh.Positions.Add(pts[0]);
mesh.Positions.Add(pts[1]);
mesh.Positions.Add(pts[2]);
mesh.Positions.Add(pts[5]);
mesh.Positions.Add(pts[6]);

mesh.TriangleIndices.Add(0);
mesh.TriangleIndices.Add(1);
mesh.TriangleIndices.Add(2);
mesh.TriangleIndices.Add(2);
mesh.TriangleIndices.Add(1);
mesh.TriangleIndices.Add(3);
mesh.TriangleIndices.Add(2);
mesh.TriangleIndices.Add(3);
mesh.TriangleIndices.Add(4);

// Face2 (0,1,4,7,3):
```

```
mesh.Positions.Add(pts[0]);
mesh.Positions.Add(pts[1]);
mesh.Positions.Add(pts[3]);
mesh.Positions.Add(pts[4]);
mesh.Positions.Add(pts[7]);

mesh.TriangleIndices.Add(5);
mesh.TriangleIndices.Add(7);
mesh.TriangleIndices.Add(9);
mesh.TriangleIndices.Add(5);
mesh.TriangleIndices.Add(9);
mesh.TriangleIndices.Add(6);
mesh.TriangleIndices.Add(6);
mesh.TriangleIndices.Add(9);
mesh.TriangleIndices.Add(8);

// Face3 (0,2,8,9,3):
mesh.Positions.Add(pts[0]);
mesh.Positions.Add(pts[2]);
mesh.Positions.Add(pts[3]);
mesh.Positions.Add(pts[8]);
mesh.Positions.Add(pts[9]);

mesh.TriangleIndices.Add(10);
mesh.TriangleIndices.Add(11);
mesh.TriangleIndices.Add(13);
mesh.TriangleIndices.Add(10);
mesh.TriangleIndices.Add(13);
mesh.TriangleIndices.Add(14);
mesh.TriangleIndices.Add(10);
mesh.TriangleIndices.Add(14);
mesh.TriangleIndices.Add(12);

// Face4 (1,4,10,11,5):
mesh.Positions.Add(pts[1]);
mesh.Positions.Add(pts[4]);
mesh.Positions.Add(pts[5]);
mesh.Positions.Add(pts[10]);
mesh.Positions.Add(pts[11]);

mesh.TriangleIndices.Add(15);
mesh.TriangleIndices.Add(16);
mesh.TriangleIndices.Add(18);
mesh.TriangleIndices.Add(15);
mesh.TriangleIndices.Add(18);
mesh.TriangleIndices.Add(17);
mesh.TriangleIndices.Add(17);
mesh.TriangleIndices.Add(18);
mesh.TriangleIndices.Add(19);

// Face5 (2,6,12,14,8):
mesh.Positions.Add(pts[2]);
mesh.Positions.Add(pts[6]);
mesh.Positions.Add(pts[8]);
```

```
mesh.Positions.Add(pts[12]);
mesh.Positions.Add(pts[14]);

mesh.TriangleIndices.Add(20);
mesh.TriangleIndices.Add(21);
mesh.TriangleIndices.Add(22);
mesh.TriangleIndices.Add(21);
mesh.TriangleIndices.Add(24);
mesh.TriangleIndices.Add(22);
mesh.TriangleIndices.Add(21);
mesh.TriangleIndices.Add(23);
mesh.TriangleIndices.Add(24);

// Face6 (3,9,15,13,7):
mesh.Positions.Add(pts[3]);
mesh.Positions.Add(pts[7]);
mesh.Positions.Add(pts[9]);
mesh.Positions.Add(pts[13]);
mesh.Positions.Add(pts[15]);

mesh.TriangleIndices.Add(25);
mesh.TriangleIndices.Add(27);
mesh.TriangleIndices.Add(26);
mesh.TriangleIndices.Add(26);
mesh.TriangleIndices.Add(27);
mesh.TriangleIndices.Add(28);
mesh.TriangleIndices.Add(28);
mesh.TriangleIndices.Add(27);
mesh.TriangleIndices.Add(29);

// Face7 (4,7,13,16,10):
mesh.Positions.Add(pts[4]);
mesh.Positions.Add(pts[7]);
mesh.Positions.Add(pts[10]);
mesh.Positions.Add(pts[13]);
mesh.Positions.Add(pts[16]);

mesh.TriangleIndices.Add(30);
mesh.TriangleIndices.Add(31);
mesh.TriangleIndices.Add(32);
mesh.TriangleIndices.Add(32);
mesh.TriangleIndices.Add(31);
mesh.TriangleIndices.Add(34);
mesh.TriangleIndices.Add(34);
mesh.TriangleIndices.Add(31);
mesh.TriangleIndices.Add(33);

// Face8 (5,11,17,12,6):
mesh.Positions.Add(pts[5]);
mesh.Positions.Add(pts[6]);
mesh.Positions.Add(pts[11]);
mesh.Positions.Add(pts[12]);
mesh.Positions.Add(pts[17]);
```

```
mesh.TriangleIndices.Add(35);
mesh.TriangleIndices.Add(37);
mesh.TriangleIndices.Add(39);
mesh.TriangleIndices.Add(35);
mesh.TriangleIndices.Add(39);
mesh.TriangleIndices.Add(38);
mesh.TriangleIndices.Add(35);
mesh.TriangleIndices.Add(38);
mesh.TriangleIndices.Add(36);

// Face9 (8,14,18,15,9):
mesh.Positions.Add(pts[8]);
mesh.Positions.Add(pts[9]);
mesh.Positions.Add(pts[14]);
mesh.Positions.Add(pts[15]);
mesh.Positions.Add(pts[18]);

mesh.TriangleIndices.Add(40);
mesh.TriangleIndices.Add(42);
mesh.TriangleIndices.Add(44);
mesh.TriangleIndices.Add(40);
mesh.TriangleIndices.Add(44);
mesh.TriangleIndices.Add(43);
mesh.TriangleIndices.Add(40);
mesh.TriangleIndices.Add(43);
mesh.TriangleIndices.Add(41);

// Face10 (10,16,19,17,11):
mesh.Positions.Add(pts[10]);
mesh.Positions.Add(pts[11]);
mesh.Positions.Add(pts[16]);
mesh.Positions.Add(pts[17]);
mesh.Positions.Add(pts[19]);

mesh.TriangleIndices.Add(45);
mesh.TriangleIndices.Add(47);
mesh.TriangleIndices.Add(49);
mesh.TriangleIndices.Add(45);
mesh.TriangleIndices.Add(49);
mesh.TriangleIndices.Add(46);
mesh.TriangleIndices.Add(46);
mesh.TriangleIndices.Add(49);
mesh.TriangleIndices.Add(48);

// Face11 (12,17,19,18,14):
mesh.Positions.Add(pts[12]);
mesh.Positions.Add(pts[14]);
mesh.Positions.Add(pts[17]);
mesh.Positions.Add(pts[18]);
mesh.Positions.Add(pts[19]);

mesh.TriangleIndices.Add(50);
mesh.TriangleIndices.Add(52);
mesh.TriangleIndices.Add(54);
```

```
mesh.TriangleIndices.Add(50);
mesh.TriangleIndices.Add(54);
mesh.TriangleIndices.Add(53);
mesh.TriangleIndices.Add(50);
mesh.TriangleIndices.Add(53);
mesh.TriangleIndices.Add(51);

// Face12 (13,15,18,19,16):
mesh.Positions.Add(pts[13]);
mesh.Positions.Add(pts[15]);
mesh.Positions.Add(pts[16]);
mesh.Positions.Add(pts[18]);
mesh.Positions.Add(pts[19]);

mesh.TriangleIndices.Add(55);
mesh.TriangleIndices.Add(56);
mesh.TriangleIndices.Add(58);
mesh.TriangleIndices.Add(55);
mesh.TriangleIndices.Add(58);
mesh.TriangleIndices.Add(59);
mesh.TriangleIndices.Add(55);
mesh.TriangleIndices.Add(59);
mesh.TriangleIndices.Add(57);

mesh.Freeze();
return mesh;
            }
        }
    }
```

In this class, you define two field members, including the sideLength and center, as well as their corresponding public properties. The SideLength property can be considered as a scaling factor for the edge length of the dodecahedron. You can use this property to control the size of the dodecahedron object.

Since each of the 12 faces of the dodecahedron is a pentagonal surface, you need three triangles to represent each pentagonal face. For each face, you add five vertices to the Positions collection of the MeshGeometry3D object, and then define the three triangles by assigning TriangleIndices with a proper configuration of the vertex order in the Positions collection.

You can see that even though the dodecahedron object has only 20 vertices, you need to add 60 vertices to the Postions collection to avoid using shared vertices for different pentagonal surfaces.

Finally, you use the get-only property of the MeshGeomery3D type named Mesh3D to create a new MeshGeometry3D object by calling the GetMesh3D method, and return that object. Every time the Mesh3D property in the IcosahedronGeometry class is accessed, it returns a new MeshGeometry3D object by calling the GetMesh3D method based on the current settings of the properties defined in your class.

Testing DodecahedronGeometry

You can use the DodecahedromGeomtry class in a XAML file by defining a DodecahedronGeometry object in the Resources section of the XAML file. If you want to use it in code, you can simply create an instance of your custom class and assign the Geometry property of a GeometryModel3D object using the Mesh3D property of your custom geometry class.

Let's use an example to illustrate how to use the DodecahedronGeometry class in XAML. This procedure is similar to that used in the previous example. Add a new WPF Window to the project Chapter11 and call it DodecahedronGeometryTest. Here is the XAML file of this example:

```
<Window x:Class="Chapter11.DodecahedronGeometryTest"
    xmlns="http://schemas.microsoft.com/winfx
        /2006/xaml/presentation"
    xmlns:x="http://schemas.microsoft.com/winfx/2006/xaml"
    xmlns:local="clr-namespace:Geometries"
    Title="Dodecahedron Geometry Test" Height="300"
    Width="300">

    <Window.Resources>
        <local:DodecahedronGeometry x:Key="dodecahedron"
            Center="0,0,0" SideLength="0.4"/>
    </Window.Resources>

    <Viewport3D>
        <ContainerUIElement3D>
            <ModelUIElement3D>
                <Model3DGroup>

                    <!-- Create first dodecahedron: -->
                    <GeometryModel3D Geometry=
                        "{Binding Source={StaticResource
                            dodecahedron},Path=Mesh3D}">

                        <!-- Set material: -->
                        <GeometryModel3D.Material>
                            <DiffuseMaterial
                                Brush="SteelBlue">
                            </DiffuseMaterial>
                        </GeometryModel3D.Material>
                    </GeometryModel3D>

                    <!-- Create second dodecahedron: -->
                    <GeometryModel3D Geometry=
                        "{Binding Source={StaticResource
                            dodecahedron},Path=Mesh3D}">

                        <!-- Set material: -->
                        <GeometryModel3D.Material>
                            <DiffuseMaterial
                                Brush="Goldenrod">
```

```
                        </DiffuseMaterial>
                    </GeometryModel3D.Material>

                    <!-- Set transforms: -->
                    <GeometryModel3D.Transform>
                        <Transform3DGroup>
                            <TranslateTransform3D
                                OffsetZ="-2"/>
                            <ScaleTransform3D ScaleX="0.7"
                                            ScaleY="0.7"
                                            ScaleZ="0.7"/>
                            <RotateTransform3D>
                              <RotateTransform3D.Rotation>
                                <AxisAngleRotation3D
                                    x:Name="rotate2"
                                    Axis="0,0,1"/>
                              </RotateTransform3D.Rotation>
                            </RotateTransform3D>
                        </Transform3DGroup>
                    </GeometryModel3D.Transform>
                </GeometryModel3D>

                <!-- Set light source: -->
                <DirectionalLight Color="Gray"
                    Direction="-1,-2,-2" />
                <AmbientLight Color="Gray"/>

                <!-- Set rotation for Model3DGroup: -->
                <Model3DGroup.Transform>
                    <RotateTransform3D>
                        <RotateTransform3D.Rotation>
                            <AxisAngleRotation3D
                                x:Name="rotate"
                                Axis="0,1,0"/>
                        </RotateTransform3D.Rotation>
                    </RotateTransform3D>
                </Model3DGroup.Transform>
            </Model3DGroup>
        </ModelUIElement3D>
    </ContainerUIElement3D>

    <!-- Set camera: -->
    <Viewport3D.Camera>
        <PerspectiveCamera Position="2,3,3"
                        LookDirection="-2,-3,-3"
                        UpDirection="0,1,0"/>
    </Viewport3D.Camera>
</Viewport3D>

<Window.Triggers>
    <EventTrigger RoutedEvent="Window.Loaded">
        <BeginStoryboard>
            <Storyboard>
                <DoubleAnimation
```

```
            Storyboard.TargetName="rotate"
            Storyboard.TargetProperty="Angle"
            From="0" To="360" Duration="0:0:5"
            RepeatBehavior="Forever"/>

        <DoubleAnimation
            Storyboard.TargetName="rotate2"
            Storyboard.TargetProperty="Angle"
            From="0" To="360" Duration="0:0:2"
            RepeatBehavior="Forever"/>
        </Storyboard>
      </BeginStoryboard>
    </EventTrigger>
  </Window.Triggers>
</Window>
```

In the Window Resources section, you define a dodecahedron geometry using the custom DodecahedronGeometry. Within the GeometryModel3D element you can then reference this resource with data binding, and create two dodecahedron objects. You perform a series of transforms on the second dodecahedron, including translation, scaling, and rotation. This way, you change the size and location of the second dodecahedron from the original model defined in the resource.

The XAML file also applies two animations for the rotation transform on these dodecahedron objects. One animation is applied to the Model3DGroup, which contains both dodecahedron objects. This animation rotates both objects as a single group. You also apply the animation to the rotation transform on the second dodecahedron that spins around its own (0, 0, 1) axis.

Figure 11-7 shows the results of running this example.

Soccer Ball Geometry

A soccer ball shape is a truncated icosahedron. It can be constructed from a regular icosahedron with the 12 vertices truncated (cut off) so that one third of each edge is cut off at each of both ends. This creates a soccer ball shape that has 12 pentagonal faces, 20 hexagonal faces, 60 vertices, and 90 edges.

The coordinates of these 60 vertices can also be expressed in terms of the golden ratio $\varphi = (1 + \sqrt{5})/2$:

$$(0, \pm 1, \pm 3\varphi)$$
$$(\pm 1, \pm 3\varphi, 0)$$
$$(\pm 3\varphi, 0, \pm 1)$$
$$(\pm 2, \pm(1 + 2\varphi), \pm \varphi)$$
$$(\pm(1 + 2\varphi), \pm \varphi, \pm 2)$$

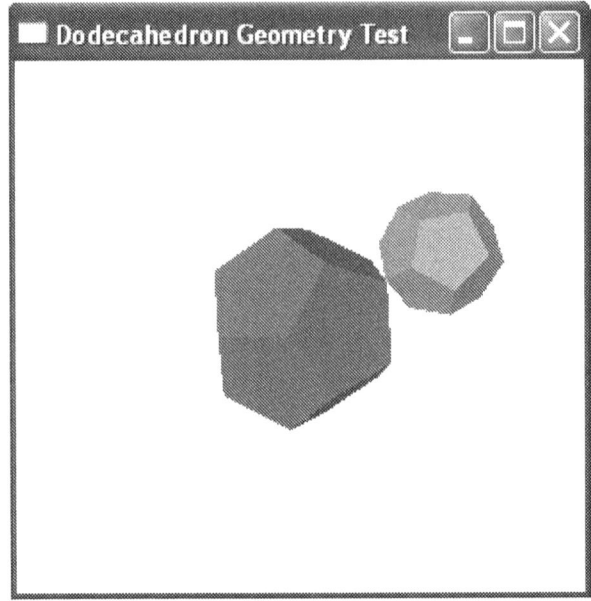

Figure 11-7 Dodecahedra created using custom geometry.

$$(\pm\varphi, \pm 2, \pm(1+2\varphi))$$
$$(\pm 1, \pm(2+\varphi), \pm 2\varphi)$$
$$(\pm(2+\varphi), \pm 2\varphi, \pm 1)$$
$$(\pm 2\varphi, \pm 1, \pm(2+\varphi))$$

Using the fact of $\varphi^2 = \varphi + 1$, you can easily verify that all the vertices are on a sphere, centered at the origin, with a radius equal to $\sqrt{9\varphi + 10}$. The edges have a length of 2.

SoccerGeometry Class

You can see that a soccer ball geometry is much more complex than an icosahedron or a dodecahedron. If you really want to create a soccer ball (not just geometry), you also need to paint the pentagonal faces and hexagonal faces with different colors! Thus, the SoccerGeometry class is required to return not only the mesh geometry for all the faces (pentagons + hexagons) but also the mesh geometries for pentagon-only and hexagon-only faces. This capability of returning different types of mesh geometries from the SoccerGeometry class allows you to specify different materials (or colors) for the pentagonal faces and hexagonal faces, respectively.

Now let's begin by writing the code for the soccer ball geometry. Add a new class called SoccerGeometry to the project Chapter11, and change its namespace from Chapter11 to Geometries. The procedure to create the custom

SoccerGeometry class is the same as you did for the Dodecahedron in the previous section. The difference is in the algorithm used to create the mesh geometry. Here is the code listing of this class:

```csharp
using System;
using System.Windows;
using System.Windows.Media;
using System.Windows.Media.Media3D;

namespace Geometries
{
    public class SoccerGeometry
    {
        // Define private fields:
        private double sideLength = 1.0;
        private Point3D center = new Point3D();

        // Define public properties:
        public double SideLength
        {
            get { return sideLength; }
            set { sideLength = value; }
        }

        public Point3D Center
        {
            get { return center; }
            set { center = value; }
        }

        // Get-only property generates MeshGeometry3D object:
        public MeshGeometry3D Mesh3D
        {
            get { return GetMesh3D(); }
        }

        // Get-only property generates MeshGeometry3D object:
        public MeshGeometry3D PentagonMesh3D
        {
            get { return GetPentagonMesh3D(); }
        }

        // Get-only property generates MeshGeometry3D object:
        public MeshGeometry3D HexagonMesh3D
        {
            get { return GetHexagonMesh3D(); }
        }

        private MeshGeometry3D GetMesh3D()
        {
            MeshGeometry3D mesh = new MeshGeometry3D();

            Point3D[] pts = GetVortices();
```

```
// Face1 (hexagon):
mesh.Positions.Add(pts[29]);
mesh.Positions.Add(pts[42]);
mesh.Positions.Add(pts[46]);
mesh.Positions.Add(pts[40]);
mesh.Positions.Add(pts[28]);
mesh.Positions.Add(pts[22]);

mesh.TriangleIndices.Add(0);
mesh.TriangleIndices.Add(1);
mesh.TriangleIndices.Add(2);
mesh.TriangleIndices.Add(0);
mesh.TriangleIndices.Add(2);
mesh.TriangleIndices.Add(3);
mesh.TriangleIndices.Add(0);
mesh.TriangleIndices.Add(3);
mesh.TriangleIndices.Add(4);
mesh.TriangleIndices.Add(0);
mesh.TriangleIndices.Add(4);
mesh.TriangleIndices.Add(5);

// Face2 (hexagon):
mesh.Positions.Add(pts[29]);
mesh.Positions.Add(pts[22]);
mesh.Positions.Add(pts[11]);
mesh.Positions.Add(pts[8]);
mesh.Positions.Add(pts[14]);
mesh.Positions.Add(pts[26]);

mesh.TriangleIndices.Add(6);
mesh.TriangleIndices.Add(7);
mesh.TriangleIndices.Add(8);
mesh.TriangleIndices.Add(6);
mesh.TriangleIndices.Add(8);
mesh.TriangleIndices.Add(9);
mesh.TriangleIndices.Add(6);
mesh.TriangleIndices.Add(9);
mesh.TriangleIndices.Add(10);
mesh.TriangleIndices.Add(6);
mesh.TriangleIndices.Add(10);
mesh.TriangleIndices.Add(11);

// Face3 (pentagon):
mesh.Positions.Add(pts[29]);
mesh.Positions.Add(pts[26]);
mesh.Positions.Add(pts[34]);
mesh.Positions.Add(pts[44]);
mesh.Positions.Add(pts[42]);

mesh.TriangleIndices.Add(12);
mesh.TriangleIndices.Add(13);
mesh.TriangleIndices.Add(14);
mesh.TriangleIndices.Add(12);
mesh.TriangleIndices.Add(14);
```

```
        mesh.TriangleIndices.Add(15);
        mesh.TriangleIndices.Add(12);
        mesh.TriangleIndices.Add(15);
        mesh.TriangleIndices.Add(16);

        ..... // You need to perform triangulation for
        ..... // 32 pentagonal and hexagonal faces here.

        mesh.Freeze();
        return mesh;
    }

    private MeshGeometry3D GetHexagonMesh3D()
    {
        MeshGeometry3D mesh = new MeshGeometry3D();

        Point3D[] pts = GetVortices();

        // Face1 (hexagon):
        mesh.Positions.Add(pts[29]);
        mesh.Positions.Add(pts[42]);
        mesh.Positions.Add(pts[46]);
        mesh.Positions.Add(pts[40]);
        mesh.Positions.Add(pts[28]);
        mesh.Positions.Add(pts[22]);

        mesh.TriangleIndices.Add(0);
        mesh.TriangleIndices.Add(1);
        mesh.TriangleIndices.Add(2);
        mesh.TriangleIndices.Add(0);
        mesh.TriangleIndices.Add(2);
        mesh.TriangleIndices.Add(3);
        mesh.TriangleIndices.Add(0);
        mesh.TriangleIndices.Add(3);
        mesh.TriangleIndices.Add(4);
        mesh.TriangleIndices.Add(0);
        mesh.TriangleIndices.Add(4);
        mesh.TriangleIndices.Add(5);

        // Face2 (hexagon):
        mesh.Positions.Add(pts[29]);
        mesh.Positions.Add(pts[22]);
        mesh.Positions.Add(pts[11]);
        mesh.Positions.Add(pts[8]);
        mesh.Positions.Add(pts[14]);
        mesh.Positions.Add(pts[26]);

        mesh.TriangleIndices.Add(6);
        mesh.TriangleIndices.Add(7);
        mesh.TriangleIndices.Add(8);
        mesh.TriangleIndices.Add(6);
        mesh.TriangleIndices.Add(8);
        mesh.TriangleIndices.Add(9);
        mesh.TriangleIndices.Add(6);
```

```
        mesh.TriangleIndices.Add(9);
        mesh.TriangleIndices.Add(10);
        mesh.TriangleIndices.Add(6);
        mesh.TriangleIndices.Add(10);
        mesh.TriangleIndices.Add(11);

        ..... // You need to perform triangulation for
        ..... // 20 hexagonal faces here.

        mesh.Freeze();
        return mesh;
}

private MeshGeometry3D GetPentagonMesh3D()
{
        MeshGeometry3D mesh = new MeshGeometry3D();

        Point3D[] pts = GetVortices();

        // Face1 (pentagon):
        mesh.Positions.Add(pts[29]);
        mesh.Positions.Add(pts[26]);
        mesh.Positions.Add(pts[34]);
        mesh.Positions.Add(pts[44]);
        mesh.Positions.Add(pts[42]);

        mesh.TriangleIndices.Add(0);
        mesh.TriangleIndices.Add(1);
        mesh.TriangleIndices.Add(2);
        mesh.TriangleIndices.Add(0);
        mesh.TriangleIndices.Add(2);
        mesh.TriangleIndices.Add(3);
        mesh.TriangleIndices.Add(0);
        mesh.TriangleIndices.Add(3);
        mesh.TriangleIndices.Add(4);

        // Face2 (pentagon):
        mesh.Positions.Add(pts[22]);
        mesh.Positions.Add(pts[28]);
        mesh.Positions.Add(pts[20]);
        mesh.Positions.Add(pts[10]);
        mesh.Positions.Add(pts[11]);

        mesh.TriangleIndices.Add(5);
        mesh.TriangleIndices.Add(6);
        mesh.TriangleIndices.Add(7);
        mesh.TriangleIndices.Add(5);
        mesh.TriangleIndices.Add(7);
        mesh.TriangleIndices.Add(8);
        mesh.TriangleIndices.Add(5);
        mesh.TriangleIndices.Add(8);
        mesh.TriangleIndices.Add(9);

        ..... // You need to perform triangulation for
```

```
      ….. // 12 pentagonal faces here.

      mesh.Freeze();
      return mesh;
}

private Point3D[] GetVortices()
{
      Point3D[] pts = new Point3D[60];

pts[0] = new Point3D(-1.00714, 0.153552, 0.067258);
pts[1] = new Point3D(-0.960284, 0.0848813, -0.33629);
pts[2] = new Point3D(-0.95172, -0.153552, 0.33629);
pts[3] = new Point3D(-0.860021, 0.529326, 0.150394);
pts[4] = new Point3D(-0.858, -0.290893, -0.470806);
pts[5] = new Point3D(-0.849436, -0.529326, 0.201774);
pts[6] = new Point3D(-0.802576, -0.597996, -0.201774);
pts[7] = new Point3D(-0.7842, 0.418215, -0.502561);
pts[8] = new Point3D(-0.749174, -0.0848813, 0.688458);
pts[9] = new Point3D(-0.722234, 0.692896, -0.201774);
pts[10] = new Point3D(-0.657475, 0.597996, 0.502561);
pts[11] = new Point3D(-0.602051, 0.290893, 0.771593);
pts[12] = new Point3D(-0.583675, -0.692896, 0.470806);
pts[13] = new Point3D(-0.57963, -0.333333, -0.771593);
pts[14] = new Point3D(-0.52171, -0.418215, 0.771593);
pts[15] = new Point3D(-0.505832, 0.375774, -0.803348);
pts[16] = new Point3D(-0.489955, -0.830237, -0.33629);
pts[17] = new Point3D(-0.403548, 0.0, -0.937864);
pts[18] = new Point3D(-0.381901, 0.925138, -0.201774);
pts[19] = new Point3D(-0.35217, -0.666667, -0.688458);
pts[20] = new Point3D(-0.317142, 0.830237, 0.502561);
pts[21] = new Point3D(-0.271054, -0.925138, 0.33629);
pts[22] = new Point3D(-0.227464, 0.333333, 0.937864);
pts[23] = new Point3D(-0.224193, -0.9938, -0.067258);
pts[24] = new Point3D(-0.179355, 0.993808, 0.150394);
pts[25] = new Point3D(-0.165499, 0.608015, -0.803348);
pts[26] = new Point3D(-0.147123, -0.375774, 0.937864);
pts[27] = new Point3D(-0.103533, 0.882697, -0.502561);
pts[28] = new Point3D(-0.0513806, 0.666667, 0.771593);
pts[29] = new Point3D(0.0000000, 0.0, 1.021);
pts[30] = new Point3D(0.0000000, 0.0, -1.021);
pts[31] = new Point3D(0.05138, -0.666667, -0.771593);
pts[32] = new Point3D(0.103533, -0.882697, 0.502561);
pts[33] = new Point3D(0.147123, 0.375774, -0.937864);
pts[34] = new Point3D(0.165499, -0.608015, 0.803348);
pts[35] = new Point3D(0.179355, -0.993808, -0.150394);
pts[36] = new Point3D(0.224193, 0.993808, 0.067258);
pts[37] = new Point3D(0.227464, -0.333333, -0.937864);
pts[38] = new Point3D(0.271054, 0.925138, -0.33629);
pts[39] = new Point3D(0.317142, -0.830237, -0.502561);
pts[40] = new Point3D(0.352168, 0.666667, 0.688458);
pts[41] = new Point3D(0.381901, -0.925138, 0.201774);
pts[42] = new Point3D(0.403548, 0.0, 0.937864);
pts[43] = new Point3D(0.489955, 0.830237, 0.33629);
```

```
pts[44] = new Point3D(0.505832, -0.375774, 0.803348);
pts[45] = new Point3D(0.521710, 0.418215, -0.771593);
pts[46] = new Point3D(0.579632, 0.333333, 0.771593);
pts[47] = new Point3D(0.583675, 0.692896, -0.470806);
pts[48] = new Point3D(0.602051, -0.290893, -0.771593);
pts[49] = new Point3D(0.657475, -0.597996, -0.502561);
pts[50] = new Point3D(0.722234, -0.692896, 0.201774);
pts[51] = new Point3D(0.749174, 0.0848813, -0.688458);
pts[52] = new Point3D(0.784200, -0.418215, 0.502561);
pts[53] = new Point3D(0.802576, 0.597996, 0.201774);
pts[54] = new Point3D(0.849436, 0.529326, -0.201774);
pts[55] = new Point3D(0.858000, 0.290893, 0.470806);
pts[56] = new Point3D(0.860021, -0.529326, -0.150394);
pts[57] = new Point3D(0.951720, 0.153552, -0.33629);
pts[58] = new Point3D(0.960284, -0.0848813, 0.33629);
pts[59] = new Point3D(1.007140, -0.153552, -0.067258);

    for (int i = 0; i < 60; i++)
    {
        pts[i] = new Point3D(pts[i].X * SideLength,
                             pts[i].Y * SideLength,
                             pts[i].Z * SideLength);
        pts[i] += (Vector3D)Center;
    }

    return pts;
}
}
}
```

In this class, you define two field members, including the sideLength and center, as well as their corresponding public properties. The SideLength property can be considered as a scaling factor for the edge length of the soccer ball geometry. You can use this property to control the size of the soccer ball.

As mentioned previously, you need to generate three different types of MeshGeometry3D objects: Mesh3D, PentagonMesh3D, and HexagonMesh3D, which are three get-only properties. These properties are used to create MeshGeometry3D objects for all the faces (pentagons + hexagons), pentagon-only faces, and hexagon-only faces by calling the GetMesh3D, GetPentagonMesh3D, and GetHexagonMesh3D methods respectively.

You need three or four triangles to represent each pentagonal or hexagonal face. For each pentagonal face, you add five vertices to the Positions collection of the MeshGeometry3D object. Similarly, for each hexagonal face, you add six vertices to the Positions collection. Then you define the triangles by assigning TriangleIndices with a proper vertex order comfiguration in the Positions collection.

For the 12 pentagon-only faces, you need to add 60 vertices to the Postions collection in order to avoid using shared vertices for different pentagonal surfaces. For the 20 hexagon-only faces, 120 vertices need to be added to the Positions collection. For the total 32 faces of the soccer geometry, you need to add 180 vertices to the Positions collection. This triangulation process is too long to be listed here in this book, so I omit these details in the above code listing. You can view the complete source code by opening the SoccerGeometry class from project Chapter11 with Visual Studio 2008.

The coordinates for the 60 vertices of the soccer geometry used here are not directly calculated using the golden ratio. Instead, I took the data file from a Fortran program that has been used to create soccer ball geomentry. The length for all the edges is scaled by a scaling factor of SideLength which is a public property defined at the beginning of the SoccerGeometry class.

Testing SoccerGeometry

You can use the SoccerGeometry class in a XAML file to create a soccer ball by defining a SoccerGeometry object in the Resources section of the XAML file. If you want to use it in code, you can simply create an instance of your custom class and assign the Geometry property of a GeometryModel3D object using the Mesh3D property of your custom geometry class.

Let's use an example to illustrate how to use the SoccerGeometry class in XAML. This procedure is similar to that used in the previous examples. Add a new WPF Window to the project Chapter11 and call it SoccerGeometryTest. Here is the XAML file of this example:

```
<Window x:Class="Chapter11.SoccerGeometryTest"
    xmlns="http://schemas.microsoft.com/winfx
        /2006/xaml/presentation"
    xmlns:x="http://schemas.microsoft.com/winfx/2006/xaml"
    xmlns:local="clr-namespace:Geometries"
    Title="Soccer Geometry Test" Height="300" Width="300">

    <Window.Resources>
        <local:SoccerGeometry x:Key="soccer"
                        Center="0,0,0"
                        SideLength="0.7"/>
    </Window.Resources>

    <Viewport3D>
        <ContainerUIElement3D>
            <ModelUIElement3D>
                <Model3DGroup>

                    <!-- Create soccer1: -->
                    <GeometryModel3D Geometry=
                        "{Binding Source={StaticResource
                            soccer},Path=HexagonMesh3D}">

                        <!-- Set material for hexagons: -->
                        <GeometryModel3D.Material>
                            <DiffuseMaterial Brush="White">
                            </DiffuseMaterial>
                        </GeometryModel3D.Material>
```

```xml
    </GeometryModel3D>

    <GeometryModel3D Geometry=
        "{Binding Source={StaticResource
            soccer},Path=PentagonMesh3D}">
        <!-- Set material for pentagons: -->
        <GeometryModel3D.Material>
            <DiffuseMaterial Brush="Black">
            </DiffuseMaterial>
        </GeometryModel3D.Material>
    </GeometryModel3D>

    <!-- Create soccer2: -->
    <GeometryModel3D Geometry=
        "{Binding Source={StaticResource
            soccer},Path=Mesh3D}">

        <!-- Set material: -->
        <GeometryModel3D.Material>
            <DiffuseMaterial
                Brush="LightCoral">
            </DiffuseMaterial>
        </GeometryModel3D.Material>

        <!-- Set Transforms: -->
        <GeometryModel3D.Transform>
            <Transform3DGroup>
                <TranslateTransform3D
                    OffsetZ="-2.5"/>
                <ScaleTransform3D ScaleX="0.5"
                                  ScaleY="0.5"
                                  ScaleZ="0.5"/>
                <RotateTransform3D>
                  <RotateTransform3D.Rotation>
                      <AxisAngleRotation3D
                          x:Name="rotate2"
                          Axis="0,0,1"/>
                  </RotateTransform3D.Rotation>
                </RotateTransform3D>
            </Transform3DGroup>
        </GeometryModel3D.Transform>
    </GeometryModel3D>

    <!-- Set light source: -->
    <DirectionalLight Color="Gray"
                 Direction="-1,-1,-1" />
    <AmbientLight Color="Gray"/>

    <!--Rotation of Model3DGroup -->
    <Model3DGroup.Transform>
        <RotateTransform3D>
            <RotateTransform3D.Rotation>
                <AxisAngleRotation3D
                    x:Name="rotate"
```

```
                                Axis="0,1,0"/>
                    </RotateTransform3D.Rotation>
                </RotateTransform3D>
            </Model3DGroup.Transform>
        </Model3DGroup>
    </ModelUIElement3D>
</ContainerUIElement3D>

<!-- Set camera: -->
<Viewport3D.Camera>
    <PerspectiveCamera Position="2,3,3"
                       LookDirection="-2,-3,-3"
                       UpDirection="0,1,0"/>
</Viewport3D.Camera>
</Viewport3D>

<Window.Triggers>
    <EventTrigger RoutedEvent="Window.Loaded">
        <BeginStoryboard>
            <Storyboard>
                <DoubleAnimation
                    Storyboard.TargetName="rotate"
                    Storyboard.TargetProperty="Angle"
                    From="0" To="360" Duration="0:0:5"
                    RepeatBehavior="Forever"/>

                <DoubleAnimation
                    Storyboard.TargetName="rotate2"
                    Storyboard.TargetProperty="Angle"
                    From="0" To="360" Duration="0:0:2"
                    RepeatBehavior="Forever"/>
            </Storyboard>
        </BeginStoryboard>
    </EventTrigger>
</Window.Triggers>
</Window>
```

To create the soccer ball, you define a soccer geometry using the custom SoccerGeometry in the Window Resources section. Pay close attention to how you create the soccer ball. Within the GeometryModel3D element you reference this resource twice; first you bind the Geometry property of the GeometryModel3D to the HexagonMesh3D, and paint the hexagonal faces with the white color by specifying its material using a white brush. Then you bind the PentagonMesh3D to the Geometry property of another GeometryModel3D object and paint the pentagonal faces with a black color through its material definition. The soccer ball is formed with these two GeometryModel3D objects. You also create a soccer ball with a single color by binding the Mesh3D to the Geometry property of the GeometryModel3D. In this case, only a single material needs to be specified for both the pentagonal and the hexagonal faces. You also perform a series of transforms on the second soccer ball, including translation, scaling, and rotation. This way, you can change the size and location of the second soccer ball from the original model defined in the resource.

The XAML file also applies two animations for the rotation transform on these soccer balls. One animation is applied to the Model3DGroup that contains both soccer balls. This animation rotates both objects as a single group. You also apply the animation to the rotation transform on the second soccer ball that spins around its own (0, 0, 1) axis.

This application generates the results shown in Figure 11-8.

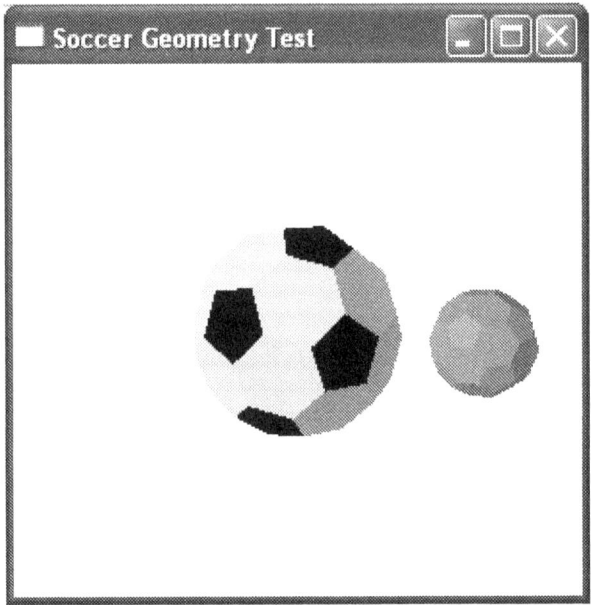

Figure 11-8 Soccer balls created using custom geometry.

In this chapter, you have created a variety of custom geometry classes. The custom classes can be used as a resource in XAML files that can be referred in your markup with a data binding. This provides a quick way to define custom geometry classes that are suitable for use as a shareable resource in a XAML file. You can even animate and transform the GeometryModel3D or Model3DGroup that makes use of these custom objects.

However, the properties defined in your custom geometry class can't be directly animated or changed by the user of your program. For example, you can't animate the SideLength and Center properties defined in your SoccerGeometry class, because WPF only allows one to animate the dependency properties. For example, you can't make the SideLength and Center properties of a SoccerGeometry the targets of data binding, indicating that these properties can't be controlled using a slider control.

In order to avoid these limitations, you need to change the properties defined in the custom geometry classes to corresponding dependency properties. Please note that even though you create the custom geometry class using dependency properties, this class still can't used directly in XAML files. It can only be used as the Window Resoures. I'll not discuss this approach in thie book.

In the next chapter, you'll learn how to create custom 3D shape classes using dependency properties. These custom 3D shapes can be used the same way as 2D shapes; i.e., they can be used directly in XAML files and their dependency properties can be animated and changed directly by the user.

Chapter 12
Custom 3D Shapes

In Chapter 11, you learned how to write custom geometry classes for basic 3D shapes. Although these geometry classes can be used as a shareable resource, they can't be used directly in XAML files. You may ask if one can go a step farther along this direction. The answer is yes. In this chapter, you'll learn how to write custom 3D shape classes that can be used in the same way as the 2D shapes, such as the Line, Rectangle, and Ellipse. You can use these custom 3D shape classes to implement a powerful 3D model library.

In .NET 3.0, WPF only has one unsealed class, called ModelVisual3D, in the entire System.Windows.Media.Media3D namespace. This class is purposely made available for inheritance. In .NET 3.5, WPF has one more class, UIElement3D, that allows you to create your own elements, which can respond to input, focus, and eventing. In this chapter, I'll show you how to create custom shape classes that derive from the UIElement3D class.

Deriving from UIElement3D

UIElement3D itself is an abstract class deriving from Visual3D. You can create a 3D custom shape that can derive from the UIElement3D class:

```
Public class CustomShape : UIElement3D
{
    .....
}
```

Even though the UIElement3D class is declared as an abstract class, it contains no any abstract method that you need to override. What you need to do is to define the dependency properties for the CustomShape to control how your shape looks using standard C# WPF code. Then you need to call the InvalidateModel method whenever any of your dependency properties changes. Here the InvalidateModel method is similar to the InvalidateVisual method existing for the 2D UIElement. Calling the InvalidateModel method indicates that the 3D model representing the UIElement 3D object has changed and should be updated.

For example, suppose the CustomShape has a Center dependency property, defined using the following code snippet:

```
public static readonly DependencyProperty CenterProperty =
    DependencyProperty.Register("Center",
    typeof(Point3D), typeof(Dodecahedron),
    new PropertyMetadata(new Point3D(0.0, 0.0, 0.0),
    PropertyChanged));

public Point3D Center
{
    get { return (Point3D)GetValue(CenterProperty); }
    set { SetValue(CenterProperty, value); }
}

private static void PropertyChanged(DependencyObject d,
    DependencyPropertyChangedEventArgs e)
{
    CustomShape cs = (CustomShape)d;
    cs.InvalidateModel();
}
```

You can see that the Center dependency property is associated with a PropertyChanged handler. Inside this handler, you call the InvalidateModel method whenever you change the Center property.

In response to the InvalidateModel, the OnUpdateModel method will be called to update the 3D model that represents the custom shape object. In this way, you can make multiple changes to properties that affect the visual appearance of the UIElement3D object and only make one final change to the model, rather than having to regenerate it each time a change is made.

You may wonder how WPF actually changes the 3D model. In .NET 3.5, Visual3D exposes a protected CLR property Visual3DModel, which represents the 3D model for the object. In order to set the visual representation for the Visual3D, you need to specify this property. There is one subtle point about setting this property. Just like with render data, setting this property will not set up the links necessary for things such as data bindings to work. To make this work properly, you need to have a dependency property for the model itself.

The code for the OnUpdateModel method is shown below, as well as the Model dependency property:

```
protected override void OnUpdateModel()
{
    GeometryModel3D model = new GeometryModel3D();

    model.Geometry = GetMesh3D();
    model.Material = new DiffuseMaterial(Brushes.Blue);

        Model = model;
```

```
}

// The Model property for your custom shape:
private static readonly DependencyProperty
    ModelProperty = DependencyProperty.Register(
        "Model", typeof(Model3D), typeof(CustomShape),
        new PropertyMetadata(ModelPropertyChanged));

private static void ModelPropertyChanged(
    DependencyObject d, DependencyPropertyChangedEventArgs e)
{
    CustomShape cs = (CustomShape)d;
    cs.Visual3DModel = (Model3D)e.NewValue;
}

private Model3D Model
{
    get { return (Model3D)GetValue(ModelProperty); }
    set { SetValue(ModelProperty, value); }
}
```

The custom shape that you create using this approach inherits many advanced features from UIElement3D, including input, focus, and eventing. For example, if you want to create a CustomShape object that responds to mouse events, you can simply use the following statement:

```
<local:CustomShape MouseDown="OnMouseDown"/>
```

And then in the code-behind file, you can implement the corresponding MouseDown event handler:

```
Private void OnMouseDown(object sender,
                         MouseButtonEventArgs e)
{
    // Add action code here.
}
```

If you have experience dealing with 2D event handlers, then this should immediately look familiar. Your CustomShape object can handle the same routed events that a 2D UIElement deals with. Thus, with your custom shape object, you can have the same great functionality that UIElement provides to 2D, but now in the 3D world.

Following the above description, you should be able to write the code for custom 3D shapes. You can also reuse the custom geometry classes, which you created in Chapter 11, to create your custom shape classes, because you don't need to regenerate the triangular meshes for the various 3D geometries.

Now, start with a new WPF Window project and name it Chapter12. Add all eight custom geometry classes from the project Chapter11 to the current project. You will use these geometry classes to create your custom 3D shapes in the following sections.

Cube Shape

In this section, you'll learn how to create a simple custom cube shape that can be used the same way as 2D shapes.

Cube Shape Class

Open project Chapter12, add a new class to the project, change its namespace to Shapes, and name it Cube. The following is the code listing of this class:

```csharp
using System;
using System.Windows;
using System.Windows.Media;
using System.Windows.Media.Media3D;
using Geometries;

namespace Shapes
{
    public class Cube : UIElement3D
    {
        protected override void OnUpdateModel()
        {
            GeometryModel3D model = new GeometryModel3D();
            CubeGeometry geometry = new CubeGeometry();
            geometry.Width = Width;
            geometry.Length = Length;
            geometry.Height = Height;
            geometry.Center = Center;

            model.Geometry = geometry.Mesh3D;
            model.Material = Material;

            Model = model;
        }

        // The Model property for the cube:
        private static readonly DependencyProperty
            ModelProperty = DependencyProperty.Register(
                "Model", typeof(Model3D), typeof(Cube),
                new PropertyMetadata(ModelPropertyChanged));

        private static void ModelPropertyChanged(
            DependencyObject d,
            DependencyPropertyChangedEventArgs e)
        {
            Cube cube = (Cube)d;
            cube.Visual3DModel = (Model3D)e.NewValue;
        }

        private Model3D Model
        {
            get { return (Model3D)GetValue(ModelProperty); }
```

```
        set { SetValue(ModelProperty, value); }
    }

    // The material of the cube:
    public static readonly DependencyProperty
        MaterialProperty =
        DependencyProperty.Register(
            "Material", typeof(Material), typeof(Cube),
            new PropertyMetadata(
            new DiffuseMaterial(Brushes.Blue),
            PropertyChanged));

    public Material Material
    {
        get {return (Material)GetValue(MaterialProperty);}
        set { SetValue(MaterialProperty, value); }
    }

    // The side length of the Cube:
    public static readonly DependencyProperty
        LengthProperty = DependencyProperty.Register(
            "Length", typeof(double), typeof(Cube),
            new PropertyMetadata(1.0, PropertyChanged));

    public double Length
    {
        get { return (double)GetValue(LengthProperty); }
        set { SetValue(LengthProperty, value); }
    }

    // The side width of the Cube:
    public static readonly DependencyProperty
        WidthProperty = DependencyProperty.Register(
            "Width", typeof(double), typeof(Cube),
            new PropertyMetadata(1.0, PropertyChanged));

    public double Width
    {
        get { return (double)GetValue(WidthProperty); }
        set { SetValue(WidthProperty, value); }
    }

    // The side height of the Cube:
    public static readonly DependencyProperty
        HeightProperty = DependencyProperty.Register(
            "Height", typeof(double), typeof(Cube),
            new PropertyMetadata(1.0, PropertyChanged));

    public double Height
    {
        get { return (double)GetValue(HeightProperty); }
        set { SetValue(HeightProperty, value); }
    }
```

```
// The center of the cube:
public static readonly DependencyProperty
    CenterProperty = DependencyProperty.Register(
        "Center", typeof(Point3D), typeof(Cube),
        new PropertyMetadata(
        new Point3D(0.0, 0.0, 0.0), PropertyChanged));

public Point3D Center
{
    get { return (Point3D)GetValue(CenterProperty); }
    set { SetValue(CenterProperty, value); }
}


private static void PropertyChanged(DependencyObject
    d, DependencyPropertyChangedEventArgs e)
{
    Cube cube = (Cube)d;
    cube.InvalidateModel();
}
    }
}
```

You may notice that at the beginning, you add a using statement:

```
Using Geometries;
```

This allows you to directly access all of the geometry classes under the Geometries namespace. Inside the OnUpdateModel method, you specify properties of CubeGeometry using corresponding dependency properties defined in the current Cube class. Then, you attach the Mesh3D property of CubeGeometry to the Geometry property of the current model. In this way, you can reuse the CubeGeometry class to create your custom cube shape.

Next, you define the standard dependency properties for the cube shape, including material, length, width, height, and center. All of these dependency properties are associated with a PropertyChanged handler, which will be called whenever the properties are changed.

Testing Cube Shape

Now, you can create the cube shape using the Cube class directly in the XAML files, just like you create a 2D shape. Of course, you can also use it in code by creating an instance of your Cube class, specifying its dependency properties, and adding it directly to the Viewport3D

Let's use an example to illustrate how to use the Cube class in XAML. Add a new WPF Window to the project Chapter12 and name it CubeShapeTest. Here is the XAML file of this example:

```
<Window x:Class="Chapter12.CubeShapeTest"
    xmlns="http://schemas.microsoft.com/winfx
        /2006/xaml/presentation"
```

```
xmlns:x="http://schemas.microsoft.com/winfx/2006/xaml"
xmlns:local="clr-namespace:Shapes"
Title="Test Cube Shapes" Height="400" Width="300">

<Grid Margin="5">
    <Grid.RowDefinitions>
        <RowDefinition Height="100*" />
        <RowDefinition Height="300*" />
    </Grid.RowDefinitions>
    <Grid Grid.Row="0">
        <Grid.RowDefinitions>
            <RowDefinition Height="*" />
            <RowDefinition Height="*" />
            <RowDefinition Height="*" />
            <RowDefinition Height="*" />
        </Grid.RowDefinitions>
        <Grid.ColumnDefinitions>
            <ColumnDefinition Width="73*" />
            <ColumnDefinition Width="205*" />
        </Grid.ColumnDefinitions>

        <!-- Control the size of the cube: -->
        <Slider Grid.Column ="1" Name="slider1"
                Value="{Binding ElementName=cube,
                    Path=Length}"
                    Minimum="0.1" Maximum="4"/>
        <Slider Grid.Row="1" Grid.Column ="1"
            Name="slider2" Margin="0"
                Value="{Binding ElementName=cube,
                    Path=Width}"
                    Minimum="0.1" Maximum="4"/>
        <Slider Grid.Row="2" Grid.Column ="1"
            Name="slider3" Margin="0"
                Value="{Binding ElementName=cube,
                    Path=Height}"
                    Minimum="0.1" Maximum="4"/>

        <!-- Animation: -->
        <Button Grid.Row="3" Grid.Column ="1"
            Content="Rotate the Blue Cube" Width="130">
            <Button.Triggers>
                <EventTrigger RoutedEvent="Button.Click">
                    <BeginStoryboard>
                        <Storyboard
                            RepeatBehavior="Forever">
                <DoubleAnimation
                    Storyboard.TargetName="rotate1"
                    Storyboard.TargetProperty="Angle"
                       From="0" To="360" Duration="0:0:5"/>

                <DoubleAnimation
                    Storyboard.TargetName="rotate2"
                    Storyboard.TargetProperty="Angle"
                       From="0" To="360" Duration="0:0:5"/>
```

```
                              </Storyboard>
                        </BeginStoryboard>
                    </EventTrigger>
                </Button.Triggers>
            </Button>

            <Label Margin="0" Grid.Row="0"
                Name="label1">Length</Label>
            <Label Margin="0" Grid.Row="1"
                Name="label2">Width</Label>
            <Label Margin="0" Grid.Row="2"
                Name="label3">Height</Label>
            <Label Margin="0" Grid.Row="3"
                Name="label4">Animation</Label>
        </Grid>

        <Viewport3D Grid.Row="1">

            <!-- Set camera: -->
            <Viewport3D.Camera>
                <PerspectiveCamera Position="4,7,6"
                                   LookDirection="-4,-7,-6"
                                   UpDirection="0,1,0" />
            </Viewport3D.Camera>

            <!-- Add the gold cube: -->
            <local:Cube x:Name="cube">
                <local:Cube.Material>
                    <DiffuseMaterial>
                        <DiffuseMaterial.Brush>
                            <SolidColorBrush  Color="Gold"/>
                        </DiffuseMaterial.Brush>
                    </DiffuseMaterial>
                </local:Cube.Material>
                <local:Cube.Transform>
                    <RotateTransform3D>
                        <RotateTransform3D.Rotation>
                            <AxisAngleRotation3D
                                x:Name="rotate1" Axis="0,1,0"/>
                        </RotateTransform3D.Rotation>
                    </RotateTransform3D>
                </local:Cube.Transform>
            </local:Cube>

            <!-- Add the blue cube: -->
            <local:Cube>
                <local:Cube.Material>
                    <DiffuseMaterial>
                        <DiffuseMaterial.Brush>
                            <SolidColorBrush  Color="LightBlue"/>
                        </DiffuseMaterial.Brush>
                    </DiffuseMaterial>
                </local:Cube.Material>
```

```
        <local:Cube.Transform>
            <Transform3DGroup>
                <TranslateTransform3D OffsetZ="-3"/>
                <RotateTransform3D>
                    <RotateTransform3D.Rotation>
                        <AxisAngleRotation3D
                            x:Name="rotate2"
                            Axis="0,1,0"/>
                    </RotateTransform3D.Rotation>
                </RotateTransform3D>
            </Transform3DGroup>
        </local:Cube.Transform>
    </local:Cube>

    <!-- Set the light source: -->
    <ModelVisual3D>
        <ModelVisual3D.Content>
            <Model3DGroup>
                <Model3DGroup.Children>
                    <DirectionalLight Color="White"
                        Direction="-1,-2,-3"/>
                </Model3DGroup.Children>
            </Model3DGroup>
        </ModelVisual3D.Content>
    </ModelVisual3D>
        </Viewport3D>
    </Grid>
</Window>
```

In this XAML file, you include a namespace for the custom shape:

```
xmlns:local="clr-namespace:Shapes"
```

Then you can add the custom shape to the Viewport3D exactly like you add any UIElement3D object:

```
<Viewport3D>
    <local:Cube x:Name="cube1"...>
    ......
    </local:Cube>
    ......
</ViewPort3D>
```

You also create several sliders that are used to change the size of the cube interactively by binding the Value property of the sliders to the corresponding the dependency properties of the cube.

Figure 12-1 shows the results of running this application. Now you can change the size by moving the sliders with your mouse, or you can rotate both shapes by clicking the Rotate Cubes button.

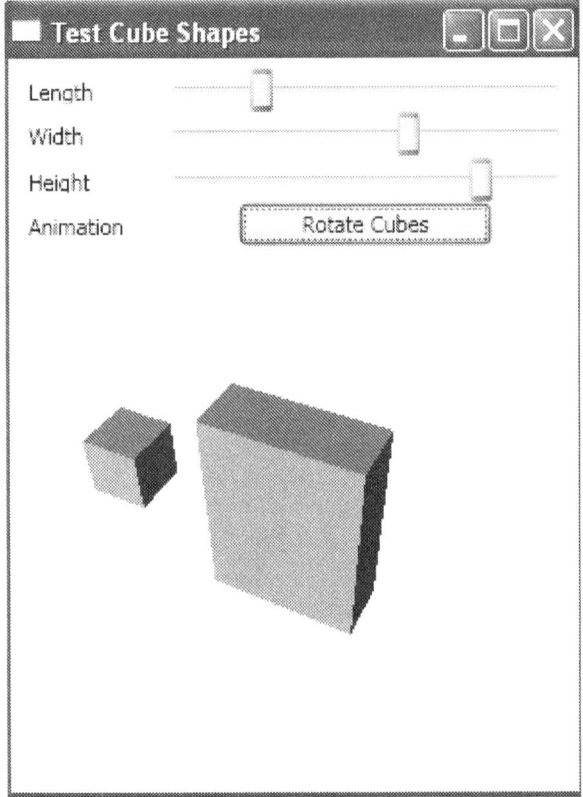

Figure 12-1 Cube created using the Custom shape class.

Ellipsoid Shape

In this section, you will create an ellipsoid shape that can be used the same way as 2D shapes.

Ellipsoid Shape Class

Add a new class to the project Chapter12, change its namespace to Shapes, and name it Ellipsoid. The following is the code listing of this class:

```
using System;
using System.Windows;
using System.Windows.Media;
using System.Windows.Media.Media3D;
using Geometries;

namespace Shapes
{
    public class Ellipsoid : UIElement3D
```

```
{
    protected override void OnUpdateModel()
    {
        GeometryModel3D model = new GeometryModel3D();
        EllipsoidGeometry geometry =
            new EllipsoidGeometry();
        geometry.XLength = XLength;
        geometry.YLength = YLength;
        geometry.ZLength = ZLength;
        geometry.ThetaDiv = ThetaDiv;
        geometry.PhiDiv = PhiDiv;
        geometry.Center = Center;
        model.Geometry = geometry.Mesh3D;
        model.Material = Material;
        Model = model;
    }

    // The Model property for the Ellipsoid:
    private static readonly DependencyProperty
        ModelProperty = DependencyProperty.Register(
        "Model", typeof(Model3D), typeof(Ellipsoid),
        new PropertyMetadata(ModelPropertyChanged));

    private static void ModelPropertyChanged(
        DependencyObject d,
        DependencyPropertyChangedEventArgs e)
    {
        Ellipsoid ellipsoid = (Ellipsoid)d;
        ellipsoid.Visual3DModel = (Model3D)e.NewValue;
    }

    private Model3D Model
    {
        get { return (Model3D)GetValue(ModelProperty); }
        set { SetValue(ModelProperty, value); }
    }

    // The material of the Ellipsoid:
    public static readonly DependencyProperty
        MaterialProperty = DependencyProperty.Register(
        "Material", typeof(Material), typeof(Ellipsoid),
        new PropertyMetadata(
            new DiffuseMaterial(Brushes.Blue),
            PropertyChanged));

    public Material Material
    {
        get {return (Material)GetValue(MaterialProperty);}
        set { SetValue(MaterialProperty, value); }
    }

    // The x length of the Ellipsoid:
    public static readonly DependencyProperty
        XLengthProperty = DependencyProperty.Register(
```

```
            "XLength", Typeof(double), typeof(Ellipsoid),
            new PropertyMetadata(1.0, PropertyChanged));

    public double XLength
    {
        get { return (double)GetValue(XLengthProperty); }
        set { SetValue(XLengthProperty, value); }
    }

    // The y length of the Ellipsoid:
    public static readonly DependencyProperty
        YLengthProperty = DependencyProperty.Register(
        "YLength", typeof(double), typeof(Ellipsoid),
        new PropertyMetadata(1.0, PropertyChanged));

    public double YLength
    {
        get { return (double)GetValue(YLengthProperty); }
        set { SetValue(YLengthProperty, value); }
    }

    // The z length of the Ellipsoid:
    public static readonly DependencyProperty
        ZLengthProperty = DependencyProperty.Register(
        "ZLength", typeof(double), typeof(Ellipsoid),
        new PropertyMetadata(1.0, PropertyChanged));

    public double ZLength
    {
        get { return (double)GetValue(ZLengthProperty); }
        set { SetValue(ZLengthProperty, value); }
    }

    // The ThetaDiv of the Ellipsoid:
    public static readonly DependencyProperty
        ThetaDivProperty = DependencyProperty.Register(
        "ThetaDiv", typeof(int), typeof(Ellipsoid),
        new PropertyMetadata(20, PropertyChanged));

    public int ThetaDiv
    {
        get { return (int)GetValue(ThetaDivProperty); }
        set { SetValue(ThetaDivProperty, value); }
    }

    // The PhiDiv of the Ellipsoid:
    public static readonly DependencyProperty
        PhiDivProperty = DependencyProperty.Register(
        "PhiDiv", typeof(int), typeof(Ellipsoid),
        new PropertyMetadata(20, PropertyChanged));

    public int PhiDiv
    {
        get { return (int)GetValue(PhiDivProperty); }
```

```
            set { SetValue(PhiDivProperty, value); }
        }

        // The center of the Ellipsoid:
        public static readonly DependencyProperty
            CenterProperty = DependencyProperty.Register(
            "Center", typeof(Point3D), typeof(Ellipsoid),
            new PropertyMetadata(new Point3D(0.0, 0.0, 0.0),
            PropertyChanged));

        public Point3D Center
        {
            get { return (Point3D)GetValue(CenterProperty); }
            set { SetValue(CenterProperty, value); }
        }

        private static void PropertyChanged(
            DependencyObject d,
            DependencyPropertyChangedEventArgs e)
        {
            Ellipsoid ellipsoid = (Ellipsoid)d;
            ellipsoid.InvalidateModel();
        }
    }
}
```

The structure of this class is similar to that of the Cube class discussed in the previous section. Inside the OnUpdateModel method, you specify properties of the EllipsoidGeometry using the corresponding dependency properties defined in the current Ellipsoid class. Then, you attach the Mesh3D property of EllipsoidGeometry to the Geometry property of the current model. This way, you can reuse the EllipsoidGeometry class in creating your custom shape.

Next, you define the standard dependency properties for the ellipsoid shape, All of these dependency properties are associated with a PropertyChanged handler, which will be called whenever the properties are changed.

Testing Ellipsoid Shape

Now, you can create the Ellipsoid shape using the Ellipsoid class directly in the XAML files, just like you create a 2D shape. Of course, you can also use it in code by creating an instance of your Ellipsoid class, specifying its dependency properties, and directly adding it to the Viewport3D

Here, I'll show you how to use the Ellipsoid class in XAML. Add a new WPF Window to the project Chapter12 and name it EllipsoidShapeTest. The XAML file of this example is similar to that used to demonstrate the Cube shape. You can view the complete source code by opening the EllipsoidShapeTest.xaml file. The difference is that you need to add the ellipsoid shapes to Viewport3D:

```
<Viewport3D>
    <local:Ellipsoid x:Name="ellipsoid1"...>
```

```
    .....
    </local:Ellipsoid>
    .....
</ViewPort3D>
```

You also create several sliders that are used to change the size of the gold ellipsoid interactively by binding the Value property of the sliders to the corresponding dependency properties of the ellipsoid.

Figure 12-2 shows the results of running this application. Now, you can change the size of the gold ellipsoid by moving the sliders with your mouse. You can also rotate the blue ellipsoid by clicking the Rotate the Blue Ellipsoid button.

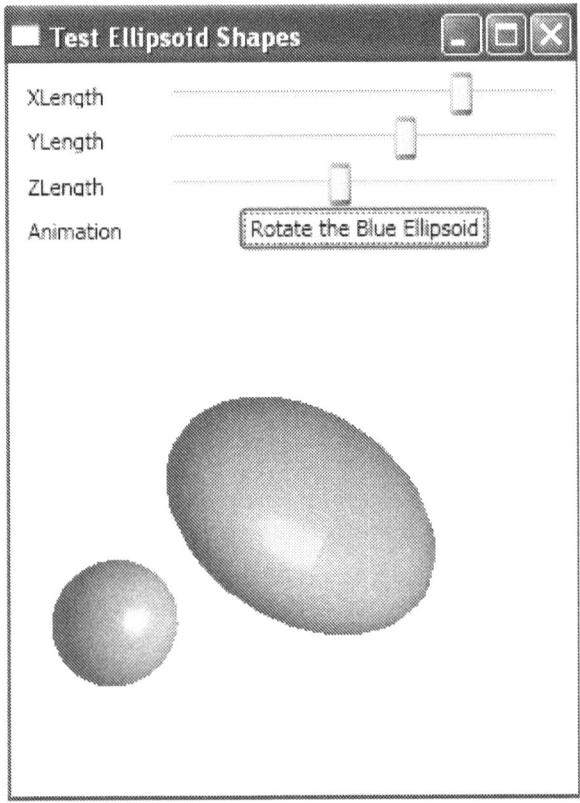

Figure 12-2 Ellipsoids created using the custom shape class.

Cylinder Shape

In this section, you will implement a custom cylinder class and learn how to use it in XAML files.

Cylinder Shape Class

Add a new class to the project Chapter12, change its namespace to Shapes, and name it Cylinder. The following is the code listing of this class:

```
using System;
using System.Windows;
using System.Windows.Media;
using System.Windows.Media.Media3D;
using Geometries;

namespace Shapes
{
    public class Cylinder : UIElement3D
    {
        protected override void OnUpdateModel()
        {
            GeometryModel3D model = new GeometryModel3D();
            CylinderGeometry geometry =
                new CylinderGeometry();
            geometry.Rin = Rin;
            geometry.Rout = Rout;
            geometry.Height = Height;
            geometry.ThetaDiv = ThetaDiv;
            geometry.Center = Center;
            model.Geometry = geometry.Mesh3D;
            model.Material = Material;
            Model = model;
        }

        // The Model property for the Cylinder:
        private static readonly DependencyProperty
            ModelProperty = DependencyProperty.Register(
            "Model", typeof(Model3D), typeof(Cylinder),
            new PropertyMetadata(ModelPropertyChanged));

        private static void ModelPropertyChanged(
            DependencyObject d,
            DependencyPropertyChangedEventArgs e)
        {
            Cylinder cylinder = (Cylinder)d;
            cylinder.Visual3DModel = (Model3D)e.NewValue;
        }

        private Model3D Model
        {
            get { return (Model3D)GetValue(ModelProperty); }
            set { SetValue(ModelProperty, value); }
        }

        // The material of the Cylinder:
        public static readonly DependencyProperty
            MaterialProperty = DependencyProperty.Register(
            "Material", typeof(Material), typeof(Cylinder),
```

```
                new PropertyMetadata(
                    new DiffuseMaterial(Brushes.Blue),
                    PropertyChanged));

        public Material Material
        {
            get {return (Material)GetValue(MaterialProperty);}
            set { SetValue(MaterialProperty, value); }
        }

        // The inner radius of the Cylinder:
        public static readonly DependencyProperty
            RinProperty = DependencyProperty.Register(
            "Rin", typeof(double), typeof(Cylinder),
            new PropertyMetadata(0.0, PropertyChanged));

        public double Rin
        {
            get { return (double)GetValue(RinProperty); }
            set { SetValue(RinProperty, value); }
        }

        // The outer radius of the Cylinder:
        public static readonly DependencyProperty
            RoutProperty = DependencyProperty.Register(
            "Rout", typeof(double), typeof(Cylinder),
            new PropertyMetadata(1.0, PropertyChanged));

        public double Rout
        {
            get { return (double)GetValue(RoutProperty); }
            set { SetValue(RoutProperty, value); }
        }

        // The height of the Cylinder:
        public static readonly DependencyProperty
            HeightProperty = DependencyProperty.Register(
            "Height", typeof(double), typeof(Cylinder),
            new PropertyMetadata(1.0, PropertyChanged));

        public double Height
        {
            get { return (double)GetValue(HeightProperty); }
            set { SetValue(HeightProperty, value); }
        }

        // The ThetaDiv of the Cylinder:
        public static readonly DependencyProperty
            ThetaDivProperty = DependencyProperty.Register(
            "ThetaDiv", typeof(int), typeof(Cylinder),
            new PropertyMetadata(20, PropertyChanged));

        public int ThetaDiv
        {
```

```
            get { return (int)GetValue(ThetaDivProperty); }
            set { SetValue(ThetaDivProperty, value); }
        }

        // The center of the Cylinder:
        public static readonly DependencyProperty
            CenterProperty = DependencyProperty.Register(
            "Center", typeof(Point3D), typeof(Cylinder),
            new PropertyMetadata(new Point3D(0.0, 0.0, 0.0),
            PropertyChanged));

        public Point3D Center
        {
            get { return (Point3D)GetValue(CenterProperty); }
            set { SetValue(CenterProperty, value); }
        }

        private static void PropertyChanged(
            DependencyObject d,
            DependencyPropertyChangedEventArgs e)
        {
            Cylinder cylinder = (Cylinder)d;
            cylinder.InvalidateModel();
        }
    }
}
```

The structure of this class is also similar to that of the Cube class discussed previously. Inside the OnUpdateModel method, you specify properties of CylinderGeometry using the corresponding dependency properties that are defined in the current Cylinder class. Then, you attach the Mesh3D property of CylinderGeometry to the Geometry property of the current model. This way, you can reuse the CylinderGeometry class to help you create the custom shape.

Next, you define the standard dependency properties for your Cylinder shape, All of these dependency properties are associated with a PropertyChanged handler, which will be called whenever the properties are changed.

Testing Cylinder Shape

Now, you can create a cylinder shape using the Cylinder class directly in the XAML files, just like you create a 2D shape. Of course, you can also use it in code by creating an instance of the Cylinder class, specifying its dependency properties, and adding it to the Viewport3D

Here, I'll show you how to use the Cylinder class in XAML. Add a new WPF Window to the project Chapter12 and name it CylinderShapeTest. The XAML file of this example is also similar to that used in demonstrating the Cube shape. You can view the code by opening the CylinderShapeTest.xaml file. The difference is that you need to add the Cylinder shapes to Viewport3D:

```
<Viewport3D>
    <local:Cylinder x:Name="cylinder1"...>
    .....
    </local:Cylinder>
    .....
</ViewPort3D>
```

You also create several sliders that are used to change the size of the cylinder interactively by binding the Value property of the sliders to the corresponding dependency properties of the object.

Figure 12-3 shows the results of running this application. Now you can change the size of the cylinder by moving the sliders with your mouse, and also you can rotate it by clicking the Rotate the Cylinder button.

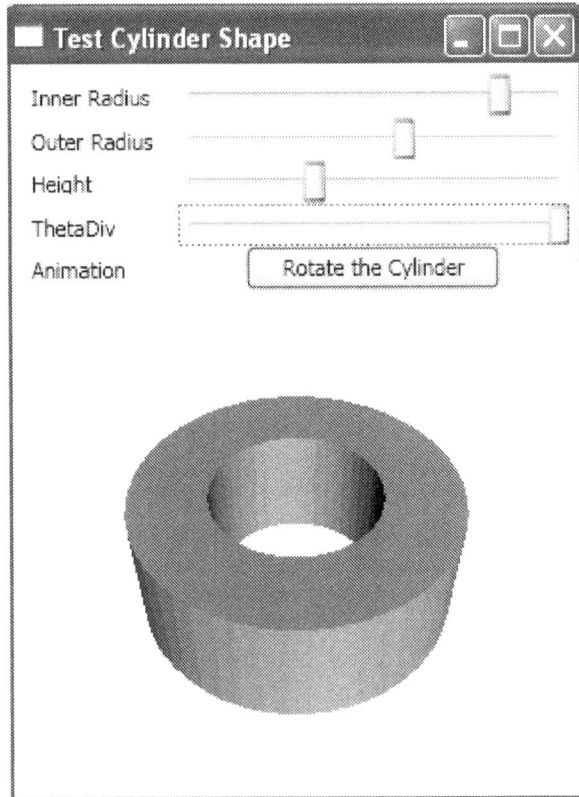

Figure 12-3 Cylinder created using the custom shape class.

Cone Shape

In this section, you'll learn how to implement a custom cone shape class and how to use it in XAML files.

Cone Shape Class

Add a new class to the project Chapter12, change its namespace to Shapes, and name it Cone. The following is the code listing of this class:

```
using System.Windows;
using System.Windows.Media;
using System.Windows.Media.Media3D;
using Geometries;

namespace Shapes
{
    public class Cone : UIElement3D
    {
        protected override void OnUpdateModel()
        {
            GeometryModel3D model = new GeometryModel3D();
            ConeGeometry geometry = new ConeGeometry();
            geometry.Rtop = Rtop;
            geometry.Rbottom = Rbottom;
            geometry.Height = Height;
            geometry.ThetaDiv = ThetaDiv;
            geometry.Center = Center;
            model.Geometry = geometry.Mesh3D;
            model.Material = Material;
            Model = model;
        }

        // The Model property for the Cone:
        private static readonly DependencyProperty
            ModelProperty = DependencyProperty.Register(
            "Model", typeof(Model3D), typeof(Cone),
            new PropertyMetadata(ModelPropertyChanged));

        private static void ModelPropertyChanged(
            DependencyObject d,
            DependencyPropertyChangedEventArgs e)
        {
            Cone cone = (Cone)d;
            cone.Visual3DModel = (Model3D)e.NewValue;
        }

        private Model3D Model
        {
            get { return (Model3D)GetValue(ModelProperty); }
            set { SetValue(ModelProperty, value); }
        }

        // The material of the Cone:
        public static readonly DependencyProperty
            MaterialProperty = DependencyProperty.Register(
            "Material", typeof(Material), typeof(Cone),
            new PropertyMetadata(
            new DiffuseMaterial(Brushes.Blue),
```

```
        PropertyChanged));

    public Material Material
    {
        get {return (Material)GetValue(MaterialProperty);}
        set { SetValue(MaterialProperty, value); }
    }

    // The top radius of the Cone:
    public static readonly DependencyProperty
        RtopProperty = DependencyProperty.Register(
        "Rtop", typeof(double), typeof(Cone),
        new PropertyMetadata(0.0, PropertyChanged));

    public double Rtop
    {
        get { return (double)GetValue(RtopProperty); }
        set { SetValue(RtopProperty, value); }
    }

    // The bottom radius of the Cone:
    public static readonly DependencyProperty
        RbottomProperty = DependencyProperty.Register(
        "Rbottom", typeof(double), typeof(Cone),
        new PropertyMetadata(1.0, PropertyChanged));

    public double Rbottom
    {
        get { return (double)GetValue(RbottomProperty); }
        set { SetValue(RbottomProperty, value); }
    }

    // The height of the Cone:
    public static readonly DependencyProperty
        HeightProperty = DependencyProperty.Register(
        "Height", typeof(double), typeof(Cone),
        new PropertyMetadata(1.0, PropertyChanged));

    public double Height
    {
        get { return (double)GetValue(HeightProperty); }
        set { SetValue(HeightProperty, value); }
    }

    // The ThetaDiv of the Cone:
    public static readonly DependencyProperty
        ThetaDivProperty = DependencyProperty.Register(
        "ThetaDiv", typeof(int), typeof(Cone),
        new PropertyMetadata(20, PropertyChanged));

    public int ThetaDiv
    {
        get { return (int)GetValue(ThetaDivProperty); }
        set { SetValue(ThetaDivProperty, value); }
```

```
        }

        // The center of the Cone:
        public static readonly DependencyProperty
            CenterProperty = DependencyProperty.Register(
            "Center", typeof(Point3D), typeof(Cone),
            new PropertyMetadata(new Point3D(0.0, 0.0, 0.0),
            PropertyChanged));

        public Point3D Center
        {
            get { return (Point3D)GetValue(CenterProperty); }
            set { SetValue(CenterProperty, value); }
        }

        private static void PropertyChanged(
            DependencyObject d,
            DependencyPropertyChangedEventArgs e)
        {
            Cone cone = (Cone)d;
            cone.InvalidateModel();
        }
    }
}
```

The structure of this class is similar to that of the Cube class discussed previously. Inside the OnUpdateModel method, you specify properties of the ConeGeometry using the corresponding dependency properties that are defined in the current Cone class. Then, you attach the Mesh3D property of ConeGeometry to the Geometry property of the current model. This way, you can reuse the ConeGeometry class in the creation of your custom shape.

Next, you define the standard dependency properties for the Cone shape, All of these dependency properties are associated with a PropertyChanged handler, which will be called whenever the properties are changed.

Testing Cone Shape

Now, you can create the cone shape using the Cone class directly in the XAML files, just like you create a 2D shape. Of course, you can also use it in code by creating an instance of the Cone class, specifying its dependency properties, and adding it to the Viewport3D

Here I'll show you how to use Cone class in XAML. Add a new WPF Window to the project Chapter12 and name it ConeShapeTest. The XAML file of this example is similar to that used in demonstrating the Cube shape. You can view the code by opening the ConeShapeTest.xaml file. The difference is that you need to add the Cone shapes to Viewport3D:

```
<Viewport3D>
    <local:Cone x:Name="cone1"...>
    ......
    </local:Cone>
    ......
</ViewPort3D>
```

You also create several sliders that are used to interactively change the size of the cone by binding the Value property of the sliders to the corresponding dependency properties of the object.

Figure 12-4 shows the results of running this application. Now you can change the size of the cone by moving the sliders with your mouse, and also you can rotate it by clicking the Rotate the Cone Shape button.

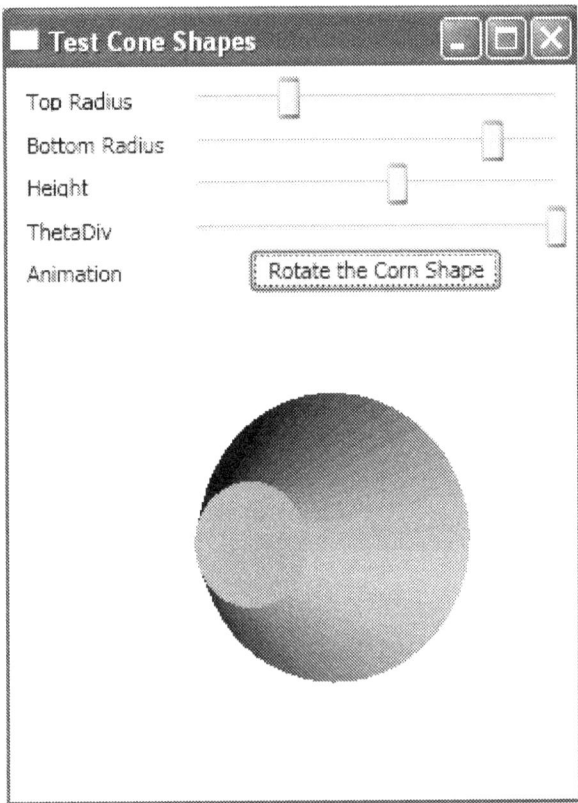

Figure 12-4 Cone created using the custom shape class.

Torus Shape

In this section, you'll learn how to implement a custom torus class and how to use it in XAML files.

Torus Shape Class

Add a new class to the project Chapter12 and name it Torus. The following is the code listing of this class:

```
using System;
using System.Windows;
using System.Windows.Media;
using System.Windows.Media.Media3D;
using Geometries;

namespace Shapes
{
    public class Torus : UIElement3D
    {
        protected override void OnUpdateModel()
        {
            GeometryModel3D model = new GeometryModel3D();
            TorusGeometry geometry = new TorusGeometry();
            geometry.R1 = R1;
            geometry.R2 = R2;
            geometry.UDiv = UDiv;
            geometry.VDiv = VDiv;
            geometry.Center = Center;
            model.Geometry = geometry.Mesh3D;
            model.Material = Material;
            Model = model;
        }

        // The Model property for the Torus:
        private static readonly DependencyProperty
            ModelProperty = DependencyProperty.Register(
            "Model", typeof(Model3D), typeof(Torus),
            new PropertyMetadata(ModelPropertyChanged));

        private static void ModelPropertyChanged(
            DependencyObject d,
            DependencyPropertyChangedEventArgs e)
        {
            Torus torus = (Torus)d;
            torus.Visual3DModel = (Model3D)e.NewValue;
        }

        private Model3D Model
        {
            get { return (Model3D)GetValue(ModelProperty); }
            set { SetValue(ModelProperty, value); }
        }

        // The material of the Torus:
        public static readonly DependencyProperty
            MaterialProperty = DependencyProperty.Register(
            "Material", typeof(Material), typeof(Torus),
            new PropertyMetadata(
```

```
        new DiffuseMaterial(Brushes.Blue),
        PropertyChanged));

public Material Material
{
    get {return (Material)GetValue(MaterialProperty);}
    set { SetValue(MaterialProperty, value); }
}

// The radius of the Tube:
public static readonly DependencyProperty
    R1Property = DependencyProperty.Register(
    "R1", typeof(double), typeof(Torus),
    new PropertyMetadata(1.0, PropertyChanged));

public double R1
{
    get { return (double)GetValue(R1Property); }
    set { SetValue(R1Property, value); }
}

// The radius of the Torus:
public static readonly DependencyProperty
    R2Property = DependencyProperty.Register(
    "R2", typeof(double), typeof(Torus),
    new PropertyMetadata(0.3, PropertyChanged));

public double R2
{
    get { return (double)GetValue(R2Property); }
    set { SetValue(R2Property, value); }
}

// The UDiv of the Torus:
public static readonly DependencyProperty
    UDivProperty = DependencyProperty.Register(
    "UDiv", typeof(int), typeof(Torus),
    new PropertyMetadata(20, PropertyChanged));

public int UDiv
{
    get { return (int)GetValue(UDivProperty); }
    set { SetValue(UDivProperty, value); }
}

// The VDiv of the Torus:
public static readonly DependencyProperty
    VDivProperty = DependencyProperty.Register(
    "VDiv", typeof(int), typeof(Torus),
    new PropertyMetadata(20, PropertyChanged));

public int VDiv
{
    get { return (int)GetValue(VDivProperty); }
```

```
            set { SetValue(VDivProperty, value); }
        }

        // The center of the Torus:
        public static readonly DependencyProperty
            CenterProperty = DependencyProperty.Register(
            "Center", typeof(Point3D), typeof(Torus),
            new PropertyMetadata(new Point3D(0.0, 0.0, 0.0),
            PropertyChanged));

        public Point3D Center
        {
            get { return (Point3D)GetValue(CenterProperty); }
            set { SetValue(CenterProperty, value); }
        }


        private static void PropertyChanged(
            DependencyObject d,
            DependencyPropertyChangedEventArgs e)
        {
            Torus torus = (Torus)d;
            torus.InvalidateModel();
        }
    }
}
```

The structure of this class is also similar to that of the Cube class discussed previously. Inside the OnUpdateModel method, you specify properties of the TorusGeometry using the corresponding dependency properties that are defined in the current Torus class. Then, you attach the Mesh3D property of the TorusGeometry to the Geometry property of the current model. This way, you can reuse the TorusGeometry class to create the custom shape.

Next, you define the standard dependency properties for the Torus shape, All of these dependency properties are associated with a PropertyChanged handler, which will be called whenever the properties are changed.

Testing Torus Shape

Now, you can create a torus shape using the Torus class directly in the XAML files, just like you create a 2D shape. Of course, you can also use it in code by creating an instance of the Torus class, specifying its dependency properties, and adding it to the Viewport3D

Here I'll show you how to use the Torus class in XAML. Add a new WPF Window to the project Chapter12 and name it TorusShapeTest. The XAML file of this example is similar to that used in demonstrating the Cube shape. You can view the code by opening the TorusShapeTest.xaml file. The difference is that you need to add the Torus shapes to Viewport3D:

```
<Viewport3D>
    <local:Torus x:Name="torus1"...>
    .....
    </local:Torus>
    .....
</ViewPort3D>
```

Again, this XAML file also creates several sliders that are used to change the size of the torus interactively by binding the Value property of the sliders to the corresponding dependency properties of the object.

Figure 12-5 shows the results of running this application. Now you can change the size of the torus by moving the sliders with your mouse, and also you can rotate it by clicking the Rotate the Torus Shape button.

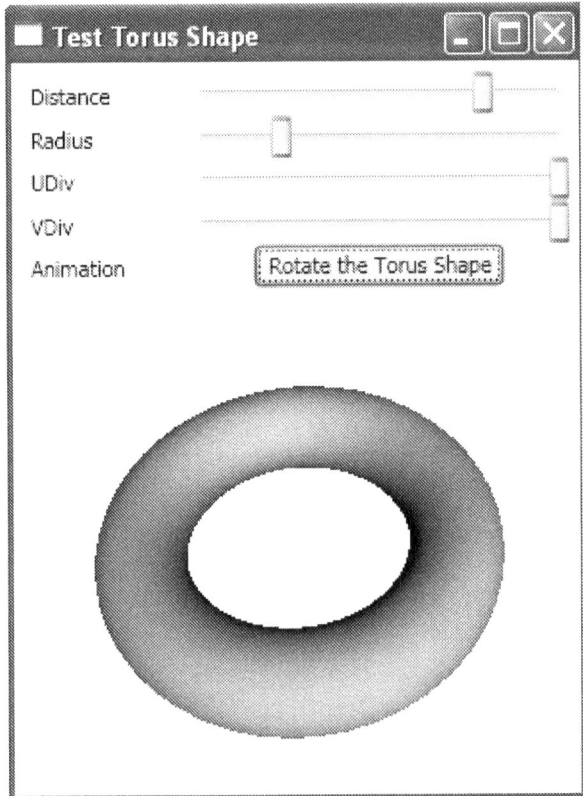

Figure 12-5 Torus created using the custom shape class.

Icosahedron Shape

In this section, you'll implement a custom icosahedron class and demonstrate how to use it in XAML files.

Icosahedron Shape Class

Add a new class to the project Chapter12, change its namespace to Shapes, and name it Icosahedron. The following is the code listing of this class:

```
using System;
using System.Windows;
using System.Windows.Media;
using System.Windows.Media.Media3D;
using Geometries;

namespace Shapes
{
    public class Icosahedron : UIElement3D
    {
        protected override void OnUpdateModel()
        {
            GeometryModel3D model = new GeometryModel3D();
            IcosahedronGeometry geometry =
                new IcosahedronGeometry();
            geometry.SideLength = SideLength;
            geometry.Center = Center;
            model.Geometry = geometry.Mesh3D;
            model.Material = Material;
            Model = model;
        }

        // The Model property for the model:
        private static readonly DependencyProperty
            ModelProperty = DependencyProperty.Register(
            "Model", typeof(Model3D), typeof(Icosahedron),
            new PropertyMetadata(ModelPropertyChanged));

        private static void ModelPropertyChanged(
            DependencyObject d,
            DependencyPropertyChangedEventArgs e)
        {
            Icosahedron icosahedron = (Icosahedron)d;
            icosahedron.Visual3DModel = (Model3D)e.NewValue;
        }

        private Model3D Model
        {
            get { return (Model3D)GetValue(ModelProperty); }
            set { SetValue(ModelProperty, value); }
        }

        // The material of the model:
        public static readonly DependencyProperty
            MaterialProperty = DependencyProperty.Register(
            "Material", typeof(Material), typeof(Icosahedron),
            new PropertyMetadata(
            new DiffuseMaterial(Brushes.Blue),
            PropertyChanged));
```

```
public Material Material
{
    get {return (Material)GetValue(MaterialProperty);}
    set { SetValue(MaterialProperty, value); }
}

// The side length of the model:
public static readonly DependencyProperty
    SideLengthProperty = DependencyProperty.Register(
    "SideLength", typeof(double), typeof(Icosahedron),
    new PropertyMetadata(1.0, PropertyChanged));

public double SideLength
{
    get {return (double)GetValue(SideLengthProperty);}
    set { SetValue(SideLengthProperty, value); }
}

// The center of the model:
public static readonly DependencyProperty
    CenterProperty = DependencyProperty.Register(
    "Center", typeof(Point3D), typeof(Icosahedron),
    new PropertyMetadata(new Point3D(0.0, 0.0, 0.0),
    PropertyChanged));

public Point3D Center
{
    get { return (Point3D)GetValue(CenterProperty); }
    set { SetValue(CenterProperty, value); }
}

private static void PropertyChanged(
    DependencyObject d,
    DependencyPropertyChangedEventArgs e)
{
    Icosahedron icosahedron = (Icosahedron)d;
    icosahedron.InvalidateModel();
}
        }
    }
```

Again, the structure of this class is similar to that of the Cube class discussed previously. Inside the OnUpdateModel method, you specify properties of IcosahedronGeometry using the corresponding dependency properties that are defined in the current Icosahedron class. Then, you attach the Mesh3D property of IcosahedronGeometry to the Geometry property of the current model. This way, you can reuse the IcosahedronGeometry class to create the custom shape.

Next, you define the standard dependency properties for the Icosahedron shape, All of these dependency properties are associated with a PropertyChanged handler, which will be called whenever the properties are changed.

Testing Icosahedron Shape

Now, you can create an icosahedron shape directly in the XAML files using the Icosahedron class, just like you create a 2D shape. Of course, you can also use it in code by creating an instance of your icosahedron class, specifying its dependency properties, and adding it to the Viewport3D

Here, I'll show you how to use the Icosahedron class in XAML. Add a new WPF Window to the project Chapter12 and name it IcosahedronShapeTest. The XAML file of this example is similar to that used in demonstrating the Cube shape. You can view the code by opening the IcosahedronShapeTest.xaml file. The difference is that you need to add the Icosahedron shapes to Viewport3D:

```
<Viewport3D>
    <local:Icosahedron x:Name="icosahedron1"...>
    ......
    </local:Icosahedron>
    ......
</ViewPort3D>
```

You also create a slider that is used to change the size of the icosahedron interactively by binding the Value property of the slider to the corresponding dependency properties of the object.

Figure 12-6 shows the results of running this application. Now you can change the size of the icosahedron by moving the slider with your mouse, or you can rotate it by clicking the Rotate the Icosahedron button.

Dodecahedron Shape

In this section, you'll learn how to implement a custom dodecahedron class and how to use it in XAML files.

Dodecahedron Shape Class

Add a new class to the project Chapter12, change its namespace to Shapes, and name it Dodecahedron. The code of this class is almost identical to the Icosahedron class discussed in the previous section. Both classes contain the same number of dependency properties, including Material, Center, and SideLength.

The difference occurs inside the OnUpdateModel method, where you must specify properties of DodecahedronGeometry using the corresponding dependency properties that are defined in the Dodecahedron class. Then, you attach the Mesh3D property of DodecahedronGeometry to the Geometry property of the current model. This way, you can reuse the DodecahedronGeometry class to create your custom shape. You can look at the complete source code by opening the Dodecahedron.cs file.

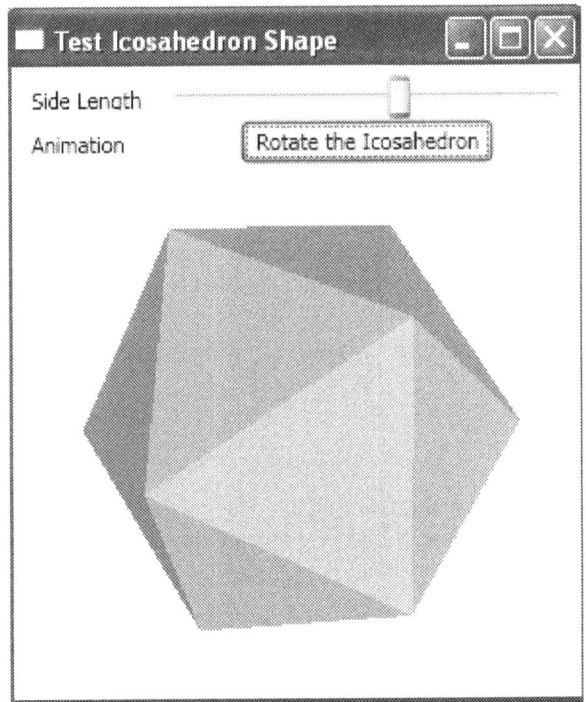

Figure 12-6 Icosahedron created using the custom shape class.

Testing Dodecahedron Shape

Now, you can create the dodecahedron shape using the Dodecahedron class directly in the XAML files, just like you create a 2D shape. Of course, you can also use it in code by creating an instance of the Dodecahedron class, specifying its dependency properties, and directly adding it to Viewport3D

Here, I'll show you how to use the Dodecahedron class in XAML. Add a new WPF Window to the project Chapter12 and name it DodecahedronShapeTest. The XAML file of this example is similar to that used in demonstrating the Cube shape. You can view the code by opening the DodecahedronShapeTest.xaml file. The difference is that you need to add the Dodecahedron shapes to Viewport3D:

```
<Viewport3D>
    <local:Dodecahedron x:Name="dodecahedron1"...>
    ......
    </local:Dodecahedron>
    ......
</ViewPort3D>
```

You also create a slider that is used to change the size of the dodecahedron interactively by binding the Value property of the slider to the corresponding dependency properties of the object.

Figure 12-7 shows the results of running this application. Now you can change the size of the dodecahedron by moving the slider with your mouse, and you can also rotate it by clicking the Rotate the Dodecahedron button.

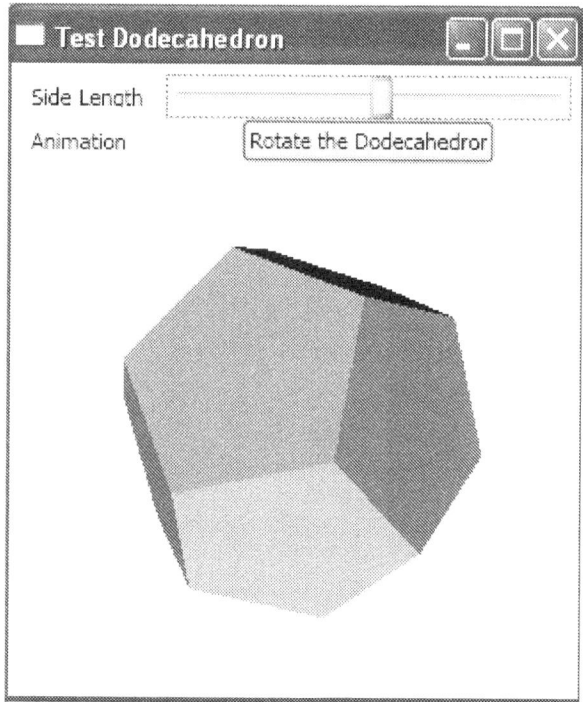

Figure 12-7 Dodecahedron created using the custom shape class.

Soccer Shape

In this section, you'll learn how to implement a custom soccer class and how to use it in XAML files.

Soccer Shape Class

Add a new class to the project Chapter12, change its namespace to Shapes, and name it Soccer. The code of this class is little different from previous models. Here is the code for the soccer shape:

```
using System;
using System.Windows;
using System.Windows.Media;
```

```csharp
using System.Windows.Media.Media3D;
using Geometries;

namespace Shapes
{
    public class Soccer : UIElement3D
    {
        protected override void OnUpdateModel()
        {
            if (IsDifferentMaterial == true)
            {
                Model3DGroup group = new Model3DGroup();
                SoccerGeometry geometry =
                    new SoccerGeometry();
                geometry.SideLength = SideLength;
                geometry.Center = Center;

                GeometryModel3D pentagonModel =
                    new GeometryModel3D();
                pentagonModel.Geometry =
                    geometry.PentagonMesh3D;
                pentagonModel.Material = PentagonMaterial;
                group.Children.Add(pentagonModel);

                GeometryModel3D hexagonModel =
                    new GeometryModel3D();
                hexagonModel.Geometry =
                    geometry.HexagonMesh3D;
                hexagonModel.Material = HexagonMaterial;
                group.Children.Add(hexagonModel);

                Model = group;
            }

            else if (IsDifferentMaterial == false)
            {
                GeometryModel3D model = new GeometryModel3D();
                SoccerGeometry geometry =
                    new SoccerGeometry();
                geometry.SideLength = SideLength;
                geometry.Center = Center;
                model.Geometry = geometry.Mesh3D;
                model.Material = Material;
                Model = model;
            }
        }

        // The Model property for the model:
        private static readonly DependencyProperty
            ModelProperty = DependencyProperty.Register(
            "Model", typeof(Model3D), typeof(Soccer),
            new PropertyMetadata(ModelPropertyChanged));

        private static void ModelPropertyChanged(
```

```
      DependencyObject d,
      DependencyPropertyChangedEventArgs e)
{
      Soccer soccer = (Soccer)d;
      soccer.Visual3DModel = (Model3D)e.NewValue;
}

private Model3D Model
{
      get { return (Model3D)GetValue(ModelProperty); }
      set { SetValue(ModelProperty, value); }
}

// The material of the entire model:
public static readonly DependencyProperty
      MaterialProperty = DependencyProperty.Register(
      "Material", typeof(Material), typeof(Soccer),
      new PropertyMetadata(
      new  DiffuseMaterial(Brushes.Blue),
      PropertyChanged));

public Material Material
{
      get {return (Material)GetValue(MaterialProperty);}
      set { SetValue(MaterialProperty, value); }
}

// The material of the pentagons:
public static readonly DependencyProperty
      PentagonMaterialProperty =
      DependencyProperty.Register("PentagonMaterial",
          typeof(Material), typeof(Soccer),
          new PropertyMetadata(
          new DiffuseMaterial(Brushes.Black),
          PropertyChanged));

public Material PentagonMaterial
{
      get { return (Material)GetValue(
          PentagonMaterialProperty); }
      set { SetValue(PentagonMaterialProperty, value); }
}

// The material of the hexagons:
public static readonly DependencyProperty
      HexagonMaterialProperty =
      DependencyProperty.Register("HexagonMaterial",
          typeof(Material), typeof(Soccer),
          new PropertyMetadata(
          new DiffuseMaterial(Brushes.White),
          PropertyChanged));

public Material HexagonMaterial
{
```

```csharp
        get { return (Material)GetValue(
            HexagonMaterialProperty); }
        set { SetValue(HexagonMaterialProperty, value); }
    }

    // The side length of the model:
    public static readonly DependencyProperty
        SideLengthProperty = DependencyProperty.Register(
        "SideLength", typeof(double), typeof(Soccer),
        new PropertyMetadata(1.0, PropertyChanged));

    public double SideLength
    {
        get {return (double)GetValue(SideLengthProperty);}
        set { SetValue(SideLengthProperty, value); }
    }

    // The center of the model:
    public static readonly DependencyProperty
        CenterProperty = DependencyProperty.Register(
        "Center", typeof(Point3D), typeof(Soccer),
        new PropertyMetadata(new Point3D(0.0, 0.0, 0.0),
        PropertyChanged));

    public Point3D Center
    {
        get { return (Point3D)GetValue(CenterProperty); }
        set { SetValue(CenterProperty, value); }
    }

    // The different material:
    public static readonly DependencyProperty
        IsDifferentMaterialProperty =
        DependencyProperty.Register("IsDifferentMaterial",
            typeof(bool), typeof(Soccer),
            new PropertyMetadata(false, PropertyChanged));

    public bool IsDifferentMaterial
    {
        get { return (bool)GetValue(
            IsDifferentMaterialProperty); }
        set { SetValue(
            IsDifferentMaterialProperty, value); }
    }

    private static void PropertyChanged(
        DependencyObject d,
        DependencyPropertyChangedEventArgs e)
    {
        Soccer soccer = (Soccer)d;
        soccer.InvalidateModel();
    }
  }
}
```

The biggest difference occurs inside the OnUpdateModel method, where you define two soccer models: one painted with two different colors, and the other painted with a single color. Both the HexagonGeometry and PentagonGeometry are added to the Model3DGroup to set the model. You also define a bool dependency property, IsDifferentMaterial, which provides the option of whether you want to paint the soccer with a single or two different colors.

Testing Soccer Shape

Now, you can create a soccer ball shape using the Soccer class directly in the XAML files, just like you create a 2D shape. Of course, you can also use it in code by creating an instance of your Soccer class, specifying its dependency properties, and adding it to the Viewport3D

Here I'll show you how to use Soccer class in XAML. Add a new WPF Window to the project Chapter12 and name it SoccerShapeTest. The XAML file of this example is similar to that used in demonstrating the Cube shape. You can view the code by opening the SoccerShapeTest.xaml file. The difference is that you need to add the Soccer ball shapes to Viewport3D:

```
<Viewport3D>
    <local:Soccer x:Name="soccer1"...>
    .....
    </local:Soccer>
    .....
</ViewPort3D>
```

Here, you add two soccer balls to Viewport3D: one ball is painted black-and-white colors and the other is painted a light-blue color. You also create a slider that is used to change the size of the black-white soccer ball interactively by binding the slider's Value property to the corresponding dependency properties of the object.

Figure 12-8 shows the results of running this application. Now you can change the size of the black-and-white ball by moving the slider with your mouse, and also you can rotate both soccer balls by clicking the Rotate Soccer Balls button.

Combining Shape

In the previous sections, you implemented several custom shape classes for the basic 3D shapes. In fact, it is possible for one to write a compex custom shape class that combines multiple basic geometries. In this section, you'll create such a composite shape class, which can be used in XAML files the same way that the basic custom shape classes are used.

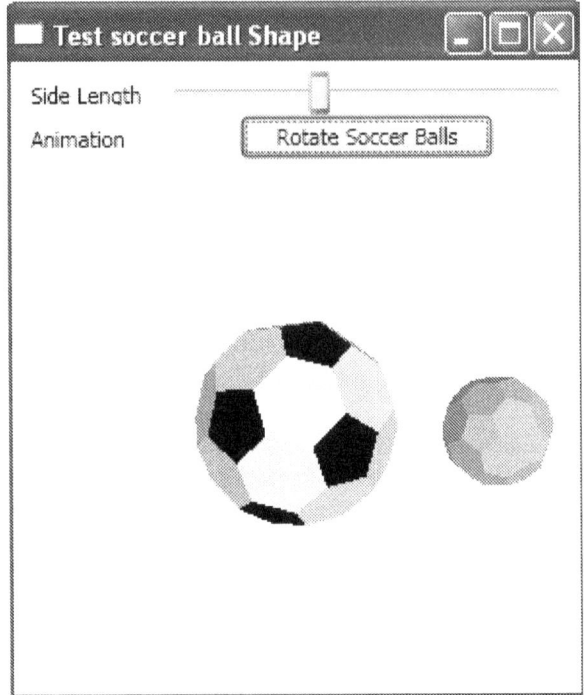

Figure 12-8 Soccer balls created using the custom shape class.

Combining Shape Class

Add a new class to the project Chapter12, change its namespace to Shapes, and name it CombineShape. The code of this class is little different from previous models. Here is the code of this class:

```
using System;
using System.Windows;
using System.Windows.Media;
using System.Windows.Media.Media3D;
using Geometries;

namespace Shapes
{
    class CombineShape : UIElement3D
    {
        protected override void OnUpdateModel()
        {
            Model3DGroup group = new Model3DGroup();
            TorusGeometry torus = new TorusGeometry();
            CylinderGeometry cylinder =
                new CylinderGeometry();

            GeometryModel3D torusModel =
```

```
                new GeometryModel3D();
        torus.R1 = 0.6 * Dimension;
        torus.R2 = 0.1 * Dimension;
        torus.Center = Center +
            new Vector3D(0, Dimension / 4, 0);
        torusModel.Geometry = torus.Mesh3D;
        torusModel.Material = TorusMaterial;
        group.Children.Add(torusModel);

        torusModel = new GeometryModel3D();
        torus.R1 = 0.65 * Dimension;
        torus.R2 = 0.2 * Dimension;
        torus.Center = Center +
            new Vector3D(0, -Dimension / 4, 0);
        torusModel.Geometry = torus.Mesh3D;
        torusModel.Material = TorusMaterial;
        group.Children.Add(torusModel);

        GeometryModel3D cylinderModel =
            new GeometryModel3D();
        cylinder.Rin = 0.4 * Dimension;
        cylinder.Rout = 0.5 * Dimension;
        cylinder.Height = 1.5 * Dimension;
        cylinder.Center = Center;
        cylinderModel.Geometry = cylinder.Mesh3D;
        cylinderModel.Material = CylinderMaterial;
        group.Children.Add(cylinderModel);

        Model = group;
    }

    // The Model property for the model:
    private static readonly DependencyProperty
        ModelProperty = DependencyProperty.Register(
        "Model", typeof(Model3D), typeof(CombineShape),
        new PropertyMetadata(ModelPropertyChanged));

    private static void ModelPropertyChanged(
        DependencyObject d,
        DependencyPropertyChangedEventArgs e)
    {
        CombineShape combine = (CombineShape)d;
        combine.Visual3DModel = (Model3D)e.NewValue;
    }

    private Model3D Model
    {
        get { return (Model3D)GetValue(ModelProperty); }
        set { SetValue(ModelProperty, value); }
    }

    // The material of the  cylinder model:
    public static readonly DependencyProperty
        CylinderMaterialProperty =
```

```
        DependencyProperty.Register("CylinderMaterial",
            typeof(Material), typeof(CombineShape),
        new PropertyMetadata(
        new DiffuseMaterial(Brushes.Blue),
        PropertyChanged));

public Material CylinderMaterial
{
    get { return (Material)GetValue(
          CylinderMaterialProperty); }
    set { SetValue(CylinderMaterialProperty, value); }
}

// The material of the  torus model:
public static readonly DependencyProperty
    TorusMaterialProperty =
    DependencyProperty.Register("TorusMaterial",
    typeof(Material), typeof(CombineShape),
    new PropertyMetadata(
    new DiffuseMaterial(Brushes.Blue),
    PropertyChanged));

public Material TorusMaterial
{
    get { return (Material)GetValue(
          TorusMaterialProperty); }
    set { SetValue(TorusMaterialProperty, value); }
}

// The dimensionof the model:
public static readonly DependencyProperty
    DimensionProperty = DependencyProperty.Register(
    "Dimension", typeof(double), typeof(CombineShape),
    new PropertyMetadata(2.0, PropertyChanged));

public double Dimension
{
    get { return (double)GetValue(DimensionProperty);}
    set { SetValue(DimensionProperty, value); }
}

// The center of the model:
public static readonly DependencyProperty
    CenterProperty = DependencyProperty.Register(
    "Center", typeof(Point3D), typeof(CombineShape),
    new PropertyMetadata(new Point3D(0.0, 0.0, 0.0),
    PropertyChanged));

public Point3D Center
{
    get { return (Point3D)GetValue(CenterProperty); }
    set { SetValue(CenterProperty, value); }
}
```

```
        private static void PropertyChanged(
            DependencyObject d,
            DependencyPropertyChangedEventArgs e)
        {
            CombineShape combine = (CombineShape)d;
            combine.InvalidateModel();
        }
    }
}
```

Here you create a composite shape using a cylinder geometry and two torus geometries. There is no limitation on the number of geometries you can use in your model. You can paint these geometries using the same material or using several different materials. In this example, you paint the two torus geometries with the TorusMaterial, and paint the cylinder geometry with the CylinderMaterial. All of the size parameters for the torus and cylinder are related to a single dependency property, Dimension, which allows you to control the size of the composite shape using a single parameter. Inside the OnUpdateModel method, you perform various transforms on the geometries in order to build your custom model.

Testing Combining Shape

Now, you can create a composite shape using the CombineShape class directly in the XAML files, just like you create a 2D shape. Of course, you can also use it in code by creating an instance of your CombineShape class, specifying its dependency properties, and adding it to the Viewport3D

Here I'll show you how to use the CombineShape class in XAML. Add a new WPF Window to the project Chapter12 and name it CombineShapeTest. The XAML file of this example is similar to that used in demonstrating the Cube shape. You can view the code by opening the CombineShapeTest.xaml file. The difference is that you need to add the combining shapes to Viewport3D:

```
<Viewport3D>
    <local:CombineShape x:Name="model"...>
    ......
    </local:CombineShape>
    ......
</ViewPort3D>
```

Here, you add a combined shape to Viewport3D. You also create a slider that is used to interactively change the size of the shape by binding the slider's Value property to the corresponding dependency properties of the object.

Figure 12-9 shows the results of running this application. Now you can change the size of the composite shape by moving the slider with your mouse, and also you can rotate it by clicking the Rotate the Shape button.

In this chapter, you learned how to write custom shape classes for various 3D objects. Following the procedures presened here, you should now be able to create your own 3D shape class library for other 3D shape structures. The advantage of this approach is that you can use the custom shape classes directly in the XAML file as children of the Viewport3D element.

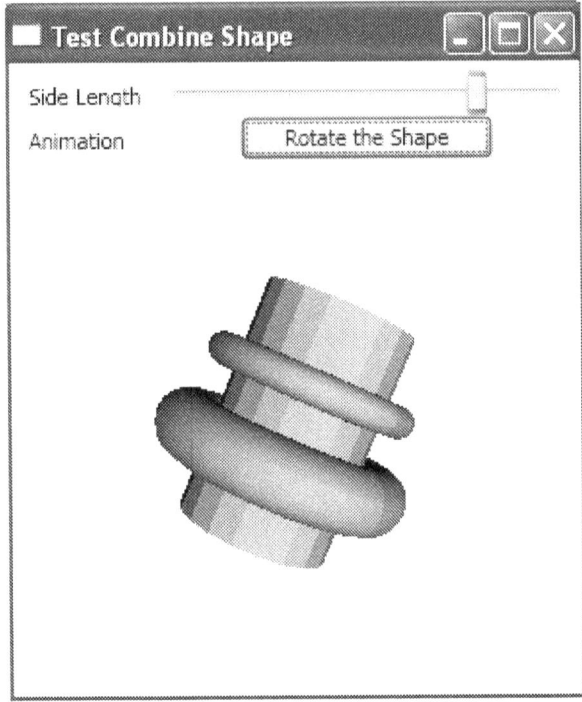

Figure 12-9 Composite shape created using the custom shape class.

Chapter 13
3D Surfaces

This chapter will show you how to create various surfaces in 3D space. Surfaces play an important role in various applications like computer graphics, virtual reality, computer games, and 3D data visualizations. The chapter begins by describing data structures and the algorithm you use to manipulate and display simple surfaces. Using this technique, you can create a variety of simple surfaces, including surfaces containing random data.

The chapter then covers several specialized techniques that you can use to create all sorts of complex surfaces, including parametric, extruded, and rotated surfaces.

Simple Surfaces

Mathematically, a surface draws a Z function on a surface for each X and Y coordinate in a region of interest. For each X and Y value, a simple surface can have at most one Z value. Complex surfaces can have multiple Z values for each pair of X and Y values, and will be discussed later in this chapter.

The coordinate system in WPF is oriented so that the Y axis gives the viewing "up" direction. To be consistent with the WPF notation, we'll consider surfaces defined by functions that return a Y value (instead of a Z value) for each X and Z coordinate in a region of interest. To translate a function from a system that gives Z as a function of X and Y, simply reverse the roles of the Y and Z axis.

You can define a simple surface by the Y-coordinates of points above a rectangular grid in the X-Z plane. The surface is formed by joining adjacent points using straight lines. Simple surfaces are useful for visualizing 2D data arrays (matrices) that are too large to display in numerical form, and for graphing functions of two variables.

Typically, a surface is formed using rectangular meshes. However, WPF only provides triangles as the basic units to represent any surface in 3D. In order to represent a surface using traditional rectangles, you need to write your own class or methods.

Rectangular Meshes

In this section, you'll learn how to write your own class and methods that allow you to create rectangular meshes. Since this class provides a common technique for generating rectangular meshes that can be used not only in simple surfaces, but in other types of complex surfaces as well, you'll implement it in a general Utility class.

Start with a new WPF project and name it Chapter13. Add a new class to this project and call it Utility. Here is the code listing of this class:

```
using System;
using System.Collections.Generic;
using System.Windows;
using System.Windows.Media;
using System.Windows.Media.Media3D;
using System.Windows.Controls;
using _3DTools;

namespace Chapter13
{
    public class Utility
    {
        public static void CreateRectangleFace(
            Point3D p0, Point3D p1, Point3D p2, Point3D p3,
            Color surfaceColor, Viewport3D viewport)
        {
            MeshGeometry3D mesh = new MeshGeometry3D();
            mesh.Positions.Add(p0);
            mesh.Positions.Add(p1);
            mesh.Positions.Add(p2);
            mesh.Positions.Add(p3);
            mesh.TriangleIndices.Add(0);
            mesh.TriangleIndices.Add(1);
            mesh.TriangleIndices.Add(2);
            mesh.TriangleIndices.Add(2);
            mesh.TriangleIndices.Add(3);
            mesh.TriangleIndices.Add(0);

            SolidColorBrush brush = new SolidColorBrush();
            brush.Color = surfaceColor;
            Material material = new DiffuseMaterial(brush);
            GeometryModel3D geometry =
                new GeometryModel3D(mesh, material);
            ModelVisual3D model = new ModelVisual3D();
            model.Content = geometry;
            viewport.Children.Add(model);
        }
```

```
public static void CreateWireframe(
    Point3D p0, Point3D p1, Point3D p2, Point3D p3,
    Color lineColor, Viewport3D viewport)
{
    ScreenSpaceLines3D ssl = new ScreenSpaceLines3D();

    ssl.Points.Add(p0);
    ssl.Points.Add(p1);
    ssl.Points.Add(p1);
    ssl.Points.Add(p2);
    ssl.Points.Add(p2);
    ssl.Points.Add(p3);
    ssl.Points.Add(p3);
    ssl.Points.Add(p0);
    ssl.Color = lineColor;
    ssl.Thickness = 2;
    viewport.Children.Add(ssl);
}

public static Point3D GetNormalize(Point3D pt,
    double xmin, double xmax,
    double ymin, double ymax,
    double zmin, double zmax)
{
    pt.X = -1 + 2 * (pt.X - xmin) / (xmax - xmin);
    pt.Y = -1 + 2 * (pt.Y - ymin) / (ymax - ymin);
    pt.Z = -1 + 2 * (pt.Z - zmin) / (zmax - zmin);
    return pt;
}
    }
}
```

This class includes three static public methods. The CreateRectangleFace method takes four vertex points as its inputs. Inside this method, the rectangular face is constructed using two triangles. You can specify the color and theViewport3D in which the rectangular face resides.

The CreateWireframe method also takes four vertices as its inputs. Here, you directly draw a rectangular mesh instead of a triangular one. When this method is called, it will create a rectangular wireframe for your surfaces.

The GetNormalize method is used to map the region of your surface into a region of [-1, 1], which gives you a better view on your screen.

SimpleSurface Class

The simplest way to store surface data is to use a 2D array. For each point (X, Z) in the region defined for the surface, the (X, Z) entry in the array gives the Y coordinate of the corresponding point on the surface.

Creating simple surfaces is easy. Add a new class called SimpleSurface to the project Chapter13. Here is the code listing of this class:

```csharp
using System;
using System.Collections.Generic;
using System.Windows;
using System.Windows.Media;
using System.Windows.Media.Media3D;
using System.Windows.Controls;

namespace Chapter13
{
    public class SimpleSurface
    {
        public delegate Point3D Function(double x, double z);

        private double xmin = -3;
        private double xmax = 3;
        private double ymin = -8;
        private double ymax = 8;
        private double zmin = -3;
        private double zmax = 3;
        private int nx = 30;
        private int nz = 30;
        private Color lineColor = Colors.Black;
        private Color surfaceColor = Colors.White;
        private Point3D center = new Point3D();
        private bool isHiddenLine = false;
        private bool isWireframe = true;
        private Viewport3D viewport3d = new Viewport3D();

        public bool IsWireframe
        {
            get { return isWireframe; }
            set { isWireframe = value; }
        }

        public bool IsHiddenLine
        {
            get { return isHiddenLine; }
            set { isHiddenLine = value; }
        }

        public Color LineColor
        {
            get { return lineColor; }
            set { lineColor = value; }
        }

        public Color SurfaceColor
        {
            get { return surfaceColor; }
            set { surfaceColor = value; }
        }

        public double Xmin
        {
```

```
    get { return xmin; }
    set { xmin = value; }
}

public double Xmax
{
    get { return xmax; }
    set { xmax = value; }
}

public double Ymin
{
    get { return ymin; }
    set { ymin = value; }
}

public double Ymax
{
    get { return ymax; }
    set { ymax = value; }
}

public double Zmin
{
    get { return zmin; }
    set { zmin = value; }
}

public double Zmax
{
    get { return zmax; }
    set { zmax = value; }
}

public int Nx
{
    get { return nx; }
    set { nx = value; }
}

public int Nz
{
    get { return nz; }
    set { nz = value; }
}

public Point3D Center
{
    get { return center; }
    set { center = value; }
}

public Viewport3D Viewport3d
{
```

```
        get { return viewport3d; }
        set { viewport3d = value; }
    }

public void CreateSurface(Function f)
{
    double dx = (Xmax - Xmin) / Nx;
    double dz = (Zmax - Zmin) / Nz;
    if (Nx < 2 || Nz < 2)
        return;

    Point3D[,] pts = new Point3D[Nx, Nz];
    for (int i = 0; i < Nx; i++)
    {
        double x = Xmin + i * dx;
        for (int j = 0; j < Nz; j++)
        {
            double z = Zmin + j * dz;
            pts[i, j] = f(x, z);
            pts[i, j] += (Vector3D)Center;
            pts[i, j] = Utility.GetNormalize(
                pts[i, j], Xmin, Xmax,
                Ymin, Ymax, Zmin, Zmax);
        }
    }

    Point3D[] p = new Point3D[4];
    for (int i = 0; i < Nx - 1; i++)
    {
        for (int j = 0; j < Nz - 1; j++)
        {
            p[0] = pts[i, j];
            p[1] = pts[i, j + 1];
            p[2] = pts[i + 1, j + 1];
            p[3] = pts[i + 1, j];

            //Create rectangular face:
            if (IsHiddenLine == false)
                Utility.CreateRectangleFace(
                    p[0], p[1], p[2], p[3],
                    SurfaceColor, Viewport3d);

            // Create wireframe:
            if (IsWireframe == true)
                Utility.CreateWireframe(
                    p[0], p[1], p[2], p[3],
                    LineColor, Viewport3d);
        }
    }
}
```

First, you define a public delegate function that allows users to import their own functions or data, which will be used to draw the surface. Then, you define several fields and their corresponding public properties. The Nx and Nz properties define the 2D data grid in the X-Z plane. Two bool properties, IsHiddenLine and IsWireframe, are used to control whether the hidden lines or wireframes appear on your surface. The default value is false for IsHiddenLine (without hidden lines), and true for IsWireframe (with wireframe).

Inside the CreateSurface method, you first populate a 2D point array with the delegate function f(x, z) on the 2D data grid, then normalize the data of this array into the region [-1, 1] by calling the GetNormalize method from the Utility class. Next, you define a rectangular mesh using four adjacent vertex points, then call the CreateRectangleFace and CreateWireframe methods from the Utility class to create the rectangular mesh. The entire surface is then created when you run over all the grid points.

Creating Simple Surfaces

Here you'll create some simple surfaces using the SimpleSurface class presented in the previous section. Add a new WPF Window application to the project Chapter13 and name it SimpleSurfaceTest. Here is the XAML file of this example:

```xml
<Window x:Class="Chapter13.SimpleSurfaceTest"
    xmlns="http://schemas.microsoft.com/winfx
        /2006/xaml/presentation"
    xmlns:x="http://schemas.microsoft.com/winfx/2006/xaml"
  Title="Simple Surface Test" Height="300" Width="300">

    <Grid>
        <Viewport3D Name="viewport">
            <Viewport3D.Camera>
                <PerspectiveCamera Position="3,3,2"
                        LookDirection="-3,-3,-2"
                        UpDirection="0,1,0"/>
            </Viewport3D.Camera>

            <ModelVisual3D>
                <ModelVisual3D.Content>
                    <Model3DGroup>
                        <AmbientLight Color="White"/>
                    </Model3DGroup>
                </ModelVisual3D.Content>
            </ModelVisual3D>
        </Viewport3D>
    </Grid>
</Window>
```

This file defines the camera and light source inside the Viewport3D named viewport. Notice that an AmbientLight source is used here which shows the object's original color. You can play with different light sources to see how they affect the appearance of your surface.

A simple surface is created in the code-behind file:

```
using System;
using System.Windows;
using System.Windows.Input;
using System.Windows.Controls;
using System.Windows.Media;
using System.Windows.Media.Media3D;

namespace Chapter13
{
    public partial class SimpleSurfaceTest : Window
    {
        private SimpleSurface ss = new SimpleSurface();

        public SimpleSurfaceTest()
        {
            InitializeComponent();

            ss.IsHiddenLine = false;
            ss.Viewport3d = viewport;
            AddSinc();
        }

        private void AddSinc()
        {
            ss.Xmin = -8;
            ss.Xmax = 8;
            ss.Zmin = -8;
            ss.Zmax = 8;
            ss.Ymin = -1;
            ss.Ymax = 1;
            ss.CreateSurface(Sinc);
        }

        private Point3D Sinc(double x, double z)
        {
            double r = Math.Sqrt(x * x + z * z) + 0.00001;
            double y = Math.Sin(r) / r;
            return new Point3D(x, y, z);
        }
    }
}
```

Here, you first create a SimpleSurface instance, and then specify the Viewport3d property of this instance with the viewport defined in the XAML file. Next, you define a Sinc function, which is called directly by the CreateSurface method. Inside the AddSinc method, you also specify the data range of interest.

Figure 13-1 shows the results of running this application.

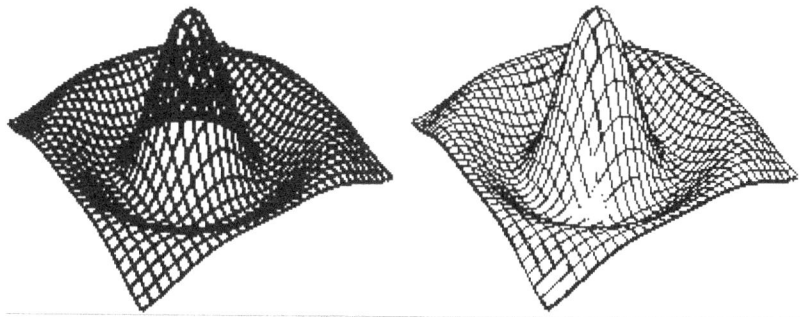

Figure 13-1 Simple surfaces with (left) and without (right) hidden lines.

You can easily create simple surfaces using other functions. For example, you can create a peak surface using a peak function:

```
private void AddPeaks()
{
    ss.Xmin = -3;
    ss.Xmax = 3;
    ss.Zmin = -3;
    ss.Zmax = 3;
    ss.Ymin = -8;
    ss.Ymax = 8;
    ss.CreateSurface(Peaks);
}

private Point3D Peaks(double x, double z)
{
double y = 3 * Math.Pow((1 - x), 2) *
Math.Exp(-x * x - (z + 1) * (z + 1)) -
    10 * (0.2 * x - Math.Pow(x, 3) -
    Math.Pow(z, 5)) * Math.Exp(-x * x - z * z) -
    1 / 3 * Math.Exp(-(x + 1) * (x + 1) - z * z);
    return new Point3D(x, y, z);
}
```

This function generates the surfaces shown in Figure 13-2.

You can even create a surface using a random function:

```
private void AddRandomSurface()
{
    ss.Xmin = -8;
    ss.Xmax = 8;
    ss.Zmin = -8;
    ss.Zmax = 8;
    ss.Ymin = -1;
    ss.Ymax = 1;
    ss.CreateSurface(RandomSurface);
}

private Random rand = new Random();
private Point3D RandomSurface(double x, double z)
```

```
{
    double r = Math.Sqrt(x * x + z * z) + 0.00001;
    double y = Math.Sin(r) / r  +
              0.2 * rand.NextDouble();
    return new Point3D(x, y, z);
}
```

This function produces the surfaces shown in Figure 13-3.

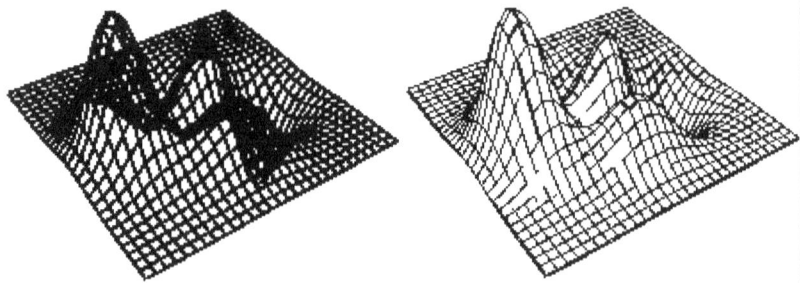

Figure 13-2 Peak surfaces with (left) and without (right) hidden lines.

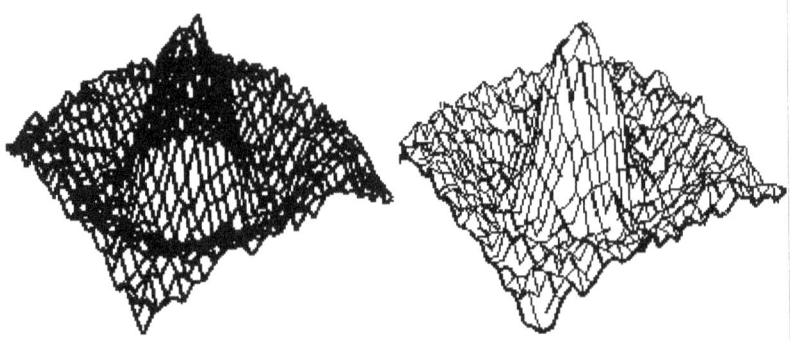

Figure 13-3 Random surfaces with (left) and without (right) hidden lines.

Parametric Surfaces

In the previous section, you learned how to create simple surfaces. A key feature of this type of surface is that there is at most one Y value for each pair of X and Z values. However, sometimes you may want to create a complex surface of a certain shape. This kind of complex surface can't be represented by a simple function. For certain values of X and Z, this surface has more than one Y value. This means that you can't use the approach discussed in the previous sections to store and display the data.

One way to represent this type of surface is to use a set of the parametric equations. These equations define the X, Y, and Z coordinates of points on the surface in terms of the parametric variables u and v. There are many complex surfaces that can be represented using parametric equations. For example, sphere, torus, and quadric surfaces are all parametric surfaces.

ParametricSurface Class

In this section, you'll write a ParametricSurface class that can be used to create parametric surfaces. Add a new class called ParametricSurface to the project Chapter13. Here is the code listing of this class:

```
using System;
using System.Collections.Generic;
using System.Windows;
using System.Windows.Media;
using System.Windows.Media.Media3D;
using System.Windows.Controls;

namespace Chapter13
{
    public class ParametricSurface
    {
        public delegate Point3D Function(double u, double v);

        private int nu = 30;
        private int nv = 30;
        private double umin = -3;
        private double umax = 3;
        private double vmin = -8;
        private double vmax = 8;
        private double xmin = -1;
        private double xmax = 1;
        private double ymin = -1;
        private double ymax = 1;
        private double zmin = -1;
        private double zmax = 1;
        private Color lineColor = Colors.Black;
        private Color surfaceColor = Colors.White;
        private Point3D center = new Point3D();
        private bool isHiddenLine = false;
        private bool isWireframe = true;
        private Viewport3D viewport3d = new Viewport3D();

        public bool IsWireframe
        {
            get { return isWireframe; }
            set { isWireframe = value; }
        }

        public bool IsHiddenLine
        {
            get { return isHiddenLine; }
            set { isHiddenLine = value; }
        }
```

```
public Color LineColor
{
    get { return lineColor; }
    set { lineColor = value; }
}

public Color SurfaceColor
{
    get { return surfaceColor; }
    set { surfaceColor = value; }
}

public double Umin
{
    get { return umin; }
    set { umin = value; }
}

public double Umax
{
    get { return umax; }
    set { umax = value; }
}

public double Vmin
{
    get { return vmin; }
    set { vmin = value; }
}

public double Vmax
{
    get { return vmax; }
    set { vmax = value; }
}

public int Nu
{
    get { return nu; }
    set { nu = value; }
}

public int Nv
{
    get { return nv; }
    set { nv = value; }
}

public double Xmin
{
    get { return xmin; }
    set { xmin = value; }
}
```

```
public double Xmax
{
    get { return xmax; }
    set { xmax = value; }
}

public double Ymin
{
    get { return ymin; }
    set { ymin = value; }
}

public double Ymax
{
    get { return ymax; }
    set { ymax = value; }
}

public double Zmin
{
    get { return zmin; }
    set { zmin = value; }
}

public double Zmax
{
    get { return zmax; }
    set { zmax = value; }
}

public Point3D Center
{
    get { return center; }
    set { center = value; }
}

public Viewport3D Viewport3d
{
    get { return viewport3d; }
    set { viewport3d = value; }
}

public void CreateSurface(Function f)
{
    double du = (Umax - Umin) / (Nu - 1);
    double dv = (Vmax - Vmin) / (Nv - 1);
    if (Nu < 2 || Nv < 2)
        return;

    Point3D[,] pts = new Point3D[Nu, Nv];
    for (int i = 0; i < Nu; i++)
    {
        double u = Umin + i * du;
```

```
        for (int j = 0; j < Nv; j++)
        {
            double v = Vmin + j * dv;
            pts[i, j] = f(u, v);
            pts[i, j] += (Vector3D)Center;
            pts[i, j] = Utility.GetNormalize(
                pts[i, j], Xmin, Xmax,
                Ymin, Ymax, Zmin, Zmax);
        }
    }

    Point3D[] p = new Point3D[4];
    for (int i = 0; i < Nu - 1; i++)
    {
        for (int j = 0; j < Nv - 1; j++)
        {
            p[0] = pts[i, j];
            p[1] = pts[i, j + 1];
            p[2] = pts[i + 1, j + 1];
            p[3] = pts[i + 1, j];

            //Create rectangular face:
            if (IsHiddenLine == false)
                Utility.CreateRectangleFace(
                    p[0], p[1], p[2], p[3],
                    SurfaceColor, Viewport3d);

            // Create wireframe:
            if (IsWireframe == true)
                Utility.CreateWireframe(
                    p[0], p[1], p[2], p[3],
                    LineColor, Viewport3d);
        }
    }
}
}
```

The structure of this class is basically similar to that of the SimpleSurface class, except that you define the delegate function using the parametric variables u and v instead of x and z. You also define the umin, umax, vmin, and vmax fields and their corresponding properties to specify the parameter region of interest. This means that in the parametric u-v space, you create a constant u-v grid (with equal spacing in the u and v directions). The delegate function f(u, v) in this space has at most one value for each pair of u and v. Thus, you actually create a simple surface in the u-v space using an approach similar to the one used to create simple surfaces. The trick to creating a parametric surface is to map the simple surface in the u-v space back to the X-Y-Z coordinate system. This mapping is governed by the parametric equations. The resulting surface in the real world space can be very different than that in the parametric space.

Creating Parametric Surfaces

Here, I'll demonstrate how to create some common parametric surfaces using the ParametricSurface class presented in the previous section. Add a new WPF Windows application to the project Chapter13 and name it ParametricSurfaceTest. The XAML file of this example is the same as that used to create simple surfaces. In the following, you will create several parametric surfaces in code.

Helicoid Surface

A helicoid is a trace of a line. For any point on the surface, there is a line on the surface passing through it. Helicoids are shaped like screws and can be described by the following parametric equations in the Cartesian coordinate system:

$$x = u \cos v$$

$$y = v$$

$$z = u \sin v$$

You can easily create a helicoid surface using the ParametricSurface class in code:

```
using System;
using System.Windows;
using System.Windows.Input;
using System.Windows.Controls;
using System.Windows.Media;
using System.Windows.Media.Media3D;

namespace Chapter13
{
    public partial class ParametricSurfaceTest : Window
    {
        private ParametricSurface ps =
            new ParametricSurface();

        public ParametricSurfaceTest()
        {
            InitializeComponent();
            ps.IsHiddenLine = false;
            ps.Viewport3d = viewport;
            AddHelicoid();
        }

        private void AddHelicoid()
        {
            ps.Umin = 0;
            ps.Umax = 1;
            ps.Vmin = -3 * Math.PI;
            ps.Vmax = 3 * Math.PI;
```

```
        ps.Nv = 100;
        ps.Nu = 10;
        ps.Ymin = ps.Vmin;
        ps.Ymax = ps.Vmax;
        ps.CreateSurface(Helicoid);
    }

    private Point3D Helicoid(double u, double v)
    {
        double x = u * Math.Cos(v);
        double z = u * Math.Sin(v);
        double y = v;
        return new Point3D(x, y, z);
    }
  }
}
```

The Helicoid method defines a delegate function in terms of the parameters u and v, and returns the Point3D object in X-Y-Z coordinates. Inside the AddHelicoid method, you specify the parameter region and call the CreateSurface method using the Helicoid function to create the parametric surface.

Figure 13-4 shows the result of running this example.

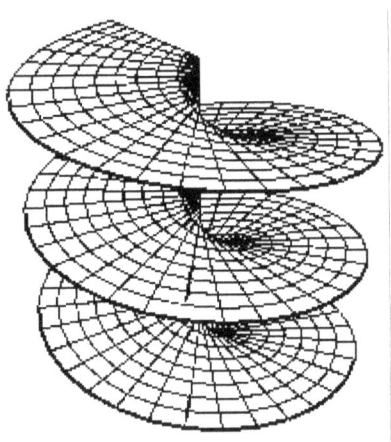

Figure 13-4 Helicoid surface.

Sphere Surface

You can also create a sphere surface using the ParametricSurface class. This can be done by simply replacing the Helicoid and AddHelicoid methods of the previous code listing with the following two code snippet:

```
private void AddSphere()
{
    ps.Umin = 0;
```

```
            ps.Umax = 2 * Math.PI;
            ps.Vmin = -0.5 * Math.PI;
            ps.Vmax = 0.5 * Math.PI;
            ps.Nu = 20;
            ps.Nv = 20;
            ps.CreateSurface(Sphere);
        }

        private Point3D Sphere(double u, double v)
        {
            double x = Math.Cos(v) * Math.Cos(u);
            double z = Math.Cos(v) * Math.Sin(u);
            double y = Math.Sin(v);
            return new Point3D(x, y, z);
        }
```

This generates the results shown in Figure 13-5. You can see that the current results provide a better surface appearance than the sphere created in Chapter 10 using triangular meshes.

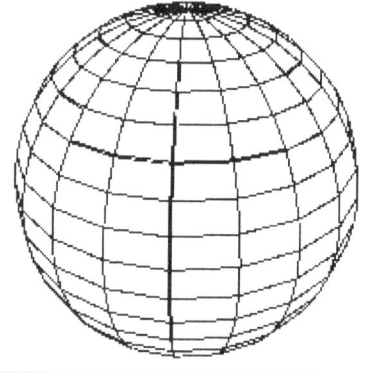

Figure 13-5 Sphere surface.

Torus Surface

You can also use the ParametricSurface class to create a torus surface with the following methods:

```
        private void AddTorus()
        {
            ps.Umin = 0;
            ps.Umax = 2 * Math.PI;
            ps.Vmin = 0;
            ps.Vmax = 2 * Math.PI;
            ps.Nu = 50;
            ps.Nv = 20;
            ps.CreateSurface(Torus);
        }
```

```
private Point3D Torus(double u, double v)
{
    double x = (1 + 0.3 * Math.Cos(v)) * Math.Cos(u);
    double z = (1 + 0.3 * Math.Cos(v)) * Math.Sin(u);
    double y = 0.3 * Math.Sin(v);
    return new Point3D(x, y, z);
}
```

This gives the result shown in Figure 13-6.

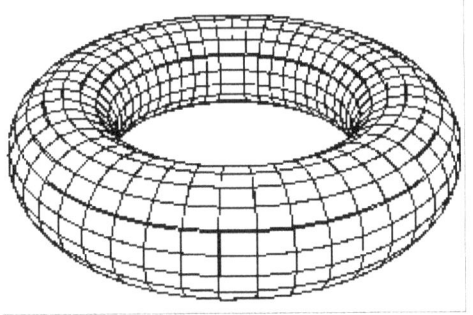

Figure 13-6 Torus surface.

Quadric Surfaces

You can also easily create various quadric surfaces using the ParametricSurface class. For example, consider the following four irreducible quadrics:

- Hyperboloid – described by the following parametric equations:

$$x = a \cos u \cosh v$$
$$y = b \sinh v$$
$$z = c \sin u \cosh v$$

- Paraboloid – described by the following parametric equations:

$$x = av \cosh u$$
$$y = v^2$$
$$z = bv \sinh u$$

- Elliptic cone – described by the following parametric equations:

$$x = av \cos u$$
$$y = bv$$
$$z = cv \sin u$$

- Elliptic cylinder – described by the following parametric equations:

$$x = a\cos u$$

$$y = v$$

$$z = b\sin u$$

where a, b, and c are constants. The corresponding methods can be easily implemented by using the above parameteric equations. You can view the complete source code by opening the file ParametricSurfaceTest.xaml.cs.

Figure 13-7 shows the results of these quadric surfaces created using the ParametricSurface class.

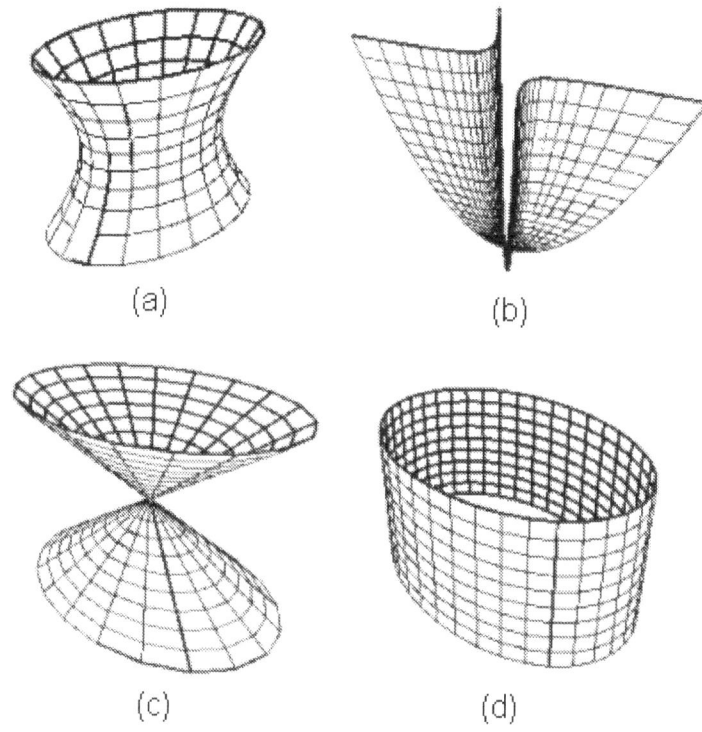

(a)

(b)

(c)

(d)

Figure 13-7 Quadric surfaces: (a) Hyperboloid, (b) Paraboloid, (c) Elliptic cone, and (d) Elliptic cylinder.

Extruded Surfaces

In 3D graphics, you can perform an extrusion by moving a base curve through space along a generating path. When you move the base curve along the generating path, the curve sweeps out a 3D surface. This type of surface is called an extruded surface. The cross sections of the surface look like the base curve that you are moving.

For example, if you move a line segment in the direction perpendicular to it, you'll sweep out a rectangle. In this case, the cross sections of the surface are line segments.

The generating path is not limited to a straight line. It can also be a longer path or a curved path. The base curve can be any kind of curve. Extruded surfaces have several interesting features. First, each of the areas that make up the surface is a parallelogram. Each time the base curve is moved along the generating path, the points along the curve are moved a fixed distance and direction determined by the generating path. Since the distance and direction are the same for any two adjacent points along the curve, the line segments connecting the points' new and old positions are parallel. Because these segments are also the same length, connecting any two of these segments gives a parallelogram.

Another interesting feature of extruded surfaces is that you can create the same surface either by moving the base curve along the generating path or by moving the generating path along the base curve. You can create extruded surfaces using either approach.

Like the simple surfaces described earlier in this chapter, extruded surfaces are generated from a set of data points. As you did when you created simple surfaces, you can implement a ExtrudeSurface class that stores, manipulates, and displays extruded surfaces.

ExtrudeSurface Class

In order to create the ExtrudeSurface class, you need two sets of data points: one set of data points is created along the base curve, and the other is created along the generating path. These two sets of data points can be defined using two List objects, which allow the user to specify the base curve and the generating path.

Add a new ExtrudeSurface class to the project Chapter13. Here is the code listing of this class:

```
using System;
using System.Collections.Generic;
using System.Windows;
using System.Windows.Media;
using System.Windows.Media.Media3D;
using System.Windows.Controls;
using _3DTools;

namespace Chapter13
{
    public class ExtrudeSurface
    {
        private List<Point3D> curvePoints =
                        new List<Point3D>();
        private List<Point3D> pathPoints =
                        new List<Point3D>();
```

```
private double xmin = -1;
private double xmax = 1;
private double ymin = -1;
private double ymax = 1;
private double zmin = -1;
private double zmax = 1;
private Color lineColor = Colors.Black;
private Color surfaceColor = Colors.White;
private Point3D center = new Point3D();
private bool isHiddenLine = false;
private bool isWireframe = true;
private Viewport3D viewport3d = new Viewport3D();

public bool IsWireframe
{
    get { return isWireframe; }
    set { isWireframe = value; }
}

public bool IsHiddenLine
{
    get { return isHiddenLine; }
    set { isHiddenLine = value; }
}

public Color LineColor
{
    get { return lineColor; }
    set { lineColor = value; }
}

public Color SurfaceColor
{
    get { return surfaceColor; }
    set { surfaceColor = value; }
}

public List<Point3D> CurvePoints
{
    get { return curvePoints; }
    set { curvePoints = value; }
}

public List<Point3D> PathPoints
{
    get { return pathPoints; }
    set { pathPoints = value; }
}

public double Xmin
{
    get { return xmin; }
    set { xmin = value; }
}
```

```csharp
public double Xmax
{
    get { return xmax; }
    set { xmax = value; }
}

public double Ymin
{
    get { return ymin; }
    set { ymin = value; }
}

public double Ymax
{
    get { return ymax; }
    set { ymax = value; }
}

public double Zmin
{
    get { return zmin; }
    set { zmin = value; }
}

public double Zmax
{
    get { return zmax; }
    set { zmax = value; }
}

public Point3D Center
{
    get { return center; }
    set { center = value; }
}

public Viewport3D Viewport3d
{
    get { return viewport3d; }
    set { viewport3d = value; }
}

public void CreateSurface()
{
    double dx, dy, dz;

    // create all points used to create
    // extruded surface:
    Point3D[,] pts = new Point3D[PathPoints.Count,
                              CurvePoints.Count];
    for (int i = 0; i < PathPoints.Count; i++)
    {
        // Calculate offsets for path points:
```

```
dx = PathPoints[i].X - PathPoints[0].X;
dy = PathPoints[i].Y - PathPoints[0].Y;
dz = PathPoints[i].Z - PathPoints[0].Z;

for (int j = 0; j < CurvePoints.Count; j++)
{
    pts[i, j].X = CurvePoints[j].X + dx;
    pts[i, j].Y = CurvePoints[j].Y + dy;
    pts[i, j].Z = CurvePoints[j].Z + dz;
    pts[i, j] += (Vector3D)Center;
    pts[i, j] = Utility.GetNormalize(
        pts[i, j], Xmin, Xmax,
        Ymin, Ymax, Zmin, Zmax);
}
}

Point3D[] p = new Point3D[4];
for (int i = 0; i < PathPoints.Count - 1; i++)
{
    for (int j = 0; j < CurvePoints.Count - 1;
        j++)
    {
        p[0] = pts[i, j];
        p[1] = pts[i + 1, j];
        p[2] = pts[i + 1, j + 1];
        p[3] = pts[i, j + 1];

        //Create rectangular face:
        if (IsHiddenLine == false)
            Utility.CreateRectangleFace(
                p[0], p[1], p[2], p[3],
                SurfaceColor, Viewport3d);

        // Create wireframe:
        if (IsWireframe == true)
            Utility.CreateWireframe(
                p[0], p[1], p[2], p[3],
                LineColor, Viewport3d);
    }
}
}
}
```

This class begins by defining two Point3D Lists: curvePoints and pathPoints, which will be used to define the base curve and the generating path. The other fields and corresponding properties are similar to those used in creating simple surfaces.

Inside the CreateSurface method, you compute the positions of the points on the surface using the CurvePoints and PathPoints objects. As long as all of the points on the surface are obtained, you can process them the same way you did when you created simple surfaces.

Creating Extruded Surfaces

It is easy to create extruded surfaces using the ExtrudeSurface class. Add a new WPF Window application to the project Chapter13 and name it ExtrudeSurfaceTest. The XAML file of this example is the same as that used to create simple surfaces. The following is the code-behind file of this example:

```
using System;
using System.Windows;
using System.Windows.Input;
using System.Windows.Controls;
using System.Windows.Media;
using System.Windows.Media.Media3D;

namespace Chapter13
{
    public partial class ExtrudeSurfaceTest : Window
    {
        private ExtrudeSurface es = new ExtrudeSurface();

        public ExtrudeSurfaceTest()
        {
            InitializeComponent();

            es.Viewport3d = viewport;
            es.IsHiddenLine = false;
            AddExtrudeSurface1();
            //AddExtrudeSurface2();
        }

        // Extruded surface:
        private void AddExtrudeSurface1()
        {
            for (int i = 0; i < 17; i++)
            {
                double angle = i * Math.PI / 16 +
                    3 * Math.PI / 2;
                es.CurvePoints.Add(
                    new Point3D(Math.Cos(angle),
                    0, Math.Sin(angle)));
            }

            for (int i = 0; i < 33; i++)
            {
                es.PathPoints.Add(new Point3D(
                    Math.Cos(i * Math.PI / 12),
                    i * Math.PI / 12, 0));
            }
            es.Xmin = -3;
            es.Xmax = 3;
            es.Ymin = 5;
            es.Ymax = 20;
            es.Zmin = -3;
```

```
            es.Zmax = 5;
            es.CreateSurface();
        }

        // Another Extruded surface:
        private void AddExtrudeSurface2()
        {
            for (int i = 0; i < 17; i++)
            {
                double angle = i * Math.PI / 8;
                es.CurvePoints.Add(new Point3D(
                    1 + 0.3 * Math.Cos(angle), 0,
                    0.3 * Math.Sin(angle)));
            }

            for (int i = 0; i < 45; i++)
            {
                double angle = i * Math.PI / 16;
                es.PathPoints.Add(new Point3D(
                    1.3*Math.Cos(angle), angle,
                    1.3*Math.Sin(angle)));
            }
            es.Xmin = -3;
            es.Xmax = 3;
            es.Ymin = 5;
            es.Ymax = 30;
            es.Zmin = -3;
            es.Zmax = 3;
            es.CreateSurface();
        }
    }
}
```

Here you create two extruded surfaces. The first surface is generated by moving a semicircle (the base curve) along a Cosine path (the generating path). The other surface is created by moving a cirle (the base curve) along a helix path (the generating path).

Figure 13-8 shows the results of running this example.

Surfaces of Revolution

When you create an extruded surface, you move a base curve along a generating path. On the other hand, in order to create a surface of revolution, you simply rotate a base curve around an axis of rotation. Figure 13-9 shows a surface of revolution with the base curve drawn in heavy lines. To create this surface, the base curve is rotated around the Y axis.

Creating a surface of revolution is similar to creating an extruded surface. In both cases, you take a base curve and repeatedly transform it. You can produce a surface of revolution by rotating the base curve around any axis in 3D space.

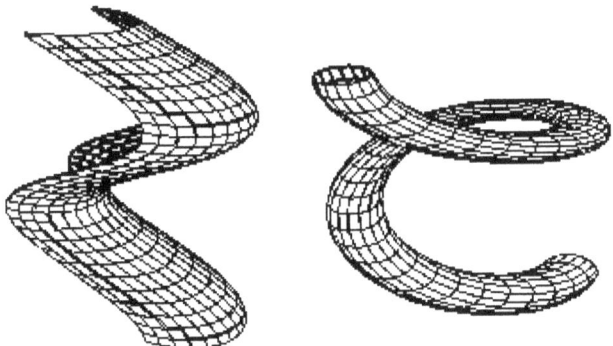

Figure 13-8 Extruded surfaces in WPF.

In practice, however, it is much easier to rotate the base curve around the coordinate axes. If you want to rotate a curve around some other axis, you can first apply translations and rotations until the axis coincides with a coordinate axis. After you perform the rotation of the base curve around the coordinate axis, you then simply translate and rotate the axis back to its original position. These transform operations are described in detail in Chapter 9.

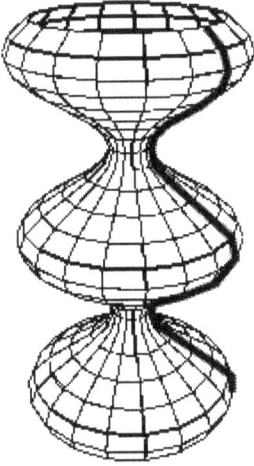

Figure 13-9 A surface of revolution created by rotating a base curve (heavy lines) around the Y axis.

RotateSurface Class

In this section, you'll implement a RotateSurface class, which can be used to create surfaces of revolution. Add a new class called RotateSurface to the project Chapter13. Here is the code listing of this class:

```
using System;
using System.Collections.Generic;
```

```csharp
using System.Windows;
using System.Windows.Media;
using System.Windows.Media.Media3D;
using System.Windows.Controls;
using _3DTools;

namespace Chapter13
{
    public class RorateSurface
    {
        private List<Point3D> curvePoints =
                            new List<Point3D>();
        private int thetaDiv = 20;
        private double xmin = -1;
        private double xmax = 1;
        private double ymin = -1;
        private double ymax = 1;
        private double zmin = -1;
        private double zmax = 1;
        private Color lineColor = Colors.Black;
        private Color surfaceColor = Colors.White;
        private Point3D center = new Point3D();
        private bool isHiddenLine = false;
        private bool isWireframe = true;
        private Viewport3D viewport3d = new Viewport3D();

        public bool IsWireframe
        {
            get { return isWireframe; }
            set { isWireframe = value; }
        }

        public int ThetaDiv
        {
            get { return thetaDiv; }
            set { thetaDiv = value; }
        }

        public bool IsHiddenLine
        {
            get { return isHiddenLine; }
            set { isHiddenLine = value; }
        }

        public Color LineColor
        {
            get { return lineColor; }
            set { lineColor = value; }
        }

        public Color SurfaceColor
        {
            get { return surfaceColor; }
            set { surfaceColor = value; }
```

```csharp
        }

        public List<Point3D> CurvePoints
        {
            get { return curvePoints; }
            set { curvePoints = value; }
        }

        public double Xmin
        {
            get { return xmin; }
            set { xmin = value; }
        }

        public double Xmax
        {
            get { return xmax; }
            set { xmax = value; }
        }

        public double Ymin
        {
            get { return ymin; }
            set { ymin = value; }
        }

        public double Ymax
        {
            get { return ymax; }
            set { ymax = value; }
        }

        public double Zmin
        {
            get { return zmin; }
            set { zmin = value; }
        }

        public double Zmax
        {
            get { return zmax; }
            set { zmax = value; }
        }

        public Point3D Center
        {
            get { return center; }
            set { center = value; }
        }

        public Viewport3D Viewport3d
        {
            get { return viewport3d; }
            set { viewport3d = value; }
```

```
}

private Point3D GetPosition(double r,
    double y, double theta)
{
    double x = r * Math.Cos(theta);
    double z = -r * Math.Sin(theta);
    return new Point3D(x, y, z);
}

public void CreateSurface()
{
    // create all points used to create surfaces
    // of revolution around the Y axis:
    Point3D[,] pts = new Point3D[ThetaDiv,
        CurvePoints.Count];
    for (int i = 0; i < ThetaDiv; i++)
    {
        double theta =
            i * 2 * Math.PI / (ThetaDiv - 1);
        for (int j = 0; j < CurvePoints.Count; j++)
        {
            double x = CurvePoints[j].X;
            double z = CurvePoints[j].Z;
            double r = Math.Sqrt(x * x + z * z);

            pts[i, j] = GetPosition(r,
                CurvePoints[j].Y, theta);
            pts[i, j] += (Vector3D)Center;
            pts[i, j] = Utility.GetNormalize(
                pts[i, j], Xmin, Xmax,
                Ymin, Ymax, Zmin, Zmax);
        }
    }

    Point3D[] p = new Point3D[4];
    for (int i = 0; i < ThetaDiv - 1; i++)
    {
        for (int j = 0; j < CurvePoints.Count - 1;
            j++)
        {
            p[0] = pts[i, j];
            p[1] = pts[i + 1, j];
            p[2] = pts[i + 1, j + 1];
            p[3] = pts[i, j + 1];

            //Create rectangular face:
            if (IsHiddenLine == false)
                Utility.CreateRectangleFace(
                    p[0], p[1], p[2], p[3],
                    SurfaceColor, Viewport3d);

            // Create wireframe:
            if (IsWireframe == true)
```

```
                            Utility.CreateWireframe(
                            p[0], p[1], p[2], p[3],
                            LineColor, Viewport3d);
                    }
                }
            }
        }
    }
}
```

This class begins by defining a Point3D list object called curvePoints, which will be used to create the base curve. The other fields and corresponding properties are similar to those used in creating simple surfaces.

Inside the CreateSurface method, you compute the positions of the points on the surface by using the CurvePoints and GetPostion methods. The GetPosition method computes the positions of the points on the surface when the base curve is rotated around the Y axis. As long as all of the points on the surface are obtained, you can process them the same way you processed simple surfaces.

Creating Surfaces of Revelution

It is easy to create surfaces of revolution using the RotateSurface class. Add a new WPF Window application to the project Chapter13 and name it RotateSurfaceTest. The XAML file of this example is the same as that used to create simple surfaces. The following is the code-behind file of this example:

```
using System;
using System.Windows;
using System.Windows.Input;
using System.Windows.Controls;
using System.Windows.Media;
using System.Windows.Media.Media3D;

namespace Chapter13
{
    public partial class RotateSurfaceTest : Window
    {
        private RorateSurface rs = new RorateSurface();

        public RotateSurfaceTest()
        {
            InitializeComponent();

            rs.Viewport3d = viewport;
            rs.IsHiddenLine = false;
            AddRotateSurface();
            //AddSphereSurface();
            //AddTorusSurface();
        }

        // Rotated surface:
        private void AddRotateSurface()
```

```
{
    for (int i = 0; i < 33; i++)
    {
        double y = i * Math.PI / 12;
        double siny = Math.Sin(y);
        rs.CurvePoints.Add(new Point3D(0.2 +
            siny * siny, y, 0));
    }
    rs.Xmin = -3;
    rs.Xmax = 3;
    rs.Ymin = 5;
    rs.Ymax = 15;
    rs.Zmin = -3;
    rs.Zmax = 3;
    rs.CreateSurface();
}

// Sphere surface:
private void AddSphereSurface()
{
    for (int i = 0; i < 11; i++)
    {
        double theta = -Math.PI / 2 +
            i * Math.PI / 10;
        rs.CurvePoints.Add(
            new Point3D(Math.Cos(theta),
            Math.Sin(theta), 0));
    }
    rs.Xmin = -2;
    rs.Xmax = 2;
    rs.Ymin = 0;
    rs.Ymax = 4;
    rs.Zmin = -2;
    rs.Zmax = 2;
    rs.CreateSurface();
}

// Torus surface:
private void AddTorusSurface()
{
    for (int i = 0; i < 21; i++)
    {
        double theta = i * Math.PI / 10;
        Point3D pt = new Point3D(
            0.3 * Math.Cos(theta),
            0.3 * Math.Sin(theta), 0);
        pt += new Vector3D(1, 0, 0);
        rs.CurvePoints.Add(pt);
    }
    rs.Xmin = -2;
    rs.Xmax = 2;
    rs.Ymin = 0;
    rs.Ymax = 4;
    rs.Zmin = -2;
```

```
                    rs.Zmax = 2;
                    rs.CreateSurface();
            }
        }
    }
```

This code creates three surfaces of revolution. The first surface is created by rotating a sine squared function around the Y axis, which is shown in Figure 13-9. The second surface represents a sphere, which is created by rotating a semicircle around the Y axis. The third surface represents a torus, which is produced by rotating a circle around the Y axis.

The sphere and torus surfaces generated using this approach are shown in Figure 13-10.

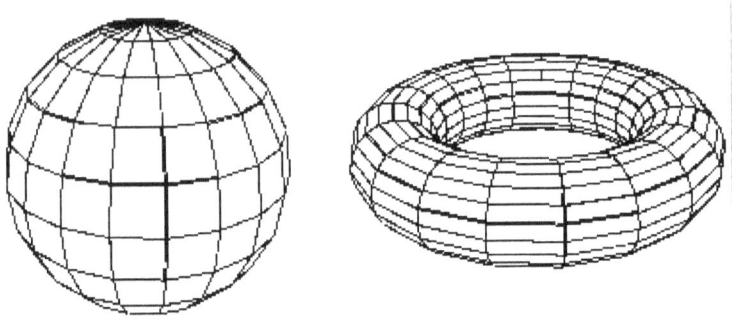

Figure 13-10 Sphere and torus created using the RotateSurface class.

You can see that the sphere and torus surfaces can be produced using several different methods, which provides flexibity when you need to create these surfaces – you can choose the approach most suitable for your application.

Surface Shading

In the previous sections, we created surfaces using the rectangular mesh lines. In some applications, however, you may want to paint the surfaces with different color and shading effects. In this section, you'll learn how to paint surfaces with different color, shading, and lighting effects. When you are considering surface shading here, you won't draw mesh lines on the surfaces.

SurfaceShading Class

In this section, you'll write a SurfaceShading class, which can be used to create surfaces with lighting and shading effects. Add a new class called SurfaceShading to the project Chapter13. Here is the code listing of this class:

```
using System;
using System.Collections.Generic;
using System.Windows;
```

```
using System.Windows.Media;
using System.Windows.Media.Media3D;
using System.Windows.Controls;

namespace Chapter13
{
    public class SurfaceShading
    {
        public delegate Point3D Function(double u, double v);

        private MaterialGroup materialGroup =
                            new MaterialGroup();
        private Material backMaterial = new DiffuseMaterial();
        private int nu = 30;
        private int nv = 30;
        private double umin = -3;
        private double umax = 3;
        private double vmin = -8;
        private double vmax = 8;
        private double xmin = -1;
        private double xmax = 1;
        private double ymin = -1;
        private double ymax = 1;
        private double zmin = -1;
        private double zmax = 1;
        private Point3D center = new Point3D();
        private Viewport3D viewport3d = new Viewport3D();

        public Material BackMaterial
        {
            get { return backMaterial; }
            set { backMaterial = value; }
        }

        public MaterialGroup MaterialGroup
        {
            get { return materialGroup; }
            set { materialGroup = value; }
        }

        public double Umin
        {
            get { return umin; }
            set { umin = value; }
        }

        public double Umax
        {
            get { return umax; }
            set { umax = value; }
        }

        public double Vmin
        {
```

```
            get { return vmin; }
            set { vmin = value; }
        }

        public double Vmax
        {
            get { return vmax; }
            set { vmax = value; }
        }

        public int Nu
        {
            get { return nu; }
            set { nu = value; }
        }

        public int Nv
        {
            get { return nv; }
            set { nv = value; }
        }

        public double Xmin
        {
            get { return xmin; }
            set { xmin = value; }
        }

        public double Xmax
        {
            get { return xmax; }
            set { xmax = value; }
        }

        public double Ymin
        {
            get { return ymin; }
            set { ymin = value; }
        }

        public double Ymax
        {
            get { return ymax; }
            set { ymax = value; }
        }

        public double Zmin
        {
            get { return zmin; }
            set { zmin = value; }
        }

        public double Zmax
        {
```

```
        get { return zmax; }
        set { zmax = value; }
}

public Point3D Center
{
    get { return center; }
    set { center = value; }
}

public Viewport3D Viewport3d
{
    get { return viewport3d; }
    set { viewport3d = value; }
}

public void CreateSurface(Function f)
{
    double du = (Umax - Umin) / (Nu - 1);
    double dv = (Vmax - Vmin) / (Nv - 1);
    if (Nu < 2 || Nv < 2)
        return;

    Point3D[,] pts = new Point3D[Nu, Nv];
    for (int i = 0; i < Nu; i++)
    {
        double u = Umin + i * du;
        for (int j = 0; j < Nv; j++)
        {
            double v = Vmin + j * dv;
            pts[i, j] = f(u, v);
            pts[i, j] += (Vector3D)Center;
            pts[i, j] = GetNormalize(pts[i, j]);
        }
    }

    Point3D[] p = new Point3D[4];
    for (int i = 0; i < Nu - 1; i++)
    {
        for (int j = 0; j < Nv - 1; j++)
        {
            p[0] = pts[i, j];
            p[1] = pts[i, j + 1];
            p[2] = pts[i + 1, j + 1];
            p[3] = pts[i + 1, j];

            CreateRectangleFace(p[0], p[1], p[2], p[3]);
        }
    }
}

public void CreateRectangleFace(Point3D p0,
    Point3D p1, Point3D p2, Point3D p3)
{
```

```
MeshGeometry3D mesh = new MeshGeometry3D();
mesh.Positions.Add(p0);
mesh.Positions.Add(p1);
mesh.Positions.Add(p2);
mesh.Positions.Add(p3);
mesh.TriangleIndices.Add(0);
mesh.TriangleIndices.Add(1);
mesh.TriangleIndices.Add(2);
mesh.TriangleIndices.Add(2);
mesh.TriangleIndices.Add(3);
mesh.TriangleIndices.Add(0);

GeometryModel3D geometry =
    new GeometryModel3D(mesh, MaterialGroup);
geometry.BackMaterial = BackMaterial;
ModelVisual3D model = new ModelVisual3D();
model.Content = geometry;
Viewport3d.Children.Add(model);
}

public Point3D GetNormalize(Point3D pt)
{
    pt.X = -1 + 2 * (pt.X - Xmin) / (Xmax - Xmin);
    pt.Y = -1 + 2 * (pt.Y - Ymin) / (Ymax - Ymin);
    pt.Z = -1 + 2 * (pt.Z - Zmin) / (Zmax - Zmin);
    return pt;
}
}
}
```

This class creates surfaces based on the parametric approach discussed earlier. In order to obtain a better color and lighting effect, you use a MaterialGroup to specify the Material property of the surfaces. The MaterialGroup can contain multiple materials. You also define a BackMaterial property for the surface because parametric surface is usually not a closed surface. In order to see the back side of your surface, you need to specify the BackMaterial property of the surface.

Creating Shaded Surfaces

It is easy to create surfaces with shading effects using the SurfaceShading class. Add a new WPF Window application to the project Chapter13 and name it SurfaceShadingTest. Here is the XAML file of this example:

```
<Window x:Class="Chapter13.SurfaceShadingTest"
    xmlns="http://schemas.microsoft.com/winfx
        /2006/xaml/presentation"
    xmlns:x="http://schemas.microsoft.com/winfx/2006/xaml"
    Title="Surface Shading" Height="300" Width="300">

    <Grid>
        <Viewport3D Name="viewport">
```

```
<Viewport3D.Camera>
    <PerspectiveCamera Position="6,4,4"
                       LookDirection="-6,-4,-4"
                       UpDirection="0,1,0"/>
</Viewport3D.Camera>

<ModelUIElement3D>
    <Model3DGroup>
        <AmbientLight Color="Gray"/>
        <DirectionalLight Color="Gray"
                          Direction="-1,0,-1"/>
        <DirectionalLight Color="Gray"
                          Direction="1,-1,-1"/>
    </Model3DGroup>
</ModelUIElement3D>
            </Viewport3D>
        </Grid>
</Window>
```

This XAML file sets the camera and light sources. Note that three light sources are used to illuminate the surfaces in order to get a better lighting effect. The following is the code-behind file of this example:

```
using System;
using System.Windows;
using System.Windows.Input;
using System.Windows.Controls;
using System.Windows.Media;
using System.Windows.Media.Media3D;

namespace Chapter13
{
    public partial class SurfaceShadingTest : Window
    {
        private SurfaceShading ss;

        public SurfaceShadingTest()
        {
            InitializeComponent();
            AddHyperboloid();
            AddEllipticCone();
            AddEllipticCylinder();
        }

        // Hyperboloid surface:
        private void AddHyperboloid()
        {
            ss = new SurfaceShading();

            Material material =
                new DiffuseMaterial(Brushes.Red);
            ss.MaterialGroup.Children.Add(material);
            material =
                new SpecularMaterial(Brushes.Yellow, 60);
```

```
        ss.MaterialGroup.Children.Add(material);
        material = new DiffuseMaterial(Brushes.SteelBlue);
        ss.BackMaterial = material;

        ss.Viewport3d = viewport;
        ss.Center = new Point3D(0, 0, 2);
        ss.Umin = 0;
        ss.Umax = 2 * Math.PI;
        ss.Vmin = -1;
        ss.Vmax = 1;
        ss.Nu = 30;
        ss.Nv = 30;
        ss.CreateSurface(Hyperboloid);
    }
    private Point3D Hyperboloid(double u, double v)
    {
        double x = 0.3 * Math.Cos(u) * Math.Cosh(v);
        double z = 0.5 * Math.Sin(u) * Math.Cosh(v);
        double y = Math.Sinh(v);
        return new Point3D(x, y, z);
    }

    //Elliptic cone:
    private void AddEllipticCone()
    {
        ss = new SurfaceShading();

        Material material =
            new DiffuseMaterial(Brushes.Green);
        ss.MaterialGroup.Children.Add(material);
        material =
            new SpecularMaterial(Brushes.LightGreen, 60);
        ss.MaterialGroup.Children.Add(material);
        material = new DiffuseMaterial(Brushes.SteelBlue);
        ss.BackMaterial = material;

        ss.Viewport3d = viewport;
        ss.Center = new Point3D(0, 0, 0);
        ss.Umin = 0;
        ss.Umax = 2 * Math.PI;
        ss.Vmin = -1;
        ss.Vmax = 1;
        ss.Nu = 30;
        ss.Nv = 30;
        ss.CreateSurface(EllipticCone);
    }
    private Point3D EllipticCone(double u, double v)
    {
        double x = 1.2 * v * Math.Cos(u);
        double z = 0.8 * v * Math.Sin(u);
        double y = 0.9 * v;
        return new Point3D(x, y, z);
    }
```

```
//Elliptic cylinder:
private void AddEllipticCylinder()
{
    ss = new SurfaceShading();

    Material material =
        new DiffuseMaterial(Brushes.Goldenrod);
    ss.MaterialGroup.Children.Add(material);
    material =
        new SpecularMaterial(
                Brushes.LightGoldenrodYellow, 60);
    ss.MaterialGroup.Children.Add(material);
    material = new DiffuseMaterial(Brushes.SteelBlue);
    ss.BackMaterial = material;

    ss.Viewport3d = viewport;
    ss.Center = new Point3D(0, 1, -2);
    ss.Umin = 0;
    ss.Umax = 2 * Math.PI;
    ss.Vmin = -0.5;
    ss.Vmax = 0.5;
    ss.Nu = 40;
    ss.Nv = 10;
    ss.CreateSurface(EllipticCylinder);
}
private Point3D EllipticCylinder(double u, double v)
{
    ss.Viewport3d = viewport;
    double x = 1.2 * Math.Cos(u);
    double z = 0.8 * Math.Sin(u);
    double y = 2 * v;
    return new Point3D(x, y, z);
}
    }
}
```

In this class, you create three surfaces with different materials. These three surfaces are the hyperboloid, elliptic cone, and elliptic cylinder surfaces.

Figure 13-11 shows the results of running this application.

In this chapter, we emphasized the algorithm used to create various surfaces, and left some important topics untouched. For example, you may want your surfaces to have a colormap scaled with the Y values and a colorbar. If you are interested in this topic, you can refer to my other book, *Practical Charts and Graphics*, where you'll find in-depth discussion on surface colormaps, color bars, and various surface charts.

We also haven't discussed two kinds of parametric surfaces: Bezier and B-spline surfaces. These surfaces are 3D counterparts to 2D Bezier curves and B-spines. Following the procedures presented here, you should be able to create these two particular kinds of surfaces without any difficulty.

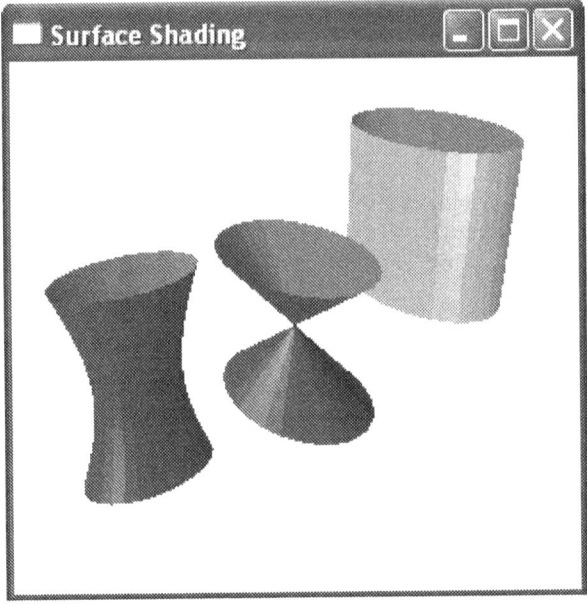

Figure 13-11 Shaded surfaces in WPF.

Chapter 14
3D Model Manipulation

In the previous chapters, we concentrated on the creation of various 3D models, including implementation of custom geometry and shape classes. In order to display these 3D models on the screen, you need to define the light sources and materials. This chapter will cover topics on manipulating 3D models, and provide more detailed information about WPF light model and material definition. It will also explain the lighting and shading effects, texture mapping, direct 3D model interaction, and 2D elements on 3D surfaces.

Lighting and Shading

In order to create realistically shaded 3D objects, WPF uses a lighting model. The interaction between light and an object is a complex physical process. Photons can be absorbed, reflected, or transmitted when they strike the surface of an object. The physical law that decribes how light interacts with an object is very complicated. It involves many factors, such as the brightness of the light, light source types (point or surface), the surface roughness of the object, and the amount of light reflected off other objects into the object you are considering. To simulate this interaction process using the knowledge of physics would be far too computationally time-consuming. WPF, instead, uses a simplified light model to emulate the real-world lighting process. WPF light model provides the following simplifications:

- Light effects are calculated for objects individually. This means that the light reflected from one object will not reflect off another object. Thus, an object will not cast a shadow on another object, no matter where it is placed.

- Lighting is calculated at the vertices of each triangle and then interpolated over the surface of the triangle. In other words, WPF determines the light strength at each vertex and blends that to fill in the triangle. This creates a problem that an object with relatively few triangles may not be illuminated correctly. To achieve a better lighting effect, you need to divide your models into a large number of triangles.

Depending on the effect you want to achieve, in some situations, you may need to work around these issues by combining multiple light sources, using different materials, and even writing your own ray tracing routine. In fact, to obtain a better lighting effect you want is part of the art of 3D scene design.

Light Sources

In the WPF lighting model, the light in a scene comes from several light sources that can be individually turned on and off. Some light comes from a particular direction or position, and some light is scattered about the scene. WPF provides four light classes, all of them derive from the abstract Light class.

- DirectionalLight class – Provides a directional light source, also known as an infinite light source, which radiates light in a single direction from infinitely far away. The rays of this light source can be considered parallel. Since they have no position in space, directional lights have infinite range and their intensity doesn't diminish over distance.

- AmbientLight class – Provides a low density light that arises from reflections of light on all nearby surfaces in an environment. It provides a rough approximation of the general brightness of a surface. Ambient light appears to come from every direction with equal intensity, and thus illuminates every part of an object uniformly.

- PointLight class – Provides a point light source that radiates light equally in every direction from a sinle point in space. The intensity of light naturally decreases with distance according to the inverse square law. WPF implements a generalization of this concept that allows you to control the intensity of light radiated by a point light source using the reciprocal of a quadratic polynomial.

  Suppose that a point light source is placed at a point P0. The intensity I of light reaching a point P1 in space is given by

  $$I = \frac{I_0}{c_0 + c_1 d + c_2 d^2}$$

  where I_0 is the intensity of light at P0, d is the distance between P0 and P1, and c_0, c_1, and c_2 are defined as the constant, linear, and quadratic attenuation constants. WPF allows you to specify these attenuation constants to control the intensity of a point light source.

- SpotLight class – Provides a spot light source that is similar to a point light source but has a preferred direction of radiation. The intensity of a spot light is not only attenuated over distance in the same way as the PointLight source does, but also attenuated by an additional exponential factor, named the spot light effect. The spot light source radiates light outward in a cone, starting from a single point.

In addition to attenuation constants, spot light also defines two properties of type Double named InnerConeAngle and OuterConeAngle. Within the InnerConeAngle, the light is affected by its angle to the vertex normals and the attenuation factor. Outside of the OuterConeAngle, the light has no effect. Between the InnerConeAngle and OuterConeAngle, the light falls off in intensity.

Testing Light Sources

In this section, We'll demonstrate the lighting effect using different light sources described in the previous section. Start with a new WPF Window project and name it Chapter14. Add the EllipsoidGeometry class from the project Chapter11 to the current project, which will be used to create sphere shapes. Add a new WPF Window to the current project and call it LightSourceTest. Here is the XAML file of this example:

```xaml
<Window x:Class="Chapter14.LightSourceTest"
    xmlns="http://schemas.microsoft.com/winfx
        /2006/xaml/presentation"
    xmlns:x="http://schemas.microsoft.com/winfx/2006/xaml"
    xmlns:local="clr-namespace:Geometries"
    Title="Light Source Test" Height="380" Width="400">

    <Window.Resources>
        <local:EllipsoidGeometry x:Key="sphere"
                                 PhiDiv="50"
                                 ThetaDiv="50"/>
        <PerspectiveCamera x:Key="camera"
                           Position="3,3,3"
                           LookDirection="-1,-1,-1"
                           UpDirection="0,1,0"/>
        <DiffuseMaterial x:Key="material" Brush="LightBlue"/>
    </Window.Resources>

    <Grid>
        <Grid.ColumnDefinitions>
            <ColumnDefinition/>
            <ColumnDefinition/>
        </Grid.ColumnDefinitions>
        <Grid.RowDefinitions>
            <RowDefinition Height="Auto"/>
            <RowDefinition Height="150*" />
            <RowDefinition Height="Auto"/>
            <RowDefinition Height="150*"/>
        </Grid.RowDefinitions>

        <TextBlock Grid.Column="0" Grid.Row="0"
            Text="Directional light"
            TextAlignment="Center" Margin="5"/>
```

```
<Viewport3D Grid.Column="0" Grid.Row="1"
    Camera="{Binding Source={StaticResource camera}}">
    <ContainerUIElement3D>
        <ModelUIElement3D>
            <Model3DGroup>
                <GeometryModel3D Geometry="{Binding
                    Source={StaticResource sphere},
                        Path=Mesh3D}"
                    Material="{Binding Source=
                        {StaticResource material}}"/>
                <!-- Set light source: -->
                <DirectionalLight Color="White"
                    Direction="-1,-1,-1" />
            </Model3DGroup>
        </ModelUIElement3D>
    </ContainerUIElement3D>
</Viewport3D>

<TextBlock Grid.Column="1" Grid.Row="0"
    Text="Ambient light" TextAlignment="Center"
    Margin="5"/>
<Viewport3D Grid.Column="1" Grid.Row="1"
    Camera="{Binding Source={StaticResource camera}}">
    <ContainerUIElement3D>
        <ModelUIElement3D>
            <Model3DGroup>
                <GeometryModel3D Geometry=
                    "{Binding Source={StaticResource
                        sphere},Path=Mesh3D}"
                    Material="{Binding Source=
                        {StaticResource material}}"/>
                <!-- Set light source: -->
                <AmbientLight Color="White"/>
            </Model3DGroup>
        </ModelUIElement3D>
    </ContainerUIElement3D>
</Viewport3D>

<TextBlock Grid.Column="0" Grid.Row="2"
    Text="Point light" TextAlignment="Center"
    Margin="5"/>
<Viewport3D Grid.Column="0" Grid.Row="3"
    Camera="{Binding Source={StaticResource camera}}">
    <ContainerUIElement3D>
        <ModelUIElement3D>
            <Model3DGroup>
                <GeometryModel3D Geometry=
                    "{Binding Source={StaticResource
                        sphere},Path=Mesh3D}"
                    Material="{Binding Source=
                        {StaticResource material}}"/>
                <!-- Set light source: -->
                <PointLight Position="2,2,2"
                    ConstantAttenuation="1"
```

```
                    QuadraticAttenuation="0.01"/>
            </Model3DGroup>
        </ModelUIElement3D>
    </ContainerUIElement3D>
</Viewport3D>

<TextBlock Grid.Column="1" Grid.Row="2"
    Text="Spot light" TextAlignment="Center"
    Margin="5"/>
<Viewport3D Grid.Column="1" Grid.Row="3"
    Camera="{Binding Source={StaticResource camera}}">
    <ContainerUIElement3D>
        <ModelUIElement3D>
            <Model3DGroup>
                <GeometryModel3D Geometry=
                    "{Binding Source={StaticResource
                        sphere},Path=Mesh3D}"
                    Material="{Binding Source=
                        {StaticResource material}}"/>
                <!-- Set light source: -->
                <SpotLight Position="2,2,2"
                    Direction="-1,-1,-1"
                    InnerConeAngle="20"
                    OuterConeAngle="30"/>
            </Model3DGroup>
        </ModelUIElement3D>
    </ContainerUIElement3D>
</Viewport3D>
        </Grid>
    </Window>
```

This XAML file creates four spheres, each with a different light source. It is crucial to remember that the lighting effects, especially from PointLight and SpotLight, are determined based on the vertices of the triangular mesh. If you define a coarse mesh with only a few trangles on your sphere surface, the illumination of the entire face of that triangle from a PointLight source will be based on the angles that the light makes with the three vertex normals. Depending on where that PointLight is placed, you might not even see any difference in illumination over the entire face of that triangle. So, to precisely control the lighting effect, it is necessary to create a dense mesh for the sphere surface that may consist of hundreds or even thousands of triangles. In the current example, each sphere contains 5000 triangles.

Figure 14-1 shows the results of this example. You can see from this figure that the directional light gives a more realistic view of the object. The Ambient light source provides a uniform light that has no shading effect. The sphere looks light blue uniformly in all directions. The PointLight mimics a light bulb that emits light in all directions. You can see that the brightest spot is the place where the light rays from the PointLight strike the sphere perpendicularly. The SpotLight behaves more or less like a flashlight. The light rays strike the spherical surface with different angles, but the light is restricted to a cone.

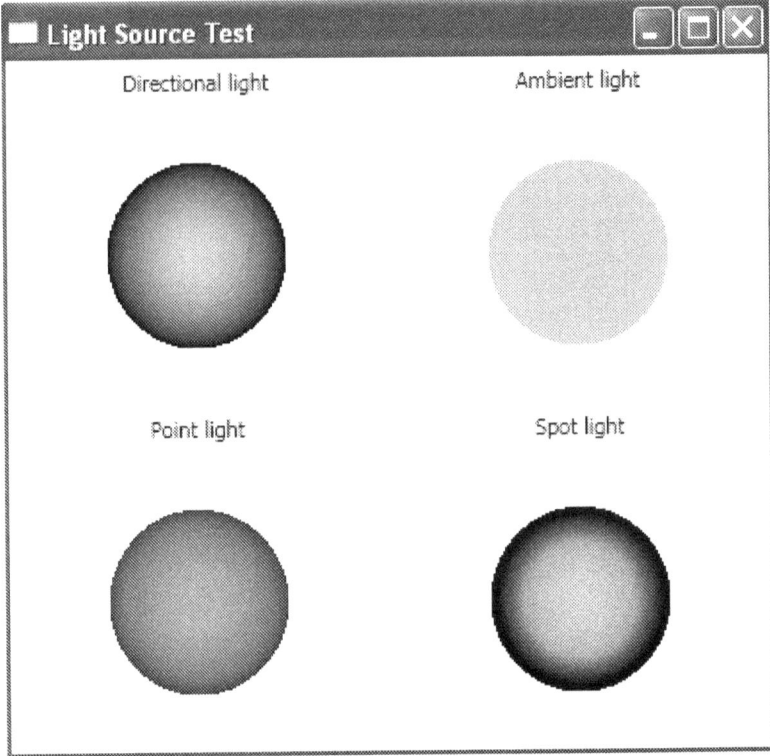

Figure 14-1 Spheres lighted with different light sources.

Shading

WPF uses triangles to simulate the surface of a 3D object. There are several techniques available to smooth out the edges between the triangles when you shade them. The two most common techniques are Gouraud shading and Phong shading.

In Gouraud shading, also called intensity interpolation shading, you begin by creating surface normal vectors at each vertex of each triangle. In WPF, you can compute these normals as you generate the surface. For example, when you create a sphere of radius r, the normal vector at the point (x, y, z) on the sphere is (x/r, y/r, z/r). You can store these normals by specifying the Normals property of MeshGeometry3D.

It is easy to calculate the normal for a general surface. The following method can be used to calculate a normal that is perpendicular to the surface of a triangle based on its three points:

```
private Vector3D GetNormal(Point3D p0, Point3D p1, Point3D p2)
{
Vector3D v1 =
    new Vector3D(p1.X - p0.X, p1.Y - p0.Y, p1.Z - p0.Z);
```

```
Vector3D v2 =
    new Vector3D(p2.X - p1.X, p2.Y - p1.Y, p2.Z - p1.Z);
    return Vector3D.CrossProduct(v1, v2);
}
```

If you don't explicitly specify the Normals property, WPF will calculate a set of vertex normals for you. It calculates a normal at each vertex by taking average of the normals of the surrounding triangles that share the same vertex. For most of the examples in this book, we have defined the Positions collections so that only triangles in the same plane share vertices, which usually results in a smooth shaded surface.

Using the vertex normals and the lighting model equations, you can calculate the color values for each vertex. You can then use interpolation to find the colors for the other points inside the triangle. As the colors vary smoothly across the triangle, they produce a smoother image than what you would get if you give every point in the triangle the same color. For example, you can use this interpolation technique to create a smoother image of a sphere using fewer data points than what you would need without Gouraud shading.

The Phong shading also uses vertex normals to create smooth shading. The Gouraud shading uses the vertex normals to compute vertex colors. It then interpolates using those colors to find the colors of the points inside a triangle. On the other hand, the Phong shading interpolates color using the vertex normals to find normals for each point in a triangle. It then uses these normals to compute the points' colors individually.

The most time-consuming part of both methods is computing the color of a point for a given surface normal. Interpolating colors or normal vectors is relatively fast. Phong shading computes the color of each individual point, whereas Gouraud shading computes only the colors of the vertices. It is thus expected that Phong shading achieves better shading effect at a slower speed when compared to Gouraud shading.

If you think the WPF built-in shading model is not good enough for your applications, you can implement your own shading model based on the Gouraud or Phong shading technique. The WPF default shading model is used in this book.

Materials

The WPF lighting model simulates an object's color from the percentage of the red, green, and blue light it reflects. For example, a perfectly red sphere surface reflects all the incoming red light and absorbs all the green and blue light that strikes on it. WPF uses the Material property to define the surface of 3D objects. You use the Material property to specify the color of the object and define how the material responds to light.

WPF provides four Material classes, all of which derive from the abstract Material class. These four classes are DiffuseMaterial, SpecularMaterial,

EmissiveMaterial, and MaterialGroup. The MaterialGroup class lets you combine more than one material into one material group. The materials are then layered overtop of one another in the order they are added to the MaterialGroup. Remember that the order of materials in the MaterialGroup is very important. If you alter the oder of materials, you would obtain a totally different lighting effect.

Diffuse Materials

The DiffuseMaterial class creates a flat, matte surface. It diffuses light evenly in all directions. It is the most commonly used material type because its behavior is closer to a real-world surface.

When using DiffuseMaterial, you focus mainly on its Brush property becaue this property defines the color of a surface. The DiffuseMaterial class has some additional properties, including Color and AmbientColor. The default values for both properties are White. The Color and AmbientColor Properties, together with the Bush property and the angle of the DirectionalLight source, govern the extent to which the material reflects light. The Color property indicates the amount of reflected light from a DirectionalLight source, and the AmbientColor property indicates the amount of reflected light from the AmbientLight source.

Let's look at an example that demonstrates how these two color properties affect the lighting effect. Add a new WPF Window to the project Chapter14 and name it DiffuseMaterialTest. The structure of the XAML file is very similar to that used in the previous example. Here I only list the geometry models, materials, and light sources. You can view the complete XAML code by opening the DiffiseMaterialTest.xaml file.

```
.....
<GeometryModel3D Geometry="{Binding Source=
    {StaticResource sphere},Path=Mesh3D}">
    <GeometryModel3D.Material>
        <DiffuseMaterial Brush="LightGray" Color="White"/>
    </GeometryModel3D.Material>
</GeometryModel3D>
<!-- Set light source: -->
<DirectionalLight Color="White" Direction="-1,-1,-1" />
.....
<GeometryModel3D Geometry="{Binding Source=
    {StaticResource sphere},Path=Mesh3D}">
    <GeometryModel3D.Material>
        <DiffuseMaterial Brush="LightGray" Color="Red"/>
    </GeometryModel3D.Material>
</GeometryModel3D>
<!-- Set light source: -->
<DirectionalLight Color="White" Direction="-1,-1,-1" />
.....
<GeometryModel3D Geometry="{Binding Source=
    {StaticResource sphere},Path=Mesh3D}">
    <GeometryModel3D.Material>
```

```
        <DiffuseMaterial Brush="LightGray"
                         AmbientColor="White"/>
    </GeometryModel3D.Material>
</GeometryModel3D>
<!-- Set light source: -->
<AmbientLight Color="White"/>
.....
<GeometryModel3D Geometry="{Binding Source=
    {StaticResource sphere},Path=Mesh3D}">
    <GeometryModel3D.Material>
        <DiffuseMaterial Brush="LightGray"
            AmbientColor="Red"/>
    </GeometryModel3D.Material>
</GeometryModel3D>
<!-- Set light source: -->
<AmbientLight Color="White"/>
.....
```

This example generates results shown in Figure 14-2.

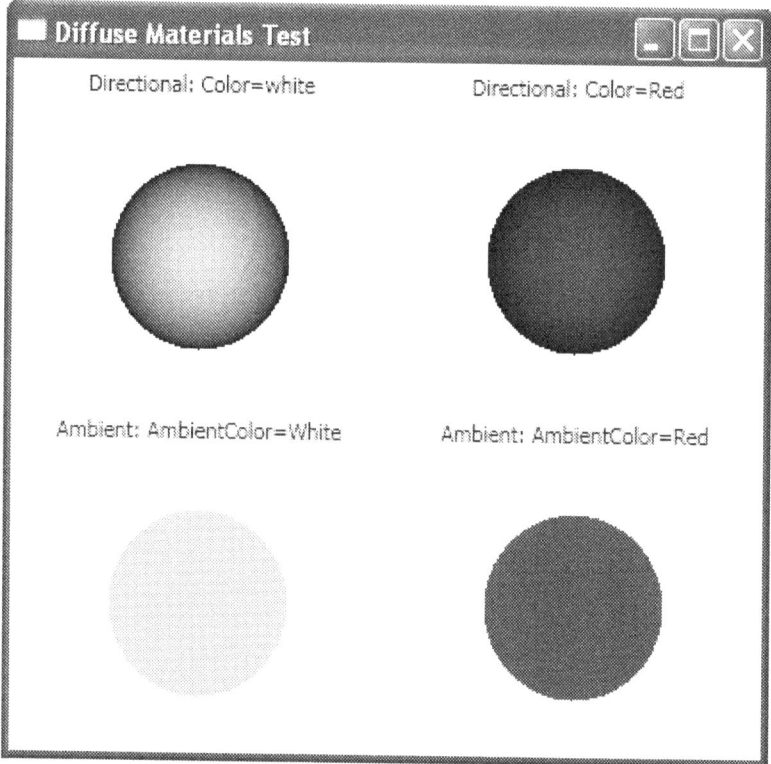

Figure 14-2 Spheres with different Color property of DiffuseMaterial and Different light sources.

You can see that each of these four sphere has a very different lighting effect. The Brush property of the DiffuseMaterial is the same for all of the apheres: Brush="LightGray". The first two spheres also have the same light source of DirectionalLight with a Color property of White. The difference between the first two spheres is the Color property of the DiffuseMaterial, one is set to White and the other set to Red. This means that the surface of the first sphere reflects all light, resulting in the shading and lighting effect with Brush's color. On the other hand, the second sphere reflects only the red light, indicating that only the red component of Brush's color can be reflected. That is why the second sphere has a red color. You can imagine the Color property of the DiffuseMaterial as indicating what light the object reflects, but think of the Brush property as a kind of color filter that lets colors through or blocks them. More interestingly, if you set the Brush property to Green for the second sphere, the sphere will become black since there is no light gets reflected (there is no red component in a green brush!).

Similarly, you can analyze the last two spheres that have the AmbientLight source. The AmbientColor property is set to White for one sphere and Red for the other. That is why one sphere shows the color of brush (LightGray) and the other displays a red color.

Specular and Emissive Materials

In addition to the uniform diffuse material, WPF also provides SpecularMaterial and EmissiveMaterial classes. The SpecularMaterial creates a glossy, highlighted look. It reflects light back directly like a mirror.

EmissiveMaterial is intended to minic a surface that radiates light, such as a light bulb or glowing hot metal. This doesn't mean that the surface becomes a light source that illuminates other objects. Instead, a surface covered with EmissiveMaterial just shows a visible color in the absence of all light sources. In the presence of light, EmissiveMaterial adds to the brightness of the object provided by the underlying DiffuseMaterial.

Remember that both SpecularMetarial and EmissiveMaterial are intended to be used in conjunction with DiffuseMaterial objects within a MaterialGroup. Usually one or more DiffuseMaterial objects come first in the MaterialGroup, followed by an EmissiveMaterial or SpecularMaterial element, or even both. If you want to use EmissiveMaterial or SpecularMaterial by itself, simply put the material on top of a DiffuseMaterial element with Brush set to Black. For EmissiveMaterial, you can simply remove the light source from your system. In the absence of light sources, the object always shows the brush's color of the EmissiveMaterial regardless of the Brush property of the underlying DiffuseMaterial.

Let's look at an example that demonstrates how the SpecularMaterial and Emissive affect the lighting and shading effects. Add a new WPF Window to the project Chapter14 and name it SpecularEmissiveTest. The structure of the XAML file is very similar to that used in the LightSourceTest example. Here I only list the geometry models, materials, and light sources. You can view the complete XAML code by opening the SpecularEmissiveTest.xaml file.

```
......
<GeometryModel3D Geometry=
    "{Binding Source={StaticResource sphere},Path=Mesh3D}">
    <GeometryModel3D.Material>
        <MaterialGroup>
            <DiffuseMaterial Brush="Red"/>
            <SpecularMaterial SpecularPower="20"
                Brush="Yellow"/>
        </MaterialGroup>
    </GeometryModel3D.Material>
</GeometryModel3D>
<!-- Set light source: -->
<DirectionalLight Color="White" Direction="-1,-1,-1" />
......
<GeometryModel3D Geometry=
    "{Binding Source={StaticResource sphere},Path=Mesh3D}">
    <GeometryModel3D.Material>
        <MaterialGroup>
            <DiffuseMaterial Brush="Black"/>
            <SpecularMaterial Brush="Red" SpecularPower="5"/>
        </MaterialGroup>
    </GeometryModel3D.Material>
</GeometryModel3D>
<!-- Set light source: -->
<DirectionalLight Color="White" Direction="-1,-1,-1" />
......
<GeometryModel3D Geometry=
    "{Binding Source={StaticResource sphere},Path=Mesh3D}">
    <GeometryModel3D.Material>
        <MaterialGroup>
            <DiffuseMaterial Brush="Yellow"/>
            <EmissiveMaterial Brush="Red"/>
        </MaterialGroup>
    </GeometryModel3D.Material>
</GeometryModel3D>
<!-- Set light source: -->
<DirectionalLight Color="White" Direction="-1,-1,-1" />
......
<GeometryModel3D Geometry=
    "{Binding Source={StaticResource sphere},Path=Mesh3D}">
    <GeometryModel3D.Material>
        <MaterialGroup>
            <DiffuseMaterial Brush="Yellow"/>
            <EmissiveMaterial Brush="Red"/>
        </MaterialGroup>
    </GeometryModel3D.Material>
</GeometryModel3D>
<!-- Remove light source: -->
<!--<DirectionalLight Color="White" Direction="-1,-1,-1" />-->
......
```

Figure 14-3 show results of running this example. The top two spheres are covered with a SpecularMaterial on top of a DiffuseMaterial. The SpecularMaterial has a SpecularPower property, which is set to 100 in this example. This property indicates the focus of the reflection. A high number makes the reflective area small, similar to a mirror. When SpecularPower gets small, SpecularMaterial behaves more like DiffuseMaterial. You can examine how the lighting effect changes when you vary the SpecularPower property.

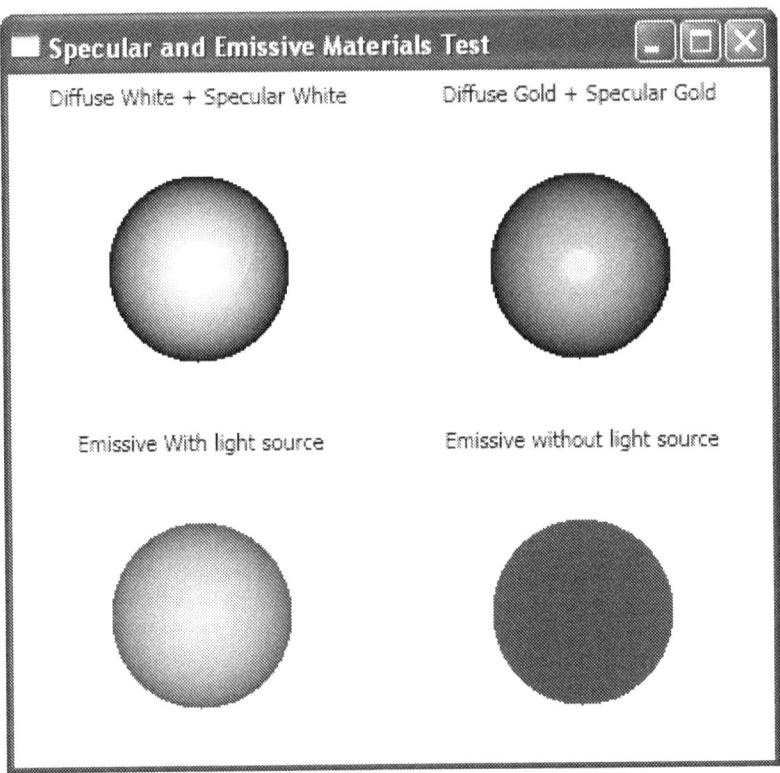

Figure 14-3 Spheres with specular (top) and emissive (bottom) materials.

In the first sphere, the Brush property is set to White for both the SpecularMaterial and DiffuseMaterial. A white brush for both materials is sometimes used to simulate plastic surface. You can simulate a metal surface with DiffuseMetarial and SpecularMaterial brushes that are similar, as it is demonstrated for the second sphere where both brushes are set to Gold.

The two spheres at the bottom in the figure are covered with EissiveMaterial on top of DiffuseMaterial. For both spheres, the DiffuseMaterial has a yellow brush and the EmissiveMaterial has a red brush. The difference is that one has a light source and the other doesn't. For the one with the light source, the EmissiveMaterial adds (red) brightness to the underlying DiffuseMaterial (yellow). When the light source is turned off, the yellow color from the

DiffuseMaterial disappears, while the red color from the EmissiveMaterial is still visible.

Texture Mapping

So far, you have painted 3D objects with solid color brushes. In this section, I'll show you how to use other brushes to decorate 3D models. These brushes include linear gradient, radial gradient, image, and tile brushes, which encompass bitmap images, drawings, and even visuals. These brushes have been used to paint 2D graphics in Chapter 5.

When using any brush other than a SolidColorBrush to paint a 3D object, you need to provide information about texture coordinates, which tells WPF how to map 2D contents of the brush onto the 3D surface. Depending on your applications, you can tile the brush content, extract just a part of it, and stretch it to fit curved and angular surfaces.

To set up a texture mapping, you need to create corresponding point in texture coordinates for each coordinate in your 3D Positions collection. Note that the point in TextureCoordinates collection is a 2D point because the content of a brush is always 2D. The following sections show you how to use various brushes to paint 3D objects.

Using LinearGradientBrush

In this section, you'll paint a 3D cube shape using a LinearGradientBrush. In order to paint the cube with a LinearGradientBrush, you need to establish a correspondence between the 3D vertices of the cube and the 2D relative coordinates of the brush (from 0 to 1).

Suppose you define a LinearGradientBrush using the following code snippet:

```
<LinearGradientBrush>
    <GradientStop Offset="0" Color="Yellow"/>
    <GradientStop Offset="1" Color="Red"/>
</LinearGradientBrush>
```

The default StartPoint and EndPoint values are (0, 0) and (1, 1). The gradient begins from the upper-left corner with yellow and ends at the lower-right corner with red. You can use the rectangle of this brush to paint a corresponding rectangular face in the 3D mesh, as it is shown on the top of Figure 14-4. In this case, you can define the MeshGeometry3D as following:

```
<MeshGeometry3D Positions="-1 1 1,-1 -1 1,1 -1 1,1 1 1"
                TriangleIndices="0 1 2,2 3 0"
                TextureCoordinates="0 0,0 1,1 1,1 0" />
```

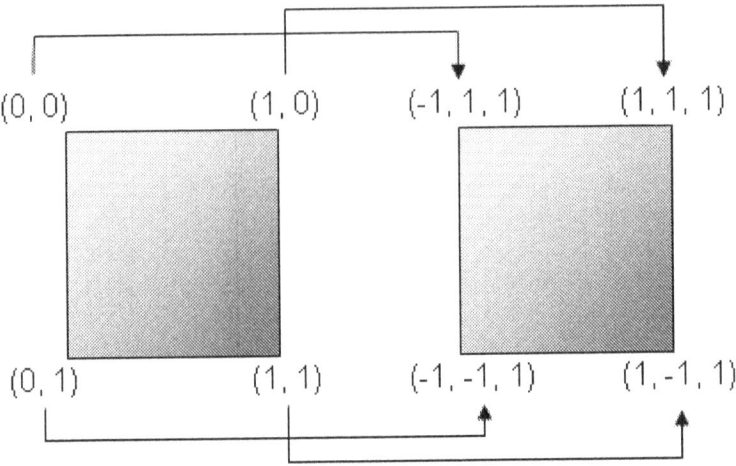

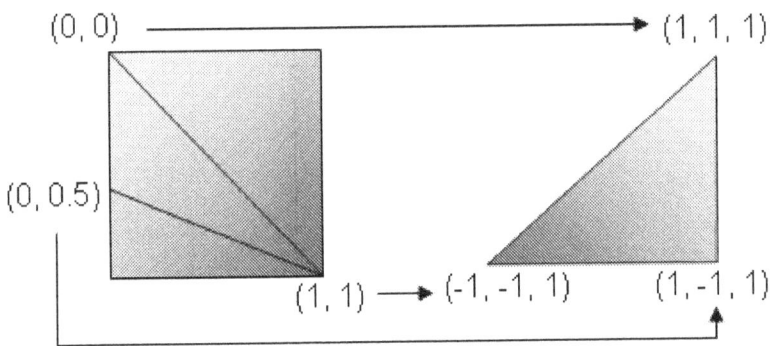

Figure 14-4 Mapping between brush coordinates and points of 3D mesh.

You can also directly paint a 3D triangular mesh using any triangular subset of the brush, as illustrated at the bottom of Figure 14-4. The selected subset of the brush is stretched to fit the entire 3D triangle. In this case, you can define the MeshGeometry3D using the following statements:

```
<MeshGeometry3D Positions="-1 -1 1,1 -1 1,1 1 1"
                TriangleIndices="0 1 2"
                TextureCoordinates="1 1,0 0.5,0 0" />
```

Note that the brush is a 2D rectangle with four vertices, and the triangular mesh consists of three vertices. It is impossible to specify TextureCoordinates values such that an entire rectangular brush fits in a single triangle. Thus, a subset of the brush should be used in this case.

Let's consider an example that paints a 3D cube shape using a LinearGradientBrush. Add a new WPF Window to the project Chapter14 and name it LinearBrushMap. Here is the XAML file of this example:

```xml
<Window x:Class="Chapter14.LinearBrushMap"
    xmlns="http://schemas.microsoft.com/winfx
    /2006/xaml/presentation"
    xmlns:x="http://schemas.microsoft.com/winfx/2006/xaml"
Title="Texture Map with Linear Gradient Brush"
    Height="300" Width="300">
    <Grid>
        <Viewport3D>
            <ModelUIElement3D>
                <Model3DGroup>
                    <GeometryModel3D>
                        <GeometryModel3D.Geometry>
                            <MeshGeometry3D
                                Positions=
            "-1  1  1, 1  1  1, 1  1 -1,-1  1 -1,
             -1 -1  1,-1 -1 -1, 1 -1 -1, 1 -1  1,
             -1  1  1,-1 -1  1, 1 -1  1, 1  1  1,
              1  1  1, 1 -1  1, 1 -1 -1, 1  1 -1,
              1  1 -1, 1 -1 -1,-1 -1 -1,-1  1 -1,
             -1  1 -1,-1 -1 -1,-1 -1  1,-1  1  1"
                                TriangleIndices=
                                    "0  1  2, 2  3  0,
                                     4  5  6, 6  7  4,
                                     8  9 10,10 11  8,
                                    12 13 14,14 15 12,
                                    16 17 18,18 19 16,
                                    20 21 22,22 23 20"
                                TextureCoordinates=
                                    "0 0,1 0,1 1,0 1,
                                     0 0,1 0,1 1,0 1,
                                     0 0,1 0,1 1,0 1,
                                     0 0,1 0,1 1,0 1,
                                     0 0,1 0,1 1,0 1,
                                     0 0,1 0,1 1,0 1"/>
                        </GeometryModel3D.Geometry>

                        <!-- Set LinearGradientBrush: -->
                        <GeometryModel3D.Material>
                            <DiffuseMaterial>
                                <DiffuseMaterial.Brush>
    <LinearGradientBrush StartPoint="0,0" EndPoint="0,1">
        <GradientStop Color="Yellow" Offset="0.2"/>
        <GradientStop Color="Red" Offset="1"/>
                                </LinearGradientBrush>
                                </DiffuseMaterial.Brush>
                            </DiffuseMaterial>
                        </GeometryModel3D.Material>

                        <!-- Set rotation transform for animation: -->
                        <GeometryModel3D.Transform>
                            <RotateTransform3D>
                                <RotateTransform3D.Rotation>
                                    <AxisAngleRotation3D
                                        x:Name="rotate"
```

```
                                        Axis="0 1 0"/>
                        </RotateTransform3D.Rotation>
                    </RotateTransform3D>
                </GeometryModel3D.Transform>
            </GeometryModel3D>

            <!-- Set light source: -->
            <DirectionalLight Color="White"
                Direction="-1,-1.2,-1.4"/>
        </Model3DGroup>
    </ModelUIElement3D>

    <!-- Set camera: -->
    <Viewport3D.Camera>
        <PerspectiveCamera Position="4 4 4"
            LookDirection="-1 -1 -1"
            UpDirection="0 1 0"/>
    </Viewport3D.Camera>
</Viewport3D>

<!-- Set Animation: -->
<Grid.Triggers>
    <EventTrigger RoutedEvent="Grid.Loaded">
        <BeginStoryboard>
            <Storyboard>
                <DoubleAnimation
                    Storyboard.TargetName="rotate"
                    Storyboard.TargetProperty="Angle"
                    From="0" To="360"
                    Duration="0:0:10"
                    RepeatBehavior="Forever"/>
            </Storyboard>
        </BeginStoryboard>
    </EventTrigger>
</Grid.Triggers>
        </Grid>
    </Window>
```

Note that the linear gradient brush is attached to the DiffuseMaterial's Brush property. Here you define a 2D point TextureCoordinates for each vertex in the Positions collection.

Figure 14-5 shows the result of running this example.

Using RadialGradientBrush

You can also use a RadialGradientBrush to paint a 3D shape. Here you will cover a 3D cube using this brush. In this case, you want the center of the brush to be at the center of each face of the cube.

Figure 14-5 Cube painted with a linear gradient brush.

Suppose you define a RadialGradientBrush like this:

```
<RadialGradientBrush>
    <GradientStop Color="Yellow" Offset="0"/>
    <GradientStop Color="Red" Offset="1"/>
</RadialGradientBrush>
```

The gradient starts from the center at (0.5, 0.5) with yellow and ends at the four corners with red, as shown on the left of Figure 14-6.

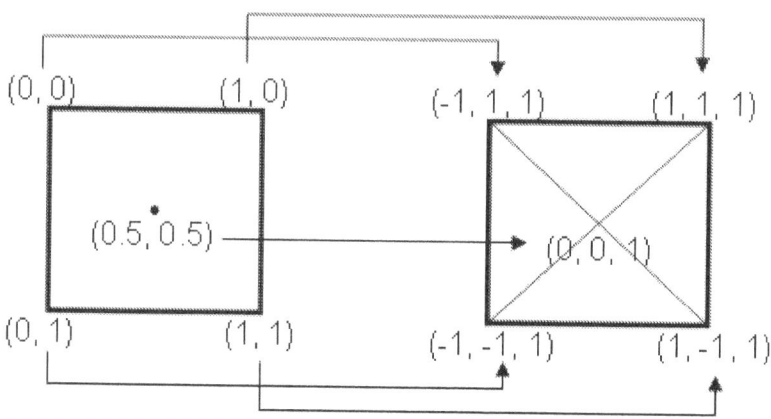

Figure 14-6 Mapping between texture coordinates and 3D vertices.

In order to paint the cube with such a radial brush, each face of the cube (shown on the right) needs also to have a center vertex. Thus, each face needs four triangles. In this case, you define the MeshGeometry3D as the following:

```
<MeshGeometry3D Positions="0 0 1,-1 1 1,-1 -1 1,1 -1 1,1 1 1"
                TraingleIndices="0 1 2,0 2 3,0 3 4,0 4 1"
                TextureCorrdinates="0.5 0.5,0 0,1 1 1,1 0"/>
```

This way, you establish a one-to-one correspondence between the TextureCoordiantes and 3D vertices of the cube.

With the above information, you are ready to paint the cube with a radial gradient brush. Add a new WPF Window to the project Chapter14 and name it RadialBrushMap. The structure of the XAML file of this example is similar to the previous example. The difference is that you need to redefine the 3D mesh, texture coordinates, and the RadialGradientBrush:

```
.....
<MeshGeometry3D
          Positions=
              "0   1   0,-1  1   1, 1  1   1, 1   1 -1,-1   1 -1,
               0  -1   0,-1  -1  1,-1  -1 -1, 1  -1 -1, 1 -1  1,
               0   0   1,-1  1   1,-1  -1  1, 1  -1  1, 1  1  1,
               0   0  -1,-1  -1 -1,-1   1 -1, 1  -1, 1 -1 -1,
              -1   0   0,-1  1   1,-1   1 -1,-1 -1,-1 -1  1,
               1   0   0, 1  1   1, 1  1 -1  1, 1 -1 -1, 1  1 -1"
          TriangleIndices=
              "0   1   2, 0   2   3, 0   3   4, 0   4   1,
               5   6   7, 5   7   8, 5   8   9, 5   9   6,
              10  11  12,10  12  13,10  13  14,10  14  11,
              15  16  17,15  17  18,15  18  19,15  19  16,
              20  21  22,20  22  23,20  23  24,20  24  21,
              25  26  27,25  27  28,25  28  29,25  29  26"
          TextureCoordinates=
              "0.5 0.5,0  0,1  0,1  1,0  1,
               0.5 0.5,0  0,1  0,1  1,0  1,
               0.5 0.5,0  0,1  0,1  1,0  1,
               0.5 0.5,0  0,1  0,1  1,0  1,
               0.5 0.5,0  0,1  0,1  1,0  1,
               0.5 0.5,0  0,1  0,1  1,0  1" />
      </GeometryModel3D.Geometry>

  <!-- Set RadialGradientBrush: -->
  <GeometryModel3D.Material>
      <DiffuseMaterial>
          <DiffuseMaterial.Brush>
              <RadialGradientBrush>
                  <GradientStop Color="Yellow" Offset="0"/>
                  <GradientStop Color="Red" Offset="1"/>
              </RadialGradientBrush>
          </DiffuseMaterial.Brush>
      </DiffuseMaterial>
  </GeometryModel3D.Material>
  .....
```

This example generates the result shown in Figure 14-7.

Figure 14-7 Cube painted using a radial gradient brush.

Using Image and Tile Brushes

You can also use an ImageBrush to put a picture on a cube. A bitmap can be easily applied to a cube. Add a new WPF Window to the project Chapter14 and name it ImageBrushMap. This example uses the similar XAML file that has been used in the LinearBrushMap example. All you need to do is simply replace the LinearGradientBrush with an ImageBrush:

```
.....
<!-- Set ImageBrush: -->
<GeometryModel3D.Material>
    <DiffuseMaterial>
        <DiffuseMaterial.Brush>
            <ImageBrush ImageSource="Flower.jpg" />
        </DiffuseMaterial.Brush>
    </DiffuseMaterial>
</GeometryModel3D.Material>
.....
```

In this example, the ImageBrush with a flower image is used to paint the cube. Depending on the TextureCoordinates you choose, you could stretch the image, wrapping it over the entire cube, or you could put a separate copy of it on each side, as you have done in this example. Figure 14-8 shows the result of running this example.

You can even paint the cube using a tile image brush:

```
<GeometryModel3D.Material>
    <DiffuseMaterial>
        <DiffuseMaterial.Brush>
            <ImageBrush ImageSource="Flower.jpg"
                Viewport="0 0 0.25 0.25"
                TileMode="Tile"/>
        </DiffuseMaterial.Brush>
    </DiffuseMaterial>
</GeometryModel3D.Material>
```

This generates the result shown in Figure 14-9.

Figure 14-8 Cube painted with a flower image.

Figure 14-9 Cube painted using a tile image brush.

It is also possible to use other brushes to paint 3D objects, including DrawingBrush and VisualBrush. The procedure using the drawing and visual brushes to paint 3D objects is similar to using ImageBrush. Remember that even though you can use the VisualBrush to put 2D elements, panels, and controls on 3D models, these are not functional controls. They are only the images of elements and controls. If you want actually functional controls on 3D objects, you need to use a new class, Viewport2DVisual3D, which is available in .NET 3.5. This will be a topic of next section.

2D Elements on 3D Surfaces

As you learned earlier in this chapter, you can use texture mapping to put 2D brush content on a 3D surface. This technique can be used to place gradient patterns and images on a 3D shape. Using a VisualBrush, you can even take the visual appearance of 2D elements, and place it in your 3D scene.

As you already know, the VisualBrush can copy the visual appearance of a 2D element, but it doesn't actually have the functionality of the element. If you use the VisualBrush to put the visual for a button on a 3D surface, you would end up with a 3D image of the button. In other words, you would not be able to click it.

Viewport2DVisual3D Class

In order to put actually functional 2D elements on a 3D surface, you need to use the Viewport2DVisual3D class. This class allows you to put interactive 2D elements on a 3D surface. Viewport2DVisual3D, which derives from the Visual3D class, has three main dependency properties, Visual, Geometry, and Material.

The Visual property is the 2D Visual that will be placed on the 3D surface. Geometry is the 3D geometry for the Viewport2DVisual3D, and the Material property describes the look of the 3D object. You can use any material you want. To place Visual on the material that you choose to use, simply set the Viewport2DVisual3D.IsVisualHostMaterial attached property to true.

Using Viewport2DVisual3D

Using the Viewport2DVisual3D class, you can take any WPF element, and place it in a 3D surface, and interact with it. The elements placed using this approach retain all the WPF features you are used to, including layout, style, templates, mouse event, drag-and-drop, etc.

Here, we consider an example that places some 2D elements (TextBlock, Button, and TextBox) on three faces of a cube. Of course, you can easily put any 2D element on any face of a 3D object following the procedure presented in this example.

Add a new WPF Window to the project Chapter14 and name it Viewport2DVisual3DTest. Here is the XAML file of this example:

```
<Window x:Class="Chapter14.Viewport2DVisual3DTest"
    xmlns="http://schemas.microsoft.com/winfx
    /2006/xaml/presentation"
    xmlns:x="http://schemas.microsoft.com/winfx/2006/xaml"
    Title="2D Elements on 3D Surfaces"
    Height="320" Width="300">
    <Grid Margin="5">
        <Grid.Resources>
            <PerspectiveCamera x:Key="camera"
                            Position="3 3 3"
                            LookDirection="-1 -1 -1"
                            UpDirection="0 1 0"/>
        </Grid.Resources>

        <Grid.RowDefinitions>
            <RowDefinition></RowDefinition>
            <RowDefinition Height="Auto"></RowDefinition>
        </Grid.RowDefinitions>
```

```
<!-- Create a slider used to control rotation -->
<Slider Name="slider" Margin="5" Grid.Row="1"
        Minimum="0" Maximum="360"
        Orientation="Horizontal"/>

<Viewport3D Camera="{Binding
    Source={StaticResource camera}}">
    <ContainerUIElement3D>
        <ModelUIElement3D>
            <Model3DGroup>
                <GeometryModel3D>
                    <GeometryModel3D.Geometry>
                        <MeshGeometry3D
                        Positions=
            "-1  1  1, 1  1  1, 1  1 -1,-1  1 -1,
             -1 -1  1,-1 -1 -1, 1 -1 -1, 1 -1  1,
             -1  1  1,-1 -1  1, 1 -1  1, 1  1  1,
              1  1  1, 1 -1  1, 1 -1 -1, 1  1 -1,
              1  1 -1, 1 -1 -1,-1 -1 -1,-1  1 -1,
             -1  1 -1,-1 -1 -1,-1 -1  1,-1  1  1"
                        TriangleIndices=
                        "0  1  2, 2  3  0,
                         4  5  6, 6  7  4,
                         8  9 10,10 11  8,
                        12 13 14,14 15 12,
                        16 17 18,18 19 16,
                        20 21 22,22 23 20"
                        TextureCoordinates=
                        "0 0,1 0,1 1,0 1,
                         0 0,1 0,1 1,0 1,
                         0 0,1 0,1 1,0 1,
                         0 0,1 0,1 1,0 1,
                         0 0,1 0,1 1,0 1,
                         0 0,1 0,1 1,0 1"/>
                    </GeometryModel3D.Geometry>

                    <GeometryModel3D.Material>
                        <DiffuseMaterial>
                            <DiffuseMaterial.Brush>
        <LinearGradientBrush StartPoint="0,0" EndPoint="0,1">
            <GradientStop Color="Yellow" Offset="0.2"/>
            <GradientStop Color="Red" Offset="1"/>
        </LinearGradientBrush>
                            </DiffuseMaterial.Brush>
                        </DiffuseMaterial>
                    </GeometryModel3D.Material>

                    <GeometryModel3D.Transform>
                        <RotateTransform3D>
                            <RotateTransform3D.Rotation>
            <AxisAngleRotation3D
        Angle="{Binding ElementName=slider, Path=Value}"
                Axis="0 1 0"/>
                            </RotateTransform3D.Rotation>
```

```xml
                  </RotateTransform3D>
                </GeometryModel3D.Transform>
              </GeometryModel3D>

              <!-- Set light source: -->
              <DirectionalLight Color="White"
                  Direction="-1,-1.2,-1.4"/>
          </Model3DGroup>
        </ModelUIElement3D>
      </ContainerUIElement3D>
  </Viewport3D>

    <Viewport3D Camera="{Binding
        Source={StaticResource camera}}">

    <!-- Set light source: -->
    <ContainerUIElement3D>
        <ModelUIElement3D>
            <DirectionalLight Color="White"
                Direction="-1,-1.2,-1.4"/>
        </ModelUIElement3D>
    </ContainerUIElement3D>

    <!-- Add 2D elements on front surface: -->
    <Viewport2DVisual3D>
        <Viewport2DVisual3D.Geometry>
            <MeshGeometry3D
                Positions="-1 1 1,-1 -1 1,1 -1 1,1 1 1"
                TriangleIndices="0,1,2 2,3,0"
                TextureCoordinates="0 0,0 1,1 1,1 0"/>
        </Viewport2DVisual3D.Geometry>

        <Viewport2DVisual3D.Material>
            <DiffuseMaterial
                Viewport2DVisual3D.IsVisualHostMaterial=
                "true" Brush="White" />
        </Viewport2DVisual3D.Material>

        <!-- Add 2D elements: -->
        <Border BorderBrush="LightBlue"
            BorderThickness="1">
            <StackPanel Margin="10">
                <TextBlock Margin="5"
                    Foreground="Blue">
                    Front Surface</TextBlock>
                <Button Margin="5"
                  Click="FrontButton_Click"
                  Foreground="Blue">Click Me</Button>
                <TextBox Margin="5"
                    Foreground="Blue">
                    Front Text:</TextBox>
            </StackPanel>
        </Border>
```

```
                    <!-- Set rotation transform: -->
                    <Viewport2DVisual3D.Transform>
                        <RotateTransform3D>
                            <RotateTransform3D.Rotation>
                                <AxisAngleRotation3D
     Angle="{Binding ElementName=slider, Path=Value}"
                                    Axis="0 1 0"/>
                            </RotateTransform3D.Rotation>
                        </RotateTransform3D>
                    </Viewport2DVisual3D.Transform>
                </Viewport2DVisual3D>

                <!-- Add 2D elements on right surface: -->
                <Viewport2DVisual3D>
                    <Viewport2DVisual3D.Geometry>
                        <MeshGeometry3D
                            Positions="1 1 1,1 -1 1,1 -1 -1,1 1 -1"
                            TriangleIndices="0,1,2 2,3,0"
                            TextureCoordinates="0 0,0 1,1 1,1 0"/>
                    </Viewport2DVisual3D.Geometry>

                    <Viewport2DVisual3D.Material>
                        <DiffuseMaterial
                        Viewport2DVisual3D.IsVisualHostMaterial=
                        "true" Brush="White" />
                    </Viewport2DVisual3D.Material>

                    <!-- Add 2D elements: -->
                    <Border BorderBrush="LightBlue"
                        BorderThickness="1">
                        <StackPanel Margin="10">
                            <TextBlock Margin="5"
                                Foreground="Blue">
                                Right Surface</TextBlock>
                            <Button Margin="5"
                                Click="RightButton_Click"
                                Foreground="Blue">Click Me</Button>
                            <TextBox Margin="5"
                                Foreground="Blue">
                                Right Text:</TextBox>
                        </StackPanel>
                    </Border>

                    <!-- Set rotation transform: -->
                    <Viewport2DVisual3D.Transform>
                        <RotateTransform3D>
                            <RotateTransform3D.Rotation>
                                <AxisAngleRotation3D
     Angle="{Binding ElementName=slider, Path=Value}"
                                        Axis="0 1 0"/>
                            </RotateTransform3D.Rotation>
                        </RotateTransform3D>
                    </Viewport2DVisual3D.Transform>
                </Viewport2DVisual3D>
```

```xml
<!-- Add 2D elements on top surface: -->
<Viewport2DVisual3D>
    <Viewport2DVisual3D.Geometry>
        <MeshGeometry3D
            Positions="-1 1 1,1 1 1,1 1 -1,-1 1 -1"
            TriangleIndices="0,1,2 2,3,0"
            TextureCoordinates="0 0,0 1,1 1,1 0"/>
    </Viewport2DVisual3D.Geometry>

    <Viewport2DVisual3D.Material>
        <DiffuseMaterial
        Viewport2DVisual3D.IsVisualHostMaterial=
        "true" Brush="White" />
    </Viewport2DVisual3D.Material>

    <!-- Add 2D elements: -->
    <Border BorderBrush="LightBlue"
        BorderThickness="1">
        <StackPanel Margin="10">
            <TextBlock Margin="5"
                Foreground="Blue">
                Top Surface</TextBlock>
            <Button Margin="5"
                Click="TopButton_Click"
                Foreground="Blue">
                Click Me</Button>
            <TextBox Margin="5"
                Foreground="Blue">
                Top Text:</TextBox>
        </StackPanel>
    </Border>

    <!-- Set rotation transform: -->
    <Viewport2DVisual3D.Transform>
        <RotateTransform3D>
            <RotateTransform3D.Rotation>
                <AxisAngleRotation3D
Angle="{Binding ElementName=slider, Path=Value}"
                    Axis="0 1 0"/>
            </RotateTransform3D.Rotation>
        </RotateTransform3D>
    </Viewport2DVisual3D.Transform>
</Viewport2DVisual3D>
            </Viewport3D>
        </Grid>
</Window>
```

The corresponding code-behind file of this example is responsible for the button's click event handling:

```csharp
using System;
using System.Windows;
using System.Windows.Media;
```

```
namespace Chapter14
{
    public partial class Viewport2DVisual3DTest : Window
    {
        public Viewport2DVisual3DTest()
        {
            InitializeComponent();
        }

        private void FrontButton_Click(object sender,
            RoutedEventArgs e)
        {
            MessageBox.Show(
                "I am a 2D button on the front surface.");
        }

        private void RightButton_Click(object sender,
            RoutedEventArgs e)
        {
            MessageBox.Show(
                "I am a 2D button on the right surface.");
        }

        private void TopButton_Click(object sender,
            RoutedEventArgs e)
        {
            MessageBox.Show(
                "I am a 2D button on the top surface.");
        }
    }
}
```

This example is based on the previous LinearBrushMap example. The key step is that you must add two Viewport3D objects to your application: one Viewport3D holds your 3D object – the cube in this example, and the other holds Viewport2DVisual3D objects. There are three Viewport2DVisual3D objects in this example, which are added to the front, right, and top surfaces of the cube. If you use a single Viewport3D to hold both the cube and Viewport2DVisual3D object, you would end up with images of the 2D elements without functionalities, just like you paint a 3D surface using a VisualBrush.

Another point I should point out is that to obain consistent behavior, you should use the same camera, light source, and transformations for both the cube and Viewport2DVisual3D objects.

In this example, the Geometry property of the Viewport2DVisual3D is specified by a mesh that mirrors a single face of the cube. The TextureCoordinates of the mesh define how 2D elements should be mapped onto 3D surface. The Visual property of Viewport2DVisual3D sets the elements that will be mapped onto 3D surface. You can use only a single element, but it is perfectly valid to use a container panel to wrap multiple elements together. This example uses a Border that contains a StackPanel with three child elements, a TextBlock, a Button, and a TextBox.

Finally, this example uses a RotateTransform3D to allow the user to turn the cube around using a slider. Both the cube and Viewport2DVisual3D objects use the same RotateTransform3D, so the cube and 2D elements move together.

Figure 14-10 shows the result of this example. Now, you can interact directly with 2D elements. You can click the buttons and enter the text into TextBox.

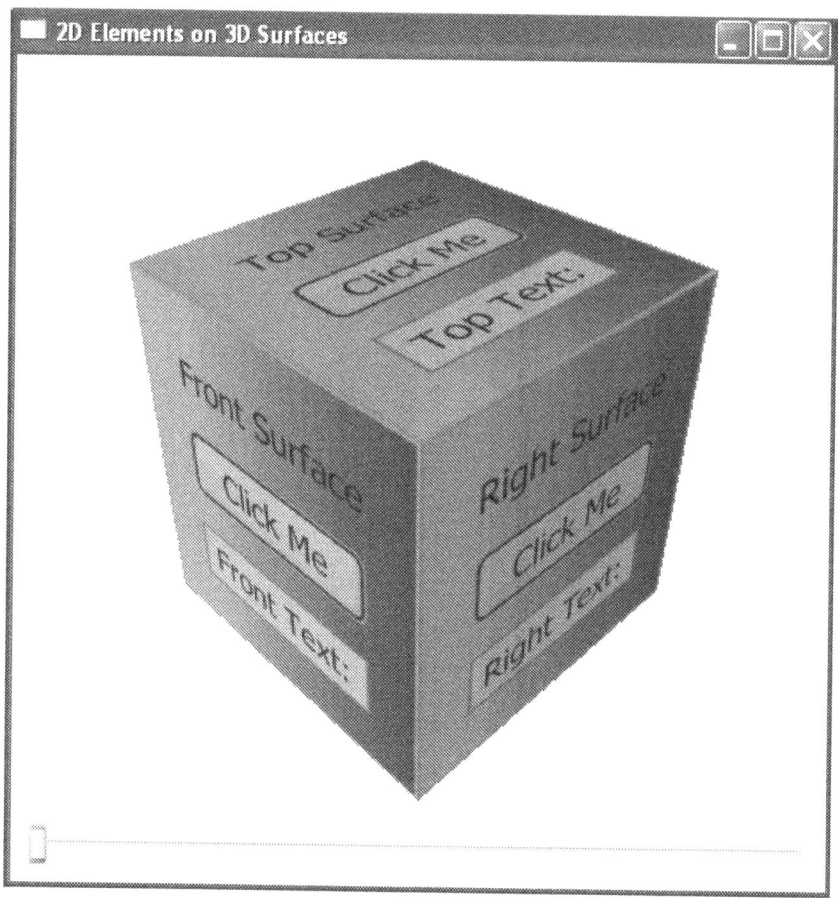

Figure 14-10 2D elements on 3D surfaces.

Interacting with 3D Models

Sometimes, you may want to allow the user to interact with your 3D objects using the mouse. This requires you to make the 3D objects dynamic, meaning that the 3D objects should respond to mouse events by the user.

In this section, you'll learn how to manipulate 3D objects using mouse and how to perform hit testing for 3D objects.

Hit-Testing for 3D Geometries

Even though mouse events for 3D objects are different than those for 2D elements, WPF does provide 3D hit-testing support. In 2D case, your program gets the 2D point of the mouse and determines the 2D object under that point. In 3D case, you can use the 3D hit-testing support by handling a mouse event in Viewport3D (such as MouseUp or MouseDown) and calling the VisualTreeHelper.HitTest method to determine which the underlying 3D object is hit.

Specifically, when working with 3D objects, your can obtain the 3D model at the mouse coordinates. When performing hit-testing in 3D, you use an asynchronous callback mechanism. This means that you can respond to multiple hits on the same click without having to write any additional code. For example, if your mouse click actually clicks into two overlapping 3D objects, the hit test callback method will fire twice. With the specific 3D object (such as ModelUIElement3D or ModelVisual3D) you can also obtain the GeometryModel3D, the MeshGeometry3D, the coordinates of the particular triangle, and weights that indicate the precise point within that triangle.

3D hit-testing essentially works the same way as that 2D hit-testing does works, except you need to project a ray from the camera into the scene. If a 3D hit test occurs somewhere along that ray, the program triggers a hit test result. Note that the 3D hit-testing is based on ModelUIElement3D or ModelVisual3D objects. If the user clicks the mouse over an area of a Viewport3D where no 3D object is located, you can't determine what 3D point corresponds to that click.

Let's consider an example that shows you how to perform a hit test on two 3D objects, a torus and a sphere that are created using the custom TorusGeometry class. When the user clicks over the torus or the sphere, it returns the coordinates of the mesh vertex that is clicked. Add a new WPF Window to the project Chapter14 and name it HitTest3D. Also add the TorusGeometry.cs class from the project Chapter11 to the current project. You can reuse the torus geometry from this class and don't need to recreate the model. Here is the XAML file of this example:

```
<Window x:Class="Chapter14.HitTest3D"
    xmlns="http://schemas.microsoft.com/winfx
    /2006/xaml/presentation"
    xmlns:x="http://schemas.microsoft.com/winfx/2006/xaml"
    xmlns:local="clr-namespace:Geometries"
    Title="HitTest3D" Height="300" Width="300">

    <Window.Resources>
        <local:TorusGeometry x:Key="torus" UDiv="40" VDiv="40"
            R1="1" R2="0.3" Center="0 0 0.5"/>
        <local:TorusGeometry x:Key="sphere" UDiv="40"
```

```xml
                VDiv="40" R1="0" R2="0.8" Center="0 0 -3"/>
        <PerspectiveCamera x:Key="camera"
                           Position="2,3,4"
                           LookDirection="-2,-3,-4"
                           UpDirection="0,1,0"/>
    </Window.Resources>

    <Grid>
        <Grid.RowDefinitions>
            <RowDefinition/>
            <RowDefinition Height="Auto"/>
        </Grid.RowDefinitions>

        <Viewport3D Name="viewport3d" MouseDown="OnMouseDown"
            Camera="{Binding Source={StaticResource camera}}">
            <ContainerUIElement3D>
                <ModelUIElement3D x:Name="model3d">
                    <Model3DGroup>

                        <!-- Create a red torus: -->
                        <GeometryModel3D x:Name="torusMesh"
Geometry="{Binding Source={StaticResource torus},
                           Path=Mesh3D}">
                            <GeometryModel3D.Material>
                                <MaterialGroup>
                                    <DiffuseMaterial Brush="Red"/>
        <SpecularMaterial Brush="Yellow" SpecularPower="30"/>
                                </MaterialGroup>
                            </GeometryModel3D.Material>
                        </GeometryModel3D>

                        <!-- Create a blue torus: -->
                        <GeometryModel3D x:Name="sphereMesh"
Geometry="{Binding Source={StaticResource sphere},
                           Path=Mesh3D}">
                            <GeometryModel3D.Material>
                                <MaterialGroup>
                                    <DiffuseMaterial Brush="DarkBlue"/>
        <SpecularMaterial Brush="LightBlue" SpecularPower="30"/>
                                </MaterialGroup>
                            </GeometryModel3D.Material>
                        </GeometryModel3D>

                        <!-- Set light source: -->
                        <AmbientLight Color="#555555"/>
                        <DirectionalLight Color="#CCCCCC"
                            Direction="-1,-2,-3" />
                    </Model3DGroup>
                </ModelUIElement3D>
            </ContainerUIElement3D>
        </Viewport3D>
        <TextBlock x:Name="textBlock" Text="Mesh Point = "
            Grid.Row="1" Margin="10"/>
    </Grid>
```

```
    </Window>
```

Here you define a torus and a sphere geometries in Window.Resources. Note that the sphere is created using the same TorusGeometry by setting its R1 property to zero. The Viewport3D and GeometryModel3D for torus and sphere are named viewport3d, torusMesh, and sphereMesh, respectively, which will be used in code. You also add a MouseDown event to the viewport3d. The TextBlock will be used to display the coordinates of the mesh point when it is clicked.

The corresponding C# code of this example implements the hit-testing:

```csharp
using System;
using System.Windows;
using System.Windows.Input;
using System.Windows.Media;
using System.Windows.Media.Media3D;

namespace Chapter14
{
    public partial class HitTest3D : Window
    {
        public HitTest3D()
        {
            InitializeComponent();
        }
        private void OnMouseDown(object sender,
            MouseButtonEventArgs e)
        {
            Point mousePoint = e.GetPosition(viewport3d);
            HitTestResult result =
                VisualTreeHelper.HitTest(viewport3d,
                                         mousePoint);
            RayMeshGeometry3DHitTestResult mesh =
                result as RayMeshGeometry3DHitTestResult;

            if (mesh != null)
            {
                // Get mesh coordinates:
                double x = Math.Round(mesh.PointHit.X, 4);
                double y = Math.Round(mesh.PointHit.Y, 4);
                double z = Math.Round(mesh.PointHit.Z, 4);
                Point3D pt = new Point3D(x, y, z);

                string text = "(" + pt.ToString() + ")";
                if (mesh.MeshHit == torusMesh.Geometry)
                    text = "Torus - Mesh Point = " + text;
                else if (mesh.MeshHit == sphereMesh.Geometry)
                    text = "Sphere - Mesh Point = " + text;
                textBlock.Text = text;
            }
        }
    }
}
```

In order to obtain the information about the mesh of the 3D objects, you cast the HitTestResult to the RayMeshGeometry3DHitTestResult object. Then you use the MeshHit property of this object to determine which specific mesh (torusMesh or sphereMesh) was hit. The coordinates of the mesh vertex is given by the PointHit property. Thus, the 3D hit-testing provides detailed information about your 3D objects. It provides not only which geometry model was hit, but also the coordinates of that specific mesh vertex.

Figure 14-11shows the result of running this application. The text underneath displays the model (torus or sphere) and mesh vertex coordinates, when the user clicks the corresponding 3D model on the screen using the mouse.

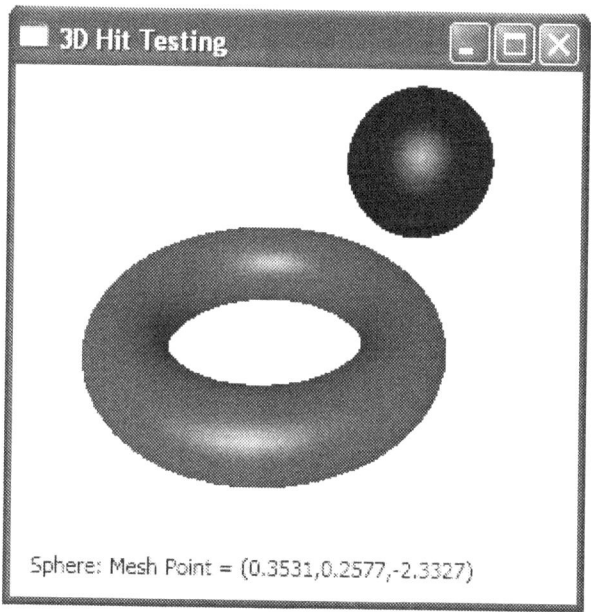

Figure 14-11 Hit-testing for custom 3D geometries.

Hit-Testing for 3D Shapes

You can also perform a similar hit test for 3D custom shapes that you have created in Chapter 12. Add a new WPF Window to the project Chapter14 and name it HitTestShape3D. Also add the custom shape classes, Ellipsoid.cs and Torus.cs, from the project Chapter12 to the current project. Here is the XAML file of this example:

```
<Window x:Class="Chapter14.HitTestShape3D"
    xmlns="http://schemas.microsoft.com/winfx
    /2006/xaml/presentation"
    xmlns:x="http://schemas.microsoft.com/winfx/2006/xaml"
    xmlns:local="clr-namespace:Shapes"
    Title="Hit Test for 3D Shapes" Height="320" Width="300">
```

```
<Grid>
    <Grid.RowDefinitions>
        <RowDefinition/>
        <RowDefinition Height="Auto"/>
    </Grid.RowDefinitions>

    <Viewport3D Name="viewport3d" MouseDown="OnMouseDown">
        <Viewport3D.Camera>
            <PerspectiveCamera
                    Position="2,3,4"
                    LookDirection="-2,-3,-4"
                    UpDirection="0,1,0"/>
        </Viewport3D.Camera>

        <!-- Add a red ellipsoid shape: -->
        <local:Ellipsoid x:Name="ellipsoid"
            Center="0,0.2,-2.5" XLength="1" YLength="0.7"
            ZLength="0.5" PhiDiv="50" ThetaDiv="50">
            <local:Ellipsoid.Material>
                <MaterialGroup>
                    <DiffuseMaterial Brush="Red"/>
                    <SpecularMaterial Brush="Yellow"
                        SpecularPower="30"/>
                </MaterialGroup>
            </local:Ellipsoid.Material>
        </local:Ellipsoid>

        <!-- Add a green torus shape: -->
        <local:Torus x:Name="torus" Center="0.3,0.3,1"
            R1="1" R2="0.3" UDiv="50" VDiv="50">
            <local:Torus.Material>
                <MaterialGroup>
                    <DiffuseMaterial Brush="Green"/>
                    <SpecularMaterial Brush="LightGreen"
                        SpecularPower="30"/>
                </MaterialGroup>
            </local:Torus.Material>
        </local:Torus>

        <ModelUIElement3D>
                <Model3DGroup>
                    <!-- Set light source: -->
                    <AmbientLight Color="#555555"/>
                    <DirectionalLight Color="#CCCCCC"
                        Direction="-1,-2,-3" />
                </Model3DGroup>
            </ModelUIElement3D>
    </Viewport3D>
    <TextBlock x:Name="textBlock" Text="Mesh Point = "
        Grid.Row="1" Margin="10"/>
</Grid>
</Window>
```

Here you create an ellipsoid and a torus shapes, named ellipsoid and torus, using the custom shape classes. These shapes are ready for hit testing. The C# portion of this example is listed below:

```
using System;
using System.Windows;
using System.Windows.Input;
using System.Windows.Media;
using System.Windows.Media.Media3D;
using System.Windows.Media.Animation;
using Shapes;

namespace Chapter14
{
    public partial class HitTestShape3D : Window
    {
        public HitTestShape3D()
        {
            InitializeComponent();
        }

        private void OnMouseDown(object sender,
            MouseButtonEventArgs e)
        {
            Point mousePoint = e.GetPosition(viewport3d);
            HitTestResult result =
                VisualTreeHelper.HitTest(viewport3d,
                mousePoint);
            RayMeshGeometry3DHitTestResult mesh =
                result as RayMeshGeometry3DHitTestResult;
            Point3DAnimation pa = new Point3DAnimation();

            if (mesh != null)
            {
                // Get mesh coordinates:
                double x = Math.Round(mesh.PointHit.X, 3);
                double y = Math.Round(mesh.PointHit.Y, 3);
                double z = Math.Round(mesh.PointHit.Z, 3);
                Point3D pt = new Point3D(x, y, z);

                string text = "(" + pt.ToString() + ")";
                if (result.VisualHit == ellipsoid)
                {
                    text = "Ellipsoid (red): Mesh Point =
                            " + text;
                    pa.From = ellipsoid.Center;
                    pa.To = pt;
                    pa.Duration = TimeSpan.FromSeconds(0.2);
                    pa.AutoReverse = true;
                    ellipsoid.BeginAnimation(
                        Ellipsoid.CenterProperty, pa);
                }
                else if (result.VisualHit == torus)
                {
```

```
                        text = "Torus (green): Mesh Point =
                                " + text;
                    pa.From = torus.Center;
                    pa.To = pt;
                    pa.Duration = TimeSpan.FromSeconds(0.2);
                    pa.AutoReverse = true;
                    torus.BeginAnimation(
                            Torus.CenterProperty, pa);
                }
                textBlock.Text = text;
            }
        }
    }
}
```

You can see that the property VisualHit of HitTestResult can be used to identify which shape is clicked. Furthermore, you can use MeshHit property to determine which specific mesh was hit. If a shape has been hit, the code creates and starts a new animation that moves the Center of the clicked shape toward the hit point, and returns back to its original location.

Figure 14-12 shows the result of this example.

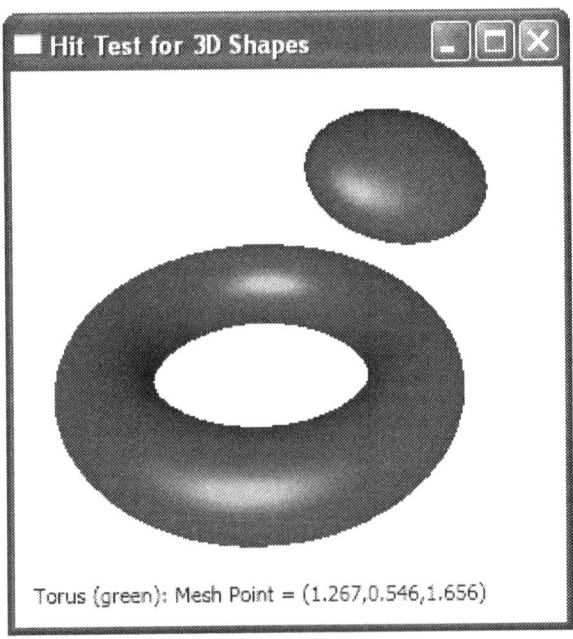

Figure 14-12 Hit-testing for custom 3D shapes.

Rotating 3D Objects with Mouse

For any program that creates 3D models, the user usually requests it to be able to rotate the objects with the mouse. One of the most commonly used techniques for rotating 3D objects via the mouse is known as a Virtual Trackball. This approach has been found widely used in many 3D graphics and CAD tools. Although WPF doesn't provide a built-in implementation of a virtual trackball, the WPF 3D team has released a free simple class that perform this function. This class has been included in the 3DTools library, which has been used in Chapter 10.

The principle of the virtual trackball is simple. It mimics the paradigm of holding an object in your hand and inspecting it. You can easily rotate the objects about any axis. A virtual trackball technique converts 2D mouse movements into 3D rotations. This is done by projecting the position of the mouse onto an imaginary sphere behind the Viewport3D object as shown in Figure 14-13.

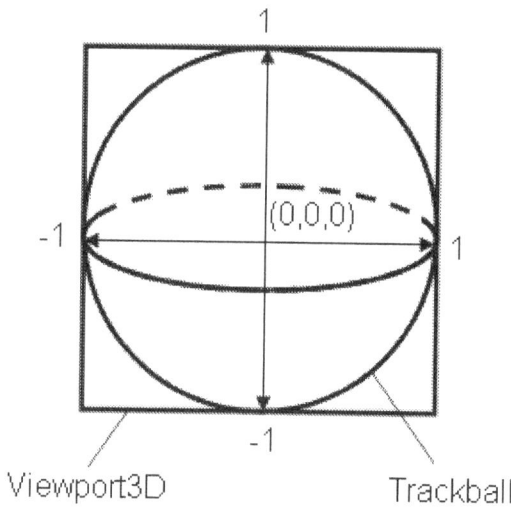

Figure 14-13 Trackball = imaginary sphere inside Viewport3D.

When the user clicks over a point on that sphere and then moves the mouse with the button down, the sphere together with the 3D objects on the Viewport3D rotate so that the clicked point stays under the mouse cursor all the time.

Although the virtual trackball appears to rotate the sphere and 3D objects, it actually works by moving the camera. The camera always remains a constant distance (usually the distance is set to one) from the center point of the Viewport3D. Basically, the camera is moved along a contour of the sphere. Here, I willn't get into the detailed implementation of the virtual trackball, instead, I simply show you how to use the Trackball class included in the 3DTools library.

Using the virtual trackball is very easy in XAML files. All you need to do is wrap your Viewport3D in the TrackballDecorator class. This class is also included in the 3DTools library, so you will need to add an XML namespace for it:

```
xmlns:tool3d="clr-namespace:_3DTools;assembly=3DTools"
```

Then you can easily add the TrackballDecorator to your XAML file:

```
<tool3d:TrackballDecorator>
    <Viewport3D>
    .....
    </Viewport3D>
</tool3D:TrackballDecorator>
```

Once you take this step, the virtual trackball functionality is automatically available.

Let's consider an example that shows how to use the Trackball class. Add a new WPF Window to the project Chapter14 and name it TrackballTest. Here is the XAML file of this example:

```
<Window x:Class="Chapter14.TrackballTest"
    xmlns="http://schemas.microsoft.com/winfx
    /2006/xaml/presentation"
    xmlns:x="http://schemas.microsoft.com/winfx/2006/xaml"
    xmlns:local="clr-namespace:Shapes"
    xmlns:tool3d="clr-namespace:_3DTools;assembly=3DTools"
    Title="Trackball Test" Height="300" Width="300">

    <Grid>
        <tool3d:TrackballDecorator>
            <Viewport3D>

                <!--Set camera: -->
                <Viewport3D.Camera>
                    <PerspectiveCamera x:Name="camera"
                        LookDirection="-1,-1,-1"
                        UpDirection="0,1,0"
                        Position="2.5,2.5,2.5"/>
                </Viewport3D.Camera>

                <!-- Add coordinate axes: -->
                <tool3d:ScreenSpaceLines3D
                    Points="0 0 0,1.5 0 0"
                    Color="Red" Thickness="2"/>
                <tool3d:ScreenSpaceLines3D
                    Points="0 0 0,0 1.5 0"
                    Color="Green" Thickness="2"/>
                <tool3d:ScreenSpaceLines3D
                    Points="0 0 0,0 0 1.5"
                    Color="Blue" Thickness="2"/>

                <ContainerUIElement3D>
                    <ModelUIElement3D>
```

```xml
        <Model3DGroup>
            <AmbientLight Color="LightGray"/>
            <DirectionalLight Color="Gray"
                Direction="-1,-1,-1"/>
            <DirectionalLight Color="Gray"
                Direction="1,-1,-1"/>
        </Model3DGroup>
    </ModelUIElement3D>

    <!-- Add an ellipsoid: -->
    <local:Ellipsoid XLength="0.3"
        YLength="0.6" ZLength="0.3"
        ThetaDiv="50"
        PhiDiv="50" Center="1,0,-1">
        <local:Ellipsoid.Material>
            <MaterialGroup>
                <DiffuseMaterial>
                    <DiffuseMaterial.Brush>
                        <SolidColorBrush
                            Color="Green" />
                    </DiffuseMaterial.Brush>
                </DiffuseMaterial>

                <SpecularMaterial
                    SpecularPower="30">
                    <SpecularMaterial.Brush>
                        <SolidColorBrush
                            Color="LightGreen"/>
                    </SpecularMaterial.Brush>
                </SpecularMaterial>
            </MaterialGroup>
        </local:Ellipsoid.Material>
    </local:Ellipsoid>

    <!-- Add a torus: -->
    <local:Torus R1="0.7" R2="0.2"
        UDiv="50" VDiv="50">
        <local:Torus.Material>
            <MaterialGroup>
                <DiffuseMaterial>
                    <DiffuseMaterial.Brush>
<SolidColorBrush Color="DarkGoldenrod" />
                    </DiffuseMaterial.Brush>
                </DiffuseMaterial>

                <SpecularMaterial
                    SpecularPower="30">
                    <SpecularMaterial.Brush>
<SolidColorBrush Color="LightGoldenrodYellow"/>
                    </SpecularMaterial.Brush>
                </SpecularMaterial>
            </MaterialGroup>
        </local:Torus.Material>
    </local:Torus>
```

```
                    </ContainerUIElement3D>
                </Viewport3D>
            </tool3d:TrackballDecorator>
        </Grid>
    </Window>
```

The Viewport3D contains several 3D objects, including coordinate axes, an ellipsoid, and a torus. The ellipsoid and torus are created using the custom 3D shape classes implemented in Chapter 12. Finally the Viewport3D is embedded into the TrackballDecorator tags.

Figure 14-14 shows the result of running this application. Now you can rotate the 3D scene (including all 3D objects) by simply clicking with your mouse and dragging.

Following the virtual trackball technique, you can easily implement 3D pan and zoom by properly moving the camera. Thus, it is easy to develop a sophisticated 3D graphics packages and 3D CAD tools in the WPF platform.

I also implement another trackball example called TrackballSurface that allows you to rotate quadric shaded surfaces created in Chapter 13 with your mouse.

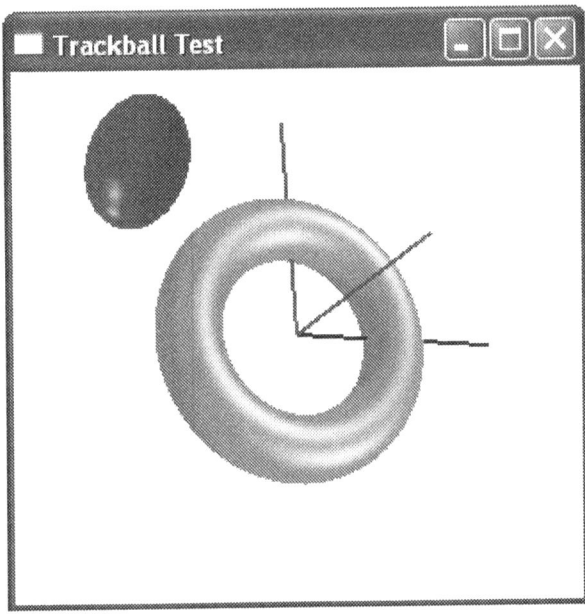

Figure 14-14 Rotating 3D objects with the virtual trackball.

Index

.

.NET 3.0, xx, 209, 435, 444, 445, 535
.NET 3.5, xix, xx, 209, 435, 445, 535, 536, 634
.NET framework, xvii, xviii, xix, 1, 316

2

2D chart, xxi, 331
2D charting application, 22
2D drawing, xx, 87, 114, 117, 143, 148, 181, 434, 436, 437
2D graphics, xvii, xx, 1, 13, 87, 88, 379, 433, 434, 627
2D line charts, xxi, 331, 378
2D matrices, xx, 43
2D shape, xviii, 540, 547, 551, 555, 559, 563, 564, 569, 573
2D space, 13, 28, 43, 44, 47, 48, 51, 69, 70, 288, 442
2D transforms, 43, 69
2D viewport, 28

3

3D applications, 434, 439
3D charts, 433
3D coordinate system, xvii
3D geometry, xxi, 469, 635
3D graphics, xvii, xviii, xxi, xxii, 1, 379, 403, 411, 433, 434, 435, 436, 440, 593, 649, 652
3D hit-testing, 642

3D model, xxii, 402, 433, 434, 437, 439, 449, 535, 536, 642
3D models, xviii, xxi, xxii, 436, 615, 627, 634, 649
3D object, 395, 396, 397, 399, 400, 411, 418, 420, 421, 425, 426, 433, 434, 435, 436, 437, 438, 441, 620, 635, 640, 642
3D objects, xxi, 379, 394, 402, 403, 411, 415, 420, 434, 435, 438, 441, 573, 615, 621, 627, 634, 641, 642, 645, 649, 652
3D Point Structures, 379
3D scene, 433, 434, 435, 440, 441, 616, 634, 652
3D shape, xviii, xxi, 435, 436, 438, 464, 467, 469, 497, 535, 573, 630, 634, 652
3D shapes, xxi, 433, 435, 444, 467, 469, 535, 537, 569, 648
3D space, 379, 384, 404, 406, 420, 437, 440, 445, 452, 464, 497, 575, 599
3D support, 433, 434
3D surface, 331, 593, 627, 634, 635, 640
3D surfaces, xviii, xxii, 615, 641
3D Transform Matrix, 420
3D transformations, 379, 433
3D transforms, 379, 420, 428
3D vectors, xxi
3DTools, 445, 446, 448, 449, 450, 576, 594, 601, 649, 650

A

AccelerationRatio, 218, 221, 222, 223, 224, 234, 235, 241, 243
affine, 70, 380, 381, 382, 384
AmbientLight, 413, 422, 440, 475, 481, 488, 496, 503, 511, 520, 530, 581, 611, 616, 618, 622, 623, 624, 643, 646, 651
animation classes, 209, 210, 211, 213, 252
animation facilities, xxi
animations, 1, 78, 131, 210, 211, 212, 213, 214, 215, 217, 218, 219, 224, 231, 235, 240, 242, 243, 244, 245, 246, 249, 250, 254, 256, 257, 271, 296, 505, 512, 521, 532
AnimationSpeed, 222
AnimationTimeline, 133, 217, 240, 250
ArcSegment class, 97
arrowhead, 68, 125, 127, 128, 130, 131
ArrowLine, 121, 125, 126, 127, 128, 131, 132, 134
attributes, 3, 6, 7, 88
AutoReverse property, 220
axis limits, 27, 29, 293, 317, 323, 334, 336, 361
AxisAngleRotation3D, 420, 426, 427, 431, 443, 446, 474, 475, 481, 487, 488, 494, 495, 496, 502, 503, 510, 511, 520, 530, 542, 543, 629, 636, 638, 639
axonometric projections, 395, 397, 399

B

BackMaterial property, 439, 610
BeginAnimation method, 213, 215, 217, 224, 240
BeginTime property, 217, 221
Bezier curves, 96, 613
Bezier lines, 96
BezierSegment object, 98
binary tree, 307, 310
BinaryTree, 307, 308, 309

bitmap, 3, 150, 189, 190, 316, 627, 633
Bitmap effects, 189, 190, 193
BounceBall, 299, 303
bouncing ball, 297, 299, 306
brush transformations, 196
brushes, xxi, 137, 150, 151, 158, 161, 173, 198, 204, 438, 439, 444, 626, 627, 634
BrushTransformExample, 198

C

Camera class, 441
Camera property, 434, 441
camera setting, 413, 433
camera Space, 402
canvas control, 19, 22, 24
Canvas control, 336
Canvas.Loaded event, 215
Center property, 89, 165, 240, 243, 256, 536
chart canvas, xxi, 336, 337, 339
chart control, 359, 361, 371, 373, 375
chart controls, xix, 376, 378
chart elements, xxi, 331
Chart2DSystem, 22, 23, 25, 29
Charts, xxi, 22, 331, 334, 375, 378, 399, 613
ChartStyle, 334, 335, 337, 339, 340, 341, 343, 344
ChartStyleGridlines class, 361, 371
Children property, 434
ClipToBounds property, 21
code-behind, 2, 4, 5, 6, 7, 12, 24, 26, 38, 39, 55, 56, 58, 66, 75, 106, 113, 131, 140, 144, 211, 233, 242, 255, 259, 271, 292, 302, 308, 318, 326, 332, 340, 349, 356, 360, 361, 367, 371, 374, 376, 385, 388, 413, 418, 423, 425, 427, 429, 430, 433, 436, 450, 453, 458, 460, 464, 582, 598, 604, 611
CodeOnly, 8, 10
coefficient of restitution, 297

collision, xxi, 263, 296, 297, 298, 299, 304, 306
color animation, 11
color maps, xix, 158, 244, 246
Color property, 151, 154, 210, 244, 246, 622, 623, 624
Color structure, 137, 139, 151, 152
color system, xxi, 137
ColorAnimation, 11, 210, 211, 216, 217, 219, 226, 227
ColorDialog control, 142
ColorExample, 139, 140
ColorMap class, 158
ColormapBrush, 158, 159, 162, 163, 164, 165, 169
ColormapBrushExample, 161, 162, 163
ColorPickerDialog, 142, 143, 148, 149, 151, 152, 153
ColorPickerExample, 143, 145
colors, 2, 91, 137, 138, 150, 151, 153, 154, 156, 157, 158, 161, 165, 173, 215, 323, 438, 444, 447, 452, 522, 569, 621
Colors class, 138, 139, 141, 142, 151, 152
CombinedGeometry class, 92, 116
CombinedGeometryExample, 93
CombinedGeometryMode property, 95
CombineShape, 570, 571, 572, 573
CombineShapeTest, 573
CombineTransformAnimation, 236, 239
CombineTransformation, 430
combining transformation, 429, 430
combining transforms, 50
complex numbers, 315
composite transforms, 236, 238, 430
CompositionTarget.Rendering event, 254, 256, 274, 286, 296, 306
Cone, 461, 489, 493, 552, 553, 554, 555, 556
cone class, 552

cone geometry, 489, 490
cone shapes, 461, 463, 464, 497, 498
ConeGeometry, 490, 493, 497, 553, 555
ConeGeometryTest, 493
ConeShapeTest, 555
ContainerUIElement3D, 412, 413, 422, 423, 435, 440, 443, 444, 474, 475, 480, 481, 487, 488, 493, 496, 501, 504, 510, 511, 519, 520, 529, 531, 618, 619, 636, 637, 643, 650, 652
coordinate systems, xx, 13, 43, 69, 420
coordinate transformation, xix
CopyPixel method, 316
coupled spring system, xxi, 263, 274, 275, 276
Cube, 447, 449, 450, 469, 473, 538, 539, 540, 541, 542, 543, 544, 547, 551, 555, 559, 562, 563, 564, 569, 573, 631, 633, 634
CubeGeometry, 469, 470, 472, 473, 476, 538, 540
CubeGeometryTest, 473
CubeShapeTest, 540
custom 3D geometries, xviii, 645
custom 3D shape classes, xxii, 535
custom animation, xxi, 249, 250, 252, 253
custom ColorDialog, 142
custom coordinate system, 17, 18, 19, 21, 22, 28, 29
custom geometries, xxi
custom geometry class, 469, 473, 480, 486, 493, 501, 509, 519, 529, 532
custom shapes, xx, 121, 130, 131, 467, 645
custom user control, xxi, 359
CustomShape, 131, 132, 535, 536, 537
Cylinder, 456, 457, 458, 460, 487, 548, 549, 550, 551, 552
cylinder class, 548
cylinder geometry, 482, 573

cylinder shape, 456, 457, 551
CylinderGeometry, 483, 486, 487, 489, 549, 551, 570
CylinderGeometryTest., 487
CylinderShapeTest.xaml, 551
cylindrical coordinate system, 456, 457, 461, 463, 489

D

dash styles, 349
data binding, xviii, xxi, 10, 11, 80, 81, 83, 88, 100, 359, 360, 361, 366, 469, 476, 482, 489, 497, 505, 512, 521, 532
Data property, 87, 100
data visualization, 331, 433
DataCollection, 334, 336, 337, 339, 340, 341, 342, 343, 350, 352, 356
DataSeries class, 334, 337, 371
DataSeries object, 341
DecelerationRatio, 218, 221, 222, 223, 224, 234, 235, 241, 243
dependency properties, 78, 84, 86, 123, 125, 130, 252, 359, 360, 361, 366, 371, 532, 535, 540, 543, 547, 548, 551, 552, 555, 556, 559, 560, 562, 563, 564, 565, 569, 573, 635
dependency property, 126, 127, 158, 210, 213, 215, 360, 361, 536, 569, 573
DependencyObject class, 366
determinant, 54, 382
device-independent pixels, 2, 13, 14, 15, 26, 27, 334, 336, 349, 402
DiffuseMaterialTest, 622
dimetric projection, 398
Direct3D, xvii, xviii, 1, 407
DirectionalLight, 413, 422, 440, 443, 450, 475, 481, 488, 496, 503, 511, 520, 530, 543, 611, 616, 618, 622, 624, 625, 630, 637, 643, 646, 651
DirectX, xviii, 2, 433, 441

DispatcherTimer, 250, 257, 258, 260
DLL assembly, 253, 476
dodecahedron class, 563
DodecahedronGeometry, 513, 519, 521, 563
DodecahedronGeometryTest, 519
DodecahedronShapeTest, 564
double animation, 11
DoubleAnimation class, 210, 215, 253
drag force, 287, 288, 289, 296
DragMoving, 110, 112, 115, 116
DrawingBrush, 150, 181, 182, 183, 184, 187, 188, 197, 198, 199, 204, 207, 634
DrawingBrushGridline, 181, 182
DrawingGroup, 71, 181, 182, 183, 185, 198, 199
DrawingImageExample, 185
DrawingVisual, 184
Duration property, 218
dynamic layout, 2

E

ellipse shape, 35, 97, 241
EllipseShape, 35
Ellipsoid class, 547
ellipsoid geometry, 477, 497
ellipsoid shape, 544, 547, 646
EllipsoidGeometry, 477, 480, 482, 545, 547, 617
EllipsoidGeometryTest, 480
EllipsoidShapeTest, 547
equation of motion, 264, 265, 267, 288
event handler, 7, 27, 75, 254, 256, 257, 261, 262, 274, 286, 296, 306, 436, 445, 537
event handlers, 4, 7, 8, 10, 74, 117, 322, 372, 435, 436, 537
event trigger, 10, 189, 213, 214, 215, 228
event triggers, 11, 12, 225, 227, 236
extruded surface, 594, 596, 599
ExtrudeSurface, 594, 598

F

FillRule property, 41, 91, 92, 102
FirstWPFProgram, 5, 6, 7, 8, 10
fractal, 306, 307, 315, 324
fractals, xxi, 306, 307, 315
fractional dimension, 306
FrameworkElement, 71, 74, 81, 83, 214
FrameworkElement class, 74
FreefallDoubleAnimation, 250, 251, 252, 253
frustum, 406, 407, 409, 410, 411, 418, 441

G

games, xxi, 263, 433, 575
GDI+, xvii, 1, 142, 316, 378
Geometry class, 87, 88
Geometry classes, xx, 89
geometry mesh, 449, 472
geometry objects, 87
Geometry objects, 87, 88, 89, 113, 116
Geometry property, 435, 438, 476, 480, 482, 486, 489, 493, 497, 501, 505, 509, 512, 519, 529, 531, 540, 547, 551, 555, 559, 562, 563, 640
Geometry3D object, 436
GeometryDrawing, 181, 182, 183, 185, 186, 188, 195, 198, 199
GeometryGroup class, 92
GeometryGroup object, 90
GeometryGroupExample, 90
GeometryModel3D class, 438
GetPixel, 316
golf balls, 287
GolfGame, 289, 292, 296
Gouraud shading, 621
GradientStop objects, 154
graphical operations, xx
graphics algorithms, xix
graphics applications, xvii, xviii, xix, 43, 50, 115, 121, 158, 403
graphics objects, xx, xxi, 13, 15, 19, 20, 21, 24, 26, 27, 29, 30, 31, 43, 64, 137, 379, 428, 434

graphics programming, xvii, xviii, xix, xx, 13
Grid control, 4, 181, 183, 342, 375
gridlines, 73, 181, 183, 184, 342, 343, 346, 349, 351, 368, 369, 372

H

helicoid, 589
HitTest method, 117, 119, 642
HitTest3D, 642, 644
HitTestCallback method, 120
HitTestExample, 117, 118, 119
hit-testing, 117, 118, 119, 120, 642, 644, 645
HitTestShape3D, 645, 647
homogeneous coordinate system, xx, 47, 70, 380, 381, 382, 384, 404, 408, 420
homogeneous coordinates, 47, 48, 49, 51, 52, 53, 63, 75, 379, 384, 402

I

icosahedron class, 560, 563
IcosahedronGeometry, 506, 509, 510, 512, 518, 561, 562
IcosahedronGeometryTest, 510
IcosahedronShapeTest, 563
illumination, 619
ImageBrush, 150, 175, 176, 177, 178, 179, 180, 181, 195, 197, 199, 201, 202, 207, 291, 633, 634
ImageBrushMap, 633
ImageBrushTile, 179
ImageSource property, 175
intensity, 440, 616, 617, 620
interactive 2D, xx, xxii, 87, 117, 148, 635
Interactive2DDrawing, 103, 104, 106
InteractiveStoryboard, 225
IntersectionDetail property, 120
Invert method, 54, 56, 383
isometric projection, 397

J

Julia set, 323, 324, 330
JuliaSet, 323, 324, 326, 330

K

Key frame animations, 211
key-frame animation, 244, 246
KeySpline property, 247

L

LayoutTransform property, 74
legend, xxi, 331, 339, 351, 354,
    357, 358, 359
Legend class, 352
Light class, 616
Light effects, 615
light source, 192, 413, 422, 433,
    434, 437, 440, 443, 444, 447,
    449, 450, 453, 475, 481, 488,
    496, 503, 511, 520, 530, 543,
    581, 615, 616, 618, 619, 622,
    623, 624, 625, 626, 630, 637,
    640, 643, 646
light sources, xxii, 434, 440, 582,
    611, 615, 616, 617, 620, 622,
    623, 624, 625
lighting, xxi, xxii, 150, 436, 439,
    440, 473, 606, 610, 611, 615,
    616, 617, 619, 621, 622, 624,
    626
lighting effect, 434, 619, 624
Lights, 440
LightSourceTest, 617, 624
line chart, 331, 332, 334, 339, 340,
    342, 351, 358, 359, 372, 373,
    374, 375, 376, 378
Line class, 31
LinearBrushMap, 628, 629, 633,
    640
LinearGradientBrush, 150, 153,
    154, 155, 156, 157, 158, 159,
    160, 161, 165, 169, 196, 199,
    200, 204, 205, 206, 232, 233,
    242, 244, 245, 246, 258, 302,
    627, 628, 629, 633, 636
LinearGradientBrushExample, 154

LineChartControl, 359, 361, 362,
    363, 364, 365, 366, 367, 371,
    372, 373, 374, 375, 376
LineChartExample, 339, 340
LineChartWithGridlines, 342, 349,
    350
LineChartWithLegend, 355, 356
LineCurveExample.xaml, 98
LineInCustomSystem, 16
LineInDefaultSystem, 14
LookDirection property, 442

M

Mandelbrot set, 315, 316, 322, 323
MandelbrotSet, 316, 317, 318, 330
markup, xxi, 10, 36, 55, 58, 73, 88,
    91, 97, 98, 131, 139, 143, 154,
    162, 213, 219, 220, 229, 245,
    254, 258, 317, 340, 359, 360,
    372, 433, 469, 532, 574
Material class, 439, 621
MaterialGroup, 439, 481, 501, 502,
    503, 607, 610, 611, 612, 613,
    622, 624, 625, 643, 646, 651
materials, xxii, 211, 434, 436, 439,
    476, 522, 573, 610, 613, 615,
    616, 622, 625, 626
matrices, xx, xxi, 43, 45, 47, 48, 50,
    53, 54, 56, 57, 63, 70, 379, 380,
    381, 383, 386, 387, 403, 404,
    409, 411, 413, 414, 415, 417,
    418, 420, 423, 441, 575
matrix inversion, 56, 386
matrix manipulation, xix
matrix multiplication, 56, 57, 386
matrix operations, 43, 45, 54, 55,
    57, 382, 383, 385
matrix structure, 53, 57, 70, 75, 382,
    420
Matrix structure, 54, 55, 69
matrix transforms, 58, 63, 130, 394
Matrix3D inversion, 386
Matrix3D structure, 381, 382, 383,
    387, 420
Matrix3DOperation, 385, 386
Matrix3DTransforms, 388, 389,
    392

MatrixCamera, 409, 412, 413, 414, 415, 417, 419, 422, 423, 441
MatrixCamera class, 409, 417, 423, 441
MatrixOperation, 55, 56
MatrixTransform class, 70, 71, 75
MatrixTransform3D class, 420, 428, 429
MediaTimeline, 217
MeshGeometry3D class, 436, 469
MeshGeometry3D object, 437, 438, 470, 473, 478, 479, 480, 484, 486, 491, 492, 493, 499, 500, 506, 509, 513, 518, 523, 528
mini-language, 100, 101, 102
Model3D, 435, 537, 538, 545, 549, 553, 557, 561, 566, 567, 571
Model3DGroup collection, 449
ModelUIElement3D, 412, 413, 422, 423, 433, 435, 436, 440, 443, 444, 449, 450, 473, 474, 475, 476, 480, 481, 487, 488, 493, 496, 501, 504, 510, 511, 519, 520, 529, 531, 611, 618, 619, 629, 630, 636, 637, 642, 643, 646, 650, 651
ModelVisual3D, 433, 435, 436, 440, 444, 445, 449, 473, 535, 543, 576, 581, 610, 642
mouse click events, 106, 113
mouse events, 92, 106, 114, 115, 435, 537, 641, 642
MouseButtonEventArgs object, 114
multiplications, 56, 386
Multiply method, 54, 383
multi-view projection, 395

N

Normals property, 436, 437, 620, 621

O

ObjectMatrixTransforms, 71, 74
ODE solver, 265, 267, 272
ODEs, 263, 264, 265, 267, 268, 275, 286, 288, 296

ODESolver, 266, 267, 272, 274, 275, 283, 286, 294, 296
Offset property, 154
opacity mask, 194
Opacity property, 161, 194, 210
OpacityMask property, 194, 196
OpacityMaskExample, 194
OpenGL, xvii, 1, 407, 416, 433, 441
ordinary differential equations, 263
ordinary differiential equations, xxi
orthographic projection, 397, 415, 416, 417, 418, 419, 424
Orthographic projection, 395, 419
orthographic transform, 416, 417
OrthographicCamera, 417, 418, 419, 423, 441
OrthographicCamera class, 417, 418, 419, 423
OrthographicProjection, 418

P

Panel class, 13
Panning, 19, 29, 30
ParallelTimeline, 217
ParametricSurface, 585, 589, 590, 592, 593
ParametricSurfaceTest, 589, 593
path animation, 240, 241, 243
Path class, 87
PathAnimationExample, 240, 241, 242
path-based animation, 211
PathFigure object, 96, 97
PathFigure objects, 96
PathFigureCollection, 100, 101
PathGeometry class, 96, 97
PathGeometry object, 96, 211
PathSegment class, 96
pendulum, xxi, 263, 267, 268, 271, 272, 274
Pendulum Simulator, 268, 269, 274
per-frame animation, 249, 254, 256, 271, 281, 292
perpendicular line, 64, 66, 68, 69
PerpendicularLine, 64, 66

perspective projection, 382, 384, 399, 400, 401, 402, 406, 409, 411, 413, 414, 415, 418, 441
PerspectiveCamera, 409, 411, 415, 423, 441, 442, 443, 446, 450, 475, 482, 488, 496, 504, 511, 520, 531, 542, 581, 611, 617, 630, 635, 643, 646, 650
PerspectiveCamera class, 409, 411, 415
PerspectiveProjection, 411, 414
Phong shading, 620, 621
Photons, 615
physical based animation, xxi
physics models, xxi, 263
physics-based animation, 249, 256
PixelFormat, 323
PlaceShapes, 36
Point3D object, 382, 384, 385, 393, 424, 436, 480, 500, 590
Point3D structure, 379, 380, 381
Point4D, 379, 381, 382, 383, 384, 387
PointLight, 440, 616, 618, 619
points, 13, 15, 16, 22, 27, 31, 37, 38, 41, 44, 47, 48, 55, 64, 66, 68, 96, 97, 98, 100, 102, 115, 123, 153, 154, 244, 247, 315, 334, 337, 341, 349, 384, 394, 400, 401, 407, 415, 436, 437, 438, 445, 455, 473, 575, 577, 581, 584, 594, 596, 597, 603, 604, 620, 621, 628
Polygon class, 38
PolygonFillRule, 40
Polygons, 38, 39, 40
Polyline class, 37, 38
Polylines, 37, 38, 39
Position property, 442
Positions collection, 436, 473, 480, 486, 492, 500, 509, 518, 528, 627, 630
Positions property, 438
projectiles, xxi, 287, 296
projections, xxi, 379, 394, 395, 396, 397, 398, 399, 400, 406, 411, 415, 418, 421

PropertyChanged handler, 536, 540, 547, 551, 555, 559, 562

Q

quadric surfaces, 585, 592, 593
quaternion, 391, 392, 426, 427
QuaternionRotation3D, 426, 427

R

RadialBrushMap, 632
RadialColormapBrush, 169, 173, 175, 176
RadialColormapBrushExample, 173, 174
RadialGradientBrush, 150, 165, 166, 167, 168, 169, 170, 171, 172, 173, 195, 199, 200, 201, 206, 225, 241, 248, 252, 279, 630, 631, 632
RayMeshGeometry3DHitTestResult, 644, 645, 647
real-world applications, xix, 21, 33, 64, 138, 158
real-world coordinate, 26, 334, 336
real-world graphics, 22
Rectangle class, 33
RectangleShape, 33
rectangular mesh, xxii, 577, 581, 606
rectangular meshes, 575, 576
recursive method, 307, 310, 315
reflection, xx, 19, 43, 46, 47, 49, 102, 103, 150, 189, 194, 405, 626
RelativeTransform, 71, 196, 197, 200, 201, 202, 203, 204, 206, 207
rendering area, 13, 22, 24, 26, 29, 30
RenderTransform property, 74, 79, 80, 81, 82, 83, 86, 117, 228, 229, 236, 302
RepeatBehavior property, 220, 227
resolution-independent layout, 2
resources, xxi, 4, 8, 190, 438, 469, 482, 489, 497, 505, 512

Resources, 90, 91, 198, 199, 207, 225, 230, 236, 238, 258, 269, 277, 289, 290, 300, 411, 413, 421, 423, 446, 447, 473, 474, 476, 480, 482, 486, 487, 489, 493, 497, 501, 505, 509, 510, 512, 519, 521, 529, 531, 617, 635, 642, 643, 644
rolling ball, 231, 235
RollingBall, 231, 233
RotateAt method, 57, 62, 393
RotateSurface, 600, 604, 606
RotateSurfaceTest, 604
RotateTransform class, 80
RotateTransformation, 427
RotateTransforms, 81
RotateTransfrom3D class, 421
rotation, xx, xxi, 14, 46, 47, 49, 50, 54, 55, 57, 58, 61, 62, 68, 70, 75, 80, 81, 84, 86, 97, 103, 105, 198, 204, 205, 206, 207, 228, 231, 236, 241, 242, 379, 382, 383, 387, 388, 391, 392, 393, 394, 402, 403, 404, 420, 421, 426, 427, 428, 430, 431, 443, 444, 447, 474, 481, 487, 488, 494, 495, 496, 502, 503, 505, 510, 511, 512, 520, 521, 531, 532, 599, 600, 629, 636, 638, 639
RoutedEvent property, 214
rubberband, 113
Runge-Kutta method, xxi, 264, 265, 268, 275, 288, 292

S

ScaleInCustomSystem, 19
ScaleTransform class, 70, 76
ScaleTransform3D class, 421
ScaleTransformation, 79, 83, 421, 423, 425, 427, 429, 430
ScaleTransforms, 76
scaling, xx, 14, 19, 20, 21, 27, 30, 43, 44, 45, 47, 48, 49, 50, 54, 58, 60, 74, 76, 79, 228, 379, 382, 383, 388, 390, 398, 402, 405, 423, 509, 518, 528, 529

ScreenSpaceLines3D class, 445, 449, 453
screen-specific resolution, xviii, 1
SetMatrixCamera method, 414, 418, 424
SetOrthographic, 418, 419, 424
SetOrthographicOffCenter, 417, 418
SetPerspectiveFov, 410, 411, 414, 424
SetPerspectiveOffCenter, 410
SetPerspetive, 410
SetPixel, 316
SetViewMatrix, 405, 414, 419, 424
shading, xxii, 606, 610, 615, 619, 620, 621, 624
Shape class, 31, 87, 88, 115, 121, 125
Shape objects, 87, 88
shere shape, 453
SimpleAnimation, 211, 212, 214, 218
SimpleLineChart, 332, 333
SimpleSurface, 577, 578, 581, 582
SimpleSurfaceTest, 581, 582
SimpleTriangle, 442
Skew method, 63
skew transform, 63, 82, 83, 228, 428
SkewTransform class, 81
SkewTransforms, 82
snowflake, 310, 311, 312, 315
SnowFlake, 311, 312, 314
soccer ball geometry, 522, 528
soccer class, 565
SoccerGeometry, 522, 523, 529, 531, 532, 566
SoccerGeometryTest, 529
SoccerShapeTest, 569
SolidColorBrush, 11, 106, 132, 137, 140, 141, 145, 148, 150, 151, 152, 153, 154, 194, 198, 210, 216, 217, 437, 439, 448, 542, 576, 627, 651
SolidColorBrushExample, 151, 152
SpecularEmissiveTest, 624
SpecularPower property, 626

SpeedRatio, 218, 221, 223, 224
Sphere, 453, 454, 590, 591, 605, 606, 644
sphere geometry, 477, 482
spherical coordinate system, 453
SplineKeyFrameAnimation, 247
SpotLight, 440, 616, 619
spring simulator, 274
StackPanel control, 58, 388
Star shape, 121, 123, 124, 131, 134
storyboard, 80, 81, 82, 213, 214, 215, 216, 217, 221, 224, 225, 228, 229
Storyboard, 11, 77, 79, 80, 81, 82, 85, 99, 100, 134, 213, 214, 215, 216, 217, 219, 220, 221, 223, 224, 225, 226, 227, 229, 230, 236, 237, 238, 240, 245, 246, 248, 249, 252, 475, 482, 488, 489, 496, 497, 504, 511, 520, 521, 531, 541, 542, 630
StoryboardInCode, 215, 216, 218, 221
StreamGeometry, 88, 100, 101, 102
Stretch property, 24, 37, 177
superball, 298, 306
surface of revolution, 464, 497, 599, 600
surface roughness, 615
Surfaces, 438, 575, 581, 584, 589, 592, 593, 598, 599, 604, 634, 635
SurfaceShading, 606, 607, 610, 611, 612, 613
SurfaceShadingTest, 610, 611

T

tennis ball, 298, 306
TestLineChartControl, 373, 374
text canvas, xxi
TextBlock control, 6
texture maps, xxii
TextureCoordinates property, 437
tick marks, 347, 349, 351, 369
TileBrush, 178, 197

TileMode, 178, 179, 180, 181, 182, 183, 188, 189, 202, 203, 204, 207, 633
Timeline, 213, 217, 218, 219, 220, 221
TimelineGroup, 217, 218
timer-based animation, 210, 249, 250, 254, 256
timing behaviors, 218
torus, 444, 464, 465, 466, 467, 497, 500, 505, 556, 557, 559, 560, 570, 571, 572, 573, 585, 591, 606, 642, 643, 644, 645, 646, 647, 648, 651, 652
Torus, 464, 465, 467, 497, 501, 505, 506, 556, 557, 558, 559, 560, 591, 592, 605, 644, 645, 646, 648, 651
TorusGeometry, 497, 498, 500, 501, 505, 557, 559, 570, 642, 644
TorusGeometryTest, 501
TorusShapeTest, 559
trackball method, xxii
TrackballDecorator, 650, 652
TrackballSurface, 652
TrackballTest, 650
Tranckball, 649
Transform classes, 69, 70, 75
transform matrix, 44, 47, 53, 70, 71, 75, 379, 384, 402, 405, 406, 409, 417, 421, 428, 429
Transform3D class, 420
Transform3DGroup class, 429, 430
TransformGroup class, 83, 84
TranslateTransform class, 79
TranslateTransform3D class, 425
TranslateTransformation, 425
TranslateTransforms, 79
translation, xx, xxi, 17, 19, 43, 47, 48, 50, 53, 54, 58, 60, 61, 69, 70, 71, 75, 79, 80, 116, 117, 228, 229, 231, 235, 379, 382, 383, 384, 387, 388, 390, 391, 402, 403, 404, 405, 412, 413, 420, 425, 428, 521, 531
triangle indices, 438, 479, 486, 492, 500

triangle meshes, 455
TriangleIndices property, 438
triangulation, 455, 460, 464, 477, 490, 492, 497, 509, 525, 526, 529
trimetric projection, 398
truncated icosahedron, 521

U

UI element, 2
UIElement, 71, 75, 83, 87, 88, 121, 187, 189, 435, 436, 535, 537
UIElement3D, 435, 436, 449, 535, 536, 537, 538, 543, 544, 549, 553, 557, 561, 566, 570
UIElement3D class, 435, 535
UpDirection property, 442
user controls, 1, 19, 71, 358, 359
user interface, xvii, xviii, 2, 64, 66, 68, 73, 78, 90, 137, 144, 184, 209, 257, 259, 268, 275, 289, 359, 413, 423, 424, 425

V

vector graphics, 1
Vector3D object, 380, 382, 384, 390, 391, 392, 442
vectors, xx, 43, 44, 48, 51, 55, 404, 405, 437, 620, 621
View Frustum, 406
view matrix, 403, 404
view transform, 403, 415, 418
Viewport2DVisual3D, 634, 635, 637, 638, 639, 640, 641
Viewport2DVisual3DTest, 635
Viewport3D class, 434
Viewport3D object, 433, 649
Visual Studio, xix, xx, 3, 4, 5, 14, 359, 430, 445, 529
VisualBrush, 150, 187, 188, 189, 194, 196, 197, 199, 203, 204, 207, 439, 634, 640
VisualBrushExample, 187

W

Window element, 4
Window resource, 447

Windows API, xvii
Windows application, 1, 331
Windows Forms, xvii, xix, 1, 2, 3, 5, 6, 8, 10
wireframe, 444, 445, 446, 447, 448, 449, 452, 456, 577, 580, 581, 588, 597, 603
Wireframe, 445, 446
WPF 3D, xviii, 433, 434, 435, 436, 438, 444, 445, 649
WPF animation, 12, 209, 210, 249, 250, 254, 256
WPF application, xviii, xx, 3, 6, 8, 10, 16, 31, 64, 78, 84, 103, 142, 161, 173, 209, 252, 372, 430, 434, 467
WPF applications, xviii, xix, xxi, 1, 2, 3, 10, 13, 43, 142, 150, 158, 186, 209, 359, 469
WPF coordinate system, 13, 16, 26, 27, 29
WPF Graphics, i, iii, iv, xvii, xviii, xx, xxi, 13, 433
WPF programming, xix, xx
WPF Window application, 4, 581, 589, 598, 604, 610

X

XAML files, xx, xxi, xxii, 2, 3, 131, 213, 253, 339, 467, 469, 480, 486, 493, 501, 509, 519, 529, 532, 535, 540, 547, 548, 551, 552, 555, 556, 559, 560, 563, 564, 565, 569, 573, 650
XamlOnly, 10, 11
XAML-only, 10, 12
XML namespace, 253, 372, 475, 650
XML namespaces, 4
xmlns attribute, 4
X-Y line chart, 332

Z

zoom in, 20, 29, 306, 317, 322, 324, 330
zoom out, 20
Zooming, 19, 29

You Need the eBook

Your purchase of this book qualifies you to buy the PDF eBook for only $12. Take the weightless companion with you anywhere.

We believe this book will prove so indispensable that you'll want to carry it with you everywhere, which is why we are offering the eBook version for only $12 to customers who purchase this book now. The eBook version includes full-color figures that have much better looking than black-white figures in the paperback book.

Once you purchase your book, getting the $12 companion eBook is simple:

- Visit www.authors.unicadpublish.com/~jack_xu

- Go to download area of this book

- Answer a randomly generated question about this title correctly, and you'll be directed to the link, from which you can buy your eBook for only $12

Also Available from Dr. Jack Xu:

For .NET developers, creating professional charts and graphics in your C# applications is now easier than ever before. Practical C# Charts and Graphics is the perfect guide to learning all the basics for creating advanced chart and graphics applications in C#. The book clearly explains practical chart and graphics methods and their underlying algorithms. The book contains:

- Overview of GDI+ graphics capabilities and mathematical basics of computer charting and graphics.
- Step-by-step procedures to create a variety of 2D and 3D charts and graphics with complete ready-to-run C# code for each application.
- Powerful 2D and 3D chart packages and user controls that can be directly used in your C# applications or can be easily modified to create your own sophisticated charts and graphics packages.
- Detailed procedures to create C# spreadsheet-like chart and graphics applications.
- Introduction for how to use Microsoft's Excel charts in your C# applications.

For details, see www.authors.unicadpublish.com/~jack_xu

www.ingramcontent.com/pod-product-compliance
Lightning Source LLC
Chambersburg PA
CBHW021022210326
41598CB00016B/884